Pocket Encyclopedia of Real Estate

CONTEMPORARY
BOOKS, INC.
CHICAGO

Published by Contemporary Books, Inc.
180 North Michigan Avenue, Chicago, Illinois 60601
Manufactured in the United States of America
Library of Congress Catalog Card Number: 82-45428
International Standard Book Number: 0-8092-5671-1

Published simultaneously in Canada by
Beaverbooks, Ltd.
150 Lesmill Road
Don Mills, Ontario M3B 2T5
Canada

This edition published by arrangement with Delphi
    Information Sciences Corporation.

Table of Contents

A

ABANDONMENT — An action indicating the voluntary surrender of a right. For instance, the failure to use a right-of-way or easement for a long period of time.

ABATEMENT — A decrease in the amount of noise, value, rent, etc.

ABC SOIL — Three-layered soil. A(upper), B(middle), C(lower).

ABSENTEE LANDLORD — An owner who rents out his property and does not live on any portion of it.

ABSORPTION RATE — The period of time it takes to completely sell the lots in a new subdivision or to rent the units in an apartment building; considered part of a builder's or developer's costs.

ABSTRACT OF TITLE — A past history of ownership of a particular property examined by an attorney to determine if there are any defects which would prevent passage or transfer of clear title to the next owner.

ABUTTING — Adjoinging, adjacent, bordering.

ACCELERATED DEPRECIATION — Fast depreciation of property in the early years of ownership rather than spreading it evenly over the total time allowed.

ACCELERATION CLAUSE — A statement in a mortgage or deed of trust giving the lender the right to call all monies owed to him to be immediately due and payable upon the occurrence of a certain event, such as a late payment or transfer of title.

ACCEPTANCE — Agreement to the terms and price of a contract or sale agreement through the act of signing the document.

ACCESSIBILITY — The ease with which the property can be reached by those people and vehicles essential to the intended use of said property.

ACCESSION — The legal addition to an owner's property of land deposited by flood water, etc.

ACCESS RIGHT — The right of entrance to and exit from one's property.

ACCOMMODATION PARTY — One who signs a negotiable instrument without receiving any benefit therefrom, so that another party may obtain a loan.

ACCORD — A compromise agreement in which a creditor accepts an amount different from that which was originally claimed as owing.

ACCOUNTS PAYABLE — An accounting term referring to money owed to creditors in return for goods and services performed.

ACCOUNTS RECEIVABLE — An accounting term referring to money which is due to be received for goods and services rendered to another firm or individual.

ACCRETION — The gradual deposit of land onto a riverbank or shore created by the movement of water which may be added to an owner's adjoining property.

ACCRUE — To accumulate, increase.

ACCRUED DEPRECIATION — For tax purposes, the amount of credit given toward the replacement of a structure or other asset; the remaining value of a property.

ACKNOWLEDGEMENT — A signed, voluntary affirmation before an authorized official (usually a notary public) verifying identity.

ACQUISITION APPRAISAL — A determination of the market value of property to be acquired by the government through condemnation (eminent domain) so that the owners may receive just compensation.

ACQUISITION COSTS — Costs in addition to the purchase price of real property such as escrow fees, lender's fees and title insurance.

ACRE — A measure of land area; 1/640th of a square mile, 160 sq. rods, 43,560 sq. ft., or approximately 209' x 209'.

ACREAGE CONTROL — A federal regulation limiting the number of acres which may be planted with crops having federal price supports.

ACTION TO QUIET TITLE — A legal proceeding to determine ownership of real property; does not cure defects.

ACTIVE LICENSEE — A real estate associate (agent) actively engaged in the business of selling other people's real property under the auspices of a broker.

ACT OF GOD — A destructive act of nature such as earthquakes, floods and storms as distinguished from damage caused by man.

ACTUAL AGE — The historical age of a building or structure regardless of its physical condition (see economic age).

ACTUAL CASH VALUE — The market value.

ACTUAL NOTICE — Expressed or implied notification.

ADDENDUM — An addition to a sale agreement, escrow instructions, contract, etc.; may be an amendment of conditions.

ADDITIONAL DEPOSIT — A second, usually a more substantial deposit made by the buyer after acceptance by the seller of an offer to purchase; establishes buyer's earnest desire to purchase.

ADJOINING — Adjacent to, abutting, next to.

ADJUDICATION — A court decision or judgment.

ADJUSTED COST BASIS — The original cost of an asset (real property), plus improvement costs, less depreciation.

ADJUSTED GROSS INCOME — The total amount of rent received on income property at 100% occupancy less a vacancy factor.

AD VALOREM — A tax imposed on real property, based on current market value.

ADVANCE COMMITTMENT — See Committment.

ADVANCE FEE — A fee paid in advance by the seller to the broker to cover advertising and promotion costs; the fee is nonrefundable and is credited against commissions in the event of sale. Typically used when large properties require big promotion budgets.

ADVANCES — Money paid in advance by the lender (mortgagee, beneficiary) to cover carrying charges (taxes and insurance) and other obligations of the borrower (mortgagor, trustor) needed to protect the secured property.

ADVERSE LAND USE — A use of land which devalues the surrounding land, such as a truck terminal in the midst of a residential community.

ADVERSE POSSESSION — A method of acquiring title to property after a period of years of use by taking possession of it under an owner's objections. When permission is given by an owner to another for use, adverse possession does not exist.

AEOLIAN SOIL — A type of soil composed of windblown materials; wind transported deposits.

AERATION ZONE — The upper zone of ground water where moisture is retained in the soil for use by plants; the excess seeps into the lower saturation zone.

AESTHETIC VALUE — Property value derived from the beauty of the surroundings or of improvements made.

AFFIDAVIT — A written statement or declaration made under oath before an official with the authority to administer such an affirmation (such as a notary public).

AFFINITY — A relationship by marriage, not by blood; any group with special, common interests (clubs, churches, schools, etc.) is an affinity group.

AFFIRMATION — A sworn statement used where the affiant has religious or moral objections to taking an oath.

A-FRAME — A structure in the shape of a capital letter "A", commonly seen in mountain resort areas.

AFTER ACQUIRED PROPERTY — In reference to a judgment lien, the lien will attach to property of the debtor obtained after the judgment.

AFTER ACQUIRED TITLE — A legal principal which automatically gives title to the grantee (the deed has been completed and delivered) once the grantor obtains title to the property.

AGENCY — A relationship where one party (the principal)

delegates to another (the agent) the authority to represent him/her in business transactions.

AGENCY AGREEMENT (LISTING) — An agreement between the seller of real property and a real estate broker wherein the broker's commission is protected against a sale by other agents, but not by the seller; often referred to as a non-exclusive agency agreement.

AGENCY BY ESTOPPEL (OSTENSIBLE AGENCY) — A legal, agency relationship created by proof of action when the principal causes another to believe that a third party is his agent or by negligence allows his agent to act in an un-authorized capacity.

AGENCY COUPLED WITH INTEREST — A non-revocable contractual agreement whereby the agent receives an interest or share in the property (a broker agrees to find land for a developer in return for an exclusive listing to sell the finished structures; referred to as a list-back). Illegal in some states.

AGENT — A person who is authorized to represent or act for another in a business matter.

AGRARIAN — Pertaining to the land or to division and distribution.

AGREEMENT — An understanding between two people with regard to the rights and obligations of each in a given situation, concerning a given subject.

AGREEMENT OF SALE — A written contract between the buyer and seller where both parties are in full agreement on the terms and conditions of sale.

AGRICULTURAL LIEN — A claim against crops only, as payment for supplies used to grow the crops.

AGRICULTURAL PROPERTY — Land which is zoned and/or used for growing crops and raising livestock.

A HORIZON — The top layer of soil, the content of which is affected by water seeping through it.

A.I.R. (AMERICAN INDUSTRIAL REAL ESTATE ASSOCIATION) — An association of real estate associates and brokers mainly dealing in industrial properties.

AIR RIGHTS — The rights to use the space above a property; land ownership includes air rights, though these may be sold later.

AIR SPACE — That part of a condominium which an owner holds exclusive title to, along with joint ownership in common areas; legally described cube of air.

ALCOVE — A small, recessed part of a room.

ALIAS — Another name by which a person is known; (AKA) also known as.

ALIENATION — The transfer of title to property from one party to another.

ALIENATION CLAUSE — A clause within a loan instrument (note) calling for immediate payment of the balance of the debt upon transfer of title to the secured property; also known as a "due-on-sale" clause.

ALLEY INFLUENCE — An appraisal term referring to the effect of an adjoining alley upon the value of a property.

ALL INCLUSIVE DEED OF TRUST — A second deed of trust which is subordinate to, but includes the face value of the first deed of trust. Also referred to as a wrap around mortgage.

ALLOTMENT — A small plot of land given or sold to farmers for cultivation as an additional source of income prior to World War II.

ALLUVION — Soil deposited by accretion.

A.L.T.A. (AMERICAN LAND TITLE ASSOCIATION) — A group of title insurance companies which has standardized forms to establish uniform coverage throughout the industry; offers extended coverage.

ALTERATIONS — Remodeling the interior or exterior of a structure without changing the exterior dimensions.

AMENDMENT — A change in the terms or conditions of an agreement that does not enter the main idea or substance.

AMENITY — An attractive or desirable improvement to a property or setting that adds value to real estate, such as a pool, built-ins, or a view.

AMORTIZATION — The repayment of a debt in equal

installments which are applied to principal and interest over a specific period of time to arrive at a zero balance.

ANCILLARY — Subordinate to, supplementary.

ANNEX — An addition to a main building; to join or add.

ANNEXATION — Permanent additions to real property such as the United States annexing the Louisana Territory.

ANNUAL PERCENTAGE RATE (A.P.R.) — The actual annual interest rate paid on a loan; disclosure is a requirement under federal truth-in-lending laws.

ANNUITY — A regular stream of equal payments (or income) paid periodically for a specified period of time.

ANNUITY METHOD — A method of appraisal using future estimated net income before depreciation and discounting it to determine present value.

ANNUM — A year.

ANTENUPTIAL AGREEMENT — An agreement made before marriage establishing the property rights of both parties during the marriage and in the event of death or divorce.

ANTICIPATION — A method of appraisal basing value on estimated future benefits.

APARTMENT HOTEL — A lodging which offers a combination of features characteristic of hotels and apartments; residents receive maid service, etc., but may stay for long periods of time, paying on a monthly or weekly basis.

APARTMENT HOUSE — A structure containing two or more separate residential units which are rented or leased to tenants.

APPARENT AUTHORITY — A condition existing when an agent appears to have more authority than he/she has in fact, as a result of actions (or lack of) by the principal.

APPOINTMENTS — Fixtures, furnishings and equipment in a building which may affect its value; prearranged meetings at appointed times.

APPORTIONMENT — Pro-rating of costs between seller and buyer, usually as of date of possession.

APPRAISAL — An estimate or opinion of value based on analysis of pertinent data by a qualified appraiser.

APPRAISAL METHODS — The three most common approaches are: the market data (comparable approach), the cost approach and the income approach.

APPRECIATION — An increase in the value of property from improvements made, the elimination of negative factors or economic conditions other than inflation; rate of appreciation is determined by supply and demand.

APPROPRIATION — Taking public property for private use, such as water from a stream.

APPROVED ATTORNEY — An attorney whose opinion is accepted by title companies where state laws require examination of the chain of ownership or title before insurance is issued.

APPURTENANCE — Something belonging to the land and conveyed with it upon transfer of title, such as a building or fixtures.

APPURTENANT EASEMENT — The right to gain access to one's property by going through land belonging to another.

APRON — The flared portion of a driveway that meets the street; a windowsill; anything that widens out.

AQUATIC RIGHTS — Rights to use oceans and waterways; including use of soil, navigation and fishing rights.

AQUEDUCT — A pipeline or channel for carrying water; may be open or underground.

ARABLE — Land suitable for farming.

ARBITRAGE — The difference between interest rates on the original and secondary mortgages in a wrap-around-mortgage; the purchase of money and securities in one market and sale of them in another for profit.

ARBITRARY MAP — A map drawn by a title company and arbitrarily divided into number lots, to describe their location; documents are filed by these numbers.

ARBITRATION CLAUSE — A clause in a lease agreement where the rent is negotiated, requiring the decision of a third party (arbiter) in the event of a dispute; used in other contracts as well.

ARCH — A concave, curved construction spanning a doorway or other opening.

ARCHITECTURE — The art of structural design; the style in which a structure is designed and built.

AREAWAY — A cellar or room below ground level.

AREA ZONING (BULK ZONING) — Zoning which establishes the ratio of improvements per unit of land area and the distance of buildings to the street.

ARMAGEDDON CLAUSE — Determines who is responsible for insurance until date of possession; shields against unforseen disasters, such as floods, tornados, etc.

ARREARS — Backpayments made after a due date.

ARTESIAN WELL — A deep well in which water is under pressure and rises to the top without being pumped.

ARTIST'S CONCEPTION (RENDERING) — A perceived, unscaled drawing of a real estate development, used to promote the project or make a sale.

ASBESTOS — A fire resistant fiber used as insulation.

AS-IS CONDITION — Property and buildings sold or leased with no guarantees as to their condition, defects, etc.

ASPECT — The appearance or view of an object.

ASSEMBLAGE — The combining of adjoining properties under one ownership for a specific use, such as creating a large piece of commercial property from a group of formerly residential properties to build a shopping center, etc.

ASSESS — To appraise, to give an opinion of the value of property in question; usually for tax purposes.

ASSESSED VALUE — A valuation of property by the tax assessor.

ASSESSMENT — The amount of tax levied.

ASSETS — Anything owned by a company or an individual which can be sold to repay debts.

ASSIGNMENT — The signing over of title, rights and ownership interest in property to another person, etc.

ASSUMPTION — The taking over by a buyer of a seller's existing mortgage obligations and/or liabilities.

ATTACHMENT — Seizure by court order of property belonging to the defendant in a law suit as security in the event of a money judgment.

ATTESTATION CLAUSE — A written statement by witnesses confirming that a document has been properly signed.

ATTIC — The space between the ceiling of the top story and the roof of a building.

ATTORNEY-IN-FACT — A disinterested party who is authorized by another to represent him/her in matters specified by the power of attorney.

ATTRACTIVE NUISANCE — Something on a property of danger to children which may attract them, but which they must be protected from, such as a swimming pool.

AUTOMATIC APPRAISER — An equation to compute the upper limits of value on apartment houses with more than 20 units using a 10% vacancy factor and a 35% expense ration.

AVERAGE DAILY TRAFFIC — The normal number of vehicles passing a particular point during a 24 hour period.

AVULSION — The sudden washing away of land and its deposit on land belonging to another. Ownership is determined by original boundaries.

AWARD — The sum of money paid for condemned property; the acceptance of a bid for construction by a contractor.

AZIMUTH — In surveying, the horizontal distance between true north and the object in question (expressed in degrees).

AZONAL SOIL — Soil not composed of distinct layers.

B

BACKFILL — Dirt used to support a structure or to fill in an excavated area.

BACK TITLE LETTER — A letter sent to an attorney by a title insurance company stating the condition of title as of a specified date; the lawyer begins his title examination as of that date (in states where this procedure is necessary); also a starter or back title certificate.

BACK-UP ORDER — An alternate offer to purchase property, made in case the primary offer falls through.

BACKWATER — Water in a stream which stops in its flow or runs back toward its source due to an obstruction (dam, etc.).

BALLOON NOTE — A note requiring a series of periodic payments that do not fully pay the loan and a large principal (balloon) payment at the end of the term.

BALOON PAYMENT — The final installment paid at the end of the term of a note; used only when preceding installments were not sufficient to pay off the note in full.

BANK — The elevated sides of a river or ditch; a financial institution.

BANKRUPT — One who is declared unable to pay current debts by a court; proceedings may be initiated by the debtor or his/her creditors.

BANKRUPTCY — A procedure of federal law to seize the property of a debtor and divide it among his creditors.

BASE — The lowest visible, load-bearing portion of a structure.

BASE AND MERIDIAN — Imaginary lines used by surveyors to find and describe the location of public or private lands.

BASEBOARD — A flat board or molding which covers or laps the joint where the interior wall and floor meet.

BASEBOARD HEATING — A type of room heating using units along the perimeter of the area, either above or replacing the baseboards.

BASE MAP — A map showing relevant physical features and boundary lines on which more detailed information is later plotted.

BASEMENT — The lowest story of a building, usually below ground level.

BASE PROPERTY — The amount of land which must be owned by a cattle rancher before he/she may obtain a permit to use public grazing lands.

BASE RENT — The minimum rent due under a percentage lease which also requires payment of a percentage of gross income.

BASE TITLE — The product of a title investigation, usually covering a large area in expectation of future sales, for internal use by a title insurance company.

BASE YEAR — The year used as a starting point for calculating rent increases which are based on changes in the operating expenses of the owner.

BASIS — The original cost of a property, including expenses for capital improvements less depreciation taken or allowed. The final figure is called adjusted basis.

BASIS POINT — .01% yielded annually; a financial term describing changes in the market price of bonds, notes and other instruments.

BATT — Insulation strips between the vertical supports of a wall.

BATTURE LAND — The land between the water's edge and the bank of a river when the water level is below normal.

BAY — The open space between two walls or columns (rows of) forming a room-like area; an inlet along the shoreline; a protruding structure.

BAY WINDOW — A window in a small structure which protrudes from the main building.

BEAM — A horizontal or vertical load-bearing member of a structure.

BEARING WALL — A wall capable of supporting weight in addition to its own.

BEDROOM COMMUNITY — A residential area from which people commute to work.

BEFORE AND AFTER METHOD — An appraisal method for determining the award due to an owner when only part of his/her property is condemned; if the remaining land is worth less per square foot after condemnation, the owner is paid for the loss in value; this method is also used to determine changes in property value due to remodeling or modernization.

BELT HIGHWAY — See By-pass.

BENCH MARK — A mark used by surveyors which is permanently affixed to the ground to denote the height of that point in relation to sea level.

BENEFICIAL ESTATE — An estate in which legal ownership has not yet been transferred to the beneficiary or where the will requests a postponement of the title transfer.

BENEFICIAL INTEREST — The ownership of property through a right to legal title rather than through actual possession of title, as in a land contract; also equitable title, equitable ownership.

BENEFICIAL USE — A principle pertaining to the allocation of water rights which favors those who will use it in the best way.

BENEFICIARY — One who benefits (receives money, etc.) from the actions of another such as the creation of a trust; the lender involved in a note or deed of trust.

BENEFICIARY'S DEMAND — A written request by a beneficiary under a deed of trust (the lender) demanding the funds needed to pay off the note and transfer title to the new owner.

BENEFICIARY'S STATEMENT — A statement by the lender (beneficiary under deed of trust) containing the relevant information needed by one taking over an existing deed of trust (such as monthly payment, unpaid balance and interest rate).

BENEFIT OF THE BARGAIN — A doctrine by which a defrauded buyer may collect the difference between the actual and the falsified value of the property purchased, regardless of the actual loss suffered.

BENEFITS — An increase in the value of property, due to the condemnation of adjoining or neighboring land.

BEQUEATH — The act of giving property by will.

BERM — A continuous mound of earth used as the shoulder of a road, as a support for pipes, the sides of drainage ditch, etc.; a terrace on a long slope; a long narrow mound of earth in front of an industrial park used to camouflage its existence.

BETTERMENT — An improvement to property or structure other than a repair which increases the value of the property.

B HORIZON — The layer of soil beneath the upper layer, the content of which is also affected by water seepage.

BI — A prefix which means "twice in" or "every two" as in biannual.

BID — An offer to purchase (as in an auction) or to perform services (as with construction); usually made in competition with others.

BIENNIAL — Something which occurs every two years; lasts for two years.

BILATERAL (RECIPROCAL) CONTRACT — A contract in which all parties pledge to perform certain actions/services for each other (failure to perform is considered breach of contract).

BI-LEVEL — A split 2-level house (structure).

BILL OF SALE — A written document used as evidence of the transfer of title from one person to another of personal property.

BINDER — A receipt for deposit left with the seller by the prospective buyer as evidence of intention to purchase the property (if it contains terms and is signed by the seller, it is a contract); a temporary insurance policy; a committment to issue title insurance.

BIRD-DOGGING — Getting the first lead on a potential investor, home buyer, loan customer, etc., which is turned over to an authorized salesperson to make the pitch.

BLACK ACRE — Refers to a fictitious name describing a property when it's description is incomplete or vague.

BLANKET MORTGAGE — A mortgage encompassing several separate pieces of real property owned by one mortgagor, such as all the lots in a subdivision owned by a developer.

BLIGHTED AREA — A run-down area in which property values are declining.

BLIND AD — An advertisement that does not reveal who placed it (may not be legal for licensed brokers).

BLIND CORNER — A corner with vegetation (shrubs, etc.) or structures that block the motorist's view of traffic traveling at right angles.

BLIND POOL — The offering of investment opportunities in unspecified property, depending on the general partner to locate and assemble the investment package.

BLOCK — A brick; a rectangular area bordered by streets; part of the legal description of lots in a subdisivion; an enclosed pulley.

BLOCK BUSTING — An illegal method of inducing sales (often below market value) by telling residents of an area that people of a different race, religion, ancestry, etc., are moving in which will cause a decline in property values.

BLUE LAWS — Laws regulating moral conduct; in some New England and Southern states the hours during which business may be conducted are regulated.

BLUEPRINT — A photographic print of a master plan for a house, subdivision, shopping center, etc., reproduced on paper with a blue background.

BLUE SKY LAWS — State laws requiring the registration of securities and disclosure of all relevant information to the state securities commissioner; they protect inexperienced investors from fraud.

BOARDFOOT — A unit of lumber measurement equaling 12" x 12" x 1".

BOARDING HOUSE — Lodging where meal service is provided and included in the rental charge.

BOARD OF EQUALIZATION — The state body responsible for consistency in assessing real property for taxes.

BONA FIDE PURCHASER — One who buys property in good faith for a fair price without knowledge of other claims against it.

BOND — An agreement by an insurance firm which protects the insured against loss or default on a contract by another; an interest bearing, negotiable instrument issued by private companies or the government (federal or local) which are secured by the assets of that body and used to finance long-term debt.

BONUS CLAUSE — A statement in a contract which entitles one to additional compensation if services are performed before a specified date.

BOOK VALUE — The estimated market price of a property based on cost plus capital expenditures for improvements, minus depreciation.

BOOT — Additional money, property or mortgage relief given to compensate for the difference in value when two properties are exchanged.

BORING TEST — A method of collecting soil samples by drilling into the earth, used to study the weight-bearing capacity of subterranean soil.

BOROUGH — A division of a city with some authority over local affairs; an incorporated township; a division of the state of Alaska.

BORROW PIT — A depression in the ground left after the removal of landfill material.

BOTTOM LAND — Low lying land in a valley, near a waterway (such as a river or creek) or between areas of high ground; land subject to flooding.

BOULEVARD — A wide major street, frequently having a tree-lined center divider.

BOUNDARY — The legally defined perimeter (physical outer limits) of a piece of land.

BREACH OF CONTRACT — Failure to fulfill any of the terms and/or conditions specified in a contract without a legal excuse.

BREACH OF COVENANT — Violation of a written agreement, usually in reference to established conditions or restrictions.

BREACH OF WARRANTY — Occurs when the physical conditions of the land or the condition of title are not as stated in the contract of sale.

BREAK-EVEN POINT — The income level (of a business or investment) where expenses have barely been covered; no profit or loss has been realized.

BREAST-HEIGHT — 4½ feet above the ground; the level at which the diameter of a tree is measured; abbr. D.B.H. (diameter breast height).

BREEZEWAY — A roofed connection between a house and garage, which is screened rather than walled-in to allow a breeze to blow through; diminishes the risk of fire spreading from garage to house.

BRICK — A block of clay which has been moulded and baked, used with cement to build.

BRIDGE LOAN — A short-term mortgage given on one property in order to purchase another without contingencies; funds from the sale of the first property must be used to pay-off the loan; may also be converted to a second mortgage on the property purchased.

BRIDLE PATH — A small road (usually unpaved) used for horseback riding usually established by easement in the original conditions, covenants and restrictions of a subdivided property to cover all the parcels.

BROKERAGE — The business of acting on behalf of another (principal) for a fee or commission; the fee itself.

BROKER, REAL ESTATE — The state licensed individual, who after passing an examination, is charged with the responsibility of overseeing the actions of licensed real estate associates within his/her own business.

BROOM CLEAN — A term which states that a building has been swept clean; describes the physical condition of a structure when turned over to the new buyer (or tenant).

BUFFER ZONE — A piece of land separating two other pieces which are being used differently (such as industrial land near a residential area).

BUILDING — Any enclosed, permanent structure for the purpose of sheltering animals, goods or people.

BUILDING AND LOAN ASSOCIATION — A financial institution which uses savings deposits collected from members to finance the purchase and improvement of real estate.

BUILDING CODE — The set of laws regulating the design and construction of buildings (which includes building materials, repairs, remodeling, intended uses of the structure, etc.).

BUILDING CONTRACT — A legally binding written agreement which establishes the terms and conditions (such as price and completion date) under which a structure is to be built.

BUILDING LINE (SETBACK LINE) — A boundary set by zoning law, beyond which further construction is prohibited; prevents construction too close to the street and other neighboring buildings; creates uniformity and enhances value.

BUILDING PAPER — A waterproof, fiber reinforced paper used as thermal insulation and a vapor barrier in construction of floors, walls, or roofs.

BUILDING PERMIT — Permission to build or make improvements, granted in writing by local government.

BUILDING RESIDUAL TECHNIQUE — A method of appraising income property (land with a building that is rented out) which separates the amount of net income earned by the structure from the value of the land, to determine the value of the whole property; can be used in figuring accrued depreciation.

BUILDING RESTRICTIONS — Limitations on construction relating to size and type of structure imposed by government zoning acts or private parties (when stated in the deed by a former owner or when land is leased).

BUILD TO SUIT — A leasing arrangement whereby the lessor builds or makes improvements to fit the specifications of the tenant in return for a lease commitment (usually long term).

BUILT-INS — Fixtures, appliances, such as stove, dishwasher, etc., and furnishings (shelves and cabinets) which are permanently attached to a building and are included in the property when sold.

BULK ZONING — See area zoning.

BUNDLE OF RIGHTS — The group of rights that pass with ownership of property; includes the right to assign, transfer, sell, encumber, use, enjoy, etc.

BUSINESS CYCLE — Recurring fluctuations in prosperity; the pattern of increases and decreases in economic activity.

BUSINESS OPORTUNITY — A business for sale which may include real estate.

BUTT JOINT — A square connection or joint formed when two boards (members) intersect at right angles.

BUYER'S MARKET — A condition in which there are more properties up for sale than there are potential buyers, hence, terms of purchase are more favorable for buyers.

BUY-SELL AGREEMENT — An agreement between business partners that one party will buy and another will sell an interest in the business at a specified price in the event of a specified occurrence.

BY-LAWS — The rules adopted by an association or corporation governing its general organization and management.

BY-PASS — A highway that passes around the outer perimeter of a city or town to avoid heavy traffic flow in the central business area.

C

CABANA — A small open structure located on a beach or near a swimming pool, used for changing clothes; Spanish word for cabin.

CABINET WORK — Inside carpentry work that is attached or built-in to a structure; usually sanded, varnished and/or painted to a smooth finish.

CADASTRAL MAP — A map showing the legal boundaries and ownership of real estate, used in the title recording to define its limits.

C.A.E. (Certified Assessment Evaluator) — An assessor certified by the International Association of Assessing Officers after completion of training and testing to evaluate property values for tax purposes.

CAISSON — A protective, sealed chamber in which men perform construction labor for underwater foundations and structures.

CALL — The designations used in a metes and bounds description of property for one angle or the distance of a line. Sample: E 75° S 45' (1 call).

CAMBER — The curving of a load-bearing, structural support to give it added strength.

CAMINO — The Spanish word for street; Camino Real means highway.

CANCELLATION CLAUSE — A stated agreement in a contract specifying the terms under which the parties may terminate it.

CANTILEVER — A strong, inflexible structural span which supports itself from one end only.

CANTILEVER BRIDGE — Characterized by two over-hanging supports connecting to each other or a suspended span.

CAPACITY — An individual's legal ability to form a valid contract or conduct business, determined by age, soundness of mind or designated authority (such as through power of attorney).

CAPE COD HOUSE — A steep-roofed, rectangular style of architecture characterized by dorm windows and a central chimney originating in 18th century New England.

CAPITA — People counted individually; per capita means per person.

CAPITAL — A person's or corporation's wealth available to generate more income.

CAPITAL ASSETS — Resources of a fixed nature such as machinery and equipment, or the value of one's interest or equity in real or personal property which can be borrowed against to create more wealth, or which in and of itself generates income.

CAPITAL CHARGES — Money needed to make payments of principal and interest on investments.

CAPITAL EXPENDITURES — Funds expended for the improvement or repair of real property structures or equipment held for long term investment. (Usually in excess of $100 on property retained longer than a year).

CAPITAL GAINS — The taxable difference on capital assets between cost (less depreciation) and sales price, after deduction of expenses for repairs and improvements.

CAPITALIZATION — A method of arriving at the current market value of an investment such as income property, using a commonly accepted rate of return on similar properties, then capitalizing net operating income by dividing it by the accepted rate of capitalization.

C

CAPITALIZATION APPROACH — A method used in appraisal to determine the present value of rental property by discounting the estimated net income to be received over the estimated life of the structure.

CAPITALIZATION RATE — (Cap Rate) The discount percentage rate used in the capitalization or income approach to determine the present value of income property or improvements to it.

CAPITALIZE — Arriving at the current value of money to be derived from estimated or fixed future income.

CAPITALIZED VALUE — The appraised value of property using the capitalization approach.

CAPITAL STOCK — The inferred worth of a corporation determined by the amount of money invested by shareholders.

CAPITAL SURPLUS — Surplus money derived from sources other than earned income; such as the profit from the sale at a premium of a corporation's own stock or donated stock.

CAPRICIOUS VALUE — An appraisal term for the seemingly arbitrary or emotional value of property which does not reflect fair market value.

CARAVAN — A regular inspection tour of newly listed properties by a brokerage sales staff.

CARPORT — A shelter without walls for parking cars, sometimes attached to structures.

CARRYING CHARGES — Taxes, interest and other charges due on a building under construction or vacant in a period when it is not generating income.

CASE LAW — Law arrived at by a judge's decision.

CASH ACCOUNTING — A seldom used method of recording revenues and expenses when the transfer of cash takes place, rather than in the period when the funds were earned or the expenses incurred.

CASH ASSETS — Funds on hand for conducting daily business.

CASH DISCOUNT — A reduction in a bill offered as an incentive to pay it prior to a certain date.

CASH FLOW — Income derived over and above all expenses and debt service, including depreciation allowances.

CASHIER'S CHECK — A check issued by a bank against it's own funds rather than a depositor's; usually required instead of a personal check in real estate transactions.

CASH OUT — A term used in listings to indicate a seller's desire for full payment of his equity or interest upon closing of a sale; in a contract or purchase money mortgage, the early repayment of the balance owing.

CASH RENT — Rent paid in cash rather than with a percentage of the crops of goods produced on the land.

CASH SALE — A sale where the full purchase price is paid in cash or by check.

CASING — The frame and trim molding around doors, windows cabinets; a section of pipe.

CATTLE GUARD — Widely spaced metal bars set in the earth over which cattle will not walk.

CATWALK — A narrow, permanent bridge or elevated footpath leading to otherwise inaccessible areas, such as the ceiling of a stage.

CAUSEWAY — An elevated passage or road over lowlands or water.

CAVEAT EMPTOR — A legal phrase which means "Let the buyer beware" and implies that the buyer takes the risk when purchasing items (without the protection of warranties) and should inspect them carefully prior to purchase.

CAVITY WALL — A hollow wall, usually of stone with a continuous "dead-space" in the center which provides thermal insulation.

CC&R'S — (Covenants, Conditions & Restrictions) Limitations placed on property to assure uniformity in use.

CELLAR — The floor of a building which lies fully or partially beneath ground level; usually used as storage area.

CEMENT BLOCK — A concrete building block.

C

CENTRAL ASSESSMENT — A method of stabilizing assessments; used when property under one ownership is located in several assessment districts (as with public utilities).

CENTRAL BUSINESS DISTRICT — The downtown area of a city where major businesses, government offices and professional services are located.

CENTRAL CITY — A city in the center of a cluster of other cities; the center or downtown area of a city.

CERTIFICATE OF DEPOSIT — (Time Certificate of Deposit or C.D.). A type of savings account where withdrawals are restricted and funds (above a stated minimum amount) are kept for a specified length of time in return for a higher interest rate than what is offered on passbook accounts.

CERTIFICATE OF ELIGIBILITY — A document issued by the Veterans Admission stating that a person is eligible for a VA guaranteed real estate loan.

CERTIFICATE OF OCCUPANCY — A document from a government building department which states that a structure was built or remodeled in compliance with regulations and is ready for occupancy.

CERTIFICATE OF REDEMPTION — A document showing that an owner has bought back (redeemed) his property after its sale by court order.

CERTIFICATE OF SALE — (Certificate of Purchase). A document given to the buyer at a sale by court order allowing transfer of title to begin when the sale is confirmed by the court, if the previous owner does not buy it back (redeem it).

CERTIFICATE OF TITLE — A written statement by an attorney which affirms that the ownership of property is established as indicated by the title documents (used only in some areas).

CERTIFIED CHECK — A personal check which a bank guarantees payment of, by holding funds in the person's account and refusing to accept stop payments.

CERTIFIED COPY — A copy which is guaranteed to be accurate by one holding the original.

CERTIFIED COMMERCIAL INVESTMENT MEMBER — (CCIM) A designation given by the Real Estate National Marketing Institute to real estate associates achieving a particular level of knowledge through training and tests on the subjects of exchanging, leasing, managing developing and syndicating commercial and investment real estate.

CERTIFIED PROPERTY MANAGER (CPM) — The highest title bestowed on professional real estate managers by the Institute of Real Estate Management of the National Association of Realtors after completion of certain requirements.

CERTIFIED RESIDENTIAL BROKER — (CRB) The designation given to real estate associates active in real estate management after achieving a level of competence demonstrated through testing and training.

CESSPOOL — An underground pit for storing sewage.

CHAIN OF TITLE — The historical order of all events or actions affecting the ownership of a piece of real estate.

CHAIN, ENGINEER'S — A chain of 100 wire links, each one foot long.

CHAIN, SURVEYOR'S — A chain four rods or 66 feet long, each link being 7.92 inches in length. One acre is equal to 10 square chains.

CHAIN STORE — One of a series of centrally owned and managed retail outlets which are similar in appearance, inventory and service.

CHANGE OF NAME — A legal process by which a person or corporation may change their name and which is reflected on documents executed prior to the change using the words "alias", "AKA" (also known as), "formerly" or "WATA" (who acquired title as).

CHANNEL — A gutter or decorative groove; a tube or pipe; a natural waterway (or the deep, navigable part); a means of communicating.

CHANNELIZATION — The direction of traffic flow through an area by means of islands, one-way streets, signs, etc.

CHATTEL — An article of personal property.

CHATTEL MORTGAGE — A loan secured by personal property.

CHATTEL PERSONAL — Movable personal property.

CHATTEL REAL — Any interest in real estate less than ownership, such as a lease.

CHECK ROW — A means of planting vegetation to form a checkerboard pattern.

CHIMNEY — A fireproof, vertical structure, extending above the roof of a building which carries smoke from a fireplace or furnace to the outside air.

CHIMNEY BACK — The fireproof rear wall which lines a fireplace, chimney or furnace.

C HORIZON — The substratum or layer of rock lying beneath the A and B horizons which is not affected by surface conditions.

CHOSE IN ACTION — The right to possession or to legal action required to gain possession of anything held by another (includes repayment of debt).

CHOSE IN POSSESSION — Actual possession of a thing as opposed to the right to possess.

CIENAGA — A swamp or marsh formed by hidden springs (Spanish).

CINDER BLOCK — A lightweight brick or block formed from a mixture of ashes and an adhesive substance (cement); used for walls and partitions.

CIRCLEHEAD WINDOW — A semicircular, decorative window (immovable) used above a door to admit light.

CIRCUIT BREAKER — An electrical safety device which automatically shuts off the current (by opening or "breaking" the circuit) in the event of an overload; differs from a fuse in that it does not need replacement after the circuit is broken.

CIRCULATING FIREPLACE — A fireplace containing a metal form and air ducts that distribute heat through convection (difference in air density).

CIRCULATION PATTERN — The pattern of regular traffic flow between residential and business areas.

CIRCUMFERENTIAL HIGHWAY — (By-pass). A highway which skirts the outer area of a city to avoid heavily congested traffic areas.

CISTERN — A storage tank for rain water, either above or below ground.

CITY — Generally, a large incorporated town; specifically, a municipality with a state charter, operated by the vote of elected representatives.

CITY PLAN — A large, detailed map of a city showing streets and important urban features (such as major buildings and parks).

CIVIL ACTION — A legal action not related to criminal acts.

CIVIL LAW — Laws regarding private rights, established by a state or nation for its own jurisdiction; law derived from old Roman Laws.

CLAIM — A statement or allegation; a declaration of a right or a demand.

CLAPBOARD — Exterior wooden siding on frame houses, consisting of overlapped (on the long edges) horizontal boards.

CLARIFIER — An underground purification system which neutralizes toxic wastes in water before it is channeled to a sewer or septic tank.

CLASS ACTION — A legal proceeding initiated on behalf of a group of people with a similar claim against a single person or entity (i.e. corporation).

CLASSIFIED PROPERTY TAX — A tax on real property which varies in rate according to how it will be used as described by zoning classification.

CLEARANCE — Distance allowed (either vertically or horizontally) for the passage of a vehicle beneath a structure, or between other structural elements to allow for placement of unobstructed movement (such as between a door and its frame); the clearing of land in preparation for improvements.

CLEAR HEADWAY — The distance from the floor to the top of a door frame or other overhead framing support.

CLEAR LUMBER — High quality wood lacking knots or other blemishes.

C

CLEAR SPAN — An interior floor area free of support columns, walls or posts, located between such structural supports.

CLEAR TITLE — (Marketable Title) Evidence of ownership which is free of defects such as undisclosed financial liens or pending legal proceedings; title without clouds.

CLERESTORY — The upper part of a wall with windows which allow light into a room with a high ceiling (most common in churches or cathedrals).

CLOSING — The completion of a real estate transaction when all documents are recorded and title has passed to the buyer; a general sales reference to the point where the buyer is asked to purchase; the last dimension (or call) given in a metes and bounds description of a property.

CLOSING COSTS — Expenses incurred by both buyer and seller in closing a real estate transaction, such as loan fees, mortgage insurance, inspections and document filing, which must be added to the purchase price or subtracted from funds received.

CLOSING STATEMENT — (Settlement Statement). A final, detailed account prepared by an escrow agent, lender or other closing agent of all cash received, charges and credits involved in closing a real estate transaction which lists the final settlement between buyer and seller.

CLOUD ON TITLE — (Cloud) Any claim, lien or document which makes the title (evidence of ownership) to real property seem dubious and renders it unmarketable until the "cloud" is removed by a quit claim deed or legal action.

CLOVERLEAF — A cloverleaf-shaped intersection (used for freeways) which facilitates the intersecting of traffic without the use of signal lights by routing vehicles over loop-shaped ramps onto roads at different levels.

CLOVERLEAFING — The solicitation of new listings or buyers in a cloverleaf pattern around a property which has already been sold or listed.

CLUSTER HOUSING — The construction of houses in a development on abnormally small lots with a large, common recreation area.

CO-ADMINISTRATOR — One who is named with another (or others) to manage the estate of a person who dies leaving no will.

COAST — Land bordering on or near an ocean.

COSTAL COMMISSION — A committee established to regulate construction along coastal areas.

CODE — A complete body of laws, thoroughly covering a specific subject, such as a building code.

CODE OF ETHICS — Standards of conduct in regard to fair treatment and responsibility toward the public by professionals.

CODICIL — An attachment or addendum to a will.

CO-EXECUTOR — A person named to share the responsibility for carrying out the terms of a will.

COFFERDAM — A temporary caisson.

COINSURANCE — An insurance policy, generally covering a large risk, which uses more than one insurer to diffuse the risk (each assumes a portion of the liability).

COLLAPSIBLE CORPORATION — A company which is sold, generating funds from the capital gains on the stock rather than through the profitable sale of its product. An example would be when a corporation develops a revolutionary battery-powered car; then instead of selling the car they sell the corporation.

COLLATERAL — Personal or real property accompanying a mortgage as security for the loan; proper meaning is parallel or along-side (i.e. Cousins to cousins in line of descent).

COLLECTOR STREET — Arterial street leading to main highway.

COLOR OF TITLE — Ownership right which appears to be clear but which is actually flawed through improper passing of title.

COLUMN FOOTINGS — The foot or base for a structural support usually made of concrete.

COMBED (STRIATED) PLYWOOD — Interior plywood with parallel grooves.

COMBINATION DOOR — Exterior doors with glass or screen inserts that can be changed for variations in weather.

COMBINATION SEWER — A dual sewer used for both raw sewage and run-off.

COMBINATION WINDOW — A window in which glass or screen inserts may be interchanged for various weather conditions.

COMMERCIAL ACRE — The actual amount of land used for building after dedication of streets and park areas in a subdivision.

COMMERCIAL BANK — An institution where checking accounts as well as savings and loan services are offered. Usually involved in short term financing for construction and personal property as compared to a savings and loan institution making long-term mortgages on real property.

COMMERCIAL PROPERTY — Business zoned property.

COMMINGLING — The deliberate or inadvertent combining of business operating funds with money deposited as down-payments on real estate. Money held on deposit should be placed in a separate trust account, otherwise the broker may lose his license.

COMMISSION — The percentage of a sale price or rental on real estate charged by the brokerage firm for services rendered.

COMMITMENT — A statement in writing made by lenders to borrowers that they will loan a certain amount of money at a particular rate of interest; a statement contained in a preliminary title report that indicates a title insurance company is willing to insure title to real property.

COMMON AREA — The land owned jointly with other title holders in planned unit developments, subdivisions or condominums, usually managed by a homeowner's association.

COMMON ELEMENTS — The undivided interest of condominium or planned unit development owner's in exterior walls, elevators, recreational facilities, etc.

COMMON LAW — See Case Law.

COMMON PROFITS — The money left over after payment of expenses for operation of a business or homeowner's association which provides for maintenance of common areas.

COMMON PROPERTY — Public land in which all persons are free to enjoy equal rights, such as a park.

COMMUNITY PROPERTY — Property acquired jointly by both husband and wife, and owned in common.

COMPACTION — The compacting together of layers of earth which may result from lack of organic, humus material in the soil or from heavy equipment packing it down. Compacted ground does not readily absorb moisture and may inhibit percolation of sewage. Tests are required prior to issuance of a building permit to determine compaction.

COMPACTOR, TRASH — An appliance, sometimes built in to a home, for compressing paper and tin-can waste materials.

COMPARABLES — Real estate of similar size and kind compared to a subject property in order to arrive at a market value.

COMPARATIVE METHOD — Method of appraisal using price per square foot comparisons to determine cost of replacement.

COMPASS ROOF — An arched roof formed from rafters, collar beams and trusses.

COMPENSATING BALANCE — Money deposited with a lender, by a borrower or third party, to create a line of credit or enhance the borrower's standing in order to secure a loan.

COMPENSATION — Money received for the taking of one's property through condemnation or for damages resulting from injury or abuse to one's rights.

COMPETENT — The legal capacity to act or form contracts as established by age or soundness of mind.

COMPLETION BOND — Posted by a developer or land-owner to assure parties of interest that the property will be free of liens and assessments after completion of structures according to specifications.

COMPONENT CONSTRUCTION — A method of mass manufacturing structures or portions thereof; referred to as modular construction or prefabrication.

COMPOUND INTEREST — Interest paid on accrued interest along with the principal balance.

COMPREHENSIVE COMMUNITY PLAN — An overall city or town zoning plan projecting future use of property in order to eliminate spot zoning and preserve valuable farm land; a plan for zoning that coordinates compatible uses of land in a given area.

COMPUTER LISTING — Listing information fed into a central computer bank for use by a large number of brokers.

CONCAVE — A 180° or less angle or curve.

CONCILIATION AGREEMENT — An agreement made by a party charged with discrimination or a similar illegal act to compensate for injuries to the damaged party; an affirmative action such as renting or selling to an injured party who has been discriminated against.

CONCRETE — A combination of cement and aggregates blended with water and poured into a form, hardening as it dries.

CONDEMNATION — The government process of taking private land for public use while paying equitable compensation for it.

CONDENSATION — Particles of moisture forming on a surface as a result of temperature changes.

CONDITION — The act of limiting or restricting the use or sale of property by placing conditions on the transfer of title; making it subject to an event occurring or not occurring.

CONDITIONAL COMMITMENT — A tentative agreement by a lender to loan money on real property subject to approval of the buyer. (Most commonly associated with FHA loans.)

CONDITIONAL SALES CONTRACT — (Land Contract) A contract under which the seller retains title to the property until the conditions of sale have been met and the balance of money owed has been paid in full.

CONDOMINIUM — One of two or more residential units where the interior air space and walls are owned individually in fee simple, while the ground, exterior walls and other structures are owned in common with other title holders, their interests therein being undivided.

CONDOMINIUM OWNER'S ASSOCIATION — A group of owners whose association is established under the Covenants, Conditions and Restrictions of a condominium subdivision plan in order to provide for maintenance and use of common property, such as exterior walls, roofs and recreational facilities.

CONDUIT — A pipe or other channel used to protect electrical wires or carry water.

CONFIGURATION — The arrangement or form of materials making a pattern.

CONFORMITY, PRINCIPLE OF — An appraising term stating that uniformity of structures throughout a certain area produces highest value.

CONGRUOUS — In appraisal, a property which is in harmony with its surroundings.

CONSEQUENTIAL DAMAGE — A monetary award made to an injured party as the result of loss in value to property through the act of an adjoining property owner or public body.

CONSERVATION — The protecting of natural resources such as forests, farm land, etc., through government regulation.

CONSIDERATION — A fee, which may be anything of legal value which is used to bind a contract by attracting another party to enter into it.

CONSTANT PAYMENT MORTGAGE — The repayment of a loan in equal monthly installments, part of which is applied to interest and the remainder to principal.

CONSTRUCTION COST — Total expenses of building, such as land, labor, materials, profits and overhead.

CONSTRUCTION LOAN — A loan, usually short-term, used to finance the original building of a structure on vacant land, or additions thereto.

CONSTRUCTIVE EVICTION — The interference by a

landlord of a tenant's right to use leased property; not an actual eviction; the right of possession of a third party which prohibits a buyer from quiet enjoyment of the property granted by the seller.

CONSUMATE — In real estate, the closing of a sale at which time a seller's interest is passed to the buyer through a deed, contract or other instrument of conveyance.

C

CONTACT CEILING — A ceiling which is attached directly to the materials above it rather than to furring strips.

CONTIGUOUS — Adjoining or nearby.

CONTINGENCY — A condition in a contract or agreement which must occur before the instrument becomes binding, such as "subject to adequate financing".

CONTINGENT FEES — A charge to be made for services and paid only if certain conditions are met, such as a real estate commission which is paid only if the property is sold.

CONTINUATION — Bringing a title search up to the current date.

CONTRACT — A written promise which is legally enforceable when made between competent parties, to perform or refrain from performing particular acts.

CONTRACTOR — The individual or entity who is paid to take overall responsibility for all phases in the construction process of a building or a development.

CONTRACTUAL LIEN — A lien, such as a mortgage or deed of trust, placed on a property voluntarily by its owner.

CONTROL DATA — Information which is used to isolate the reasons for a difference in value when comparing similar real properties.

CONVECTION — The movement of air caused by differences in air or water temperatures. For instance, in heating, lighter warm air rises to displace cold air, which has more density.

CONVENTIONAL LOAN — Mortgage money obtained through a savings and loan or bank which is not insured by a government program such as FHA or VA.

CONVERSION — The changing of one type of property into another. For instance, converting a multiple unit apartment complex into a condominium subdivision in order to sell the units individually. Legal process must be followed.

CONVEX — A curve or angle in excess of 180°.

CONVEYANCE — A document through which an interest in real estate is transferred, such as deed or mortgage.

COOPERATING BROKER — A broker who sells another broker's listing and receives part of the commission.

COOPERATIVE APARTMENT — An apartment where the right to occupy is purchased as stock from a corporation owning the complex in its entirety.

CO-ORDINATES — In surveying for legal descriptions, the designations given for intersecting points, planes or lines.

COPING — A protective covering on top of a wall, curved to shed water.

CORE — The inner layer of plywood.

CORE SPACE — The calculated amount of floor space that is considered rentable in an office building.

CORK TILE — A floor covering made of granulated bark and synthetics that is sealed with a protective coating.

CORNER BEAD — A metal strip sealed into corners with plaster to give it strength.

CORNER BOARDS — On a wood structure, the trim board against which the exterior siding is fitted to corners.

CORNER INFLUENCE — The difference in real estate values between a lot situated on or near a corner intersected by two streets, as compared to a lot fronted by one street.

CORNICE — An ornamental trim or molding around the top of a wall, window or door.

CORPORATION — An association of people considered by law as separate entity formed to conduct business.

CORPORATION COCK — A valve placed near the main gas or water service line.

CORPOREAL PROPERTY — Real or personal property that can be touched, as compared to incorporeal property, such as an idea.

CORRECTION DEED — A deed issued to correct a factual error.

CORRECTION LINES — The line used in government surveys, at 24 mile intervals, to allow for corrections needed because of earth curvature, usually a full 6 miles between north and south range lines.

CORRUGATED — Wrinkled, ridged or grooved material, such as glass, aluminum, paneling, etc.

COST APPROACH — The estimated reproduction cost of property, including land and minus depreciation for appraisal purposes.

COST OF REPRODUCTION — The cost of duplicating property using similar materials.

COTENANCY — Refers to tenancy in common or joint tenancy.

COTTAGE — A small rural or summer dwelling.

COUNSELOR — An attorney; in real estate the designation given to someone with expertise and experience by the American Society of Real Estate Counselors.

COUNTER FLASHING — A sheet metal strip used on roof peaks and valleys to prevent water leakage.

COUNTER OFFER — An adjunct to a sales agreement which specifies additional terms under which a seller or buyer would agree to accept an original offer to sell or buy.

COUNTER SINK — The boring of a depression in wood which allows the head of a screw to be flush with the surface.

COURT — A small enclosed area bordered by two or more walls; a room where legal proceedings are held; a short street or cul de sac.

COVE LIGHTING — Hidden lighting.

COVENANT — A written promise between parties.

COVENANT OF QUIET ENJOYMENT — A promise made by a seller or lessor to a buyer or lessee warranting freedom from disturbance caused by defective title.

COVENANTS, CONDITIONS AND RESTRICTIONS
— (CC&R's) See page 23.

COWL — The covering or hood over a vent pipe or soil stack which protects against the entrance of moisture.

CRADLING — The support frame for a curved or vaulted ceiling.

CRATERING — Collapsed paint film caused by trapped air bubbles during application.

CRAWL — The movement of wet paint created by poor bonding with the surface.

CRAWL SPACE — An interior area of space in a structure that permits access to plumbing and heating fixtures.

CREATIVE SELLING — Establishing a market for property by locating a buyer who has need of it.

CREDIT — The ability of a borrower to repay based on past history.

CREDITOR — A person or entity to whom money is owed.

CREDIT REPORT — A report on the past credit history of a person desiring to borrow money to establish his ability to repay.

CREDIT UNION — An association of depositors who buy stock in the cooperative enabling them to borrow money at a lower rate of interest on short-term loans, and receive a higher rate of interest on deposits.

CRIPPLE STUD — A short length of wood in a building frame beneath a window or above a door.

CROSS BEAM — A support beam running across the center of a building or structure.

CROSS VENTILATION — The movement of air through a building created by windows and doors being placed on opposite sides of a room.

CRUISE — An estimate of the amount and kind of standing timber on a parcel of land required to establish property value.

CRV (CERTIFICATE OF REASONABLE VALUE) — A Veteran's Administration appraisal required prior to their guaranteeing a loan.

CUBBY — A small hiding place, room or storage area.

CUL DE SAC — A short, pear-shaped street opening at one end only.

CURB CUTS — The section of curb removed to make a flared driveway entrance.

CURLING — The curving or warping of wood caused by moisture absorption or improper drying.

D

CURRENT ASSETS — The amount of cash on hand or expected to be received within a short period of time from accounts receivable.

CURRENT LIABILITIES — Debts payable within a short period of time.

CURTAIL SCHEDULE — The amounts and dates of principal payments due on a loan balance.

CUSTOM BUILDER — One who has been hired to build a structure according to a buyer's design specifications.

CUT-OVER LAND — Forest land which has had the original growth of timber removed.

CUTS — The changing of land configuration by removal or addition of earth in order to construct roads, buildings or flood-control terraces.

CYCLICAL MOVEMENT — The change in national economic conditions as a reflection of supply and demand for money and goods; from recession to boom period to recession again.

D

DAMAGES — The monetary value attached to an injury resulting from the loss of property through condemnation or otherwise.

DAMP COURSE — A moisture barrier of tile, metal or dense limestone, etc., used to prevent upward or downward seepage.

DAMPER — In a fireplace or furnace, the flat disc which can be turned to regulate air flow over the fire.

DAMPING MATERIAL — A sound absorbing material used to reduce noise radiation.

DATA PLANT — A lender's, appraiser's or title insurance company's stock of information on real estate.

DATE OF AGREEMENT — If not stated on the face of the agreement, the date signed, recorded or established by award.

DATE OF COMPLETION — The date an owner may occupy the premises after certification by an architect that the terms of the contract have been substantially completed.

DATUM LINE — A line established by building codes from which heights and depths are measured.

DAY — A section in a leaded or stained glass window.

DAYLIGHT GLASS — A blue glass that absorbs radiation through the red spectrum to give a daylight effect.

DBA — (Doing Business As) Refers to the name under which a business operates.

DEAD AIR SPACE — Air that cannot circulate, such as between the panes of a double-glassed (thermal) window.

DEAD BOLT — A sliding bar lock, usually operated by a handle or door key.

DEAD-END STREET — A street that ends and does not lead to another street.

DEAD LOAD — The fixed weight of a structure and its attached equipment and fixtures.

DEAD RENT — The base rent of a commercial space charged in conjunction with a percentage lease.

DEAD WALL — An empty wall.

DEALER — An Internal Revenue Service designation for someone who buys and sells real estate as a business as opposed to an investor, the profit from which is taxed as ordinary income rather than capital gains.

DEBENTURES — A loan obligation issued without security at a fixed rate of interest to be repaid after a term of years or upon termination of the company.

DEBIT — A sum of money owed to another party; an accounting term.

DEBTOR'S POSITION — The amount of an owner's interest in property over and above the amount of liens outstanding.

DEBT SERVICE — On real property, the amount owed for mortgages or trust deeds.

DECENTRALIZATION — Movement of businesses and people to the suburbs from a central business area.

DECK — A flat, usually unenclosed surface.

DECLARATION OF RESTRICTIONS — A document filed by a developer to regulate a subdivision.

DECLARATION OF TRUST — A document in which one party promises to hold legal title for use of another.

DECLINING BALANCE — See Depreciation .

DEDICATION — The donation of private property to the public for use as streets, parks, etc.

DEED — A document used to transfer title of real property.

DEED MONEY ESCROW — A third party escrow with whom money is deposited until the seller delivers a deed to property.

DEED OF TRUST — See Trust Deed .

DEED, QUITCLAIM — A deed without warrants; passes a grantor's interest only.

DEED, WARRANTY — A deed in which a grantor insures a grantee that title is free to pass.

DEED RESTRICTIONS — A deed which binds all future owners of a property to abide by its restrictions for use of the property.

DEFAULT — The failure of a party or parties to abide by the terms of a contract; i.e. mortgage, deed of trust, sale agreement, etc.

DEFAULT JUDGMENT — A judgment arrived at when someone fails to appear in court as required.

DEFEASANCE — A deed containing conditions which, if met, will cancel the conveyance.

DEFECTIVE TITLE — Title which has been transferred under false pretenses or does not contain all the necessary elements to make a contract binding.

DEFECT OF RECORD — A publicly recorded encumbrance such as an easement, mortgage, judgment, deed of trust or other lien.

DEFERRED COMMISSION — An earned commission on which payment is delayed.

DEFERRED MAINTENANCE — The existing need for repairs on property.

DEFERRED PAYMENTS — Future installments on debt.

DEFICIENCY JUDGMENT — The difference between the amount received on a foreclosure sale and the borrower's liability, if the sale does not entirely cure the debt. Judgment is made for the total amount from which the amount received is subtracted.

DEFLATION — As opposed to inflation, money becomes more valuable.

DEGREE — A one point measure in a circle of 360°; 60 minutes 1 degree.

DEHUMIDIFIER — A machine that removes moisture from the air.

DELIVERY — The actual transfer of the right of possession which takes place upon recording of the deed, or delivering it to a buyer or his representative.

DEMAND — The need for material goods as established by the number of people wishing to purchase; the written statement of a lender indicating the amount owing on a mortgage or trust deed.

DEMAND NOTE — A promissory note which becomes due upon request by the lender, rather than at a specified time.

DEMISE — The assignment of one's interest in an estate (real property) for a period of years, for life or at will.

DEMOGRAPHY — The study of population figures which is used to determine a market for a particular product or store.

DEN — A small room used for work or leisure.

DENSITY — The amount of people in a particular area.

DEPARTMENT OF HOUSING AND URBAN DEVELOPMENT — (HUD) The federal department responsible for public housing, urban renewal, model cities, rehabilitation under which jurisdiction the Federal Housing Administration, the Government National Mortgage Association and the Office of Interstate Land Sales Registration is under.

DEPARTMENT OF REAL ESTATE — The state government department that regulates and licenses persons involved in the business of real estate.

DEPLETION — The loss of value to an asset caused by waste or exhaustion.

DEPOSIT — Money placed with a seller or his representative by a buyer to show sincere desire to purchase property; referred to as earnest money.

DEPRECIATION — The declining value of a structure. The loss from original value is determined by age and deterioriation; on income producing property, it may be deducted for income tax purposes. Various methods are used.

DEPRECIATION RATE — The rate at which a property (excluding land) is declining in value.

DEPRESSION — A period in a business cycle when the supply of a product exceeds the demand bringing about lower productivity and prices and higher unemployment.

DEPTH CURVE — A graph used in appraisal which shows the decreasing value of a lot from front footage to rear footage.

DESCENT — As determined by law, the person or persons in a line of succession who become owners of property after someone's death.

DESIST AND REFRAIN — A command by someone of public authority stating that a particular act must be stopped and refrained from in the future.

DETACHED DWELLING — A building or housing unit that is separated by open space; single family detached housing as compared to attached condominium units.

DETERIORATION — The slow aging of a structure through wear and tear caused by exposure to weather and constant use.

DEVELOPED AREA — Land on which structures have been built.

DEVELOPER — Usually an owner of land who creates a subdivision from raw land by providng for public utilities, streets, etc., after which lots are sold to builders.

DEVELOPMENT — An area of land on which homes or other buildings may be built after installation of streets, sewers and other utilities.

DEVILING — Making plaster rough.

DEVISE — Real property passed down through a will.

DIAGONAL — A timber placed at an opposing angle to another.

DIFFUSED LIGHT — Light emitted indirectly and not from one dominating source.

DIFFUSER — Any apparatus that spreads light or sound.

DILUVIUM — Deposits of earth resulting from flooding.

DIMENSION SHINGLES — Shingles all of one size.

DIMMER — A device that controls levels of light by varying the electrical current.

DIRECT ACTING THERMOSTAT — A thermostat which shuts off or turns on when a particular temperature is reached.

DIRECTIONAL GROWTH — The pattern of growth that a community appears to be following; considered by lenders making mortgages based on the future value of real property.

DIRECT REDUCTION MORTGAGE — Mortgages on which fixed amounts are paid on the principal while the amount paid on interest varies according to the balance owed; unequal installment mortgages.

DISBURSEMENT — The distribution of money upon the closing of a sale or during the course of an escrow.

DISCOUNT — Reducing the face value of negotiable paper or instrument in order to sell it; prepaid interest by the seller which allows the lender a profit margin on resale.

DISCRIMINATION — Making a decision which shows favor based on a person's affiliation with a group or class of people.

DISINTERMEDIATION — The private investment by individuals of their own money in government bonds or corporate securities which creates a scarcity of mortgage money. Savings and loan associations and banks depend on the deposits of private investors for money to loan on mortgages.

DISPOSAL FIELD — The series of clay tiles and gravel through which sanitary wastes from a septic tank drain and filter out.

DISSOLUTION — The act of canceling or annulling a contract or business arrangement.

DISTRESS SALE — The forced sale of property because of financial problems, foreclosure or to settle an estate.

DIVIDED INTEREST — The separate interests of an owner, mortgagee or lessee in the same property.

DIVIDER — A decorative room partitioning device in the form of wood dowels or bookshelves, etc., that sets apart or divides a particular area of a room, such as the entryway from the living room.

DOCUMENTARY TAX STAMPS — A revenue stamp which represents the amount of fee paid for transferring title from one owner to the next, charged by the state; not a recording fee.

DOCUMENTARY TRANSFER TAX — A tax charged by the state or county for transfer of title based on the sale price of property.

DOMINANT ESTATE — (Tenement) The property which receives the benefit of an easement; dominates the property giving the easement (servient tenement).

DOUBLE DECLINING BALANCE — An accelerated method of depreciation which uses 125%, 150% or 200% of the straight line rate in the early years of a property life.

DOUBLE ESCROW — Used when one person is both buying and selling the same property within a few day's time or concurrently and uses the money from the sale to make the purchase; not legal in some states.

DOWNPAYMENT — The amount of a buyer's original investment in property; the balance is financed.

DOWNZONING — Zoning which decreases the number of units per acre that may be built, such as occurs when multi-family is rezoned to single family residential.

DRAGNET CLAUSE — Establishes real property as collateral for an existing debt in a mortgage or deed of trust.

DRAW — Loan money received by a borrower after completion of particular stages of construction; money paid on the basis of future income.

DRY MORTGAGE — A mortgage which becomes a lien against the property only and not a liability of the borrower.

DUAL AGENCY — Occurring when both buyer and seller are represented by one broker, each paying a commission; both parties must be made aware of the dual representation.

DUE ON SALE CLAUSE — (Alienation) Requires that the loan be paid in full upon the occurrence of a certain event, such as transfer of title.

DUPLEX — A two unit dwelling.

DURESS — Pressure applied to another party in order to force them to perform an act, such as signing a contract. Illegal; makes the contract void.

DWELLING UNIT — A shelter occupied by one family unit; usually refers to apartment houses.

E

EARLY AMERICAN — Commonly refers to a style of furniture or decor which includes antiques.

EARNEST MONEY — Money deposited as a partial downpayment on real property to demonstrate an earnest desire to purchase it.

EARNINGS — Money acquired for the performance of labor or a service.

EASEMENT — The right to cross over or through another's property.

EASEMENT APPURTENANT — The actual easement granted to another property for the benefit of its owner which passes with title and actually is attached to the property.

EASEMENT IN GROSS — An easement granted to a company rather than an individual property, such as for public utilities.

EASEMENT OF NECESSITY — A right-of-way granted by court order to create access, usually for landlocked property.

ECONOMIC BASE ANALYSIS — A measurement of population and employment patterns to determine future economic values of real estate.

ECONOMIC LIFE — The term of time over which a structure is estimated to be profitably useable; the remainder thereof.

ECONOMIC OBSOLESCENCE — Actual depreciation of property created by economic, social or environmental factors and not caused by the property itself.

ECONOMIC RENT — Rent that is established by supply and demand, the market rental value of a property.

EFFECTIVE AGE — Age established by the condition of property rather than its actual age, considering the need for rehabilitation or maintenance.

EFFECTIVE GROSS INCOME — Total rental income received before deduction of expenses, allowing for vacancies.

EFFICIENCY UNIT — A one room apartment with kitchen and bedroom combined.

EFFLUENT — Sewage after it has been partially treated; water running from a main stream.

EGRESS — A property exit.

EJECTMENT — The act of legally removing someone from property or enforcing the terms of the right to possess.

ELECTION OF REMEDIES — A choice of alternative actions by the injured party upon breach of a contract.

EMBLEMENTS — Crops grown by a tenant which may be removed upon expiration of a lease.

EMPTY-NESTER — A parent or parents whose children have grown up and left the family unit.

EMINENT DOMAIN — The power vested in a government body to take private property for public use.

ENCROACHMENT — The partial or whole, unauthorized construction of a fence, building or other structure on another's property.

ENCUMBRANCE — A voluntary or involuntary lien or liability placed on real property as security for a debt.

ENDORSEMENT — The assignment by the holder of a negotiable instrument, such as a note or check, to another by affixing their signature to the back.

ENTITY — An association or body of people acting as one, such as a corporation or government; a separated being, not an individual.

ENVIRONMENT — The area around a property which may affect its value.

ENVIRONMENTAL DEFICIENCY — A detrimental factor which has an affect on property value, such as poorly planned zoning, inadequate street or sewer facilities, etc.

ENVIRONMENTAL IMPACT — The effect that a commercial or residential development, etc., will have on surrounding facilities or resources, such as the effect of increased population and their use of water, sewers, schools.

ENVIRONMENTAL PROTECTION AGENCY — (EPA) The federal agency charged with protecting natural resources.

EQUAL CREDIT OPPORTUNITY ACT — The federal law which prohibits lenders from discriminating against women applying for loans; their income contributions must be considered in the qualifying process, irregardless of whether they are of child-bearing age.

EQUALIZATION BOARD — See Board of Equalization.

EQUAL RIGHT OF POSSESSION — Granted to all parties of interest under a tenancy in common deed.

EQUITABLE CONVERSION — The law that establishes the title of an owner purchasing property under contract prior to it being paid in full.

EQUITABLE SERVITUDE — The doctrine that establishes an owner's right to enforce the covenants, conditions and restrictions of a developed area for uniform useage; the right of a homeowner in a tract of single family dwellings to enforce conformity in unit size or prevent the building of a multi-family structure.

EQUITABLE TITLE — Ownership without legal title, such as a vendee under a land contract.

EQUITY — The amount of an owner's free and clear interest in real property; the difference between the amount owed on it and the market value; a legal interpretation of fairness not based on the law alone.

EQUITY OF REDEMPTION — The right of a party in default to pay back payments owed on principal, interest and costs.

EQUITY PURCHASER — A buyer who assumes or takes over an existing mortgage or deed of trust, and whose downpayment equals the seller's equity.

ERRORS AND OMISSIONS INSURANCE — Covers mistakes, errors and negligence which might occur in the selling and listing actions of a broker or sales agents.

ESCALATION CLAUSE — A clause in a lease, option or mortgage which calls for an increase in rent, sale price or interest rate according to the current rate of inflation, market value or expenses.

ESCHEAT — The reverting of title to property to the state when the owner dies and there are no known heirs.

ESCROW — A neutral entity acting upon instructions of two or more interested principals; a holder and disburser of funds and documents for the benefit of others.

ESTATE — The degree of interest a person has in real property.

ESTIMATE OF VALUE — An opinion of worth given by a real estate associate not certified as an appraiser, as to the current market value of real property.

ESTOPPEL — The inability to impose a legal right because of a prior action to assert a claim, defense or right.

EXCHANGE — The concurrent and reciprocal transfer of real property for the purpose of deferring taxes owed on gain; to qualify as a tax-free exchange, certain guidelines must be followed.

EXCLUSIVE AGENCY AGREEMENT — A listing agreement in which a seller obligates himself to pay a commission to a specified brokerage firm if the sale is made; the owner reserves the right to sell the property himself without paying a commission.

EXCLUSIVE RIGHT TO SELL AGREEMENT — A listing agreement whereby the seller obligates himself to pay a commission to a specified brokerage firm, irregardless of who makes the sale; the owner does not reserve the right to sell the property himself without paying a commission.

EXECUTORY CONTRACT — An agreement whose terms are not entirely fulfilled at the time of sale, such as a land contract.

EXISTING MORTGAGE — The balance of a mortgage on real property.

EXPOSURE — The amount of advertising done, or the amount of potential buyers and renters notified of a property for sale or rent; the view toward which a property faces, such as east, west, etc.

EXPRESS — Clearly defined.

EXPROPRIATION — The taking of private property by an entity such as a government. See emminent domain.

EXTENDED COVERAGE — Coverage of casualty due to losses not ordinarily included in a standard insurance policy.

EXTENDER CLAUSE — An automatic renewal clause in a listing agreement.

F

FAE — Forced air electric furnace.

FAG — Forced air gas furnace.

FACE BRICK — A shiny exterior brick of even quality and size.

FACE VALUE — The amount stated on the face of a note or mortgage, not considering discount.

FACTOR — A discount note, mortgage or contract buyer; an agent who acts on behalf of a principal; a buyer of accounts receivable at a discount.

FAIR VALUE — The price a purchaser is warranted in paying for a property, not necessarily the price at which it is sold or market value.

FAIR CREDIT REPORTING ACT — The federal act which grants an individual the right to see the contents of his file at a credit bureau and which governs the recording of inaccurate information in that file.

FAIR MARKET VALUE — The estimated price arrived at by making comparisons with other similar properties that a seller and buyer may agree upon.

FALSE ADVERTISING — Any advertising which misrepresents a real property in some way; cause for the revocation of a broker's or sales agent's license.

FAMILY ROOM — A second but less formal living room in a home.

FANNIE MAE — Federal National Mortgage Association. A wholesale buyer for first mortgages (secondary lender).

FARM — In real estate, an area in which a salesperson cultivates contacts for the purpose of obtaining listings, etc.

FEASIBILITY SURVEY — A study of an area which is being considered for development to determine the probability of financial success.

FEDERAL FAIR HOUSING LAW — That portion of the Civil Rights Act prohibiting racial and other types of discrimination concered with housing.

FEDERAL HOME LOAN BANK — A bank or savings and loan chartered under the Federal Home Bank Act of 1932 which may obtain funds for first mortgages on homes from regional banks who have a fairly constant supply of money; they contain the word "federal" in their name.

FEDERAL HOUSING ADMINISTRATION — (FHA) An agency under the control of the Housing and Urban Development Commission authorized to insure first mortgages on homes so that lenders are able to make larger loans to individuals than they would qualify for under conventional financing.

FEDERAL NATIONAL MORTGAGE CORPORATION — See Fannie Mae.

FEDERAL SAVINGS AND LOAN ASSOCIATION — See Federal Home Loan Bank.

FEDERAL TAX LIEN — A claim against property for taxes that are outstanding, such as estate or income; not automatically cleared by a foreclosure proceeding.

F

FEE — A non-refundable charge for a service rendered; refers to a type of ownership in real property.

FEE SIMPLE ABSOLUTE — The greatest interest one may possess in real property; the most complete and least restricted.

FELT PAPER — A black, tarred paper used for insulation and as a sub-layer beneath a roof.

F.H.A. — See Federal Housing Administration.

FHLMC — (Freddie Mac). Federal Home Loan Mortgage Corporation which buys first mortgages insured by the government and conventionally; a wholesale first mortgage buyer or secondary lender.

FICTITIOUS DOCUMENT — A document which has standard use within a state or county; to save expenses, a standard form is filed and all later similar documents recorded or used incorporate its general terms and provisions.

FIDUCIARY — An implied relationship of trust.

FIELD TILE — Tiles laid beneath a structure to prevent water seepage upward into a foundation.

FILE — The act of recording an original legal document with a government body, making it part of the public record.

FILTERING DOWN PROCESS — Original high quality homes owned by high and middle income occupants that have, through obsolescence, become available to lower income families.

FINANCIAL INFORMATION SHEET — A form used by real estate associates to gather information from potential buyers to establish their ability to purchase a particular property.

FINANCIAL STATEMENT — Lists a person's or company's assets and liabilities; required by lending institutions for use in conjunction with an application, credit report, etc., to qualify a borrower for a loan.

FINANCING COSTS — The cost of borrowing money, including interest and loan fees.

FINANCE FEE — Loan fee.

FINANCING STATEMENT — A document recording a

lien, used in place of a chattel mortgage, inventory lien or pledge in some states.

FINDER'S FEE — Compensation paid to a party for locating property; normally considered a commission which may be paid only to licensed real estate associates.

FIRE WALL — An inner wall filled with fire-retardant material to prohibit the spread of fire, such as between a home and an attached garage.

FIRM COMMITMENT — A definite assurance that an event will occur, such as a loan will be granted, title insurance will be issued, a sale will transpire.

F

FIRST MORTGAGE — A mortgage on property whose rights are superior to all others; the first mortgage to be recorded on property.

FIRST RIGHT OF REFUSAL — The lessee's right given by the lessor to have the first opportunity to purchase a property under specific terms and conditions.

FIRST USER — The first owner of property and is the first to put the improvements to use; a tax term signifying higher rates of depreciation.

FIXED ASSETS — Buildings or heavy machinery needed to operate a business and which are permanent in nature.

FIXED CHARGES — Interest or other recurring charges.

FIXING-UP EXPENSES — Those expenses incurred for wallpaper, paint, etc., to ready a property for sale; must be paid for within 90 days prior to sale agreement or 30 days thereafter, to qualify as tax deductible.

FIXTURES — Appliances, drapery rods, fireplace screens, etc., which are attached to real property by means of hardware and which are considered legally to be a part of that property and may not be removed upon sale, except by exclusion in an agreement or removal prior to offering a property for sale.

FLASHING — The metal sheathing used around chimneys and vent pipes to prevent water seepage.

FLAG LOT — A lot formed in the shape of a flag with pole.

FLAT — An antequated term for a one level living unit which has been replaced by duplex, triplex, four-plex, etc.

FLEXIBLE PAYMENT MORTGAGE — A loan on which payment installments are unequal and which takes into consideration a borrower's current financial position and his ability to make larger payments in future years. Either the interest rate or the principal payments may gradually increase.

FLIGHT PATTERN — The pattern an airplane flys when landing or taking off from an airport.

FLOAT RATE — An interest rate that is not fixed at one percentage but which "floats" between points.

FLOOD INSURANCE — A federally subsidized flood insurance required by lenders in areas where there is a risk of floods.

FLOODPLANE — Low-lying land adjacent to rivers subject to flooding.

FLOOR FURNACE — A radiant heat furnace placed in a floor.

FLOOR LOAN — The lowest amount a lender commits itself to loan on a commercial structure based on the degree of occupancy by tenants.

FLOOR TIME — The rotated time a sales agent spends in a real estate office answering the telephone and dealing with walk-in customers, usually established monthly.

FLOWAGE EASEMENT — The common law easement which provides for passage of water from high ground across lower ground.

FLUE — A chimney channel through which gases and fumes escape from a furnace.

FNMA — See Fannie Mae.

FOOTING — The cement base of a foundation wall, usually partially or wholly buried, which supports and secures the main structure.

FORBEARANCE — An arrangement worked out by a borrower in default on payments to satisfy a mortgage or deed of trust, in exchange for the lender refraining from legal action.

FORCED AIR FURNACE — A furnace with a fan installed in it to blow the heated air throughout a structure.

FORCED SALE — The sale of property, usually at less than full market value, because of financial hardship when a mortgage or deed of trust is in default.

FORECLOSURE — The elimination of all rights of ownership and interest in a property through legal process after said owner has failed to satisfy the terms of a mortgage, trust deed or contract.

FORFEITURE — Giving up the right to something of value, such as consideration or downpayment, under specified conditions. A lessee may forfeit a downpayment under a lease/option agreement by not exercising the option within the specified time period.

FORGERY — Illegally duplicating, altering or falsifying documents.

FORMICA — A trade name for a vinyl (synthetic) material used on countertops, paneling, etc, inside a structure.

FORUM SHOPPING CLAUSE — A clause in an agreement or contract which specifies the state and the laws which will govern it.

FOYER — The entryway of a home or other building.

FRACTIONAL APPRAISAL — The separate appraisal of a particular interest in property, such as the leasehold interest or the value of improvements.

FRAME CONSTRUCTION — Wooden structural supports on which the exterior of a building is mounted.

FRAMEHOUSE — A house built with wood supports and exterior wood siding.

FRANCHISE — Individual ownership of a business combined with central control. The individual owner pays for the use of the name and often gets benefits of advertising.

FRAUD — Misrepresentation, by an act or a statement, in order to trick another party for the purpose of gain.

FREE AND CLEAR — Real estate which has no liens and encumbrances attached to it.

FREEHOLD — An interest in real property that has no specified or exact termination date, such as a life estate that will terminate upon the death of a named party.

FRONT FOOT COST — A valuation of real estate which is based on the amount of footage along a main road; used in commercial real estate appraisal.

FRONT MONEY — The amount of money a developer has available in cash for expenses and land costs prior to development of a project, as opposed to the amount he needs to borrow to complete it.

FULL DISCLOSURE — The act of a seller or broker which informs a buyer of all known defects or other pertinent information which may affect his decision to purchase a particular property.

FULL PERFORMANCE — Occurs when all parties have complied with the terms of an agreement or contract.

FUNCTIONAL — The use of property for its originally intended purpose.

FUNCTIONAL OBSOLESCENCE — The lack of use of property for its originally intended purpose due to improvements or advancements made since its creation.

FUNDS — Available money.

FURNITURE AND FIXTURES — Refers to business furniture and fixtures which may be depreciated.

FURRING — Leveling wood or metal strips on which wall panels or ceiling tiles may be mounted.

FUSE — A glass enclosed metal strip which melts when an electrical circuit is overloaded, breaking the current, rather than letting it overheat to a danger level.

FUTURE ACQUIRED PROPERTY — A clause in loan agreement or mortgage which states that property acquired after the initial signing will be encumbered as additional security.

FUTURE ADVANCE CLAUSE — Permits a borrower to obtain more money on a loan security at some future date without negotiating a new instrument or mortgaging additional property.

FUTURE BENEFITS — Anticipated benefits an owner will receive.

FUTURE INTEREST — A current interest in property without the right of possession until a later time.

G

GAIN — Taxable profit.

GAP FINANCING — Temporary financing of the difference between a floor loan and the total amount required for an investment. Bridges the gap of time involved between a sale and closing and permits a buyer to utilize his equity in one property to purchase another, prior to the final sale of the first.

GARBAGE DISPOSAL — Located beneath a sink, it is a small tank device with teeth that grinds large chunks of garbage into small pieces which may be flushed into a sewer with water, for disposal.

GARDEN APARTMENT — A multiple dwelling unit which allows room for a lawn and garden areas outdoors.

GARNISHMENT — A legal cure for a debt which allows a creditor to take money or property belonging to a debtor when it is in the possession of a third party, such as wages owed by an employer to an employee (debtor). Must follow legal process.

GENERAL BENEFITS — Benefits created by the condemnation of property, not actually taken.

GENERAL CONTRACTOR — The main contractor for a building or project who may hire smaller more specialized subcontractors to perform actual labor, etc.; the primary project coordinator.

GENERAL INDEX — A book which lists liens against individuals which may have an effect on the purchase of real property, such as a lien against a borrower which may diminish his ability to repay a long term mortgage; used by title insurance companies.

GENERAL LIEN — Rather than attaching to a specific property, a general lien attaches to all property of a particular person; must be pre-arranged by agreement.

GENERAL PLAN RESTRICTIONS — See Covenants, Conditions and Restrictions.

GEODETIC SYSTEM — A system of nationwide survey marks (bench) at longitude and latitude points, created by the federal government.

GEORGIAN ARCHITECTURE — Characterized by windows on the first floor which almost touch the ground.

GERRYMANDER — A method of establishing political power for an illegal purpose, such as to prevent racial integration.

GIFT DEED — A deed given for nominal consideration.

G.I. LOAN — See Veteran's Administration.

GINGERBREAD WORK — Intricately designed woodwork on homes built in the late 1800's and early 1900's.

GIRDER — A metal support for the floor of a building or other structure, such as a bridge.

GLASS BLOCK — A decorative, hollow glass building block, not used for support.

GLASS-WOOL INSULATION — A spun-glass heat insulator.

GNMA — Government National Mortgage Association. A secondary lender or wholesale mortgage buyer specializing in FHA loans. Also called Ginnie Mae.

GOOD FAITH — An act performed on the basis of trust and with no intent to misrepresent or defraud.

GOOD WILL — The intangible value of a business based upon past utilization or purchase of services or goods by its customers who will return to do repeat business.

GORE — A triangle-shaped piece of land.

GOVERNMENT LOTS — Waterfront property or other odd pieces of land which could not be divided evenly into government survey sections.

GOVERNMENT NATIONAL MORTGAGE ASSOCIATION — See GNMA.

GOVERNMENT PATENT — The original method of conveying government-owned land to individuals.

GOVERNMENT SURVEY — The survey by the government that created or established townships and sections.

GRACE PERIOD — A short period of time during which a late payment may be paid without being considered delinquent.

GRADE — The angle at which land slopes, determined by degrees.

GRADED LEASE — A lease in which rent payments are increased gradually at specified time periods.

GRADED TAX — A tax rate that places greater value on land and less on improvements in order to encourage development.

G.R.I. — Graduate, Realtors Institute. A designation given by the National Board of Realtors to a licensee who successfully completes their educational program.

GRADUATED LEASE — A lease agreement where rent increases are stepped-up gradually over a period of time.

G

GRANDFATHER CLAUSE — A common term given to the law that permits the continued use of a property according to older laws which have been changed to outlaw that particular use, such as the sale of a lot which does not conform to present day zoning laws, but which was subdivided in the records prior to the change in zoning laws.

GRAND LIST — New England tax roll.

GRANT — Give or transfer.

GRANT DEED — A general type of deed, containing warranties, used to transfer real property.

GRANTEE — One who is given title under a deed.

GRANTOR — One who is gives title to another under a deed.

GRANTOR-GRANTEE INDEX — The county records of real property transfers according to names, rather than descriptions.

GRATUITY — A voluntary reward to another in exchange for a service, such as a tip.

GRAVITY FURNACE — A furnace whose heat moves or flows as a result in differences in air density between warm and cold; one moves toward the other naturally.

GRAYING OF AMERICA — The increase in ratios of older people to young in America created by the fact that more people are surviving to age 75.

GREEN BELT — An area in a subdivision preserved for grass, etc.

GREEN LUMBER — Wood that is not fully dried or has been recently cut and not kiln dried; tends to warp if used prematurely in construction.

GREENSBORO PLAN — A plan designed to speed the process of obtaining an FHA loan.

GRID — An overlay of horizontal lines used to coordinate statistics.

GRIDIRON PATTERN — A rectangular or square plan of streets in a subdivision.

GROSS — Total amount before deductions.

GROSS ACRE — A full acre of 43,560 sq. ft. before deducting the amount used for streets, etc.

GROSS AREA — A measurement calculated from the exterior dimensions of a building.

GROSS EFFECTIVE INCOME — See adjusted gross income.

GROSS INCOME — Total income before deductions.

GROSS INCOME MULTIPLIER — A general appraising rule of thumb which when multiplied by the annual gross income of a property will estimate the market value.

GROSS LEASE — A lease under which a lessor pays for all or part of the expenses of the leased area, such as insurance, taxes, etc.

GROSS PROFIT — Profit figured prior to deduction of expenses.

GROUND LEASE — Lease of ground space without buildings.

GROUND RENT — Rent paid for raw land only.

GROUND WATER — Water in the top layer of earth and subsoil.

GUARANTEED SALE — A guarantee in a listing agreement which states that after a specified length of time, if the subject property has not been sold, the brokerage firm will buy it, under particular terms and conditions, usually at a substantial discount from the listed price.

GUARANTEED MORTGAGE — A mortgage whose

principal and interest is guaranteed to be repaid to the original lender by a secondary lender who charges a fee for managing the mortgage and making the guarantee.

GYPSUM — Hydrated calcium sulphate, an ingredient used in plaster and cement.

H

HABENDUM — A statement in a legal document which describes the type of ownership, such as life or fee estate.

HABITABLE — Of a condition fit to live in.

HACIENDA — A house or an establishment, such as a farm or an estate.

HALF BATH — A bathroom with a commode and sink only.

HALF-TIMBERED — The decorative effect of exposed timbers associated with Spanish, Italian or Bavarian architecture.

HAND — The width of an average size man's hand, usually 4 inches.

HANGOUT — The amount of time difference between a lease and a loan term, such as occurs when a lender makes a loan for 15 years to a lessee whose lease will expire in 10 years. The 5 year difference is referred to as a hangout.

HARD MONEY MORTGAGE — A mortgage given in return for cash, as opposed to a purchase money mortgage incurred to facilitate the sale of real property.

HARDPAN — A packed, non-porous soil layer that is difficult for water or a shovel to penetrate.

HARDWOOD — Wood from slow growing trees such as maple, oak and walnut.

HARMONIOUS — In balance, coordinated.

HEADER — A beam or stud which fits horizontally over a doorway to stablize the frame.

HEARTH — The floor of a fireplace.

HEATER — Usually refers to a floor or space heater rather than a furnace.

HEAT PUMP — A combination heating, cooling apparatus which exchanges warm air for cold, and vice versa.

HEIGHT DENSITY — The maximum allowed height of a building as established by zoning restrictions.

HEIR — One who receives the estate of a deceased person who left no will.

HEREDITAMENTS — Inheritable property.

HETEROGENEOUS — An area of assorted types and styles of property which detracts from overall value.

HIDDEN RISK — The potential for a flaw in title that is not easily detected, such as would be created by a forged signature on a deed.

HIGHEST AND BEST USE — The utilization of land in a manner that would generate the greatest return on investment on it.

HIGH-RISE — An apartment building with a great number of levels, as opposed to a low-rise with four stories or less.

HIGHWAY FRONTAGE — For the purpose of estimating real property value, the amount of footage that fronts a main road or highway.

HIP ROOF — A pyramid-shaped roof familiar to church steeples and garages.

HISTORICAL COST — The original construction cost of a building.

HISTORIC STRUCTURE — A designation established under the Tax Reform Act of 1976 to make available tax incentives for the preservation of old buildings or structures.

HOLDBACK — Part of a loan held by the lender until certain conditions have been met, such as to bring a property to good repair under FHA or VA appraisal specifications.

HOLDER IN DUE COURSE — The holder of a note or check that is no longer good.

HOLD HARMLESS AGREEMENT — See indemnity agreement.

HOLDING ESCROW — An escrow established to hold a deed until fulfillment of the terms under a land contract; may also be used to collect payments due under the contract and pay encumbrance such as taxes and insurance.

HOLDING PERIOD — The amount of time a taxpayer holds a property before resale; determines whether it is a long or short term capital gain for tax purposes.

HOLD OVER TENANT — A tenant who occupies property beyond the term of a lease.

HOME OWNERS' ASSOCIATION — An association of owners in a condominium, planned unit or residential subdivision established to provide management for and maintenance of property in which they own an undivided, common interest.

HOW — Homeowners' Warranty. A program of insurance under the National Association of Home Builders that provides protection to a new home buyer for 10 years against defects in construction.

HOMESTEAD EXEMPTION — A reduction in property tax set by statute in some states for older homeowners; may also exempt a personal residence from claims of creditors.

HOME WARRANTY INSURANCE — Insurance, normally purchased by a seller, to protect a buyer from failures in plumbing, heating and electrical apparatus during their first year of residence.

HOMOGENEOUS — Of similar kind and style; in estimating property value, conformity of use and style enhance overall worth.

HORIZONTAL PROPERTY LAW — The label for the first condominium law which was created in Puerto Rico.

HOT TUB — An open-topped tank approximately 4 to 6 feet in diameter filled with hot, circulating water for relaxation and recreation.

HOT WATER HEATING SYSTEM — Warm air generated from hot water heated in a boiler and circulated through a system of pipes.

HOUSE RULES — Regulations established by a condominum or planned unit development homeowners' association through their board of directors to promote harmonious use of the common ground and facilities.

HOUSE SEWER — A home's public sewer service.

HOUSING STARTS — Houses on which construction has been started; counted to determine the potential supply and demand for money, material and labor.

HUD — See Department of Housing and Urban Development.

HUMIDIFIER — An apparatus commonly attached to furnaces to add moisture to dry, heated air in a building.

HUNDRED PERCENT LOCATION — The best location possible for a particular building project or the land of greatest value in a given area; an appraisal term.

HYDROGRAPH — An apparatus which measures the depth or flow of water in a well or stream.

HYPOTHECATE — The pledging of a specific piece of property as security for a loan without actually giving up possession of it.

I

ILLUVIATION — See eluviation.

IMPLIED — Indirectly inferred.

IMPLIED AGENCY — Established by the conduct of a principal rather than by written agreement.

IMPLIED CONTRACT — A contract in which the terms are not expressly stated but which all parties understand by inference.

IMPLIED WARRANTY OF HABITABILITY — The inferred responsibility of a landlord to maintain rented premises in a habitable condition.

IMPOUND ACCOUNT — See Reserve account.

IMPROVED LAND — Land either on site improvements or off-site utilities, such as sewer, water and electrical power.

IMPROVED VALUE — The combined total worth of land and its improvements.

IMPROVEMENTS — Structures, buildings or facilities placed on or in land, including streets, sewers, water lines, etc.

IMPUTED INTEREST — An interest rate established by law when it has not been stated on the face of a negotiable instrument.

INACTIVE LICENSEE — A real estate agent who has

voluntarily placed his license in an inactive state with the real estate commission, rather than activating it by placing it with a broker's office.

INCHOATE — Not completely finished.

INCINERATOR — An enclosed trash burner usually located indoors.

INCOME — Money received for services performed or as profit or gain from an investment.

INCOME APPROACH — Estimating income after expenses on a rental or income property to determine its value; an appraisal method.

INCOME AVERAGING — Averaging income over several years to reduce the tax rate rather than paying taxes on the full amount earned during one year.

INCOME PRICE RATIO — Equals the net income divided by the sales price of a property.

INCOME PROPERTY — Any property which is not totally occupied by an owner as his personal residence and which is used to produce income, such as a rental property.

INCOMPETENT — The inability because of mental defect to manage one's personal or business affairs with intelligent reasoning, thereby disqualifying them from entering into legally binding contracts.

INCORPOREAL RIGHTS — The right to access rather than to possession, such as through an esement; an intangible right.

INCREASING AND DIMINISHING RETURNS — An economic theory based on increased productivity resulting in increased profit, and vice versa. When an increase in production is proportionately greater than the addition, the return increases; the return will diminish if production is proportionately less than the addition.

INCREMENT — An additional increase.

INCUMBRANCE — See Encumbrance.

INCURABLE DEPRECIATION — Diminished value of property caused when it becomes too expensive to repair it; there is no cure for it.

INDEMNITY CLAUSE — An clause in an agreement which guarantees one party they will be held harmless (not responsible) for any damages or expenses resulting from the actions by another party to the agreement.

INDENTURE DEED — A deed signed by the buyer (grantee) as well as the seller (grantor) agreeing to specific terms and conditions, such as to abide by the covenants and conditions stated or to assume liability for a mortgage on the property covered.

INDEPENDENT APPRAISAL — An appraisal made by a disinterested neutral party for a fee.

INDEPENDENT CONTRACTOR — Any person who does not receive a set salary or hourly wage, but rather a commission or fee for services performed and who is independently responsible for payment of their own taxes (self-employed); most real estate salespeople are independent contractors.

INDEX LEASE — A lease arrangement that provides for increases in rent according to increases in the consumer price index.

INDIVIDUAL RETIREMENT ACCOUNT — A savings program for self-employed (independent contractors) individuals which provides them with retirement funds in later years by sheltering a portion of current income from taxes when it is deposited in an IRA account.

INDIRECT CONSTRUCTION COSTS — Costs not directly paid out for material and labor, such as loan fees and interest, taxes and insurance.

INDORSEMENT — See Endorsement.

INDUSTRIAL MULTIPLE — See Multiple listing.

INDUSTRIAL PARK — A subdivided industrial area customized to the needs of its users.

INDUSTRIAL TAX EXEMPTION — A tax break given to entice businesses or industry into an area.

INFLATION — A period of rapid increase in costs of products and services, lessening the value of money.

INGRESS AND EGRESS — Access to and from land.

IN GROSS — An easement given to a person rather than one which is attached to and passes with land.

INJUNCTION — A court order which halts or prevents a particular action from occurring.

INLIQUIDITY — The inability of assets to be easily or quickly sold for cash.

INNER CITY — An economic rather than geographic location; an area of a large city that is occupied by low-income residents, usually plaqued by a high crime rate as a result of unrest.

IN PERPETUITY — Lasting forever.

IN PERSONAM — Affecting particular people rather than property.

INSOLVENCY — Inability to repay debt.

INSPECTION — Viewing goods or property to detect potential defects.

INSTALLMENT CONTRACT — An agreement providing for possession of property prior to paying for it in full and which establishes a payment program, usually monthly.

INSTALLMENT NOTE — A promissory note which is to be repaid over a period of time, rather than in one lump sum.

INSTALLMENT SALE — A tax term referring to a qualified sale; a land contract repaid over two years or more and which accepts no more than 30% of the purchase price during the first year and 30% during the second year, the balance to be repaid thereafter.

INSTITUTE OF REAL ESTATE MANAGEMENT — The training school which offers Certified Property Manager (C.P.M.) designations to qualified individuals.

INSTITUTIONAL LENDERS — Lenders who are in the business of loaning money, as opposed to private individuals or companies lending to employees.

INSTRUMENT — A deed, mortgage, lease or promissory note used to convey an interest in property.

INSULATION — A material that prevents the transfer of heat, cold, sound or electricity, such as glass.

INSURABLE INTEREST — An interest in property, which if destroyed would cause a financial loss.

INSURANCE RISK — The degree of hazard involved in insuring a particular property which determines the cost of insuring.

INSURED MORTGAGE — Insurance purchased by a borrower to guarantee a mortgagee (lender) that in the event of default, the mortgage balance will be fully repaid.

INTANGIBLE — Something which has a value but cannot be physically touched, such as business goodwill or an easement.

INTEREST — Rent paid for the use of money; a legal share or right in an item of value.

INTEREST EXTRA RATE — Interest charged on a note according to the decrease in principal balance; payments decrease on interest, but remain equal on principal.

INTEREST INCLUDED NOTE — Equal monthly installment payments on which the amount applied to interest decreases while the amount applied to principal increases.

INTEREST RATE — An annual percentage of a loan amount, charged as a fee for the use of the money.

INTERIM FINANCING — See Gap financing.

INTERIOR LOT — A lot in a subdivision, not on a corner.

INTERPLEADER — A legal action filed by a neutral party to settle a dispute or a claim between two opposing parties who have an interest in the same property.

INTERSTATE LAND SALES — Federal regulation regarding the sale of land to buyers residing in other states, which allows them three days to rescind a purchase agreement after signing it.

INTER VIVOS — Involving living persons.

INTESTATE — Without a will.

INTRINSIC VALUE — The worth of an item itself; such as the worth of the paper a deed is printed on rather than the value of the property stated in it.

INURE — To be used.

INVENTORY — A list of merchandise or property.

INVERSE CONDEMNATION — Property not actually taken by the government, but which loses value as a result of the taking of nearby property; the loss must be compensated for just as though it were condemned.

INVESTMENT — Utilizing money in a manner that will cause the original amount to increase.

INVESTMENT CREDIT — A federal tax regulation that allows 10% of the amount invested in equipment to be used for business, as a deduction from taxes otherwise owed; the equipment must have an economic life of seven years or longer.

INVESTMENT INTEREST — Interest costs on business investments.

INVESTMENT PROPERTY — Property purchased to increase income and at the same time shelter it from high tax rates by taking advantage of depreciation and expense deductions.

INVESTMENT TRUST — A business which sells stock in itself to generate money for investment in real estate, stocks, etc.

INVESTMENT YIELD — The amount of money gained compared to the amount of money initially placed in an investment.

INVOLUNTARY CONVERSION — Exchanging condemned property for other real property without paying a tax on the gain, within three years of the actual taking.

INVOLUNTARY LIEN — A lien made against property without the owner's consent, such as in a tax lien, judgment, etc.

IRA — See Individual Retirement Account.

IRON-SAFE CLAUSE — A fire insurance policy clause that requires records to be kept in a fire-proof safe.

IRREVOCABLE — An agreement that may not be rescinded.

IRRIGATION DISTRICT — A local authority empowered to levy assessments in exchange for supplying irrigation water.

JACK POST — A support post used in older houses to raise sagging floors or level them; the jack itself screws up or down inside the post.

JACOB'S LADDER — A suspended wooden ladder with rope sides used for attic access, etc.

JACUZZI — A trade name for a ceramic tiled pool of hot circulating water usually attached to a swimming pool or built into a bathroom.

JERRY-BUILT — A building or structure of inferior quality.

JOINDER — Binding together by some legal process.

JOINT AND SEVERAL — A debt which a creditor may sue either one party separately or several jointly for repayment.

JOINT NOTE — A promissory note signed by more than one party who may be held liable for payment.

JOINT PROTECTION POLICY — Title insurance which insures both the lender and the owner together.

JOINT TENANCY — Equal rights of ownership of the same property, by two or more title holders (joint tenants) whose interest automatically passes after death to the other owners.

JOINTURE — An agreement between a man and his wife that entitles her to a life estate in property after his death.

JUDGMENT — A court decision awarding the payment of money which may be satisfied by placing a lien on property.

JUDICIAL FORECLOSURE — The court ordered sale of real property which has been defaulted upon, in order to remove liens against it.

JUNIOR LIEN — A lien which takes second place to another recorded lien.

JUNIOR MORTGAGE — A mortgage of secondary status to another mortgage.

JUST COMPENSATION — The amount paid to a property owner under condemnation proceedings.

JUSTIFIED PRICE — The price an informed and prudent buyer would be warranted in paying for property; may not be market price.

K

KEOGH PLAN — A plan allowing self-employed people to deposit money into a retirement fund account and defer paying income tax upon it until it is withdrawn after they reach retirement age when their income bracket will be substantially lower.

KEY LOT — A strategically located lot important to the best utilization of an adjoining lot; its location increases its value.

KEYMAN INSURANCE — Insurance placed on an important business figure based on his value to the company and the loss which would be incurred by his absence; required by some lenders making loans to small companies with a few key people running the operation.

KICKERS — Equity participation required by a lender before making a loan, such as the payment of rent, profit or extra interest to the lender; may violate usury laws.

KIN — Blood relatives.

KNOCK DOWN — Portable window frames or partitions which are easily taken apart for moving.

J
K
L

L

LACHES — Time delays which extend a legal action or claim beyond the limits allowed under the statute of limitations in order to bring about the loss of another's right to make a claim or pursue legal action.

LALLY COLUMNS — Steel support columns filled with cement.

LAMINATE — Layering of materials as a means of construction or for its own protection, such as plywood glued together in layers or plastic covering a surface.

LAND BANK — Property purchased to preserve it for future development, by a government body.

LAND CONTRACT — An installment agreement involving the sale of land, with or without improvements. The seller (vendor) retains title until fully paid, while the buyer (vendee) is said to have equitable title during the term of the agreement.

LAND GRANT — Land given by the federal government to a local government, business or person.

LAND LEASEBACK — Land leased back by a seller from a buyer who in addition subordinates his interest so that 100% financing may be obtained for both the land and the development of it.

LANDLOCKED PARCEL — A piece of land that has no legal means of being entered or exited; frequently created by leftover land condemned to build a highway.

LANDOWNER'S ROYALTY — The owner's percentage of interest in oil and gas removed from his property on a lease agreement.

LAND RESIDUAL TECHNIQUE — An appraisal method used to determine the value of land without its improvements.

LAND-SERVICE ROAD — A road usually running parallel to a limited access highway, which serves the property adjacent to it and connects parcels otherwise cut-off by the highway.

LAND TRUST CERTIFICATE — A document which states that land is being held by a trustee for the benefit of an owner.

LAND USE INTENSITY — The percentage ratio of land to buildings, allowed by zoning laws.

LAND USE PLANNING — Local development of a plan for the future use of land within its jurisdiction, established by zoning laws.

LAND VALUE MAP — A map showing the value of property in a given area according to square footage, front footage or acres.

LAP SIDING — Long boards, usually cedar, which overlap to create exterior siding for a building.

LATE CHARGE — A charge made for payments that are overdue after a grace period.

LATENT DEFECT BOND — A bond required by F H A

assuring a borrower that any defects resulting from poor construction which may be undetected until after closing will be taken care of by the builder or prior owner.

LATERAL — A projection receiving support from that which it adjoins.

LATERAL SUPPORT — A landowner's right to the natural support of adjoining land which may not be hampered by the adjoining owner removing or weakening in any way that support.

LAYOUT — A plan showing the arrangement of rooms in a building, etc.

LEACHING — Filtering sewage wastes through porous materials, such as sand, gravel, tile, etc.

LEAD LENDER — A lender who services and processes a loan, but who may find a larger lender to actually finance the loan.

LEASE — An agreement where a renter establishes a legal interest in property for a specified period of time under certain conditions, and for consideration (rent).

LEASEBACK — A pre-arranged lease agreement between a buyer and seller under which the property purchased is leased back to the seller.

LEASEHOLD — An interest in property established under a lease agreement for a fixed period of time; the lease itself is considered personal property.

LEASEHOLD INTEREST — The difference between the amount of remaining interest a lessee might have in property according to the total rent owed under the lease, and the amount the lessee would have to pay to rent like property.

LEASEHOLD VALUE — The worth of a leasehold interest under a long term lease when the amount paid is less than what a lessee would have to pay to lease a similar property.

LEASE WITH OPTION TO BUY — A lease under which a lessee has the future right to purchase the leased property under specified conditions.

LEGAL DESCRIPTION — A legally accepted method of identifying property, such as lot, block and subdivision or a metes and bounds description.

LEGAL OWNER — The person or persons whose names are specified on the last deed executed granting them title even though they may have passed possession on to another who has right of possession under a land contract. A land contract owner is said to have equitable title while the land contract holder has legal title.

LEGAL RATE OF INTEREST — A rate of interest whose limit is established by law, usually state statute.

LENDER — Anyone who loans money to another; under a deed of trust the mortgagee (beneficiary).

LESSEE — The (tenant) party who has right of possession under a lease.

LESSEE'S INTEREST — The appraised value of a lessee's interest in order to determine its worth for assignment or sale.

LESSOR — The owner who grants the tenant the right to possess or occupy his property in return for rent under a lease agreement.

LETTER OF ATTORNMENT — A written statement from an owner to a tenant informing the tenant that the property has been sold and future rent should be paid to the new owner.

LETTER OF CREDIT — A letter from a bank commiting itself to lend a specified amount to a specified person on specific terms.

LETTER OF INTENT — Not an offer, but a letter from a developer, lessee, buyer or other interested party stating their intention to purchase, etc.; used to project sales in a large development project, such as a condominium subdivision, for the purpose of assuring a lender of its financial feasibility.

LETTING — Leasing.

LEVEL PAYMENT MORTGAGE — See Interest included note.

LEVERAGE — A financing tool used by investors which enables them to use a small amount of their own money in conjunction with a large amount of borrowed money to purchase property for gain.

LIABILITY — Debt or obligation.

LIABLE — Owing.

LICENSE — Direct or indirect permission granting another the right to perform an act on behalf of a third party or oneself.

LICENSE EXAMINATION — The test which determines whether a person is knowledgeable enough about a particular subject, i.e. real estate, insurance, to be granted the right to perform services on behalf of another.

LIEN — A debt attached to property and considered an encumbrance to clear title.

LIEN WAIVER — A subcontractor's waiver of his right to place a mechanic's lien against property for materials and labor performed, so that the general contractor may draw against a construction loan.

LIFE ESTATE — An interest in property, such as to occupy or possess, granted for the life of a specific person, upon whose death the right reverts to the grantor or his heirs.

LIFE INTEREST — See life estate.

LIGHT AND AIR EASEMENT — An easement obtained from an adjoining land owner to protect against the obstruction of light and air which would result if a building or structure was constructed on the property granting the easement.

LIGHT INDUSTRY — Non-polluting manufacturers or businesses.

LIGHT WELL — The outside pit or well around a basement window which provides light and air to it.

LIKE IN KIND PROPERTY — Investment property for investment property, as referred to in an exchange of real estate.

LIMITATION OF ACTION — The legally limited time period in which a claim or court action may take place to settle a dispute.

LIMITED ACCESS HIGHWAY — A highway that restricts access to intervals of one mile or greater.

LIMITED COMMON ELEMENTS — Areas in a condominium subdivision that are owned as undivided interests but which are physically restricted in use, such as a parking space belonging to a particular unit or a storage area.

LINE OF CREDIT — The amount of money a businessman or investor might obtain from a lender without a credit check, to use for business purposes.

LIQUID ASSETS — Assets which may be quickly sold or exchanged for cash.

LIQUIDATED DAMAGES — By prearrangement, the amount established in a contract to be paid as damages by the party breaching a contract.

LIS PENDENS — A recorded notice that legal action is pending against the subject property and anyone who purchases it will be bound by the decision arrived at.

LIST-BACK — Real estate located by a licensed agent for a developer who purchases it without paying a commission on the condition that the property when subdivided into lots and improved will be listed with the agent, who will then derive a commission from its sale.

LISTING — A written agreement between an owner of real property and a brokerage firm which specifies the conditions upon which a sale may be made and lists facts pertinent to the property, at the same time providing that a commission will be paid in exchange for the brokerage firm securing a firm sale on the property.

LISTING AGENT — The broker's representative who obtains a listing agreement with the seller, as opposed to the selling agent who may represent another brokerage.

LITTORAL — Involving the shore of lakes and oceans.

LIVE LOAD — The weight of everything in a building, including people and furniture, which it is built to support, versus the dead weight (fixed) of the building itself.

LIVING TRUST — A trust established by a living person from which he benefits during his lifetime; a testamentary trust takes effect after death.

LOAD-BEARING — The support capacity of a lateral or vertical column or beam.

LOAN — The act of lending a specified sum of money based on a promise to repay said money, including interest.

LOAN COMMITMENT — See Commitment.

LOAN CORRESPONDENT — An intermediary who processes and services a loan for another institution who actually lends the funds for a mortgage.

LOAN PACKAGE — All of the documents and information necessary for a lender to make a decision as to whether or not to make a loan, such as credit report, job verification, appraisal, etc.

LOAN POLICY — A policy issued for the benefit of a lender and paid for by a borrower, to insure against loss which might occur as a result of defective title or loss of priority.

LOAN TO VALUE RATIO — The amount of money a lender is willing to loan in comparison to the property value which determines the rate of interest to be charged.

LOAN RELIEF — In an exchange of real property it would be referred to as boot or the extra amount received as a result of a lower mortgage balance.

LOCAL IMPROVEMENT DISTRICT — See Improvement District.

LOCATION — In appraising value, a property geographically well-situated for its intended use.

LOCK-IN — A clause in a loan security agreement which states a time period during which a loan may not be repaid without penalty.

LOFT — An open area reached by a stairway or ladder without partitions but with a protective railing enclosing it.

LONG TERM CAPITAL GAIN — Profit on a property that has been held for a specified period of time prior to resale, usually 1 year or more. The IRS treats this gain at a special rate as opposed to ordinary income.

LONG TERM FINANCING — A mortgage which extends over a period of ten years or more rather than short-term interim or construction financing.

LONG TERM LEASE — A lease with a term of ten years or more. Some areas of the country consider long term to be five years or more.

LOOSE MONEY — An economic term referring to the availability of money; borrowers qualify for more money under fewer restrictions when mortgage money is loose.

LOSS FACTOR — In commercially leased floor space, the difference between square footage rented and that which can actually be used; loss may result from an area taken up by support columns.

LOSS OF ACCESS — Loss of the ingress or egress to property resulting from condemnation of property for a limited access highway, etc.

LOSS PAYABLE CLAUSE — In an insurance policy, the clause which names the persons or parties to whom funds will be paid in the event of loss, according to their priority of interest.

LOT, BLOCK AND SUBDIVISION — A legal description of property in reference to its situation in a recorded subdivision.

M

MADE-LAND — Land that has been artificially created by movement of fill dirt.

MAGGIE MAE — Mortgage Guaranty Insurance Corporation. A mortgage insurer and secondary market for insured mortgages.

MANUFACTURED LOT — A lot with utilities and streets provided for and which has been approved by the local regulating office.

M.A.I. — Member Appraisal Institute. A designation given after training and examination by the American Institute of Real Estate Appraisers.

MAINTENANCE FEE — A monthly charge for caring for and repairing the commonly owned areas in a condominium subdivision or planned unit development.

MAINTENANCE RESERVE — Funds set aside for replacement and repair of structures and facilities.

MAJOR PARTITION — The division of one parcel of land into 2 or 3 lots, including a provision for roads, during 1 calendar year. May vary in different areas.

MAKER — A borrower who signs a note.

MANAGEMENT AGREEMENT- An agreement between an owner of investment property and the firm or individual hired to oversee it. Also referred to as property management.

MARGINAL — An unstable investment; borderline between making money and losing it.

MARK-UP — A percentage of cost added to the original cost to arrive at a sales price.

MARKETABILITY — Capable of being sold at current value.

MARKETABLE TITLE — Title free and clear of known risks and problems, which can be easily transferred.

MARKET DATA APPROACH — An appraisal method in which similar properties are compared for size, price, location, etc. to arrive at price or value of the subject property. Also called Market Value Approach.

MARKET PRICE — Anticipated or actual sales price.

MARKET RENT — The open market rental value of a property as opposed to the actual rent.

MARKET VALUE — The worth of a property as established by the willingness of a buyer to purchase it and a seller to sell it under terms accepted by both, both being fully informed of market conditions.

MARKET VALUE APPROACH — See Market Data Approach.

MASS APPRAISING — An appraisal made of an entire area for the purpose of assessing property taxes.

MASTER DEED — The recorded main deed of a condominium subdivision granting title to common areas which automatically becomes part of the deed granted for an individual unit by reference to it.

MASTER LEASE — The main lease of a building which governs leases or sub-leases which follow it.

MASTER PLAN — An overall zoning plan for an entire city or region.

MATERIALMAN — A supplier of construction materials.

M

MATURITY — The date on which the final balance of a note, mortgage, etc., falls due.

MAXIMUM RENT — Rent regulated by law.

MEANDER LINES — Surveying lines along rivers to measure curves.

MECHANIC'S LIEN — A lien attached to property by recording it, for materials or labor used in its improvement.

MEETING OF THE MINDS — Mutual agreement to the terms in a contract.

MERCURY SWITCH — A silent wall switch which makes electrical contact through mercury.

MERGE — Combining two entities into one.

MERGE LINE — A line, for appraisal purposes, which divides a lot having frontage on two streets, at a point which would give each lot its greatest value.

MERIDIAN — A surveying line circling the earth, spaced 24 miles apart at the equator and crossing the poles.

METAMORPHIC ROCK — A major type of rock, created by changes in heat and pressure.

METES AND BOUNDS — A measurement of boundaries using points, angles, distance and direction for legal descriptions.

M.G.I.C. — See Mortgage Guaranty Insurance Corporation.

MICRORELIEF — A farm appraisal term used for low-lying configurations of topography, such as dunes, channels, or mounds.

MILL CONSTRUCTION — The use of fire resistant materials in construction, such as masonry, heavy timbers, brick, etc.

MILLWORK — Manufactured portions of buildings, such as window sashes and doors.

MINERAL RIGHTS — Separate rights of ownership of ores, such as gold, silver and iron beneath the ground, apart from ownership of surface land.

MINERAL WOOL — Rock wool produced by the application of steam under pressure with molten rock; used for insulation.

MINIMUM LOT — The least amount of square footage

required for a lot to be approved under local zoning laws.

MINIMUM PROPERTY REQUIREMENTS — An FHA term for specifications that require a property to be well-built, well-located and livable before loan approval will be granted or underwritten.

MINIMUM RENTAL — The least amount of fixed rent to be paid under a lease agreement which may call for a percentage of the gross profit, etc.

MINOR PARTITION — The division of one parcel into 2 or 3 lots during one calendar year without providing for streets. May vary in different areas.

MISNOMER — A mistake in the use of a name.

MISPLACED IMPROVEMENTS — Improvements made on land for a use that is less than its highest and best use.

MISREPRESENTATION — The direct or indirect representation of a fact, through statement or conduct, which is inaccurate; if it misleads a buyer into the purchase of property he might not otherwise buy, the misrepresentation may be a cause for a damage suit or the rescission of a contract.

MOBIL HOME — Manufactured housing which may or may not be moved once it reaches a destination, depending on its size and portability.

MOBIL HOME PARK — An area where mobil home owners may rent space connected to public utilities to park their units.

MODEL HOME — Usually a decorated sample home in a subdivision which is used to reflect the quality and style of building available for interested buyers.

MODERNIZATION — Bringing the exterior or interior of a structure up-to-date in design and function.

MODULAR HOUSE — A house whose components have been manufactured and assembled prior to being placed on a foundation.

MOISTURE BARRIER — The use of plastic sheeting or a coating to prevent the transfer of moisture from the ground into a structure; prohibits condensation.

MONEY MARKET — The current availability of money for lending on short or long term financing projects.

MONTH-TO-MONTH TENANCY — Occupation of a rental unit without benefit of a lease; the tenant and owner must each give one another 30 days notice prior to termination of occupancy.

MORATORIUM — A tool used by local governments to stop construction in an area until its effect on facilities can be fully studied.

MORTGAGE — The instrument which secures (hypothecates) real property in the name of a lender until a loan (mortgage) is fully paid.

MORTGAGE BANKER — A lender who actually loans his own funds to a borrower rather than acting as an intermediary (broker).

MORTGAGE BROKER — An intermediary agent who brings borrowers and lenders together for a fee.

MORTGAGE BOND — A bond offered for sale by a corporation to raise money for its operation; the bond is secured by a mortgage on real property belonging to the corporation.

MORTGAGE CERTIFICATE — A document issued to an investor who buys a portion of a mortgage.

MORTGAGE COMPANY — See Mortgage Broker.

MORTGAGE DISCOUNT — Prepaid interest charged by a lender to a seller when FHA or VA financing is to be obtained; the actual rate charged the borrower is established by FHA-VA and does not allow a margin of profit to the lender when the mortgage is resold to a secondary lender. Discount points allow for a profit margin.

MORTGAGEE — The lender of funds who receives the mortgage.

MORTGAGE LIFE INSURANCE — A life insurance policy for the mortgagor (borrower) which covers the term of the mortgage and provides for repayment of the loan upon a mortgagor's death or serious injury.

MORTGAGEE'S POLICY — A title insurance policy for the benefit of the lender, insuring against defective title or loss of priority of the mortgage.

MORTGAGE SERVICING — Caring for the responsibilities of mortgage lending, such as collecting installment payments, releasing liens, initiating foreclosure upon default, etc. May be done by a service company hired by the original lender.

MORTGAGE WAREHOUSING — Holding a mortgage for a period of time until the market for reselling it improves and a greater profit may be made.

MORTGAGOR — The borrower of funds who voluntarily gives a mortgage.

MORTISE — Notches cut in wood for the purpose of joining two pieces together.

MUD ROOM — A small room or hallway near a back entrance where coats and boots are hung.

MULTIFAMILY DWELLING — A structure which houses more than one family, such as an apartment house or duplex.

MULTIPLE EXCHANGE — Three or more transfers of real property simultaneously by separate owners with one another.

MULTIPLE LISTING SERVICE — A business organization which a brokerage firm may join for a fee which disburses information on listing agreements over a large area to a number of brokerage firms for the purpose of exposing property for sale to a larger market.

MUNIMENTS OF TITLE — An owner's written evidence of title.

MUTUAL SAVINGS BANK — A bank owned by its depositors which loans its funds on a long term basis.

MUTUAL MORTGAGE INSURANCE FUND — A source from which government insured loans are repaid to lenders, upon default by the borrower.

N

NAR — (National Association of Realtors). An organization formed in 1908 consisting of individuals involved in the business of real estate, dedicated to the improvement or real estate training and ethics.

NAREB — National Association of Real Estate Boards. A trade organization which includes real estate brokers, appraisers, property managers, etc.

NATIONAL ASSOCIATION OF REAL ESTATE BROKERS — An organization of black real estate brokers who refer to themselves as "Realists".

NATURAL RESOURCES — Land, timber, water, people, minerals.

NEGATIVE CASH FLOW — The amount of money owner's must use out of their own pockets to meet expenses when the income from an investment is insufficient to cover them.

NEGOTIABLE INSTRUMENT — Legal instruments which may be assigned, transferred or sold, such as stocks, bonds, notes, mortgages.

NET ACRE — The amount of actual acreage that may be used for building lots after installation of streets, sidewalks, etc.

NET AFTER TAXES — The amount of money remaining after expenses and income taxes have been paid, received from investment property.

NET BEFORE TAXES — The amount of money remaining after expenses before income taxes are paid, received from investment property.

NET EARNINGS — The amount of income or profit derived after payment of expenses, which may or may not include depreciation.

NET GROUND LEASE — The net amount received for leasing raw land.

NET INCOME — See Net Earnings.

NET INCOME MULTIPLIER — The sales price divided by the net income equals the net income multiplier.

NET LEASE — In addition to a fixed rent, a lease which calls for payment of taxes, insurance, etc., by the lessee.

NET LISTING — A listing agreement in which the seller specifies a fixed net amount he wants to receive upon sale of property and the brokerage firm receives a sum in addition to that for services rendered. Not legal in some states.

NET LOSS — The difference between income received and expenses, when expenses are greater.

NET PROFIT — See Net After Taxes.

NET RENTAL — The amount received as rent over and above the expenses of the property.

NET WORTH — The value of assets over and above the liabilities of an individual or business.

"NO BONUS" CLAUSE — A clause in a lease that states a lessee may not be awarded more than the actual value of improvements he makes in the event of condemnation or taking through eminent domain.

NO GROWTH ZONING — Zoning regulations which prohibit or restrict the fast commercial and residential growth of a city or town; generally a reflection of the attitude of people responsible for decision-making such as the city council.

NOMINAL CONSIDERATION — A reasonable amount of money or other valuable security, not necessarily a reflection of true market value.

NOMINEE — An unnamed representative of a grantee in a deed.

NONCONFORMING USE — A property whose current use does not reflect current zoning regulations.

NONJUDICIAL FORECLOSURE SALE — A real property sale by a trustee empowered under a deed of trust to foreclose without going through a court action.

N

NONRECOURSE LOAN — A loan which cannot incur a deficiency judgment, the loan becomes a liability against the property and not the borrower.

NONRECURRING EXPENSE — Expenses created as a result of a natural disaster, etc., such as a flood, which are not likely to reoccur.

NOTARY PUBLIC — One who acts as an agent of the government to officially attest to the authenticity of signatures, and in some cases documents; also administers oaths.

NOTE — A written promise by one party to pay another party a specific sum of money at a specified time; may or may not be secured by a mortgage or trust deed.

NOTICE OF ACTION — Lis Pendens. A recorded notice to interested parties that a particular property is subject to upcoming or current litigation, a lien or defective title.

NOTICE OF COMPLETION — A legal notice posted on a completed building by a local building inspector stating that the property has been properly completed according to code. When and if it is recorded will determine the validity of a mechanic's lien.

NOTICE OF DEFAULT — A filed notice to interested parties that a borrower owes backpayments on a mortgage attached to the property.

NOTICE OF NONRESPONSIBILITY — When work is requested or hired by a tenant, a mechanic's lien may not be attached to the property if the owner files a notice stating he did not contract for the services rendered.

NOTORIOUS POSSESSION — When an owner's property is being used without his permission, but with his knowledge, possession is said to be notorious; required to establish adverse possession.

NOVATION — Replacing old borrowers with new ones under the same obligation, such as an assumption, or replacing an old contract with a new one using the same borrowers.

NUNCUPATIVE WILL — A will given orally, just prior to a person's death, before witnesses; may not be legally binding.

O

OCCUPANCY AGREEMENT — A written agreement between a seller and buyer, whereby for additional consideration (rent), possession of the property is given to the buyer prior to closing; usually arranged on a day-by-day rental agreement.

OFFER — A written proposal of an offer to purchase, containing specified price and terms, which an owner may turn into a contract by accepting through his signature.

OFFERING SHEET — A lender's brief summary of a loan proposal.

OFFICE EXCLUSIVE — A listing which is not submitted to a cooperative multiple listing service on the written request of the seller; only the broker or broker's salespeople will be allowed to show the property and make a sale; not ethical if the broker belongs to the National Association of Realtors.

OFFICE OF INTERSTATE LAND SALES REGISTRATION — A HUD agency established to prevent fraud and misrepresentation on all property sold to out-of-state buyers; deals primarily with the promotion and sale of recreation property.

OFFSET STATEMENT — Statements given to purchasers of rental property, stating the terms and rent of a tenant and listing the balance of existing mortgages on the property.

OFF-SITE IMPROVEMENTS — Installation of streets, sewers, sidewalks, electrical power, and water for the benefit of adjoining property.

ONE HOUR DOOR — A door constructed to resist fire for at least one hour.

ON-SITE IMPROVEMENTS — Structures or buildings placed on a property of a permanent nature.

OPEN-END MORTGAGE — A mortgage which may have additional sums added to it as the value of the property increases, based on the owner's equity.

OPEN HOUSE — A house for sale which is open to viewing by prospective buyers without an appointment; usually on Saturday or Sunday afternoon.

OPEN HOUSING — Housing available for all types and kinds of buyers without discrimination.

OPEN LISTING — A listing which obligates a seller to pay a commission when a specified broker makes a sale, but which reserves the right of the seller to sell his own property without paying a commission; open listings may be given to any number of brokers on the same property.

O

OPEN SPACE — Land set aside, preserved or used for farming, recreation, conservation, etc.; in condominium subdivisions or planned unit developments or housing developments, the land which is jointly owned in common for the benefit of all.

OPERATING EXPENSES — Ordinary expenses of operating an income property, such as taxes, insurance, upkeep, utilities, etc.

OPERATIVE BUILDER — A builder who builds a home on the speculation that he will find a buyer for it upon completion.

OPTION — An agreement which gives a party the right to purchase or lease a particular property, at a specified price for a specified period of time; usually a deposit or a portion of the rent applies to the downpayment or is forfeited when the option is not exercised.

OPTIONEE — The person receiving the option; prospective buyer.

OPTIONOR — The person granting the option; owner.

ORAL CONTRACT — A spoken agreement; may not be binding in regard to real estate transactions.

ORDINANCE — A law or statute imposed by a municipal body or county.

ORDINARY AND BUSINESS EXPENSE — Business expenses for rent, supplies, etc., which may be deducted during the tax year in which they are paid, rather than spread over a period of years, such as a capital expense.

ORDINARY INCOME — As opposed to capital gains, income derived during a tax year, such as for wages, salaries, or business profit which is taxed at regular rates, rather than at a reduced rate.

ORDINARY REPAIRS — Maintenance repairs on a structure to keep it in good condition.

ORIENTATION — Deciding the best relationship of a structure to the land on which it is to be placed.

ORIGINAL COST — The current owner's purchase price of property.

ORIGINATION FEE — See Loan Fee.

OR MORE CLAUSE — A clause which enables a borrower to repay a loan early, with no prepayment penalty.

OSTENSIBLE AGENCY — An agency established by law when one party acts as principal on behalf of another without written authority, but with suggested authority.

OUTLAWED CLAIM — A claim that is no longer valid, if the time allowed by statute has passed, for making it.

OVERALL PROPERTY TAX LIMITATION — A fixed percentage of actual value which may be levied against a property for taxes.

OVERIMPROVEMENT — Improvements made to property in a poor location, which may not be recovered upon sale.

OVERRIDE — A percentage of sales over and above a stated lease rental.

OWNER OF RECORD — An owner whose title is recorded in county records.

OWNERSHIP — The right to assign, sell, use or enjoy possession of property over all others, except as restricted by zoning restrictions, liens or easements.

OWNER'S POLICY — Title insurance granted to an owner rather than a lender.

P

PACKAGE MORTGAGE — A lien on personal property, as well as real property.

PAPER — Refers to any negotiable instrument taken as part payment for real property, such as a land contract, deed of trust, mortgage, etc.

PAR — Usual, ordinary; the amount stated on the face of an instrument, such as a note or mortgage.

PARCEL — A legally described piece of land area.

PARITY CLAUSE — Enables a mortgage or trust deed to cover several notes with no order of preference.

PAROL EVIDENCE — Admissible oral evidence when the content of a contract is unclear.

PARTIALLY DISCLOSED PRINCIPAL — When a third party acts on behalf of a second party, without telling the first party who the second party is, even though they may discern another party is involved.

PARTIAL RELEASE CLAUSE — Used by subdividers to release lots individually from an overall mortgage, upon their sale.

PARTICIPATION — In exchange for making a loan, a percentage of the profit and inteest in land given a lender by a developer.

P

PARTITIONING — Dividing real property into two or more parcels.

PART PERFORMANCE — Less than full performance under a contract, which is acceptable to the parties involved.

PARTY WALL — A wall owned jointly or in common with other owners.

PASSIVE INVESTOR — An investor who contributes money but not time to a real estate project.

PATENT — The original method of conveyance of title from the government to private owners.

PAYMENT BOND — A bond purchased by a general contractor stating that payments to subcontractors and for materials will be made in full and no mechanic's liens will be filed.

PAYOFF — The amount owed on an existing loan or lien which will be paid off on a closing.

PERCENTAGE LEASE — See Overage Income.

PERCOLATION — Perk Test. Required prior to construction of a septic tank to determine the soil's ability to absorb water.

PERFECTING TITLE — Clearing claims or defects.

PERFORMANCE BOND — A builder's bond insuring the project will be finished.

PERIODIC TENANCY — A lease that runs from period to period, year to year, or month to month, until notice of cancellation by either party.

PERMANENT MORTGAGE — A mortgage of 10 years or longer.

PERPETUITY — In reference to real estate, 21 years after the death of a specified person.

PERSONAL PROPERTY — Property other than real property.

PIGGYBACK LOAN — A single mortgage with two or more lenders involved, loaning portions of the total amount.

PLANNED UNIT DEVELOPMENT — A subdivision of 5 or more units where the land beneath the unit is individually owned in addition to common areas, jointly owned.

PLANNING COMMISSION — The agency of a local or county government which recommends approval or disapproval of proposed building projects in their jurisdiction; a higher authority such as the city council makes the final decision based on the advice of the Planning Commission.

PLANS AND SPECS — Written and drawn instructions of a planned building or development project showing electrical, mechanical and construction diagrams and detailing finishes, colors, materials and workmanship.

PLAT — Plat map. A map of a subdivision, showing single lots and street layouts.

PLEDGE — Placing on deposit, a security for a debt, such as a sum of money equal to a mortgage deposited with the lender.

PLOT — Area designated for an improvement.

PLOT PLAN — A map showing where improvements are to be placed on a parcel of land.

PLOTTAGE INCREMENT — Joining small parcels together to form a large parcel for the purpose of increasing value.

P.M.I. — Private Mortgage Insurance. Covers part of the first mortgage on 90 - 100% loans, enabling the lender to loan a greater percentage of the sales price; paid for by borrower.

POCKET LISTING — A listing withheld from other sales people so that the listing agent or broker has the first opportunity to sell the property; discouraged by most brokers.

POINTS — See Discount Points.

POINT OF BEGINNING — P.O.B. The beginning and ending of a metes and bounds description.

POSSESSION — Physically in control of property, real or personal, lawfully or unlawfully.

POSSIBILITY OF REVERTER — A condition in a contract or deed which states that if property is not used according to terms specified, title will return to the original owner or heirs.

POTABLE — Water fit to drink.

POWER OF SALE — A foreclosure which may take place without court action, as granted under a deed of trust or mortgage.

PRE-CLOSING — The gathering of all documents necessary to final closing of a real estate transaction.

PRELIMINARY COSTS — Expenses which occur prior to actual building, such as feasibility studies, construction loan charges, and legal counsel.

PRELIMINARY TITLE REPORT — A report which may be requested by the lender or borrower prior to closing which discloses defects of record and liens of record, as well as other pertinent information; also states whether or not title insurance will be issued by the company making the report.

PREPAID EXPENSES — Items which will be pro-rated between seller and buyer at closing, such as taxes and insurance.

PREPAYMENT PENALTY — See Or More Clause.

PRE-QUALIFYING — Establishing the capability of a buyer to obtain a large enough mortgage prior to making an offer to buy on their behalf.

PRE-SALE — Sales solicited prior to the beginning of construction in order to obtain a construction loan commitment.

PRESCRIPTIVE EASEMENT — An easement granted by law after land has been openly and continuously used and it can be assumed a prior easement had been given, though not recorded.

PRESENTATION — Soliciting a listing from a seller by presenting him with information about a broker's services and performance.

PRIME RATE — The lowest rate charged by banks or commercial lenders on short-term loans to their best qualified customers.

PRIME TENANT — A financially sound business tenant who will occupy a large amount of space in a commercial development and whose presence will make the project feasible to a lender.

PRINCIPAL — One granting authority to another; the original or remaining balance of a note or mortgage, etc.

PRINCIPAL BROKER — The broker charged with overall responsibility of a brokerage firm; a principal broker may have

10 offices each staffed with a broker, referred to as associate brokers.

PRIORITY LIEN — A lien established on the records as having first priority over other liens.

PRIVATE MORTGAGE INSURANCE — See P.M.I.

PRIVITY — The relationship between parties in a real estate transaction, such as grantor to grantee.

PROCESSING — Preparing a loan and/or other documents for a closing.

PROCURING CAUSE — The effort that is responsible for causing an event, such as a broker obtaining a sale under an open listing entitles him to a commission.

PROFIT — The gain of money after payment of expenses.

PROMISSORY NOTE — See Note.

PROPERTY LINE — The measured border lines of a parcel of land.

PROPERTY MANAGEMENT — The enterprise of overseeing or being responsible for income property for a fee; involves renting, maintaining, etc.

PROPERTY REPORT — A complete summary of information of property offered for sale to out of state buyers as required by the Interstate Land Sales Full Disclosure Act.

PROPERTY TAX — An assessment against real property generally based on a percentage of estimated market value.

PROPERTY VALUE — The estimated market value of property based on comparable sales of similar property.

PROPRIETARY LEASE — Refers to a cooperative apartment lease; owners purchase stock in a corporation which entitles them to lease a unit.

PRO RATE — Division of expenses, such as taxes, between seller and buyer, at the time of sale.

PROSPECT — A person interested in buying, selling or leasing property, who has not actually done so.

PUBLIC OFFERING STATEMENT — A disclosure of all facts about a subdivision, as required by state subdivision laws.

P

PUBLIC RECORDS — A recorded record of all documents filed such as liens, deeds, easements, etc. with the county or other local body which are open to public inspection.

PUFFER — A phony bidder at an auction attempting to raise the price of property for sale.

PUFFING — Overstating aspects of real property to enhance its appeal.

PUNCH LIST — A list of construction flaws arrived at by the purchaser and builder for correction, prior to closing.

PURCHASE AGREEMENT — A contract to sell and buy real property according to terms set forth therein.

PURCHASE MONEY MORTGAGE — The seller becomes the lender, taking back a mortgage on a portion of the sales price as part payment.

PURCHASER'S POLICY — See Owner's Policy.

PYRAMID — To build an estate by multiple acquisitions of properties utilizing the initial properties for a base for further investment.

Q

QUALIFIED BUYER — One who has a good credit rating, adequate downpayment, verifiable job and can afford the amount of mortgage payment he has in mind as determined from financial information gathered prior to showing the property.

QUALIFIED ACCEPTANCE — A tentative acceptance based on further conditions; a counteroffer; neither of which is legally binding until all terms are accepted by both seller and buyer.

QUANTITY SURVEY METHOD — An estimated cost of construction based on the amount of labor and materials needed.

QUIET ENJOYMENT — A right of ownership; the right to enjoy property in peace.

QUIET TITLE — A legal action to cease all claims.

QUITCLAIM DEED — A deed that passes on an interest in real property with no warranties attached.

QUORUM — A majority of interested parties needed to vote on rules and regulations; required to establish rules and regulations for condominium subdivision.

R

RADIANT HEATING — See Hot water heating.

RATABLE ESTATE — A property whose worth may be estimated for assessment purposes.

RATE OF RETURN — The amount of profit earned based on a percentage on investment made during one year.

RATIFICATION — Agreeing to an act after it has taken place in order to make it legal or give it authority, such as a minor ratifying a contract made prior to his becoming of legal age.

RAW LAND — Bare land without improvements.

READY, WILLING AND ABLE — Refers to the point in time when a broker's commission is considered earned; when he procures a buyer who is ready, willing and able to meet all of the seller's terms and price under the listing agreement.

REAL ESTATE — Land and anything permanently affixed to it, such as fences and structures, and any fixtures attached to those structures.

REAL ESTATE INVESTMENT TRUST — REIT. An association of investors formed under a trust agreement, who derive 90% of their income for the trust from real estate; 100 persons or less following income tax laws and federal regulations who form an association for the purpose of real estate investment.

REAL ESTATE LICENSE — A license issued by a state to a qualified broker or salesperson who successfuly completed tests for the same.

REAL ESTATE SECURITY — Stock owned by an investor in a real estate investment trust or corporation dealing in real estate investment.

REALIST — Also called Realtist. Designation of the National Association of Real Estate Brokers.

REALTOR — A member of the Board of the National Association of Real Estate Boards.

Q
R

REALTY — Real property.

REBATE — Part of a purchase price returned as reward for making the purchase or for prompt or early payment of a bill.

RECAPTURE — Money regained that was part of the original investment, upon the sale of the investment.

RECAPTURE CLAUSE — A lease agreement clause that establishes terms for repossession of property or provides for receiving part of the profit over and above a fixed rent amount.

RECAPTURE OF DEPRECIATION — Extra depreciation taken on investment property over and above the normal straight-line rate, the taxes for which are recovered on sale of the property.

RECASTING — Redoing an existing loan for a borrower owing backpayments in order to avoid default and foreclosure; the interest rate and term may be readjusted to lower payments.

RECEIPT — A written note or clause stating that something has been received, such as a receipt for a deposit of money.

RECIPROCITY — An agreement with another state whereby licensed attorneys and real estate brokers may legally conduct business in more than one state in exchange for the same privilege.

RECONCILIATION — A balancing of different methods of appraisal to determine a final estimate of value for a property.

RECONVEYANCE — Releasing title to an original owner after clearing a debt under a mortgage or deed of trust.

RECORDING — Placing on file in the public record of the county, documents which pertain to real property transfers, liens, etc.

RECOURSE — Action against the borrower himself for repayment of a mortgage balance and not just against the property encumbered.

REDDENDUM — A clause in a deed, lease or other assignment instrument which reserves some right for the assignor.

REDEMPTION — The right of a defaulted prior owner to regain title to his property within a period of time after foreclosure upon payment of the mortgage balance and related expenses.

RED HERRING — A term for a security which has been filed with the state but not yet approved; a red stamp on the left margin states it may not be sold until registration is approved; hence the name red herring.

RED LINING — The practice of lenders refusing to loan on high risk properties in certain outlined inner city or core areas; illegal in some states.

REFERRAL — Recommending to a real estate associate the name of a friend or acquaintance who may be interested in selling or buying real estate.

REFINANCE — Increasing or adding to the original principal amount of a mortgage by the same borrower through the same or another lender.

REFORMATION — Changing a deed or a document to correct an error or fraud.

REGRESSION — The appraisal factor which determines that the value of a better quality property is affected by the location of nearby properties of lesser value.

REGISTRAR OF DEEDS — The county official, usually called the recorder, who is responsible for real estate documents on public file.

REGULATION Z — A portion of the Truth-in-Lending law which states that a purchaser on credit be informed of all expenses involved with the application for credit and subsequent loan.

REINSTATEMENT — Bringing a defaulted note or mortgage up-to-date by paying back-payments.

REINSURANCE — Apportioning liability among several insurers to lessen the risk.

REISSUE RATE — A reduced rate on title insurance that has recently been issued on the same property with a prior owner.

R.E.I.T. — See Real Estate Investment Trust.

R

RELATION-BACK DOCTRINE — In the event of death of a grantor while a deed, documents and purchase money are in escrow, the prior date of signing the initial agreement to sell takes priority; the death of the grantor does not automatically terminate the transaction.

RELEASE — A recorded document which states that a lien or mortgage has been satisfied and the property is released from liability thereon.

RELEASE CLAUSE — When there are several parcels named in one mortgage, each may be singly released by prior agreement, upon payment of a specified amount.

RELICTION — An addition of land created by receding water of a lake, or other body of water.

RELIEF MAP — A map showing surface elevations.

REMAINDER ESTATE — An estate created simultaneously with another estate, but which does not take effect until termination of the other estate, such as the heir who receives an estate upon the death of a party who had a life estate interest.

REMAINING ECONOMIC LIFE — The balance of time remaining during which a structure is said to have economic worth as determined by appraisal; the full economic life of a wood structure is said to be 30 years and the balance remaining after 10 years would be 20.

REMISE — A term used in a quitclaim deed to terminate a prior interest.

REMNANT — A small, usually irregular or landlocked parcel, left after the majority of a parcel has been used for the purpose taken, such as under eminent domain.

RENEGOTIATION CLAUSE — A clause found in a long term lease which calls for negotiating the rent after a period of time.

RENEWAL OPTION — A lessee's option stated in a lease which allows him to renew a lease agreement for another period of time at a renegotiated rental rate.

RENTABLE AREA — The amount of space in a commercial building which can actually be used as rented area, excluding stairways, restrooms, halls, etc.

RENTAL AGENT — One who is paid a fee to find a residence for a renter, or a property for a tenant.

RENTAL POOL — A group of apartment units which may be rented out and whose owners share the income and expenses as a group rather than individually.

RENT CONTROLS — Restrictive legislation controlling maximum rental rates owner's may charge on their available units.

REPLACEMENT FUND — A pool of money contributed to by members of a homeowner's association in a condominium subdivision, planned unit development, etc., which provides for replacement of commonly owned property, such as the roof or exterior siding.

REPLACEMENT COST — An appraisal method for determing value by substituting a like property.

REPRODUCION COST — The appraisal of property by estimating the cost to replace it.

RERECORDING — See Correction Deed.

RECISION OF A CONTRACT — Withdrawing from a contract, as though one never existed.

RESERVE — An amount of money set aside to pay future expenses, such as property taxes, insurance, etc.

RESIDENTIAL BUILDING RATE — The number of housing units began in one year, per 1000 population.

RESPA — Real Estate Settlement Procedures Act. Requires informing a borrower who will be obtaining a federally insured loan, of all costs involved.

RESPONDEAT SUPERIOR — The idea that a broker (principal) is responsible for the acts of others acting on his authority, such as a real estate agent.

RESTRAINT OF ALIENATION — Restrictions involving the resale of property.

RESUBDIVISION — Changing a prior established subdivision.

RETAINING WALL — A barrier to retain earth.

RETALIATORY EVICTION — An eviction by a landlord against a tenant who has complained about poor maintenance or need repairs on an apartment or other rental unit; not legal in some states.

R

REVENUE STAMPS — A stamp on a conveying instrument which reflects a state tax on the sale of property.

REVERSION — The giving back of rights in an estate to a grantor or heirs after the decease of the party holding possession, as in a life estate.

REVOCABLE — The right of cancellation of an agreement.

RIGHT OF REDEMPTION — See Redemption.

RIGHT OF SURVIVORSHIP — Under a joint tenancy deed, the right of the surviving tenant to the property of a deceased tenant.

RIGHT OF WAY — A right of entry and exit across land belonging to another through an easement granted under condemnation or by agreement.

RIPARIAN — Rights commonly attached to land which borders a river, stream or body of water, such as the right to use the water for boating, swimming, etc, and the right to claim the land deposited by alluvium.

RISK CAPITAL — Money invested as speculation that a property will increase in value.

RISK RATING — The process of rating by lenders, the ability of people and property to repay the amount of mortgage applied for to determine the amount or risk involved.

ROCK WOOL — Molten rock fiber insulation, made through application of steam to the rock.

ROLL-OVER PAPER — Interim or bridge financing which may be turned into long term financing after the short term note falls due.

ROOM COUNT — The determination of the number of rooms in a residence for sale, which usually excludes the bathrooms.

ROW HOUSES — The forerunner of the condominium or townshouse where common walls are shared between owners of single units.

RUNNING WITH THE LAND — Attached to land and its transfer of ownership, such as an easement.

S

SAFETY CLAUSE — A listing clause which states that should a buyer who was made aware of property for sale though the efforts of a broker, purchase said property after expiration of the listing, the seller will remain liable for a commission on the sale.

SALE-LEASEBACK — See Leaseback.

SALES-ASSESSMENT RATIO — The ratio of sales price to assessed value.

SALES CONTRACT — See Purchase Agreement.

SALESPERSON — A licensed real estate associate operating under the auspices of a broker.

SALVAGE VALUE — The worth of a building which is to be moved to another site.

SANDWICH LEASE — A leasehold interest that has been sub-leased to a third party; the lessee's lease between the first and third party.

SANITARY SEWER — A public sewer for wastes, as opposed to a storm sewer which carries rain water.

SATISFACTION OF MORTGAGE — See Release.

SAVINGS AND LOAN ASSOCIATION — A federally or state chartered and regulated association which pays interest on deposits and makes long term first mortgages.

SCARCITY — The amount of a product available in relation to the demand for it.

SCENIC EASEMENT — An easement purchased or condemned in order to preserve a natural beauty, such as a view.

SCOPE OF AUTHORITY — The range of authority which an agent has over a principal; it may be implied or apparent.

SCRIBING — Marking wood for cutting to attain an accurate fit.

SEASONED LOAN — A loan that has been in existence long enough to establish the borrower's credit worthiness.

SECONDARY FINANCING — A second loan on a property which has priority under the first mortgage; not established by first recording, but by agreement.

SECONDARY LENDER — A wholesale mortgage buyer who purchases first mortgages from banks and savings and loan associations, enabling them to restock their money supply and loan more money.

S

SECONDARY MORTGAGE MARKET — See Secondary Lender.

SECOND MORTGAGE — See Secondary Financing.

SECURED PARTY — The lender under a mortgage or deed of trust.

SECURITY — Real or personal property collateral used to back up a mortgage or lien, which gives the lender tangible property that may be sold upon default to pay off the indebtedness.

SELLING AGENT — The agent who secures a buyer for a seller, not necessarily the same as the listing agent and may not be associated with the listing broker.

SEPARATE PROPERTY — Individual property belonging solely to a husband or wife in which the other has no legal interest.

SEPTIC TANK — A cement tank buried in the ground into which household sewage drains and is broken down into liquids and gases.

SEQUESTRATION, WRIT OF — A court order which empowers someone to take custody of another's personal or real property.

SERVICE PROPERTY — A property used for public service, such as a school or museum.

SERVICE ROAD — A road parallel to a limited access highway which serves adjacent property.

SERVIENT TENEMENT — Land over which an easement has been granted to another property.

SET BACK — The amount of distance from a boundary line to where a building may be constructed as regulated by zoning restrictions.

SETTLEMENT STATEMENT — See Closing Statement.

SEVERALTY — A property owned by one individual separately.

SEVERANCE DAMAGE — Loss in value to the remaining property, after a portion has been taken in condemnation.

SHAREHOLDER — An individual or entity owning shares in a corporation.

SHEET EROSION — Washing away of earth by water action.

SHERIFF'S DEED — A deed granted to a buyer by the sheriff after a foreclosure sale.

SHORT TERM DOCUMENT — A shortened version of a legal document which makes reference to a master document on file whose terms are included as part of the total agreement.

SHORT TERM CAPITAL GAIN — Gain from the sale of a property or a security not held long enough to qualify as a long term investment; usually property sold in less than 1 year after purchase. The gain is taxable as ordinary income.

SHORT TERM LEASE — A lease agreement whose term is less than 10 years; the term varies in different areas.

SIGNED, SEALED AND DELIVERED — An expression meaning that the document has been signed by interested parties and copies have been delivered to interested parties. The seal refers to application of a notary, corporation or government official seal, if required.

SIMPLE INTEREST — Interest charged on principal and not interest charged on interest, as in compound interest.

SIMULTANEOUS ISSUE — An owner's and a lender's title insurance policies issued at the same time, thereby reducing the charge for the lender's policy.

SINGLE FAMILY DWELLING — A house designed and zoned for use by a single family unit on a lot owned with it, as opposed to a multi-family unit or condominium where the land is owned as one parcel and the units are joined together.

SINKING FUND — Money reserved for the repair and maintenance of investment property.

SLANDER OF TITLE — False statements made by a second party to a third party regarding a first party's ownership; when the first party suffers a loss as a result of slander of title, a legal claim for damages may be sustained.

SOFT MONEY — Money disbursed for expenses or a second mortgage which does not increase in value through appreciation, as would money invested as a downpayment.

SOIL PIPE AND STACK — A pipe which carries waste

S

materials from a house and which is ventilated by a vertical pipe which allows for release of sewer gases.

SOLAR HEATING — Sun radiated heat.

SOUND VALUE — An insurance term which estimates actual value at the time of loss by fire.

SPECIAL ASSESSMENT — Liens placed against a property for off-site improvements such as sewers, streets, sidewalks.

SPECIAL BENEFITS — Additional benefits to property resulting from the taking of a part of the property by eminent domain.

SPECIAL PURPOSE PROPERTY — Property that is not suitable for more than one use without costly changes being made, such as a church.

SPECIFICATIONS — A building contractor's detailed instructions and drawings.

SPECIFIC PERFORMANCE — A legal action to enforce the terms of an agreement.

SPECIMEN TREE — A tree planted singly rather than as part of a group, because of its distinct beauty.

SPECULATOR — An investor in the business of buying and selling real property for profit.

SPENDABLE INCOME — The amount of income left after deduction of expenses, taxes and debt service.

SPENDTHRIFT TRUST — A trust established to pay income to its beneficiary and to avoid claims against a beneficiary by creditors. The beneficiary may not sell or transfer property in the trust.

SPIN-OFF — A method of controlling a real estate development, by selling assets to a subsidiary corporation which then disburses stock to shareholders according to their interest.

SPLIT-LEVEL HOUSE — A house with more than one elevation, such as a tri-level.

SPLIT-RATE — The value of improvements on land established separately from the land itself, for the purpose of determining a capitalization rate.

SPOT LOAN — A loan granted on one unit of a condominium

by a lender not familiar through previous loans with the subdivision; additional expenses may be involved for analyzing the risk.

SPOT ZONING — Erratic zoning of land with no long-range plan in mind.

SQUARE FOOT METHOD — A method of estimating rent or land value according to the square footage cost.

SRA — Society of Real Estate Appraisers. An association of professional appraisers who admit members according to their training, experience and education.

STANDARD COVERAGE POLICY — A title insurance policy which covers defects of record only.

STANDARD DEPTH — The average depth of a subdivided lot.

STANDBY COMMITMENT — A lender's commitment for a loan of 1 to 5 years after completion of a building project, in case other long term financing cannot be obtained.

STANDING LOAN — A loan on which installment payments are made on interest only; the principal amount is not repaid until the final due date.

START CARD — An escrow account card which shows the date opened, the names of the parties involved, etc.

STARTER — The latest title policy issued on a particular property; an attorney searches the title from that date forward before issuing a letter of opinion or back title letter converning the condition of title.

STATEMENT OF INFORMATION — A form filled out by buyer and seller which enables a title insurance company to determine if there are liens or judgments against either party; usually requested when one of the parties has a common name such as John Smith.

STATUTE — A law legislated by a state or federal body, as opposed to one established by court action.

STATUTE OF FRAUDS — A state law that requires contracts for real property to be in writing.

STATUTE OF LIMITATIONS — The law that determines the legal period during which a valid claim may be filed.

S

STATUTORY LIEN — A lien provided for by law rather than by agreement, such as for taxes, judgments, etc.

STATUTORY RESERVE — Money which banks and savings and loan associations are required to set aside to meet regular business obligations.

STEP-UP LEASE — A lease which provides for increases in rent periodically.

STOCK COOPERATIVE — See Cooperative.

STORM SEWER — A drainage pipe for rainwater.

STRAIGHT LINE DEPRECIATION — Depreciating property at a fixed rate annually over its economic life.

STAIGHT NOTE — A note that requires repayment to be made on demand rather than through installment payments.

STRAIGHT TERM MORTGAGE — A mortgage in which the principal amount is paid at the end of the term.

STRIP CENTER — A string of small retail stores or businesses who share a parking area.

SUBCONTRACTOR — The specialized contractor hired by the general contractor to furnish labor and materials on a building project, such as electrial or plumbing installations.

SUBJECT TO CLAUSE — A clause in a deed or contract specifying that the new buyer is purchasing the property subject to an existing mortgage, which may be called due by the lender according to the terms of the mortgage.

SUBLEASE — A lease given by a lessee to a third party.

SUBORDINATION — A clause in a deed or contract whereby a seller agrees to grant first priority to another lender's mortgage in order to secure a loan for construction by the buyer.

SUBSURFACE RIGHTS — Oil, gas and mineral rights.

SUBURBAN — A residential and small business area on the outer extremities of a larger city.

SUCCESSION — The transfer of property as specified in a will.

SUMP PUMP — An underground pump which pumps water upward to a drain.

SUNBELT — Southern states exposed to sunshine through the majority of the year.

SUPPLY AND DEMAND — An economic theory upon which prices for products and service are determined; the greater the demand is over the available supply of a product, the greater in price the product becomes.

SURETY — One who insures that a debt or claim for damages will be paid, such as a co-signer on a mortgage or an insurance company.

SURFACE RIGHTS — A right or easement granted with mineral rights, enabling the possessor of the mineral rights to drill or mine through the surface.

SWEAT EQUITY — The creation of an interest in property by a buyer prior to closing whereby he is allowed to perform labor to improve the property in order to obtain financing.

SURFACE WATER — See Ground Water.

SURVIVORSHIP — See Right of Survivorship.

SYNDICATION — Bringing together a group of people according to state regulations for the purpose of investing in real property or securities as a business.

T

TAKE-OUT COMMITMENT — A lender's written statement that a short-term construction loan may be converted to long-term financing after completion of the project.

TANDEM PLAN — The resale of first mortgages to GNMA, who in turn resells them to FNMA at a discount; increases the supply of funds available for lending on first mortgages.

TANGIBLE VALUE — The physical worth of a structure, as opposed to the value of a mortgage placed on it.

TAX ABATEMENT — A tax assessment decrease.

TAX BASE — The total assessed value of all the property in a given area which determines the rate at which an individual property is assessed.

TAX DEED — A deed issued to a government body upon non-payment of taxes for a period of time; the deed issued to a purchaser of property through a tax sale.

T

TAX EXEMPTION — Freedom from taxation of property owned by non-profit organizations or qualified elderly individuals.

TAX SHELTER — Personal or real property invested in for income producing purposes which offers tax advantages.

TAX STAMP — See Revenue Stamp.

TAX-STOP CLAUSE — Increases in rent under a lease agreement which go to pay for increases in taxes on the property.

TENANCY BY THE ENTIRETY — A type of deed which states that the rights of one spouse in the ownership of a piece of property automatically pass to a spouse surviving the death of the other.

TENANCY IN COMMON — Property owned jointly by two or more people with no right of survivorship.

TENDER — An offer on the part of one party to an agreement to fulfill the terms of the agreement in full; if rejected by the other party, it becomes a breach of contract.

TENURE — The status of one's ownership or title in property in relation to another person's interest in the same property; a less than fee interest in real property.

TERMITE INSPECTION — A determination after examination by a licensed inspector as to whether or not termites are present in a structure.

TERMS — The mutually agreed upon conditions written into a contract, such as a sales agreement, mortgage, etc.

TERRA COTTA — Unglazed fired earth (clay) used for roof and floor tiles.

TESTIMONIUM CLAUSE — A deed clause which acknowledges through the presence of a witness that the right parties are signing the instrument of conveyance.

THERMAL WINDOW — A double-paned window with dead air space between, for insulating purposes.

THIRD PARTY — A reference term in a legal instrument which indicates the involvement of a third person not a party to the contract.

THREE-QUARTERS BATH — A bathroom with a commode, sink and shower.

TIGHT MONEY — An economic reference to the lack of availability of money for lending during periods of high interest rates or recession.

TILLABLE LAND — Cleared land, suitable for farming.

TIMBER — A marketable tree, cut or uncut.

TIMELINESS — The importance of fulfilling the terms of a contract by the date mentioned in the agreement, i.e. "Time is of the essence".

TIME-SHARING — Sharing ownership in a recreational or resort condominium according to time, for example 1 week per year would be a 1/52 · interest. Various plans are available.

TITLE — Proof of ownership in real property.

TITLE INSURANCE — A policy of insurance which protects an owner or other party of interest against defects in title created by improper parties signing an instrument of conveyance, fraud, incompetency, etc.

TITLE SEARCH — A search of public records, etc., by a title company or attorney to establish the condition of title prior to a transfer of ownership.

TOPOGRAPHICAL SURVEY — A survey of land to determine its elevation levels in relation to sea level.

TORRENS SYSTEM — A registration of land ownership, bearing the name of its originator.

TOWNHOUSE — A 2-level unit of a row house or condominium subdivision.

TOWNSHIP — Thirty-six square miles as determined by federal survey.

TRACK RECORD — Past history of performance.

TRACT — Subdivision.

TRADE FIXTURES — Business equipment attached to real property which may be removed at the time of sale of the real property.

TRANSFER — Passing the ownership of property to another.

TRANSFER TAX — See Revenue Stamps.

T

TRANSOM — A horizontal crossbeam over a door or window.

TRAP — The curved section of pipe beneath a sink which traps grease and other objects going down the drain.

TRIPLE NET LEASE — A lease arrangement under which the lessee pays the expenses of the property, such as taxes and insurance, as well as the cost of maintenance and repairs, in addition to a base rent; called net, net, net.

TRI-PLEX — A 3-unit apartment dwelling.

TRUST — A relationship established for the benefit of one or more parties, but actually managed by another, called the trustee.

TRUST ACCOUNT — A neutral account at a bank established by a third party to hold funds of a first or second party, such as the account in which a buyer's deposit on real estate is held until the time of closing.

TRUST DEED — A deed used in the same manner as a mortgage to secure property for a debt; a trustee holds title for the trustor (owner-borrower) and is empowered to sell the property in the event of default, and pay off the (lender-beneficiary) from the funds.

TRUSTOR — The owner-borrower under a deed of trust who grants title to a trustee.

TURN KEY — A rental arrangement of business property where the tenant furnishes only the furniture, inventory and telephone and the landlord prepares the premises itself for a business operation.

TURN-OVER — The rate at which business inventory sells.

U

UNAVOIDABLE CAUSE — A delay in the performance of an agreement or contract, created by an unforseen event such as death of a party, or the loss of papers pertaining to the contract.

UNBALANCED IMPROVEMENT — An improvement to real property which is not suitable to its location, and which may adversely affect its value.

UNCONSCIONABLE CONTRACT — A contract which obviously favors one party to the agreement only.

UNDER-LEASE — A sub-lease which does not include all of the originally leased property or which terminates prior to the full term of the original lease.

UNDERLYING FINANCING — An existing, prior mortgage or deed of trust on a property resold on contract.

UNDERWRITER — A lender or insurer who solicits business according to the rate of risk involved.

UNDIVIDED INTEREST — A commonly shared interest in real property where the owners have equal rights of possession and use, such as the recreational facilities and common area of a condominium subdivision.

UNDUE INFLUENCE — Pressure or force used to induce another to act against their own free will.

UNEARNED INCREMENT — Increased property value as a result of the area surrounding it being ungraded.

UNENCUMBERED PROPERTY — Propery cleared of debt, and free to be transferred.

UNENFORCIBLE CONTRACT — A contract whose form does not abide by legal statute, for instance, is not in writing, does not show consideration, etc.

UNFINISHED BUILDING SPACE — An incomplete building which may require plumbing or heating fixtures, etc.

UNIFORM COMMERCIAL CODE — A group of nationally conforming laws which regulate personal and real property transactions.

UNILATERAL CONTRACT — A contract agreement whereby one party promises to perform an act for another, in exchange for consideration.

UNIMPROVED LAND — Bare land.

UNIT COST — Square foot cost.

UNIT VALUE RATIO — The percentage of value of one unit to the total project, for example, one condominium unit to the whole subdivision.

UNIT RULE — In condemnation proceedings, property valued as a whole.

UNITY OF TIME, TITLE, INTEREST & POSSESSION — Under joint tenancy, all interests must be equal.

UNLAWFUL DETAINER — Unlawful possession of another's property, such as a tenant continuing to live in an apartment after right of tenancy was terminated.

UNMARKETABLE TITLE — Encumbered or defective title.

UNRECORDED INSTRUMENT — Legal documents pertaining to real estate which are not recorded with the county, i.e., a deed, mortgage, easement, etc., are valid between the parties, but not protected by state statutes.

UPSET PRICE — Lowest price at which a property may be sold through foreclosure.

URBAN RENEWAL — Improving functionally obsolescent portions of a city with government financing.

USABLE AREA — That portion of rented space which is actually usable, excluding stairways and restrooms, etc.

USE DENSITY — See Density.

USEFUL LIFE — For appraisal or tax purposes, the time period during which a building or structure is economically feasible to use per owner.

USE TAX — A tax levied on goods purchased in another state.

USURY — Excessive interest charged, over and above legal limits.

UTILITY ROOM — A room which may contain one or all of the following: washer, dryer, water heater, furnace, cleaning materials.

V

VACANCY FACTOR — The anticipated amount of income that will be lost during one year from rental property units remaining empty for a period of time.

VACANT LAND — Land without structures.

VALID — Properly executed according to law.

VALUABLE CONSIDERATION — See Consideration.

VALUE — See Market Value.

VAPOR BARRIER — A material such as plastic, rubber or tinfoil which retards or prevents the transfer of moisture from the earth or air into a structure.

VARIABLE INTEREST RATE — A flexible rate of interest which increases or decreases according to current market rates.

VARIANCE — Permission given by a zoning authority to use property for a purpose other than what it is currently zoned for, such as building a tri-plex in an area zoned for single family residences.

VAULTED CEILING — A ceiling open all the way to the roof supports, usually displaying open beams.

VENDEE — Land contract buyer.

VENDOR — Land contract seller.

VENT PIPE — See Soil Pipe and Stack.

VENTURE CAPITAL — Money invested in high risk projects which demands a higher rate of interest for its use.

VENUE — Official jurisdiction.

VERIFICATION — A written or oral statement as to the truth of a matter, document or individual.

VESTED — Rights granted to an owner of property under the legal document conveying them.

VETERAN'S ADMINISTRATION — The authority guaranteeing repayment of loans made to eligible veterans for home mortgages.

VISUAL RIGHTS — The right to clearly see an upcoming hazard, unobstructed, such as the right of a car driver to view traffic at an intersection takes precedence over the right of a property owner to allow a shrub to grow tall blocking the view.

VOID — Not legally enforceable.

VOIDABLE — May be annulled.

VOLUNTARY LIEN — A lien placed on property with an owner's permission.

W

WAIVE — Giving up the right to make a claim.

WAREHOUSING — Holding a mortgage until the market for its resale improves; a fee may be charged to a borrower to offset a lender's mortgage costs. Warehousing occurs during tight money markets when discount rates charged by wholesale (secondary) mortgage buyers to first mortgage lenders exceeds their profit margin, forcing them to hold mortgages until rates drop.

WARRANTY — A clause in a deed which states that a grantor guarantees a grantee the right of quiet enjoyment and possession of the subject property, free of hindrances which may be created by other parties of interest; title policies assure the same rights.

WASTING ASSETS — Assets which decrease in value through use and over a period of time, such as business equipment or a franchise.

WEAR AND TEAR — The normal decrease in value created by regular usage, such as wear and tear on carpet in a commercially leased office space; the lessor would usually be responsible for its replacement.

WEIR BOX — An apparatus that measures the flow of water through an irrigation canal.

WILD INTEREST — An interest in property which may not be properly reflected in public records due to an incorrect legal description or a changed name.

WILD LAND — Uncultivated land in its original state.

WITHOUT RECOURSE — A type of mortgage which is secured by the property alone and does not become a liability of the borrower.

WITNESS — A neutral third party called upon to view (witness) the signing by interested parties of deeds, wills, or other legal documents.

WORKING CAPITAL — Money needed to operate a business from day to day; may be derived by borrowing against accounts receivable or liquidating assets.

WORKING DRAWING — See Specifications.

WRAP-AROUND MORTGAGE — A mortgage which encompasses another mortgage or mortgages, which are usually at lower rates of interest. The mortgagee holding the wrap-around mortgage charges a higher rate of interest and makes a profit on the difference. Enables investors to earn interest (profit) on other lender's money.

WRIT OF EJECTMENT — Written instructions of a court directing the repossession of leased or rented property from a tenant.

WRIT OF EXECUTION — Written instructions directing that a court order judgment be fulfilled.

X

"X" — A mark used in place of a signature on a legal document by a person who is unable to write their name; must be witnessed.

X-BRACING — Cross braces in a wall.

Y

YIELD — The net annual income of a property in relation to an investor's initial downpayment equals the yield.

Z

ZERO LOT LINE — The front boundary of a lot, to which a commercial building might be constructed, such as to the sidewalk.

ZONING — Locally designated areas establishing the use of property, and the size, height and location of structures placed on it, as defined by zoning ordinances.

10.000%　MONTHLY AMORTIZING PAYMENTS

AMOUNT OF LOAN	NUMBER OF YEARS IN TERM							
	1	2	3	4	5	6	7	8
$ 50	4.40	2.31	1.62	1.27	1.07	.93	.84	.76
100	8.80	4.62	3.23	2.54	2.13	1.86	1.67	1.52
200	17.59	9.23	6.46	5.08	4.25	3.71	3.33	3.04
300	26.38	13.85	9.69	7.61	6.38	5.56	4.99	4.56
400	35.17	18.46	12.91	10.15	8.50	7.42	6.65	6.07
500	43.96	23.08	16.14	12.69	10.63	9.27	8.31	7.59
600	52.75	27.69	19.37	15.22	12.75	11.12	9.97	9.11
700	61.55	32.31	22.59	17.76	14.88	12.97	11.63	10.63
800	70.34	36.92	25.82	20.30	17.00	14.83	13.29	12.14
900	79.13	41.54	29.05	22.83	19.13	16.68	14.95	13.66
1000	87.92	46.15	32.27	25.37	21.25	18.53	16.61	15.18
2000	175.84	92.29	64.54	50.73	42.50	37.06	33.21	30.35
3000	263.75	138.44	96.81	76.09	63.75	55.58	49.81	45.53
4000	351.67	184.58	129.07	101.46	84.99	74.11	66.41	60.70
5000	439.58	230.73	161.34	126.82	106.24	92.63	83.01	75.88
6000	527.50	276.87	193.61	152.18	127.49	111.16	99.61	91.05
7000	615.42	323.02	225.88	177.54	148.73	129.69	116.21	106.22
8000	703.33	369.16	258.14	202.91	169.98	148.21	132.81	121.40
9000	791.25	415.31	290.41	228.27	191.23	166.74	149.42	136.57
10000	879.16	461.45	322.68	253.63	212.48	185.26	166.02	151.75
11000	967.08	507.60	354.94	278.99	233.72	203.79	182.62	166.92
12000	1055.00	553.74	387.21	304.36	254.97	222.32	199.22	182.09
13000	1142.91	599.89	419.48	329.72	276.22	240.84	215.82	197.27
14000	1230.83	646.03	451.75	355.08	297.46	259.37	232.42	212.44
15000	1318.74	692.18	484.01	380.44	318.71	277.89	249.02	227.62
16000	1406.66	738.32	516.28	405.81	339.96	296.42	265.62	242.79
17000	1494.58	784.47	548.55	431.17	361.20	314.94	282.23	257.97
18000	1582.49	830.61	580.81	456.53	382.45	333.47	298.83	273.14
19000	1670.41	876.76	613.08	481.89	403.70	352.00	315.43	288.31
20000	1758.32	922.90	645.35	507.26	424.95	370.52	332.03	303.49
21000	1846.24	969.05	677.62	532.62	446.19	389.05	348.63	318.66
22000	1934.15	1015.19	709.88	557.98	467.44	407.57	365.23	333.84
23000	2022.07	1061.34	742.15	583.34	488.69	426.10	381.83	349.01
24000	2109.99	1107.48	774.42	608.71	509.93	444.63	398.43	364.18
25000	2197.90	1153.63	806.68	634.07	531.18	463.15	415.03	379.36
26000	2285.82	1199.77	838.95	659.43	552.43	481.68	431.64	394.53
27000	2373.73	1245.92	871.22	684.79	573.68	500.20	448.24	409.71
28000	2461.65	1292.06	903.49	710.16	594.92	518.73	464.84	424.88
29000	2549.57	1338.21	935.75	735.52	616.17	537.25	481.44	440.06
30000	2637.48	1384.35	968.02	760.88	637.42	555.78	498.04	455.23
31000	2725.40	1430.50	1000.29	786.25	658.66	574.31	514.64	470.40
32000	2813.31	1476.64	1032.55	811.61	679.91	592.83	531.24	485.58
33000	2901.23	1522.79	1064.82	836.97	701.16	611.36	547.84	500.75
34000	2989.15	1568.93	1097.09	862.33	722.40	629.88	564.45	515.93
35000	3077.06	1615.08	1129.36	887.70	743.65	648.41	581.05	531.10
40000	3516.64	1845.80	1290.69	1014.51	849.89	741.04	664.05	606.97
45000	3956.22	2076.53	1452.03	1141.32	956.12	833.67	747.06	682.84
50000	4395.80	2307.25	1613.36	1268.13	1062.36	926.30	830.06	758.71
55000	4835.38	2537.98	1774.70	1394.95	1168.59	1018.93	913.07	834.58
60000	5274.96	2768.70	1936.04	1521.76	1274.83	1111.56	996.08	910.45
65000	5714.54	2999.43	2097.37	1648.57	1381.06	1204.18	1079.08	986.33
70000	6154.12	3230.15	2258.71	1775.39	1487.30	1296.81	1162.09	1062.20
75000	6593.70	3460.87	2420.04	1902.20	1593.53	1389.44	1245.09	1138.07
80000	7033.28	3691.60	2581.38	2029.01	1699.77	1482.07	1328.10	1213.94
85000	7472.86	3922.32	2742.72	2155.82	1806.00	1574.70	1411.11	1289.81
90000	7912.43	4153.05	2904.05	2282.64	1912.24	1667.33	1494.11	1365.68
95000	8352.01	4383.77	3065.39	2409.45	2018.47	1759.96	1577.12	1441.55
100000	8791.59	4614.50	3226.72	2536.26	2124.71	1852.59	1660.12	1517.42
105000	9231.17	4845.22	3388.06	2663.08	2230.94	1945.22	1743.13	1593.29
110000	9670.75	5075.95	3549.40	2789.89	2337.18	2037.85	1826.14	1669.16
115000	10110.23	5306.67	3710.73	2916.70	2443.42	2130.48	1909.14	1745.03
120000	10549.91	5537.40	3872.07	3043.52	2549.65	2223.11	1992.15	1820.90
125000	10989.49	5768.12	4033.40	3170.33	2655.89	2315.73	2075.15	1896.78
130000	11429.07	5998.85	4194.74	3297.14	2762.12	2408.36	2158.16	1972.65
135000	11868.65	6229.57	4356.08	3423.95	2868.36	2500.99	2241.16	2048.52
140000	12308.23	6460.29	4517.41	3550.77	2974.59	2593.62	2324.17	2124.39
145000	12747.81	6691.02	4678.75	3677.58	3080.83	2686.25	2407.18	2200.26
150000	13187.39	6921.74	4840.08	3804.39	3187.06	2778.88	2490.18	2276.13
155000	13626.97	7152.47	5001.42	3931.21	3293.30	2871.51	2573.19	2352.00
160000	14066.55	7383.19	5162.75	4058.02	3399.53	2964.14	2656.19	2427.87

114

MONTHLY AMORTIZING PAYMENTS 10.000%

AMOUNT OF LOAN	NUMBER OF YEARS IN TERM							
	9	10	15	20	25	30	35	40
$ 50	.71	.67	.54	.49	.46	.44	.43	.43
100	1.41	1.33	1.08	.97	.91	.88	.86	.85
200	2.82	2.65	2.15	1.94	1.82	1.76	1.72	1.70
300	4.23	3.97	3.23	2.90	2.73	2.64	2.58	2.55
400	5.64	5.29	4.30	3.87	3.64	3.52	3.44	3.40
500	7.04	6.61	5.38	4.83	4.55	4.39	4.30	4.25
600	8.45	7.93	6.45	5.80	5.46	5.27	5.16	5.10
700	9.86	9.26	7.53	6.76	6.37	6.15	6.02	5.95
800	11.27	10.58	8.60	7.73	7 27	7.03	6.88	6.80
900	12.68	11.90	9.68	8.69	8 18	7.90	7.74	7.65
1000	14.08	13.22	10.75	9.66	9.09	8.78	8.60	8.50
2000	28.16	26.44	21.50	19.31	18.18	17.56	17.20	16.99
3000	42.24	39.65	32.24	28.96	27.27	26.33	25.80	25.48
4000	56.32	52.87	42.99	38.61	36.35	35.11	34.39	33.97
5000	70.40	66.08	53.74	48.26	45.44	43.88	42.99	42.46
6000	84.48	79.30	64.48	57.91	54.53	52.66	51.59	50.95
7000	98.56	92.51	75.23	67.56	63.61	61.44	60.18	59.45
8000	112.63	105.73	85.97	77.21	72.70	70.21	68.78	67.94
9000	126.71	118.94	96.72	86.86	81.79	78.99	77.38	76.43
10000	140.79	132.16	107.47	96.51	90.88	87.76	85.97	84.92
11000	154.87	145.37	118.21	106.16	99.96	96.54	94.57	93.41
12000	168.95	158.59	128.96	115.81	109.05	105.31	103.17	101.90
13000	183.03	171.80	139.70	125.46	118.14	114.09	111.76	110.39
14000	197.11	185.02	150.45	135.11	127.22	122.87	120.36	118.89
15000	211.19	198.23	161.20	144.76	136.31	131.64	128.96	127.38
16000	225.26	211.45	171.94	154.41	145.40	140.42	137.55	135.87
17000	239.34	224.66	182.69	164.06	154.48	149.19	146.15	144.36
18000	253.42	237.88	193.43	173.71	163.57	157.97	154.75	152.85
19000	267.50	251.09	204.18	183.36	172.66	166.74	163.34	161.34
20000	281.58	264.31	214.93	193.01	181.75	175.52	171.94	169.83
21000	295.66	277.52	225.67	202.66	190.83	184.30	180.54	178.33
22000	309.74	290.74	236.42	212.31	199.92	193.07	189.13	186.82
23000	323.81	303.95	247.16	221.96	209.01	201.85	197.73	195.31
24000	337.89	317.17	257.91	231.61	218.09	210.62	206.33	203.80
25000	351.97	330.38	268.66	241.26	227.18	219.40	214.92	212.29
26000	366.05	343.60	279.40	250.91	236.27	228.17	223.52	220.78
27000	380.13	356.81	290.15	260.56	245.35	236.95	232.12	229.27
28000	394.21	370.03	300.89	270.21	254.44	245.73	240.71	237.77
29000	408.29	383.24	311.64	279.86	263.53	254.50	249.31	246.26
30000	422.37	396.46	322.39	289.51	272.62	263.28	257.91	254.75
31000	436.44	409.67	333.13	299.16	281.70	272.05	266.50	263.24
32000	450.52	422.89	343.88	308.81	290.79	280.83	275.10	271.73
33000	464.60	436.10	354.62	318.46	299.88	289.60	283.70	280.22
34000	478.68	449.32	365.37	328.11	308.96	298.38	292.29	288.71
35000	492.76	462.53	376.12	337.76	318.05	307.16	300.89	297.21
40000	563.15	528.61	429.85	386.01	363.49	351.03	343.87	339.66
45000	633.55	594.68	483.58	434.26	408.92	394.91	386.86	382.12
50000	703.94	660.76	537.31	482.52	454.36	438.79	429.84	424.58
55000	774.33	726.83	591.04	530.77	499.79	482.67	472.82	467.04
60000	844.73	792.91	644.77	579.02	545.23	526.55	515.81	509.49
65000	915.12	858.98	698.50	627.27	590.66	570.43	558.79	551.95
70000	985.51	925.06	752.23	675.52	636.10	614.31	601.78	594.41
75000	1055.91	991.14	805.96	723.77	681.53	658.18	644.76	636.86
80000	1126.30	1057.21	859.69	772.02	726.97	702.06	687.74	679.32
85000	1196.69	1123.29	913.42	820.27	772.40	745.94	730.73	721.78
90000	1267.09	1189.36	967.15	868.52	817.84	789.82	773.71	764.24
95000	1337.48	1255.44	1020.88	916.78	863.27	833.70	816.69	806.69
100000	1407.87	1321.51	1074.61	965.03	908.71	877.58	859.68	849.15
105000	1478.27	1387.59	1128.34	1013.28	954.14	921.46	902.66	891.61
110000	1548.66	1453.66	1182.07	1061.53	999.58	965.33	945.64	934.07
115000	1619.05	1519.74	1235.80	1109.78	1045.01	1009.21	988.63	976.52
120000	1689.45	1585.81	1289.53	1158.03	1090.45	1053.09	1031.61	1018.98
125000	1759.84	1651.89	1343.26	1206.28	1135.88	1096.97	1074.60	1061.44
130000	1830.23	1717.96	1396.99	1254.53	1181.32	1140.85	1117.58	1103.89
135000	1900.63	1784.04	1450.72	1302.78	1226.75	1184.73	1160.56	1146.35
140000	1971.02	1850.12	1504.45	1351.04	1272.19	1228.61	1203.55	1188.81
145000	2041.41	1916.19	1558.18	1399.29	1317.62	1272.48	1246.53	1231.27
150000	2111.81	1982.27	1611.91	1447.54	1363.06	1316.36	1289.51	1273.72
155000	2182.20	2048.34	1665.64	1495.79	1408.49	1360.24	1332.50	1316.18
160000	2252.59	2114.42	1719.37	1544.04	1453.93	1404.12	1375.48	1358.64

115

10.250% MONTHLY AMORTIZING PAYMENTS

AMOUNT OF LOAN	NUMBER OF YEARS IN TERM							
	1	2	3	4	5	6	7	8
$ 50	4.41	2.32	1.62	1.28	1.07	.94	.84	.77
100	8.81	4.63	3.24	2.55	2.14	1.87	1.68	1.54
200	17.61	9.26	6.48	5.10	4.28	3.74	3.35	3.07
300	26.41	13.88	9.72	7.65	6.42	5.60	5.02	4.60
400	35.22	18.51	12.96	10.20	8.55	7.47	6.70	6.13
500	44.02	23.14	16.20	12.75	10.69	9.33	8.37	7.66
600	52.82	27.76	19.44	15.29	12.83	11.20	10.04	9.19
700	61.63	32.39	22.67	17.84	14.96	13.06	11.72	10.72
800	70.43	37.01	25.91	20.39	17.10	14.93	13.39	12.25
900	79.23	41.64	29.15	22.94	19.24	16.79	15.06	13.78
1000	88.04	46.27	32.39	25.49	21.38	18.66	16.74	15.31
2000	176.07	92.53	64.77	50.97	42.75	37.31	33.47	30.62
3000	264.10	138.79	97.16	76.45	64.12	55.96	50.20	45.93
4000	352.13	185.05	129.54	101.94	85.49	74.61	66.93	61.23
5000	440.17	231.31	161.93	127.42	106.86	93.27	83.66	76.54
6000	528.20	277.57	194.31	152.90	128.23	111.92	100.39	91.85
7000	616.23	323.83	226.70	178.38	149.60	130.57	117.12	107.15
8000	704.26	370.00	259.08	203.87	170.97	149.22	133.85	122.46
9000	792.29	416.35	291.47	229.35	192.34	167.87	150.58	137.77
10000	880.33	462.61	323.85	254.83	213.71	186.53	167.31	153.07
11000	968.36	508.87	356.24	280.32	235.08	205.18	184.04	168.38
12000	1056.39	555.13	388.62	305.80	256.45	223.83	200.77	183.69
13000	1144.42	601.39	421.01	331.28	277.82	242.48	217.50	198.99
14000	1232.46	647.65	453.39	356.76	299.19	261.14	234.23	214.30
15000	1320.49	693.91	485.78	382.25	320.56	279.79	250.96	229.61
16000	1408.52	740.17	518.16	407.73	341.93	298.44	267.70	244.91
17000	1496.55	786.43	550.54	433.21	363.30	317.09	284.43	260.22
18000	1584.58	832.69	582.93	458.70	384.67	335.74	301.16	275.53
19000	1672.62	878.95	615.31	484.18	406.04	354.40	317.89	290.83
20000	1760.65	925.21	647.70	509.66	427.41	373.05	334.62	306.14
21000	1848.68	971.47	680.08	535.14	448.78	391.70	351.35	321.45
22000	1936.71	1017.73	712.47	560.63	470.15	410.35	368.08	336.75
23000	2024.75	1063.99	744.85	586.11	491.52	429.00	384.81	352.06
24000	2112.78	1110.25	777.24	611.59	512.89	447.66	401.54	367.37
25000	2200.81	1156.51	809.62	637.08	534.26	466.31	418.27	382.67
26000	2288.84	1202.78	842.01	662.56	555.63	484.96	435.00	397.98
27000	2376.87	1249.04	874.39	688.04	577.00	503.61	451.73	413.29
28000	2464.91	1295.30	906.78	713.52	598.37	522.27	468.46	428.59
29000	2552.94	1341.56	939.16	739.01	619.74	540.92	485.19	443.90
30000	2640.97	1387.82	971.55	764.49	641.11	559.57	501.92	459.21
31000	2729.00	1434.08	1003.93	789.97	662.48	578.22	518.65	474.51
32000	2817.04	1480.34	1036.32	815.46	683.85	596.87	535.39	489.82
33000	2905.07	1526.60	1068.70	840.94	705.22	615.53	552.12	505.13
34000	2993.10	1572.86	1101.08	866.42	726.59	634.18	568.85	520.44
35000	3081.13	1619.12	1133.47	891.90	747.96	652.83	585.58	535.74
40000	3521.29	1850.42	1295.39	1019.32	854.82	746.09	669.23	612.28
45000	3961.45	2081.72	1457.32	1146.73	961.67	839.35	752.88	688.81
50000	4401.62	2313.02	1619.24	1274.15	1068.52	932.61	836.54	765.34
55000	4841.78	2544.33	1781.16	1401.56	1175.37	1025.87	920.19	841.88
60000	5281.94	2775.63	1943.09	1528.97	1282.22	1119.13	1003.84	918.41
65000	5722.10	3006.93	2105.01	1656.39	1389.07	1212.40	1087.50	994.95
70000	6162.26	3238.23	2266.93	1783.80	1495.92	1305.66	1171.15	1071.48
75000	6602.42	3469.53	2428.86	1911.22	1602.77	1398.92	1254.80	1148.01
80000	7042.58	3700.84	2590.78	2038.63	1709.63	1492.18	1338.46	1224.55
85000	7482.74	3932.14	2752.70	2166.04	1816.48	1585.44	1422.11	1301.08
90000	7922.90	4163.44	2914.63	2293.46	1923.33	1678.70	1505.76	1377.61
95000	8363.06	4394.74	3076.55	2420.87	2030.18	1771.96	1589.42	1454.15
100000	8803.23	4626.04	3238.47	2548.29	2137.03	1865.22	1673.07	1530.68
105000	9243.39	4857.35	3400.40	2675.70	2243.88	1958.48	1756.72	1607.22
110000	9683.55	5088.65	3562.32	2803.11	2350.73	2051.74	1840.38	1683.75
115000	10123.71	5319.95	3724.24	2930.53	2457.59	2145.00	1924.03	1760.28
120000	10563.87	5551.25	3886.17	3057.94	2564.44	2238.26	2007.68	1836.82
125000	11004.03	5782.55	4048.09	3185.36	2671.29	2331.52	2091.34	1913.35
130000	11444.19	6013.86	4210.01	3312.77	2778.14	2424.79	2174.99	1989.89
135000	11884.35	6245.16	4371.94	3440.18	2884.99	2518.05	2258.64	2066.42
140000	12324.51	6476.46	4533.86	3567.60	2991.84	2611.31	2342.30	2142.95
145000	12764.67	6707.76	4695.78	3695.01	3098.69	2704.57	2425.95	2219.49
150000	13204.84	6939.06	4857.71	3822.43	3205.54	2797.83	2509.60	2296.02
155000	13645.00	7170.37	5019.63	3949.84	3312.40	2891.09	2593.25	2372.55
160000	14085.16	7401.67	5181.56	4077.26	3419.25	2984.35	2676.91	2449.09

116

AMOUNT OF LOAN	NUMBER OF YEARS IN TERM							
	9	10	15	20	25	30	35	40
$ 50	.72	.67	.55	.50	.47	.45	.44	.44
100	1.43	1.34	1.09	.99	.93	.90	.88	.87
200	2.85	2.68	2.18	1.97	1.86	1.80	1.76	1.74
300	4.27	4.01	3.27	2.95	2.78	2.69	2.64	2.61
400	5.69	5.35	4.36	3.93	3.71	3.59	3.52	3.48
500	7.11	6.68	5.45	4.91	4.64	4.49	4.40	4.35
600	8.53	8.02	6.54	5.89	5.56	5.38	5.28	5.22
700	9.96	9.35	7.63	6.88	6.49	6.28	6.16	6.09
800	11.38	10.69	8.72	7.86	7.42	7.17	7.04	6.96
900	12.80	12.02	9.81	8.84	8.34	8.07	7.91	7.82
1000	14.22	13.36	10.90	9.82	9.27	8.97	8.79	8.69
2000	28.43	26.71	21.80	19.64	18.53	17.93	17.58	17.38
3000	42.65	40.07	32.70	29.45	27.80	26.89	26.37	26.07
4000	56.86	53.42	43.60	39.27	37.06	35.85	35.16	34.76
5000	71.08	66.77	54.50	49.09	46.32	44.81	43.95	43.45
6000	85.29	80.13	65.40	58.90	55.59	53.77	52.74	52.13
7000	99.51	93.48	76.30	68.72	64.85	62.73	61.52	60.82
8000	113.72	106.84	87.20	78.54	74.12	71.69	70.31	69.51
9000	127.93	120.19	98.10	88.35	83.38	80.65	79.10	78.20
10000	142.15	133.54	109.00	98.17	92.64	89.62	87.89	86.89
11000	156.36	146.90	119.90	107.99	101.91	98.58	96.68	95.58
12000	170.58	160.25	130.80	117.80	111.17	107.54	105.47	104.26
13000	184.79	173.61	141.70	127.62	120.43	116.50	114.26	112.95
14000	199.01	186.96	152.60	137.44	129.70	125.46	123.04	121.64
15000	213.22	200.31	163.50	147.25	138.96	134.42	131.83	130.33
16000	227.44	213.67	174.40	157.07	148.23	143.38	140.62	139.02
17000	241.65	227.02	185.30	166.88	157.49	152.34	149.41	147.70
18000	255.86	240.38	196.20	176.70	166.75	161.30	158.20	156.39
19000	270.08	253.73	207.10	186.52	176.02	170.26	166.99	165.08
20000	284.29	267.08	218.00	196.33	185.28	179.23	175.78	173.77
21000	298.51	280.44	228.89	206.15	194.55	188.19	184.56	182.46
22000	312.72	293.79	239.79	215.97	203.81	197.15	193.35	191.15
23000	326.94	307.14	250.69	225.78	213.07	206.11	202.14	199.83
24000	341.15	320.50	261.59	235.60	222.34	215.07	210.93	208.52
25000	355.37	333.85	272.49	245.42	231.60	224.03	219.72	217.21
26000	369.58	347.21	283.39	255.23	240.86	232.99	228.51	225.90
27000	383.79	360.56	294.29	265.05	250.13	241.95	237.30	234.59
28000	398.01	373.91	305.19	274.87	259.39	250.91	246.08	243.27
29000	412.22	387.27	316.09	284.68	268.66	259.87	254.87	251.96
30000	426.44	400.62	326.99	294.50	277.92	268.84	263.66	260.65
31000	440.65	413.98	337.89	304.31	287.18	277.80	272.45	269.34
32000	454.87	427.33	348.79	314.13	296.45	286.76	281.24	278.03
33000	469.08	440.68	359.69	323.95	305.71	295.72	290.03	286.72
34000	483.30	454.04	370.59	333.76	314.98	304.68	298.82	295.40
35000	497.51	467.39	381.49	343.58	324.24	313.64	307.60	304.09
40000	568.58	534.16	435.99	392.66	370.56	358.45	351.55	347.53
45000	639.65	600.93	490.48	441.74	416.88	403.25	395.49	390.97
50000	710.73	667.70	544.98	490.83	463.20	448.06	439.43	434.41
55000	781.80	734.47	599.48	539.91	509.52	492.86	483.38	477.86
60000	852.87	801.24	653.98	588.99	555.83	537.67	527.32	521.30
65000	923.94	868.01	708.47	638.07	602.15	582.47	571.26	564.74
70000	995.01	934.78	762.97	687.16	648.47	627.28	615.20	608.18
75000	1066.09	1001.55	817.47	736.24	694.79	672.08	659.15	651.62
80000	1137.16	1068.32	871.97	785.32	741.11	716.89	703.09	695.06
85000	1208.23	1135.09	926.46	834.40	787.43	761.69	747.03	738.50
90000	1279.30	1201.86	980.96	883.48	833.75	806.50	790.98	781.94
95000	1350.37	1268.63	1035.46	932.57	880.07	851.30	834.92	825.38
100000	1421.45	1335.40	1089.96	981.65	926.39	896.11	878.86	868.82
105000	1492.52	1402.16	1144.45	1030.73	972.71	940.91	922.80	912.26
110000	1563.59	1468.93	1198.95	1079.81	1019.03	985.72	966.75	955.71
115000	1634.66	1535.70	1253.45	1128.89	1065.35	1030.52	1010.69	999.15
120000	1705.74	1602.47	1307.95	1177.98	1111.66	1075.33	1054.63	1042.59
125000	1776.81	1669.24	1362.44	1227.06	1157.98	1120.13	1098.57	1086.03
130000	1847.88	1736.01	1416.94	1276.14	1204.30	1164.94	1142.52	1129.47
135000	1918.95	1802.78	1471.44	1325.22	1250.62	1209.74	1186.46	1172.91
140000	1990.02	1869.55	1525.94	1374.31	1296.94	1254.55	1230.40	1216.35
145000	2061.10	1936.32	1580.43	1423.39	1343.26	1299.35	1274.35	1259.79
150000	2132.17	2003.09	1634.93	1472.47	1389.58	1344.16	1318.29	1303.23
155000	2203.24	2069.86	1689.43	1521.55	1435.90	1388.96	1362.23	1346.67
160000	2274.31	2136.63	1743.93	1570.63	1482.22	1433.77	1406.17	1390.11

10.500% MONTHLY AMORTIZING PAYMENTS

AMOUNT OF LOAN	NUMBER OF YEARS IN TERM							
	1	2	3	4	5	6	7	8
$ 50	4.41	2.32	1.63	1.29	1.08	.94	.85	.78
100	8.82	4.64	3.26	2.57	2.15	1.88	1.69	1.55
200	17.63	9.28	6.51	5.13	4.30	3.76	3.38	3.09
300	26.45	13.92	9.76	7.69	6.45	5.64	5.06	4.64
400	35.26	18.56	13.01	10.25	8.60	7.52	6.75	6.18
500	44.08	23.19	16.26	12.81	10.75	9.39	8.44	7.73
600	52.89	27.83	19.51	15.37	12.90	11.27	10.12	9.27
700	61.71	32.47	22.76	17.93	15.05	13.15	11.81	10.81
800	70.52	37.11	26.01	20.49	17.20	15.03	13.49	12.36
900	79.34	41.74	29.26	23.05	19.35	16.91	15.18	13.90
1000	88.15	46.38	32.51	25.61	21.50	18.78	16.87	15.45
2000	176.30	92.76	65.01	51.21	42.99	37.56	33.73	30.89
3000	264.45	139.13	97.51	76.82	64.49	56.34	50.59	46.33
4000	352.60	185.51	130.01	102.42	85.98	75.12	67.45	61.77
5000	440.75	231.89	162.52	128.02	107.47	93.90	84.31	77.21
6000	528.90	278.26	195.02	153.63	128.97	112.68	101.17	92.65
7000	617.05	324.64	227.52	179.23	150.46	131.46	118.03	108.09
8000	705.19	371.01	260.02	204.83	171.96	150.24	134.89	123.53
9000	793.34	417.39	292.53	230.44	193.45	169.02	151.75	138.97
10000	881.49	463.77	325.03	256.04	214.94	187.79	168.61	154.41
11000	969.64	510.14	357.53	281.64	236.44	206.57	185.47	169.85
12000	1057.79	556.52	390.03	307.25	257.93	225.35	202.33	185.29
13000	1145.94	602.89	422.54	332.85	279.43	244.13	219.19	200.73
14000	1234.09	649.27	455.04	358.45	300.92	262.91	236.05	216.17
15000	1322.23	695.65	487.54	384.06	322.41	281.69	252.92	231.61
16000	1410.38	742.02	520.04	409.66	343.91	300.47	269.78	247.05
17000	1498.53	788.40	552.55	435.26	365.40	319.25	286.64	262.49
18000	1586.68	834.77	585.05	460.87	386.90	338.03	303.50	277.93
19000	1674.83	881.15	617.55	486.47	408.39	356.81	320.36	293.37
20000	1762.98	927.53	650.05	512.07	429.88	375.58	337.22	308.81
21000	1851.13	973.90	682.56	537.68	451.38	394.36	354.08	324.25
22000	1939.27	1020.28	715.06	563.28	472.87	413.14	370.94	339.69
23000	2027.42	1066.65	747.56	588.88	494.36	431.92	387.80	355.13
24000	2115.57	1113.03	780.06	614.49	515.86	450.70	404.66	370.57
25000	2203.72	1159.41	812.57	640.09	537.35	469.48	421.52	386.01
26000	2291.89	1205.78	845.07	665.69	558.85	488.26	438.38	401.45
27000	2380.02	1252.16	877.57	691.30	580.34	507.04	455.24	416.89
28000	2468.17	1298.53	910.07	716.90	601.83	525.82	472.10	432.33
29000	2556.31	1344.91	942.58	742.50	623.33	544.60	488.96	447.77
30000	2644.46	1391.29	975.08	768.11	644.82	563.37	505.83	463.21
31000	2732.61	1437.66	1007.58	793.71	666.32	582.15	522.69	478.65
32000	2820.76	1484.04	1040.08	819.31	687.81	600.93	539.55	494.09
33000	2908.91	1530.41	1072.59	844.92	709.30	619.71	556.41	509.53
34000	2997.06	1576.79	1105.09	870.52	730.80	638.49	573.27	524.97
35000	3085.21	1623.17	1137.59	896.12	752.29	657.27	590.13	540.41
40000	3525.95	1855.05	1300.10	1024.14	859.76	751.16	674.43	617.61
45000	3966.69	2086.93	1462.61	1152.16	967.23	845.06	758.74	694.81
50000	4407.44	2318.81	1625.13	1280.17	1074.70	938.95	843.04	772.01
55000	4848.18	2550.69	1787.64	1408.19	1182.17	1032.85	927.34	849.21
60000	5288.92	2782.57	1950.15	1536.21	1289.64	1126.74	1011.65	926.41
65000	5729.66	3014.45	2112.66	1664.22	1397.11	1220.64	1095.95	1003.61
70000	6170.41	3246.33	2275.18	1792.24	1504.58	1314.53	1180.25	1080.81
75000	6611.15	3478.21	2437.69	1920.26	1612.05	1408.43	1264.56	1158.01
80000	7051.89	3710.09	2600.20	2048.28	1719.52	1502.32	1348.86	1235.21
85000	7492.64	3941.97	2762.71	2176.29	1826.99	1596.22	1433.16	1312.41
90000	7933.38	4173.85	2925.22	2304.31	1934.46	1690.11	1517.47	1389.61
95000	8374.12	4405.73	3087.74	2432.33	2041.93	1784.01	1601.77	1466.81
100000	8814.87	4637.61	3250.25	2560.34	2149.40	1877.90	1686.07	1544.01
105000	9255.61	4869.49	3412.76	2688.36	2256.86	1971.80	1770.38	1621.21
110000	9696.35	5101.37	3575.27	2816.38	2364.33	2065.69	1854.68	1698.41
115000	10137.09	5333.25	3737.79	2944.39	2471.80	2159.59	1938.98	1775.61
120000	10577.84	5565.13	3900.30	3072.41	2579.27	2253.48	2023.29	1852.81
125000	11018.58	5797.01	4062.81	3200.43	2686.74	2347.38	2107.59	1930.01
130000	11459.32	6028.89	4225.32	3328.44	2794.21	2441.27	2191.89	2007.21
135000	11900.07	6260.77	4387.83	3456.46	2901.68	2535.17	2276.20	2084.41
140000	12340.81	6492.65	4550.35	3584.48	3009.15	2629.06	2360.50	2161.61
145000	12781.55	6724.53	4712.86	3712.50	3116.62	2722.96	2444.80	2238.81
150000	13222.30	6956.41	4875.37	3840.51	3224.09	2816.85	2529.11	2316.01
155000	13663.04	7188.29	5037.88	3968.53	3331.56	2910.75	2613.41	2393.21
160000	14103.78	7420.17	5200.40	4096.55	3439.03	3004.64	2697.71	2470.41

118

AMOUNT OF LOAN	NUMBER OF YEARS IN TERM							
	9	10	15	20	25	30	35	40
$ 50	.72	.68	.56	.50	.48	.46	.45	.45
100	1.44	1.35	1.11	1.00	.95	.92	.90	.89
200	2.88	2.70	2.22	2.00	1.89	1.83	1.80	1.78
300	4.31	4.05	3.32	3.00	2.84	2.75	2.70	2.67
400	5.75	5.40	4.43	4.00	3.78	3.66	3.60	3.56
500	7.18	6.75	5.53	5.00	4.73	4.58	4.50	4.45
600	8.62	8.10	6.64	6.00	5.67	5.49	5.39	5.34
700	10.05	9.45	7.74	6.99	6.61	6.41	6.29	6.22
800	11.49	10.80	8.85	7.99	7.56	7.32	7.19	7.11
900	12.92	12.15	9.95	8.99	8.50	8.24	8.09	8.00
1000	14.36	13.50	11.06	9.99	9.45	9.15	8.99	8.89
2000	28.71	26.99	22.11	19.97	18.89	18.30	17.97	17.78
3000	43.06	40.49	33.17	29.96	28.33	27.45	26.95	26.66
4000	57.41	53.98	44.22	39.94	37.77	36.59	35.93	35.55
5000	71.76	67.47	55.27	49.92	47.21	45.74	44.91	44.43
6000	86.11	80.97	66.33	59.91	56.66	54.89	53.89	53.32
7000	100.46	94.46	77.38	69.89	66.10	64.04	62.87	62.20
8000	114.81	107.95	88.44	79.88	75.54	73.18	71.86	71.09
9000	129.16	121.45	99.49	89.86	84.98	82.33	80.84	79.98
10000	143.51	134.94	110.54	99.84	94.42	91.48	89.82	88.86
11000	157.86	148.43	121.60	109.83	103.86	100.63	98.80	97.75
12000	172.22	161.93	132.65	119.81	113.31	109.77	107.78	106.63
13000	186.57	175.42	143.71	129.79	122.75	118.92	116.76	115.52
14000	200.92	188.91	154.76	139.78	132.19	128.07	125.74	124.40
15000	215.27	202.41	165.81	149.76	141.63	137.22	134.73	133.29
16000	229.63	215.90	176.87	159.75	151.07	146.36	143.71	142.18
17000	243.97	229.39	187.92	169.73	160.52	155.51	152.69	151.06
18000	258.32	242.89	198.98	179.71	169.96	164.66	161.67	159.95
19000	272.67	256.38	210.03	189.70	179.40	173.81	170.65	168.83
20000	287.02	269.87	221.08	199.68	188.84	182.95	179.63	177.72
21000	301.37	283.37	232.14	209.66	198.28	192.10	188.61	186.60
22000	315.72	296.86	243.19	219.65	207.72	201.25	197.59	195.49
23000	330.07	310.36	254.25	229.63	217.17	210.40	206.58	204.38
24000	344.43	323.85	265.30	239.62	226.61	219.54	215.56	213.26
25000	358.78	337.34	276.35	249.60	236.05	228.69	224.54	222.15
26000	373.13	350.84	287.41	259.58	245.49	237.84	233.52	231.03
27000	387.48	364.33	298.46	269.57	254.93	246.98	242.50	239.92
28000	401.83	377.82	309.52	279.55	264.38	256.13	251.48	248.80
29000	416.18	391.32	320.57	289.54	273.82	265.28	260.46	257.69
30000	430.53	404.81	331.62	299.52	283.26	274.43	269.45	266.58
31000	444.88	418.30	342.68	309.50	292.70	283.57	278.43	275.46
32000	459.23	431.80	353.73	319.49	302.14	292.72	287.41	284.35
33000	473.58	445.29	364.79	329.47	311.58	301.87	296.39	293.23
34000	487.93	458.78	375.84	339.45	321.03	311.02	305.37	302.12
35000	502.29	472.28	386.89	349.44	330.47	320.16	314.35	311.00
40000	574.04	539.74	442.16	399.36	377.68	365.90	359.26	355.43
45000	645.79	607.21	497.43	449.28	424.89	411.64	404.17	399.86
50000	717.55	674.68	552.70	499.19	472.10	457.37	449.07	444.29
55000	789.30	742.15	607.97	549.11	519.30	503.11	493.98	488.72
60000	861.06	809.61	663.24	599.03	566.51	548.85	538.89	533.15
65000	932.81	877.08	718.51	648.95	613.72	594.59	583.79	577.58
70000	1004.57	944.55	773.78	698.87	660.93	640.32	628.70	622.00
75000	1076.32	1012.02	829.05	748.79	708.14	686.06	673.61	666.43
80000	1148.07	1079.48	884.32	798.71	755.35	731.80	718.51	710.86
85000	1219.83	1146.95	939.59	848.63	802.56	777.53	763.42	755.29
90000	1291.58	1214.42	994.86	898.55	849.77	823.27	808.33	799.72
95000	1363.34	1281.89	1050.13	948.47	896.98	869.01	853.23	844.15
100000	1435.09	1349.35	1105.40	998.38	944.19	914.74	898.14	888.58
105000	1506.85	1416.82	1160.67	1048.30	991.40	960.48	943.05	933.00
110000	1578.60	1484.29	1215.94	1098.22	1038.60	1006.22	987.95	977.43
115000	1650.35	1551.76	1271.21	1148.14	1085.81	1051.96	1032.86	1021.86
120000	1722.11	1619.22	1326.48	1198.06	1133.02	1097.69	1077.77	1066.29
125000	1793.86	1686.69	1381.75	1247.98	1180.23	1143.43	1122.67	1110.72
130000	1865.62	1754.16	1437.02	1297.90	1227.44	1189.17	1167.58	1155.15
135000	1937.37	1821.63	1492.29	1347.82	1274.65	1234.90	1212.49	1199.57
140000	2009.13	1889.09	1547.56	1397.74	1321.86	1280.64	1257.39	1244.00
145000	2080.88	1956.56	1602.83	1447.66	1369.07	1326.38	1302.30	1288.43
150000	2152.63	2024.03	1658.10	1497.57	1416.28	1372.11	1347.21	1332.86
155000	2224.39	2091.50	1713.37	1547.49	1463.49	1417.85	1392.11	1377.29
160000	2296.14	2158.96	1768.64	1597.41	1510.70	1463.59	1437.02	1421.72

10.750%   MONTHLY AMORTIZING PAYMENTS

AMOUNT OF LOAN	NUMBER OF YEARS IN TERM							
	1	2	3	4	5	6	7	8
$ 50	4.42	2.33	1.64	1.29	1.09	.95	.85	.78
100	8.83	4.65	3.27	2.58	2.17	1.90	1.70	1.56
200	17.66	9.30	6.53	5.15	4.33	3.79	3.40	3.12
300	26.48	13.95	9.79	7.72	6.49	5.68	5.10	4.68
400	35.31	18.60	13.05	10.29	8.65	7.57	6.80	6.23
500	44.14	23.25	16.32	12.87	10.81	9.46	8.50	7.79
600	52.96	27.90	19.58	15.44	12.98	11.35	10.20	9.35
700	61.79	32.55	22.84	18.01	15.14	13.24	11.90	10.91
800	70.62	37.20	26.10	20.58	17.30	15.13	13.60	12.46
900	79.44	41.85	29.36	23.16	19.46	17.02	15.30	14.02
1000	88.27	46.50	32.63	25.73	21.62	18.91	17.00	15.58
2000	176.54	92.99	65.25	51.45	43.24	37.82	33.99	31.15
3000	264.80	139.48	97.87	77.18	64.86	56.72	50.98	46.73
4000	353.07	185.97	130.49	102.90	86.48	75.63	67.97	62.30
5000	441.33	232.46	163.11	128.63	108.09	94.54	84.96	77.87
6000	529.60	278.96	195.73	154.35	129.71	113.44	101.95	93.45
7000	617.86	325.45	228.35	180.07	151.33	132.35	118.94	109.02
8000	706.13	371.94	260.97	205.80	172.95	151.26	135.94	124.60
9000	794.39	418.43	293.59	231.52	194.57	170.16	152.93	140.17
10000	882.66	464.92	326.21	257.25	216.18	189.07	169.92	155.74
11000	970.92	511.42	358.83	282.97	237.80	207.97	186.91	171.32
12000	1059.19	557.91	391.45	308.70	259.42	226.88	203.90	186.89
13000	1147.45	604.40	424.07	334.42	281.04	245.79	220.89	202.47
14000	1235.72	650.89	456.69	360.14	302.66	264.69	237.88	218.04
15000	1323.98	697.38	489.31	385.87	324.27	283.60	254.87	233.61
16000	1412.25	743.87	521.93	411.59	345.89	302.51	271.87	249.19
17000	1500.51	790.37	554.55	437.32	367.51	321.41	288.86	264.76
18000	1588.78	836.86	587.17	463.04	389.13	340.32	305.85	280.34
19000	1677.04	883.35	619.79	488.77	410.75	359.22	322.84	295.91
20000	1765.31	929.84	652.41	514.49	432.36	378.13	339.83	311.48
21000	1853.57	976.33	685.03	540.21	453.98	397.04	356.82	327.06
22000	1941.84	1022.83	717.65	565.94	475.60	415.94	373.81	342.63
23000	2030.10	1069.32	750.28	591.66	497.22	434.85	390.80	358.20
24000	2118.37	1115.81	782.90	617.39	518.84	453.76	407.80	373.78
25000	2206.63	1162.30	815.52	643.11	540.45	472.66	424.79	389.35
26000	2294.90	1208.79	848.14	668.84	562.07	491.57	441.78	404.93
27000	2383.16	1255.29	880.76	694.56	583.69	510.47	458.77	420.50
28000	2471.43	1301.78	913.38	720.28	605.31	529.38	475.76	436.07
29000	2559.69	1348.27	946.00	746.01	626.93	548.29	492.75	451.65
30000	2647.96	1394.76	978.62	771.73	648.54	567.19	509.74	467.22
31000	2736.22	1441.25	1011.24	797.46	670.16	586.10	526.73	482.80
32000	2824.49	1487.74	1043.86	823.18	691.78	605.01	543.73	498.37
33000	2912.75	1534.24	1076.48	848.91	713.40	623.91	560.72	513.94
34000	3001.02	1580.73	1109.10	874.63	735.02	642.82	577.71	529.52
35000	3089.28	1627.22	1141.72	900.35	756.63	661.72	594.70	545.09
40000	3530.61	1859.68	1304.82	1028.98	864.72	756.26	679.66	622.96
45000	3971.93	2092.14	1467.93	1157.60	972.81	850.79	764.61	700.83
50000	4413.26	2324.60	1631.03	1286.22	1080.90	945.32	849.57	778.70
55000	4854.58	2557.06	1794.13	1414.84	1188.99	1039.85	934.52	856.57
60000	5295.91	2789.52	1957.23	1543.46	1297.08	1134.38	1019.48	934.44
65000	5737.24	3021.98	2120.33	1672.08	1405.17	1228.91	1104.44	1012.31
70000	6178.56	3254.43	2283.44	1800.70	1513.26	1323.44	1189.39	1090.18
75000	6619.89	3486.89	2446.54	1929.33	1621.35	1417.98	1274.35	1168.05
80000	7061.21	3719.35	2609.64	2057.95	1729.44	1512.51	1359.31	1245.92
85000	7502.54	3951.81	2772.74	2186.57	1837.53	1607.04	1444.26	1323.79
90000	7943.86	4184.27	2935.85	2315.19	1945.62	1701.57	1529.22	1401.66
95000	8385.19	4416.73	3098.95	2443.81	2053.71	1796.10	1614.18	1479.53
100000	8826.51	4649.19	3262.05	2572.43	2161.80	1890.63	1699.13	1557.40
105000	9267.84	4881.65	3425.15	2701.05	2269.89	1985.16	1784.09	1635.26
110000	9709.16	5114.11	3588.25	2829.68	2377.98	2079.70	1869.04	1713.13
115000	10150.49	5346.57	3751.36	2958.30	2486.07	2174.23	1954.00	1791.00
120000	10591.82	5579.03	3914.46	3086.92	2594.16	2268.76	2038.96	1868.87
125000	11033.14	5811.49	4077.56	3215.54	2702.25	2363.29	2123.91	1946.74
130000	11474.47	6043.95	4240.66	3344.16	2810.34	2457.82	2208.87	2024.61
135000	11915.79	6276.41	4403.77	3472.78	2918.43	2552.35	2293.83	2102.48
140000	12357.12	6508.86	4566.87	3601.40	3026.52	2646.88	2378.78	2180.35
145000	12798.44	6741.32	4729.97	3730.03	3134.61	2741.42	2463.74	2258.22
150000	13239.77	6973.78	4893.07	3858.65	3242.70	2835.95	2548.70	2336.09
155000	13681.09	7206.24	5056.18	3987.27	3350.79	2930.48	2633.65	2413.96
160000	14122.42	7438.70	5219.28	4115.89	3458.88	3025.01	2718.61	2491.83

AMOUNT OF LOAN	NUMBER OF YEARS IN TERM							
	9	10	15	20	25	30	35	40
$ 50	.73	.69	.57	.51	.49	.47	.46	.46
100	1.45	1.37	1.13	1.02	.97	.94	.92	.91
200	2.90	2.73	2.25	2.04	1.93	1.87	1.84	1.82
300	4.35	4.10	3.37	3.05	2.89	2.81	2.76	2.73
400	5.80	5.46	4.49	4.07	3.85	3.74	3.68	3.64
500	7.25	6.82	5.61	5.08	4.82	4.67	4.59	4.55
600	8.70	8.19	6.73	6.10	5.78	5.61	5.51	5.46
700	10.15	9.55	7.85	7.11	6.74	6.54	6.43	6.36
800	11.60	10.91	8.97	8.13	7.70	7.47	7.35	7.27
900	13.04	12.28	10.09	9.14	8.66	8.41	8.26	8.18
1000	14.49	13.64	11.21	10.16	9.63	9.34	9.18	9.09
2000	28.98	27.27	22.42	20.31	19.25	18.67	18.36	18.17
3000	43.47	40.91	33.63	30.46	28.87	28.01	27.53	27.26
4000	57.96	54.54	44.84	40.61	38.49	37.34	36.71	36.34
5000	72.45	68.17	56.05	50.77	48.11	46.68	45.88	45.42
6000	86.93	81.81	67.26	60.92	57.73	56.01	55.06	54.51
7000	101.42	95.44	78.47	71.07	67.35	65.35	64.23	63.59
8000	115.91	109.08	89.68	81.22	76.97	74.68	73.41	72.68
9000	130.40	122.71	100.89	91.38	86.59	84.02	82.58	81.76
10000	144.89	136.34	112.10	101.53	96.21	93.35	91.76	90.84
11000	159.37	149.98	123.31	111.68	105.84	102.69	100.93	99.93
12000	173.86	163.61	134.52	121.83	115.46	112.02	110.11	109.01
13000	188.35	177.25	145.73	131.98	125.08	121.36	119.28	118.10
14000	202.84	190.88	156.94	142.14	134.70	130.69	128.46	127.18
15000	217.33	204.51	168.15	152.29	144.32	140.03	137.63	136.26
16000	231.81	218.15	179.36	162.44	153.94	149.36	146.81	145.35
17000	246.30	231.78	190.57	172.59	163.56	158.70	155.98	154.43
18000	260.79	245.41	201.78	182.75	173.18	168.03	165.16	163.52
19000	275.28	259.05	212.99	192.90	182.80	177.37	174.33	172.60
20000	289.77	272.68	224.19	203.05	192.42	186.70	183.51	181.68
21000	304.25	286.32	235.40	213.20	202.04	196.04	192.68	190.77
22000	318.74	299.95	246.61	223.36	211.67	205.37	201.86	199.85
23000	333.23	313.58	257.82	233.51	221.29	214.71	211.03	208.94
24000	347.72	327.22	269.03	243.66	230.91	224.04	220.21	218.02
25000	362.21	340.85	280.24	253.81	240.53	233.38	229.38	227.10
26000	376.69	354.49	291.45	263.96	250.15	242.71	238.56	236.19
27000	391.18	368.12	302.66	274.12	259.77	252.04	247.73	245.27
28000	405.67	381.75	313.87	284.27	269.39	261.38	256.91	254.36
29000	420.16	395.39	325.08	294.42	279.01	270.71	266.08	263.44
30000	434.65	409.02	336.29	304.57	288.63	280.05	275.26	272.52
31000	449.13	422.65	347.50	314.73	298.25	289.38	284.43	281.61
32000	463.62	436.29	358.71	324.88	307.87	298.72	293.61	290.69
33000	478.11	449.92	369.92	335.03	317.50	308.05	302.78	299.78
34000	492.60	463.56	381.13	345.18	327.12	317.39	311.96	308.86
35000	507.09	477.19	392.34	355.34	336.74	326.72	321.13	317.94
40000	579.53	545.36	448.38	406.10	384.84	373.40	367.01	363.36
45000	651.97	613.53	504.43	456.86	432.95	420.07	412.88	408.78
50000	724.41	681.70	560.48	507.62	481.05	466.75	458.76	454.20
55000	796.85	749.87	616.53	558.38	529.16	513.42	504.64	499.62
60000	869.29	818.04	672.57	609.14	577.26	560.09	550.51	545.04
65000	941.73	886.21	728.62	659.90	625.37	606.77	596.38	590.46
70000	1014.17	954.38	784.67	710.67	673.47	653.44	642.26	635.88
75000	1086.61	1022.55	840.72	761.43	721.57	700.12	688.13	681.30
80000	1159.05	1090.71	896.76	812.19	769.68	746.79	734.01	726.72
85000	1231.49	1158.88	952.81	862.95	817.78	793.46	779.88	772.14
90000	1303.93	1227.05	1008.86	913.71	865.89	840.14	825.76	817.56
95000	1376.37	1295.22	1064.91	964.47	913.99	886.81	871.63	862.98
100000	1448.81	1363.39	1120.95	1015.23	962.10	933.49	917.51	908.40
105000	1521.25	1431.56	1177.00	1066.00	1010.20	980.16	963.38	953.82
110000	1593.69	1499.73	1233.05	1116.76	1058.31	1026.83	1009.26	999.24
115000	1666.13	1567.90	1289.10	1167.52	1106.41	1073.51	1055.13	1044.66
120000	1738.57	1636.07	1345.14	1218.28	1154.52	1120.18	1101.01	1090.08
125000	1811.01	1704.24	1401.19	1269.04	1202.62	1166.86	1146.88	1135.50
130000	1883.45	1772.41	1457.24	1319.80	1250.73	1213.53	1192.76	1180.92
135000	1955.89	1840.58	1513.28	1370.56	1298.83	1260.20	1238.63	1226.34
140000	2028.33	1908.75	1569.33	1421.33	1346.93	1306.88	1284.51	1271.76
145000	2100.77	1976.92	1625.38	1472.09	1395.04	1353.55	1330.38	1317.18
150000	2173.21	2045.09	1681.43	1522.85	1443.14	1400.23	1376.26	1362.60
155000	2245.65	2113.25	1737.47	1573.61	1491.25	1446.90	1422.13	1408.02
160000	2318.09	2181.42	1793.52	1624.37	1539.35	1493.58	1468.01	1453.44

11.000% MONTHLY AMORTIZING PAYMENTS

AMOUNT OF LOAN	NUMBER OF YEARS IN TERM							
	1	2	3	4	5	6	7	8
$ 50	4.42	2.34	1.64	1.30	1.09	.96	.86	.79
100	8.84	4.67	3.28	2.59	2.18	1.91	1.72	1.58
200	17.68	9.33	6.55	5.17	4.35	3.81	3.43	3.15
300	26.52	13.99	9.83	7.76	6.53	5.72	5.14	4.72
400	35.36	18.65	13.10	10.34	8.70	7.62	6.85	6.29
500	44.20	23.31	16.37	12.93	10.88	9.52	8.57	7.86
600	53.03	27.97	19.65	15.51	13.05	11.43	10.28	9.43
700	61.87	32.63	22.92	18.10	15.22	13.33	11.99	11.00
800	70.71	37.29	26.20	20.68	17.40	15.23	13.70	12.57
900	79.55	41.95	29.47	23.27	19.57	17.14	15.42	14.14
1000	88.39	46.61	32.74	25.85	21.75	19.04	17.13	15.71
2000	176.77	93.22	65.48	51.70	43.49	38.07	34.25	31.42
3000	265.15	139.83	98.22	77.54	65.23	57.11	51.37	47.13
4000	353.53	186.44	130.96	103.39	86.97	76.14	68.49	62.84
5000	441.91	233.04	163.70	129.23	108.72	95.18	85.62	78.55
6000	530.29	279.65	196.44	155.08	130.46	114.21	102.74	94.26
7000	618.68	326.26	229.18	180.92	152.20	133.24	119.86	109.96
8000	707.06	372.87	261.91	206.77	173.94	152.28	136.98	125.67
9000	795.44	419.48	294.65	232.61	195.69	171.31	154.11	141.38
10000	883.82	466.08	327.39	258.46	217.43	190.35	171.23	157.09
11000	972.20	512.69	360.13	284.31	239.17	209.38	188.35	172.80
12000	1060.58	559.30	392.87	310.15	260.91	228.41	205.47	188.51
13000	1148.97	605.91	425.61	336.00	282.66	247.45	222.60	204.21
14000	1237.35	652.51	458.35	361.84	304.40	266.48	239.72	219.92
15000	1325.73	699.12	491.09	387.69	326.14	285.52	256.84	235.63
16000	1414.11	745.73	523.82	413.53	347.88	304.55	273.96	251.34
17000	1502.49	792.34	556.56	439.38	369.63	323.58	291.09	267.05
18000	1590.87	838.95	589.30	465.22	391.37	342.62	308.21	282.76
19000	1679.26	885.55	622.04	491.07	413.11	361.65	325.33	298.47
20000	1767.64	932.16	654.78	516.92	434.85	380.69	342.45	314.17
21000	1856.02	978.77	687.52	542.76	456.60	399.72	359.58	329.88
22000	1944.40	1025.38	720.26	568.61	478.34	418.75	376.70	345.59
23000	2032.78	1071.99	753.00	594.45	500.08	437.79	393.82	361.30
24000	2121.16	1118.59	785.73	620.30	521.82	456.82	410.94	377.01
25000	2209.55	1165.20	818.47	646.14	543.57	475.86	428.07	392.72
26000	2297.93	1211.81	851.21	671.99	565.31	494.89	445.19	408.42
27000	2386.31	1258.42	883.95	697.83	587.05	513.93	462.31	424.13
28000	2474.69	1305.02	916.69	723.68	608.79	532.96	479.43	439.84
29000	2563.07	1351.63	949.43	749.53	630.54	551.99	496.56	455.55
30000	2651.45	1398.24	982.17	775.37	652.28	571.03	513.68	471.26
31000	2739.84	1444.85	1014.91	801.22	674.02	590.06	530.80	486.97
32000	2828.22	1491.46	1047.64	827.06	695.76	609.10	547.92	502.67
33000	2916.60	1538.06	1080.38	852.91	717.50	628.13	565.05	518.38
34000	3004.98	1584.67	1113.12	878.75	739.25	647.16	582.17	534.09
35000	3093.36	1631.28	1145.86	904.60	760.99	666.20	599.29	549.80
40000	3535.27	1864.32	1309.55	1033.83	869.70	761.37	684.90	628.34
45000	3977.18	2097.36	1473.25	1163.05	978.41	856.54	770.51	706.88
50000	4419.09	2330.40	1636.94	1292.28	1087.13	951.71	856.13	785.43
55000	4861.00	2563.44	1800.63	1421.51	1195.84	1046.88	941.74	863.97
60000	5302.90	2796.48	1964.33	1550.74	1304.55	1142.05	1027.35	942.51
65000	5744.81	3029.51	2128.02	1679.96	1413.26	1237.22	1112.96	1021.05
70000	6186.72	3262.55	2291.72	1809.19	1521.97	1332.39	1198.58	1099.59
75000	6628.63	3495.59	2455.41	1938.42	1630.69	1427.56	1284.19	1178.14
80000	7070.54	3728.63	2619.10	2067.65	1739.40	1522.73	1369.80	1256.68
85000	7512.45	3961.67	2782.80	2196.87	1848.11	1617.90	1455.41	1335.22
90000	7954.35	4194.71	2946.49	2326.10	1956.82	1713.07	1541.02	1413.76
95000	8396.26	4427.75	3110.18	2455.33	2065.54	1808.24	1626.64	1492.31
100000	8838.17	4660.79	3273.88	2584.56	2174.25	1903.41	1712.25	1570.85
105000	9280.08	4893.83	3437.57	2713.78	2282.96	1998.58	1797.86	1649.39
110000	9721.99	5126.87	3601.26	2843.01	2391.67	2093.75	1883.47	1727.93
115000	10163.90	5359.91	3764.96	2972.24	2500.38	2188.92	1969.09	1806.47
120000	10605.80	5592.95	3928.65	3101.47	2609.10	2284.09	2054.70	1885.02
125000	11047.71	5825.98	4092.34	3230.70	2717.81	2379.26	2140.31	1963.56
130000	11489.62	6059.02	4256.04	3359.92	2826.52	2474.44	2225.92	2042.10
135000	11931.53	6292.06	4419.73	3489.15	2935.23	2569.61	2311.53	2120.64
140000	12373.44	6525.10	4583.43	3618.38	3043.94	2664.78	2397.15	2199.18
145000	12815.35	6758.14	4747.12	3747.61	3152.66	2759.95	2482.76	2277.73
150000	13257.25	6991.18	4910.81	3876.83	3261.37	2855.12	2568.37	2356.27
155000	13699.16	7224.22	5074.51	4006.06	3370.08	2950.29	2653.98	2434.81
160000	14141.07	7457.26	5238.20	4135.29	3478.79	3045.46	2739.59	2513.35

122

AMOUNT OF LOAN	NUMBER OF YEARS IN TERM							
	9	10	15	20	25	30	35	40
$ 50	.74	.69	.57	.52	.50	.48	.47	.47
100	1.47	1.38	1.14	1.04	.99	.96	.94	.93
200	2.93	2.76	2.28	2.07	1.97	1.91	1.88	1.86
300	4.39	4.14	3.41	3.10	2.95	2.86	2.82	2.79
400	5.86	5.51	4.55	4.13	3.93	3.81	3.75	3.72
500	7.32	6.89	5.69	5.17	4.91	4.77	4.69	4.65
600	8.78	8.27	6.82	6.20	5.89	5.72	5.63	5.57
700	10.24	9.65	7.96	7.23	6.87	6.67	6.56	6.50
800	11.71	11.02	9.10	8.26	7.85	7.62	7.50	7.43
900	13.17	12.40	10.23	9.29	8.83	8.58	8.44	8.36
1000	14.63	13.78	11.37	10.33	9.81	9.53	9.37	9.29
2000	29.26	27.56	22.74	20.65	19.61	19.05	18.74	18.57
3000	43.88	41.33	34.10	30.97	29.41	28.57	28.11	27.85
4000	58.51	55.11	45.47	41.29	39.21	38.10	37.48	37.14
5000	73.13	68.88	56.83	51.61	49.01	47.62	46.85	46.42
6000	87.76	82.66	68.20	61.94	58.81	57.14	56.22	55.70
7000	102.39	96.43	79.57	72.26	68.61	66.67	65.59	64.99
8000	117.01	110.21	90.93	82.58	78.41	76.19	74.96	74.27
9000	131.64	123.98	102.30	92.90	88.22	85.71	84.33	83.55
10000	146.26	137.76	113.66	103.22	98.02	95.24	93.70	92.83
11000	160.89	151.53	125.03	113.55	107.82	104.76	103.07	102.12
12000	175.52	165.31	136.40	123.87	117.62	114.28	112.44	111.40
13000	190.14	179.08	147.76	134.19	127.42	123.81	121.81	120.68
14000	204.77	192.86	159.13	144.51	137.22	133.33	131.18	129.97
15000	219.39	206.63	170.49	154.83	147.02	142.85	140.55	139.25
16000	234.02	220.41	181.86	165.16	156.82	152.38	149.92	148.53
17000	248.64	234.18	193.23	175.48	166.62	161.90	159.29	157.82
18000	263.27	247.96	204.59	185.80	176.43	171.42	168.66	167.10
19000	277.90	261.73	215.96	196.12	186.23	180.95	178.03	176.38
20000	292.52	275.51	227.32	206.44	196.03	190.47	187.40	185.66
21000	307.15	289.28	238.69	216.76	205.83	199.99	196.77	194.95
22000	321.77	303.06	250.06	227.09	215.63	209.52	206.14	204.23
23000	336.40	316.83	261.42	237.41	225.43	219.04	215.51	213.51
24000	351.03	330.61	272.79	247.73	235.23	228.56	224.87	222.80
25000	365.65	344.38	284.15	258.05	245.03	238.09	234.24	232.08
26000	380.28	358.16	295.52	268.37	254.83	247.61	243.61	241.36
27000	394.90	371.93	306.89	278.70	264.64	257.13	252.98	250.64
28000	409.53	385.71	318.25	289.02	274.44	266.66	262.35	259.93
29000	424.15	399.48	329.62	299.34	284.24	276.18	271.72	269.21
30000	438.78	413.26	340.98	309.66	294.04	285.70	281.09	278.49
31000	453.41	427.03	352.35	319.98	303.84	295.23	290.46	287.78
32000	468.03	440.81	363.72	330.31	313.64	304.75	299.83	297.06
33000	482.66	454.58	375.08	340.63	323.44	314.27	309.20	306.34
34000	497.28	468.36	386.45	350.95	333.24	323.79	318.57	315.63
35000	511.91	482.13	397.81	361.27	343.04	333.32	327.94	324.91
40000	585.04	551.01	454.64	412.88	392.05	380.93	374.79	371.32
45000	658.17	619.88	511.47	464.49	441.06	428.55	421.64	417.74
50000	731.30	688.76	568.30	516.10	490.06	476.17	468.48	464.15
55000	804.43	757.63	625.13	567.71	539.07	523.78	515.33	510.57
60000	877.56	826.51	681.96	619.32	588.07	571.40	562.18	556.98
65000	950.69	895.38	738.79	670.93	637.08	619.02	609.03	603.40
70000	1023.82	964.26	795.62	722.54	686.08	666.63	655.88	649.81
75000	1096.94	1033.13	852.45	774.15	735.09	714.25	702.72	696.23
80000	1170.07	1102.01	909.28	825.76	784.10	761.86	749.57	742.64
85000	1243.20	1170.88	966.11	877.37	833.10	809.48	796.42	789.06
90000	1316.33	1239.76	1022.94	928.97	882.11	857.10	843.27	835.47
95000	1389.46	1308.63	1079.77	980.58	931.11	904.71	890.11	881.88
100000	1462.59	1377.51	1136.60	1032.19	980.12	952.33	936.96	928.30
105000	1535.72	1446.38	1193.43	1083.80	1029.12	999.94	983.81	974.71
110000	1608.85	1515.26	1250.26	1135.41	1078.13	1047.56	1030.66	1021.13
115000	1681.98	1584.13	1307.09	1187.02	1127.14	1095.18	1077.51	1067.54
120000	1755.11	1653.01	1363.92	1238.63	1176.14	1142.79	1124.35	1113.96
125000	1828.24	1721.88	1420.75	1290.24	1225.15	1190.41	1171.20	1160.37
130000	1901.37	1790.76	1477.58	1341.85	1274.15	1238.03	1218.05	1206.79
135000	1974.50	1859.63	1534.41	1393.46	1323.16	1285.64	1264.90	1253.20
140000	2047.63	1928.51	1591.24	1445.07	1372.16	1333.26	1311.75	1299.62
145000	2120.75	1997.38	1648.07	1496.68	1421.17	1380.87	1358.59	1346.03
150000	2193.88	2066.26	1704.90	1548.29	1470.17	1428.49	1405.44	1392.45
155000	2267.01	2135.13	1761.73	1599.90	1519.18	1476.11	1452.29	1438.86
160000	2340.14	2204.01	1818.56	1651.51	1568.19	1523.72	1499.14	1485.28

11.250% MONTHLY AMORTIZING PAYMENTS

AMOUNT OF LOAN	NUMBER OF YEARS IN TERM							
	1	2	3	4	5	6	7	8
$ 50	4.43	2.34	1.65	1.30	1.10	.96	.87	.80
100	8.85	4.68	3.29	2.60	2.19	1.92	1.73	1.59
200	17.70	9.35	6.58	5.20	4.38	3.84	3.46	3.17
300	26.55	14.02	9.86	7.80	6.57	5.75	5.18	4.76
400	35.40	18.69	13.15	10.39	8.75	7.67	6.91	6.34
500	44.25	23.37	16.43	12.99	10.94	9.59	8.63	7.93
600	53.10	28.04	19.72	15.59	13.13	11.50	10.36	9.51
700	61.95	32.71	23.01	18.18	15.31	13.42	12.08	11.10
800	70.80	37.38	26.29	20.78	17.50	15.33	13.81	12.68
900	79.65	42.06	29.58	23.38	19.69	17.25	15.53	14.26
1000	88.50	46.73	32.86	25.97	21.87	19.17	17.26	15.85
2000	177.00	93.45	65.72	51.94	43.74	38.33	34.51	31.69
3000	265.50	140.18	98.58	77.91	65.61	57.49	51.77	47.54
4000	354.00	186.90	131.43	103.87	87.47	76.65	69.02	63.38
5000	442.50	233.62	164.29	129.84	109.34	95.82	86.28	79.22
6000	530.99	280.35	197.15	155.81	131.21	114.98	103.53	95.07
7000	619.49	327.07	230.01	181.77	153.08	134.14	120.78	110.91
8000	707.99	373.80	262.86	207.74	174.94	153.30	138.04	126.75
9000	796.49	420.52	295.72	233.71	196.81	172.47	155.29	142.60
10000	884.99	467.24	328.58	259.68	218.68	191.63	172.55	158.44
11000	973.49	513.97	361.43	285.64	240.55	210.79	189.80	174.28
12000	1061.98	560.69	394.29	311.61	262.41	229.95	207.06	190.13
13000	1150.48	607.42	427.15	337.58	284.28	249.12	224.31	205.97
14000	1238.98	654.14	460.01	363.54	306.15	268.28	241.56	221.82
15000	1327.48	700.86	492.86	389.51	328.01	287.44	258.82	237.66
16000	1415.98	747.59	525.72	415.48	349.88	306.60	276.07	253.50
17000	1504.48	794.31	558.58	441.45	371.75	325.77	293.33	269.35
18000	1592.97	841.04	591.44	467.41	393.62	344.93	310.58	285.19
19000	1681.47	887.76	624.29	493.38	415.48	364.09	327.83	301.03
20000	1769.97	934.48	657.15	519.35	437.35	383.25	345.09	316.88
21000	1858.47	981.21	690.01	545.31	459.22	402.41	362.34	332.72
22000	1946.97	1027.93	722.86	571.28	481.09	421.58	379.60	348.56
23000	2035.47	1074.66	755.72	597.25	502.95	440.74	396.85	364.41
24000	2123.96	1121.38	788.58	623.22	524.82	459.90	414.11	380.25
25000	2212.46	1168.10	821.44	649.18	546.69	479.06	431.36	396.09
26000	2300.96	1214.83	854.29	675.15	568.56	498.23	448.61	411.94
27000	2389.46	1261.55	887.15	701.12	590.42	517.39	465.87	427.78
28000	2477.96	1308.28	920.01	727.08	612.29	536.55	483.12	443.63
29000	2566.46	1355.00	952.86	753.05	634.16	555.71	500.38	459.47
30000	2654.95	1401.72	985.72	779.02	656.02	574.88	517.63	475.31
31000	2743.45	1448.45	1018.58	804.99	677.89	594.04	534.88	491.16
32000	2831.95	1495.17	1051.44	830.95	699.76	613.20	552.14	507.00
33000	2920.45	1541.90	1084.29	856.92	721.63	632.36	569.39	522.84
34000	3008.95	1588.62	1117.15	882.89	743.49	651.53	586.65	538.69
35000	3097.45	1635.34	1150.01	908.85	765.36	670.69	603.90	554.53
40000	3539.94	1868.96	1314.29	1038.69	874.70	766.50	690.17	633.75
45000	3982.43	2102.58	1478.58	1168.52	984.03	862.31	776.44	712.97
50000	4424.92	2336.20	1642.87	1298.36	1093.37	958.12	862.71	792.18
55000	4867.41	2569.82	1807.15	1428.20	1202.71	1053.94	948.98	871.40
60000	5309.90	2803.44	1971.44	1558.03	1312.04	1149.75	1035.26	950.62
65000	5752.40	3037.06	2135.73	1687.87	1421.38	1245.56	1121.53	1029.84
70000	6194.89	3270.68	2300.01	1817.70	1530.72	1341.37	1207.80	1109.06
75000	6637.38	3504.30	2464.30	1947.54	1640.05	1437.18	1294.07	1188.27
80000	7079.87	3737.92	2628.58	2077.37	1749.39	1532.99	1380.34	1267.49
85000	7522.36	3971.54	2792.87	2207.21	1858.73	1628.81	1466.61	1346.71
90000	7964.85	4205.16	2957.16	2337.04	1968.06	1724.62	1552.88	1425.93
95000	8407.34	4438.78	3121.44	2466.88	2077.40	1820.43	1639.15	1505.15
100000	8849.84	4672.40	3285.73	2596.71	2186.74	1916.24	1725.42	1584.36
105000	9292.33	4906.02	3450.01	2726.55	2296.07	2012.05	1811.69	1663.58
110000	9734.82	5139.64	3614.30	2856.39	2405.41	2107.87	1897.96	1742.80
115000	10177.31	5373.26	3778.59	2986.22	2514.75	2203.68	1984.23	1822.02
120000	10619.80	5606.88	3942.87	3116.06	2624.08	2299.49	2070.51	1901.24
125000	11062.29	5840.50	4107.16	3245.89	2733.42	2395.30	2156.78	1980.45
130000	11504.79	6074.12	4271.45	3375.73	2842.76	2491.11	2243.05	2059.67
135000	11947.28	6307.74	4435.73	3505.56	2952.09	2586.93	2329.32	2138.89
140000	12389.77	6541.36	4600.02	3635.40	3061.43	2682.74	2415.59	2218.11
145000	12832.26	6774.98	4764.30	3765.23	3170.76	2778.55	2501.86	2297.32
150000	13274.75	7008.60	4928.59	3895.07	3280.10	2874.36	2588.13	2376.54
155000	13717.24	7242.22	5092.88	4024.91	3389.44	2970.17	2674.40	2455.76
160000	14159.74	7475.84	5257.16	4154.74	3498.77	3065.98	2760.67	2534.98

124

AMOUNT OF LOAN	NUMBER OF YEARS IN TERM							
	9	10	15	20	25	30	35	40
$ 50	.74	.70	.58	.53	.50	.49	.48	.48
100	1.48	1.40	1.16	1.05	1.00	.98	.96	.95
200	2.96	2.79	2.31	2.10	2.00	1.95	1.92	1.90
300	4.43	4.18	3.46	3.15	3.00	2.92	2.87	2.85
400	5.91	5.57	4.61	4.20	4.00	3.89	3.83	3.80
500	7.39	6.96	5.77	5.25	5.00	4.86	4.79	4.75
600	8.86	8.36	6.92	6.30	5.99	5.83	5.74	5.69
700	10.34	9.75	8.07	7.35	6.99	6.80	6.70	6.64
800	11.82	11.14	9.22	8.40	7.99	7.78	7.66	7.59
900	13.29	12.53	10.38	9.45	8.99	8.75	8.61	8.54
1000	14.77	13.92	11.53	10.50	9.99	9.72	9.57	9.49
2000	29.53	27.84	23.05	20.99	19.97	19.43	19.13	18.97
3000	44.30	41.76	34.58	31.48	29.95	29.14	28.70	28.45
4000	59.06	55.67	46.10	41.98	39.93	38.86	38.26	37.94
5000	73.83	69.59	57.62	52.47	49.92	48.57	47.83	47.42
6000	88.59	83.51	69.15	62.96	59.90	58.28	57.39	56.90
7000	103.36	97.42	80.67	73.45	69.88	67.99	66.96	66.38
8000	118.12	111.34	92.19	83.95	79.86	77.71	76.52	75.87
9000	132.88	125.26	103.72	94.44	89.85	87.42	86.09	85.35
10000	147.65	139.17	115.24	104.93	99.83	97.13	95.65	94.83
11000	162.41	153.09	126.76	115.42	109.81	106.84	105.22	104.31
12000	177.18	167.01	138.29	125.92	119.79	116.56	114.78	113.80
13000	191.94	180.92	149.81	136.41	129.78	126.27	124.35	123.28
14000	206.71	194.84	161.33	146.90	139.76	135.98	133.91	132.76
15000	221.47	208.76	172.86	157.39	149.74	145.69	143.48	142.24
16000	236.24	222.68	184.38	167.89	159.72	155.41	153.04	151.73
17000	251.00	236.59	195.90	178.38	169.71	165.12	162.61	161.21
18000	265.76	250.51	207.43	188.87	179.69	174.83	172.17	170.69
19000	280.53	264.43	218.95	199.36	189.67	184.54	181.74	180.17
20000	295.29	278.34	230.47	209.86	199.65	194.26	191.30	189.66
21000	310.06	292.26	242.00	220.35	209.64	203.97	200.87	199.14
22000	324.82	306.18	253.52	230.84	219.62	213.68	210.43	208.62
23000	339.59	320.09	265.04	241.33	229.60	223.40	220.00	218.10
24000	354.35	334.01	276.57	251.83	239.58	233.11	229.56	227.59
25000	369.12	347.93	288.09	262.32	249.56	242.82	239.13	237.07
26000	383.88	361.84	299.61	272.81	259.55	252.53	248.69	246.55
27000	398.64	375.76	311.14	283.30	269.53	262.25	258.26	256.03
28000	413.41	389.68	322.66	293.80	279.51	271.96	267.82	265.52
29000	428.17	403.59	334.18	304.29	289.49	281.67	277.39	275.00
30000	442.94	417.51	345.71	314.78	299.48	291.38	286.95	284.48
31000	457.70	431.43	357.23	325.27	309.46	301.10	296.52	293.96
32000	472.47	445.35	368.76	335.77	319.44	310.81	306.08	303.45
33000	487.23	459.26	380.28	346.26	329.42	320.52	315.65	312.93
34000	502.00	473.18	391.80	356.75	339.41	330.23	325.21	322.41
35000	516.76	487.10	403.33	367.24	349.39	339.95	334.78	331.90
40000	590.58	556.68	460.94	419.71	399.30	388.51	382.60	379.31
45000	664.40	626.27	518.56	472.17	449.21	437.07	430.43	426.72
50000	738.23	695.85	576.18	524.63	499.12	485.64	478.25	474.13
55000	812.05	765.43	633.79	577.10	549.04	534.20	526.08	521.55
60000	885.87	835.02	691.41	629.56	598.95	582.76	573.90	568.96
65000	959.69	904.60	749.03	682.02	648.86	631.32	621.73	616.37
70000	1033.51	974.19	806.65	734.48	698.77	679.89	669.55	663.79
75000	1107.34	1043.77	864.26	786.95	748.68	728.45	717.38	711.20
80000	1181.16	1113.36	921.88	839.41	798.60	777.01	765.20	758.61
85000	1254.98	1182.94	979.50	891.87	848.51	825.58	813.02	806.02
90000	1328.80	1252.53	1037.12	944.34	898.42	874.14	860.85	853.44
95000	1402.62	1322.11	1094.73	996.80	948.33	922.70	908.67	900.85
100000	1476.45	1391.69	1152.35	1049.26	998.24	971.27	956.50	948.26
105000	1550.27	1461.28	1209.97	1101.72	1048.16	1019.83	1004.32	995.68
110000	1624.09	1530.86	1267.58	1154.19	1098.07	1068.39	1052.15	1043.09
115000	1697.91	1600.45	1325.20	1206.65	1147.98	1116.96	1099.97	1090.50
120000	1771.73	1670.03	1382.82	1259.11	1197.89	1165.52	1147.80	1137.91
125000	1845.56	1739.62	1440.44	1311.58	1247.80	1214.08	1195.62	1185.33
130000	1919.38	1809.20	1498.05	1364.04	1297.72	1262.64	1243.45	1232.74
135000	1993.20	1878.79	1555.67	1416.50	1347.63	1311.21	1291.27	1280.15
140000	2067.02	1948.37	1613.29	1468.96	1397.54	1359.77	1339.10	1327.57
145000	2140.84	2017.95	1670.90	1521.43	1447.45	1408.33	1386.92	1374.98
150000	2214.67	2087.54	1728.52	1573.89	1497.36	1456.90	1434.75	1422.39
155000	2288.49	2157.12	1786.14	1626.35	1547.28	1505.46	1482.57	1469.80
160000	2362.31	2226.71	1843.76	1678.81	1597.19	1554.02	1530.40	1517.22

125

MONTHLY AMORTIZING PAYMENTS

AMOUNT OF LOAN	NUMBER OF YEARS IN TERM							
	1	2	3	4	5	6	7	8
$ 50	4.44	2.35	1.65	1.31	1.10	.97	.87	.80
100	8.87	4.69	3.30	2.61	2.20	1.93	1.74	1.60
200	17.73	9.37	6.60	5.22	4.40	3.86	3.48	3.20
300	26.59	14.06	9.90	7.83	6.60	5.79	5.22	4.80
400	35.45	18.74	13.20	10.44	8.80	7.72	6.96	6.40
500	44.31	23.43	16.49	13.05	11.00	9.65	8.70	7.99
600	53.17	28.11	19.79	15.66	13.20	11.58	10.44	9.59
700	62.04	32.79	23.09	18.27	15.40	13.51	12.18	11.19
800	70.90	37.48	26.39	20.88	17.60	15.44	13.91	12.79
900	79.76	42.16	29.68	23.49	19.80	17.37	15.65	14.39
1000	88.62	46.85	32.98	26.09	22.00	19.30	17.39	15.98
2000	177.24	93.69	65.96	52.18	43.99	38.59	34.78	31.96
3000	265.85	140.53	98.93	78.27	65.98	57.88	52.16	47.94
4000	354.47	187.37	131.91	104.36	87.98	77.17	69.55	63.92
5000	443.08	234.21	164.89	130.45	109.97	96.46	86.94	79.90
6000	531.70	281.05	197.86	156.54	131.96	115.75	104.32	95.88
7000	620.31	327.89	230.84	182.63	153.95	135.04	121.71	111.86
8000	708.93	374.73	263.81	208.72	175.95	154.33	139.10	127.84
9000	797.54	421.57	296.79	234.81	197.94	173.63	156.48	143.82
10000	886.16	468.41	329.77	260.90	219.93	192.92	173.87	159.80
11000	974.77	515.25	362.74	286.98	241.92	212.21	191.26	175.78
12000	1063.39	562.09	395.72	313.07	263.92	231.50	208.64	191.76
13000	1152.00	608.93	428.69	339.16	285.91	250.79	226.03	207.74
14000	1240.62	655.77	461.67	365.25	307.90	270.08	243.42	223.72
15000	1329.23	702.61	494.65	391.34	329.89	289.37	260.80	239.70
16000	1417.85	749.45	527.62	417.43	351.89	308.66	278.19	255.67
17000	1506.46	796.29	560.60	443.52	373.88	327.95	295.57	271.65
18000	1595.08	843.13	593.57	469.61	395.87	347.25	312.96	287.63
19000	1683.69	889.97	626.55	495.70	417.86	366.54	330.35	303.61
20000	1772.31	936.81	659.53	521.79	439.86	385.83	347.73	319.59
21000	1860.92	983.65	692.50	547.87	461.85	405.12	365.12	335.57
22000	1949.54	1030.49	725.48	573.96	483.84	424.41	382.51	351.55
23000	2038.15	1077.33	758.45	600.05	505.83	443.70	399.89	367.53
24000	2126.77	1124.17	791.43	626.14	527.83	462.99	417.28	383.51
25000	2215.38	1171.01	824.41	652.23	549.82	482.28	434.67	399.49
26000	2304.00	1217.85	857.38	678.32	571.81	501.58	452.05	415.47
27000	2392.61	1264.69	890.36	704.41	593.81	520.87	469.44	431.45
28000	2481.23	1311.53	923.33	730.50	615.80	540.16	486.83	447.43
29000	2569.84	1358.37	956.31	756.59	637.79	559.45	504.21	463.41
30000	2658.46	1405.21	989.29	782.68	659.78	578.74	521.60	479.39
31000	2747.07	1452.05	1022.26	808.76	681.78	598.03	538.99	495.37
32000	2835.69	1498.90	1055.24	834.85	703.77	617.32	556.37	511.34
33000	2924.30	1545.74	1088.21	860.94	725.76	636.61	573.76	527.32
34000	3012.92	1592.58	1121.19	887.03	747.75	655.90	591.14	543.30
35000	3101.53	1639.42	1154.17	913.12	769.75	675.20	608.53	559.28
40000	3544.61	1873.62	1319.05	1043.57	879.71	771.65	695.46	639.18
45000	3987.68	2107.82	1483.93	1174.01	989.67	868.11	782.40	719.08
50000	4430.76	2342.02	1648.81	1304.46	1099.64	964.56	869.33	798.97
55000	4873.83	2576.22	1813.69	1434.90	1209.60	1061.02	956.26	878.87
60000	5316.91	2810.42	1978.57	1565.35	1319.56	1157.47	1043.19	958.77
65000	5759.98	3044.63	2143.45	1695.79	1429.52	1253.93	1130.12	1038.66
70000	6203.06	3278.83	2308.33	1826.24	1539.49	1350.39	1217.06	1118.56
75000	6646.13	3513.03	2473.21	1956.68	1649.45	1446.84	1303.99	1198.46
80000	7089.21	3747.23	2638.09	2087.13	1759.41	1543.30	1390.92	1278.35
85000	7532.28	3981.43	2802.97	2217.57	1869.38	1639.75	1477.85	1358.25
90000	7975.36	4215.63	2967.85	2348.02	1979.34	1736.21	1564.79	1438.15
95000	8418.44	4449.83	3132.73	2478.46	2089.30	1832.66	1651.72	1518.05
100000	8861.51	4684.04	3297.61	2608.91	2199.27	1929.12	1738.65	1597.94
105000	9304.59	4918.24	3462.49	2739.35	2309.23	2025.58	1825.58	1677.84
110000	9747.66	5152.44	3627.37	2869.80	2419.19	2122.03	1912.52	1757.74
115000	10190.74	5386.64	3792.25	3000.24	2529.15	2218.49	1999.45	1837.63
120000	10633.81	5620.84	3957.13	3130.69	2639.12	2314.94	2086.38	1917.53
125000	11076.89	5855.04	4122.01	3261.13	2749.08	2411.40	2173.31	1997.43
130000	11519.96	6089.25	4286.89	3391.58	2859.04	2507.86	2260.24	2077.32
135000	11963.04	6323.45	4451.77	3522.02	2969.01	2604.31	2347.18	2157.22
140000	12406.11	6557.65	4616.65	3652.47	3078.97	2700.77	2434.11	2237.12
145000	12849.19	6791.85	4781.53	3782.91	3188.93	2797.22	2521.04	2317.01
150000	13292.26	7026.05	4946.41	3913.36	3298.90	2893.68	2607.97	2396.91
155000	13735.34	7260.25	5111.29	4043.80	3408.86	2990.13	2694.91	2476.81
160000	14178.41	7494.46	5276.17	4174.25	3518.82	3086.59	2781.84	2556.70

126

AMOUNT OF LOAN	NUMBER OF YEARS IN TERM							
	9	10	15	20	25	30	35	40
$ 50	.75	.71	.59	.54	.51	.50	.49	.49
100	1.50	1.41	1.17	1.07	1.02	1.00	.98	.97
200	2.99	2.82	2.34	2.14	2.04	1.99	1.96	1.94
300	4.48	4.22	3.51	3.20	3.05	2.98	2.93	2.91
400	5.97	5.63	4.68	4.27	4.07	3.97	3.91	3.88
500	7.46	7.03	5.85	5.34	5.09	4.96	4.89	4.85
600	8.95	8.44	7.01	6.40	6.10	5.95	5.86	5.81
700	10.44	9.85	8.18	7.47	7.12	6.94	6.84	6.78
800	11.93	11.25	9.35	8.54	8.14	7.93	7.81	7.75
900	13.42	12.66	10.52	9.60	9.15	8.92	8.79	8.72
1000	14.91	14.06	11.69	10.67	10.17	9.91	9.77	9.69
2000	29.81	28.12	23.37	21.33	20.33	19.81	19.53	19.37
3000	44.72	42.18	35.05	32.00	30.50	29.71	29.29	29.05
4000	59.62	56.24	46.73	42.66	40.66	39.62	39.05	38.74
5000	74.52	70.30	58.41	53.33	50.83	49.52	48.81	48.42
6000	89.43	84.36	70.10	63.99	60.99	59.42	58.57	58.10
7000	104.33	98.42	81.78	74.66	71.16	69.33	68.33	67.78
8000	119.23	112.48	93.46	85.32	81.32	79.23	78.09	77.47
9000	134.14	126.54	105.14	95.98	91.49	89.13	87.85	87.15
10000	149.04	140.60	116.82	106.65	101.65	99.03	97.62	96.83
11000	163.95	154.66	128.51	117.31	111.82	108.94	107.38	106.52
12000	178.85	168.72	140.19	127.98	121.98	118.84	117.14	116.20
13000	193.75	182.78	151.87	138.64	132.15	128.74	126.90	125.88
14000	208.66	196.84	163.55	149.31	142.31	138.65	136.66	135.56
15000	223.56	210.90	175.23	159.97	152.48	148.55	146.42	145.25
16000	238.46	224.96	186.92	170.63	162.64	158.45	156.18	154.93
17000	253.37	239.02	198.60	181.30	172.80	168.35	165.94	164.61
18000	268.27	253.08	210.28	191.96	182.97	178.26	175.70	174.30
19000	283.17	267.14	221.96	202.63	193.13	188.16	185.47	183.98
20000	298.08	281.20	233.64	213.29	203.30	198.06	195.23	193.66
21000	312.98	295.26	245.32	223.96	213.46	207.97	204.99	203.34
22000	327.89	309.31	257.01	234.62	223.63	217.87	214.75	213.03
23000	342.79	323.37	268.69	245.28	233.79	227.77	224.51	222.71
24000	357.69	337.43	280.37	255.95	243.96	237.67	234.27	232.39
25000	372.60	351.49	292.05	266.61	254.12	247.58	244.03	242.08
26000	387.50	365.55	303.73	277.28	264.29	257.48	253.79	251.76
27000	402.40	379.61	315.42	287.94	274.45	267.38	263.55	261.44
28000	417.31	393.67	327.10	298.61	284.62	277.29	273.32	271.12
29000	432.21	407.73	338.78	309.27	294.78	287.19	283.08	280.81
30000	447.11	421.79	350.46	319.93	304.95	297.09	292.84	290.49
31000	462.02	435.85	362.14	330.60	315.11	307.00	302.60	300.17
32000	476.92	449.91	373.83	341.26	325.28	316.90	312.36	309.86
33000	491.83	463.97	385.51	351.93	335.44	326.80	322.12	319.54
34000	506.73	478.03	397.19	362.59	345.60	336.70	331.88	329.22
35000	521.63	492.09	408.87	373.26	355.77	346.61	341.64	338.90
40000	596.15	562.39	467.28	426.58	406.59	396.12	390.45	387.32
45000	670.67	632.68	525.69	479.90	457.42	445.64	439.25	435.73
50000	745.19	702.98	584.10	533.22	508.24	495.15	488.06	484.15
55000	819.71	773.28	642.51	586.54	559.06	544.67	536.86	532.56
60000	894.22	843.58	700.92	639.86	609.89	594.18	585.67	580.97
65000	968.74	913.88	759.33	693.18	660.71	643.69	634.47	629.39
70000	1043.26	984.17	817.74	746.51	711.53	693.21	683.28	677.80
75000	1117.78	1054.47	876.15	799.83	762.36	742.72	732.09	726.22
80000	1192.30	1124.77	934.56	853.15	813.18	792.24	780.89	774.63
85000	1266.82	1195.07	992.97	906.47	864.00	841.75	829.70	823.04
90000	1341.33	1265.36	1051.38	959.79	914.83	891.27	878.50	871.46
95000	1415.85	1335.66	1109.79	1013.11	965.65	940.78	927.31	919.87
100000	1490.37	1405.96	1168.19	1066.43	1016.47	990.30	976.11	968.29
105000	1564.89	1476.26	1226.60	1119.76	1067.30	1039.81	1024.92	1016.70
110000	1639.41	1546.55	1285.01	1173.08	1118.12	1089.33	1073.72	1065.12
115000	1713.93	1616.85	1343.42	1226.40	1168.94	1138.84	1122.53	1113.53
120000	1788.44	1687.15	1401.83	1279.72	1219.77	1188.35	1171.33	1161.94
125000	1862.96	1757.45	1460.24	1333.04	1270.59	1237.87	1220.14	1210.36
130000	1937.48	1827.75	1518.65	1386.36	1321.41	1287.38	1268.94	1258.77
135000	2012.00	1898.04	1577.06	1439.69	1372.24	1336.90	1317.75	1307.19
140000	2086.52	1968.34	1635.47	1493.01	1423.06	1386.41	1366.56	1355.60
145000	2161.04	2038.64	1693.88	1546.33	1473.88	1435.93	1415.36	1404.01
150000	2235.55	2108.94	1752.29	1599.65	1524.71	1485.44	1464.17	1452.43
155000	2310.07	2179.23	1810.70	1652.97	1575.53	1534.96	1512.97	1500.84
160000	2384.59	2249.53	1869.11	1706.29	1626.36	1584.47	1561.78	1549.26

MONTHLY AMORTIZING PAYMENTS

AMOUNT OF LOAN	NUMBER OF YEARS IN TERM							
	1	2	3	4	5	6	7	8
$ 50	4.44	2.35	1.66	1.32	1.11	.98	.88	.81
100	8.88	4.70	3.31	2.63	2.22	1.95	1.76	1.62
200	17.75	9.40	6.62	5.25	4.43	3.89	3.51	3.23
300	26.62	14.09	9.93	7.87	6.64	5.83	5.26	4.84
400	35.50	18.79	13.24	10.49	8.85	7.77	7.01	6.45
500	44.37	23.48	16.55	13.11	11.06	9.72	8.76	8.06
600	53.24	28.18	19.86	15.73	13.28	11.66	10.52	9.67
700	62.12	32.87	23.17	18.35	15.49	13.60	12.27	11.29
800	70.99	37.57	26.48	20.97	17.70	15.54	14.02	12.90
900	79.86	42.27	29.79	23.60	19.91	17.48	15.77	14.51
1000	88.74	46.96	33.10	26.22	22.12	19.43	17.52	16.12
2000	177.47	93.92	66.20	52.43	44.24	38.85	35.04	32.24
3000	266.20	140.88	99.29	78.64	66.36	58.27	52.56	48.35
4000	354.93	187.83	132.39	104.85	88.48	77.69	70.08	64.47
5000	443.66	234.79	165.48	131.06	110.60	97.11	87.60	80.58
6000	532.40	281.75	198.58	157.27	132.71	116.53	105.12	96.70
7000	621.13	328.70	231.67	183.48	154.83	135.95	122.64	112.82
8000	709.86	375.66	264.77	209.70	176.95	155.37	140.16	128.93
9000	798.59	422.62	297.86	235.91	199.07	174.79	157.68	145.05
10000	887.32	469.57	330.96	262.12	221.19	194.21	175.20	161.16
11000	976.06	516.53	364.05	288.33	243.31	213.63	192.72	177.28
12000	1064.79	563.49	397.15	314.54	265.42	233.05	210.24	193.39
13000	1153.52	610.44	430.24	340.75	287.54	252.47	227.76	209.51
14000	1242.25	657.40	463.34	366.96	309.66	271.89	245.28	225.63
15000	1330.98	704.36	496.43	393.17	331.78	291.31	262.79	241.74
16000	1419.72	751.31	529.53	419.39	353.90	310.73	280.31	257.86
17000	1508.45	798.27	562.62	445.60	376.02	330.15	297.83	273.97
18000	1597.18	845.23	595.72	471.81	398.13	349.57	315.35	290.09
19000	1685.91	892.18	628.81	498.02	420.25	368.99	332.87	306.21
20000	1774.64	939.14	661.91	524.23	442.37	388.41	350.39	322.32
21000	1863.37	986.10	695.00	550.44	464.49	407.83	367.91	338.44
22000	1952.11	1033.05	728.10	576.65	486.61	427.25	385.43	354.55
23000	2040.84	1080.01	761.19	602.86	508.73	446.67	402.95	370.67
24000	2129.57	1126.97	794.29	629.08	530.84	466.10	420.47	386.78
25000	2218.30	1173.93	827.38	655.29	552.96	485.52	437.99	402.90
26000	2307.03	1220.88	860.48	681.50	575.08	504.94	455.51	419.02
27000	2395.77	1267.84	893.57	707.71	597.20	524.36	473.03	435.13
28000	2484.50	1314.80	926.67	733.92	619.32	543.78	490.55	451.25
29000	2573.23	1361.75	959.76	760.13	641.44	563.20	508.07	467.36
30000	2661.96	1408.71	992.86	786.34	663.55	582.62	525.58	483.48
31000	2750.69	1455.67	1025.95	812.55	685.67	602.04	543.10	499.59
32000	2839.43	1502.62	1059.05	838.77	707.79	621.46	560.62	515.71
33000	2928.16	1549.58	1092.14	864.98	729.91	640.88	578.14	531.83
34000	3016.89	1596.54	1125.24	891.19	752.03	660.30	595.66	547.94
35000	3105.62	1643.49	1158.33	917.40	774.15	679.72	613.18	564.06
40000	3549.28	1878.28	1323.81	1048.46	884.74	776.82	700.78	644.64
45000	3992.94	2113.06	1489.28	1179.51	995.33	873.92	788.37	725.22
50000	4436.60	2347.85	1654.76	1310.57	1105.92	971.03	875.97	805.79
55000	4880.26	2582.63	1820.23	1441.62	1216.51	1068.13	963.57	886.37
60000	5323.92	2817.41	1985.71	1572.68	1327.10	1165.23	1051.16	966.95
65000	5767.58	3052.20	2151.18	1703.74	1437.70	1262.33	1138.76	1047.53
70000	6211.24	3286.98	2316.66	1834.79	1548.29	1359.44	1226.36	1128.11
75000	6654.90	3521.77	2482.13	1965.85	1658.88	1456.54	1313.95	1208.69
80000	7098.56	3756.55	2647.61	2096.91	1769.47	1553.64	1401.55	1289.27
85000	7542.21	3991.33	2813.08	2227.96	1880.06	1650.74	1489.15	1369.85
90000	7985.87	4226.12	2978.56	2359.02	1990.65	1747.84	1576.74	1450.43
95000	8429.53	4460.90	3144.03	2490.07	2101.25	1844.95	1664.34	1531.01
100000	8873.19	4695.69	3309.51	2621.13	2211.84	1942.05	1751.94	1611.58
105000	9316.85	4930.47	3474.98	2752.19	2322.43	2039.15	1839.53	1692.16
110000	9760.51	5165.25	3640.46	2883.24	2433.02	2136.25	1927.13	1772.74
115000	10204.17	5400.04	3805.93	3014.30	2543.61	2233.35	2014.73	1853.32
120000	10647.83	5634.82	3971.41	3145.36	2654.20	2330.46	2102.32	1933.90
125000	11091.49	5869.61	4136.88	3276.41	2764.80	2427.56	2189.92	2014.48
130000	11535.15	6104.39	4302.36	3407.47	2875.39	2524.66	2277.52	2095.06
135000	11978.81	6339.17	4467.83	3538.52	2985.98	2621.76	2365.11	2175.64
140000	12422.47	6573.96	4633.31	3669.58	3096.57	2718.87	2452.71	2256.22
145000	12866.13	6808.74	4798.78	3800.64	3207.16	2815.97	2540.31	2336.80
150000	13309.79	7043.53	4964.26	3931.69	3317.75	2913.07	2627.90	2417.37
155000	13753.45	7278.31	5129.73	4062.75	3428.34	3010.17	2715.50	2497.95
160000	14197.11	7513.09	5295.21	4193.81	3538.94	3107.27	2803.10	2578.53

128

AMOUNT OF LOAN	NUMBER OF YEARS IN TERM							
	9	10	15	20	25	30	35	40
$ 50	.76	.72	.60	.55	.52	.51	.50	.50
100	1.51	1.43	1.19	1.09	1.04	1.01	1.00	.99
200	3.01	2.85	2.37	2.17	2.07	2.02	2.00	1.98
300	4.52	4.27	3.56	3.26	3.11	3.03	2.99	2.97
400	6.02	5.69	4.74	4.34	4.14	4.04	3.99	3.96
500	7.53	7.11	5.93	5.42	5.18	5.05	4.98	4.95
600	9.03	8.53	7.11	6.51	6.21	6.06	5.98	5.94
700	10.54	9.95	8.29	7.59	7.25	7.07	6.98	6.92
800	12.04	11.37	9.48	8.67	8.28	8.08	7.97	7.91
900	13.54	12.79	10.66	9.76	9.32	9.09	8.97	8.90
1000	15.05	14.21	11.85	10.84	10.35	10.10	9.96	9.89
2000	30.09	28.41	23.69	21.68	20.70	20.19	19.92	19.77
3000	45.14	42.61	35.53	32.52	31.05	30.29	29.88	29.66
4000	60.18	56.82	47.37	43.35	41.40	40.38	39.84	39.54
5000	75.22	71.02	59.21	54.19	51.74	50.48	49.79	49.42
6000	90.27	85.22	71.05	65.03	62.09	60.57	59.75	59.31
7000	105.31	99.43	82.89	75.86	72.44	70.66	69.71	69.19
8000	120.35	113.63	94.74	86.70	82.79	80.76	79.67	79.00
9000	135.40	127.83	106.58	97.54	93.14	90.85	89.63	88.96
10000	150.44	142.03	118.42	108.38	103.48	100.95	99.58	98.84
11000	165.48	156.24	130.26	119.21	113.83	111.04	109.54	108.73
12000	180.53	170.44	142.10	130.05	124.18	121.13	119.50	118.61
13000	195.57	184.64	153.94	140.89	134.53	131.23	129.46	128.49
14000	210.62	198.85	165.78	151.72	144.88	141.32	139.42	138.38
15000	225.66	213.05	177.62	162.56	155.22	151.42	149.37	148.26
16000	240.70	227.25	189.47	173.40	165.57	161.51	159.33	158.14
17000	255.75	241.46	201.31	184.24	175.92	171.60	169.29	168.03
18000	270.79	255.66	213.15	195.07	186.27	181.70	179.25	177.91
19000	285.83	269.86	224.99	205.91	196.62	191.79	189.21	187.79
20000	300.88	284.06	236.83	216.75	206.96	201.89	199.16	197.68
21000	315.92	298.27	248.67	227.58	217.31	211.98	209.12	207.56
22000	330.96	312.47	260.51	238.42	227.66	222.08	219.08	217.45
23000	346.01	326.67	272.36	249.26	238.01	232.17	229.04	227.33
24000	361.05	340.88	284.20	260.09	248.36	242.26	239.00	237.21
25000	376.10	355.08	296.04	270.93	258.70	252.36	248.95	247.10
26000	391.14	369.28	307.88	281.77	269.05	262.45	258.91	256.98
27000	406.18	383.48	319.72	292.61	279.40	272.55	268.87	266.86
28000	421.23	397.69	331.56	303.44	289.75	282.64	278.83	276.75
29000	436.27	411.89	343.40	314.28	300.10	292.73	288.79	286.63
30000	451.31	426.09	355.24	325.12	310.44	302.83	298.74	296.51
31000	466.36	440.30	367.09	335.95	320.79	312.92	308.70	306.40
32000	481.40	454.50	378.93	346.79	331.14	323.02	318.66	316.28
33000	496.44	468.70	390.77	357.63	341.49	333.11	328.62	326.17
34000	511.49	482.91	402.61	368.47	351.84	343.20	338.57	336.05
35000	526.53	497.11	414.45	379.30	362.18	353.30	348.53	345.93
40000	601.75	568.12	473.66	433.49	413.92	403.77	398.32	395.35
45000	676.97	639.14	532.86	487.67	465.66	454.24	448.11	444.77
50000	752.19	710.15	592.07	541.86	517.40	504.71	497.90	494.19
55000	827.40	781.17	651.28	596.04	569.14	555.18	547.69	543.61
60000	902.62	852.18	710.48	650.23	620.88	605.65	597.48	593.02
65000	977.84	923.20	769.69	704.41	672.62	656.12	647.27	642.44
70000	1053.06	994.21	828.90	758.60	724.36	706.59	697.06	691.86
75000	1128.28	1065.23	888.10	812.79	776.10	757.06	746.85	741.28
80000	1203.49	1136.24	947.31	866.97	827.84	807.53	796.64	790.70
85000	1278.71	1207.26	1006.52	921.16	879.58	858.00	846.43	840.11
90000	1353.93	1278.27	1065.72	975.34	931.32	908.47	896.22	889.53
95000	1429.15	1349.28	1124.93	1029.53	983.06	958.94	946.01	938.95
100000	1504.37	1420.30	1184.14	1083.71	1034.80	1009.41	995.80	988.37
105000	1579.58	1491.31	1243.34	1137.90	1086.54	1059.89	1045.59	1037.79
110000	1654.80	1562.33	1302.55	1192.08	1138.28	1110.36	1095.38	1087.21
115000	1730.02	1633.34	1361.76	1246.27	1190.02	1160.83	1145.17	1136.62
120000	1805.24	1704.36	1420.96	1300.45	1241.76	1211.30	1194.96	1186.04
125000	1880.46	1775.37	1480.17	1354.64	1293.50	1261.77	1244.75	1235.46
130000	1955.67	1846.39	1539.38	1408.82	1345.24	1312.24	1294.54	1284.88
135000	2030.89	1917.40	1598.58	1463.01	1396.98	1362.71	1344.33	1334.30
140000	2106.11	1988.42	1657.79	1517.19	1448.72	1413.18	1394.12	1383.71
145000	2181.33	2059.43	1717.00	1571.38	1500.46	1463.65	1443.91	1433.13
150000	2256.55	2130.45	1776.20	1625.57	1552.20	1514.12	1493.70	1482.55
155000	2331.76	2201.46	1835.41	1679.75	1603.94	1564.59	1543.49	1531.97
160000	2406.98	2272.48	1894.62	1733.94	1655.68	1615.06	1593.28	1581.39

12.000%　MONTHLY AMORTIZING PAYMENTS

AMOUNT OF LOAN	NUMBER OF YEARS IN TERM							
	1	2	3	4	5	6	7	8
$ 50	4.45	2.36	1.67	1.32	1.12	.98	.89	.82
100	8.89	4.71	3.33	2.64	2.23	1.96	1.77	1.63
200	17.77	9.42	6.65	5.27	4.45	3.92	3.54	3.26
300	26.66	14.13	9.97	7.91	6.68	5.87	5.30	4.88
400	35.54	18.83	13.29	10.54	8.90	7.83	7.07	6.51
500	44.43	23.54	16.61	13.17	11.13	9.78	8.83	8.13
600	53.31	28.25	19.93	15.81	13.35	11.74	10.60	9.76
700	62.20	32.96	23.26	18.44	15.58	13.69	12.36	11.38
800	71.08	37.66	26.58	21.07	17.80	15.65	14.13	13.01
900	79.97	42.37	29.90	23.71	20.03	17.60	15.89	14.63
1000	88.85	47.08	33.22	26.34	22.25	19.56	17.66	16.26
2000	177.70	94.15	66.43	52.67	44.49	39.11	35.31	32.51
3000	266.55	141.23	99.65	79.01	66.74	58.66	52.96	48.76
4000	355.40	188.30	132.86	105.34	88.98	78.21	70.62	65.02
5000	444.25	235.37	166.08	131.67	111.23	97.76	88.27	81.27
6000	533.10	282.45	199.29	158.01	133.47	117.31	105.92	97.52
7000	621.95	329.52	232.51	184.34	155.72	136.86	123.57	113.77
8000	710.80	376.59	265.72	210.68	177.96	156.41	141.23	130.03
9000	799.64	423.67	298.93	237.01	200.21	175.96	158.88	146.28
10000	888.49	470.74	332.15	263.34	222.45	195.51	176.53	162.53
11000	977.34	517.81	365.36	289.68	244.69	215.06	194.19	178.79
12000	1066.19	564.89	398.58	316.01	266.94	234.61	211.84	195.04
13000	1155.04	611.96	431.79	342.34	289.18	254.16	229.49	211.29
14000	1243.89	659.03	465.01	368.68	311.43	273.71	247.14	227.54
15000	1332.74	706.11	498.22	395.01	333.67	293.26	264.80	243.80
16000	1421.59	753.18	531.43	421.35	355.92	312.81	282.45	260.05
17000	1510.43	800.25	564.65	447.68	378.16	332.36	300.10	276.30
18000	1599.28	847.33	597.86	474.01	400.41	351.91	317.75	292.56
19000	1688.13	894.40	631.08	500.35	422.65	371.46	335.41	308.81
20000	1776.98	941.47	664.29	526.68	444.89	391.01	353.06	325.06
21000	1865.83	988.55	697.51	553.02	467.14	410.56	370.71	341.31
22000	1954.68	1035.62	730.72	579.35	489.38	430.11	388.37	357.57
23000	2043.53	1082.69	763.93	605.68	511.63	449.66	406.02	373.82
24000	2132.38	1129.77	797.15	632.02	533.87	469.21	423.67	390.07
25000	2221.22	1176.84	830.36	658.35	556.12	488.76	441.32	406.33
26000	2310.07	1223.92	863.58	684.68	578.36	508.31	458.98	422.58
27000	2398.92	1270.99	896.79	711.02	600.61	527.86	476.63	438.83
28000	2487.77	1318.06	930.01	737.35	622.85	547.41	494.28	455.08
29000	2576.62	1365.14	963.22	763.69	645.09	566.96	511.93	471.34
30000	2665.47	1412.21	996.43	790.02	667.34	586.51	529.59	487.59
31000	2754.32	1459.28	1029.65	816.35	689.58	606.06	547.24	503.84
32000	2843.17	1506.36	1062.86	842.69	711.83	625.61	564.89	520.10
33000	2932.02	1553.43	1096.08	869.02	734.07	645.16	582.55	536.35
34000	3020.86	1600.50	1129.29	895.36	756.32	664.71	600.20	552.60
35000	3109.71	1647.58	1162.51	921.69	778.56	684.26	617.85	568.85
40000	3553.96	1882.94	1328.58	1053.36	889.78	782.01	706.11	650.12
45000	3998.20	2118.31	1494.65	1185.03	1001.01	879.76	794.38	731.38
50000	4442.44	2353.68	1660.72	1316.70	1112.23	977.51	882.64	812.65
55000	4886.69	2589.05	1826.79	1448.37	1223.45	1075.27	970.91	893.91
60000	5330.93	2824.41	1992.86	1580.04	1334.67	1173.02	1059.17	975.18
65000	5775.18	3059.78	2158.94	1711.70	1445.89	1270.77	1147.43	1056.44
70000	6219.42	3295.15	2325.01	1843.37	1557.12	1368.52	1235.70	1137.70
75000	6663.66	3530.52	2491.08	1975.04	1668.34	1466.27	1323.96	1218.97
80000	7107.91	3765.88	2657.15	2106.71	1779.56	1564.02	1412.22	1300.23
85000	7552.15	4001.25	2823.22	2238.38	1890.78	1661.77	1500.49	1381.50
90000	7996.40	4236.62	2989.29	2370.05	2002.01	1759.52	1588.75	1462.76
95000	8440.64	4471.98	3155.36	2501.72	2113.23	1857.27	1677.01	1544.02
100000	8884.88	4707.35	3321.44	2633.39	2224.45	1955.02	1765.28	1625.29
105000	9329.13	4942.72	3487.51	2765.06	2335.67	2052.78	1853.54	1706.55
110000	9773.37	5178.09	3653.58	2896.73	2446.89	2150.53	1941.81	1787.82
115000	10217.62	5413.45	3819.65	3028.40	2558.12	2248.28	2030.07	1869.08
120000	10661.86	5648.82	3985.72	3160.07	2669.34	2346.03	2118.33	1950.35
125000	11106.10	5884.19	4151.79	3291.73	2780.56	2443.78	2206.60	2031.61
130000	11550.35	6119.56	4317.87	3423.40	2891.78	2541.53	2294.86	2112.87
135000	11994.59	6354.92	4483.94	3555.07	3003.01	2639.28	2383.12	2194.14
140000	12438.84	6590.29	4650.01	3686.74	3114.23	2737.03	2471.39	2275.40
145000	12883.08	6825.66	4816.08	3818.41	3225.45	2834.78	2559.65	2356.67
150000	13327.32	7061.03	4982.15	3950.08	3336.68	2932.53	2647.91	2437.93
155000	13771.57	7296.39	5148.22	4081.75	3447.89	3030.28	2736.18	2519.20
160000	14215.81	7531.76	5311.29	4213.42	3559.12	3128.04	2824.44	2600.46

130

MONTHLY AMORTIZING PAYMENTS 12.000%

AMOUNT OF LOAN	NUMBER OF YEARS IN TERM							
	9	10	15	20	25	30	35	40
$ 50	.76	.72	.61	.56	.53	.52	.51	.51
100	1.52	1.44	1.21	1.11	1.06	1.03	1.02	1.01
200	3.04	2.87	2.41	2.21	2.11	2.06	2.04	2.02
300	4.56	4.31	3.61	3.31	3.16	3.09	3.05	3.03
400	6.08	5.74	4.81	4.41	4.22	4.12	4.07	4.04
500	7.60	7.18	6.01	5.51	5.27	5.15	5.08	5.05
600	9.12	8.61	7.21	6.61	6.32	6.18	6.10	6.06
700	10.63	10.05	8.41	7.71	7.38	7.21	7.11	7.06
800	12.15	11.48	9.61	8.81	8.43	8.23	8.13	8.07
900	13.67	12.92	10.81	9.91	9.48	9.26	9.14	9.08
1000	15.19	14.35	12.01	11.02	10.54	10.29	10.16	10.09
2000	30.37	28.70	24.01	22.03	21.07	20.58	20.32	20.17
3000	45.56	43.05	36.01	33.04	31.60	30.86	30.47	30.26
4000	60.74	57.39	48.01	44.05	42.13	41.15	40.63	40.34
5000	75.93	71.74	60.01	55.06	52.67	51.44	50.78	50.43
6000	91.11	86.09	72.02	66.07	63.20	61.72	60.94	60.51
7000	106.29	100.43	84.02	77.08	73.73	72.01	71.09	70.60
8000	121.48	114.78	96.02	88.09	84.26	82.29	81.25	80.68
9000	136.66	129.13	108.02	99.10	94.80	92.58	91.40	90.77
10000	151.85	143.48	120.02	110.11	105.33	102.87	101.56	100.85
11000	167.03	157.82	132.02	121.12	115.86	113.15	111.72	110.94
12000	182.22	172.17	144.03	132.14	126.39	123.44	121.87	121.02
13000	197.40	186.52	156.03	143.15	136.92	133.72	132.03	131.11
14000	212.58	200.86	168.03	154.16	147.46	144.01	142.18	141.19
15000	227.77	215.21	180.03	165.17	157.99	154.30	152.34	151.28
16000	242.95	229.56	192.03	176.18	168.52	164.58	162.49	161.36
17000	258.14	243.91	204.03	187.19	179.05	174.87	172.65	171.45
18000	273.32	258.25	216.04	198.20	189.59	185.16	182.80	181.53
19000	288.51	272.60	228.04	209.21	200.12	195.44	192.96	191.62
20000	303.69	286.95	240.04	220.22	210.65	205.73	203.11	201.70
21000	318.87	301.29	252.04	231.23	221.18	216.01	213.27	211.79
22000	334.06	315.64	264.04	242.24	231.71	226.30	223.43	221.87
23000	349.24	329.99	276.04	253.25	242.25	236.59	233.58	231.96
24000	364.43	344.34	288.05	264.27	252.78	246.87	243.74	242.04
25000	379.61	358.68	300.05	275.28	263.31	257.16	253.89	252.13
26000	394.80	373.03	312.05	286.29	273.84	267.44	264.05	262.21
27000	409.98	387.38	324.05	297.30	284.38	277.73	274.20	272.30
28000	425.16	401.72	336.05	308.31	294.91	288.02	284.36	282.38
29000	440.35	416.07	348.05	319.32	305.44	298.30	294.51	292.47
30000	455.53	430.42	360.06	330.33	315.97	308.59	304.67	302.55
31000	470.72	444.76	372.06	341.34	326.50	318.87	314.83	312.64
32000	485.90	459.11	384.06	352.35	337.04	329.16	324.98	322.72
33000	501.08	473.46	396.06	363.36	347.57	339.45	335.14	332.81
34000	516.27	487.81	408.06	374.37	358.10	349.73	345.29	342.89
35000	531.45	502.15	420.06	385.39	368.63	360.02	355.45	352.98
40000	607.37	573.89	480.07	440.44	421.29	411.45	406.22	403.40
45000	683.30	645.62	540.08	495.49	473.96	462.88	457.00	453.83
50000	759.22	717.36	600.09	550.55	526.62	514.31	507.78	504.25
55000	835.14	789.10	660.10	605.60	579.28	565.74	558.56	554.68
60000	911.06	860.83	720.11	660.66	631.94	617.17	609.33	605.10
65000	986.98	932.57	780.11	715.71	684.60	668.60	660.11	655.53
70000	1062.90	1004.30	840.12	770.77	737.26	720.03	710.89	705.95
75000	1138.82	1076.04	900.13	825.82	789.92	771.46	761.67	756.38
80000	1214.74	1147.77	960.14	880.87	842.58	822.90	812.44	806.80
85000	1290.66	1219.51	1020.15	935.93	895.25	874.33	863.22	857.23
90000	1366.59	1291.24	1080.16	990.98	947.91	925.76	914.00	907.65
95000	1442.51	1362.98	1140.16	1046.04	1000.57	977.19	964.78	958.08
100000	1518.43	1434.71	1200.17	1101.09	1053.23	1028.62	1015.55	1008.50
105000	1594.35	1506.45	1260.18	1156.15	1105.89	1080.05	1066.33	1058.93
110000	1670.27	1578.19	1320.19	1211.20	1158.55	1131.48	1117.11	1109.35
115000	1746.19	1649.92	1380.20	1266.25	1211.21	1182.91	1167.89	1159.78
120000	1822.11	1721.66	1440.19	1321.31	1263.87	1234.34	1218.66	1210.20
125000	1898.03	1793.39	1500.22	1376.36	1316.54	1285.77	1269.44	1260.63
130000	1973.96	1865.13	1560.22	1431.42	1369.20	1337.20	1320.22	1311.05
135000	2049.88	1936.86	1620.23	1486.47	1421.86	1388.63	1371.00	1361.48
140000	2125.80	2008.60	1680.24	1541.53	1474.52	1440.06	142..77	1411.90
145000	2201.72	2080.33	1740.25	1596.58	1527.18	1491.49	1472.55	1462.33
150000	2277.64	2152.07	1800.26	1651.63	1579.84	1542.92	1523.33	1512.75
155000	2353.56	2223.80	1860.27	1706.69	1632.50	1594.35	1574.11	1563.18
160000	2429.48	2295.54	1920.27	1761.74	1685.16	1645.79	1624.88	1613.60

131

12.250% MONTHLY AMORTIZING PAYMENTS

AMOUNT OF LOAN	NUMBER OF YEARS IN TERM							
	1	2	3	4	5	6	7	8
$ 50	4.45	2.36	1.67	1.33	1.12	.99	.89	.82
100	8.90	4.72	3.34	2.65	2.24	1.97	1.78	1.64
200	17.80	9.44	6.67	5.30	4.48	3.94	3.56	3.28
300	26.69	14.16	10.01	7.94	6.72	5.91	5.34	4.92
400	35.59	18.88	13.34	10.59	8.95	7.88	7.12	6.56
500	44.49	23.60	16.67	13.23	11.19	9.85	8.90	8.20
600	53.38	28.32	20.01	15.88	13.43	11.81	10.68	9.84
700	62.28	33.04	23.34	18.52	15.66	13.78	12.46	11.48
800	71.18	37.76	26.67	21.17	17.90	15.75	14.23	13.12
900	80.07	42.48	30.01	23.82	20.14	17.72	16.01	14.76
1000	88.97	47.20	33.34	26.46	22.38	19.69	17.79	16.40
2000	177.94	94.39	66.67	52.92	44.75	39.37	35.58	32.79
3000	266.90	141.58	100.01	79.38	67.12	59.05	53.37	49.18
4000	355.87	188.77	133.34	105.83	89.49	78.73	71.15	65.57
5000	444.83	235.96	166.67	132.29	111.86	98.41	88.94	81.96
6000	533.80	283.15	200.01	158.75	134.23	118.09	106.73	98.35
7000	622.77	330.34	233.34	185.20	156.60	137.77	124.51	114.74
8000	711.73	377.53	266.68	211.66	178.97	157.45	142.30	131.13
9000	800.70	424.72	300.01	238.12	201.34	177.13	160.09	147.52
10000	889.66	471.91	333.34	264.57	223.71	196.81	177.87	163.91
11000	978.63	519.10	366.68	291.03	246.09	216.49	195.66	180.30
12000	1067.59	566.29	400.01	317.49	268.46	236.17	213.45	196.69
13000	1156.56	613.48	433.34	343.94	290.83	255.85	231.23	213.08
14000	1245.53	660.67	466.68	370.40	313.20	275.53	249.02	229.47
15000	1334.49	707.86	500.01	396.86	335.57	295.21	266.81	245.86
16000	1423.46	755.05	533.35	423.31	357.94	314.89	284.59	262.25
17000	1512.42	802.24	566.68	449.77	380.31	334.57	302.38	278.64
18000	1601.39	849.43	600.01	476.23	402.68	354.25	320.17	295.03
19000	1690.35	896.62	633.35	502.68	425.05	373.93	337.95	311.42
20000	1779.32	943.81	666.68	529.14	447.42	393.61	355.74	327.82
21000	1868.29	991.00	700.02	555.60	469.80	413.29	373.53	344.21
22000	1957.25	1038.19	733.35	582.05	492.17	432.97	391.31	360.60
23000	2046.22	1085.38	766.68	608.51	514.54	452.66	409.10	376.99
24000	2135.18	1132.57	800.02	634.97	536.91	472.34	426.89	393.38
25000	2224.15	1179.76	833.35	661.42	559.28	492.02	444.67	409.77
26000	2313.12	1226.95	866.68	687.88	581.65	511.70	462.46	426.16
27000	2402.08	1274.14	900.02	714.34	604.02	531.38	480.25	442.55
28000	2491.05	1321.33	933.35	740.79	626.39	551.06	498.03	458.94
29000	2580.01	1368.52	966.69	767.25	648.76	570.74	515.82	475.33
30000	2668.98	1415.71	1000.02	793.71	671.13	590.42	533.61	491.72
31000	2757.94	1462.90	1033.35	820.16	693.51	610.10	551.39	508.11
32000	2846.91	1510.09	1066.69	846.62	715.88	629.78	569.18	524.50
33000	2935.88	1557.29	1100.02	873.08	738.25	649.46	586.97	540.89
34000	3024.84	1604.48	1133.36	899.53	760.62	669.14	604.75	557.28
35000	3113.81	1651.67	1166.69	925.99	782.99	688.82	622.54	573.67
40000	3558.64	1887.62	1333.36	1058.28	894.84	787.22	711.47	655.63
45000	4003.47	2123.57	1500.03	1190.56	1006.70	885.62	800.41	737.58
50000	4448.29	2359.52	1666.70	1322.84	1118.55	984.03	889.34	819.53
55000	4893.12	2595.47	1833.37	1455.13	1230.41	1082.43	978.27	901.48
60000	5337.95	2831.42	2000.04	1587.41	1342.26	1180.83	1067.21	983.44
65000	5782.78	3067.37	2166.70	1719.69	1454.12	1279.23	1156.14	1065.39
70000	6227.61	3303.33	2333.37	1851.98	1565.97	1377.64	1245.07	1147.34
75000	6672.44	3539.28	2500.04	1984.26	1677.83	1476.04	1334.01	1229.29
80000	7117.27	3775.23	2666.71	2116.55	1789.68	1574.44	1422.94	1311.25
85000	7562.10	4011.18	2833.38	2248.83	1901.54	1672.84	1511.88	1393.20
90000	8006.93	4247.13	3000.05	2381.11	2013.39	1771.24	1600.81	1475.15
95000	8451.75	4483.08	3166.72	2513.40	2125.25	1869.65	1689.74	1557.10
100000	8896.58	4719.04	3333.39	2645.68	2237.10	1968.05	1778.68	1639.06
105000	9341.41	4954.99	3500.06	2777.96	2348.96	2066.45	1867.61	1721.01
110000	9786.24	5190.94	3666.73	2910.25	2460.81	2164.85	1956.54	1802.96
115000	10231.07	5426.89	3833.40	3042.53	2572.67	2263.26	2045.48	1884.91
120000	10675.90	5662.84	4000.07	3174.82	2684.52	2361.66	2134.41	1966.87
125000	11120.73	5898.79	4166.74	3307.10	2796.38	2460.06	2223.34	2048.82
130000	11565.56	6134.74	4333.40	3439.38	2908.23	2558.46	2312.28	2130.77
135000	12010.39	6370.70	4500.07	3571.67	3020.09	2656.86	2401.21	2212.72
140000	12455.21	6606.65	4666.74	3703.95	3131.94	2755.27	2490.14	2294.68
145000	12900.04	6842.60	4833.41	3836.23	3243.80	2853.67	2579.08	2376.63
150000	13344.87	7078.55	5000.08	3968.52	3355.65	2952.07	2668.01	2458.58
155000	13789.70	7314.50	5166.75	4100.80	3467.51	3050.47	2756.94	2540.53
160000	14234.53	7550.45	5333.42	4233.08	3579.36	3148.88	2845.88	2622.49

MONTHLY AMORTIZING PAYMENTS 12.250%

AMOUNT OF LOAN	NUMBER OF YEARS IN TERM							
	9	10	15	20	25	30	35	40
$ 50	.77	.73	.61	.56	.54	.53	.52	.52
100	1.54	1.45	1.22	1.12	1.08	1.05	1.04	1.03
200	3.07	2.90	2.44	2.24	2.15	2.10	2.08	2.06
300	4.60	4.35	3.65	3.36	3.22	3.15	3.11	3.09
400	6.14	5.80	4.87	4.48	4.29	4.20	4.15	4.12
500	7.67	7.25	6.09	5.60	5.36	5.24	5.18	5.15
600	9.20	8.70	7.30	6.72	6.44	6.29	6.22	6.18
700	10.73	10.15	8.52	7.83	7.51	7.34	7.25	7.21
800	12.27	11.60	9.74	8.95	8.58	8.39	8.29	8.23
900	13.80	13.05	10.95	10.07	9.65	9.44	9.32	9.26
1000	15.33	14.50	12.17	11.19	10.72	10.48	10.36	10.29
2000	30.66	28.99	24.33	22.38	21.44	20.96	20.71	20.58
3000	45.98	43.48	36.49	33.56	32.16	31.44	31.07	30.87
4000	61.31	57.97	48.66	44.75	42.87	41.92	41.42	41.15
5000	76.63	72.46	60.82	55.93	53.59	52.40	51.77	51.44
6000	91.96	86.96	72.98	67.12	64.31	62.88	62.13	61.73
7000	107.28	101.45	85.15	78.30	75.03	73.36	72.48	72.01
8000	122.61	115.94	97.31	89.49	85.74	83.84	82.83	82.30
9000	137.93	130.43	109.47	100.68	96.46	94.32	93.19	92.59
10000	153.26	144.92	121.63	111.86	107.18	104.79	103.54	102.87
11000	168.59	159.42	133.80	123.05	117.90	115.27	113.90	113.16
12000	183.91	173.91	145.96	134.23	128.61	125.75	124.25	123.45
13000	199.24	188.40	158.12	145.42	139.33	136.23	134.60	133.73
14000	214.56	202.89	170.29	156.60	150.05	146.71	144.96	144.02
15000	229.89	217.38	182.45	167.79	160.77	157.19	155.31	154.31
16000	245.21	231.88	194.61	178.98	171.48	167.67	165.66	164.59
17000	260.54	246.37	206.78	190.16	182.20	178.15	176.02	174.88
18000	275.86	260.86	218.94	201.35	192.92	188.63	186.37	185.17
19000	291.19	275.35	231.10	212.53	203.64	199.11	196.73	195.46
20000	306.52	289.84	243.26	223.72	214.35	209.58	207.08	205.74
21000	321.84	304.34	255.43	234.90	225.07	220.06	217.43	216.03
22000	337.17	318.83	267.59	246.09	235.79	230.54	227.79	226.32
23000	352.49	333.32	279.75	257.27	246.51	241.02	238.14	236.60
24000	367.82	347.81	291.92	268.46	257.22	251.50	248.49	246.89
25000	383.14	362.30	304.08	279.65	267.94	261.98	258.85	257.18
26000	398.47	376.80	316.24	290.83	278.66	272.46	269.20	267.46
27000	413.79	391.29	328.41	302.02	289.38	282.94	279.56	277.75
28000	429.12	405.78	340.57	313.20	300.09	293.42	289.91	288.04
29000	444.45	420.27	352.73	324.39	310.81	303.89	300.26	298.32
30000	459.77	434.76	364.89	335.57	321.53	314.37	310.62	308.61
31000	475.10	449.26	377.06	346.76	332.25	324.85	320.97	318.90
32000	490.42	463.75	389.22	357.95	342.96	335.33	331.32	329.18
33000	505.75	478.24	401.38	369.13	353.68	345.81	341.68	339.47
34000	521.07	492.73	413.55	380.32	364.40	356.29	352.03	349.76
35000	536.40	507.22	425.71	391.50	375.12	366.77	362.38	360.05
40000	613.03	579.68	486.52	447.43	428.70	419.16	414.15	411.48
45000	689.65	652.14	547.34	503.36	482.29	471.56	465.92	462.91
50000	766.28	724.60	608.15	559.29	535.88	523.95	517.69	514.35
55000	842.91	797.06	668.97	615.22	589.46	576.35	569.46	565.78
60000	919.54	869.52	729.78	671.14	643.05	628.74	621.23	617.22
65000	996.17	941.98	790.60	727.07	696.64	681.14	673.00	668.65
70000	1072.79	1014.44	851.41	783.00	750.23	733.53	724.76	720.09
75000	1149.42	1086.90	912.23	838.93	803.81	785.93	776.53	771.52
80000	1226.05	1159.36	973.04	894.86	857.40	838.32	828.30	822.95
85000	1302.68	1231.82	1033.86	950.78	910.99	890.72	880.07	874.39
90000	1379.30	1304.28	1094.67	1006.71	964.57	943.11	931.84	925.82
95000	1455.93	1376.74	1155.49	1062.64	1018.16	995.51	983.61	977.26
100000	1532.56	1449.20	1216.30	1118.57	1071.75	1047.90	1035.38	1028.69
105000	1609.19	1521.66	1277.12	1174.50	1125.34	1100.30	1087.14	1080.13
110000	1685.82	1594.12	1337.93	1230.43	1178.92	1152.69	1138.91	1131.56
115000	1762.44	1666.58	1398.75	1286.35	1232.51	1205.09	1190.68	1182.99
120000	1839.07	1739.04	1459.56	1342.28	1286.10	1257.48	1242.45	1234.43
125000	1915.70	1811.50	1520.38	1398.21	1339.68	1309.88	1294.22	1285.86
130000	1992.33	1883.96	1581.19	1454.14	1393.27	1362.27	1345.99	1337.30
135000	2068.95	1956.42	1642.01	1510.07	1446.86	1414.67	1397.76	1388.73
140000	2145.58	2028.88	1702.82	1566.00	1500.45	1467.06	1449.52	1440.17
145000	2222.21	2101.34	1763.64	1621.92	1554.03	1519.45	1501.29	1491.60
150000	2298.84	2173.80	1824.45	1677.85	1607.62	1571.85	1553.06	1543.03
155000	2375.47	2246.26	1885.27	1733.78	1661.21	1624.24	1604.83	1594.47
160000	2452.09	2318.72	1946.08	1789.71	1714.80	1676.64	1656.60	1645.90

133

12.500% MONTHLY AMORTIZING PAYMENTS

AMOUNT OF LOAN	NUMBER OF YEARS IN TERM							
	1	2	3	4	5	6	7	8
$ 50	4.46	2.37	1.68	1.33	1.13	1.00	.90	.83
100	8.91	4.74	3.35	2.66	2.25	1.99	1.80	1.66
200	17.82	9.47	6.70	5.32	4.50	3.97	3.59	3.31
300	26.73	14.20	10.04	7.98	6.75	5.95	5.38	4.96
400	35.64	18.93	13.39	10.64	9.00	7.93	7.17	6.62
500	44.55	23.66	16.73	13.29	11.25	9.91	8.97	8.27
600	53.45	28.39	20.08	15.95	13.50	11.89	10.76	9.92
700	62.36	33.12	23.42	18.61	15.75	13.87	12.55	11.58
800	71.27	37.85	26.77	21.27	18.00	15.85	14.34	13.23
900	80.18	42.58	30.11	23.93	20.25	17.84	16.13	14.88
1000	89.09	47.31	33.46	26.58	22.50	19.82	17.93	16.53
2000	178.17	94.62	66.91	53.16	45.00	39.63	35.85	33.06
3000	267.25	141.93	100.37	79.74	67.50	59.44	53.77	49.59
4000	356.34	189.23	133.82	106.32	90.00	79.25	71.69	66.12
5000	445.42	236.54	167.27	132.90	112.49	99.06	89.61	82.65
6000	534.50	283.85	200.73	159.48	134.99	118.87	107.53	99.18
7000	623.59	331.16	234.18	186.06	157.49	138.68	125.45	115.71
8000	712.67	378.46	267.63	212.64	179.99	158.49	143.37	132.24
9000	801.75	425.77	301.09	239.22	202.49	178.31	161.30	148.76
10000	890.83	473.08	334.54	265.80	224.98	198.12	179.22	165.29
11000	979.92	520.39	367.99	292.38	247.48	217.93	197.14	181.82
12000	1069.00	567.69	401.45	318.96	269.98	237.74	215.06	198.35
13000	1158.08	615.00	434.90	345.54	292.48	257.55	232.98	214.88
14000	1247.17	662.31	468.36	372.12	314.98	277.36	250.90	231.41
15000	1336.25	709.61	501.81	398.70	337.47	297.17	268.82	247.94
16000	1425.33	756.92	535.26	425.28	359.97	316.98	286.74	264.47
17000	1514.41	804.23	568.72	451.86	382.47	336.80	304.67	280.99
18000	1603.50	851.54	602.17	478.44	404.97	356.61	322.59	297.52
19000	1692.58	898.84	635.62	505.02	427.47	376.42	340.51	314.05
20000	1781.66	946.15	669.08	531.60	449.96	396.23	358.43	330.58
21000	1870.75	993.46	702.53	558.18	472.46	416.04	376.35	347.11
22000	1959.83	1040.77	735.98	584.76	494.96	435.85	394.27	363.64
23000	2048.91	1088.07	769.44	611.34	517.46	455.66	412.19	380.17
24000	2137.99	1135.38	802.89	637.92	539.96	475.47	430.11	396.70
25000	2227.08	1182.69	836.35	664.50	562.45	495.28	448.04	413.23
26000	2316.16	1230.00	869.80	691.08	584.95	515.10	465.96	429.75
27000	2405.24	1277.30	903.25	717.66	607.45	534.91	483.88	446.28
28000	2494.33	1324.61	936.71	744.24	629.95	554.72	501.80	462.81
29000	2583.41	1371.92	970.16	770.82	652.45	574.53	519.72	479.34
30000	2672.49	1419.22	1003.61	797.40	674.94	594.34	537.64	495.87
31000	2761.57	1466.53	1037.07	823.98	697.44	614.15	555.56	512.40
32000	2850.66	1513.84	1070.52	850.56	719.94	633.96	573.48	528.93
33000	2939.74	1561.15	1103.97	877.14	742.44	653.77	591.41	545.46
34000	3028.82	1608.45	1137.43	903.72	764.93	673.59	609.33	561.98
35000	3117.91	1655.76	1170.88	930.30	787.43	693.40	627.25	578.51
40000	3563.32	1892.30	1338.15	1063.20	899.92	792.45	716.85	661.16
45000	4008.73	2128.83	1505.42	1196.10	1012.41	891.51	806.46	743.80
50000	4454.15	2365.37	1672.69	1329.00	1124.90	990.56	896.07	826.45
55000	4899.56	2601.91	1839.95	1461.90	1237.39	1089.62	985.67	909.09
60000	5344.98	2838.44	2007.22	1594.80	1349.88	1188.68	1075.28	991.73
65000	5790.39	3074.98	2174.49	1727.70	1462.37	1287.73	1164.89	1074.38
70000	6235.81	3311.52	2341.76	1860.60	1574.86	1386.79	1254.49	1157.02
75000	6681.22	3548.05	2509.03	1993.50	1687.35	1485.84	1344.10	1239.67
80000	7126.63	3784.59	2676.30	2126.40	1799.84	1584.90	1433.70	1322.31
85000	7572.05	4021.13	2843.56	2259.30	1912.33	1683.96	1523.31	1404.95
90000	8017.46	4257.66	3010.83	2392.20	2024.82	1783.01	1612.92	1487.60
95000	8462.88	4494.20	3178.10	2525.10	2137.31	1882.07	1702.52	1570.24
100000	8908.29	4730.74	3345.37	2658.00	2249.80	1981.12	1792.13	1652.89
105000	9353.71	4967.27	3512.64	2790.90	2362.29	2080.18	1881.74	1735.53
110000	9799.12	5203.81	3679.90	2923.80	2474.78	2179.23	1971.34	1818.17
115000	10244.53	5440.35	3847.17	3056.70	2587.27	2278.29	2060.95	1900.82
120000	10689.95	5676.88	4014.44	3189.60	2699.76	2377.35	2150.55	1983.46
125000	11135.36	5913.42	4181.71	3322.50	2812.25	2476.40	2240.16	2066.11
130000	11580.78	6149.96	4348.98	3455.40	2924.74	2575.46	2329.77	2148.75
135000	12026.19	6386.49	4516.24	3588.30	3037.23	2674.51	2419.37	2231.39
140000	12471.61	6623.03	4683.51	3721.20	3149.72	2773.57	2508.98	2314.04
145000	12917.02	6859.56	4850.78	3854.10	3262.21	2872.63	2598.58	2396.68
150000	13362.43	7096.10	5018.05	3987.00	3374.70	2971.68	2688.19	2479.33
155000	13807.85	7332.64	5185.32	4119.90	3487.19	3070.74	2777.80	2561.97
160000	14253.26	7569.17	5352.59	4252.80	3599.68	3169.79	2867.40	2644.61

134

AMOUNT OF LOAN	NUMBER OF YEARS IN TERM							
	9	10	15	20	25	30	35	40
$ 50	.78	.74	.62	.57	.55	.54	.53	.53
100	1.55	1.47	1.24	1.14	1.10	1.07	1.06	1.05
200	3.10	2.93	2.47	2.28	2.19	2.14	2.12	2.10
300	4.65	4.40	3.70	3.41	3.28	3.21	3.17	3.15
400	6.19	5.86	4.94	4.55	4.37	4.27	4.23	4.20
500	7.74	7.32	6.17	5.69	5.46	5.34	5.28	5.25
600	9.29	8.79	7.40	6.82	6.55	6.41	6.34	6.30
700	10.83	10.25	8.63	7.96	7.64	7.48	7.39	7.35
800	12.38	11.72	9.87	9.09	8.73	8.54	8.45	8.40
900	13.93	13.18	11.10	10.23	9.82	9.61	9.50	9.45
1000	15.47	14.64	12.33	11.37	10.91	10.68	10.56	10.49
2000	30.94	29.28	24.66	22.73	21.81	21.35	21.11	20.98
3000	46.41	43.92	36.98	34.09	32.72	32.02	31.66	31.47
4000	61.88	58.56	49.31	45.45	43.62	42.70	42.22	41.96
5000	77.34	73.19	61.63	56.81	54.52	53.37	52.77	52.45
6000	92.81	87.83	73.96	68.17	65.43	64.04	63.32	62.94
7000	108.28	102.47	86.28	79.53	76.33	74.71	73.87	73.43
8000	123.75	117.11	98.61	90.90	87.23	85.39	84.43	83.92
9000	139.21	131.74	110.93	102.26	98.14	96.06	94.98	94.41
10000	154.68	146.38	123.26	113.62	109.04	106.73	105.53	104.90
11000	170.15	161.02	135.58	124.98	119.94	117.40	116.08	115.39
12000	185.62	175.66	147.91	136.34	130.85	128.08	126.64	125.88
13000	201.08	190.29	160.23	147.70	141.75	138.75	137.19	136.36
14000	216.55	204.93	172.56	159.06	152.65	149.42	147.74	146.85
15000	232.02	219.57	184.88	170.43	163.56	160.09	158.29	157.34
16000	247.49	234.21	197.21	181.79	174.46	170.77	168.85	167.83
17000	262.95	248.84	209.53	193.15	185.37	181.44	179.40	178.32
18000	278.42	263.48	221.86	204.51	196.27	192.11	189.95	188.81
19000	293.89	278.12	234.18	215.87	207.17	202.78	200.50	199.30
20000	309.36	292.76	246.51	227.23	218.08	213.46	211.06	209.79
21000	324.82	307.39	258.83	238.59	228.98	224.13	221.61	220.28
22000	340.29	322.03	271.16	249.96	239.88	234.80	232.16	230.77
23000	355.76	336.67	283.49	261.32	250.79	245.47	242.71	241.26
24000	371.23	351.31	295.81	272.68	261.69	256.15	253.27	251.75
25000	386.69	365.95	308.14	284.04	272.59	266.82	263.82	262.23
26000	402.16	380.58	320.46	295.40	283.50	277.49	274.37	272.72
27000	417.63	395.22	332.79	306.76	294.40	288.16	284.92	283.21
28000	433.10	409.86	345.11	318.12	305.30	298.84	295.48	293.70
29000	448.56	424.50	357.44	329.49	316.21	309.51	306.03	304.19
30000	464.03	439.13	369.76	340.85	327.11	320.18	316.58	314.68
31000	479.50	453.77	382.09	352.21	338.01	330.85	327.13	325.17
32000	494.97	468.41	394.41	363.57	348.92	341.53	337.69	335.66
33000	510.43	483.05	406.74	374.93	359.82	352.20	348.24	346.15
34000	525.90	497.68	419.06	386.29	370.73	362.87	358.79	356.64
35000	541.37	512.32	431.39	397.65	381.63	373.55	369.34	367.13
40000	618.71	585.51	493.01	454.46	436.15	426.91	422.11	419.57
45000	696.04	658.70	554.64	511.27	490.66	480.27	474.87	472.02
50000	773.38	731.89	616.27	568.08	545.18	533.63	527.63	524.46
55000	850.72	805.07	677.89	624.88	599.70	587.00	580.39	576.91
60000	928.06	878.26	739.52	681.69	654.22	640.36	633.16	629.36
65000	1005.40	951.45	801.14	738.50	708.74	693.72	685.92	681.80
70000	1082.73	1024.64	862.77	795.30	763.25	747.09	738.68	734.25
75000	1160.07	1097.83	924.40	852.11	817.77	800.45	791.45	786.69
80000	1237.41	1171.01	986.02	908.92	872.29	853.81	844.21	839.14
85000	1314.75	1244.20	1047.65	965.72	926.81	907.17	896.97	891.59
90000	1392.08	1317.39	1109.27	1022.53	981.32	960.54	949.73	944.03
95000	1469.42	1390.58	1170.90	1079.34	1035.84	1013.90	1002.50	996.48
100000	1546.76	1463.77	1232.53	1136.15	1090.36	1067.26	1055.26	1048.92
105000	1624.10	1536.95	1294.15	1192.95	1144.88	1120.63	1108.02	1101.37
110000	1701.44	1610.14	1355.78	1249.76	1199.39	1173.99	1160.78	1153.82
115000	1778.77	1683.33	1417.41	1306.57	1253.91	1227.35	1213.55	1206.26
120000	1856.11	1756.52	1479.03	1363.37	1308.43	1280.71	1266.31	1258.71
125000	1933.45	1829.71	1540.66	1420.18	1362.95	1334.08	1319.07	1311.15
130000	2010.79	1902.90	1602.28	1476.99	1417.47	1387.44	1371.84	1363.60
135000	2088.12	1976.08	1663.91	1533.79	1471.98	1440.80	1424.60	1416.05
140000	2165.46	2049.27	1725.54	1590.60	1526.50	1494.17	1477.36	1468.49
145000	2242.80	2122.46	1787.16	1647.41	1581.02	1547.53	1530.12	1520.94
150000	2320.14	2195.65	1848.79	1704.22	1635.54	1600.89	1582.89	1573.38
155000	2397.48	2268.84	1910.41	1761.02	1690.05	1654.25	1635.65	1625.83
160000	2474.81	2342.02	1972.04	1817.83	1744.57	1707.62	1688.41	1678.28

12.750% MONTHLY AMORTIZING PAYMENTS

AMOUNT OF LOAN	NUMBER OF YEARS IN TERM							
	1	2	3	4	5	6	7	8
$ 50	4.47	2.38	1.68	1.34	1.14	1.00	.91	.84
100	8.93	4.75	3.36	2.68	2.27	2.00	1.81	1.67
200	17.85	9.49	6.72	5.35	4.53	3.99	3.62	3.34
300	26.77	14.23	10.08	8.02	6.79	5.99	5.42	5.01
400	35.69	18.97	13.43	10.69	9.06	7.98	7.23	6.67
500	44.61	23.72	16.79	13.36	11.32	9.98	9.03	8.34
600	53.53	28.46	20.15	16.03	13.58	11.97	10.84	10.01
700	62.45	33.20	23.51	18.70	15.84	13.96	12.64	11.67
800	71.37	37.94	26.86	21.37	18.11	15.96	14.45	13.34
900	80.29	42.69	30.22	24.04	20.37	17.95	16.26	15.01
1000	89.21	47.43	33.58	26.71	22.63	19.95	18.06	16.67
2000	178.41	94.85	67.15	53.41	45.26	39.89	36.12	33.34
3000	267.61	142.28	100.73	80.12	67.88	59.83	54.17	50.01
4000	356.81	189.70	134.30	106.82	90.51	79.77	72.23	66.68
5000	446.01	237.13	167.87	133.52	113.13	99.72	90.29	83.34
6000	535.21	284.55	201.45	160.23	135.76	116.66	108.34	100.01
7000	624.41	331.98	235.02	186.93	158.38	139.60	126.40	116.68
8000	713.61	379.40	268.59	213.63	181.01	159.54	144.46	133.35
9000	802.81	426.83	302.17	240.34	203.63	179.49	162.51	150.01
10000	892.01	474.25	335.74	267.04	226.26	199.43	180.57	166.68
11000	981.21	521.67	369.32	293.74	248.88	219.37	198.62	183.35
12000	1070.41	569.10	402.89	320.45	271.51	239.31	216.68	200.02
13000	1159.61	616.52	436.46	347.15	294.13	259.26	234.74	216.69
14000	1248.81	663.95	470.04	373.86	316.76	279.20	252.79	233.35
15000	1338.01	711.37	503.61	400.56	339.38	299.14	270.85	250.02
16000	1427.21	758.80	537.18	427.26	362.01	319.08	288.91	266.69
17000	1516.41	806.22	570.76	453.97	384.64	339.03	306.96	283.36
18000	1605.61	853.65	604.33	480.67	407.26	358.97	325.02	300.02
19000	1694.81	901.07	637.90	507.37	429.89	378.91	343.08	316.69
20000	1784.01	948.49	671.48	534.08	452.51	398.85	361.13	333.36
21000	1873.21	995.92	705.05	560.78	475.14	418.80	379.19	350.03
22000	1962.41	1043.34	738.63	587.48	497.76	438.74	397.24	366.69
23000	2051.61	1090.77	772.20	614.19	520.39	458.68	415.30	383.36
24000	2140.81	1138.19	805.77	640.89	543.01	478.62	433.36	400.03
25000	2230.01	1185.62	839.35	667.59	565.64	498.56	451.41	416.70
26000	2319.21	1233.04	872.92	694.30	588.26	518.51	469.47	433.37
27000	2408.41	1280.47	906.49	721.00	610.89	538.45	487.53	450.03
28000	2497.61	1327.89	940.07	747.71	633.51	558.39	505.58	466.70
29000	2586.81	1375.31	973.64	774.41	656.14	578.33	523.64	483.37
30000	2676.01	1422.74	1007.21	801.11	678.76	598.28	541.69	500.04
31000	2765.21	1470.16	1040.79	827.82	701.39	618.22	559.75	516.70
32000	2854.41	1517.59	1074.36	854.52	724.01	638.16	577.81	533.37
33000	2943.61	1565.01	1107.94	881.22	746.64	658.10	595.86	550.04
34000	3032.81	1612.44	1141.51	907.93	769.27	678.05	613.92	566.71
35000	3122.01	1659.86	1175.08	934.63	791.89	697.99	631.98	583.38
40000	3568.01	1896.98	1342.95	1068.15	905.02	797.70	722.26	666.71
45000	4014.01	2134.11	1510.82	1201.67	1018.14	897.41	812.54	750.05
50000	4460.01	2371.23	1678.69	1335.18	1131.27	997.13	902.82	833.39
55000	4906.01	2608.35	1846.56	1468.70	1244.40	1096.84	993.10	916.73
60000	5352.01	2845.47	2014.42	1602.22	1357.52	1196.55	1083.38	1000.07
65000	5798.01	3082.60	2182.29	1735.74	1470.65	1296.26	1173.67	1083.41
70000	6244.01	3319.72	2350.16	1869.26	1583.78	1395.97	1263.95	1166.75
75000	6690.01	3556.84	2518.03	2002.77	1696.90	1495.69	1354.23	1250.08
80000	7136.01	3793.96	2685.90	2136.29	1810.03	1595.40	1444.51	1333.42
85000	7582.01	4031.09	2853.77	2269.81	1923.16	1695.11	1534.79	1416.76
90000	8028.01	4268.21	3021.63	2403.33	2036.28	1794.82	1625.07	1500.10
95000	8474.01	4505.33	3189.50	2536.85	2149.41	1894.54	1715.36	1583.44
100000	8920.01	4742.45	3357.37	2670.36	2262.54	1994.25	1805.64	1666.78
105000	9366.01	4979.58	3525.24	2803.88	2375.66	2093.96	1895.92	1750.12
110000	9812.01	5216.70	3693.11	2937.40	2488.79	2193.67	1986.20	1833.45
115000	10258.01	5453.82	3860.98	3070.92	2601.91	2293.38	2076.48	1916.79
120000	10704.01	5690.94	4028.84	3204.43	2715.04	2393.09	2166.76	2000.13
125000	11150.01	5928.07	4196.71	3337.95	2828.17	2492.81	2257.05	2083.47
130000	11596.01	6165.19	4364.58	3471.47	2941.29	2592.52	2347.33	2166.81
135000	12042.01	6402.31	4532.45	3604.99	3054.42	2692.23	2437.61	2250.15
140000	12488.01	6639.43	4700.32	3738.51	3167.55	2791.94	2527.89	2333.49
145000	12934.01	6876.55	4868.19	3872.02	3280.67	2891.65	2618.17	2416.82
150000	13380.01	7113.68	5036.05	4005.54	3393.80	2991.37	2708.45	2500.16
155000	13826.01	7350.80	5203.92	4139.06	3506.93	3091.08	2798.74	2583.50
160000	14272.01	7587.92	5371.79	4272.58	3620.05	3190.79	2889.02	2666.84

136

AMOUNT OF LOAN	NUMBER OF YEARS IN TERM							
	9	10	15	20	25	30	35	40
$ 50	.79	.74	.63	.58	.56	.55	.54	.54
100	1.57	1.48	1.25	1.16	1.11	1.09	1.08	1.07
200	3.13	2.96	2.50	2.31	2.22	2.18	2.16	2.14
300	4.69	4.44	3.75	3.47	3.33	3.27	3.23	3.21
400	6.25	5.92	5.00	4.62	4.44	4.35	4.31	4.28
500	7.81	7.40	6.25	5.77	5.55	5.44	5.38	5.35
600	9.37	8.88	7.50	6.93	6.66	6.53	6.46	6.42
700	10.93	10.35	8.75	8.08	7.77	7.61	7.53	7.49
800	12.49	11.83	10.00	9.24	8.88	8.70	8.61	8.56
900	14.05	13.31	11.24	10.39	9.99	9.79	9.68	9.63
1000	15.62	14.79	12.49	11.54	11.10	10.87	10.76	10.70
2000	31.23	29.57	24.98	23.08	22.19	21.74	21.51	21.39
3000	46.84	44.36	37.47	34.62	33.28	32.61	32.26	32.08
4000	62.45	59.14	49.96	46.16	44.37	43.47	43.01	42.77
5000	78.06	73.92	62.45	57.70	55.46	54.34	53.76	53.46
6000	93.67	88.71	74.94	69.23	66.55	65.21	64.52	64.16
7000	109.28	103.49	87.42	80.77	77.64	76.07	75.27	74.85
8000	124.89	118.28	99.91	92.31	88.73	86.94	86.02	85.54
9000	140.50	133.06	112.40	103.85	99.82	97.81	96.77	96.23
10000	156.11	147.84	124.89	115.39	110.91	108.67	107.52	106.92
11000	171.72	162.63	137.38	126.92	122.00	119.54	118.28	117.62
12000	187.33	177.41	149.87	138.46	133.09	130.41	129.03	128.31
13000	202.94	192.20	162.35	150.00	144.18	141.28	139.78	139.00
14000	218.55	206.98	174.84	161.54	155.27	152.14	150.53	149.69
15000	234.16	221.76	187.33	173.08	166.36	163.01	161.28	160.38
16000	249.77	236.55	199.82	184.61	177.45	173.88	172.04	171.08
17000	265.38	251.33	212.31	196.15	188.54	184.74	182.79	181.77
18000	280.99	266.12	224.80	207.69	199.63	195.61	193.54	192.46
19000	296.60	280.90	237.28	219.23	210.72	206.48	204.29	203.15
20000	312.21	295.68	249.77	230.77	221.82	217.34	215.04	213.84
21000	327.82	310.47	262.26	242.31	232.91	228.21	225.80	224.54
22000	343.43	325.25	274.75	253.84	244.00	239.08	236.55	235.23
23000	359.04	340.04	287.24	265.38	255.09	249.94	247.30	245.92
24000	374.65	354.82	299.73	276.92	266.18	260.81	258.05	256.61
25000	390.26	369.60	312.21	288.46	277.27	271.68	268.80	267.30
26000	405.87	384.39	324.70	300.00	288.36	282.55	279.56	278.00
27000	421.48	399.17	337.19	311.53	299.45	293.41	290.31	288.69
28000	437.09	413.96	349.68	323.07	310.54	304.28	301.06	299.38
29000	452.70	428.74	362.17	334.61	321.63	315.15	311.81	310.07
30000	468.31	443.52	374.66	346.15	332.72	326.01	322.56	320.76
31000	483.92	458.31	387.14	357.69	343.81	336.88	333.32	331.46
32000	499.53	473.09	399.63	369.22	354.90	347.75	344.07	342.15
33000	515.14	487.88	412.12	380.76	365.99	358.61	354.82	352.84
34000	530.75	502.66	424.61	392.30	377.08	369.48	365.57	363.53
35000	546.36	517.44	437.10	403.84	388.17	380.35	376.32	374.22
40000	624.41	591.36	499.54	461.53	443.63	434.68	430.08	427.68
45000	702.47	665.28	561.98	519.22	499.08	489.02	483.84	481.14
50000	780.52	739.20	624.42	576.91	554.53	543.35	537.60	534.60
55000	858.57	813.12	686.87	634.60	609.98	597.69	591.36	588.06
60000	936.62	887.04	749.31	692.29	665.44	652.02	645.12	641.52
65000	1014.67	960.96	811.75	749.98	720.89	706.36	698.88	694.98
70000	1092.72	1034.88	874.19	807.67	776.34	760.69	752.64	748.44
75000	1170.77	1108.80	936.63	865.36	831.79	815.02	806.40	801.90
80000	1248.82	1182.72	999.07	923.05	887.25	869.36	860.16	855.36
85000	1326.87	1256.64	1061.52	980.74	942.70	923.69	913.92	908.82
90000	1404.93	1330.56	1123.96	1038.44	998.15	978.03	967.68	962.28
95000	1482.98	1404.48	1186.40	1096.13	1053.60	1032.36	1021.44	1015.74
100000	1561.03	1478.40	1248.84	1153.82	1109.06	1086.70	1075.20	1069.20
105000	1639.08	1552.32	1311.28	1211.51	1164.51	1141.03	1128.96	1122.66
110000	1717.13	1626.24	1373.73	1269.20	1219.96	1195.37	1182.72	1176.12
115000	1795.18	1700.16	1436.17	1326.89	1275.42	1249.70	1236.48	1229.58
120000	1873.23	1774.08	1498.61	1384.58	1330.87	1304.04	1290.24	1283.04
125000	1951.28	1848.00	1561.05	1442.27	1386.32	1358.37	1344.00	1336.50
130000	2029.34	1921.92	1623.49	1499.96	1441.77	1412.71	1397.76	1389.96
135000	2107.39	1995.84	1685.93	1557.65	1497.23	1467.04	1451.52	1443.42
140000	2185.44	2069.76	1748.38	1615.34	1552.68	1521.38	1505.28	1496.88
145000	2263.49	2143.68	1810.82	1673.03	1608.13	1575.71	1559.04	1550.34
150000	2341.54	2217.60	1873.26	1730.72	1663.58	1630.04	1612.80	1603.80
155000	2419.59	2291.52	1935.70	1788.41	1719.04	1684.38	1666.56	1657.26
160000	2497.64	2365.44	1998.14	1846.10	1774.49	1738.71	1720.32	1710.72

AMOUNT OF LOAN	NUMBER OF YEARS IN TERM							
	1	2	3	4	5	6	7	8
$ 50	4.47	2.38	1.69	1.35	1.14	1.01	.91	.85
100	8.94	4.76	3.37	2.69	2.28	2.01	1.82	1.69
200	17.87	9.51	6.74	5.37	4.56	4.02	3.64	3.37
300	26.80	14.27	10.11	8.05	6.83	6.03	5.46	5.05
400	35.73	19.02	13.48	10.74	9.11	8.03	7.28	6.73
500	44.66	23.78	16.85	13.42	11.38	10.04	9.10	8.41
600	53.60	28.53	20.22	16.10	13.66	12.05	10.92	10.09
700	62.53	33.28	23.59	18.78	15.93	14.06	12.74	11.77
800	71.46	38.04	26.96	21.47	18.21	16.06	14.56	13.45
900	80.39	42.79	30.33	24.15	20.48	18.07	16.38	15.13
1000	89.32	47.55	33.70	26.83	22.76	20.08	18.20	16.81
2000	178.64	95.09	67.39	53.66	45.51	40.15	36.39	33.62
3000	267.96	142.63	101.09	80.49	68.26	60.23	54.58	50.43
4000	357.27	190.17	134.78	107.31	91.02	80.30	72.77	67.23
5000	446.59	237.71	168.47	134.14	113.77	100.38	90.96	84.04
6000	535.91	285.26	202.17	160.97	136.52	120.45	109.16	100.85
7000	625.23	332.80	235.86	187.80	159.28	140.52	127.35	117.66
8000	714.54	380.34	269.56	214.62	182.03	160.60	145.54	134.46
9000	803.86	427.88	303.25	241.45	204.78	180.67	163.73	151.27
10000	893.18	475.42	336.94	268.28	227.54	200.75	181.92	168.08
11000	982.50	522.97	370.64	295.11	250.29	220.82	200.12	184.88
12000	1071.81	570.51	404.33	321.93	273.04	240.89	218.31	201.69
13000	1161.13	618.05	438.03	348.76	295.79	260.97	236.50	218.50
14000	1250.45	665.59	471.72	375.59	318.55	281.04	254.69	235.31
15000	1339.76	713.13	505.41	402.42	341.30	301.12	272.88	252.11
16000	1429.08	760.67	539.11	429.24	364.05	321.19	291.08	268.92
17000	1518.40	808.22	572.80	456.07	386.81	341.26	309.27	285.73
18000	1607.72	855.76	606.50	482.90	409.56	361.34	327.46	302.54
19000	1697.03	903.30	640.19	509.73	432.31	381.41	345.65	319.34
20000	1786.35	950.84	673.88	536.55	455.07	401.49	363.84	336.15
21000	1875.67	998.38	707.58	563.38	477.82	421.56	382.04	352.96
22000	1964.99	1045.93	741.27	590.21	500.57	441.64	400.23	369.76
23000	2054.30	1093.47	774.97	617.04	523.33	461.71	418.42	386.57
24000	2143.62	1141.01	808.66	643.86	546.08	481.78	436.61	403.38
25000	2232.94	1188.55	842.35	670.69	568.83	501.86	454.80	420.19
26000	2322.25	1236.09	876.05	697.52	591.58	521.93	473.00	436.99
27000	2411.57	1283.63	909.74	724.35	614.34	542.01	491.19	453.80
28000	2500.89	1331.18	943.44	751.17	637.09	562.08	509.38	470.61
29000	2590.21	1378.72	977.13	778.00	659.84	582.15	527.57	487.42
30000	2679.52	1426.26	1010.82	804.83	682.60	602.23	545.76	504.22
31000	2768.84	1473.80	1044.52	831.66	705.35	622.30	563.96	521.03
32000	2858.16	1521.34	1078.21	858.48	728.10	642.38	582.15	537.84
33000	2947.48	1568.89	1111.91	885.31	750.86	662.45	600.34	554.64
34000	3036.79	1616.43	1145.60	912.14	773.61	682.52	618.53	571.45
35000	3126.11	1663.97	1179.29	938.97	796.36	702.60	636.72	588.26
40000	3572.70	1901.68	1347.76	1073.10	910.13	802.97	727.68	672.30
45000	4019.28	2139.39	1516.23	1207.24	1023.89	903.34	818.64	756.33
50000	4465.87	2377.10	1684.70	1341.38	1137.66	1003.71	909.60	840.37
55000	4912.46	2614.81	1853.17	1475.52	1251.42	1104.08	1000.56	924.40
60000	5359.04	2852.51	2021.64	1609.65	1365.19	1204.45	1091.52	1008.44
65000	5805.63	3090.22	2190.11	1743.79	1478.95	1304.82	1182.48	1092.48
70000	6252.21	3327.93	2358.58	1877.93	1592.72	1405.19	1273.44	1176.51
75000	6698.80	3565.64	2527.05	2012.07	1706.49	1505.56	1364.40	1260.55
80000	7145.39	3803.35	2695.52	2146.20	1820.25	1605.93	1455.36	1344.59
85000	7591.97	4041.06	2863.99	2280.34	1934.02	1706.30	1546.32	1428.62
90000	8038.56	4278.77	3032.46	2414.48	2047.78	1806.67	1637.28	1512.66
95000	8485.15	4516.48	3200.93	2548.62	2161.55	1907.04	1728.24	1596.69
100000	8931.73	4754.19	3369.40	2682.75	2275.31	2007.42	1819.20	1680.73
105000	9378.32	4991.90	3537.87	2816.89	2389.08	2107.79	1910.16	1764.77
110000	9824.91	5229.61	3706.34	2951.03	2502.84	2208.16	2001.12	1848.80
115000	10271.49	5467.31	3874.81	3085.17	2616.61	2308.53	2092.08	1932.84
120000	10718.08	5705.02	4043.28	3219.30	2730.37	2408.90	2183.04	2016.88
125000	11164.66	5942.73	4211.75	3353.44	2844.14	2509.27	2274.00	2100.91
130000	11611.25	6180.44	4380.22	3487.58	2957.90	2609.64	2364.96	2184.95
135000	12057.84	6418.15	4548.69	3621.72	3071.67	2710.01	2455.92	2268.98
140000	12504.42	6655.86	4717.16	3755.85	3185.44	2810.38	2546.88	2353.02
145000	12951.01	6893.57	4885.63	3889.99	3299.20	2910.75	2637.84	2437.06
150000	13397.60	7131.28	5054.10	4024.13	3412.97	3011.12	2728.80	2521.09
155000	13844.18	7368.99	5222.57	4158.27	3526.73	3111.49	2819.76	2605.13
160000	14290.77	7606.70	5391.04	4292.40	3640.50	3211.86	2910.72	2689.17

AMOUNT OF LOAN	NUMBER OF YEARS IN TERM							
	9	10	15	20	25	30	35	40
$ 50	.79	.75	.64	.59	.57	.56	.55	.55
100	1.58	1.50	1.27	1.18	1.13	1.11	1.10	1.09
200	3.16	2.99	2.54	2.35	2.26	2.22	2.20	2.18
300	4.73	4.48	3.80	3.52	3.39	3.32	3.29	3.27
400	6.31	5.98	5.07	4.69	4.52	4.43	4.39	4.36
500	7.88	7.47	6.33	5.86	5.64	5.54	5.48	5.45
600	9.46	8.96	7.60	7.03	6.77	6.64	6.58	6.54
700	11.03	10.46	8.86	8.21	7.90	7.75	7.67	7.63
800	12.61	11.95	10.13	9.38	9.03	8.85	8.77	8.72
900	14.18	13.44	11.39	10.55	10.16	9.96	9.86	9.81
1000	15.76	14.94	12.66	11.72	11.28	11.07	10.96	10.90
2000	31.51	29.87	25.31	23.44	22.56	22.13	21.91	21.80
3000	47.27	44.80	37.96	35.15	33.84	33.19	32.86	32.69
4000	63.02	59.73	50.61	46.87	45.12	44.25	43.81	43.59
5000	78.77	74.66	63.27	58.58	56.40	55.31	54.76	54.48
6000	94.53	89.59	75.92	70.30	67.68	66.38	65.72	65.38
7000	110.28	104.52	88.57	82.02	78.95	77.44	76.67	76.27
8000	126.03	119.45	101.22	93.73	90.23	88.50	87.62	87.17
9000	141.79	134.38	113.88	105.45	101.51	99.56	98.57	98.06
10000	157.54	149.32	126.53	117.16	112.79	110.62	109.52	108.96
11000	173.29	164.25	139.18	128.88	124.07	121.69	120.48	119.85
12000	189.05	179.18	151.83	140.59	135.35	132.75	131.43	130.75
13000	204.80	194.11	164.49	152.31	146.62	143.81	142.38	141.64
14000	220.56	209.04	177.14	164.03	157.90	154.87	153.33	152.54
15000	236.31	223.97	189.79	175.74	169.18	165.93	164.28	163.43
16000	252.06	238.90	202.44	187.46	180.46	177.00	175.24	174.33
17000	267.82	253.83	215.10	199.17	191.74	188.06	186.19	185.22
18000	283.57	268.76	227.75	210.89	203.02	199.12	197.14	196.12
19000	299.32	283.70	240.40	222.60	214.29	210.18	208.09	207.01
20000	315.08	298.63	253.05	234.32	225.57	221.24	219.04	217.91
21000	330.83	313.56	265.71	246.04	236.85	232.31	230.00	228.80
22000	346.58	328.49	278.36	257.75	248.13	243.37	240.95	239.70
23000	362.34	343.42	291.01	269.47	259.41	254.43	251.90	250.59
24000	378.09	358.35	303.66	281.18	270.69	265.49	262.85	261.49
25000	393.84	373.28	316.32	292.90	281.96	276.55	273.80	272.38
26000	409.60	388.21	328.97	304.61	293.24	287.62	284.76	283.28
27000	425.35	403.14	341.62	316.33	304.52	298.68	295.71	294.17
28000	441.11	418.08	354.27	328.05	315.80	309.74	306.66	305.07
29000	456.86	433.01	366.93	339.76	327.08	320.80	317.61	315.96
30000	472.61	447.94	379.58	351.48	338.36	331.86	328.56	326.86
31000	488.37	462.87	392.23	363.19	349.63	342.93	339.51	337.75
32000	504.12	477.80	404.88	374.91	360.91	353.99	350.47	348.65
33000	519.87	492.73	417.53	386.62	372.19	365.05	361.42	359.54
34000	535.63	507.66	430.19	398.34	383.47	376.11	372.37	370.44
35000	551.38	522.59	442.84	410.06	394.75	387.17	383.32	381.33
40000	630.15	597.25	506.10	468.64	451.14	442.48	438.08	435.81
45000	708.92	671.90	569.36	527.21	507.53	497.79	492.84	490.29
50000	787.68	746.56	632.63	585.79	563.92	553.10	547.60	544.76
55000	866.45	821.21	695.89	644.37	620.31	608.41	602.36	599.24
60000	945.22	895.87	759.15	702.95	676.71	663.72	657.12	653.71
65000	1023.99	970.52	822.41	761.53	733.10	719.03	711.88	708.19
70000	1102.75	1045.18	885.67	820.11	789.49	774.34	766.64	762.66
75000	1181.52	1119.84	948.94	878.69	845.88	829.65	821.40	817.14
80000	1260.29	1194.49	1012.20	937.27	902.27	884.96	876.16	871.62
85000	1339.06	1269.15	1075.46	995.84	958.67	940.27	930.92	926.09
90000	1417.83	1343.80	1138.72	1054.42	1015.06	995.58	985.68	980.57
95000	1496.60	1418.46	1201.99	1113.00	1071.45	1050.89	1040.44	1035.04
100000	1575.36	1493.11	1265.25	1171.58	1127.84	1106.20	1095.20	1089.52
105000	1654.13	1567.77	1328.51	1230.16	1184.23	1161.51	1149.96	1143.99
110000	1732.90	1642.42	1391.77	1288.74	1240.62	1216.82	1204.72	1198.47
115000	1811.67	1717.08	1455.03	1347.32	1297.02	1272.13	1259.48	1252.95
120000	1890.44	1791.73	1518.30	1405.90	1353.41	1327.44	1314.24	1307.42
125000	1969.20	1866.39	1581.56	1464.47	1409.80	1382.75	1369.00	1361.90
130000	2047.97	1941.04	1644.82	1523.05	1466.19	1438.06	1423.76	1416.37
135000	2126.74	2015.70	1708.08	1581.63	1522.58	1493.37	1478.52	1470.85
140000	2205.51	2090.36	1771.34	1640.21	1578.97	1548.68	1533.28	1525.32
145000	2284.28	2165.01	1834.61	1698.79	1635.37	1603.99	1588.04	1579.80
150000	2363.04	2239.67	1897.87	1757.37	1691.76	1659.30	1642.79	1634.28
155000	2441.81	2314.32	1961.13	1815.95	1748.15	1714.61	1697.55	1688.75
160000	2520.58	2388.98	2024.39	1874.53	1804.54	1769.92	1752.31	1743.23

13.250% MONTHLY AMORTIZING PAYMENTS

AMOUNT OF LOAN	NUMBER OF YEARS IN TERM							
	1	2	3	4	5	6	7	8
$ 50	4.48	2.39	1.70	1.35	1.15	1.02	.92	.85
100	8.95	4.77	3.39	2.70	2.29	2.03	1.84	1.70
200	17.89	9.54	6.77	5.40	4.58	4.05	3.67	3.39
300	26.84	14.30	10.15	8.09	6.87	6.07	5.50	5.09
400	35.78	19.07	13.53	10.79	9.15	8.09	7.34	6.78
500	44.72	23.83	16.91	13.48	11.45	10.11	9.17	8.48
600	53.67	28.60	20.29	16.18	13.73	12.13	11.00	10.17
700	62.61	33.37	23.68	18.87	16.02	14.15	12.83	11.87
800	71.55	38.13	27.06	21.57	18.31	16.17	14.67	13.56
900	80.50	42.90	30.44	24.26	20.60	18.19	16.50	15.26
1000	89.44	47.66	33.82	26.96	22.89	20.21	18.33	16.95
2000	178.87	95.32	67.63	53.91	45.77	40.42	36.66	33.90
3000	268.31	142.98	101.45	80.86	68.65	60.62	54.99	50.85
4000	357.74	190.64	135.26	107.81	91.53	80.83	73.32	67.79
5000	447.18	238.30	169.08	134.76	114.41	101.04	91.65	84.74
6000	536.61	285.96	202.89	161.72	137.29	121.24	109.97	101.69
7000	626.05	333.62	236.71	188.67	160.17	141.45	128.30	118.64
8000	715.48	381.28	270.52	215.62	183.06	161.66	146.63	135.58
9000	804.92	428.94	304.34	242.57	205.94	181.86	164.96	152.53
10000	894.35	476.60	338.15	269.52	228.82	202.07	183.29	169.48
11000	983.79	524.26	371.96	296.47	251.70	222.27	201.61	186.43
12000	1073.22	571.92	405.78	323.43	274.58	242.48	219.94	203.37
13000	1162.65	619.58	439.59	350.38	297.46	262.69	238.27	220.32
14000	1252.09	667.24	473.41	377.33	320.34	282.89	256.60	237.27
15000	1341.52	714.90	507.22	404.28	343.22	303.10	274.93	254.22
16000	1430.96	762.55	541.04	431.23	366.11	323.31	293.26	271.16
17000	1520.39	810.21	574.85	458.18	388.99	343.51	311.58	288.11
18000	1609.83	857.87	608.67	485.14	411.87	363.72	329.91	305.06
19000	1699.26	905.53	642.48	512.09	434.75	383.92	348.24	322.01
20000	1788.70	953.19	676.29	539.04	457.63	404.13	366.57	338.95
21000	1878.13	1000.85	710.11	565.99	480.51	424.34	384.90	355.90
22000	1967.57	1048.51	743.92	592.94	503.39	444.54	403.22	372.85
23000	2057.00	1096.17	777.74	619.90	526.27	464.75	421.55	389.80
24000	2146.44	1143.83	811.55	646.85	549.16	484.96	439.88	406.74
25000	2235.87	1191.49	845.37	673.80	572.04	505.16	458.21	423.69
26000	2325.30	1239.15	879.18	700.75	594.92	525.37	476.54	440.64
27000	2414.74	1286.81	913.00	727.70	617.80	545.57	494.87	457.58
28000	2504.17	1334.47	946.81	754.65	640.68	565.78	513.19	474.53
29000	2593.61	1382.13	980.63	781.61	663.56	585.99	531.52	491.48
30000	2683.04	1429.79	1014.44	808.56	686.44	606.19	549.85	508.43
31000	2772.48	1477.44	1048.26	835.51	709.32	626.40	568.18	525.37
32000	2861.91	1525.10	1082.07	862.46	732.21	646.61	586.51	542.32
33000	2951.35	1572.76	1115.88	889.41	755.09	666.81	604.83	559.27
34000	3040.78	1620.42	1149.70	916.36	777.97	687.02	623.16	576.22
35000	3130.22	1668.08	1183.51	943.32	800.85	707.23	641.49	593.16
40000	3577.39	1906.38	1352.58	1078.07	915.26	808.26	733.13	677.90
45000	4024.56	2144.68	1521.66	1212.83	1029.66	909.29	824.77	762.64
50000	4471.74	2382.97	1690.73	1347.59	1144.07	1010.32	916.41	847.38
55000	4918.91	2621.27	1859.80	1482.35	1258.47	1111.35	1008.05	932.11
60000	5366.08	2859.57	2028.87	1617.11	1372.88	1212.38	1099.69	1016.85
65000	5813.25	3097.86	2197.95	1751.87	1487.29	1313.41	1191.33	1101.59
70000	6260.43	3336.16	2367.02	1886.63	1601.69	1414.45	1282.98	1186.32
75000	6707.60	3574.46	2536.09	2021.39	1716.10	1515.48	1374.62	1271.06
80000	7154.77	3812.75	2705.16	2156.14	1830.51	1616.51	1466.26	1355.80
85000	7601.95	4051.05	2874.24	2290.90	1944.91	1717.54	1557.90	1440.53
90000	8049.12	4289.35	3043.31	2425.66	2059.32	1818.57	1649.54	1525.27
95000	8496.29	4527.64	3212.38	2560.42	2173.72	1919.60	1741.18	1610.01
100000	8943.47	4765.94	3381.45	2695.18	2288.13	2020.63	1832.82	1694.75
105000	9390.64	5004.24	3550.53	2829.94	2402.54	2121.67	1924.46	1779.48
110000	9837.81	5242.53	3719.60	2964.70	2516.94	2222.70	2016.10	1864.22
115000	10284.99	5480.83	3888.67	3099.46	2631.35	2323.73	2107.74	1948.96
120000	10732.16	5719.13	4057.74	3234.21	2745.76	2424.76	2199.38	2033.69
125000	11179.33	5957.42	4226.82	3368.97	2860.16	2525.79	2291.02	2118.43
130000	11626.50	6195.72	4395.89	3503.73	2974.57	2626.82	2382.66	2203.17
135000	12073.68	6434.02	4564.96	3638.49	3088.97	2727.85	2474.31	2287.90
140000	12520.85	6672.31	4734.03	3773.25	3203.38	2828.89	2565.95	2372.64
145000	12968.02	6910.61	4903.11	3908.01	3317.79	2929.92	2657.59	2457.38
150000	13415.20	7148.91	5072.18	4042.77	3432.19	3030.95	2749.23	2542.12
155000	13862.37	7387.20	5241.25	4177.53	3546.60	3131.98	2840.87	2626.85
160000	14309.54	7625.50	5410.32	4312.28	3661.01	3233.01	2932.51	2711.59

140

MONTHLY AMORTIZING PAYMENTS 13.250%

AMOUNT OF LOAN	NUMBER OF YEARS IN TERM							
	9	10	15	20	25	30	35	40
$ 50	.80	.76	.65	.60	.58	.57	.56	.56
100	1.59	1.51	1.29	1.19	1.15	1.13	1.12	1.11
200	3.18	3.02	2.57	2.38	2.30	2.26	2.24	2.22
300	4.77	4.53	3.85	3.57	3.45	3.38	3.35	3.33
400	6.36	6.04	5.13	4.76	4.59	4.51	4.47	4.44
500	7.95	7.54	6.41	5.95	5.74	5.63	5.58	5.55
600	9.54	9.05	7.70	7.14	6.89	6.76	6.70	6.66
700	11.13	10.56	8.98	8.33	8.03	7.89	7.81	7.77
800	12.72	12.07	10.26	9.52	9.18	9.01	8.93	8.88
900	14.31	13.58	11.54	10.71	10.33	10.14	10.04	9.99
1000	15.90	15.08	12.82	11.90	11.47	11.26	11.16	11.10
2000	31.80	30.16	25.64	23.79	22.94	22.52	22.31	22.20
3000	47.70	45.24	38.46	35.69	34.41	33.78	33.46	33.30
4000	63.60	60.32	51.27	47.58	45.87	45.04	44.61	44.40
5000	79.49	75.40	64.09	59.48	57.34	56.29	55.77	55.50
6000	95.39	90.48	76.91	71.37	68.81	67.55	66.92	66.60
7000	111.29	105.56	89.73	83.27	80.27	78.81	78.07	77.70
8000	127.19	120.64	102.54	95.16	91.74	90.07	89.22	88.79
9000	143.08	135.72	115.36	107.05	103.21	101.32	100.38	99.89
10000	158.98	150.79	128.18	118.95	114.68	112.58	111.53	110.99
11000	174.88	165.87	141.00	130.84	126.14	123.84	122.68	122.09
12000	190.78	180.95	153.81	142.74	137.61	135.10	133.83	133.19
13000	206.67	196.03	166.63	154.63	149.08	146.36	144.99	144.29
14000	222.57	211.11	179.45	166.53	160.54	157.61	156.14	155.39
15000	238.47	226.19	192.27	178.42	172.01	168.87	167.29	166.49
16000	254.37	241.27	205.08	190.31	183.48	180.13	178.44	177.58
17000	270.26	256.35	217.90	202.21	194.94	191.39	189.60	188.68
18000	286.16	271.43	230.72	214.10	206.41	202.64	200.75	199.78
19000	302.06	286.50	243.53	226.00	217.88	213.90	211.90	210.88
20000	317.96	301.58	256.35	237.89	229.35	225.16	223.05	221.98
21000	333.85	316.66	269.17	249.79	240.81	236.42	234.21	233.08
22000	349.75	331.74	281.99	261.68	252.28	247.68	245.36	244.18
23000	365.65	346.82	294.80	273.57	263.75	258.93	256.51	255.28
24000	381.55	361.90	307.62	285.47	275.21	270.19	267.66	266.37
25000	397.45	376.98	320.44	297.36	286.68	281.45	278.82	277.47
26000	413.34	392.06	333.26	309.26	298.15	292.71	289.97	288.57
27000	429.24	407.14	346.07	321.15	309.61	303.96	301.12	299.67
28000	445.14	422.21	358.89	333.05	321.08	315.22	312.27	310.77
29000	461.04	437.29	371.71	344.94	332.55	326.48	323.43	321.87
30000	476.93	452.37	384.53	356.83	344.02	337.74	334.58	332.97
31000	492.83	467.45	397.34	368.73	355.48	348.99	345.73	344.06
32000	508.73	482.53	410.16	380.62	366.95	360.25	356.88	355.16
33000	524.63	497.61	422.98	392.52	378.42	371.51	368.03	366.26
34000	540.52	512.69	435.80	404.41	389.88	382.77	379.19	377.36
35000	556.42	527.77	448.61	416.31	401.35	394.03	390.34	388.46
40000	635.91	603.16	512.70	475.78	458.69	450.31	446.10	443.95
45000	715.40	678.56	576.79	535.25	516.02	506.60	501.86	499.45
50000	794.89	753.95	640.87	594.72	573.36	562.89	557.63	554.94
55000	874.37	829.34	704.96	654.19	630.69	619.18	613.39	610.43
60000	953.86	904.74	769.05	713.66	688.03	675.47	669.15	665.93
65000	1033.35	980.13	833.13	773.13	745.36	731.76	724.91	721.42
70000	1112.84	1055.53	897.22	832.61	802.70	788.05	780.67	776.91
75000	1192.33	1130.92	961.31	892.08	860.03	844.34	836.44	832.41
80000	1271.81	1206.32	1025.39	951.55	917.37	900.62	892.20	887.90
85000	1351.30	1281.71	1089.48	1011.02	974.70	956.91	947.96	943.39
90000	1430.79	1357.11	1153.57	1070.49	1032.04	1013.20	1003.72	998.89
95000	1510.28	1432.50	1217.65	1129.96	1089.37	1069.49	1059.49	1054.38
100000	1589.77	1507.89	1281.74	1189.44	1146.71	1125.78	1115.25	1109.87
105000	1669.25	1583.29	1345.83	1248.91	1204.04	1182.07	1171.01	1165.37
110000	1748.74	1658.68	1409.92	1308.38	1261.38	1238.36	1226.77	1220.86
115000	1828.23	1734.08	1474.00	1367.85	1318.71	1294.64	1282.53	1276.36
120000	1907.72	1809.47	1538.09	1427.32	1376.05	1350.93	1338.30	1331.85
125000	1987.21	1884.87	1602.18	1486.79	1433.38	1407.22	1394.06	1387.34
130000	2066.70	1960.26	1666.26	1546.26	1490.72	1463.51	1449.82	1442.84
135000	2146.18	2035.66	1730.35	1605.74	1548.05	1519.80	1505.58	1498.33
140000	2225.67	2111.05	1794.44	1665.21	1605.39	1576.09	1561.34	1553.82
145000	2305.16	2186.44	1858.53	1724.68	1662.72	1632.38	1617.11	1609.32
150000	2384.65	2261.84	1922.61	1784.15	1720.06	1688.67	1672.87	1664.81
155000	2464.14	2337.23	1986.70	1843.62	1777.39	1744.95	1728.63	1720.30
160000	2543.62	2412.63	2050.78	1903.09	1834.73	1801.24	1784.39	1775.80

13.500% MONTHLY AMORTIZING PAYMENTS

AMOUNT OF LOAN	NUMBER OF YEARS IN TERM							
	1	2	3	4	5	6	7	8
$ 50	4.48	2.39	1.70	1.36	1.16	1.02	.93	.86
100	8.96	4.78	3.40	2.71	2.31	2.04	1.85	1.71
200	17.92	9.56	6.79	5.42	4.61	4.07	3.70	3.42
300	26.87	14.34	10.19	8.13	6.91	6.11	5.54	5.13
400	35.83	19.12	13.58	10.84	9.21	8.14	7.39	6.84
500	44.78	23.89	16.97	13.54	11.51	10.17	9.24	8.55
600	53.74	28.67	20.37	16.25	13.81	12.21	11.08	10.26
700	62.69	33.45	23.76	18.96	16.11	14.24	12.93	11.97
800	71.65	38.23	27.15	21.67	18.41	16.28	14.78	13.68
900	80.60	43.00	30.55	24.37	20.71	18.31	16.62	15.38
1000	89.56	47.78	33.94	27.08	23.01	20.34	18.47	17.09
2000	179.11	95.56	67.88	54.16	46.02	40.68	36.93	34.18
3000	268.66	143.34	101.81	81.23	69.03	61.02	55.40	51.27
4000	358.21	191.11	135.75	108.31	92.04	81.36	73.86	68.36
5000	447.77	238.89	169.68	135.39	115.05	101.70	92.33	85.45
6000	537.32	286.67	203.62	162.46	138.06	122.04	110.79	102.53
7000	626.87	334.44	237.55	189.54	161.07	142.38	129.26	119.62
8000	716.42	382.22	271.49	216.62	184.08	162.72	147.72	136.71
9000	805.97	430.00	305.42	243.69	207.09	183.06	166.19	153.80
10000	895.53	477.78	339.36	270.77	230.10	203.39	184.65	170.89
11000	985.08	525.55	373.29	297.84	253.11	223.73	203.12	187.97
12000	1074.63	573.33	407.23	324.92	276.12	244.07	221.58	205.06
13000	1164.18	621.11	441.16	352.00	299.13	264.41	240.05	222.15
14000	1253.73	668.88	475.10	379.07	322.14	284.75	258.51	239.24
15000	1343.29	716.66	509.03	406.15	345.15	305.09	276.98	256.33
16000	1432.84	764.44	542.97	433.23	368.16	325.43	295.44	273.42
17000	1522.39	812.21	576.90	460.30	391.17	345.77	313.91	290.50
18000	1611.94	859.99	610.84	487.38	414.18	366.11	332.37	307.59
19000	1701.49	907.77	644.78	514.46	437.19	386.45	350.84	324.68
20000	1791.05	955.55	678.71	541.53	460.20	406.78	369.30	341.77
21000	1880.60	1003.32	712.65	568.61	483.21	427.12	387.77	358.86
22000	1970.15	1051.10	746.58	595.68	506.22	447.46	406.23	375.94
23000	2059.70	1098.88	780.52	622.76	529.23	467.80	424.70	393.03
24000	2149.25	1146.65	814.45	649.84	552.24	488.14	443.16	410.12
25000	2238.81	1194.43	848.39	676.91	575.25	508.48	461.63	427.21
26000	2328.36	1242.21	882.32	703.99	598.26	528.82	480.09	444.30
27000	2417.91	1289.98	916.26	731.07	621.27	549.16	498.56	461.39
28000	2507.46	1337.76	950.19	758.14	644.28	569.50	517.02	478.47
29000	2597.01	1385.54	984.13	785.22	667.29	589.83	535.49	495.56
30000	2686.57	1433.32	1018.06	812.29	690.30	610.17	553.95	512.65
31000	2776.12	1481.09	1052.00	839.37	713.31	630.51	572.42	529.74
32000	2865.67	1528.87	1085.93	866.45	736.32	650.85	590.88	546.83
33000	2955.22	1576.65	1119.87	893.52	759.33	671.19	609.35	563.91
34000	3044.77	1624.42	1153.80	920.60	782.34	691.53	627.81	581.00
35000	3134.33	1672.20	1187.74	947.68	805.35	711.87	646.28	598.09
40000	3582.09	1911.09	1357.42	1083.06	920.40	813.56	738.60	683.53
45000	4029.85	2149.97	1527.09	1218.44	1035.45	915.26	830.93	768.97
50000	4477.61	2388.86	1696.77	1353.82	1150.50	1016.95	923.25	854.41
55000	4925.37	2627.74	1866.45	1489.20	1265.55	1118.65	1015.57	939.85
60000	5373.13	2866.63	2036.12	1624.58	1380.60	1220.34	1107.90	1025.29
65000	5820.89	3105.51	2205.80	1759.97	1495.64	1322.04	1200.22	1110.74
70000	6268.65	3344.40	2375.48	1895.35	1610.69	1423.73	1292.55	1196.18
75000	6716.41	3583.28	2545.15	2030.73	1725.74	1525.43	1384.87	1281.62
80000	7164.17	3822.17	2714.83	2166.11	1840.79	1627.12	1477.20	1367.06
85000	7611.93	4061.05	2884.50	2301.49	1955.84	1728.82	1569.52	1452.50
90000	8059.69	4299.94	3054.18	2436.88	2070.89	1830.51	1661.85	1537.94
95000	8507.45	4538.82	3223.86	2572.26	2185.94	1932.21	1754.17	1623.38
100000	8955.21	4777.71	3393.53	2707.64	2300.99	2033.90	1846.49	1708.82
105000	9402.97	5016.59	3563.21	2843.02	2416.04	2135.60	1938.82	1794.26
110000	9850.73	5255.48	3732.89	2978.40	2531.09	2237.29	2031.14	1879.70
115000	10298.49	5494.36	3902.56	3113.78	2646.14	2338.99	2123.47	1965.14
120000	10746.25	5733.25	4072.24	3249.16	2761.19	2440.68	2215.79	2050.58
125000	11194.01	5972.13	4241.92	3384.55	2876.24	2542.38	2308.12	2136.02
130000	11641.77	6211.02	4411.59	3519.93	2991.28	2644.07	2400.44	2221.47
135000	12089.53	6449.90	4581.27	3655.31	3106.33	2745.76	2492.77	2306.91
140000	12537.29	6688.79	4750.95	3790.69	3221.38	2847.46	2585.09	2392.35
145000	12985.05	6927.67	4920.62	3926.07	3336.43	2949.15	2677.41	2477.79
150000	13432.81	7166.56	5090.30	4061.45	3451.48	3050.85	2769.74	2563.23
155000	13880.57	7405.44	5259.97	4196.84	3566.53	3152.54	2862.06	2648.67
160000	14328.33	7644.33	5429.65	4332.22	3681.58	3254.24	2954.39	2734.11

142

MONTHLY AMORTIZING PAYMENTS 13.500%

AMOUNT OF LOAN	\multicolumn{8}{c}{NUMBER OF YEARS IN TERM}
	9	10	15	20	25	30	35	40
$ 50	.81	.77	.65	.61	.59	.58	.57	.57
100	1.61	1.53	1.30	1.21	1.17	1.15	1.14	1.14
200	3.21	3.05	2.60	2.42	2.34	2.30	2.28	2.27
300	4.82	4.57	3.90	3.63	3.50	3.44	3.41	3.40
400	6.42	6.10	5.20	4.83	4.67	4.59	4.55	4.53
500	8.03	7.62	6.50	6.04	5.83	5.73	5.68	5.66
600	9.63	9.14	7.79	7.25	7.00	6.88	6.82	6.79
700	11.23	10.66	9.09	8.46	8.16	8.02	7.95	7.92
800	12.84	12.19	10.39	9.66	9.33	9.17	9.09	9.05
900	14.44	13.71	11.69	10.87	10.50	10.31	10.22	10.18
1000	16.05	15.23	12.99	12.08	11.66	11.46	11.36	11.31
2000	32.09	30.46	25.97	24.15	23.32	22.91	22.71	22.61
3000	48.13	45.69	38.95	36.23	34.97	34.37	34.07	33.91
4000	64.17	60.91	51.94	48.30	46.63	45.82	45.42	45.22
5000	80.22	76.14	64.92	60.37	58.29	57.28	56.77	56.52
6000	96.26	91.37	77.90	72.45	69.94	68.73	68.13	67.82
7000	112.30	106.60	90.89	84.52	81.60	80.18	79.48	79.12
8000	128.34	121.82	103.87	96.59	93.26	91.64	90.83	90.43
9000	144.39	137.05	116.85	108.67	104.91	103.09	102.19	101.73
10000	160.43	152.28	129.84	120.74	116.57	114.55	113.54	113.03
11000	176.47	167.51	142.82	132.82	128.23	126.00	124.89	124.33
12000	192.51	182.73	155.80	144.89	139.88	137.45	136.25	135.64
13000	208.56	197.96	168.79	156.96	151.54	148.91	147.60	146.94
14000	224.60	213.19	181.77	169.04	163.20	160.36	158.95	158.24
15000	240.64	228.42	194.75	181.11	174.85	171.82	170.31	169.54
16000	256.68	243.64	207.74	193.18	186.51	183.27	181.66	180.85
17000	272.72	258.87	220.72	205.26	198.16	194.73	193.01	192.15
18000	288.77	274.10	233.70	217.33	209.82	206.18	204.37	203.45
19000	304.81	289.33	246.69	229.41	221.48	217.63	215.72	214.75
20000	320.85	304.55	259.67	241.48	233.13	229.09	227.07	226.06
21000	336.89	319.78	272.65	253.55	244.79	240.54	238.43	237.36
22000	352.94	335.01	285.64	265.63	256.45	252.00	249.78	248.66
23000	368.98	350.24	298.62	277.70	268.10	263.45	261.13	259.97
24000	385.02	365.46	311.60	289.77	279.76	274.90	272.49	271.27
25000	401.06	380.69	324.58	301.85	291.42	286.36	283.84	282.57
26000	417.11	395.92	337.57	313.92	303.07	297.81	295.19	293.87
27000	433.15	411.15	350.55	326.00	314.73	309.27	306.55	305.18
28000	449.19	426.37	363.53	338.07	326.39	320.72	317.90	316.48
29000	465.23	441.60	376.52	350.14	338.04	332.17	329.25	327.78
30000	481.27	456.83	389.50	362.22	349.70	343.63	340.61	339.08
31000	497.32	472.06	402.48	374.29	361.35	355.08	351.96	350.39
32000	513.36	487.28	415.47	386.36	373.01	366.54	363.31	361.69
33000	529.40	502.51	428.45	398.44	384.67	377.99	374.67	372.99
34000	545.44	517.74	441.43	410.51	396.32	389.45	386.02	384.29
35000	561.49	532.97	454.42	422.59	407.98	400.90	397.37	395.60
40000	641.70	609.10	519.33	482.95	466.26	458.17	454.14	452.11
45000	721.91	685.24	584.25	543.32	524.55	515.44	510.91	508.62
50000	802.12	761.38	649.16	603.69	582.83	572.71	567.68	565.14
55000	882.33	837.51	714.08	664.06	641.11	629.98	624.44	621.65
60000	962.54	913.65	779.00	724.43	699.39	687.25	681.21	678.16
65000	1042.76	989.79	843.91	784.80	757.67	744.52	737.98	734.67
70000	1122.97	1065.93	908.83	845.17	815.96	801.79	794.74	791.19
75000	1203.18	1142.06	973.74	905.54	874.24	859.06	851.51	847.70
80000	1283.39	1218.20	1038.66	965.90	932.52	916.33	908.28	904.21
85000	1363.60	1294.34	1103.58	1026.27	990.80	973.61	965.04	960.73
90000	1443.81	1370.47	1168.49	1086.64	1049.09	1030.88	1021.81	1017.24
95000	1524.02	1446.61	1233.41	1147.01	1107.37	1088.15	1078.58	1073.75
100000	1604.24	1522.75	1298.32	1207.38	1165.65	1145.42	1135.35	1130.27
105000	1684.45	1598.89	1363.24	1267.75	1223.93	1202.69	1192.11	1186.78
110000	1764.66	1675.02	1428.16	1328.12	1282.21	1259.96	1248.88	1243.29
115000	1844.87	1751.16	1493.07	1388.49	1340.50	1317.23	1305.65	1299.81
120000	1925.08	1827.30	1557.99	1448.85	1398.78	1374.50	1362.41	1356.32
125000	2005.29	1903.43	1622.90	1509.22	1457.06	1431.77	1419.18	1412.83
130000	2085.51	1979.57	1687.82	1569.59	1515.34	1489.04	1475.95	1469.34
135000	2165.72	2055.71	1752.74	1629.96	1573.63	1546.31	1532.71	1525.86
140000	2245.93	2131.85	1817.65	1690.33	1631.91	1603.58	1589.48	1582.37
145000	2326.14	2207.98	1882.57	1750.70	1690.19	1660.85	1646.25	1638.88
150000	2406.35	2284.12	1947.48	1811.07	1748.47	1718.12	1703.02	1695.40
155000	2486.56	2360.26	2012.40	1871.44	1806.75	1775.39	1759.78	1751.91
160000	2566.78	2436.39	2077.31	1931.80	1865.04	1832.66	1816.55	1808.42

143

13.750%   MONTHLY AMORTIZING PAYMENTS

AMOUNT OF LOAN	NUMBER OF YEARS IN TERM							
	1	2	3	4	5	6	7	8
$ 50	4.49	2.40	1.71	1.37	1.16	1.03	.94	.87
100	8.97	4.79	3.41	2.73	2.32	2.05	1.87	1.73
200	17.94	9.58	6.82	5.45	4.63	4.10	3.73	3.45
300	26.91	14.37	10.22	8.17	6.95	6.15	5.59	5.17
400	35.87	19.16	13.63	10.89	9.26	8.19	7.45	6.90
500	44.84	23.95	17.03	13.61	11.57	10.24	9.31	8.62
600	53.81	28.74	20.44	16.33	13.89	12.29	11.17	10.34
700	62.77	33.53	23.84	19.05	16.20	14.34	13.03	12.07
800	71.74	38.32	27.25	21.77	18.52	16.38	14.89	13.79
900	80.71	43.11	30.66	24.49	20.83	18.43	16.75	15.51
1000	89.67	47.90	34.06	27.21	23.14	20.48	18.61	17.23
2000	179.34	95.79	68.12	54.41	46.28	40.95	37.21	34.46
3000	269.00	143.69	102.17	81.61	69.42	61.42	55.81	51.69
4000	358.68	191.58	136.23	108.81	92.56	81.89	74.41	68.92
5000	448.35	239.48	170.29	136.01	115.70	102.37	93.02	86.15
6000	538.02	287.37	204.34	163.21	138.84	122.84	111.62	103.38
7000	627.69	335.27	238.40	190.41	161.98	143.31	130.22	120.61
8000	717.36	383.16	272.46	217.61	185.12	163.78	148.82	137.84
9000	807.03	431.06	306.51	244.82	208.25	184.25	167.42	155.07
10000	896.70	478.95	340.57	272.02	231.39	204.73	186.03	172.30
11000	986.37	526.85	374.62	299.22	254.53	225.20	204.63	189.53
12000	1076.04	574.74	408.68	326.42	277.67	245.67	223.23	206.76
13000	1165.71	622.64	442.74	353.62	300.81	266.14	241.83	223.99
14000	1255.38	670.53	476.79	380.82	323.95	286.61	260.44	241.22
15000	1345.05	718.43	510.85	408.02	347.09	307.09	279.04	258.45
16000	1434.72	766.32	544.91	435.22	370.23	327.56	297.64	275.68
17000	1524.39	814.22	578.96	462.43	393.37	348.03	316.24	292.91
18000	1614.06	862.11	613.02	489.63	416.50	368.50	334.84	310.14
19000	1703.73	910.01	647.08	516.83	439.64	388.98	353.45	327.37
20000	1793.40	957.90	681.13	544.03	462.78	409.45	372.05	344.60
21000	1883.07	1005.80	715.19	571.23	485.92	429.92	390.65	361.83
22000	1972.73	1053.69	749.24	598.43	509.06	450.39	409.25	379.05
23000	2062.40	1101.59	783.30	625.63	532.20	470.86	427.86	396.28
24000	2152.07	1149.48	817.36	652.83	555.34	491.34	446.46	413.51
25000	2241.74	1197.38	851.41	680.04	578.48	511.81	465.06	430.74
26000	2331.41	1245.27	885.47	707.24	601.61	532.28	483.66	447.97
27000	2421.08	1293.17	919.53	734.44	624.75	552.75	502.26	465.20
28000	2510.75	1341.06	953.58	761.64	647.89	573.22	520.87	482.43
29000	2600.42	1388.96	987.64	788.84	671.03	593.70	539.47	499.66
30000	2690.09	1436.85	1021.69	816.04	694.17	614.17	558.07	516.89
31000	2779.76	1484.75	1055.75	843.24	717.31	634.64	576.67	534.12
32000	2869.43	1532.64	1089.81	870.44	740.45	655.11	595.27	551.35
33000	2959.10	1580.54	1123.86	897.65	763.59	675.58	613.88	568.58
34000	3048.77	1628.43	1157.92	924.85	786.73	696.06	632.48	585.81
35000	3138.44	1676.33	1191.98	952.05	809.86	716.53	651.08	603.04
40000	3586.79	1915.80	1362.26	1088.05	925.56	818.89	744.09	689.19
45000	4035.13	2155.27	1532.54	1224.06	1041.25	921.25	837.10	775.33
50000	4483.48	2394.75	1702.82	1360.07	1156.95	1023.61	930.11	861.48
55000	4931.83	2634.22	1873.10	1496.07	1272.64	1125.97	1023.12	947.63
60000	5380.18	2873.70	2043.38	1632.08	1388.34	1228.33	1116.14	1033.78
65000	5828.52	3113.17	2213.67	1768.09	1504.03	1330.69	1209.15	1119.92
70000	6276.87	3352.65	2383.95	1904.09	1619.72	1433.05	1302.16	1206.07
75000	6725.22	3592.12	2554.23	2040.10	1735.42	1535.41	1395.17	1292.22
80000	7173.57	3831.59	2724.51	2176.10	1851.11	1637.77	1488.18	1378.37
85000	7621.92	4071.07	2894.79	2312.11	1966.81	1740.13	1581.19	1464.51
90000	8070.26	4310.54	3065.07	2448.12	2082.50	1842.50	1674.20	1550.66
95000	8518.61	4550.02	3235.36	2584.12	2198.20	1944.86	1767.21	1636.81
100000	8966.96	4789.49	3405.64	2720.13	2313.89	2047.22	1860.22	1722.96
105000	9415.31	5028.97	3575.92	2856.13	2429.58	2149.58	1953.23	1809.11
110000	9863.65	5268.44	3746.20	2992.14	2545.28	2251.94	2046.24	1895.25
115000	10312.00	5507.91	3916.48	3128.15	2660.97	2354.30	2139.26	1981.40
120000	10760.35	5747.39	4086.76	3264.15	2776.67	2456.66	2232.27	2067.55
125000	11208.70	5986.86	4257.05	3400.16	2892.36	2559.02	2325.28	2153.70
130000	11657.04	6226.34	4427.33	3536.17	3008.05	2661.38	2418.29	2239.84
135000	12105.39	6465.81	4597.61	3672.17	3123.75	2763.74	2511.30	2325.99
140000	12553.74	6705.29	4767.89	3808.18	3239.44	2866.10	2604.31	2412.14
145000	13002.09	6944.76	4938.17	3944.18	3355.14	2968.46	2697.32	2498.29
150000	13450.43	7184.23	5108.45	4080.19	3470.83	3070.82	2790.33	2584.43
155000	13898.78	7423.71	5278.74	4216.20	3586.53	3173.18	2883.34	2670.58
160000	14347.13	7663.18	5449.02	4352.20	3702.22	3275.54	2976.35	2756.73

MONTHLY AMORTIZING PAYMENTS 13.750%

AMOUNT OF LOAN	NUMBER OF YEARS IN TERM							
	9	10	15	20	25	30	35	40
$ 50	.81	.77	.66	.62	.60	.59	.58	.58
100	1.62	1.54	1.32	1.23	1.19	1.17	1.16	1.16
200	3.24	3.08	2.63	2.46	2.37	2.34	2.32	2.31
300	4.86	4.62	3.95	3.68	3.56	3.50	3.47	3.46
400	6.48	6.16	5.26	4.91	4.74	4.67	4.63	4.61
500	8.10	7.69	6.58	6.13	5.93	5.83	5.78	5.76
600	9.72	9.23	7.89	7.36	7.11	7.00	6.94	6.91
700	11.34	10.77	9.21	8.58	8.30	8.16	8.09	8.06
800	12.96	12.31	10.52	9.81	9.48	9.33	9.25	9.21
900	14.57	13.84	11.84	11.03	10.67	10.49	10.40	10.36
1000	16.19	15.38	13.15	12.26	11.85	11.66	11.56	11.51
2000	32.38	30.76	26.30	24.51	23.70	23.31	23.11	23.02
3000	48.57	46.14	39.45	36.77	35.54	34.96	34.67	34.53
4000	64.76	61.51	52.60	49.02	47.39	46.61	46.22	46.03
5000	80.94	76.89	65.75	61.28	59.24	58.26	57.78	57.54
6000	97.13	92.27	78.90	73.53	71.08	69.91	69.33	69.05
7000	113.32	107.64	92.05	85.78	82.93	81.56	80.89	80.55
8000	129.51	123.02	105.20	98.04	94.78	93.21	92.44	92.06
9000	145.69	138.40	118.35	110.29	106.62	104.87	104.00	103.57
10000	161.88	153.77	131.50	122.55	118.47	116.52	115.55	115.07
11000	178.07	169.15	144.65	134.80	130.32	128.17	127.11	126.58
12000	194.26	184.53	157.80	147.05	142.16	139.82	138.66	138.09
13000	210.44	199.90	170.95	159.31	154.01	151.47	150.22	149.59
14000	226.63	215.28	184.10	171.56	165.86	163.12	161.77	161.10
15000	242.82	230.66	197.25	183.82	177.70	174.77	173.33	172.61
16000	259.01	246.03	210.40	196.07	189.55	186.42	184.88	184.11
17000	275.20	261.41	223.55	208.32	201.40	198.07	196.44	195.62
18000	291.38	276.79	236.70	220.58	213.24	209.73	207.99	207.13
19000	307.57	292.16	249.85	232.83	225.09	221.38	219.55	218.64
20000	323.76	307.54	263.00	245.09	236.94	233.03	231.10	230.14
21000	339.95	322.92	276.15	257.34	248.78	244.68	242.66	241.65
22000	356.13	338.29	289.30	269.59	260.63	256.33	254.21	253.16
23000	372.32	353.67	302.45	281.85	272.48	267.98	265.77	264.66
24000	388.51	369.05	315.60	294.10	284.32	279.63	277.32	276.17
25000	404.70	384.42	328.75	306.36	296.17	291.28	288.88	287.68
26000	420.88	399.80	341.90	318.61	308.02	302.93	300.43	299.18
27000	437.07	415.18	355.05	330.86	319.86	314.59	311.99	310.69
28000	453.26	430.55	368.20	343.12	331.71	326.24	323.54	322.20
29000	469.45	445.93	381.35	355.37	343.56	337.89	335.10	333.70
30000	485.64	461.31	394.50	367.63	355.40	349.54	346.65	345.21
31000	501.82	476.68	407.65	379.88	367.25	361.19	358.21	356.72
32000	518.01	492.06	420.80	392.13	379.10	372.84	369.76	368.22
33000	534.20	507.44	433.95	404.39	390.94	384.49	381.32	379.73
34000	550.39	522.81	447.10	416.64	402.79	396.14	392.87	391.24
35000	566.57	538.19	460.25	428.90	414.64	407.79	404.42	402.74
40000	647.51	615.07	526.00	490.17	473.87	466.05	462.20	460.28
45000	728.45	691.96	591.75	551.44	533.10	524.31	519.97	517.81
50000	809.39	768.84	657.50	612.71	592.34	582.56	577.75	575.35
55000	890.33	845.72	723.25	673.98	651.57	640.82	635.52	632.88
60000	971.27	922.61	789.00	735.25	710.80	699.07	693.30	690.42
65000	1052.20	999.49	854.75	796.52	770.04	757.33	751.07	747.95
70000	1133.14	1076.37	920.50	857.79	829.27	815.58	808.84	805.48
75000	1214.08	1153.26	986.25	919.06	888.50	873.84	866.62	863.02
80000	1295.02	1230.14	1051.99	980.33	947.74	932.10	924.39	920.55
85000	1375.96	1307.02	1117.74	1041.60	1006.97	990.35	982.17	978.09
90000	1456.90	1383.91	1183.49	1102.87	1066.20	1048.61	1039.94	1035.62
95000	1537.83	1460.79	1249.24	1164.14	1125.44	1106.86	1097.72	1093.16
100000	1618.77	1537.67	1314.99	1225.41	1184.67	1165.12	1155.49	1150.69
105000	1699.71	1614.56	1380.74	1286.68	1243.90	1223.37	1213.26	1208.22
110000	1780.65	1691.44	1446.48	1347.95	1303.14	1281.63	1271.04	1265.76
115000	1861.59	1768.32	1512.24	1409.22	1362.37	1339.88	1328.81	1323.29
120000	1942.53	1845.21	1577.99	1470.49	1421.60	1398.14	1386.59	1380.83
125000	2023.46	1922.09	1643.74	1531.76	1480.84	1456.40	1444.36	1438.36
130000	2104.40	1998.97	1709.49	1593.03	1540.07	1514.65	1502.14	1495.90
135000	2185.34	2075.86	1775.24	1654.30	1599.30	1572.91	1559.91	1553.43
140000	2266.28	2152.74	1840.99	1715.57	1658.54	1631.16	1617.68	1610.96
145000	2347.22	2229.62	1906.74	1776.84	1717.77	1689.42	1675.46	1668.50
150000	2428.16	2306.51	1972.49	1838.11	1777.00	1747.67	1733.23	1726.03
155000	2509.09	2383.39	2038.24	1899.38	1836.24	1805.93	1791.01	1783.57
160000	2590.03	2460.27	2103.98	1960.65	1895.47	1864.19	1848.78	1841.10

145

14.000%   MONTHLY AMORTIZING PAYMENTS

AMOUNT OF LOAN	NUMBER OF YEARS IN TERM							
	1	2	3	4	5	6	7	8
$ 50	4.49	2.41	1.71	1.37	1.17	1.04	.94	.87
100	8.98	4.81	3.42	2.74	2.33	2.07	1.88	1.74
200	17.95	9.61	6.84	5.47	4.66	4.13	3.75	3.48
300	26.94	14.41	10.26	8.20	6.99	6.19	5.63	5.22
400	35.92	19.21	13.68	10.94	9.31	8.25	7.50	6.95
500	44.90	24.01	17.09	13.67	11.64	10.31	9.38	8.69
600	53.88	28.81	20.51	16.40	13.97	12.37	11.25	10.43
700	62.86	33.61	23.93	19.13	16.29	14.43	13.12	12.17
800	71.83	38.42	27.35	21.87	18.62	16.49	15.00	13.90
900	80.81	43.22	30.76	24.60	20.95	18.55	16.87	15.64
1000	89.79	48.02	34.18	27.33	23.27	20.61	18.75	17.38
2000	179.58	96.03	68.36	54.66	46.54	41.22	37.49	34.75
3000	269.37	144.04	102.54	81.98	69.81	61.82	56.23	52.12
4000	359.15	192.06	136.72	109.31	93.08	82.43	74.97	69.49
5000	448.94	240.07	170.89	136.64	116.35	103.03	93.71	86.86
6000	538.73	288.08	205.07	163.96	139.61	123.64	112.45	104.23
7000	628.51	336.10	239.25	191.29	162.88	144.25	131.19	121.61
8000	718.30	384.11	273.43	218.62	186.15	164.85	149.93	138.98
9000	808.09	432.12	307.60	245.94	209.42	185.46	168.67	156.35
10000	897.88	480.13	341.78	273.27	232.69	206.06	187.41	173.72
11000	987.66	528.15	375.96	300.60	255.96	226.67	206.15	191.09
12000	1077.45	576.16	410.14	327.92	279.22	247.27	224.89	208.46
13000	1167.24	624.17	444.31	355.25	302.49	267.88	243.63	225.83
14000	1257.02	672.19	478.49	382.58	325.76	288.49	262.37	243.21
15000	1346.81	720.20	512.67	409.90	349.03	309.09	281.11	260.58
16000	1436.60	768.21	546.85	437.23	372.30	329.70	299.85	277.95
17000	1526.39	816.22	581.02	464.56	395.57	350.30	318.59	295.32
18000	1616.17	864.24	615.20	491.88	418.83	370.91	337.33	312.69
19000	1705.96	912.25	649.38	519.21	442.10	391.51	356.07	330.06
20000	1795.75	960.26	683.56	546.53	465.37	412.12	374.81	347.44
21000	1885.53	1008.28	717.74	573.86	488.64	432.73	393.55	364.81
22000	1975.32	1056.29	751.91	601.19	511.91	453.33	412.29	382.18
23000	2065.11	1104.30	786.09	628.51	535.17	473.94	431.03	399.55
24000	2154.90	1152.31	820.27	655.84	558.44	494.54	449.77	416.92
25000	2244.68	1200.33	854.45	683.17	581.71	515.15	468.51	434.29
26000	2334.47	1248.34	888.62	710.49	604.98	535.75	487.25	451.66
27000	2424.26	1296.35	922.80	737.82	628.25	556.36	505.99	469.04
28000	2514.04	1344.37	956.98	765.15	651.52	576.97	524.73	486.41
29000	2603.83	1392.38	991.16	792.47	674.78	597.57	543.47	503.78
30000	2693.62	1440.39	1025.33	819.80	698.05	618.18	562.21	521.15
31000	2783.41	1488.40	1059.51	847.13	721.32	638.78	580.95	538.52
32000	2873.19	1536.42	1093.69	874.45	744.59	659.39	599.69	555.89
33000	2962.98	1584.43	1127.87	901.78	767.86	679.99	618.43	573.26
34000	3052.77	1632.44	1162.04	929.11	791.13	700.60	637.17	590.64
35000	3142.55	1680.46	1196.22	956.43	814.39	721.21	655.91	608.01
40000	3591.49	1920.52	1367.11	1093.06	930.74	824.23	749.61	694.87
45000	4040.43	2160.58	1538.00	1229.70	1047.08	927.26	843.31	781.72
50000	4489.36	2400.65	1708.89	1366.33	1163.42	1030.29	937.01	868.58
55000	4938.30	2640.71	1879.77	1502.96	1279.76	1133.32	1030.71	955.44
60000	5387.23	2880.78	2050.66	1639.59	1396.10	1236.35	1124.41	1042.30
65000	5836.17	3120.84	2221.55	1776.23	1512.44	1339.38	1218.11	1129.15
70000	6285.10	3360.91	2392.44	1912.86	1628.78	1442.41	1311.81	1216.01
75000	6734.04	3600.97	2563.33	2049.49	1745.12	1545.44	1405.51	1302.87
80000	7182.97	3841.04	2734.22	2186.12	1861.47	1648.46	1499.21	1389.73
85000	7631.91	4081.10	2905.10	2322.76	1977.81	1751.49	1592.91	1476.58
90000	8080.85	4321.16	3075.99	2459.39	2094.15	1854.52	1686.61	1563.44
95000	8529.78	4561.23	3246.88	2596.02	2210.49	1957.55	1780.31	1650.30
100000	8978.72	4801.29	3417.77	2732.65	2326.83	2060.58	1874.01	1737.16
105000	9427.65	5041.36	3588.66	2869.29	2443.17	2163.61	1967.71	1824.01
110000	9876.59	5281.42	3759.54	3005.92	2559.51	2266.64	2061.41	1910.87
115000	10325.52	5521.49	3930.43	3142.55	2675.85	2369.67	2155.11	1997.73
120000	10774.46	5761.55	4101.32	3279.18	2792.20	2472.69	2248.81	2084.59
125000	11223.39	6001.62	4272.21	3415.81	2908.54	2575.72	2342.51	2171.44
130000	11672.33	6241.68	4443.10	3552.45	3024.88	2678.75	2436.21	2258.30
135000	12121.27	6481.74	4613.99	3689.08	3141.22	2781.78	2529.91	2345.16
140000	12570.20	6721.81	4784.87	3825.71	3257.56	2884.81	2623.61	2432.02
145000	13019.14	6961.87	4955.76	3962.34	3373.90	2987.84	2717.31	2518.87
150000	13468.07	7201.94	5126.65	4098.98	3490.24	3090.87	2811.01	2605.73
155000	13917.01	7442.00	5297.54	4235.61	3606.58	3193.89	2904.71	2692.59
160000	14365.94	7682.07	5468.43	4372.24	3722.93	3296.92	2998.41	2779.45

146

AMOUNT OF LOAN	NUMBER OF YEARS IN TERM							
	9	10	15	20	25	30	35	40
$ 50	.82	.78	.67	.63	.61	.60	.59	.59
100	1.64	1.56	1.34	1.25	1.21	1.19	1.18	1.18
200	3.27	3.11	2.67	2.49	2.41	2.37	2.36	2.35
300	4.91	4.66	4.00	3.74	3.62	3.56	3.53	3.52
400	6.54	6.22	5.33	4.98	4.82	4.74	4.71	4.69
500	8.17	7.77	6.66	6.22	6.02	5.93	5.88	5.86
600	9.81	9.32	8.00	7.47	7.23	7.11	7.06	7.03
700	11.44	10.87	9.33	8.71	8.43	8.30	8.23	8.20
800	13.07	12.43	10.66	9.95	9.64	9.48	9.41	9.37
900	14.71	13.98	11.99	11.20	10.84	10.67	10.59	10.55
1000	16.34	15.53	13.32	12.44	12.04	11.85	11.76	11.72
2000	32.67	31.06	26.64	24.88	24.08	23.70	23.52	23.43
3000	49.01	46.58	39.96	37.31	36.12	35.55	35.28	35.14
4000	65.34	62.11	53.27	49.75	48.16	47.40	47.03	46.85
5000	81.67	77.64	66.59	62.18	60.19	59.25	58.79	58.56
6000	98.01	93.16	79.91	74.62	72.23	71.10	70.55	70.27
7000	114.34	108.69	93.23	87.05	84.27	82.95	82.30	81.98
8000	130.67	124.22	106.54	99.49	96.31	94.79	94.06	93.70
9000	147.01	139.74	119.86	111.92	108.34	106.64	105.82	105.41
10000	163.34	155.27	133.18	124.36	120.38	118.49	117.57	117.12
11000	179.68	170.80	146.50	136.79	132.42	130.34	129.33	128.83
12000	196.01	186.32	159.81	149.23	144.46	142.19	141.09	140.54
13000	212.34	201.85	173.13	161.66	156.49	154.04	152.84	152.25
14000	228.68	217.38	186.45	174.10	168.53	165.89	164.60	163.96
15000	245.01	232.90	199.77	186.53	180.57	177.74	176.36	175.68
16000	261.34	248.43	213.08	198.97	192.61	189.58	188.11	187.39
17000	277.68	263.96	226.40	211.40	204.64	201.43	199.87	199.10
18000	294.01	279.48	239.72	223.84	216.68	213.28	211.63	210.81
19000	310.35	295.01	253.04	236.27	228.72	225.13	223.38	222.52
20000	326.68	310.54	266.35	248.71	240.76	236.98	235.14	234.23
21000	343.01	326.06	279.67	261.14	252.79	248.83	246.90	245.94
22000	359.35	341.59	292.99	273.58	264.83	260.68	258.65	257.66
23000	375.68	357.12	306.31	286.01	276.87	272.53	270.41	269.37
24000	392.01	372.64	319.62	298.45	288.91	284.37	282.17	281.08
25000	408.35	388.17	332.94	310.89	300.95	296.22	293.92	292.79
26000	424.68	403.70	346.26	323.32	312.98	308.07	305.68	304.50
27000	441.01	419.22	359.58	335.76	325.02	319.92	317.44	316.21
28000	457.35	434.75	372.89	348.19	337.06	331.77	329.19	327.92
29000	473.68	450.28	386.21	360.63	349.10	343.62	340.95	339.64
30000	490.02	465.80	399.53	373.06	361.13	355.47	352.71	351.35
31000	506.35	481.33	412.84	385.50	373.17	367.32	364.46	363.06
32000	522.68	496.86	426.16	397.93	385.21	379.16	376.22	374.77
33000	539.02	512.38	439.48	410.37	397.25	391.01	387.98	386.48
34000	555.35	527.91	452.80	422.80	409.28	402.86	399.73	398.19
35000	571.68	543.44	466.11	435.24	421.32	414.71	411.49	409.90
40000	653.35	621.07	532.70	497.41	481.51	473.95	470.27	468.46
45000	735.02	698.70	599.29	559.59	541.70	533.20	529.06	527.02
50000	816.69	776.34	665.88	621.77	601.89	592.44	587.84	585.58
55000	898.36	853.97	732.46	683.94	662.07	651.68	646.63	644.13
60000	980.03	931.60	799.05	746.12	722.26	710.93	705.41	702.69
65000	1061.70	1009.24	865.64	808.29	782.45	770.17	764.19	761.25
70000	1143.36	1086.87	932.22	870.47	842.64	829.42	822.98	819.80
75000	1225.03	1164.50	998.81	932.65	902.83	888.66	881.76	878.36
80000	1306.70	1242.14	1065.40	994.82	963.01	947.90	940.54	936.92
85000	1388.37	1319.77	1131.99	1057.00	1023.20	1007.15	999.33	995.47
90000	1470.04	1397.40	1198.57	1119.17	1083.39	1066.39	1058.11	1054.03
95000	1551.71	1475.04	1265.16	1181.35	1143.58	1125.63	1116.89	1112.59
100000	1633.38	1552.67	1331.75	1243.53	1203.77	1184.88	1175.68	1171.15
105000	1715.04	1630.30	1398.33	1305.70	1263.95	1244.12	1234.46	1229.70
110000	1796.71	1707.94	1464.92	1367.88	1324.14	1303.36	1293.25	1288.26
115000	1878.38	1785.57	1531.51	1430.05	1384.33	1362.61	1352.03	1346.82
120000	1960.05	1863.20	1598.09	1492.23	1444.52	1421.85	1410.81	1405.37
125000	2041.72	1940.84	1664.68	1554.41	1504.71	1481.09	1469.60	1463.93
130000	2123.39	2018.47	1731.27	1616.58	1564.89	1540.34	1528.38	1522.49
135000	2205.05	2096.10	1797.86	1678.76	1625.08	1599.58	1587.16	1581.04
140000	2286.72	2173.74	1864.44	1740.93	1685.27	1658.83	1645.95	1639.60
145000	2368.39	2251.37	1931.03	1803.11	1745.46	1718.07	1704.73	1698.16
150000	2450.06	2329.00	1997.62	1865.29	1805.65	1777.31	1763.51	1756.72
155000	2531.73	2406.63	2064.20	1927.46	1865.83	1836.56	1822.30	1815.27
160000	2613.40	2484.27	2130.79	1989.64	1926.02	1895.80	1881.08	1873.83

14.250%   MONTHLY AMORTIZING PAYMENTS

AMOUNT OF LOAN	NUMBER OF YEARS IN TERM							
	1	2	3	4	5	6	7	8
$ 50	4.50	2.41	1.72	1.38	1.17	1.04	.95	.88
100	9.00	4.82	3.43	2.75	2.34	2.08	1.89	1.76
200	17.99	9.63	6.86	5.50	4.68	4.15	3.78	3.51
300	26.98	14.44	10.29	8.24	7.02	6.23	5.67	5.26
400	35.97	19.26	13.72	10.99	9.36	8.30	7.56	7.01
500	44.96	24.07	17.15	13.73	11.70	10.37	9.44	8.76
600	53.95	28.88	20.58	16.48	14.04	12.45	11.33	10.51
700	62.94	33.70	24.01	19.22	16.38	14.52	13.22	12.26
800	71.93	38.51	27.44	21.97	18.72	16.60	15.11	14.02
900	80.92	43.32	30.87	24.71	21.06	18.67	17.00	15.77
1000	89.91	48.14	34.30	27.46	23.40	20.74	18.88	17.52
2000	179.81	96.27	68.60	54.91	46.80	41.48	37.76	35.03
3000	269.72	144.40	102.90	82.36	70.20	62.22	56.64	52.55
4000	359.62	192.53	137.20	109.81	93.60	82.96	75.52	70.06
5000	449.53	240.66	171.50	137.27	117.00	103.70	94.40	87.58
6000	539.43	288.79	205.80	164.72	140.39	124.44	113.28	105.09
7000	629.34	336.92	240.10	192.17	163.79	145.18	132.15	122.60
8000	719.24	385.05	274.40	219.62	187.19	165.92	151.03	140.12
9000	809.15	433.18	308.70	247.07	210.59	186.66	169.91	157.63
10000	899.05	481.32	343.00	274.53	233.99	207.40	188.79	175.15
11000	988.96	529.45	377.30	301.98	257.38	228.14	207.67	192.66
12000	1078.86	577.58	411.60	329.43	280.78	248.88	226.55	210.17
13000	1168.77	625.71	445.89	356.88	304.18	269.62	245.42	227.69
14000	1258.67	673.84	480.19	384.33	327.58	290.36	264.30	245.20
15000	1348.58	721.97	514.49	411.79	350.98	311.10	283.18	262.72
16000	1438.48	770.10	548.79	439.24	374.37	331.84	302.06	280.23
17000	1528.39	818.23	583.09	466.69	397.77	352.58	320.94	297.74
18000	1618.29	866.36	617.39	494.14	421.17	373.32	339.82	315.26
19000	1708.20	914.50	651.69	521.59	444.57	394.06	358.69	332.77
20000	1798.10	962.63	685.99	549.05	467.97	414.80	377.57	350.29
21000	1888.01	1010.76	720.29	576.50	491.36	435.54	396.45	367.80
22000	1977.91	1058.89	754.59	603.95	514.76	456.28	415.33	385.31
23000	2067.82	1107.02	788.89	631.40	538.16	477.02	434.21	402.83
24000	2157.72	1155.15	823.19	658.85	561.56	497.76	453.09	420.34
25000	2247.62	1203.28	857.48	686.31	584.96	518.50	471.96	437.86
26000	2337.53	1251.41	891.78	713.76	608.35	539.24	490.84	455.37
27000	2427.43	1299.54	926.08	741.21	631.75	559.98	509.72	472.89
28000	2517.34	1347.67	960.38	768.66	655.15	580.72	528.60	490.40
29000	2607.24	1395.81	994.68	796.11	678.55	601.46	547.48	507.91
30000	2697.15	1443.94	1028.98	823.57	701.95	622.20	566.36	525.43
31000	2787.05	1492.07	1063.28	851.02	725.34	642.94	585.24	542.94
32000	2876.96	1540.20	1097.58	878.47	748.74	663.68	604.11	560.46
33000	2966.86	1588.33	1131.88	905.92	772.14	684.42	622.99	577.97
34000	3056.77	1636.46	1166.18	933.37	795.54	705.16	641.87	595.48
35000	3146.67	1684.59	1200.48	960.83	818.94	725.90	660.75	613.00
40000	3596.20	1925.25	1371.97	1098.09	935.93	829.60	755.14	700.57
45000	4045.72	2165.90	1543.47	1235.35	1052.92	933.30	849.53	788.14
50000	4495.24	2406.56	1714.96	1372.61	1169.91	1037.00	943.92	875.71
55000	4944.77	2647.21	1886.46	1509.87	1286.90	1140.70	1038.32	963.28
60000	5394.29	2887.87	2057.96	1647.13	1403.89	1244.40	1132.71	1050.85
65000	5843.82	3128.52	2229.45	1784.39	1520.88	1348.09	1227.10	1138.42
70000	6293.34	3369.18	2400.95	1921.65	1637.87	1451.79	1321.49	1225.99
75000	6742.86	3609.84	2572.44	2058.91	1754.86	1555.49	1415.88	1313.56
80000	7192.39	3850.49	2743.94	2196.17	1871.85	1659.19	1510.28	1401.13
85000	7641.91	4091.15	2915.44	2333.43	1988.84	1762.89	1604.67	1488.70
90000	8091.44	4331.80	3086.93	2470.69	2105.83	1866.59	1699.06	1576.27
95000	8540.96	4572.46	3258.43	2607.95	2222.82	1970.29	1793.45	1663.84
100000	8990.48	4813.11	3429.92	2745.21	2339.81	2073.99	1887.84	1751.41
105000	9440.01	5053.77	3601.42	2882.47	2456.80	2177.69	1982.24	1838.98
110000	9889.53	5294.42	3772.91	3019.73	2573.79	2281.39	2076.63	1926.55
115000	10339.06	5535.08	3944.41	3156.99	2690.78	2385.09	2171.02	2014.12
120000	10788.58	5775.73	4115.91	3294.25	2807.77	2488.79	2265.41	2101.69
125000	11238.10	6016.39	4287.40	3431.51	2924.76	2592.49	2359.80	2189.26
130000	11687.63	6257.04	4458.90	3568.77	3041.75	2696.18	2454.20	2276.84
135000	12137.15	6497.70	4630.39	3706.03	3158.74	2799.88	2548.59	2364.41
140000	12586.68	6738.35	4801.89	3843.29	3275.73	2903.58	2642.98	2451.98
145000	13036.20	6979.01	4973.39	3980.55	3392.72	3007.28	2737.37	2539.55
150000	13485.72	7219.67	5144.88	4117.81	3509.71	3110.98	2831.76	2627.12
155000	13935.25	7460.32	5316.38	4255.07	3626.70	3214.68	2926.16	2714.69
160000	14384.77	7700.98	5487.87	4392.33	3743.70	3318.38	3020.55	2802.26

148

AMOUNT OF LOAN	NUMBER OF YEARS IN TERM							
	9	10	15	20	25	30	35	40
$ 50	.83	.79	.68	.64	.62	.61	.60	.60
100	1.65	1.57	1.35	1.27	1.23	1.21	1.20	1.20
200	3.30	3.14	2.70	2.53	2.45	2.41	2.40	2.39
300	4.95	4.71	4.05	3.79	3.67	3.62	3.59	3.58
400	6.60	6.28	5.40	5.05	4.90	4.82	4.79	4.77
500	8.25	7.84	6.75	6.31	6.12	6.03	5.98	5.96
600	9.89	9.41	8.10	7.58	7.34	7.23	7.18	7.15
700	11.54	10.98	9.45	8.84	8.57	8.44	8.38	8.35
800	13.19	12.55	10.79	10.10	9.79	9.64	9.57	9.54
900	14.84	14.11	12.14	11.36	11.01	10.85	10.77	10.73
1000	16.49	15.68	13.49	12.62	12.23	12.05	11.96	11.92
2000	32.97	31.36	26.98	25.24	24.46	24.10	23.92	23.84
3000	49.45	47.04	40.46	37.86	36.69	36.15	35.88	35.75
4000	65.93	62.71	53.95	50.47	48.92	48.19	47.84	47.67
5000	82.41	78.39	67.43	63.09	61.15	60.24	59.80	59.59
6000	98.89	94.07	80.92	75.71	73.38	72.29	71.76	71.50
7000	115.37	109.75	94.41	88.33	85.61	84.33	83.72	83.42
8000	131.85	125.42	107.89	100.94	97.84	96.38	95.68	95.33
9000	148.33	141.10	121.38	113.56	110.07	108.43	107.64	107.25
10000	164.81	156.78	134.86	126.18	122.30	120.47	119.60	119.17
11000	181.29	172.46	148.35	138.79	134.53	132.52	131.55	131.08
12000	197.77	188.13	161.83	151.41	146.76	144.57	143.51	143.00
13000	214.25	203.81	175.32	164.03	158.99	156.61	155.47	154.92
14000	230.73	219.49	188.81	176.65	171.21	168.66	167.43	166.83
15000	247.21	235.16	202.29	189.26	183.44	180.71	179.39	178.75
16000	263.69	250.84	215.78	201.88	195.67	192.75	191.35	190.66
17000	280.17	266.52	229.26	214.50	207.90	204.80	203.31	202.58
18000	296.65	282.20	242.75	227.11	220.13	216.85	215.27	214.50
19000	313.13	297.87	256.24	239.73	232.36	228.90	227.23	226.41
20000	329.61	313.55	269.72	252.35	244.59	240.94	239.19	238.33
21000	346.09	329.23	283.21	264.97	256.82	252.99	251.14	250.25
22000	362.57	344.91	296.69	277.58	269.05	265.04	263.10	262.16
23000	379.05	360.58	310.18	290.20	281.28	277.08	275.06	274.08
24000	395.53	376.26	323.66	302.82	293.51	289.13	287.02	285.99
25000	412.01	391.94	337.15	315.43	305.74	301.18	298.98	297.91
26000	428.49	407.62	350.64	328.05	317.97	313.22	310.94	309.83
27000	444.98	423.29	364.12	340.67	330.20	325.27	322.90	321.74
28000	461.46	438.97	377.61	353.29	342.42	337.32	334.86	333.66
29000	477.94	454.65	391.09	365.90	354.65	349.36	346.82	345.58
30000	494.42	470.32	404.58	378.52	366.88	361.41	358.78	357.49
31000	510.90	486.00	418.06	391.14	379.11	373.46	370.73	369.41
32000	527.38	501.68	431.55	403.76	391.34	385.50	382.69	381.32
33000	543.86	517.36	445.04	416.37	403.57	397.55	394.65	393.24
34000	560.34	533.03	458.52	428.99	415.80	409.60	406.61	405.16
35000	576.82	548.71	472.01	441.61	428.03	421.65	418.57	417.07
40000	659.22	627.10	539.44	504.69	489.18	481.88	478.37	476.65
45000	741.62	705.48	606.87	567.78	550.32	542.11	538.16	536.24
50000	824.02	783.87	674.29	630.86	611.47	602.35	597.96	595.82
55000	906.43	862.26	741.72	693.95	672.62	662.58	657.75	655.40
60000	988.83	940.64	809.15	757.04	733.76	722.82	717.55	714.98
65000	1071.23	1019.03	876.58	820.12	794.91	783.05	777.34	774.56
70000	1153.63	1097.42	944.01	883.21	856.05	843.29	837.14	834.14
75000	1236.03	1175.80	1011.44	946.29	917.20	903.52	896.93	893.72
80000	1318.44	1254.19	1078.87	1009.38	978.35	963.75	956.73	953.30
85000	1400.84	1332.58	1146.30	1072.47	1039.49	1023.99	1016.52	1012.88
90000	1483.24	1410.96	1213.73	1135.55	1100.64	1084.22	1076.32	1072.47
95000	1565.64	1489.35	1281.16	1198.64	1161.79	1144.46	1136.11	1132.05
100000	1648.04	1567.74	1348.58	1261.72	1222.93	1204.69	1195.91	1191.63
105000	1730.45	1646.12	1416.01	1324.81	1284.08	1264.93	1255.70	1251.21
110000	1812.85	1724.51	1483.44	1387.90	1345.23	1325.16	1315.50	1310.79
115000	1895.25	1802.90	1550.87	1450.98	1406.37	1385.40	1375.29	1370.37
120000	1977.65	1881.28	1618.30	1514.07	1467.52	1445.63	1435.09	1429.95
125000	2060.05	1959.67	1685.73	1577.15	1528.66	1505.86	1494.88	1489.53
130000	2142.45	2038.06	1753.16	1640.24	1589.81	1566.10	1554.68	1549.12
135000	2224.86	2116.44	1820.59	1703.33	1650.96	1626.33	1614.47	1608.70
140000	2307.26	2194.83	1888.02	1766.41	1712.10	1686.57	1674.27	1668.28
145000	2389.66	2273.22	1955.45	1829.50	1773.25	1746.80	1734.06	1727.86
150000	2472.06	2351.60	2022.87	1892.58	1834.40	1807.04	1793.86	1787.44
155000	2554.46	2429.99	2090.30	1955.67	1895.54	1867.27	1853.65	1847.02
160000	2636.87	2508.37	2157.73	2018.76	1956.69	1927.50	1913.45	1906.60

AMOUNT OF LOAN	NUMBER OF YEARS IN TERM							
	1	2	3	4	5	6	7	8
$ 50	4.51	2.42	1.73	1.38	1.18	1.05	.96	.89
100	9.01	4.83	3.45	2.76	2.36	2.09	1.91	1.77
200	18.01	9.65	6.89	5.52	4.71	4.18	3.81	3.54
300	27.01	14.48	10.33	8.28	7.06	6.27	5.71	5.30
400	36.01	19.30	13.77	11.04	9.42	8.35	7.61	7.07
500	45.02	24.13	17.22	13.79	11.77	10.44	9.51	8.83
600	54.02	28.95	20.66	16.55	14.12	12.53	11.42	10.60
700	63.02	33.78	24.10	19.31	16.47	14.62	13.32	12.37
800	72.02	38.60	27.54	22.07	18.83	16.70	15.22	14.13
900	81.03	43.43	30.98	24.83	21.18	18.79	17.12	15.90
1000	90.03	48.25	34.43	27.58	23.53	20.88	19.02	17.66
2000	180.05	96.50	68.85	55.16	47.06	41.75	38.04	35.32
3000	270.07	144.75	103.27	82.74	70.59	62.63	57.06	52.98
4000	360.10	193.00	137.69	110.32	94.12	83.50	76.07	70.63
5000	450.12	241.25	172.11	137.89	117.65	104.38	95.09	88.29
6000	540.14	289.50	206.53	165.47	141.17	125.25	114.11	105.95
7000	630.16	337.75	240.95	193.05	164.70	146.13	133.13	123.61
8000	720.19	386.00	275.37	220.63	188.23	167.00	152.14	141.26
9000	810.21	434.25	309.79	248.21	211.76	187.87	171.16	158.92
10000	900.23	482.50	344.21	275.78	235.29	208.75	190.18	176.58
11000	990.25	530.75	378.64	303.36	258.82	229.62	209.20	194.23
12000	1080.28	579.00	413.06	330.94	282.34	250.50	228.21	211.89
13000	1170.30	627.25	447.48	358.52	305.87	271.37	247.23	229.55
14000	1260.32	675.50	481.90	386.10	329.40	292.25	266.25	247.21
15000	1350.34	723.75	516.32	413.67	352.93	313.12	285.26	264.86
16000	1440.37	772.00	550.74	441.25	376.46	334.00	304.28	282.52
17000	1530.39	820.25	585.16	468.83	399.99	354.87	323.30	300.18
18000	1620.41	868.49	619.58	496.41	423.51	375.74	342.32	317.84
19000	1710.43	916.74	654.00	523.99	447.04	396.62	361.33	335.49
20000	1800.46	964.99	688.42	551.56	470.57	417.49	380.35	353.15
21000	1890.48	1013.24	722.85	579.14	494.10	438.37	399.37	370.81
22000	1980.50	1061.49	757.27	606.72	517.63	459.24	418.39	388.46
23000	2070.52	1109.74	791.69	634.30	541.16	480.12	437.40	406.12
24000	2160.55	1157.99	826.11	661.88	564.68	500.99	456.42	423.78
25000	2250.57	1206.24	860.53	689.45	588.21	521.87	475.44	441.44
26000	2340.59	1254.49	894.95	717.03	611.74	542.74	494.45	459.09
27000	2430.61	1302.74	929.37	744.61	635.27	563.61	513.47	476.75
28000	2520.64	1350.99	963.79	772.19	658.80	584.49	532.49	494.41
29000	2610.66	1399.24	998.21	799.77	682.33	605.36	551.51	512.07
30000	2700.68	1447.49	1032.63	827.34	705.85	626.24	570.52	529.72
31000	2790.70	1495.74	1067.06	854.92	729.38	647.11	589.54	547.38
32000	2880.73	1543.99	1101.48	882.50	752.91	667.99	608.56	565.04
33000	2970.75	1592.24	1135.90	910.08	776.44	688.86	627.58	582.69
34000	3060.77	1640.49	1170.32	937.66	799.97	709.74	646.59	600.35
35000	3150.79	1688.73	1204.74	965.23	823.49	730.61	665.61	618.01
40000	3600.91	1929.98	1376.84	1103.12	941.14	834.98	760.70	706.30
45000	4051.02	2171.23	1548.95	1241.01	1058.78	939.35	855.78	794.58
50000	4501.13	2412.48	1721.05	1378.90	1176.42	1043.73	950.87	882.87
55000	4951.25	2653.72	1893.16	1516.79	1294.06	1148.10	1045.96	971.15
60000	5401.36	2894.97	2065.26	1654.68	1411.70	1252.47	1141.04	1059.44
65000	5851.47	3136.22	2237.37	1792.57	1529.34	1356.84	1236.13	1147.73
70000	6301.58	3377.46	2409.47	1930.46	1646.98	1461.21	1331.22	1236.01
75000	6751.70	3618.71	2581.58	2068.35	1764.63	1565.59	1426.30	1324.30
80000	7201.81	3859.96	2753.68	2206.24	1882.27	1669.96	1521.39	1412.59
85000	7651.92	4101.21	2925.79	2344.13	1999.91	1774.33	1616.48	1500.87
90000	8102.03	4342.45	3097.89	2482.02	2117.55	1878.70	1711.56	1589.16
95000	8552.15	4583.70	3270.00	2619.91	2235.19	1983.08	1806.65	1677.44
100000	9002.26	4824.95	3442.10	2757.80	2352.83	2087.45	1901.74	1765.73
105000	9452.37	5066.19	3614.21	2895.69	2470.47	2191.82	1996.82	1854.02
110000	9902.49	5307.44	3786.31	3033.58	2588.12	2296.19	2091.91	1942.30
115000	10352.60	5548.69	3958.42	3171.47	2705.76	2400.56	2186.99	2030.59
120000	10802.71	5789.94	4130.52	3309.36	2823.40	2504.94	2282.08	2118.88
125000	11252.82	6031.18	4302.63	3447.25	2941.04	2609.31	2377.17	2207.16
130000	11702.94	6272.43	4474.73	3585.14	3058.68	2713.68	2472.25	2295.45
135000	12153.05	6513.68	4646.84	3723.03	3176.32	2818.05	2567.34	2383.73
140000	12603.16	6754.92	4818.94	3860.92	3293.96	2922.42	2662.43	2472.02
145000	13053.27	6996.17	4991.05	3998.81	3411.61	3026.80	2757.51	2560.31
150000	13503.39	7237.42	5163.15	4136.70	3529.25	3131.17	2852.60	2648.59
155000	13953.50	7478.67	5335.26	4274.59	3646.89	3235.54	2947.69	2736.88
160000	14403.61	7719.91	5507.36	4412.48	3764.53	3339.91	3042.77	2825.17

AMOUNT OF LOAN	NUMBER OF YEARS IN TERM							
	9	10	15	20	25	30	35	40
$ 50	.84	.80	.69	.64	.63	.62	.61	.61
100	1.67	1.59	1.37	1.28	1.25	1.23	1.22	1.22
200	3.33	3.17	2.74	2.56	2.49	2.45	2.44	2.43
300	4.99	4.75	4.10	3.84	3.73	3.68	3.65	3 64
400	6.66	6.34	5.47	5.12	4.97	4.90	4.87	4.85
500	8.32	7.92	6.83	6.40	6.22	6.13	6.09	6.07
600	9.98	9.50	8.20	7.68	7.46	7.35	7.30	7.28
700	11.64	11.09	9.56	8.96	8.70	8.58	8.52	8.49
800	13.31	12.67	10.93	10.24	9.94	9.80	9.73	9.70
900	14.97	14.25	12.29	11.52	11.18	11.03	10.95	10.91
1000	16.63	15.83	13.66	12.80	12.43	12.25	12.17	12.13
2000	33.26	31.66	27.32	25.60	24.85	24.50	24.33	24.25
3000	49.89	47.49	40.97	38.40	37.27	36.74	36.49	36.37
4000	66.52	63.32	54.63	51.20	49.69	48.99	48.65	48.49
5000	83.14	79.15	68.28	64.00	62.11	61.23	60.81	60.61
6000	99.77	94.98	81.94	76.80	74.53	73.48	72.98	72.73
7000	116.40	110.81	95.59	89.60	86.96	85.72	85.14	84.85
8000	133.03	126.63	109.25	102.40	99.38	97.97	97.30	96.98
9000	149.65	142.46	122.90	115.20	111.80	110.22	109.46	109.10
10000	166.28	158.29	136.56	128.00	124.22	122.46	121.62	121.22
11000	182.91	174.12	150.21	140.80	136.64	134.71	133.78	133.34
12000	199.54	189.95	163.87	153.60	149.06	146.95	145.95	145.46
13000	216.17	205.78	177.52	166.40	161.49	159.20	158.11	157.58
14000	232.79	221.61	191.18	179.20	173.91	171.44	170.27	169.70
15000	249.42	237.44	204.83	192.00	186.33	183.69	182.43	181.82
16000	266.05	253.26	218.49	204.80	198.75	195.93	194.59	193.95
17000	282.68	269.09	232.14	217.60	211.17	208.18	206.75	206.07
18000	299.30	284.92	245.80	230.40	223.59	220.43	218.92	218.19
19000	315.93	300.75	259.45	243.20	236.02	232.67	231.08	230.31
20000	332.56	316.58	273.11	256.00	248.44	244.92	243.24	242.43
21000	349.19	332.41	286.76	268.80	260.86	257.16	255.40	254.55
22000	365.81	348.24	300.42	281.60	273.28	269.41	267.56	266.67
23000	382.44	364.06	314.07	294.40	285.70	281.65	279.72	278.80
24000	399.07	379.89	327.73	307.20	298.12	293.90	291.89	290.92
25000	415.70	395.72	341.38	320.00	310.55	306.14	304.05	303.04
26000	432.33	411.55	355.04	332.80	322.97	318.39	316.21	315.16
27000	448.95	427.38	368.69	345.60	335.39	330.64	328.37	327.28
28000	465.58	443.21	382.35	358.40	347.81	342.88	340.53	339.40
29000	482.21	459.04	396.00	371.20	360.23	355.13	352.69	351.52
30000	498.84	474.87	409.66	384.00	372.66	367.37	364.86	363.64
31000	515.46	490.69	423.31	396.80	385.08	379.62	377.02	375.77
32000	532.09	506.52	436.97	409.60	397.50	391.86	389.18	387.89
33000	548.72	522.35	450.62	422.40	409.92	404.11	401.34	400.01
34000	565.35	538.18	464.28	435.20	422.34	416.35	413.50	412.13
35000	581.98	554.01	477.93	448.00	434.76	428.60	425.66	424.25
40000	665.11	633.15	546.21	512.00	496.87	489.83	486.47	484.86
45000	748.25	712.30	614.48	576.00	558.98	551.06	547.28	545.46
50000	831.39	791.44	682.76	640.00	621.09	612.28	608.09	606.07
55000	914.53	870.58	751.03	704.00	683.19	673.51	668.90	666.68
60000	997.63	949.73	819.31	768.00	745.30	734.74	729.71	727.28
65000	1080.81	1028.87	887.58	832.00	807.41	795.97	790.52	787.89
70000	1163.95	1108.01	955.86	896.00	869.52	857.19	851.32	848.50
75000	1247.08	1187.16	1024.13	960.00	931.63	918.42	912.13	909.10
80000	1330.22	1266.30	1092.41	1024.00	993.74	979.65	972.94	969.71
85000	1413.36	1345.44	1160.68	1088.00	1055.84	1040.88	1033.75	1030.32
90000	1496.50	1424.59	1228.96	1152.00	1117.95	1102.11	1094.56	1090.92
95000	1579.64	1503.73	1297.23	1216.00	1180.06	1163.33	1155.37	1151.53
100000	1662.78	1582.87	1365.51	1280.00	1242.17	1224.56	1216.18	1212.14
105000	1745.92	1662.02	1433.78	1344.00	1304.28	1285.79	1276.98	1272.74
110000	1829.05	1741.16	1502.06	1408.00	1366.38	1347.02	1337.79	1333.35
115000	1912.19	1820.30	1570.33	1472.00	1428.49	1408.24	1398.60	1393.96
120000	1995.33	1899.45	1638.61	1536.00	1490.60	1469.47	1459.41	1454.56
125000	2078.47	1978.59	1706.88	1600.00	1552.71	1530.70	1520.22	1515.17
130000	2161.61	2057.73	1775.16	1664.00	1614.82	1591.93	1581.03	1575.78
135000	2244.75	2136.88	1843.43	1728.00	1676.92	1653.16	1641.84	1636.38
140000	2327.89	2216.02	1911.71	1792.00	1739.03	1714.38	1702.64	1696.99
145000	2411.02	2295.16	1979.98	1856.00	1801.14	1775.61	1763.45	1757.60
150000	2494.16	2374.31	2048.26	1920.00	1863.25	1836.84	1824.26	1818.20
155000	2577.30	2453.45	2116.53	1984.00	1925.36	1898.07	1885.07	1878.81
160000	2660.44	2532.59	2184.81	2048.00	1987.47	1959.29	1945.88	1939.42

14.750% MONTHLY AMORTIZING PAYMENTS

AMOUNT OF LOAN	NUMBER OF YEARS IN TERM							
	1	2	3	4	5	6	7	8
$ 50	4.51	2.42	1.73	1.39	1.19	1.06	.96	.90
100	9.02	4.84	3.46	2.78	2.37	2.11	1.92	1.79
200	18.03	9.68	6.91	5.55	4.74	4.21	3.84	3.57
300	27.05	14.52	10.37	8.32	7.10	6.31	5.75	5.35
400	36.06	19.35	13.82	11.09	9.47	8.41	7.67	7.13
500	45.08	24.19	17.28	13.86	11.83	10.51	9.58	8.91
600	54.09	29.03	20.73	16.63	14.20	12.61	11.50	10.69
700	63.10	33.86	24.19	19.40	16.57	14.71	13.41	12.47
800	72.12	38.70	27.64	22.17	18.93	16.81	15.33	14.25
900	81.13	43.54	31.09	24.94	21.30	18.91	17.25	16.03
1000	90.15	48.37	34.55	27.71	23.66	21.01	19.16	17.81
2000	180.29	96.74	69.09	55.41	47.32	42.02	38.32	35.61
3000	270.43	145.11	103.63	83.12	70.98	63.03	57.48	53.41
4000	360.57	193.48	138.18	110.82	94.64	84.04	76.63	71.21
5000	450.71	241.84	172.72	138.53	118.30	105.05	95.79	89.01
6000	540.85	290.21	207.26	166.23	141.96	126.06	114.95	106.81
7000	630.99	338.58	241.81	193.93	165.62	147.07	134.10	124.61
8000	721.13	386.95	276.35	221.64	189.28	168.08	153.26	142.41
9000	811.27	435.32	310.89	249.34	212.94	189.09	172.42	160.21
10000	901.41	483.68	345.44	277.05	236.59	210.10	191.57	178.02
11000	991.55	532.05	379.98	304.75	260.25	231.11	210.73	195.82
12000	1081.69	580.42	414.52	332.46	283.91	252.12	229.89	213.62
13000	1171.83	628.79	449.06	360.16	307.57	273.13	249.04	231.42
14000	1261.97	677.16	483.61	387.86	331.23	294.14	268.20	249.22
15000	1352.11	725.52	518.15	415.57	354.89	315.15	287.36	267.02
16000	1442.25	773.89	552.69	443.27	378.55	336.16	306.51	284.82
17000	1532.39	822.26	587.24	470.98	402.21	357.17	325.67	302.62
18000	1622.53	870.63	621.78	498.68	425.87	378.18	344.83	320.42
19000	1712.67	919.00	656.32	526.38	449.52	399.19	363.98	338.22
20000	1802.81	967.36	690.87	554.09	473.18	420.19	383.14	356.03
21000	1892.95	1015.73	725.41	581.79	496.84	441.20	402.30	373.83
22000	1983.09	1064.10	759.95	609.50	520.50	462.21	421.45	391.63
23000	2073.23	1112.47	794.49	637.20	544.16	483.22	440.61	409.43
24000	2163.37	1160.84	829.04	664.91	567.82	504.23	459.77	427.23
25000	2253.51	1209.20	863.58	692.61	591.48	525.24	478.92	445.03
26000	2343.66	1257.57	898.12	720.31	615.14	546.25	498.08	462.83
27000	2433.80	1305.94	932.67	748.02	638.80	567.26	517.24	480.63
28000	2523.94	1354.31	967.21	775.72	662.45	588.27	536.39	498.43
29000	2614.08	1402.68	1001.75	803.43	686.11	609.28	555.55	516.23
30000	2704.22	1451.04	1036.30	831.13	709.77	630.29	574.71	534.04
31000	2794.36	1499.41	1070.84	858.83	733.43	651.30	593.86	551.84
32000	2884.50	1547.78	1105.38	886.54	757.09	672.31	613.02	569.64
33000	2974.64	1596.15	1139.92	914.24	780.75	693.32	632.18	587.44
34000	3064.78	1644.52	1174.47	941.95	804.41	714.33	651.33	605.24
35000	3154.92	1692.88	1209.01	969.65	828.07	735.34	670.49	623.04
40000	3605.62	1934.72	1381.73	1108.17	946.36	840.38	766.28	712.05
45000	4056.32	2176.56	1554.44	1246.69	1064.66	945.43	862.06	801.05
50000	4507.02	2418.40	1727.16	1385.21	1182.95	1050.48	957.84	890.06
55000	4957.73	2660.24	1899.87	1523.74	1301.24	1155.53	1053.63	979.06
60000	5408.43	2902.08	2072.59	1662.26	1419.54	1260.57	1149.41	1068.07
65000	5859.13	3143.92	2245.30	1800.78	1537.83	1365.62	1245.19	1157.07
70000	6309.83	3385.76	2418.02	1939.30	1656.13	1470.67	1340.98	1246.08
75000	6760.53	3627.60	2590.73	2077.82	1774.42	1575.72	1436.76	1335.08
80000	7211.24	3869.44	2763.45	2216.34	1892.72	1680.76	1532.55	1424.09
85000	7661.94	4111.28	2936.16	2354.86	2011.01	1785.81	1628.33	1513.09
90000	8112.64	4353.12	3108.88	2493.38	2129.31	1890.86	1724.11	1602.10
95000	8563.34	4594.96	3281.59	2631.90	2247.60	1995.91	1819.90	1691.10
100000	9014.04	4836.80	3454.31	2770.42	2365.90	2100.95	1915.68	1780.11
105000	9464.75	5078.64	3627.02	2908.94	2484.19	2206.00	2011.46	1869.11
110000	9915.45	5320.48	3799.74	3047.47	2602.48	2311.05	2107.25	1958.12
115000	10366.15	5562.32	3972.45	3185.99	2720.78	2416.10	2203.03	2047.12
120000	10816.85	5804.16	4145.17	3324.51	2839.07	2521.14	2298.82	2136.13
125000	11267.55	6046.00	4317.88	3463.03	2957.37	2626.19	2394.60	2225.13
130000	11718.26	6287.84	4490.60	3601.55	3075.66	2731.24	2490.38	2314.14
135000	12168.96	6529.68	4663.31	3740.07	3193.96	2836.29	2586.17	2403.14
140000	12619.66	6771.52	4836.03	3878.59	3312.25	2941.33	2681.95	2492.15
145000	13070.36	7013.36	5008.74	4017.11	3430.55	3046.38	2777.74	2581.15
150000	13521.06	7255.20	5181.46	4155.63	3548.84	3151.43	2873.52	2670.16
155000	13971.76	7497.04	5354.17	4294.15	3667.14	3256.47	2969.30	2759.16
160000	14422.47	7738.88	5526.89	4432.67	3785.43	3361.52	3065.09	2848.17

152

AMOUNT OF LOAN	NUMBER OF YEARS IN TERM							
	9	10	15	20	25	30	35	40
$ 50	.84	.80	.70	.65	.64	.63	.62	.62
100	1.68	1.60	1.39	1.30	1.27	1.25	1.24	1.24
200	3.36	3.20	2.77	2.60	2.53	2.49	2.48	2.47
300	5.04	4.80	4.15	3.90	3.79	3.74	3.71	3.70
400	6.72	6.40	5.54	5.20	5.05	4.98	4.95	4.94
500	8.39	8.00	6.92	6.50	6.31	6.23	6.19	6.17
600	10.07	9.59	8.30	7.80	7.57	7.47	7.42	7.40
700	11.75	11.19	9.68	9.09	8.84	8.72	8.66	8.63
800	13.43	12.79	11.07	10.39	10.10	9.96	9.90	9.87
900	15.10	14.39	12.45	11.69	11.36	11.21	11.13	11.10
1000	16.78	15.99	13.83	12.99	12.62	12.45	12.37	12.33
2000	33.56	31.97	27.66	25.97	25.23	24.89	24.73	24.66
3000	50.33	47.95	41.48	38.96	37.85	37.34	37.10	36.99
4000	67.11	63.93	55.31	51.94	50.46	49.78	49.46	49.31
5000	83.88	79.91	69.13	64.92	63.08	62.23	61.83	61.64
6000	100.66	95.89	82.96	77.91	75.69	74.67	74.19	73.97
7000	117.43	111.87	96.78	90.89	88.31	87.12	86.56	86.29
8000	134.21	127.85	110.61	103.87	100.92	99.56	98.92	98.62
9000	150.99	143.83	124.43	116.86	113.54	112.01	111.29	110.95
10000	167.76	159.81	138.26	129.84	126.15	124.45	123.65	123.27
11000	184.54	175.79	152.08	142.82	138.77	136.90	136.02	135.60
12000	201.31	191.77	165.91	155.81	151.38	149.34	148.38	147.93
13000	218.09	207.75	179.73	168.79	164.00	161.79	160.75	160.25
14000	234.86	223.74	193.56	181.77	176.61	174.23	173.11	172.58
15000	251.64	239.72	207.38	194.76	189.22	186.68	185.48	184.91
16000	268.42	255.70	221.21	207.74	201.84	199.12	197.84	197.23
17000	285.19	271.68	235.03	220.73	214.45	211.57	210.21	209.56
18000	301.97	287.66	248.86	233.71	227.07	224.01	222.57	221.89
19000	318.75	303.64	262.68	246.69	239.68	236.46	234.94	234.21
20000	335.52	319.62	276.51	259.68	252.30	248.90	247.30	246.54
21000	352.29	335.60	290.33	272.66	264.91	261.34	259.66	258.87
22000	369.07	351.58	304.16	285.64	277.53	273.79	272.03	271.19
23000	385.85	367.56	317.98	298.63	290.14	286.23	284.39	283.52
24000	402.62	383.54	331.81	311.61	302.76	298.68	296.76	295.85
25000	419.40	399.52	345.63	324.59	315.37	311.12	309.12	308.17
26000	436.17	415.50	359.46	337.58	327.99	323.57	321.49	320.50
27000	452.95	431.49	373.28	350.56	340.60	336.01	333.85	332.83
28000	469.72	447.47	387.11	363.54	353.22	348.46	346.22	345.15
29000	486.50	463.45	400.93	376.53	365.83	360.90	358.58	357.48
30000	503.28	479.43	414.76	389.51	378.44	373.35	370.95	369.81
31000	520.05	495.41	428.58	402.50	391.06	385.79	383.31	382.13
32000	536.83	511.39	442.41	415.48	403.67	398.24	395.68	394.46
33000	553.60	527.37	456.23	428.46	416.29	410.68	408.04	406.79
34000	570.38	543.35	470.06	441.45	428.90	423.13	420.41	419.11
35000	587.15	559.33	483.88	454.43	441.52	435.57	432.77	431.44
40000	671.03	639.23	553.01	519.35	504.59	497.80	494.59	493.07
45000	754.91	719.14	622.13	584.26	567.66	560.02	556.42	554.71
50000	838.79	799.04	691.26	649.18	630.74	622.24	618.24	616.34
55000	922.67	878.95	760.38	714.10	693.81	684.47	680.07	677.97
60000	1006.55	958.85	829.51	779.02	756.88	746.69	741.89	739.61
65000	1090.43	1038.75	898.63	843.94	819.96	808.91	803.71	801.24
70000	1174.30	1118.66	967.76	908.85	883.03	871.14	865.54	862.87
75000	1258.18	1198.56	1036.88	973.77	946.10	933.36	927.36	924.51
80000	1342.06	1278.46	1106.01	1038.69	1009.18	995.59	989.18	986.14
85000	1425.94	1358.37	1175.13	1103.61	1072.25	1057.81	1051.01	1047.77
90000	1509.82	1438.27	1244.26	1168.52	1135.32	1120.03	1112.83	1109.41
95000	1593.70	1518.18	1313.38	1233.44	1198.40	1182.26	1174.66	1171.04
100000	1677.58	1598.08	1382.51	1298.36	1261.47	1244.48	1236.48	1232.67
105000	1761.45	1677.98	1451.63	1363.28	1324.54	1306.70	1298.30	1294.31
110000	1845.33	1757.89	1520.76	1428.20	1387.62	1368.93	1360.13	1355.94
115000	1929.21	1837.79	1589.88	1493.11	1450.69	1431.15	1421.95	1417.57
120000	2013.09	1917.69	1659.01	1558.03	1513.76	1493.38	1483.77	1479.21
125000	2096.97	1997.60	1728.13	1622.95	1576.84	1555.60	1545.60	1540.84
130000	2180.85	2077.50	1797.26	1687.87	1639.91	1617.82	1607.42	1602.47
135000	2264.73	2157.41	1866.39	1752.78	1702.98	1680.05	1669.25	1664.11
140000	2348.60	2237.31	1935.51	1817.70	1766.06	1742.27	1731.07	1725.74
145000	2432.48	2317.21	2004.64	1882.62	1829.13	1804.49	1792.89	1787.37
150000	2516.36	2397.12	2073.76	1947.54	1892.20	1866.72	1854.72	1849.01
155000	2600.24	2477.02	2142.89	2012.46	1955.28	1928.94	1916.54	1910.64
160000	2684.12	2556.92	2212.01	2077.37	2018.35	1991.17	1978.36	1972.27

15.000% MONTHLY AMORTIZING PAYMENTS

AMOUNT OF LOAN	NUMBER OF YEARS IN TERM							
	1	2	3	4	5	6	7	8
$ 50	4 52	2.43	1.74	1.40	1.19	1.06	.97	.90
100	9.03	4.85	3.47	2.79	2.38	2.12	1.93	1.80
200	18.06	9.70	6.94	5.57	4.76	4.23	3.86	3.59
300	27.08	14.55	10.40	8.35	7.14	6.35	5.79	5.39
400	36.11	19.40	13.87	11.14	9.52	8.46	7.72	7.18
500	45.13	24.25	17.34	13.92	11.90	10.58	9.65	8.98
600	54.16	29.10	20.80	16.70	14.28	12.69	11.58	10.77
700	63.19	33.95	24.27	19.49	16.66	14.81	13.51	12.57
800	72.21	38.79	27.74	22.27	19.04	16.92	15.44	14.36
900	81.24	43.64	31.20	25.05	21.42	19.04	17.37	16.16
1000	90.26	48.49	34.67	27.84	23.79	21.15	19.30	17.95
2000	180.52	96.98	69.34	55.67	47.58	42.30	38.60	35.90
3000	270.78	145.46	104.00	83.50	71.37	63.44	57.90	53.84
4000	361.04	193.95	138.67	111.33	95.16	84.59	77.19	71.79
5000	451.30	242.44	173.33	139.16	118.95	105.73	96.49	89.73
6000	541.55	290.92	208.00	166.99	142.74	126.88	115.79	107.68
7000	631.81	339.41	242.66	194.82	166.53	148.02	135.08	125.62
8000	722.07	387.90	277.33	222.65	190.32	169.17	154.38	143.57
9000	812.33	436.38	311.99	250.48	214.11	190.31	173.68	161.51
10000	902.59	484.87	346.66	278.31	237.90	211.46	192.97	179.46
11000	992.85	533.36	381.32	306.14	261.69	232.60	212.27	197.40
12000	1083.10	581.84	415.99	333.97	285.48	253.75	231.57	215.35
13000	1173.36	630.33	450.65	361.80	309.27	274.89	250.86	233.30
14000	1263.62	678.82	485.32	389.64	333.06	296.04	270.16	251.24
15000	1353.88	727.30	519.98	417.47	356.85	317.18	289.46	269.19
16000	1444.14	775.79	554.65	445.30	380.64	338.33	308.75	287.13
17000	1534.40	824.28	589.32	473.13	404.43	359.47	328.05	305.08
18000	1624.65	872.76	623.98	500.96	428.22	380.62	347.35	323.02
19000	1714.91	921.25	658.65	528.79	452.01	401.76	366.64	340.97
20000	1805.17	969.74	693.31	556.62	475.80	422.91	385.94	358.91
21000	1895.43	1018.22	727.98	584.45	499.59	444.05	405.24	376.86
22000	1985.69	1066.71	762.64	612.28	523.38	465.20	424.53	394.80
23000	2075.95	1115.20	797.31	640.11	547.17	486.34	443.83	412.75
24000	2166.20	1163.68	831.97	667.94	570.96	507.49	463.13	430.69
25000	2256.46	1212.17	866.64	695.77	594.75	528.63	482.42	448.64
26000	2346.72	1260.66	901.30	723.60	618.54	549.78	501.72	466.59
27000	2436.98	1309.14	935.97	751.44	642.33	570.92	521.02	484.53
28000	2527.24	1357.63	970.63	779.27	666.12	592.07	540.31	502.48
29000	2617.50	1406.12	1005.30	807.10	689.91	613.21	559.61	520.42
30000	2707.75	1454.60	1039.96	834.93	713.70	634.36	578.91	538.37
31000	2798.01	1503.09	1074.63	862.76	737.49	655.50	598.20	556.31
32000	2888.27	1551.58	1109.30	890.59	761.28	676.65	617.50	574.26
33000	2978.53	1600.06	1143.96	918.42	785.07	697.79	636.80	592.20
34000	3068.79	1648.55	1178.63	946.25	808.86	718.94	656.09	610.15
35000	3159.05	1697.04	1213.29	974.08	832.65	740.08	675.39	628.09
40000	3610.34	1939.47	1386.62	1113.23	951.60	845.81	771.88	717.82
45000	4061.63	2181.90	1559.94	1252.39	1070.55	951.53	868.36	807.55
50000	4512.92	2424.34	1733.27	1391.54	1189.50	1057.26	964.84	897.28
55000	4964.21	2666.77	1906.60	1530.70	1308.45	1162.98	1061.33	987.00
60000	5415.50	2909.20	2079.92	1669.85	1427.40	1268.71	1157.81	1076.73
65000	5866.80	3151.64	2253.25	1809.00	1546.35	1374.43	1254.29	1166.46
70000	6318.09	3394.07	2426.58	1948.16	1665.30	1480.16	1350.78	1256.18
75000	6769.38	3636.50	2599.90	2087.31	1784.25	1585.88	1447.26	1345.91
80000	7220.67	3878.94	2773.23	2226.46	1903.20	1691.61	1543.75	1435.64
85000	7671.96	4121.37	2946.56	2365.62	2022.15	1797.33	1640.23	1525.36
90000	8123.25	4363.80	3119.88	2504.77	2141.10	1903.06	1736.71	1615.09
95000	8574.54	4606.24	3293.21	2643.93	2260.05	2008.78	1833.20	1704.82
100000	9025.84	4848.67	3466.54	2783.08	2379.00	2114.51	1929.68	1794.55
105000	9477.13	5091.10	3639.86	2922.23	2497.95	2220.23	2026.16	1884.27
110000	9928.42	5333.54	3813.19	3061.39	2616.90	2325.96	2122.65	1974.00
115000	10379.71	5575.97	3986.52	3200.54	2735.85	2431.68	2219.13	2063.73
120000	10831.00	5818.40	4159.84	3339.69	2854.80	2537.41	2315.62	2153.45
125000	11282.29	6060.84	4333.17	3478.85	2973.75	2643.13	2412.10	2243.18
130000	11733.59	6303.27	4506.50	3618.00	3092.70	2748.86	2508.58	2332.91
135000	12184.88	6545.70	4679.82	3757.16	3211.65	2854.58	2605.07	2422.63
140000	12636.17	6788.14	4853.15	3896.31	3330.60	2960.31	2701.55	2512.36
145000	13087.46	7030.57	5026.48	4035.46	3449.54	3066.03	2798.03	2602.09
150000	13538.75	7273.00	5199.80	4174.62	3568.49	3171.76	2894.52	2691.82
155000	13990.04	7515.44	5373.13	4313.77	3687.44	3277.48	2991.00	2781.54
160000	14441.33	7757.87	5546.46	4452.92	3806.39	3383.21	3087.49	2871.27

154

MONTHLY AMORTIZING PAYMENTS 15.000%

AMOUNT OF LOAN	NUMBER OF YEARS IN TERM							
	9	10	15	20	25	30	35	40
$ 50	.85	.81	.70	.66	.65	.64	.63	.63
100	1.70	1.62	1.40	1.32	1.29	1.27	1.26	1.26
200	3.39	3.23	2.80	2.64	2.57	2.53	2.52	2.51
300	5.08	4.85	4.20	3.96	3.85	3.80	3.78	3.76
400	6.77	6.46	5.60	5.27	5.13	5.06	5.04	5.02
500	8.47	8.07	7.00	6.59	6.41	6.33	6.29	6.27
600	10.16	9.69	8.40	7.91	7.69	7.59	7.55	7.52
700	11.85	11.30	9.80	9.22	8.97	8.86	8.80	8.78
800	13.54	12.91	11.20	10.54	10.25	10.12	10.06	10.03
900	15.24	14.53	12.60	11.86	11.53	11.38	11.32	11.28
1000	16.93	16.14	14.00	13.17	12.81	12.65	12.57	12.54
2000	33.85	32.27	28.00	26.34	25.62	25.29	25.14	25.07
3000	50.78	48.41	41.99	39.51	38.43	37.94	37.71	37.60
4000	67.70	64.54	55.99	52.68	51.24	50.58	50.28	50.13
5000	84.63	80.67	69.98	65.84	64.05	63.23	62.85	62.67
6000	101.55	96.81	83.98	79.01	76.85	75.87	75.41	75.20
7000	118.48	112.94	97.98	92.18	89.66	88.52	87.98	87.73
8000	135.40	129.07	111.97	105.35	102.47	101.16	100.55	100.26
9000	152.32	145.21	125.97	118.52	115.28	113.80	113.12	112.80
10000	169.25	161.34	139.96	131.68	128.09	126.45	125.69	125.33
11000	186.17	177.47	153.96	144.85	140.90	139.09	138.25	137.86
12000	203.10	193.61	167.96	158.02	153.70	151.74	150.82	150.39
13000	220.02	209.74	181.95	171.19	166.51	164.38	163.39	162.92
14000	236.95	225.87	195.95	184.36	179.32	177.03	175.96	175.46
15000	253.87	242.01	209.94	197.52	192.13	189.67	188.53	187.99
16000	270.79	258.14	223.94	210.69	204.94	202.32	201.10	200.52
17000	287.72	274.27	237.93	223.86	217.75	214.96	213.66	213.05
18000	304.64	290.41	251.93	237.03	230.55	227.60	226.23	225.59
19000	321.57	306.54	265.93	250.20	243.36	240.25	238.80	238.12
20000	338.49	322.67	279.92	263.36	256.17	252.89	251.37	250.65
21000	355.42	338.81	293.92	276.53	268.98	265.54	263.94	263.18
22000	372.34	354.94	307.91	289.70	281.79	278.18	276.50	275.71
23000	389.26	371.08	321.91	302.87	294.60	290.83	289.07	288.25
24000	406.19	387.21	335.91	316.03	307.40	303.47	301.64	300.78
25000	423.11	403.34	349.90	329.20	320.21	316.12	314.21	313.31
26000	440.04	419.48	363.90	342.37	333.02	328.76	326.78	325.84
27000	456.96	435.61	377.89	355.54	345.83	341.40	339.34	338.38
28000	473.89	451.74	391.89	368.71	358.64	354.05	351.91	350.91
29000	490.81	467.88	405.88	381.87	371.45	366.69	364.48	363.44
30000	507.74	484.01	419.88	395.04	384.25	379.34	377.05	375.97
31000	524.66	500.14	433.88	408.21	397.06	391.98	389.62	388.50
32000	541.58	516.28	447.87	421.38	409.87	404.63	402.19	401.04
33000	558.51	532.41	461.87	434.55	422.68	417.27	414.75	413.57
34000	575.43	548.54	475.86	447.71	435.49	429.92	427.32	426.10
35000	592.36	564.68	489.86	460.88	448.30	442.56	439.89	438.63
40000	676.98	645.34	559.84	526.72	512.34	505.78	502.73	501.29
45000	761.60	726.01	629.82	592.56	576.38	569.00	565.57	563.96
50000	846.22	806.68	699.80	658.40	640.42	632.23	628.41	626.62
55000	930.84	887.35	769.78	724.24	704.46	695.45	691.25	689.28
60000	1015.47	968.01	839.76	790.08	768.50	758.67	754.09	751.94
65000	1100.09	1048.68	909.74	855.92	832.54	821.89	816.93	814.60
70000	1184.71	1129.35	979.72	921.76	896.59	885.12	879.77	877.26
75000	1269.33	1210.02	1049.70	987.60	960.63	948.34	942.61	939.92
80000	1353.95	1290.68	1119.67	1053.44	1024.67	1011.56	1005.46	1002.58
85000	1438.57	1371.35	1189.65	1119.28	1088.71	1074.78	1068.30	1065.25
90000	1523.20	1452.02	1259.63	1185.12	1152.75	1138.00	1131.14	1127.91
95000	1607.82	1532.69	1329.61	1250.96	1216.79	1201.23	1193.98	1190.57
100000	1692.44	1613.35	1399.59	1316.79	1280.84	1264.45	1256.82	1253.23
105000	1777.06	1694.02	1469.57	1382.63	1344.88	1327.67	1319.66	1315.89
110000	1861.68	1774.69	1539.55	1448.47	1408.92	1390.89	1382.50	1378.55
115000	1946.30	1855.36	1609.53	1514.31	1472.96	1454.12	1445.34	1441.21
120000	2030.93	1936.02	1679.51	1580.15	1537.00	1517.34	1508.18	1503.87
125000	2115.55	2016.69	1749.49	1645.99	1601.04	1580.56	1571.02	1566.54
130000	2200.17	2097.36	1819.47	1711.83	1665.08	1643.78	1633.86	1629.20
135000	2284.79	2178.03	1889.45	1777.67	1729.13	1707.00	1696.70	1691.86
140000	2369.41	2258.69	1959.43	1843.51	1793.17	1770.23	1759.54	1754.52
145000	2454.03	2339.36	2029.41	1909.35	1857.21	1833.45	1822.38	1817.18
150000	2538.66	2420.03	2099.39	1975.19	1921.25	1896.67	1885.22	1879.84
155000	2623.28	2500.70	2169.37	2041.03	1985.29	1959.89	1948.07	1942.50
160000	2707.90	2581.36	2239.34	2106.87	2049.33	2023.12	2010.91	2005.16

15.250% MONTHLY AMORTIZING PAYMENTS

AMOUNT OF LOAN	NUMBER OF YEARS IN TERM							
	1	2	3	4	5	6	7	8
$ 50	4.52	2.44	1.74	1.40	1.20	1.07	.98	.91
100	9.04	4.87	3.48	2.80	2.40	2.13	1.95	1.81
200	18.08	9.73	6.96	5.60	4.79	4.26	3.89	3.62
300	27.12	14.59	10.44	8.39	7.18	6.39	5.84	5.43
400	36.16	19.45	13.92	11.19	9.57	8.52	7.78	7.24
500	45.19	24.31	17.40	13.98	11.97	10.65	9.72	9.05
600	54.23	29.17	20.88	16.78	14.36	12.77	11.67	10.86
700	63.27	34.03	24.36	19.58	16.75	14.90	13.61	12.67
800	72.31	38.89	27.84	22.37	19.14	17.03	15.55	14.48
900	81.34	43.75	31.31	25.17	21.53	19.16	17.50	16.29
1000	90.38	48.61	34.79	27.96	23.93	21.29	19.44	18.10
2000	180.76	97.22	69.58	55.92	47.85	42.57	38.88	36.19
3000	271.13	145.82	104.37	83.88	71.77	63.85	58.32	54.28
4000	361.51	194.43	139.16	111.84	95.69	85.13	77.75	72.37
5000	451.89	243.03	173.94	139.79	119.61	106.41	97.19	90.46
6000	542.26	291.64	208.73	167.75	143.53	127.69	116.63	108.55
7000	632.64	340.24	243.52	195.71	167.45	148.97	136.07	126.64
8000	723.02	388.85	278.31	223.67	191.38	170.25	155.50	144.73
9000	813.39	437.45	313.10	251.62	215.30	191.53	174.94	162.82
10000	903.77	486.06	347.88	279.58	239.22	212.82	194.38	180.91
11000	994.14	534.67	382.67	307.54	263.14	234.10	213.82	199.00
12000	1084.52	583.27	417.46	335.50	287.06	255.38	233.25	217.09
13000	1174.90	631.88	452.25	363.45	310.98	276.66	252.69	235.18
14000	1265.27	680.48	487.04	391.41	334.90	297.94	272.13	253.27
15000	1355.65	729.09	521.82	419.37	358.83	319.22	291.56	271.36
16000	1446.03	777.69	556.61	447.33	382.75	340.50	311.00	289.45
17000	1536.40	826.30	591.40	475.28	406.67	361.78	330.44	307.54
18000	1626.78	874.90	626.19	503.24	430.59	383.06	349.88	325.63
19000	1717.16	923.51	660.97	531.20	454.51	404.34	369.31	343.72
20000	1807.53	972.12	695.76	559.16	478.43	425.63	388.75	361.81
21000	1897.91	1020.72	730.55	587.12	502.35	446.91	408.19	379.90
22000	1988.28	1069.33	765.34	615.07	526.27	468.19	427.63	397.99
23000	2078.66	1117.93	800.13	643.03	550.20	489.47	447.06	416.08
24000	2169.04	1166.54	834.91	670.99	574.12	510.75	466.50	434.17
25000	2259.41	1215.14	869.70	698.95	598.04	532.03	485.94	452.26
26000	2349.79	1263.75	904.49	726.90	621.96	553.31	505.37	470.35
27000	2440.17	1312.35	939.28	754.86	645.88	574.59	524.81	488.44
28000	2530.54	1360.96	974.07	782.82	669.80	595.87	544.25	506.54
29000	2620.92	1409.56	1008.85	810.78	693.72	617.15	563.69	524.63
30000	2711.29	1458.17	1043.64	838.73	717.65	638.44	583.12	542.72
31000	2801.67	1506.78	1078.43	866.69	741.57	659.72	602.56	560.81
32000	2892.05	1555.38	1113.22	894.65	765.49	681.00	622.00	578.90
33000	2982.42	1603.99	1148.01	922.61	789.41	702.28	641.44	596.99
34000	3072.80	1652.59	1182.79	950.56	813.33	723.56	660.87	615.08
35000	3163.18	1701.20	1217.58	978.52	837.25	744.84	680.31	633.17
40000	3615.06	1944.23	1391.52	1118.31	956.86	851.25	777.50	723.62
45000	4066.94	2187.25	1565.46	1258.10	1076.47	957.65	874.68	814.07
50000	4518.82	2430.28	1739.40	1397.89	1196.07	1064.06	971.87	904.52
55000	4970.70	2673.31	1913.34	1537.68	1315.68	1170.46	1069.06	994.98
60000	5422.58	2916.34	2087.28	1677.46	1435.29	1276.87	1166.24	1085.43
65000	5874.47	3159.36	2261.22	1817.25	1554.89	1383.27	1263.43	1175.88
70000	6326.35	3402.39	2435.16	1957.04	1674.50	1489.68	1360.61	1266.33
75000	6778.23	3645.42	2609.10	2096.83	1794.11	1596.08	1457.80	1356.78
80000	7230.11	3888.45	2783.04	2236.62	1913.71	1702.49	1554.99	1447.23
85000	7681.99	4131.47	2956.97	2376.40	2033.32	1808.89	1652.17	1537.69
90000	8133.87	4374.50	3130.91	2516.19	2152.93	1915.30	1749.36	1628.14
95000	8585.76	4617.53	3304.85	2655.98	2272.53	2021.70	1846.55	1718.59
100000	9037.64	4860.56	3478.79	2795.77	2392.14	2128.11	1943.73	1809.04
105000	9489.52	5103.58	3652.73	2935.56	2511.75	2234.51	2040.92	1899.49
110000	9941.40	5346.61	3826.67	3075.35	2631.35	2340.92	2138.11	1989.95
115000	10393.28	5589.64	4000.61	3215.13	2750.96	2447.32	2235.29	2080.40
120000	10845.16	5832.67	4174.55	3354.92	2870.57	2553.73	2332.48	2170.85
125000	11297.05	6075.69	4348.49	3494.71	2990.17	2660.13	2429.67	2261.30
130000	11748.93	6318.72	4522.43	3634.50	3109.78	2766.54	2526.85	2351.75
135000	12200.81	6561.75	4696.37	3774.29	3229.39	2872.94	2624.04	2442.20
140000	12652.69	6804.78	4870.31	3914.07	3349.00	2979.35	2721.22	2532.66
145000	13104.57	7047.80	5044.25	4053.86	3468.60	3085.75	2818.41	2623.11
150000	13556.45	7290.83	5218.19	4193.65	3588.21	3192.16	2915.60	2713.56
155000	14008.33	7533.86	5392.13	4333.44	3707.82	3298.56	3012.78	2804.01
160000	14460.22	7776.89	5566.07	4473.23	3827.42	3404.97	3109.97	2894.46

MONTHLY AMORTIZING PAYMENTS 15.250%

AMOUNT OF LOAN	NUMBER OF YEARS IN TERM							
	9	10	15	20	25	30	35	40
$ 50	.86	.82	.71	.67	.66	.65	.64	.64
100	1.71	1.63	1.42	1.34	1.31	1.29	1.28	1.28
200	3.42	3.26	2.84	2.68	2.61	2.57	2.56	2.55
300	5.13	4.89	4.26	4.01	3.91	3.86	3.84	3.83
400	6.83	6.52	5.67	5.35	5.21	5.14	5.11	5.10
500	8.54	8.15	7.09	6.68	6.51	6.43	6.39	6.37
600	10.25	9.78	8.51	8.02	7.81	7.71	7.67	7.65
700	11.96	11.41	9.92	9.35	9.11	9.00	8.95	8.92
800	13.66	13.03	11.34	10.69	10.41	10.28	10.22	10.20
900	15.37	14.66	12.76	12.02	11.71	11.57	11.50	11.47
1000	17.08	16.29	14.17	13.36	13.01	12.85	12.78	12.74
2000	34.15	32.58	28.34	26.71	26.01	25.69	25.55	25.48
3000	51.23	48.87	42.51	40.06	39.01	38.54	38.32	38.22
4000	68.30	65.15	56.67	53.42	52.02	51.38	51.09	50.96
5000	85.37	81.44	70.84	66.77	65.02	64.23	63.86	63.70
6000	102.45	97.73	85.01	80.12	78.02	77.07	76.64	76.43
7000	119.52	114.01	99.18	93.48	91.02	89.92	89.41	89.17
8000	136.59	130.30	113.34	106.83	104.03	102.76	102.18	101.91
9000	153.67	146.59	127.51	120.18	117.03	115.61	114.95	114.65
10000	170.74	162.87	141.68	133.53	130.03	128.45	127.72	127.39
11000	187.81	179.16	155.85	146.89	143.03	141.30	140.50	140.12
12000	204.89	195.45	170.01	160.24	156.04	154.14	153.27	152.86
13000	221.96	211.74	184.18	173.59	169.04	166.98	166.04	165.60
14000	239.04	228.02	198.35	186.95	182.04	179.83	178.81	178.34
15000	256.11	244.31	212.52	200.30	195.04	192.67	191.58	191.08
16000	273.18	260.60	226.68	213.65	208.05	205.52	204.35	203.81
17000	290.26	276.88	240.85	227.01	221.05	218.36	217.13	216.55
18000	307.33	293.17	255.02	240.36	234.05	231.21	229.90	229.29
19000	324.40	309.46	269.19	253.71	247.05	244.05	242.67	242.03
20000	341.48	325.74	283.35	267.06	260.06	256.90	255.44	254.77
21000	358.55	342.03	297.52	280.42	273.06	269.74	268.21	267.50
22000	375.62	358.32	311.69	293.77	286.06	282.59	280.99	280.24
23000	392.70	374.60	325.86	307.12	299.06	295.43	293.76	292.98
24000	409.77	390.89	340.02	320.48	312.07	308.28	306.53	305.72
25000	426.85	407.18	354.19	333.83	325.07	321.12	319.30	318.46
26000	443.92	423.47	368.36	347.18	338.07	333.96	332.07	331.19
27000	460.99	439.75	382.53	360.54	351.07	346.81	344.84	343.93
28000	478.07	456.04	396.69	373.89	364.08	359.65	357.62	356.67
29000	495.14	472.33	410.86	387.24	377.08	372.50	370.39	369.41
30000	512.21	488.61	425.03	400.59	390.08	385.34	383.16	382.15
31000	529.29	504.90	439.20	413.94	403.09	398.19	395.93	394.88
32000	546.36	521.19	453.36	427.30	416.09	411.03	408.70	407.62
33000	563.43	537.47	467.53	440.65	429.09	423.88	421.48	420.36
34000	580.51	553.76	481.70	454.01	442.09	436.72	434.25	433.10
35000	597.58	570.05	495.87	467.36	455.10	449.57	447.02	445.84
40000	682.95	651.48	566.70	534.12	520.11	513.79	510.88	509.53
45000	768.32	732.92	637.54	600.89	585.12	578.01	574.74	573.22
50000	853.69	814.35	708.38	667.65	650.13	642.23	638.60	636.91
55000	939.05	895.79	779.22	734.42	715.15	706.46	702.46	700.60
60000	1024.42	977.22	850.05	801.18	780.16	770.68	766.32	764.29
65000	1109.79	1058.66	920.89	867.95	845.17	834.90	830.17	827.98
70000	1195.16	1140.09	991.73	934.71	910.19	899.13	894.03	891.67
75000	1280.53	1221.53	1062.57	1001.48	975.20	963.35	957.89	955.36
80000	1365.89	1302.96	1133.40	1068.24	1040.21	1027.57	1021.75	1019.05
85000	1451.26	1384.39	1204.24	1135.01	1105.22	1091.79	1085.61	1082.74
90000	1536.63	1465.83	1275.08	1201.77	1170.24	1156.02	1149.47	1146.43
95000	1622.00	1547.26	1345.92	1268.54	1235.25	1220.24	1213.33	1210.12
100000	1707.37	1628.70	1416.75	1335.30	1300.26	1284.46	1277.19	1273.81
105000	1792.73	1710.13	1487.59	1402.07	1365.28	1348.69	1341.05	1337.50
110000	1878.10	1791.57	1558.43	1468.83	1430.29	1412.91	1404.91	1401.19
115000	1963.47	1873.00	1629.27	1535.60	1495.30	1477.13	1468.77	1464.88
120000	2048.84	1954.44	1700.10	1602.36	1560.31	1541.36	1532.63	1528.57
125000	2134.21	2035.87	1770.94	1669.13	1625.33	1605.58	1596.48	1592.26
130000	2219.57	2117.31	1841.78	1735.89	1690.34	1669.80	1660.34	1655.95
135000	2304.94	2198.74	1912.62	1802.66	1755.35	1734.02	1724.20	1719.64
140000	2390.31	2280.18	1983.45	1869.42	1820.37	1798.25	1788.06	1783.33
145000	2475.68	2361.61	2054.29	1936.19	1885.38	1862.47	1851.92	1847.02
150000	2561.05	2443.05	2125.13	2002.95	1950.39	1926.69	1915.78	1910.71
155000	2646.41	2524.48	2195.97	2069.72	2015.41	1990.92	1979.64	1974.40
160000	2731.78	2605.91	2266.80	2136.48	2080.42	2055.14	2043.50	2038.09

15.500% MONTHLY AMORTIZING PAYMENTS

AMOUNT OF LOAN	NUMBER OF YEARS IN TERM							
	1	2	3	4	5	6	7	8
$ 50	4.53	2.44	1.75	1.41	1.21	1.08	.98	.92
100	9.05	4.88	3.50	2.81	2.41	2.15	1.96	1.83
200	18.10	9.75	6.99	5.62	4.82	4.29	3.92	3.65
300	27.15	14.62	10.48	8.43	7.22	6.43	5.88	5.48
400	36.20	19.49	13.97	11.24	9.63	8.57	7.84	7.30
500	45.25	24.37	17.46	14.05	12.03	10.71	9.79	9.12
600	54.30	29.24	20.95	16.86	14.44	12.86	11.75	10.95
700	63.35	34.11	24.44	19.66	16.84	15.00	13.71	12.77
800	72.40	38.98	27.93	22.47	19.25	17.14	15.67	14.59
900	81.45	43.86	31.42	25.28	21.65	19.28	17.63	16.42
1000	90.50	48.73	34.92	28.09	24.06	21.42	19.58	18.24
2000	180.99	97.45	69.83	56.17	48.11	42.84	39.16	36.48
3000	271.49	146.18	104.74	84.26	72.16	64.26	58.74	54.71
4000	361.98	194.90	139.65	112.34	96.22	85.67	78.32	72.95
5000	452.48	243.63	174.56	140.43	120.27	107.09	97.90	91.18
6000	542.97	292.35	209.47	168.51	144.32	128.51	117.48	109.42
7000	633.47	341.08	244.38	196.60	168.38	149.93	137.05	127.66
8000	723.96	389.80	279.29	224.68	192.43	171.34	156.63	145.89
9000	814.45	438.53	314.20	252.77	216.48	192.76	176.21	164.13
10000	904.95	487.25	349.11	280.85	240.54	214.18	195.79	182.36
11000	995.44	535.97	384.02	308.94	264.59	235.60	215.37	200.60
12000	1085.94	584.70	418.93	337.02	288.64	257.01	234.95	218.84
13000	1176.43	633.42	453.84	365.11	312.70	278.43	254.52	237.07
14000	1266.93	682.15	488.75	393.19	336.75	299.85	274.10	255.31
15000	1357.42	730.87	523.67	421.28	360.80	321.27	293.68	273.54
16000	1447.92	779.60	558.58	449.36	384.86	342.68	313.26	291.78
17000	1538.41	828.32	593.49	477.45	408.91	364.10	332.84	310.02
18000	1628.90	877.05	628.40	505.53	432.96	385.52	352.42	328.25
19000	1719.40	925.77	663.31	533.62	457.02	406.94	371.99	346.49
20000	1809.89	974.50	698.22	561.70	481.07	428.35	391.57	364.72
21000	1900.39	1023.22	733.13	589.79	505.12	449.77	411.15	382.96
22000	1990.88	1071.94	768.04	617.87	529.18	471.19	430.73	401.20
23000	2081.38	1120.67	802.95	645.96	553.23	492.61	450.31	419.43
24000	2171.87	1169.39	837.86	674.04	577.28	514.02	469.89	437.67
25000	2262.37	1218.12	872.77	702.13	601.33	535.44	489.46	455.90
26000	2352.86	1266.84	907.68	730.21	625.39	556.86	509.04	474.14
27000	2443.35	1315.57	942.59	758.30	649.44	578.28	528.62	492.37
28000	2533.85	1364.29	977.50	786.38	673.49	599.69	548.20	510.61
29000	2624.34	1413.02	1012.41	814.47	697.55	621.11	567.78	528.85
30000	2714.84	1461.74	1047.33	842.55	721.60	642.53	587.36	547.08
31000	2805.33	1510.47	1082.24	870.64	745.65	663.95	606.93	565.32
32000	2895.83	1559.19	1117.15	898.72	769.71	685.36	626.51	583.55
33000	2986.32	1607.91	1152.06	926.81	793.76	706.78	646.09	601.79
34000	3076.82	1656.64	1186.97	954.89	817.81	728.20	665.67	620.03
35000	3167.31	1705.36	1221.88	982.98	841.87	749.62	685.25	638.26
40000	3619.78	1948.99	1396.43	1123.40	962.13	856.70	783.14	729.44
45000	4072.25	2192.61	1570.99	1263.82	1082.40	963.79	881.03	820.62
50000	4524.73	2436.23	1745.54	1404.25	1202.66	1070.88	978.92	911.80
55000	4977.20	2679.85	1920.09	1544.67	1322.93	1177.97	1076.81	1002.98
60000	5429.67	2923.48	2094.65	1685.10	1443.20	1285.05	1174.71	1094.16
65000	5882.14	3167.10	2269.20	1825.52	1563.46	1392.14	1272.60	1185.34
70000	6334.61	3410.72	2443.75	1965.95	1683.73	1499.23	1370.49	1276.52
75000	6787.09	3654.35	2618.31	2106.37	1803.99	1606.32	1468.38	1367.70
80000	7239.56	3897.97	2792.86	2246.79	1924.26	1713.40	1566.27	1458.88
85000	7692.03	4141.59	2967.41	2387.22	2044.53	1820.49	1664.16	1550.06
90000	8144.50	4385.21	3141.97	2527.64	2164.79	1927.58	1762.06	1641.24
95000	8596.97	4628.84	3316.52	2668.07	2285.06	2034.67	1859.95	1732.42
100000	9049.45	4872.46	3491.07	2808.49	2405.32	2141.75	1957.84	1823.60
105000	9501.92	5116.08	3665.63	2948.92	2525.59	2248.84	2055.73	1914.78
110000	9954.39	5359.70	3840.18	3089.34	2645.86	2355.93	2153.62	2005.96
115000	10406.86	5603.33	4014.73	3229.76	2766.12	2463.02	2251.51	2097.14
120000	10859.33	5846.95	4189.29	3370.19	2886.39	2570.10	2349.41	2188.32
125000	11311.81	6090.57	4363.84	3510.61	3006.65	2677.19	2447.30	2279.50
130000	11764.28	6334.20	4538.39	3651.04	3126.92	2784.28	2545.19	2370.67
135000	12216.75	6577.82	4712.95	3791.46	3247.19	2891.37	2643.08	2461.85
140000	12669.22	6821.44	4887.50	3931.89	3367.45	2998.45	2740.97	2553.03
145000	13121.70	7065.06	5062.05	4072.31	3487.72	3105.54	2838.87	2644.21
150000	13574.17	7308.69	5236.61	4212.73	3607.98	3212.63	2936.76	2735.39
155000	14026.64	7552.31	5411.16	4353.16	3728.25	3319.72	3034.65	2826.57
160000	14479.11	7795.93	5585.71	4493.58	3848.52	3426.80	3132.54	2917.75

158

AMOUNT OF LOAN	NUMBER OF YEARS IN TERM							
	9	10	15	20	25	30	35	40
$ 50	.87	.83	.72	.68	.66	.66	.65	.65
100	1.73	1.65	1.44	1.36	1.32	1.31	1.30	1.30
200	3.45	3.29	2.87	2.71	2.64	2.61	2.60	2.59
300	5.17	4.94	4.31	4.07	3.96	3.92	3.90	3.89
400	6.89	6.58	5.74	5.42	5.28	5.22	5.20	5.18
500	8.62	8.23	7.17	6.77	6.60	6.53	6.49	6.48
600	10.34	9.87	8.61	8.13	7.92	7.83	7.79	7.77
700	12.06	11.51	10.04	9.48	9.24	9.14	9.09	9.07
800	13.78	13.16	11.48	10.84	10.56	10.44	10.39	10.36
900	15.51	14.80	12.91	12.19	11.88	11.75	11.68	11.65
1000	17.23	16.45	14.34	13.54	13.20	13.05	12.98	12.95
2000	34.45	32.89	28.68	27.08	26.40	26.10	25.96	25.89
3000	51.68	49.33	43.02	40.62	39.60	39.14	38.93	38.84
4000	68.90	65.77	57.36	54.16	52.79	52.19	51.91	51.78
5000	86.12	82.21	71.70	67.70	65.99	65.23	64.88	64.72
6000	103.35	98.65	86.04	81.24	79.19	78.28	77.86	77.67
7000	120.57	115.09	100.38	94.78	92.39	91.32	90.84	90.61
8000	137.79	131.53	114.72	108.32	105.58	104.37	103.81	103.56
9000	155.02	147.97	129.06	121.85	118.78	117.41	116.79	116.50
10000	172.24	164.42	143.40	135.39	131.98	130.46	129.76	129.44
11000	189.46	180.86	157.74	148.93	145.18	143.50	142.74	142.39
12000	206.69	197.30	172.08	162.47	158.37	156.55	155.72	155.33
13000	223.91	213.74	186.42	176.01	171.57	169.59	168.69	168.28
14000	241.13	230.18	200.76	189.55	184.77	182.64	181.67	181.22
15000	258.36	246.62	215.10	203.09	197.97	195.68	194.64	194.16
16000	275.58	263.06	229.44	216.63	211.16	208.73	207.62	207.11
17000	292.80	279.50	243.78	230.16	224.36	221.77	220.59	220.05
18000	310.03	295.94	258.12	243.70	237.56	234.82	233.57	233.00
19000	327.25	312.39	272.46	257.24	250.76	247.86	246.55	245.94
20000	344.48	328.83	286.80	270.78	263.95	260.91	259.52	258.88
21000	361.70	345.27	301.14	284.32	277.15	273.95	272.50	271.83
22000	378.92	361.71	315.48	297.86	290.35	287.00	285.47	284.77
23000	396.15	378.15	329.82	311.40	303.55	300.04	298.45	297.72
24000	413.37	394.59	344.16	324.94	316.74	313.09	311.43	310.66
25000	430.59	411.03	358.50	338.48	329.94	326.13	324.40	323.60
26000	447.82	427.47	372.84	352.01	343.14	339.18	337.38	336.55
27000	465.04	443.91	387.18	365.55	356.34	352.22	350.35	349.49
28000	482.26	460.35	401.52	379.09	369.53	365.27	363.33	362.44
29000	499.49	476.80	415.86	392.63	382.73	378.31	376.30	375.38
30000	516.71	493.24	430.20	406.17	395.93	391.36	389.28	388.32
31000	533.93	509.68	444.54	419.71	409.13	404.41	402.26	401.27
32000	551.16	526.12	458.88	433.25	422.32	417.45	415.23	414.21
33000	568.38	542.56	473.22	446.79	435.52	430.50	428.21	427.16
34000	585.60	559.00	487.56	460.32	448.72	443.54	441.18	440.10
35000	602.83	575.44	501.90	473.86	461.92	456.59	454.16	453.04
40000	688.95	657.65	573.60	541.56	527.90	521.81	519.04	517.76
45000	775.06	739.85	645.30	609.25	593.89	587.04	583.92	582.48
50000	861.18	822.06	717.00	676.95	659.88	652.26	648.80	647.20
55000	947.30	904.26	788.70	744.64	725.86	717.49	713.68	711.92
60000	1033.42	986.47	860.40	812.33	791.85	782.72	778.56	776.64
65000	1119.53	1068.67	932.10	880.03	857.84	847.94	843.44	841.36
70000	1205.65	1150.88	1003.80	947.72	923.83	913.17	908.31	906.08
75000	1291.77	1233.08	1075.50	1015.42	989.81	978.39	973.19	970.80
80000	1377.89	1315.29	1147.20	1083.11	1055.80	1043.62	1038.07	1035.52
85000	1464.00	1397.49	1218.90	1150.80	1121.79	1108.84	1102.95	1100.24
90000	1550.12	1479.70	1290.60	1218.50	1187.78	1174.07	1167.83	1164.96
95000	1636.24	1561.91	1362.30	1286.19	1253.76	1239.30	1232.71	1229.68
100000	1722.36	1644.11	1434.00	1353.89	1319.75	1304.52	1297.59	1294.40
105000	1808.48	1726.32	1505.69	1421.58	1385.74	1369.75	1362.47	1359.12
110000	1894.59	1808.52	1577.39	1489.27	1451.72	1434.97	1427.35	1423.84
115000	1980.71	1890.73	1649.09	1556.97	1517.71	1500.20	1492.23	1488.56
120000	2066.83	1972.93	1720.79	1624.66	1583.70	1565.43	1557.11	1553.28
125000	2152.95	2055.14	1792.49	1692.36	1649.69	1630.65	1621.99	1618.00
130000	2239.06	2137.34	1864.19	1760.05	1715.67	1695.88	1686.87	1682.72
135000	2325.18	2219.55	1935.89	1827.74	1781.66	1761.10	1751.74	1747.44
140000	2411.30	2301.75	2007.59	1895.44	1847.65	1826.33	1816.62	1812.16
145000	2497.42	2383.96	2079.29	1963.13	1913.64	1891.55	1881.50	1876.88
150000	2583.53	2466.16	2150.99	2030.83	1979.62	1956.78	1946.38	1941.60
155000	2669.65	2548.37	2222.69	2098.52	2045.61	2022.01	2011.26	2006.32
160000	2755.77	2630.57	2294.39	2166.21	2111.60	2087.23	2076.14	2071.04

15.750% MONTHLY AMORTIZING PAYMENTS

AMOUNT OF LOAN	NUMBER OF YEARS IN TERM							
	1	2	3	4	5	6	7	8
$ 50	4.54	2.45	1.76	1.42	1.21	1.08	.99	.92
100	9.07	4.89	3.51	2.83	2.42	2.16	1.98	1.84
200	18.13	9.77	7.01	5.65	4.84	4.32	3.95	3.68
300	27.19	14.66	10.52	8.47	7.26	6.47	5.92	5.52
400	36.25	19.54	14.02	11.29	9.68	8.63	7.89	7.36
500	45.31	24.43	17.52	14.11	12.10	10.78	9.86	9.20
600	54.37	29.31	21.03	16.93	14.52	12.94	11.84	11.03
700	63.43	34.20	24.53	19.75	16.93	15.09	13.81	12.87
800	72.50	39.08	28.03	22.57	19.35	17.25	15.78	14.71
900	81.56	43.96	31.54	25.40	21.77	19.40	17.75	16.55
1000	90.62	48.85	35.04	28.22	24.19	21.56	19.72	18.39
2000	181.23	97.69	70.07	56.43	48.38	43.11	39.44	36.77
3000	271.84	146.54	105.11	84.64	72.56	64.67	59.16	55.15
4000	362.46	195.38	140.14	112.85	96.75	86.22	78.88	73.53
5000	453.07	244.22	175.17	141.07	120.93	107.78	98.60	91.92
6000	543.68	293.07	210.21	169.28	145.12	129.33	118.32	110.30
7000	634.29	341.91	245.24	197.49	169.30	150.89	138.04	128.68
8000	724.91	390.75	280.27	225.70	193.49	172.44	157.76	147.06
9000	815.52	439.60	315.31	253.92	217.67	193.99	177.48	165.44
10000	906.13	488.44	350.34	282.13	241.86	215.55	197.20	183.83
11000	996.74	537.29	385.38	310.34	266.04	237.10	216.92	202.21
12000	1087.36	586.13	420.41	338.55	290.23	258.66	236.64	220.59
13000	1177.97	634.97	455.44	366.77	314.42	280.21	256.36	238.97
14000	1268.58	683.82	490.48	394.98	338.60	301.77	276.08	257.35
15000	1359.19	732.66	525.51	423.19	362.79	323.32	295.80	275.74
16000	1449.81	781.50	560.54	451.40	386.97	344.88	315.52	294.12
17000	1540.42	830.35	595.58	479.62	411.16	366.43	335.24	312.50
18000	1631.03	879.19	630.61	507.83	435.34	387.98	354.96	330.88
19000	1721.64	928.04	665.65	536.04	459.53	409.54	374.68	349.26
20000	1812.26	976.88	700.68	564.25	483.71	431.09	394.40	367.65
21000	1902.87	1025.72	735.71	592.47	507.90	452.65	414.12	386.03
22000	1993.48	1074.57	770.75	620.68	532.08	474.20	433.84	404.41
23000	2084.09	1123.41	805.78	648.89	556.27	495.76	453.56	422.79
24000	2174.71	1172.25	840.81	677.10	580.46	517.31	473.28	441.17
25000	2265.32	1221.10	875.85	705.32	604.64	538.87	493.00	459.56
26000	2355.93	1269.94	910.88	733.53	628.83	560.42	512.72	477.94
27000	2446.55	1318.79	945.92	761.74	653.01	581.97	532.44	496.32
28000	2537.16	1367.63	980.95	789.95	677.20	603.53	552.16	514.70
29000	2627.77	1416.47	1015.98	818.16	701.38	625.08	571.88	533.08
30000	2718.38	1465.32	1051.02	846.38	725.57	646.64	591.60	551.47
31000	2809.00	1514.16	1086.05	874.59	749.75	668.19	611.32	569.85
32000	2899.61	1563.00	1121.08	902.80	773.94	689.75	631.04	588.23
33000	2990.22	1611.85	1156.12	931.01	798.12	711.30	650.76	606.61
34000	3080.83	1660.69	1191.15	959.23	822.31	732.86	670.48	625.00
35000	3171.45	1709.54	1226.19	987.44	846.49	754.41	690.20	643.38
40000	3624.51	1953.75	1401.35	1128.50	967.42	862.18	788.80	735.29
45000	4077.57	2197.97	1576.52	1269.56	1088.35	969.95	887.40	827.20
50000	4530.63	2442.19	1751.69	1410.63	1209.28	1077.73	986.00	919.11
55000	4983.70	2686.41	1926.86	1551.69	1330.20	1185.50	1084.60	1011.02
60000	5436.76	2930.63	2102.03	1692.75	1451.13	1293.27	1183.20	1102.93
65000	5889.82	3174.85	2277.20	1833.81	1572.06	1401.04	1281.80	1194.84
70000	6342.89	3419.07	2452.37	1974.87	1692.99	1508.82	1380.40	1286.75
75000	6795.95	3663.29	2627.53	2115.94	1813.91	1616.59	1479.00	1378.66
80000	7249.01	3907.50	2802.70	2257.00	1934.84	1724.36	1577.60	1470.57
85000	7702.08	4151.72	2977.87	2398.06	2055.77	1832.13	1676.20	1562.48
90000	8155.14	4395.94	3153.04	2539.12	2176.69	1939.90	1774.80	1654.39
95000	8608.20	4640.16	3328.21	2680.18	2297.62	2047.68	1873.40	1746.30
100000	9061.26	4884.38	3503.38	2821.25	2418.55	2155.45	1972.00	1838.21
105000	9514.33	5128.60	3678.55	2962.31	2539.47	2263.22	2070.60	1930.12
110000	9967.39	5372.82	3853.72	3103.37	2660.40	2370.99	2169.20	2022.03
115000	10420.45	5617.04	4028.88	3244.43	2781.33	2478.76	2267.80	2113.94
120000	10873.52	5861.25	4204.05	3385.49	2902.26	2586.54	2366.40	2205.85
125000	11326.58	6105.47	4379.22	3526.56	3023.18	2694.31	2465.00	2297.76
130000	11779.64	6349.69	4554.39	3667.62	3144.11	2802.08	2563.60	2389.67
135000	12232.71	6593.91	4729.56	3808.68	3265.04	2909.85	2662.20	2481.58
140000	12685.77	6838.13	4904.73	3949.74	3385.96	3017.63	2760.80	2573.49
145000	13138.83	7082.35	5079.90	4090.80	3506.89	3125.40	2859.40	2665.40
150000	13591.89	7326.57	5255.06	4231.87	3627.82	3233.17	2958.00	2757.31
155000	14044.96	7570.79	5430.23	4372.93	3748.75	3340.94	3056.60	2849.22
160000	14498.02	7815.00	5605.40	4513.99	3869.67	3448.71	3155.20	2941.14

160

MONTHLY AMORTIZING PAYMENTS 15.750%

AMOUNT OF LOAN	\multicolumn{8}{c}{NUMBER OF YEARS IN TERM}							
	9	10	15	20	25	30	35	40
$ 50	.87	.83	.73	.69	.67	.67	.66	.66
100	1.74	1.66	1.46	1.38	1.34	1.33	1.32	1.32
200	3.48	3.32	2.91	2.75	2.68	2.65	2.64	2.64
300	5.22	4.98	4.36	4.12	4.02	3.98	3.96	3.95
400	6.95	6.64	5.81	5.50	5.36	5.30	5.28	5.27
500	8.69	8.30	7.26	6.87	6.70	6.63	6.60	6.58
600	10.43	9.96	8.71	8.24	8.04	7.95	7.91	7.90
700	12.17	11.62	10.16	9.61	9.38	9.28	9.23	9.21
800	13.90	13.28	11.62	10.99	10.72	10.60	10.55	10.53
900	15.64	14.94	13.07	12.36	12.06	11.93	11.87	11.84
1000	17.38	16.60	14.52	13.73	13.40	13.25	13.19	13.16
2000	34.75	33.20	29.03	27.46	26.79	26.50	26.37	26.31
3000	52.13	49.79	43.54	41.18	40.18	39.74	39.55	39.46
4000	69.50	66.39	58.06	54.91	53.58	52.99	52.73	52.61
5000	86.88	82.98	72.57	68.63	66.97	66.24	65.91	65.76
6000	104.25	99.58	87.08	82.36	80.36	79.48	79.09	78.91
7000	121.62	116.18	101.60	96.08	93.76	92.73	92.27	92.06
8000	139.00	132.77	116.11	109.81	107.15	105.97	105.45	105.21
9000	156.37	149.37	130.62	123.53	120.54	119.22	118.63	118.36
10000	173.75	165.96	145.14	137.26	133.93	132.47	131.81	131.51
11000	191.12	182.56	159.65	150.98	147.33	145.71	144.99	144.66
12000	208.49	199.16	174.16	164.71	160.72	158.96	158.17	157.81
13000	225.87	215.75	188.68	178.43	174.11	172.21	171.35	170.96
14000	243.24	232.35	203.19	192.16	187.51	185.45	184.53	184.11
15000	260.62	248.94	217.70	205.89	200.90	198.70	197.71	197.26
16000	277.99	265.54	232.21	219.61	214.29	211.94	210.89	210.41
17000	295.36	282.13	246.73	233.34	227.68	225.19	224.07	223.56
18000	312.74	298.73	261.24	247.06	241.08	238.44	237.25	236.71
19000	330.11	315.33	275.75	260.79	254.47	251.68	250.43	249.86
20000	347.49	331.92	290.27	274.51	267.86	264.93	263.61	263.01
21000	364.86	348.52	304.78	288.24	281.26	278.17	276.79	276.16
22000	382.23	365.11	319.29	301.96	294.65	291.42	289.97	289.31
23000	399.61	381.71	333.81	315.69	308.04	304.67	303.15	302.46
24000	416.98	398.31	348.32	329.41	321.43	317.91	316.33	315.61
25000	434.36	414.90	362.83	343.14	334.83	331.16	329.51	328.76
26000	451.73	431.50	377.35	356.86	348.22	344.41	342.69	341.91
27000	469.10	448.09	391.86	370.59	361.61	357.65	355.87	355.06
28000	486.48	464.69	406.37	384.31	375.01	370.90	369.05	368.21
29000	503.85	481.28	420.88	398.04	388.40	384.14	382.23	381.36
30000	521.23	497.88	435.40	411.77	401.79	397.39	395.41	394.51
31000	538.60	514.48	449.91	425.49	415.18	410.64	408.59	407.66
32000	555.98	531.07	464.42	439.22	428.58	423.88	421.77	420.81
33000	573.35	547.67	478.94	452.94	441.97	437.13	434.95	433.96
34000	590.72	564.26	493.45	466.67	455.36	450.37	448.13	447.11
35000	608.10	580.86	507.96	480.39	468.76	463.62	461.31	460.26
40000	694.97	663.84	580.53	549.02	535.72	529.85	527.21	526.01
45000	781.84	746.82	653.09	617.65	602.69	596.08	593.11	591.76
50000	868.71	829.80	725.66	686.27	669.65	662.31	659.01	657.51
55000	955.58	912.78	798.22	754.90	736.61	728.54	724.91	723.26
60000	1042.45	995.76	870.79	823.53	803.58	794.78	790.81	789.01
65000	1129.32	1078.74	943.36	892.15	870.54	861.01	856.71	854.77
70000	1216.19	1161.71	1015.92	960.78	937.51	927.24	922.61	920.52
75000	1303.06	1244.69	1088.49	1029.41	1004.47	993.47	988.52	986.27
80000	1389.93	1327.67	1161.05	1098.03	1071.44	1059.70	1054.42	1052.02
85000	1476.80	1410.65	1233.62	1166.66	1138.40	1125.93	1120.32	1117.77
90000	1563.67	1493.63	1306.18	1235.29	1205.37	1192.16	1186.22	1183.52
95000	1650.54	1576.61	1378.75	1303.91	1272.33	1258.39	1252.12	1249.27
100000	1737.41	1659.59	1451.31	1372.54	1339.29	1324.62	1318.02	1315.02
105000	1824.28	1742.57	1523.88	1441.17	1406.26	1390.85	1383.92	1380.77
110000	1911.15	1825.55	1596.44	1509.79	1473.22	1457.08	1449.82	1446.52
115000	1998.02	1908.53	1669.01	1578.42	1540.19	1523.31	1515.72	1512.27
120000	2084.89	1991.51	1741.57	1647.05	1607.15	1589.55	1581.62	1578.02
125000	2171.76	2074.49	1814.14	1715.67	1674.12	1655.78	1647.52	1643.77
130000	2258.63	2157.47	1886.71	1784.30	1741.08	1722.01	1713.42	1709.53
135000	2345.50	2240.44	1959.27	1852.93	1808.05	1788.24	1779.32	1775.28
140000	2432.38	2323.42	2031.84	1921.55	1875.01	1854.47	1845.22	1841.03
145000	2519.25	2406.40	2104.40	1990.18	1941.97	1920.70	1911.12	1906.78
150000	2606.12	2489.38	2176.97	2058.81	2008.94	1986.93	1977.03	1972.53
155000	2692.99	2572.36	2249.53	2127.43	2075.90	2053.16	2042.93	2038.28
160000	2779.86	2655.34	2322.10	2196.06	2142.87	2119.39	2108.83	2104.03

16.000% MONTHLY AMORTIZING PAYMENTS

AMOUNT OF LOAN	NUMBER OF YEARS IN TERM							
	1	2	3	4	5	6	7	8
$ 50	4.54	2.45	1.76	1.42	1.22	1.09	1.00	.93
100	9.08	4.90	3.52	2.84	2.44	2.17	1.99	1.86
200	18.15	9.80	7.04	5.67	4.87	4.34	3.98	3.71
300	27.22	14.69	10.55	8.51	7.30	6.51	5.96	5.56
400	36.30	19.59	14.07	11.34	9.73	8.68	7.95	7.42
500	45.37	24.49	17.58	14.18	12.16	10.85	9.94	9.27
600	54.44	29.38	21.10	17.01	14.60	13.02	11.92	11.12
700	63.52	34.28	24.61	19.84	17.03	15.19	13.91	12.98
800	72.59	39.18	28.13	22.68	19.46	17.36	15.89	14.83
900	81.66	44.07	31.65	25.51	21.89	19.53	17.88	16.68
1000	90.74	48.97	35.16	28.35	24.32	21.70	19.87	18.53
2000	181.47	97.93	70.32	56.69	48.64	43.39	39.73	37.06
3000	272.20	146.89	105.48	85.03	72.96	65.08	59.59	55.59
4000	362.93	195.86	140.63	113.37	97.28	86.77	79.45	74.12
5000	453.66	244.82	175.79	141.71	121.60	108.46	99.32	92.65
6000	544.39	293.78	210.95	170.05	145.91	130.15	119.18	111.18
7000	635.12	342.75	246.10	198.39	170.23	151.85	139.04	129.71
8000	725.85	391.71	281.26	226.73	194.55	173.54	158.90	148.24
9000	816.58	440.67	316.42	255.07	218.87	195.23	178.76	166.76
10000	907.31	489.64	351.58	283.41	243.19	216.92	198.63	185.29
11000	998.04	538.60	386.73	311.75	267.50	238.62	218.49	203.82
12000	1088.78	587.56	421.89	340.09	291.82	260.31	238.35	222.35
13000	1179.51	636.53	457.05	492.20	368.43	316.14	282.00	258.21	240.88
14000	1270.24	685.49	492.20	396.77	340.46	303.69	278.07	259.41
15000	1360.97	734.45	527.36	425.11	364.78	325.38	297.94	277.94
16000	1451.70	783.41	562.52	453.45	389.09	347.07	317.80	296.47
17000	1542.43	832.38	597.67	481.79	413.41	368.77	337.66	314.99
18000	1633.16	881.34	632.83	510.13	437.73	390.46	357.52	333.52
19000	1723.89	930.30	667.99	538.47	462.05	412.15	377.38	352.05
20000	1814.62	979.27	703.15	566.81	486.37	433.84	397.25	370.58
21000	1905.35	1028.23	738.30	595.15	510.68	455.53	417.11	389.11
22000	1996.08	1077.19	773.46	623.49	535.00	477.23	436.97	407.64
23000	2086.81	1126.16	808.62	651.83	559.32	498.92	456.83	426.17
24000	2177.55	1175.12	843.77	680.17	583.64	520.61	476.69	444.70
25000	2268.28	1224.08	878.93	708.51	607.96	542.30	496.56	463.22
26000	2359.01	1273.05	914.09	736.85	632.27	563.99	516.42	481.75
27000	2449.74	1322.01	949.24	765.19	656.59	585.68	536.28	500.28
28000	2540.47	1370.97	984.40	793.53	680.91	607.38	556.14	518.81
29000	2631.20	1419.94	1019.56	821.87	705.23	629.07	576.00	537.34
30000	2721.93	1468.90	1054.72	850.21	729.55	650.76	595.87	555.87
31000	2812.66	1517.86	1089.87	878.55	753.86	672.45	615.73	574.40
32000	2903.39	1566.82	1125.03	906.89	778.18	694.14	635.59	592.93
33000	2994.12	1615.79	1160.19	935.23	802.50	715.84	655.45	611.45
34000	3084.85	1664.75	1195.34	963.57	826.82	737.53	675.32	629.98
35000	3175.59	1713.71	1230.50	991.91	851.14	759.22	695.18	648.51
40000	3629.24	1958.53	1406.29	1133.62	972.73	867.68	794.49	741.16
45000	4082.89	2203.34	1582.07	1275.32	1094.32	976.14	893.80	833.80
50000	4536.55	2448.16	1757.86	1417.02	1215.91	1084.60	993.11	926.44
55000	4990.20	2692.98	1933.64	1558.72	1337.50	1193.06	1092.42	1019.09
60000	5443.86	2937.79	2109.43	1700.42	1459.09	1301.52	1191.73	1111.73
65000	5897.51	3182.61	2285.21	1842.12	1580.68	1409.97	1291.04	1204.38
70000	6351.17	3427.42	2461.00	1983.82	1702.27	1518.43	1390.35	1297.02
75000	6804.82	3672.24	2636.78	2125.53	1823.86	1626.89	1489.66	1389.66
80000	7258.47	3917.05	2812.57	2267.23	1945.45	1735.35	1588.97	1482.31
85000	7712.13	4161.87	2988.35	2408.93	2067.04	1843.81	1688.28	1574.95
90000	8165.78	4406.68	3164.14	2550.63	2188.63	1952.27	1787.59	1667.60
95000	8619.44	4651.50	3339.92	2692.33	2310.22	2060.73	1886.90	1760.24
100000	9073.09	4896.32	3515.71	2834.03	2431.81	2169.19	1986.21	1852.88
105000	9526.75	5141.13	3691.49	2975.73	2553.40	2277.65	2085.52	1945.53
110000	9980.40	5385.95	3867.28	3117.44	2674.99	2386.11	2184.83	2038.17
115000	10434.05	5630.76	4043.06	3259.14	2796.58	2494.57	2284.14	2130.82
120000	10887.71	5875.58	4218.85	3400.84	2918.17	2603.03	2383.45	2223.46
125000	11341.36	6120.39	4394.63	3542.54	3039.76	2711.49	2482.76	2316.10
130000	11795.02	6365.21	4570.42	3684.24	3161.35	2819.94	2582.07	2408.75
135000	12248.67	6610.02	4746.20	3825.94	3282.94	2928.40	2681.38	2501.39
140000	12702.33	6854.84	4921.99	3967.64	3404.53	3036.86	2780.69	2594.04
145000	13155.98	7099.66	5097.77	4109.35	3526.12	3145.32	2880.00	2686.68
150000	13609.63	7344.47	5273.56	4251.05	3647.71	3253.78	2979.31	2779.32
155000	14063.29	7589.29	5449.35	4392.75	3769.30	3362.24	3078.62	2871.97
160000	14516.94	7834.10	5625.13	4534.45	3890.89	3470.70	3177.94	2964.61

162

AMOUNT OF LOAN	NUMBER OF YEARS IN TERM							
	9	10	15	20	25	30	35	40
$ 50	.88	.84	.74	.70	.68	.68	.67	.67
100	1.76	1.68	1.47	1.40	1.36	1.35	1.34	1.34
200	3.51	3.36	2.94	2.79	2.72	2.69	2.68	2.68
300	5.26	5.03	4.41	4.18	4.08	4.04	4.02	4.01
400	7.02	6.71	5.88	5.57	5.44	5.38	5.36	5.35
500	8.77	8.38	7.35	6.96	6.80	6.73	6.70	6.68
600	10.52	10.06	8.82	8.35	8.16	8.07	8.04	8.02
700	12.27	11.73	10.29	9.74	9.52	9.42	9.37	9.35
800	14.03	13.41	11.75	11.14	10.88	10.76	10.71	10.69
900	15.78	15.08	13.22	12.53	12.23	12.11	12.05	12.03
1000	17.53	16.76	14.69	13.92	13.59	13.45	13.39	13.36
2000	35.06	33.51	29.38	27.83	27.18	26.90	26.77	26.72
3000	52.58	50.26	44.07	41.74	40.77	40.35	40.16	40.07
4000	70.11	67.01	58.75	55.66	54.36	53.80	53.54	53.43
5000	87.63	83.76	73.44	69.57	67.95	67.24	66.93	66.79
6000	105.16	100.51	88.13	83.48	81.54	80.69	80.31	80.14
7000	122.68	117.26	102.81	97.39	95.13	94.14	93.70	93.50
8000	140.21	134.02	117.50	111.31	108.72	107.59	107.08	106.86
9000	157.73	150.77	132.19	125.22	122.30	121.03	120.47	120.21
10000	175.26	167.52	146.88	139.13	135.89	134.48	133.85	133.57
11000	192.78	184.27	161.56	153.04	149.48	147.93	147.24	146.93
12000	210.31	201.02	176.25	166.96	163.07	161.38	160.62	160.28
13000	227.83	217.77	190.94	180.87	176.66	174.82	174.01	173.64
14000	245.36	234.52	205.62	194.78	190.25	188.27	187.39	187.00
15000	262.88	251.27	220.31	208.69	203.84	201.72	200.78	200.35
16000	280.41	268.03	235.00	222.61	217.43	215.17	214.16	213.71
17000	297.93	284.78	249.68	236.52	231.02	228.61	227.54	227.07
18000	315.46	301.53	264.37	250.43	244.60	242.06	240.93	240.42
19000	332.98	318.28	279.06	264.34	258.19	255.51	254.31	253.78
20000	350.51	335.03	293.75	278.26	271.78	268.96	267.70	267.13
21000	368.04	351.78	308.43	292.17	285.37	282.40	281.08	280.49
22000	385.56	368.53	323.12	306.08	298.96	295.85	294.47	293.85
23000	403.09	385.29	337.81	319.99	312.55	309.30	307.85	307.20
24000	420.61	402.04	352.49	333.91	326.14	322.75	321.24	320.56
25000	438.14	418.79	367.18	347.82	339.73	336.19	334.62	333.92
26000	455.66	435.54	381.87	361.73	353.32	349.64	348.01	347.27
27000	473.19	452.29	396.55	375.64	366.90	363.09	361.39	360.63
28000	490.71	469.04	411.24	389.56	380.49	376.54	374.78	373.99
29000	508.24	485.79	425.93	403.47	394.08	389.98	388.16	387.34
30000	525.76	502.54	440.62	417.38	407.67	403.43	401.55	400.70
31000	543.29	519.30	455.30	431.29	421.26	416.88	414.93	414.06
32000	560.81	536.05	469.99	445.21	434.85	430.33	428.32	427.41
33000	578.34	552.80	484.68	459.12	448.44	443.77	441.70	440.77
34000	595.86	569.55	499.36	473.03	462.03	457.22	455.08	454.13
35000	613.39	586.30	514.05	486.94	475.62	470.67	468.47	467.48
40000	701.02	670.06	587.49	556.51	543.56	537.91	535.39	534.26
45000	788.64	753.81	660.92	626.07	611.50	605.15	602.32	601.05
50000	876.27	837.57	734.36	695.63	679.45	672.38	669.24	667.83
55000	963.89	921.33	807.79	765.20	747.39	739.62	736.16	734.61
60000	1051.52	1005.08	881.23	834.76	815.34	806.86	803.09	801.39
65000	1139.15	1088.84	954.66	904.32	883.28	874.10	870.01	868.18
70000	1226.77	1172.60	1028.10	973.88	951.23	941.33	936.93	934.96
75000	1314.40	1256.35	1101.53	1043.45	1019.17	1008.57	1003.86	1001.74
80000	1402.03	1340.11	1174.97	1113.01	1087.12	1075.81	1070.78	1068.52
85000	1489.65	1423.87	1248.40	1182.57	1155.06	1143.05	1137.70	1135.31
90000	1577.28	1507.62	1321.84	1252.14	1223.00	1210.29	1204.63	1202.09
95000	1664.90	1591.38	1395.27	1321.70	1290.95	1277.52	1271.55	1268.87
100000	1752.53	1675.14	1468.71	1391.26	1358.89	1344.76	1338.47	1335.65
105000	1840.16	1758.89	1542.14	1460.82	1426.84	1412.00	1405.40	1402.44
110000	1927.78	1842.65	1615.58	1530.39	1494.78	1479.24	1472.32	1469.22
115000	2015.41	1926.41	1689.01	1599.95	1562.73	1546.48	1539.24	1536.00
120000	2103.04	2010.16	1762.45	1669.51	1630.67	1613.71	1606.17	1602.78
125000	2190.66	2093.92	1835.88	1739.07	1698.62	1680.95	1673.09	1669.57
130000	2278.29	2177.68	1909.32	1808.64	1766.56	1748.19	1740.02	1736.35
135000	2365.91	2261.43	1982.75	1878.20	1834.50	1815.43	1806.94	1803.13
140000	2453.54	2345.19	2056.19	1947.76	1902.45	1882.66	1873.86	1869.91
145000	2541.17	2428.95	2129.62	2017.33	1970.39	1949.90	1940.79	1936.70
150000	2628.79	2512.70	2203.06	2086.89	2038.34	2017.14	2007.71	2003.48
155000	2716.42	2596.46	2276.49	2156.45	2106.28	2084.38	2074.63	2070.26
160000	2804.05	2680.21	2349.93	2226.01	2174.23	2151.62	2141.56	2137.04

16.250%　MONTHLY AMORTIZING PAYMENTS

AMOUNT OF LOAN	NUMBER OF YEARS IN TERM							
	1	2	3	4	5	6	7	8
$ 50	4.55	2.46	1.77	1.43	1.23	1.10	1.01	.94
100	9.09	4.91	3.53	2.85	2.45	2.19	2.01	1.87
200	18.17	9.82	7.06	5.70	4.90	4.37	4.01	3.74
300	27.26	14.73	10.59	8.55	7.34	6.55	6.01	5.61
400	36.34	19.64	14.12	11.39	9.79	8.74	8.01	7.48
500	45.43	24.55	17.65	14.24	12.23	10.92	10.01	9.34
600	54.51	29.45	21.17	17.09	14.68	13.10	12.01	11.21
700	63.60	34.36	24.70	19.93	17.12	15.29	14.01	13.08
800	72.68	39.27	28.23	22.78	19.57	17.47	16.01	14.95
900	81.77	44.18	31.76	25.63	22.01	19.65	18.01	16.81
1000	90.85	49.09	35.29	28.47	24.46	21.83	20.01	18.68
2000	181.70	98.17	70.57	56.94	48.91	43.66	40.01	37.36
3000	272.55	147.25	105.85	85.41	73.36	65.49	60.02	56.03
4000	363.40	196.34	141.13	113.88	97.81	87.32	80.02	74.71
5000	454.25	245.42	176.41	142.35	122.26	109.15	100.03	93.39
6000	545.10	294.50	211.69	170.82	146.71	130.98	120.03	112.06
7000	635.95	343.58	246.97	199.28	171.16	152.81	140.04	130.74
8000	726.80	392.67	282.25	227.75	195.61	174.64	160.04	149.41
9000	817.65	441.75	317.53	256.22	220.06	196.47	180.05	168.09
10000	908.50	490.83	352.81	284.69	244.52	218.30	200.05	186.77
11000	999.35	539.91	388.09	313.16	268.97	240.13	220.06	205.44
12000	1090.20	589.00	423.37	341.63	293.42	261.96	240.06	224.12
13000	1181.04	638.08	458.65	370.10	317.87	283.79	260.07	242.79
14000	1271.89	687.16	493.93	398.56	342.32	305.62	280.07	261.47
15000	1362.74	736.24	529.21	427.03	366.77	327.45	300.08	280.15
16000	1453.59	785.33	564.49	455.50	391.22	349.28	320.08	298.82
17000	1544.44	834.41	599.77	483.97	415.67	371.11	340.09	317.50
18000	1635.29	883.49	635.06	512.44	440.12	392.94	360.09	336.17
19000	1726.14	932.58	670.34	540.91	464.58	414.77	380.09	354.85
20000	1816.99	981.66	705.62	569.37	489.03	436.60	400.10	373.53
21000	1907.84	1030.74	740.90	597.84	513.48	458.43	420.10	392.20
22000	1998.69	1079.82	776.18	626.31	537.93	480.26	440.11	410.88
23000	2089.54	1128.91	811.46	654.78	562.38	502.09	460.11	429.56
24000	2180.39	1177.99	846.74	683.25	586.83	523.92	480.12	448.23
25000	2271.24	1227.07	882.02	711.72	611.28	545.75	500.12	466.91
26000	2362.08	1276.15	917.30	740.19	635.73	567.58	520.13	485.58
27000	2452.93	1325.24	952.58	768.65	660.18	589.41	540.13	504.26
28000	2543.78	1374.32	987.86	797.12	684.64	611.24	560.14	522.94
29000	2634.63	1423.40	1023.14	825.59	709.09	633.07	580.14	541.61
30000	2725.48	1472.48	1058.42	854.06	733.54	654.90	600.15	560.29
31000	2816.33	1521.57	1093.70	882.53	757.99	676.73	620.15	578.96
32000	2907.18	1570.65	1128.98	911.00	782.44	698.56	640.16	597.64
33000	2998.03	1619.73	1164.26	939.46	806.89	720.39	660.16	616.32
34000	3088.88	1668.81	1199.54	967.93	831.34	742.22	680.17	634.99
35000	3179.73	1717.90	1234.83	996.40	855.79	764.05	700.17	653.67
40000	3633.97	1963.31	1411.23	1138.74	978.05	873.19	800.19	747.05
45000	4088.22	2208.72	1587.63	1281.09	1100.30	982.34	900.22	840.43
50000	4542.47	2454.14	1764.03	1423.43	1222.56	1091.49	1000.24	933.81
55000	4996.71	2699.55	1940.44	1565.77	1344.81	1200.64	1100.26	1027.19
60000	5450.96	2944.96	2116.84	1708.11	1467.07	1309.79	1200.29	1120.57
65000	5905.20	3190.38	2293.24	1850.46	1589.33	1418.94	1300.31	1213.95
70000	6359.45	3435.79	2469.65	1992.80	1711.58	1528.09	1400.33	1307.33
75000	6813.70	3681.20	2646.05	2135.14	1833.84	1637.23	1500.36	1400.71
80000	7267.94	3926.62	2822.45	2277.48	1956.09	1746.38	1600.38	1494.09
85000	7722.19	4172.03	2998.85	2419.83	2078.35	1855.53	1700.41	1587.47
90000	8176.43	4417.44	3175.26	2562.17	2200.60	1964.68	1800.43	1680.85
95000	8630.68	4662.86	3351.66	2704.51	2322.86	2073.83	1900.45	1774.23
100000	9084.93	4908.27	3528.06	2846.85	2445.11	2182.98	2000.48	1867.61
105000	9539.17	5153.68	3704.47	2989.20	2567.37	2292.13	2100.50	1960.99
110000	9993.42	5399.10	3880.87	3131.54	2689.62	2401.27	2200.52	2054.37
115000	10447.66	5644.51	4057.27	3273.88	2811.88	2510.42	2300.55	2147.76
120000	10901.91	5889.92	4233.67	3416.22	2934.14	2619.57	2400.57	2241.14
125000	11356.16	6135.34	4410.08	3558.57	3056.39	2728.72	2500.59	2334.52
130000	11810.40	6380.75	4586.48	3700.91	3178.65	2837.87	2600.62	2427.90
135000	12264.65	6626.16	4762.88	3843.25	3300.90	2947.02	2700.64	2521.28
140000	12718.89	6871.58	4939.29	3985.59	3423.16	3056.17	2800.66	2614.66
145000	13173.14	7116.99	5115.69	4127.93	3545.41	3165.31	2900.69	2708.04
150000	13627.39	7362.40	5292.09	4270.28	3667.67	3274.46	3000.71	2801.42
155000	14081.63	7607.82	5468.50	4412.62	3789.92	3383.61	3100.74	2894.80
160000	14535.88	7853.23	5644.90	4554.96	3912.18	3492.76	3200.76	2988.18

AMOUNT OF LOAN	NUMBER OF YEARS IN TERM							
	9	**10**	**15**	**20**	**25**	**30**	**35**	**40**
$ 50	.89	.85	.75	.71	.69	.69	.68	.68
100	1.77	1.70	1.49	1.42	1.38	1.37	1.36	1.36
200	3.54	3.39	2.98	2.83	2.76	2.73	2.72	2.72
300	5.31	5.08	4.46	4.24	4.14	4.10	4.08	4.07
400	7.08	6.77	5.95	5.65	5.52	5.46	5.44	5.43
500	8.84	8.46	7.44	7.06	6.90	6.83	6.80	6.79
600	10.61	10.15	8.92	8.47	8.28	8.19	8.16	8.14
700	12.38	11.84	10.41	9.88	9.65	9.56	9.52	9.50
800	14.15	13.53	11.89	11.29	11.03	10.92	10.88	10.86
900	15.91	15.22	13.38	12.70	12.41	12.29	12.24	12.21
1000	17.68	16.91	14.87	14.11	13.79	13.65	13.59	13.57
2000	35.36	33.82	29.73	28.21	27.58	27.30	27.18	27.13
3000	53.04	50.73	44.59	42.31	41.36	40.95	40.77	40.69
4000	70.71	67.63	59.45	56.41	55.15	54.60	54.36	54.26
5000	88.39	84.54	74.31	70.51	68.93	68.25	67.95	67.82
6000	106.07	101.45	89.18	84.61	82.72	81.90	81.54	81.38
7000	123.74	118.36	104.04	98.71	96.50	95.55	95.13	94.95
8000	141.42	135.26	118.90	112.81	110.29	109.20	108.72	108.51
9000	159.10	152.17	133.76	126.91	124.07	122.85	122.31	122.07
10000	176.78	169.08	148.62	141.01	137.86	136.50	135.90	135.63
11000	194.45	185.99	163.48	155.11	151.64	150.15	149.49	149.20
12000	212.13	202.89	178.35	169.21	165.43	163.80	163.08	162.76
13000	229.81	219.80	193.21	183.31	179.22	177.45	176.67	176.32
14000	247.48	236.71	208.07	197.41	193.00	191.10	190.26	189.89
15000	265.16	253.62	222.93	211.51	206.79	204.75	203.85	203.45
16000	282.84	270.52	237.79	225.61	220.57	218.39	217.44	217.01
17000	300.51	287.43	252.65	239.71	234.36	232.04	231.03	230.58
18000	318.19	304.34	267.52	253.81	248.14	245.69	244.62	244.14
19000	335.87	321.25	282.38	267.91	261.93	259.34	258.21	257.70
20000	353.55	338.15	297.24	282.01	275.71	272.99	271.79	271.26
21000	371.22	355.06	312.10	296.11	289.50	286.64	285.38	284.83
22000	388.90	371.97	326.96	310.22	303.28	300.29	298.97	298.39
23000	406.58	388.88	341.82	324.32	317.07	313.94	312.56	311.95
24000	424.25	405.78	356.69	338.42	330.85	327.59	326.15	325.52
25000	441.93	422.69	371.55	352.52	344.64	341.24	339.74	339.08
26000	459.61	439.60	386.41	366.62	358.43	354.89	353.33	352.64
27000	477.29	456.51	401.27	380.72	372.21	368.54	366.92	366.21
28000	494.96	473.41	416.13	394.82	386.00	382.19	380.51	379.77
29000	512.64	490.32	430.99	408.92	399.78	395.84	394.10	393.33
30000	530.32	507.23	445.86	423.02	413.57	409.49	407.69	406.89
31000	547.99	524.14	460.72	437.12	427.35	423.13	421.28	420.46
32000	565.67	541.04	475.58	451.22	441.14	436.78	434.87	434.02
33000	583.35	557.95	490.44	465.32	454.92	450.43	448.46	447.58
34000	601.02	574.86	505.30	479.42	468.71	464.08	462.05	461.15
35000	618.70	591.77	520.16	493.52	482.49	477.73	475.64	474.71
40000	707.09	676.30	594.47	564.02	551.42	545.98	543.58	542.52
45000	795.47	760.84	668.78	634.53	620.35	614.23	611.53	610.34
50000	883.86	845.38	743.09	705.03	689.28	682.47	679.48	678.15
55000	972.24	929.91	817.40	775.53	758.20	750.72	747.43	745.97
60000	1060.63	1014.45	891.71	846.03	827.13	818.97	815.37	813.78
65000	1149.01	1098.99	966.01	916.53	896.06	887.21	883.32	881.60
70000	1237.40	1183.53	1040.32	987.04	964.98	955.46	951.27	949.41
75000	1325.78	1268.06	1114.63	1057.54	1033.91	1023.71	1019.22	1017.23
80000	1414.17	1352.60	1188.94	1128.04	1102.84	1091.95	1087.16	1085.04
85000	1502.55	1437.14	1263.25	1198.54	1171.77	1160.20	1155.11	1152.86
90000	1590.94	1521.67	1337.56	1269.05	1240.69	1228.45	1223.06	1220.67
95000	1679.33	1606.21	1411.86	1339.55	1309.62	1296.69	1291.01	1288.49
100000	1767.71	1690.75	1486.17	1410.05	1378.55	1364.94	1358.95	1356.30
105000	1856.10	1775.29	1560.48	1480.55	1447.47	1433.19	1426.90	1424.12
110000	1944.48	1859.82	1634.79	1551.06	1516.40	1501.43	1494.85	1491.93
115000	2032.87	1944.36	1709.10	1621.56	1585.33	1569.68	1562.80	1559.75
120000	2121.25	2028.90	1783.41	1692.06	1654.25	1637.93	1630.74	1627.56
125000	2209.64	2113.44	1857.72	1762.56	1723.18	1706.17	1698.69	1695.38
130000	2298.02	2197.97	1932.02	1833.06	1792.11	1774.42	1766.64	1763.19
135000	2386.41	2282.51	2006.33	1903.57	1861.04	1842.67	1834.59	1831.01
140000	2474.79	2367.05	2080.64	1974.07	1929.96	1910.91	1902.53	1898.82
145000	2563.18	2451.58	2154.95	2044.57	1998.89	1979.16	1970.48	1966.64
150000	2651.56	2536.12	2229.26	2115.07	2067.82	2047.41	2038.43	2034.45
155000	2739.95	2620.66	2303.57	2185.58	2136.74	2115.65	2106.38	2102.26
160000	2828.33	2705.20	2377.87	2256.08	2205.67	2183.90	2174.32	2170.08

16.500%　MONTHLY AMORTIZING PAYMENTS

AMOUNT OF LOAN	NUMBER OF YEARS IN TERM							
	1	2	3	4	5	6	7	8
$ 50	4.55	2.47	1.78	1.43	1.23	1.10	1.01	.95
100	9.10	4.93	3.55	2.86	2.46	2.20	2.02	1.89
200	18.20	9.85	5.72	4.92	4.40	4.03	3.77	
300	27.30	14.77	10.63	8.58	7.38	6.60	6.05	5.65
400	36.39	19.69	14.17	11.44	9.84	8.79	8.06	7.53
500	45.49	24.61	17.71	14.30	12.30	10.99	10.08	9.42
600	54.59	29.53	21.25	17.16	14.76	13.19	12.09	11.30
700	63.68	34.45	24.79	20.02	17.21	15.38	14.11	13.18
800	72.78	39.37	28.33	22.88	19.67	17.58	16.12	15.06
900	81.88	44.29	31.87	25.74	22.13	19.78	18.14	16.95
1000	90.97	49.21	35.41	28.60	24.59	21.97	20.15	18.83
2000	181.94	98.41	70.81	57.20	49.17	43.94	40.30	37.65
3000	272.91	147.61	106.22	85.80	73.76	65.91	60.45	56.48
4000	363.88	196.81	141.62	114.39	98.34	87.88	80.60	75.30
5000	454.84	246.02	177.03	142.99	122.93	109.85	100.74	94.12
6000	545.81	295.22	212.43	171.59	147.51	131.81	120.89	112.95
7000	636.78	344.42	247.84	200.18	172.10	153.78	141.04	131.77
8000	727.75	393.62	283.24	228.78	196.68	175.75	161.19	150.60
9000	818.71	442.83	318.64	257.38	221.27	197.72	181.34	169.42
10000	909.68	492.03	354.05	285.98	245.85	219.69	201.48	188.24
11000	1000.65	541.23	389.45	314.57	270.43	241.65	221.63	207.07
12000	1091.62	590.43	424.86	343.17	295.02	263.62	241.78	225.89
13000	1182.58	639.64	460.26	371.77	319.60	285.59	261.93	244.72
14000	1273.55	688.84	495.67	400.36	344.19	307.56	282.08	263.54
15000	1364.52	738.04	531.07	428.96	368.77	329.53	302.22	282.36
16000	1455.49	787.24	566.48	457.56	393.36	351.49	322.37	301.19
17000	1546.45	836.44	601.88	486.15	417.94	373.46	342.52	320.01
18000	1637.42	885.65	637.28	514.75	442.53	395.43	362.67	338.84
19000	1728.39	934.85	672.69	543.35	467.11	417.40	382.81	357.66
20000	1819.36	984.05	708.09	571.95	491.70	439.37	402.96	376.48
21000	1910.33	1033.25	743.50	600.54	516.28	461.33	423.11	395.31
22000	2001.29	1082.46	778.90	629.14	540.86	483.30	443.26	414.13
23000	2092.26	1131.66	814.31	657.74	565.45	505.27	463.41	432.96
24000	2183.23	1180.86	849.71	686.33	590.03	527.24	483.55	451.78
25000	2274.20	1230.06	885.11	714.93	614.62	549.21	503.70	470.60
26000	2365.16	1279.27	920.52	743.53	639.20	571.17	523.85	489.43
27000	2456.13	1328.47	955.92	772.12	663.79	593.14	544.00	508.25
28000	2547.10	1377.67	991.33	800.72	688.37	615.11	564.15	527.08
29000	2638.07	1426.87	1026.73	829.32	712.96	637.08	584.29	545.90
30000	2729.03	1476.08	1062.14	857.92	737.54	659.05	604.44	564.72
31000	2820.00	1525.28	1097.54	886.51	762.13	681.01	624.59	583.55
32000	2910.97	1574.48	1132.95	915.11	786.71	702.98	644.74	602.37
33000	3001.94	1623.68	1168.35	943.71	811.29	724.95	664.89	621.20
34000	3092.90	1672.88	1203.75	972.30	835.88	746.92	685.03	640.02
35000	3183.87	1722.09	1239.16	1000.90	860.46	768.89	705.18	658.84
40000	3638.71	1968.10	1416.18	1143.89	983.39	878.73	805.92	752.96
45000	4093.55	2214.11	1593.20	1286.87	1106.31	988.57	906.66	847.08
50000	4548.39	2460.12	1770.22	1429.86	1229.23	1098.41	1007.40	941.20
55000	5003.23	2706.13	1947.25	1572.84	1352.15	1208.25	1108.14	1035.32
60000	5458.06	2952.15	2124.27	1715.83	1475.08	1318.09	1208.88	1129.44
65000	5912.90	3198.16	2301.29	1858.81	1598.00	1427.93	1309.62	1223.56
70000	6367.74	3444.17	2478.31	2001.80	1720.92	1537.77	1410.36	1317.68
75000	6822.58	3690.18	2655.33	2144.78	1843.84	1647.61	1511.10	1411.80
80000	7277.42	3936.19	2832.36	2287.77	1966.77	1757.45	1611.84	1505.92
85000	7732.25	4182.20	3009.38	2430.75	2089.69	1867.29	1712.58	1600.04
90000	8187.09	4428.22	3186.40	2573.74	2212.61	1977.13	1813.32	1694.16
95000	8641.93	4674.23	3363.42	2716.72	2335.53	2086.97	1914.05	1788.28
100000	9096.77	4920.24	3540.44	2859.71	2458.46	2196.81	2014.79	1882.40
105000	9551.65	5166.25	3717.47	3002.69	2581.38	2306.65	2115.53	1976.52
110000	10006.45	5412.26	3894.49	3145.68	2704.30	2416.49	2216.27	2070.64
115000	10461.28	5658.28	4071.51	3288.66	2827.22	2526.33	2317.01	2164.76
120000	10916.12	5904.29	4248.53	3431.65	2950.15	2636.17	2417.75	2258.88
125000	11370.96	6150.30	4425.55	3574.63	3073.07	2746.01	2518.49	2353.00
130000	11825.80	6396.31	4602.57	3717.62	3195.99	2855.85	2619.23	2447.12
135000	12280.64	6642.32	4779.60	3860.60	3318.92	2965.69	2719.97	2541.24
140000	12735.47	6888.33	4956.62	4003.59	3441.84	3075.53	2820.71	2635.36
145000	13190.31	7134.35	5133.64	4146.57	3564.76	3185.37	2921.45	2729.48
150000	13645.15	7380.36	5310.66	4289.56	3687.68	3295.21	3022.19	2823.60
155000	14099.99	7626.37	5487.68	4432.54	3810.61	3405.05	3122.93	2917.72
160000	14554.83	7872.38	5664.71	4575.53	3933.53	3514.89	3223.67	3011.84

166

AMOUNT OF LOAN	NUMBER OF YEARS IN TERM							
	9	10	15	20	25	30	35	40
$ 50	.90	.86	.76	.72	.70	.70	.69	.69
100	1.79	1.71	1.51	1.43	1.40	1.39	1.38	1.38
200	3.57	3.42	3.01	2.86	2.80	2.78	2.76	2.76
300	5.35	5.12	4.52	4.29	4.20	4.16	4.14	4.14
400	7.14	6.83	6.02	5.72	5.60	5.55	5.52	5.51
500	8.92	8.54	7.52	7.15	7.00	6.93	6.90	6.89
600	10.70	10.24	9.03	8.58	8.39	8.32	8.28	8.27
700	12.49	11.95	10.53	10.01	9.79	9.70	9.66	9.64
800	14.27	13.66	12.03	11.44	11.19	11.09	11.04	11.02
900	16.05	15.36	13.54	12.87	12.59	12.47	12.42	12.40
1000	17.83	17.07	15.04	14.29	13.99	13.86	13.80	13.77
2000	35.66	34.13	30.08	28.58	27.97	27.71	27.59	27.54
3000	53.49	51.20	45.12	42.87	41.95	41.56	41.39	41.31
4000	71.32	68.26	60.15	57.16	55.93	55.41	55.18	55.08
5000	89.15	85.33	75.19	71.45	69.92	69.26	68.98	68.85
6000	106.98	102.39	90.23	85.74	83.90	83.11	82.77	82.62
7000	124.81	119.45	105.26	100.03	97.88	96.97	96.57	96.39
8000	142.64	136.52	120.30	114.32	111.86	110.82	110.36	110.16
9000	160.47	153.58	135.34	128.61	125.85	124.67	124.16	123.93
10000	178.30	170.65	150.38	142.90	139.83	138.52	137.95	137.70
11000	196.13	187.71	165.41	157.18	153.81	152.37	151.74	151.47
12000	213.96	204.78	180.45	171.47	167.79	166.22	165.54	165.24
13000	231.79	221.84	195.49	185.76	181.78	180.07	179.33	179.01
14000	249.62	238.90	210.52	200.05	195.76	193.93	193.13	192.78
15000	267.45	255.97	225.56	214.34	209.74	207.78	206.92	206.55
16000	285.28	273.03	240.60	228.63	223.72	221.63	220.72	220.32
17000	303.11	290.10	255.64	242.92	237.71	235.48	234.51	234.09
18000	320.94	307.16	270.67	257.21	251.69	249.33	248.31	247.86
19000	338.77	324.23	285.71	271.50	265.67	263.18	262.10	261.63
20000	356.59	341.29	300.75	285.79	279.65	277.03	275.90	275.40
21000	374.42	358.35	315.78	300.07	293.64	290.89	289.69	289.17
22000	392.25	375.42	330.82	314.36	307.62	304.74	303.48	302.94
23000	410.08	392.48	345.86	328.65	321.60	318.59	317.28	316.71
24000	427.91	409.55	360.90	342.94	335.58	332.44	331.07	330.48
25000	445.74	426.61	375.93	357.23	349.57	346.29	344.87	344.24
26000	463.57	443.67	390.97	371.52	363.55	360.14	358.66	358.01
27000	481.40	460.74	406.01	385.81	377.53	373.99	372.46	371.78
28000	499.23	477.80	421.04	400.10	391.51	387.85	386.25	385.55
29000	517.06	494.87	436.08	414.39	405.50	401.70	400.05	399.32
30000	534.89	511.93	451.12	428.68	419.48	415.55	413.84	413.09
31000	552.72	529.00	466.15	442.96	433.46	429.40	427.64	426.86
32000	570.55	546.06	481.19	457.25	447.44	443.25	441.43	440.63
33000	588.38	563.12	496.23	471.54	461.43	457.10	455.22	454.40
34000	606.21	580.19	511.27	485.83	475.41	470.96	469.02	468.17
35000	624.04	597.25	526.30	500.12	489.39	484.81	482.81	481.94
40000	713.18	682.57	601.49	571.57	559.30	554.06	551.79	550.79
45000	802.33	767.90	676.67	643.01	629.22	623.32	620.76	619.64
50000	891.48	853.22	751.86	714.46	699.13	692.58	689.73	688.48
55000	980.63	938.54	827.04	785.90	769.04	761.84	758.70	757.33
60000	1069.77	1023.86	902.23	857.35	838.95	831.09	827.68	826.18
65000	1158.92	1109.18	977.42	928.79	908.86	900.35	896.65	895.03
70000	1248.07	1194.50	1052.60	1000.24	978.78	969.61	965.62	963.88
75000	1337.22	1279.82	1127.79	1071.68	1048.69	1038.87	1034.60	1032.72
80000	1426.36	1365.14	1202.97	1143.13	1118.60	1108.12	1103.57	1101.57
85000	1515.51	1450.46	1278.16	1214.57	1188.51	1177.38	1172.54	1170.42
90000	1604.66	1535.79	1353.34	1286.02	1258.43	1246.64	1241.51	1239.27
95000	1693.81	1621.11	1428.53	1357.46	1328.34	1315.90	1310.49	1308.12
100000	1782.95	1706.43	1503.71	1428.91	1398.25	1385.15	1379.46	1376.96
105000	1872.10	1791.75	1578.90	1500.35	1468.16	1454.41	1448.43	1445.81
110000	1961.25	1877.07	1654.08	1571.80	1538.07	1523.67	1517.40	1514.66
115000	2050.40	1962.39	1729.27	1643.24	1607.99	1592.93	1586.38	1583.51
120000	2139.54	2047.71	1804.46	1714.69	1677.90	1662.18	1655.35	1652.36
125000	2228.69	2133.03	1879.64	1786.13	1747.81	1731.44	1724.32	1721.20
130000	2317.84	2218.35	1954.83	1857.58	1817.72	1800.70	1793.30	1790.05
135000	2406.99	2303.68	2030.01	1929.02	1887.64	1869.95	1862.27	1858.90
140000	2496.13	2389.00	2105.20	2000.47	1957.55	1939.21	1931.24	1927.75
145000	2585.28	2474.32	2180.38	2071.91	2027.46	2008.47	2000.21	1996.60
150000	2674.43	2559.64	2255.57	2143.36	2097.37	2077.73	2069.19	2065.44
155000	2763.57	2644.96	2330.75	2214.80	2167.28	2146.98	2138.16	2134.29
160000	2852.72	2730.28	2405.94	2286.25	2237.20	2216.24	2207.13	2203.14

16.750%　MONTHLY AMORTIZING PAYMENTS

AMOUNT OF LOAN	NUMBER OF YEARS IN TERM							
	1	2	3	4	5	6	7	8
$ 50	4.56	2.47	1.78	1.44	1.24	1.11	1.02	.95
100	9.11	4.94	3.56	2.88	2.48	2.22	2.03	1.90
200	18.22	9.87	7.11	5.75	4.95	4.43	4.06	3.80
300	27.33	14.80	10.66	8.62	7.42	6.64	6.09	5.70
400	36.44	19.73	14.22	11.50	9.89	8.85	8.12	7.59
500	45.55	24.67	17.77	14.37	12.36	11.06	10.15	9.49
600	54.66	29.60	21.32	17.24	14.84	13.27	12.18	11.39
700	63.77	34.53	24.87	20.11	17.31	15.48	14.21	13.29
800	72.87	39.46	28.43	22.99	19.78	17.69	16.24	15.18
900	81.98	44.40	31.98	25.86	22.25	19.90	18.27	17.08
1000	91.09	49.33	35.53	28.73	24.72	22.11	20.30	18.98
2000	182.18	98.65	71.06	57.46	49.44	44.21	40.59	37.95
3000	273.26	147.97	106.59	86.18	74.16	66.33	60.88	56.92
4000	364.35	197.29	142.12	114.91	98.88	88.43	81.17	75.89
5000	455.44	246.62	177.65	143.63	123.60	110.54	101.46	94.87
6000	546.52	295.94	213.18	172.36	148.32	132.65	121.75	113.84
7000	637.61	345.26	248.70	201.09	173.03	154.75	142.05	132.81
8000	728.69	394.58	284.23	229.81	197.75	176.86	162.34	151.78
9000	819.78	443.91	319.76	258.54	222.47	198.97	182.63	170.76
10000	910.87	493.23	355.29	287.26	247.19	221.07	202.92	189.73
11000	1001.95	542.55	390.82	315.99	271.91	243.18	223.21	208.70
12000	1093.04	591.87	426.35	344.72	296.63	265.29	243.50	227.67
13000	1184.12	641.19	461.87	373.44	321.34	287.39	263.80	246.65
14000	1275.21	690.52	497.40	402.17	346.06	309.50	284.09	265.62
15000	1366.30	739.84	532.93	430.89	370.78	331.61	304.38	284.59
16000	1457.38	789.16	568.46	459.62	395.50	353.71	324.67	303.56
17000	1548.47	838.48	603.99	488.34	420.22	375.82	344.96	322.54
18000	1639.56	887.81	639.52	517.07	444.94	397.93	365.25	341.51
19000	1730.64	937.13	675.05	545.80	469.65	420.04	385.55	360.48
20000	1821.73	986.45	710.57	574.52	494.37	442.14	405.84	379.45
21000	1912.81	1035.77	746.10	603.25	519.09	464.25	426.13	398.43
22000	2003.90	1085.09	781.63	631.97	543.81	486.36	446.42	417.40
23000	2094.99	1134.42	817.16	660.70	568.53	508.46	466.71	436.37
24000	2186.07	1183.74	852.69	689.43	593.25	530.57	487.00	455.34
25000	2277.16	1233.06	888.22	718.15	617.96	552.68	507.29	474.32
26000	2368.24	1282.38	923.74	746.88	642.68	574.78	527.59	493.29
27000	2459.33	1331.71	959.27	775.60	667.40	596.89	547.88	512.26
28000	2550.42	1381.03	994.80	804.33	692.12	619.00	568.17	531.23
29000	2641.50	1430.35	1030.33	833.06	716.84	641.10	588.46	550.21
30000	2732.59	1479.67	1065.86	861.78	741.56	663.21	608.75	569.18
31000	2823.68	1528.99	1101.39	890.51	766.27	685.32	629.04	588.15
32000	2914.76	1578.32	1136.91	919.23	790.99	707.42	649.34	607.12
33000	3005.85	1627.64	1172.44	947.96	815.71	729.53	669.63	626.10
34000	3096.93	1676.96	1207.97	976.68	840.43	751.64	689.92	645.07
35000	3188.02	1726.28	1243.50	1005.41	865.15	773.75	710.21	664.04
40000	3643.45	1972.89	1421.14	1149.04	988.74	884.28	811.67	758.90
45000	4098.88	2219.51	1598.78	1292.67	1112.33	994.81	913.13	853.76
50000	4554.31	2466.12	1776.43	1436.30	1235.92	1105.35	1014.58	948.63
55000	5009.74	2712.73	1954.07	1579.93	1359.51	1215.88	1116.04	1043.49
60000	5465.17	2959.34	2131.71	1723.56	1483.11	1326.42	1217.50	1138.35
65000	5920.60	3205.95	2309.35	1867.19	1606.70	1436.95	1318.96	1233.21
70000	6376.04	3452.56	2487.00	2010.82	1730.29	1547.49	1420.42	1328.07
75000	6831.47	3699.17	2664.64	2154.45	1853.88	1658.02	1521.87	1422.94
80000	7286.90	3945.78	2842.28	2298.07	1977.47	1768.55	1623.33	1517.80
85000	7742.33	4192.39	3019.92	2441.70	2101.06	1879.09	1724.79	1612.66
90000	8197.76	4439.01	3197.56	2585.33	2224.66	1989.62	1826.25	1707.52
95000	8653.19	4685.62	3375.21	2728.96	2348.25	2100.16	1927.71	1802.39
100000	9108.62	4932.23	3552.85	2872.59	2471.84	2210.69	2029.16	1897.25
105000	9564.05	5178.84	3730.49	3016.22	2595.43	2321.23	2130.62	1992.11
110000	10019.48	5425.45	3908.13	3159.85	2719.02	2431.76	2232.08	2086.97
115000	10474.91	5672.06	4085.77	3303.48	2842.62	2542.29	2333.54	2181.83
120000	10930.34	5918.67	4263.42	3447.11	2966.21	2652.83	2435.00	2276.70
125000	11385.17	6165.28	4441.06	3590.74	3089.80	2763.36	2536.45	2371.56
130000	11841.20	6411.89	4618.70	3734.37	3213.39	2873.90	2637.91	2466.42
135000	12296.64	6658.51	4796.34	3878.00	3336.98	2984.43	2739.37	2561.28
140000	12752.07	6905.12	4973.99	4021.63	3460.57	3094.97	2840.83	2656.14
145000	13207.50	7151.73	5151.63	4165.26	3584.17	3205.50	2942.29	2751.00
150000	13662.93	7398.34	5329.27	4308.88	3707.76	3316.03	3043.74	2845.87
155000	14118.36	7644.95	5506.91	4452.51	3831.35	3426.57	3145.20	2940.73
160000	14573.79	7891.56	5684.55	4596.14	3954.94	3537.10	3246.66	3035.59

168

MONTHLY AMORTIZING PAYMENTS 16.750%

AMOUNT OF LOAN	NUMBER OF YEARS IN TERM							
	9	10	15	20	25	30	35	40
$ 50	.90	.87	.77	.73	.71	.71	.70	.70
100	1.80	1.73	1.53	1.45	1.42	1.41	1.40	1.40
200	3.60	3.45	3.05	2.90	2.84	2.82	2.80	2.80
300	5.40	5.17	4.57	4.35	4.26	4.22	4.20	4.20
400	7.20	6.89	6.09	5.80	5.68	5.63	5.60	5.60
500	9.00	8.62	7.61	7.24	7.09	7.03	7.00	6.99
600	10.79	10.34	9.13	8.69	8.51	8.44	8.40	8.39
700	12.59	12.06	10.65	10.14	9.93	9.84	9.80	9.79
800	14.39	13.78	12.18	11.59	11.35	11.25	11.20	11.19
900	16.19	15.50	13.70	13.04	12.77	12.65	12.60	12.58
1000	17.99	17.23	15.22	14.48	14.18	14.06	14.00	13.98
2000	35.97	34.45	30.43	28.96	28.36	28.11	28.00	27.96
3000	53.95	51.67	45.64	43.44	42.54	42.17	42.00	41.93
4000	71.94	68.89	60.86	57.92	56.72	56.22	56.00	55.91
5000	89.92	86.11	76.07	72.40	70.90	70.27	70.00	69.89
6000	107.90	103.34	91.28	86.87	85.08	84.33	84.00	83.86
7000	125.88	120.56	106.50	101.35	99.26	98.38	98.00	97.84
8000	143.87	137.78	121.71	115.83	113.44	112.44	112.00	111.82
9000	161.85	155.00	136.92	130.31	127.62	126.49	126.00	125.79
10000	179.83	172.22	152.14	144.79	141.80	140.54	140.00	139.77
11000	197.81	189.44	167.35	159.27	155.98	154.60	154.00	153.74
12000	215.80	206.67	182.56	173.74	170.16	168.65	168.00	167.72
13000	233.78	223.89	197.78	188.22	184.34	182.71	182.00	181.70
14000	251.76	241.11	212.99	202.70	198.52	196.76	196.00	195.67
15000	269.74	258.33	228.20	217.18	212.70	210.81	210.00	209.65
16000	287.73	275.55	243.42	231.66	226.88	224.87	224.00	223.63
17000	305.71	292.77	258.63	246.13	241.06	238.92	238.00	237.60
18000	323.69	310.00	273.84	260.61	255.24	252.98	252.00	251.58
19000	341.67	327.22	289.06	275.09	269.42	267.03	266.00	265.56
20000	359.66	344.44	304.27	289.57	283.60	281.08	280.00	279.53
21000	377.64	361.66	319.48	304.05	297.78	295.14	294.00	293.51
22000	395.62	378.88	334.70	318.53	311.96	309.19	308.00	307.48
23000	413.60	396.10	349.91	333.00	326.14	323.25	322.00	321.46
24000	431.59	413.33	365.12	347.48	340.32	337.30	336.00	335.44
25000	449.57	430.55	380.34	361.96	354.50	351.35	350.00	349.41
26000	467.55	447.77	395.55	376.44	368.68	365.41	364.00	363.39
27000	485.53	464.99	410.76	390.92	382.86	379.46	378.00	377.37
28000	503.52	482.21	425.97	405.39	397.04	393.52	392.00	391.34
29000	521.50	499.43	441.19	419.87	411.22	407.57	406.00	405.32
30000	539.48	516.66	456.40	434.35	425.40	421.62	420.00	419.30
31000	557.46	533.88	471.61	448.83	439.58	435.68	434.00	433.27
32000	575.45	551.10	486.83	463.31	453.76	449.73	448.00	447.25
33000	593.43	568.32	502.04	477.79	467.94	463.79	462.00	461.22
34000	611.41	585.54	517.25	492.26	482.12	477.84	476.00	475.20
35000	629.39	602.76	532.47	506.74	496.30	491.89	490.00	489.18
40000	719.31	688.87	608.53	579.13	567.20	562.16	560.00	559.06
45000	809.22	774.98	684.60	651.52	638.10	632.43	630.00	628.94
50000	899.13	861.09	760.67	723.91	709.00	702.70	699.99	698.82
55000	989.04	947.20	836.73	796.31	779.90	772.97	769.99	768.70
60000	1078.96	1033.31	912.80	868.70	850.80	843.24	839.99	838.59
65000	1168.87	1119.41	988.86	941.09	921.70	913.51	909.99	908.47
70000	1258.78	1205.52	1064.93	1013.48	992.60	983.78	979.99	978.35
75000	1348.69	1291.63	1141.00	1085.87	1063.50	1054.05	1049.99	1048.23
80000	1438.61	1377.74	1217.06	1158.26	1134.40	1124.32	1119.99	1118.11
85000	1528.52	1463.85	1293.13	1230.65	1205.30	1194.59	1189.99	1187.99
90000	1618.43	1549.96	1369.19	1303.04	1276.20	1264.86	1259.99	1257.88
95000	1708.35	1636.06	1445.26	1375.43	1347.10	1335.13	1329.99	1327.76
100000	1798.26	1722.17	1521.33	1447.82	1418.00	1405.40	1399.98	1397.64
105000	1888.17	1808.28	1597.39	1520.22	1488.90	1475.67	1469.98	1467.52
110000	1978.08	1894.39	1673.46	1592.61	1559.80	1545.94	1539.98	1537.40
115000	2068.00	1980.50	1749.52	1665.00	1630.70	1616.21	1609.98	1607.29
120000	2157.91	2066.61	1825.59	1737.39	1701.60	1686.48	1679.98	1677.17
125000	2247.82	2152.71	1901.66	1809.78	1772.50	1756.75	1749.98	1747.05
130000	2337.73	2238.82	1977.72	1882.17	1843.40	1827.02	1819.98	1816.93
135000	2427.65	2324.93	2053.79	1954.56	1914.30	1897.29	1889.98	1886.81
140000	2517.56	2411.04	2129.85	2026.95	1985.20	1967.56	1959.98	1956.69
145000	2607.47	2497.15	2205.92	2099.34	2056.10	2037.83	2029.98	2026.58
150000	2697.38	2583.26	2281.99	2171.73	2127.00	2108.10	2099.97	2096.46
155000	2787.30	2669.36	2358.05	2244.13	2197.90	2178.37	2169.97	2166.34
160000	2877.21	2755.47	2434.12	2316.52	2268.80	2248.64	2239.97	2236.22

17.000%   MONTHLY AMORTIZING PAYMENTS

AMOUNT OF LOAN	NUMBER OF YEARS IN TERM							
	1	2	3	4	5	6	7	8
$ 50	4.57	2.48	1.79	1.45	1.25	1.12	1.03	.96
100	9.13	4.95	3.57	2.89	2.49	2.23	2.05	1.92
200	18.25	9.89	5.78	5.78	4.98	4.45	4.09	3.83
300	27.37	14.84	10.70	8.66	7.46	6.68	6.14	5.74
400	36.49	19.78	14.27	11.55	9.95	8.90	8.18	7.65
500	45.61	24.73	17.83	14.43	12.43	11.13	10.22	9.57
600	54.73	29.67	21.40	17.32	14.92	13.35	12.27	11.48
700	63.85	34.61	24.96	20.20	17.40	15.58	14.31	13.39
800	72.97	39.56	28.53	23.09	19.89	17.80	16.35	15.30
900	82.09	44.50	32.09	25.97	22.37	20.03	18.40	17.21
1000	91.21	49.45	35.66	28.86	24.86	22.25	20.44	19.13
2000	182.41	98.89	71.31	57.72	49.71	44.50	40.88	38.25
3000	273.62	148.33	106.96	86.57	74.56	66.74	61.31	57.37
4000	364.82	197.77	142.62	115.43	99.42	88.99	81.75	76.49
5000	456.03	247.22	178.27	144.28	124.27	111.24	102.18	95.61
6000	547.23	296.66	213.92	173.14	149.12	133.48	122.62	114.73
7000	638.44	346.10	249.57	201.99	173.97	155.73	143.06	133.86
8000	729.64	395.54	285.23	230.85	198.83	177.97	163.49	152.98
9000	820.85	444.99	320.88	259.70	223.68	200.22	183.93	172.10
10000	912.05	494.43	356.53	288.56	248.53	222.47	204.36	191.22
11000	1003.26	543.87	392.19	317.41	273.38	244.71	224.80	210.34
12000	1094.46	593.31	427.84	346.27	298.24	266.96	245.23	229.46
13000	1185.67	642.75	463.49	375.12	323.09	289.20	265.67	248.58
14000	1276.87	692.20	499.14	403.98	347.94	311.45	286.11	267.71
15000	1368.08	741.64	534.80	432.83	372.79	333.70	306.54	286.83
16000	1459.28	791.08	570.45	461.69	397.65	355.94	326.98	305.95
17000	1550.49	840.52	606.10	490.54	422.50	378.19	347.41	325.07
18000	1641.69	889.97	641.75	519.40	447.35	400.44	367.85	344.19
19000	1732.90	939.41	677.41	548.25	472.20	422.68	388.29	363.31
20000	1824.10	988.85	713.06	577.11	497.06	444.93	408.72	382.43
21000	1915.30	1038.29	748.71	605.96	521.91	467.17	429.16	401.56
22000	2006.51	1087.73	784.37	634.82	546.76	489.42	449.59	420.68
23000	2097.71	1137.18	820.02	663.67	571.61	511.67	470.03	439.80
24000	2188.92	1186.62	855.67	692.53	596.47	533.91	490.46	458.92
25000	2280.12	1236.06	891.32	721.38	621.32	556.16	510.90	478.04
26000	2371.33	1285.50	926.98	750.24	646.17	578.40	531.34	497.16
27000	2462.53	1334.95	962.63	779.09	671.02	600.65	551.77	516.28
28000	2553.74	1384.39	998.28	807.95	695.88	622.90	572.21	535.41
29000	2644.94	1433.83	1033.93	836.80	720.73	645.14	592.64	554.53
30000	2736.15	1483.27	1069.59	865.66	745.58	667.39	613.08	573.65
31000	2827.35	1532.72	1105.24	894.51	770.43	689.64	633.51	592.77
32000	2918.56	1582.16	1140.89	923.37	795.29	711.88	653.95	611.89
33000	3009.76	1631.60	1176.55	952.22	820.14	734.13	674.39	631.01
34000	3100.97	1681.04	1212.20	981.08	844.99	756.37	694.82	650.13
35000	3192.17	1730.48	1247.85	1009.93	869.85	778.62	715.26	669.26
40000	3648.20	1977.70	1426.11	1154.21	994.11	889.85	817.44	764.86
45000	4104.22	2224.91	1604.38	1298.48	1118.37	1001.08	919.62	860.47
50000	4560.24	2472.12	1782.64	1442.76	1242.63	1112.31	1021.80	956.08
55000	5016.27	2719.33	1960.91	1587.03	1366.90	1223.54	1123.97	1051.68
60000	5472.29	2966.54	2139.17	1731.31	1491.16	1334.77	1226.15	1147.29
65000	5928.31	3213.75	2317.43	1875.58	1615.42	1446.00	1328.33	1242.90
70000	6384.34	3460.96	2495.70	2019.86	1739.69	1557.23	1430.51	1338.51
75000	6840.36	3708.17	2673.96	2164.13	1863.95	1668.46	1532.69	1434.11
80000	7296.39	3955.39	2852.22	2308.41	1988.21	1779.70	1634.87	1529.72
85000	7752.41	4202.60	3030.49	2452.68	2112.47	1890.93	1737.05	1625.33
90000	8208.43	4449.81	3208.75	2596.96	2236.74	2002.16	1839.23	1720.94
95000	8664.46	4697.02	3387.01	2741.23	2361.00	2113.39	1941.41	1816.54
100000	9120.48	4944.23	3565.28	2885.51	2485.26	2224.62	2043.59	1912.15
105000	9576.50	5191.44	3743.54	3029.78	2609.53	2335.85	2145.76	2007.76
110000	10032.53	5438.65	3921.81	3174.06	2733.79	2447.08	2247.94	2103.36
115000	10488.55	5685.87	4100.07	3318.33	2858.05	2558.31	2350.12	2198.97
120000	10944.58	5933.08	4278.33	3462.61	2982.31	2669.54	2452.30	2294.58
125000	11400.60	6180.29	4456.60	3606.89	3106.58	2780.77	2554.48	2390.19
130000	11856.62	6427.50	4634.86	3751.16	3230.84	2892.00	2656.66	2485.79
135000	12312.65	6674.71	4813.12	3895.44	3355.10	3003.23	2758.84	2581.40
140000	12768.67	6921.92	4991.39	4039.71	3479.37	3114.46	2861.02	2677.01
145000	13224.69	7169.13	5169.65	4183.99	3603.63	3225.69	2963.20	2772.62
150000	13680.72	7416.34	5347.91	4328.26	3727.89	3336.92	3065.38	2868.22
155000	14136.74	7663.56	5526.18	4472.54	3852.15	3448.16	3167.55	2963.83
160000	14592.77	7910.77	5704.44	4616.81	3976.42	3559.39	3269.73	3059.44

170

AMOUNT OF LOAN	NUMBER OF YEARS IN TERM							
	9	10	15	20	25	30	35	40
$ 50	.91	.87	.77	.74	.72	.72	.72	.71
100	1.82	1.74	1.54	1.47	1.44	1.43	1.43	1.42
200	3.63	3.48	3.08	2.94	2.88	2.86	2.85	2.84
300	5.45	5.22	4.62	4.41	4.32	4.28	4.27	4.26
400	7.26	6.96	6.16	5.87	5.76	5.71	5.69	5.68
500	9.07	8.69	7.70	7.34	7.19	7.13	7.11	7.10
600	10.89	10.43	9.24	8.81	8.63	8.56	8.53	8.51
700	12.70	12.17	10.78	10.27	10.07	9.98	9.95	9.93
800	14.51	13.91	12.32	11.74	11.51	11.41	11.37	11.35
900	16.33	15.65	13.86	13.21	12.95	12.84	12.79	12.77
1000	18.14	17.38	15.40	14.67	14.38	14.26	14.21	14.19
2000	36.28	34.76	30.79	29.34	28.76	28.52	28.42	28.37
3000	54.41	52.14	46.18	44.01	43.14	42.78	42.62	42.55
4000	72.55	69.52	61.57	58.68	57.52	57.03	56.83	56.74
5000	90.69	86.90	76.96	73.35	71.89	71.29	71.03	70.92
6000	108.82	104.28	92.35	88.01	86.27	85.55	85.24	85.10
7000	126.96	121.66	107.74	102.68	100.65	99.80	99.44	99.29
8000	145.09	139.04	123.13	117.35	115.03	114.06	113.65	113.47
9000	163.23	156.42	138.52	132.02	129.41	128.32	127.85	127.65
10000	181.37	173.80	153.91	146.69	143.78	142.57	142.06	141.84
11000	199.50	191.18	169.30	161.35	158.16	156.83	156.26	156.02
12000	217.64	208.56	184.69	176.02	172.54	171.09	170.47	170.20
13000	235.78	225.94	200.08	190.69	186.92	185.34	184.67	184.39
14000	253.91	243.32	215.47	205.36	201.30	199.60	198.88	198.57
15000	272.05	260.70	230.86	220.03	215.67	213.86	213.08	212.75
16000	290.18	278.08	246.25	234.69	230.05	228.11	227.29	226.94
17000	308.32	295.46	261.64	249.36	244.43	242.37	241.49	241.12
18000	326.46	312.84	277.03	264.03	258.81	256.63	255.70	255.30
19000	344.59	330.22	292.42	278.70	273.19	270.88	269.90	269.49
20000	362.73	347.60	307.81	293.37	287.56	285.14	284.11	283.67
21000	380.86	364.98	323.20	308.03	301.94	299.40	298.32	297.85
22000	399.00	382.36	338.59	322.70	316.32	313.65	312.52	312.04
23000	417.14	399.74	353.98	337.37	330.70	327.91	326.73	326.22
24000	435.27	417.12	369.37	352.04	345.08	342.17	340.93	340.40
25000	453.41	434.50	384.76	366.71	359.45	356.42	355.14	354.59
26000	471.55	451.88	400.15	381.37	373.83	370.68	369.34	368.77
27000	489.68	469.26	415.54	396.04	388.21	384.94	383.55	382.95
28000	507.82	486.64	430.93	410.71	402.59	399.19	397.75	397.14
29000	525.95	504.02	446.32	425.38	416.97	413.45	411.96	411.32
30000	544.09	521.40	461.71	440.05	431.34	427.71	426.16	425.50
31000	562.23	538.78	477.10	454.71	445.72	441.96	440.37	439.69
32000	580.36	556.16	492.49	469.38	460.10	456.22	454.57	453.87
33000	598.50	573.54	507.88	484.05	474.48	470.48	468.78	468.05
34000	616.64	590.92	523.27	498.72	488.86	484.73	482.98	482.24
35000	634.77	608.30	538.66	513.39	503.23	498.99	497.19	496.42
40000	725.45	695.20	615.61	586.74	575.12	570.28	568.22	567.33
45000	816.13	782.09	692.56	660.07	647.01	641.56	639.24	638.25
50000	906.81	868.99	769.51	733.41	718.90	712.84	710.27	709.17
55000	997.50	955.89	846.46	806.75	790.79	784.13	781.29	780.08
60000	1088.18	1042.79	923.41	880.09	862.68	855.41	852.32	851.00
65000	1178.86	1129.69	1000.36	953.43	934.57	926.69	923.35	921.92
70000	1269.54	1216.59	1077.31	1026.77	1006.46	997.98	994.37	992.83
75000	1360.22	1303.49	1154.26	1100.11	1078.35	1069.26	1065.40	1063.75
80000	1450.90	1390.39	1231.21	1173.45	1150.24	1140.55	1136.43	1134.66
85000	1541.58	1477.29	1308.16	1246.79	1222.13	1211.83	1207.45	1205.58
90000	1632.26	1564.18	1385.11	1320.13	1294.02	1283.11	1278.48	1276.50
95000	1722.94	1651.08	1462.06	1393.47	1365.91	1354.40	1349.50	1347.41
100000	1813.62	1737.98	1539.01	1466.81	1437.80	1425.68	1420.53	1418.33
105000	1904.30	1824.88	1615.96	1540.15	1509.69	1496.96	1491.56	1489.24
110000	1994.99	1911.78	1692.91	1613.49	1581.58	1568.25	1562.58	1560.16
115000	2085.67	1998.68	1769.86	1686.83	1653.47	1639.53	1633.61	1631.08
120000	2176.35	2085.68	1846.81	1760.17	1725.36	1710.82	1704.64	1701.99
125000	2267.03	2172.48	1923.76	1833.51	1797.25	1782.10	1775.66	1772.91
130000	2357.71	2259.37	2000.71	1906.85	1869.14	1853.38	1846.69	1843.83
135000	2448.39	2346.27	2077.66	1980.19	1941.03	1924.67	1917.72	1914.74
140000	2539.07	2433.17	2154.61	2053.53	2012.92	1995.95	1988.74	1985.66
145000	2629.75	2520.07	2231.56	2126.87	2084.81	2067.23	2059.77	2056.57
150000	2720.43	2606.97	2308.51	2200.21	2156.70	2138.52	2130.79	2127.49
155000	2811.11	2693.87	2385.46	2273.55	2228.59	2209.80	2201.82	2198.41
160000	2901.80	2780.77	2462.41	2346.89	2300.48	2281.09	2272.85	2269.32

171

MONTHLY AMORTIZING PAYMENTS

AMOUNT OF LOAN	NUMBER OF YEARS IN TERM							
	1	2	3	4	5	6	7	8
$ 50	4.57	2.48	1.79	1.45	1.25	1.12	1.03	.97
100	9.14	4.96	3.58	2.90	2.50	2.24	2.06	1.93
200	18.27	9.92	7.16	5.80	5.00	4.48	4.12	3.86
300	27.40	14.87	10.74	8.70	7.50	6.72	6.18	5.79
400	36.53	19.83	14.32	11.60	10.00	8.96	8.24	7.71
500	45.67	24.79	17.89	14.50	12.50	11.20	10.30	9.64
600	54.80	29.74	21.47	17.40	15.00	13.44	12.35	11.57
700	63.93	34.70	25.05	20.29	17.50	15.68	14.41	13.49
800	73.06	39.65	28.63	23.19	19.99	17.91	16.47	15.42
900	82.20	44.61	32.20	26.09	22.49	20.15	18.53	17.35
1000	91.33	49.57	35.78	28.99	24.99	22.39	20.59	19.28
2000	182.65	99.13	71.56	57.97	49.98	44.78	41.17	38.55
3000	273.98	148.69	107.34	86.96	74.97	67.16	61.75	57.82
4000	365.30	198.25	143.11	115.94	99.95	89.55	82.33	77.09
5000	456.62	247.82	178.89	144.93	124.94	111.93	102.91	96.36
6000	547.95	297.38	214.67	173.91	149.93	134.32	123.49	115.63
7000	639.27	346.94	250.45	202.90	174.92	156.71	144.07	134.90
8000	730.59	396.50	286.22	231.88	199.90	179.09	164.65	154.17
9000	821.92	446.07	322.00	260.87	224.89	201.48	185.23	173.44
10000	913.24	495.63	357.78	289.85	249.88	223.86	205.81	192.72
11000	1004.56	545.19	393.55	318.84	274.86	246.25	226.39	211.99
12000	1095.89	594.75	429.33	347.82	299.85	268.64	246.97	231.26
13000	1187.21	644.32	465.11	376.80	324.84	291.02	267.55	250.53
14000	1278.53	693.88	500.89	405.79	349.83	313.41	288.13	269.80
15000	1369.86	743.44	536.66	434.77	374.81	335.79	308.71	289.07
16000	1461.18	793.00	572.44	463.76	399.80	358.18	329.29	308.34
17000	1552.50	842.57	608.22	492.74	424.79	380.56	349.87	327.61
18000	1643.83	892.13	644.00	521.73	449.77	402.95	370.45	346.88
19000	1735.15	941.69	679.77	550.71	474.76	425.34	391.04	366.15
20000	1826.47	991.25	715.55	579.70	499.75	447.72	411.62	385.43
21000	1917.80	1040.82	751.33	608.68	524.74	470.11	432.20	404.70
22000	2009.12	1090.38	787.10	637.67	549.72	492.49	452.78	423.97
23000	2100.44	1139.94	822.88	666.65	574.71	514.88	473.36	443.24
24000	2191.77	1189.50	858.66	695.63	599.70	537.27	493.94	462.51
25000	2283.09	1239.07	894.44	724.62	624.68	559.65	514.52	481.78
26000	2374.41	1288.63	930.21	753.60	649.67	582.04	535.10	501.05
27000	2465.74	1338.19	965.99	782.59	674.66	604.42	555.68	520.32
28000	2557.06	1387.75	1001.77	811.57	699.65	626.81	576.26	539.59
29000	2648.38	1437.32	1037.55	840.56	724.63	649.19	596.84	558.87
30000	2739.71	1486.88	1073.32	869.54	749.62	671.58	617.42	578.14
31000	2831.03	1536.44	1109.10	898.53	774.61	693.97	638.00	597.41
32000	2922.35	1586.00	1144.88	927.51	799.60	716.35	658.58	616.68
33000	3013.68	1635.57	1180.65	956.50	824.58	738.74	679.16	635.95
34000	3105.00	1685.13	1216.43	985.48	849.57	761.12	699.74	655.22
35000	3196.33	1734.69	1252.21	1014.46	874.56	783.51	720.32	674.49
40000	3652.94	1982.50	1431.10	1159.39	999.49	895.44	823.23	770.85
45000	4109.56	2230.32	1609.98	1304.31	1124.43	1007.37	926.13	867.20
50000	4566.18	2478.13	1788.87	1449.23	1249.36	1119.30	1029.03	963.56
55000	5022.79	2725.94	1967.75	1594.16	1374.30	1231.23	1131.93	1059.91
60000	5479.41	2973.75	2146.64	1739.08	1499.24	1343.16	1234.84	1156.27
65000	5936.03	3221.57	2325.53	1884.00	1624.17	1455.09	1337.74	1252.62
70000	6392.65	3469.38	2504.41	2028.92	1749.11	1567.02	1440.64	1348.98
75000	6849.26	3717.19	2683.30	2173.85	1874.04	1678.94	1543.55	1445.33
80000	7305.88	3965.00	2862.19	2318.77	1998.98	1790.87	1646.45	1541.69
85000	7762.50	4212.82	3041.07	2463.69	2123.92	1902.80	1749.35	1638.04
90000	8219.11	4460.63	3219.96	2608.61	2248.85	2014.73	1852.25	1734.40
95000	8675.73	4708.44	3398.85	2753.54	2373.79	2126.66	1955.16	1830.75
100000	9132.35	4956.25	3577.73	2898.46	2498.72	2238.59	2058.06	1927.11
105000	9588.97	5204.06	3756.62	3043.38	2623.66	2350.52	2160.96	2023.47
110000	10045.58	5451.88	3935.50	3188.31	2748.60	2462.45	2263.86	2119.82
115000	10502.20	5699.69	4114.39	3333.23	2873.53	2574.38	2366.77	2216.18
120000	10958.82	5947.50	4293.28	3478.15	2998.47	2686.31	2469.67	2312.53
125000	11415.43	6195.31	4472.16	3623.07	3123.40	2798.24	2572.57	2408.89
130000	11872.05	6443.13	4651.05	3768.00	3248.34	2910.17	2675.48	2505.24
135000	12328.67	6690.94	4829.94	3912.92	3373.28	3022.10	2778.38	2601.60
140000	12785.29	6938.75	5008.82	4057.84	3498.21	3134.03	2881.28	2697.95
145000	13241.90	7186.56	5187.71	4202.76	3623.15	3245.95	2984.18	2794.31
150000	13698.52	7434.38	5366.60	4347.69	3748.08	3357.88	3087.09	2890.66
155000	14155.14	7682.19	5545.48	4492.61	3873.02	3469.81	3189.99	2987.02
160000	14611.75	7930.00	5724.37	4637.53	3997.96	3581.74	3292.89	3083.37

AMOUNT OF LOAN	NUMBER OF YEARS IN TERM							
	9	10	15	20	25	30	35	40
$ 50	.92	.88	.78	.75	.73	.73	.73	.72
100	1.83	1.76	1.56	1.49	1.46	1.45	1.45	1.44
200	3.66	3.51	3.12	2.98	2.92	2.90	2.89	2.88
300	5.49	5.27	4.68	4.46	4.38	4.34	4.33	4.32
400	7.32	7.02	6.23	5.95	5.84	5.79	5.77	5.76
500	9.15	8.77	7.79	7.43	7.29	7.23	7.21	7.20
600	10.98	10.53	9.35	8.92	8.75	8.68	8.65	8.64
700	12.81	12.28	10.90	10.41	10.21	10.13	10.09	10.08
800	14.64	14.04	12.46	11.89	11.67	11.57	11.53	11.52
900	16.47	15.79	14.02	13.38	13.12	13.02	12.97	12.96
1000	18.30	17.54	15.57	14.86	14.58	14.46	14.42	14.40
2000	36.59	35.08	31.14	29.72	29.16	28.92	28.83	28.79
3000	54.88	52.62	46.71	44.58	43.73	43.38	43.24	43.18
4000	73.17	70.16	62.28	59.44	58.31	57.84	57.65	57.57
5000	91.46	87.70	77.84	74.30	72.89	72.30	72.06	71.96
6000	109.75	105.24	93.41	89.16	87.46	86.76	86.47	86.35
7000	128.04	122.77	108.98	104.01	102.04	101.22	100.88	100.74
8000	146.33	140.31	124.55	118.87	116.62	115.68	115.29	115.13
9000	164.62	157.85	140.11	133.73	131.19	130.14	129.70	129.52
10000	182.91	175.39	155.68	148.59	145.77	144.60	144.11	143.91
11000	201.20	192.93	171.25	163.45	160.35	159.06	158.53	158.30
12000	219.49	210.47	186.82	178.31	174.92	173.52	172.94	172.69
13000	237.78	228.01	202.38	193.16	189.50	187.98	187.35	187.08
14000	256.07	245.54	217.95	208.02	204.07	202.44	201.76	201.47
15000	274.36	263.08	233.52	222.88	218.65	216.90	216.17	215.86
16000	292.65	280.62	249.09	237.74	233.23	231.36	230.58	230.25
17000	310.94	298.16	264.65	252.60	247.80	245.82	244.99	244.64
18000	329.23	315.70	280.22	267.46	262.38	260.28	259.40	259.03
19000	347.52	333.24	295.79	282.31	276.96	274.74	273.81	273.42
20000	365.81	350.78	311.36	297.17	291.53	289.20	288.22	287.81
21000	384.10	368.31	326.92	312.03	306.11	303.66	302.63	302.20
22000	402.40	385.85	342.49	326.89	320.69	318.12	317.05	316.59
23000	420.69	403.39	358.06	341.75	335.26	332.58	331.46	330.98
24000	438.98	420.93	373.63	356.61	349.84	347.04	345.87	345.37
25000	457.27	438.47	389.19	371.47	364.42	361.50	360.28	359.76
26000	475.56	456.01	404.76	386.32	378.99	375.96	374.69	374.15
27000	493.85	473.54	420.33	401.18	393.57	390.42	389.10	388.54
28000	512.14	491.08	435.90	416.04	408.14	404.88	403.51	402.93
29000	530.43	508.62	451.46	430.90	422.72	419.34	417.92	417.32
30000	548.72	526.16	467.03	445.76	437.30	433.80	432.33	431.71
31000	567.01	543.70	482.60	460.62	451.87	448.26	446.74	446.10
32000	585.30	561.24	498.17	475.47	466.45	462.72	461.15	460.49
33000	603.59	578.78	513.73	490.33	481.03	477.18	475.57	474.88
34000	621.88	596.31	529.30	505.19	495.60	491.64	489.98	489.27
35000	640.17	613.85	544.87	520.05	510.18	506.10	504.39	503.66
40000	731.62	701.55	622.71	594.34	583.06	578.40	576.44	575.61
45000	823.08	789.24	700.55	668.63	655.94	650.70	648.50	647.57
50000	914.53	876.93	778.38	742.93	728.83	723.00	720.55	719.52
55000	1005.98	964.62	856.22	817.22	801.71	795.30	792.61	791.47
60000	1097.43	1052.32	934.06	891.51	874.59	867.60	864.66	863.42
65000	1188.88	1140.01	1011.90	965.80	947.47	939.90	936.71	935.37
70000	1280.34	1227.70	1089.73	1040.09	1020.35	1012.20	1008.77	1007.32
75000	1371.79	1315.39	1167.57	1114.39	1093.24	1084.49	1080.82	1079.27
80000	1463.24	1403.09	1245.41	1188.68	1166.12	1156.79	1152.88	1151.22
85000	1554.69	1490.78	1323.25	1262.97	1239.00	1229.09	1224.93	1223.17
90000	1646.15	1578.47	1401.09	1337.26	1311.88	1301.39	1296.99	1295.13
95000	1737.60	1666.16	1478.92	1411.55	1384.76	1373.69	1369.04	1367.08
100000	1829.05	1753.86	1556.76	1485.85	1457.65	1445.99	1441.10	1439.03
105000	1920.50	1841.55	1634.60	1560.14	1530.53	1518.29	1513.15	1510.98
110000	2011.96	1929.24	1712.44	1634.43	1603.41	1590.59	1585.21	1582.93
115000	2103.41	2016.93	1790.28	1708.72	1676.29	1662.89	1657.26	1654.88
120000	2194.86	2104.63	1868.11	1783.02	1749.17	1735.19	1729.32	1726.83
125000	2286.31	2192.32	1945.95	1857.31	1822.06	1807.49	1801.37	1798.78
130000	2377.76	2280.01	2023.79	1931.60	1894.94	1879.79	1873.42	1870.74
135000	2469.22	2367.70	2101.63	2005.89	1967.82	1952.09	1945.48	1942.69
140000	2560.67	2455.40	2179.46	2080.18	2040.70	2024.39	2017.53	2014.64
145000	2652.12	2543.09	2257.30	2154.48	2113.59	2096.68	2089.59	2086.59
150000	2743.57	2630.78	2335.14	2228.77	2186.47	2168.98	2161.64	2158.54
155000	2835.03	2718.47	2412.98	2303.06	2259.35	2241.28	2233.70	2230.49
160000	2926.48	2806.17	2490.82	2377.35	2332.23	2313.58	2305.75	2302.44

173

17.500% MONTHLY AMORTIZING PAYMENTS

AMOUNT OF LOAN	NUMBER OF YEARS IN TERM							
	1	2	3	4	5	6	7	8
$ 50	4.58	2.49	1.80	1.46	1.26	1.13	1.04	.98
100	9.15	4.97	3.60	2.92	2.52	2.26	2.08	1.95
200	18.29	9.94	7.19	5.83	5.03	4.51	4.15	3.89
300	27.44	14.91	10.78	8.74	7.54	6.76	6.22	5.83
400	36.58	19.88	14.37	11.65	10.05	9.02	8.30	7.77
500	45.73	24.85	17.96	14.56	12.57	11.27	10.37	9.72
600	54.87	29.81	21.55	17.47	15.08	13.52	12.44	11.66
700	64.01	34.78	25.14	20.39	17.59	15.77	14.51	13.60
800	73.16	39.75	28.73	23.30	20.10	18.03	16.59	15.54
900	82.30	44.72	32.32	26.21	22.61	20.28	18.66	17.48
1000	91.45	49.69	35.91	29.12	25.13	22.53	20.73	19.43
2000	182.89	99.37	71.81	58.23	50.25	45.06	41.46	38.85
3000	274.33	149.05	107.71	87.35	75.37	67.58	62.18	58.27
4000	365.77	198.74	143.61	116.46	100.49	90.11	82.91	77.69
5000	457.22	248.42	179.52	145.58	125.62	112.64	103.63	97.11
6000	548.66	298.10	215.42	174.69	150.74	135.16	124.36	116.53
7000	640.10	347.78	251.32	203.81	175.86	157.69	145.09	135.95
8000	731.54	397.47	287.22	232.92	200.98	180.21	165.81	155.37
9000	822.98	447.15	323.12	262.03	226.10	202.74	186.54	174.80
10000	914.43	496.83	359.03	291.15	251.23	225.27	207.26	194.22
11000	1005.87	546.52	394.93	320.26	276.35	247.79	227.99	213.64
12000	1097.31	596.20	430.83	349.38	301.47	270.32	248.71	233.06
13000	1188.75	645.88	466.73	378.49	326.59	292.84	269.44	252.48
14000	1280.20	695.56	502.63	407.61	351.72	315.37	290.17	271.90
15000	1371.64	745.25	538.54	436.72	376.84	337.90	310.89	291.32
16000	1463.08	794.93	574.44	465.83	401.96	360.42	331.62	310.74
17000	1554.52	844.61	610.34	494.95	427.08	382.95	352.34	330.17
18000	1645.96	894.30	646.24	524.06	452.20	405.47	373.07	349.59
19000	1737.41	943.98	682.14	553.18	477.33	428.00	393.80	369.01
20000	1828.85	993.66	718.05	582.29	502.45	450.53	414.52	388.43
21000	1920.29	1043.34	753.95	611.41	527.57	473.05	435.25	407.85
22000	2011.73	1093.03	789.85	640.52	552.69	495.58	455.97	427.27
23000	2103.18	1142.71	825.75	669.64	577.82	518.10	476.70	446.69
24000	2194.62	1192.39	861.65	698.75	602.94	540.63	497.42	466.11
25000	2286.06	1242.08	897.56	727.86	628.06	563.16	518.15	485.54
26000	2377.50	1291.76	933.46	756.98	653.18	585.68	538.88	504.96
27000	2468.94	1341.44	969.36	786.09	678.30	608.21	559.60	524.38
28000	2560.39	1391.12	1005.26	815.21	703.43	630.73	580.33	543.80
29000	2651.83	1440.81	1041.16	844.32	728.55	653.26	601.05	563.22
30000	2743.27	1490.49	1077.07	873.44	753.67	675.79	621.78	582.64
31000	2834.71	1540.17	1112.97	902.55	778.79	698.31	642.50	602.06
32000	2926.16	1589.86	1148.87	931.66	803.92	720.84	663.23	621.48
33000	3017.60	1639.54	1184.77	960.78	829.04	743.36	683.96	640.90
34000	3109.04	1689.22	1220.68	989.89	854.16	765.89	704.68	660.33
35000	3200.48	1738.90	1256.58	1019.01	879.28	788.42	725.41	679.75
40000	3657.69	1987.32	1436.09	1164.58	1004.89	901.05	829.04	776.85
45000	4114.90	2235.73	1615.60	1310.15	1130.50	1013.68	932.67	873.96
50000	4572.12	2484.15	1795.11	1455.72	1256.12	1126.31	1036.29	971.07
55000	5029.33	2732.56	1974.62	1601.30	1381.73	1238.94	1139.92	1068.17
60000	5486.54	2980.98	2154.13	1746.87	1507.34	1351.57	1243.55	1165.28
65000	5943.75	3229.39	2333.64	1892.44	1632.95	1464.20	1347.18	1262.38
70000	6400.96	3477.80	2513.15	2038.01	1758.56	1576.83	1450.81	1359.49
75000	6858.17	3726.22	2692.66	2183.58	1884.17	1689.46	1554.44	1456.60
80000	7315.38	3974.63	2872.17	2329.15	2009.78	1802.09	1658.07	1553.70
85000	7772.59	4223.05	3051.68	2474.73	2135.39	1914.72	1761.70	1650.81
90000	8229.80	4471.46	3231.19	2620.30	2261.00	2027.35	1865.33	1747.91
95000	8687.01	4719.88	3410.70	2765.87	2386.62	2139.98	1968.96	1845.02
100000	9144.23	4968.29	3590.21	2911.44	2512.23	2252.61	2072.58	1942.13
105000	9601.44	5216.70	3769.72	3057.01	2637.84	2365.24	2176.21	2039.23
110000	10058.65	5465.12	3949.23	3202.59	2763.45	2477.87	2279.84	2136.34
115000	10515.86	5713.53	4128.74	3348.16	2889.06	2590.50	2383.47	2233.44
120000	10973.07	5961.95	4308.25	3493.73	3014.67	2703.13	2487.10	2330.55
125000	11430.28	6210.36	4487.76	3639.30	3140.28	2815.76	2590.73	2427.66
130000	11887.49	6458.78	4667.27	3784.87	3265.89	2928.39	2694.36	2524.76
135000	12344.70	6707.19	4846.78	3930.45	3391.50	3041.02	2797.99	2621.87
140000	12801.91	6955.60	5026.29	4076.02	3517.11	3153.65	2901.62	2718.97
145000	13259.12	7204.02	5205.80	4221.59	3642.73	3266.28	3005.25	2816.08
150000	13716.34	7452.43	5385.31	4367.16	3768.34	3378.91	3108.87	2913.19
155000	14173.55	7700.85	5564.83	4512.73	3893.95	3491.54	3212.50	3010.29
160000	14630.76	7949.26	5744.34	4658.30	4019.56	3604.17	3316.13	3107.40

MONTHLY AMORTIZING PAYMENTS 17.500%

AMOUNT OF LOAN	NUMBER OF YEARS IN TERM							
	9	10	15	20	25	30	35	40
$ 50	.93	.89	.79	.76	.74	.74	.74	.73
100	1.85	1.77	1.58	1.51	1.48	1.47	1.47	1.46
200	3.69	3.54	3.15	3.01	2.96	2.94	2.93	2.92
300	5.54	5.31	4.73	4.52	4.44	4.40	4.39	4.38
400	7.38	7.08	6.30	6.02	5.92	5.87	5.85	5.84
500	9.23	8.85	7.88	7.53	7.39	7.34	7.31	7.30
600	11.07	10.62	9.45	9.03	8.87	8.80	8.78	8.76
700	12.92	12.39	11.03	10.54	10.35	10.27	10.24	10.22
800	14.76	14.16	12.60	12.04	11.83	11.74	11.70	11.68
900	16.61	15.93	14.18	13.55	13.30	13.20	13.16	13.14
1000	18.45	17.70	15.75	15.05	14.78	14.67	14.62	14.60
2000	36.90	35.40	31.50	30.10	29.56	29.33	29.24	29.20
3000	55.34	53.10	47.24	45.15	44.33	43.99	43.86	43.80
4000	73.79	70.80	62.99	60.20	59.11	58.66	58.47	58.39
5000	92.23	88.49	78.73	75.25	73.88	73.32	73.09	72.99
6000	110.68	106.19	94.48	90.30	88.66	87.98	87.71	87.59
7000	129.12	123.89	110.23	105.35	103.43	102.65	102.32	102.19
8000	147.57	141.59	125.97	120.40	118.21	117.31	116.94	116.78
9000	166.01	159.29	141.72	135.45	132.98	131.97	131.56	131.38
10000	184.46	176.98	157.46	150.50	147.76	146.64	146.17	145.98
11000	202.90	194.68	173.21	165.55	162.53	161.30	160.79	160.58
12000	221.35	212.38	188.95	180.60	177.31	175.96	175.41	175.17
13000	239.79	230.08	204.70	195.65	192.08	190.63	190.02	189.77
14000	258.24	247.78	220.45	210.70	206.86	205.29	204.64	204.37
15000	276.69	265.47	236.19	225.75	221.63	219.95	219.26	218.97
16000	295.13	283.17	251.94	240.80	236.41	234.62	233.87	233.56
17000	313.58	300.87	267.68	255.85	251.19	249.28	248.49	248.16
18000	332.02	318.57	283.43	270.89	265.96	263.94	263.11	262.76
19000	350.47	336.26	299.17	285.94	280.74	278.61	277.72	277.35
20000	368.91	353.96	314.92	300.99	295.51	293.27	292.34	291.95
21000	387.36	371.66	330.67	316.04	310.29	307.93	306.96	306.55
22000	405.80	389.36	346.41	331.09	325.06	322.60	321.57	321.15
23000	424.25	407.06	362.16	346.14	339.84	337.26	336.19	335.74
24000	442.69	424.75	377.90	361.19	354.61	351.92	350.81	350.34
25000	461.14	442.45	393.65	376.24	369.39	366.59	365.42	364.94
26000	479.58	460.15	409.40	391.29	384.16	381.25	380.04	379.54
27000	498.03	477.85	425.14	406.34	398.94	395.91	394.66	394.13
28000	516.47	495.55	440.89	421.39	413.71	410.58	409.27	408.73
29000	534.92	513.24	456.63	436.44	428.49	425.24	423.89	423.33
30000	553.37	530.94	472.38	451.49	443.26	439.90	438.51	437.93
31000	571.81	548.64	488.12	466.54	458.04	454.57	453.12	452.52
32000	590.26	566.34	503.87	481.59	472.81	469.23	467.74	467.12
33000	608.70	584.03	519.62	496.64	487.59	483.89	482.36	481.72
34000	627.15	601.73	535.36	511.69	502.37	498.56	496.97	496.31
35000	645.59	619.43	551.11	526.73	517.14	513.22	511.59	510.91
40000	737.82	707.92	629.84	601.98	591.02	586.54	584.68	583.90
45000	830.05	796.41	708.57	677.23	664.89	659.85	657.76	656.89
50000	922.27	884.90	787.29	752.48	738.77	733.17	730.84	729.87
55000	1014.50	973.39	866.02	827.72	812.65	806.48	803.93	802.86
60000	1106.73	1061.88	944.75	902.97	886.52	879.80	877.01	875.85
65000	1198.95	1150.37	1023.48	978.22	960.40	953.12	950.09	948.83
70000	1291.18	1238.86	1102.21	1053.46	1034.28	1026.43	1023.18	1021.82
75000	1383.41	1327.35	1180.94	1128.71	1108.15	1099.75	1096.26	1094.81
80000	1475.63	1415.84	1259.67	1203.96	1182.03	1173.07	1169.35	1167.79
85000	1567.86	1504.32	1338.40	1279.21	1255.91	1246.38	1242.43	1240.78
90000	1660.09	1592.81	1417.13	1354.45	1329.78	1319.70	1315.51	1313.77
95000	1752.31	1681.30	1495.85	1429.70	1403.66	1393.01	1388.60	1386.75
100000	1844.54	1769.79	1574.58	1504.95	1477.53	1466.33	1461.68	1459.74
105000	1936.77	1858.28	1653.31	1580.19	1551.41	1539.65	1534.76	1532.73
110000	2028.99	1946.77	1732.04	1655.44	1625.29	1612.96	1607.85	1605.71
115000	2121.22	2035.26	1810.77	1730.69	1699.16	1686.28	1680.93	1678.70
120000	2213.45	2123.75	1889.50	1805.94	1773.04	1759.60	1754.02	1751.69
125000	2305.67	2212.24	1968.23	1881.18	1846.92	1832.91	1827.10	1824.67
130000	2397.90	2300.73	2046.96	1956.43	1920.79	1906.23	1900.18	1897.66
135000	2490.13	2389.22	2125.69	2031.68	1994.67	1979.54	1973.27	1970.65
140000	2582.35	2477.71	2204.41	2106.92	2068.55	2052.86	2046.35	2043.63
145000	2674.58	2566.20	2283.14	2182.17	2142.42	2126.18	2119.43	2116.62
150000	2766.81	2654.69	2361.87	2257.42	2216.30	2199.49	2192.52	2189.61
155000	2859.03	2743.18	2440.60	2332.66	2290.18	2272.81	2265.60	2262.59
160000	2951.26	2831.67	2519.33	2407.91	2364.05	2346.13	2338.69	2335.58

MONTHLY AMORTIZING PAYMENTS

AMOUNT OF LOAN	NUMBER OF YEARS IN TERM							
	1	2	3	4	5	6	7	8
$ 50	4.58	2.50	1.81	1.47	1.27	1.14	1.05	.98
100	9.16	4.99	3.61	2.93	2.53	2.27	2.09	1.96
200	18.32	9.97	7.21	5.85	5.06	4.54	4.18	3.92
300	27.47	14.95	10.81	8.78	7.58	6.81	6.27	5.88
400	36.63	19.93	14.42	11.70	10.11	9.07	8.35	7.83
500	45.79	24.91	18.02	14.63	12.63	11.34	10.44	9.79
600	54.94	29.89	21.62	17.55	15.16	13.61	12.53	11.75
700	64.10	34.87	25.22	20.48	17.69	15.87	14.62	13.71
800	73.25	39.85	28.83	23.40	20.21	18.14	16.70	15.66
900	82.41	44.83	32.43	26.33	22.74	20.41	18.79	17.62
1000	91.57	49.81	36.03	29.25	25.26	22.67	20.88	19.58
2000	183.13	99.61	72.06	58.49	50.52	45.34	41.75	39.15
3000	274.69	149.42	108.09	87.74	75.78	68.01	62.62	58.72
4000	366.25	199.22	144.11	116.98	101.04	90.67	83.49	78.29
5000	457.81	249.02	180.14	146.23	126.29	113.34	104.36	97.86
6000	549.37	298.83	216.17	175.47	151.55	136.01	125.23	117.44
7000	640.93	348.63	252.19	204.72	176.81	158.67	146.11	137.01
8000	732.49	398.43	288.22	233.96	202.07	181.34	166.98	156.58
9000	824.05	448.24	324.25	263.21	227.32	204.01	187.85	176.15
10000	915.62	498.04	360.27	292.45	252.58	226.67	208.72	195.72
11000	1007.18	547.84	396.30	321.69	277.84	249.34	229.59	215.30
12000	1098.74	597.65	432.33	350.94	303.10	272.01	250.46	234.87
13000	1190.30	647.45	468.36	380.18	328.35	294.67	271.34	254.44
14000	1281.86	697.25	504.38	409.43	353.61	317.34	292.21	274.01
15000	1373.42	747.06	540.41	438.67	378.87	340.01	313.08	293.58
16000	1464.98	796.86	576.44	467.92	404.13	362.67	333.95	313.16
17000	1556.54	846.66	612.47	497.16	429.38	385.34	354.82	332.73
18000	1648.10	896.47	648.49	526.41	454.64	408.01	375.69	352.30
19000	1739.67	946.27	684.52	555.65	479.90	430.67	396.56	371.87
20000	1831.23	996.07	720.55	584.90	505.16	453.34	417.44	391.44
21000	1922.79	1045.88	756.57	614.14	530.42	476.01	438.31	411.02
22000	2014.35	1095.68	792.60	643.38	555.67	498.67	459.18	430.59
23000	2105.91	1145.48	828.63	672.63	580.93	521.34	480.05	450.16
24000	2197.47	1195.29	864.66	701.87	606.19	544.01	500.92	469.73
25000	2289.03	1245.09	900.68	731.12	631.45	566.67	521.79	489.30
26000	2380.59	1294.89	936.71	760.36	656.70	589.34	542.67	508.88
27000	2472.15	1344.70	972.74	789.61	681.96	612.01	563.54	528.45
28000	2563.71	1394.50	1008.76	818.85	707.22	634.67	584.41	548.02
29000	2655.28	1444.30	1044.79	848.10	732.48	657.34	605.28	567.59
30000	2746.84	1494.11	1080.82	877.34	757.73	680.01	626.15	587.16
31000	2838.40	1543.91	1116.85	906.59	782.99	702.67	647.02	606.73
32000	2929.96	1593.71	1152.87	935.83	808.25	725.34	667.89	626.31
33000	3021.52	1643.52	1188.90	965.07	833.51	748.01	688.77	645.88
34000	3113.08	1693.32	1224.93	994.32	858.76	770.67	709.64	665.45
35000	3204.64	1743.12	1260.95	1023.56	884.02	793.34	730.51	685.02
40000	3662.45	1992.14	1441.09	1169.79	1010.31	906.67	834.87	782.88
45000	4120.25	2241.16	1621.22	1316.01	1136.60	1020.01	939.23	880.74
50000	4578.06	2490.17	1801.36	1462.23	1262.89	1133.34	1043.58	978.60
55000	5035.86	2739.19	1981.50	1608.45	1389.17	1246.67	1147.94	1076.46
60000	5493.67	2988.21	2161.63	1754.68	1515.46	1360.01	1252.30	1174.32
65000	5951.47	3237.23	2341.77	1900.90	1641.75	1473.34	1356.66	1272.18
70000	6409.28	3486.24	2521.90	2047.12	1768.04	1586.67	1461.01	1370.04
75000	6867.08	3735.26	2702.04	2193.34	1894.33	1700.01	1565.37	1467.90
80000	7324.89	3984.28	2882.17	2339.57	2020.61	1813.34	1669.73	1565.76
85000	7782.69	4233.29	3062.31	2485.79	2146.90	1926.67	1774.09	1663.62
90000	8240.50	4482.31	3242.44	2632.01	2273.19	2040.01	1878.45	1761.48
95000	8698.31	4731.33	3422.58	2778.23	2399.48	2153.34	1982.80	1859.34
100000	9156.11	4980.34	3602.72	2924.46	2525.77	2266.67	2087.16	1957.20
105000	9613.92	5229.36	3782.85	3070.68	2652.06	2380.01	2191.52	2055.06
110000	10071.72	5478.38	3962.99	3216.90	2778.34	2493.34	2295.88	2152.92
115000	10529.53	5727.39	4143.12	3363.13	2904.63	2606.67	2400.23	2250.78
120000	10987.33	5976.41	4323.26	3509.35	3030.92	2720.01	2504.59	2348.64
125000	11445.14	6225.43	4503.39	3655.57	3157.21	2833.34	2608.95	2446.50
130000	11902.94	6474.45	4683.53	3801.79	3283.50	2946.67	2713.31	2544.36
135000	12360.75	6723.46	4863.66	3948.02	3409.78	3060.01	2817.66	2642.22
140000	12818.55	6972.48	5043.80	4094.24	3536.07	3173.34	2922.02	2740.08
145000	13276.36	7221.50	5223.94	4240.46	3662.36	3286.68	3026.38	2837.94
150000	13734.16	7470.51	5404.07	4386.68	3788.65	3400.01	3130.74	2935.79
155000	14191.97	7719.53	5584.21	4532.91	3914.94	3513.34	3235.10	3033.65
160000	14649.77	7968.55	5764.34	4679.13	4041.22	3626.68	3339.45	3131.51

AMOUNT OF LOAN	NUMBER OF YEARS IN TERM							
	9	10	15	20	25	30	35	40
$ 50	.94	.90	.80	.77	.75	.75	.75	.75
100	1.87	1.79	1.60	1.53	1.50	1.49	1.49	1.49
200	3.73	3.58	3.19	3.05	3.00	2.98	2.97	2.97
300	5.59	5.36	4.78	4.58	4.50	4.47	4.45	4.45
400	7.45	7.15	6.37	6.10	5.99	5.95	5.93	5.93
500	9.31	8.93	7.97	7.63	7.49	7.44	7.42	7.41
600	11.17	10.72	9.56	9.15	8.99	8.93	8.90	8.89
700	13.03	12.51	11.15	10.67	10.49	10.41	10.38	10.37
800	14.89	14.29	12.74	12.20	11.98	11.90	11.86	11.85
900	16.75	16.08	14.34	13.72	13.48	13.39	13.35	13.33
1000	18.61	17.86	15.93	15.25	14.98	14.87	14.83	14.81
2000	37.21	35.72	31.85	30.49	29.95	29.74	29.65	29.61
3000	55.81	53.58	47.78	45.73	44.93	44.61	44.47	44.42
4000	74.41	71.44	63.70	60.97	59.90	59.47	59.30	59.22
5000	93.01	89.29	79.63	76.21	74.88	74.34	74.12	74.03
6000	111.61	107.15	95.55	91.45	89.85	89.21	88.94	88.83
7000	130.21	125.01	111.48	106.69	104.83	104.07	103.76	103.64
8000	148.81	142.87	127.40	121.93	119.80	118.94	118.59	118.44
9000	167.41	160.73	143.33	137.17	134.78	133.81	133.41	133.25
10000	186.01	178.58	159.25	152.41	149.75	148.67	148.23	148.05
11000	204.61	196.44	175.18	167.66	164.73	163.54	163.06	162.85
12000	223.21	214.30	191.10	182.90	179.70	178.41	177.88	177.66
13000	241.82	232.16	207.03	198.14	194.67	193.27	192.70	192.46
14000	260.42	250.02	222.95	213.38	209.65	208.14	207.52	207.27
15000	279.02	267.87	238.87	228.62	224.62	223.01	222.35	222.07
16000	297.62	285.73	254.80	243.86	239.60	237.88	237.17	236.88
17000	316.22	303.59	270.72	259.10	254.57	252.74	251.99	251.68
18000	334.82	321.45	286.65	274.34	269.55	267.61	266.81	266.49
19000	353.42	339.30	302.57	289.58	284.52	282.48	281.64	281.29
20000	372.02	357.16	318.50	304.82	299.50	297.34	296.46	296.10
21000	390.62	375.02	334.42	320.07	314.47	312.21	311.28	310.90
22000	409.22	392.88	350.35	335.31	329.45	327.08	326.11	325.70
23000	427.82	410.74	366.27	350.55	344.42	341.94	340.93	340.51
24000	446.42	428.59	382.20	365.79	359.40	356.81	355.75	355.31
25000	465.03	446.45	398.12	381.03	374.37	371.68	370.57	370.12
26000	483.63	464.31	414.05	396.27	389.34	386.54	385.40	384.92
27000	502.23	482.17	429.97	411.51	404.32	401.41	400.22	399.73
28000	520.83	500.03	445.90	426.75	419.29	416.28	415.04	414.53
29000	539.43	517.88	461.82	441.99	434.27	431.15	429.86	429.34
30000	558.03	535.74	477.74	457.23	449.24	446.01	444.69	444.14
31000	576.63	553.60	493.67	472.48	464.22	460.88	459.51	458.95
32000	595.23	571.46	509.59	487.72	479.19	475.75	474.33	473.75
33000	613.83	589.32	525.52	502.96	494.17	490.61	489.16	488.55
34000	632.43	607.17	541.44	518.20	509.14	505.48	503.98	503.36
35000	651.03	625.03	557.37	533.44	524.12	520.35	518.80	518.16
40000	744.04	714.32	636.99	609.64	598.99	594.68	592.92	592.19
45000	837.04	803.61	716.61	685.85	673.86	669.02	667.03	666.21
50000	930.05	892.90	796.24	762.05	748.73	743.35	741.14	740.23
55000	1023.05	982.19	875.86	838.26	823.61	817.69	815.26	814.25
60000	1116.05	1071.48	955.48	914.46	898.48	892.02	889.37	888.28
65000	1209.06	1160.77	1035.11	990.67	973.35	966.35	963.48	962.30
70000	1302.06	1250.06	1114.73	1066.87	1048.23	1040.69	1037.60	1036.32
75000	1395.07	1339.35	1194.35	1143.08	1123.10	1115.02	1111.71	1110.35
80000	1488.07	1428.64	1273.98	1219.28	1197.97	1189.36	1185.83	1184.37
85000	1581.07	1517.93	1353.60	1295.49	1272.85	1263.69	1259.94	1258.39
90000	1674.08	1607.21	1433.22	1371.69	1347.72	1338.03	1334.05	1332.41
95000	1767.08	1696.50	1512.85	1447.90	1422.59	1412.36	1408.17	1406.44
100000	1860.09	1785.79	1592.47	1524.10	1497.46	1486.70	1482.28	1480.46
105000	1953.09	1875.08	1672.09	1600.31	1572.34	1561.03	1556.39	1554.48
110000	2046.09	1964.37	1751.72	1676.51	1647.21	1635.37	1630.51	1628.50
115000	2139.10	2053.66	1831.34	1752.72	1722.08	1709.70	1704.62	1702.53
120000	2232.10	2142.95	1910.96	1828.92	1796.96	1784.04	1778.74	1776.55
125000	2325.11	2232.24	1990.59	1905.13	1871.83	1858.37	1852.85	1850.57
130000	2418.11	2321.53	2070.21	1981.33	1946.70	1932.70	1926.96	1924.59
135000	2511.11	2410.82	2149.83	2057.54	2021.58	2007.04	2001.08	1998.62
140000	2604.12	2500.11	2229.46	2133.74	2096.45	2081.37	2075.19	2072.64
145000	2697.12	2589.40	2309.08	2209.95	2171.32	2155.71	2149.30	2146.66
150000	2790.13	2678.69	2388.70	2286.15	2246.19	2230.04	2223.42	2220.69
155000	2883.13	2767.98	2468.33	2362.36	2321.07	2304.38	2297.53	2294.71
160000	2976.13	2857.27	2547.95	2438.56	2395.94	2378.71	2371.65	2368.73

18.000% MONTHLY AMORTIZING PAYMENTS

AMOUNT OF LOAN	NUMBER OF YEARS IN TERM							
	1	2	3	4	5	6	7	8
$ 50	4.59	2.50	1.81	1.47	1.27	1.15	1.06	.99
100	9.17	5.00	3.62	2.94	2.54	2.29	2.11	1.98
200	18.34	9.99	7.24	5.88	5.08	4.57	4.21	3.95
300	27.51	14.98	10.85	8.82	7.62	6.85	6.31	5.92
400	36.68	19.97	14.47	11.75	10.16	9.13	8.41	7.89
500	45.84	24.97	18.08	14.69	12.70	11.41	10.51	9.87
600	55.01	29.96	21.70	17.63	15.24	13.69	12.62	11.84
700	64.18	34.95	25.31	20.57	17.78	15.97	14.72	13.81
800	73.35	39.94	28.93	23.50	20.32	18.25	16.82	15.78
900	82.52	44.94	32.54	26.44	22.86	20.53	18.92	17.76
1000	91.68	49.93	36.16	29.38	25.40	22.81	21.02	19.73
2000	183.36	99.85	72.31	58.75	50.79	45.62	42.04	39.45
3000	275.04	149.78	108.46	88.13	76.19	68.43	63.06	59.17
4000	366.72	199.70	144.61	117.50	101.58	91.24	84.08	78.90
5000	458.40	249.63	180.77	146.88	126.97	114.04	105.09	98.62
6000	550.08	299.55	216.92	176.25	152.37	136.85	126.11	118.34
7000	641.76	349.47	253.07	205.63	177.76	159.66	147.13	138.07
8000	733.44	399.40	289.22	235.00	203.15	182.47	168.15	157.79
9000	825.12	449.32	325.38	264.38	228.55	205.28	189.17	177.51
10000	916.80	499.25	361.53	293.75	253.94	228.08	210.18	197.24
11000	1008.48	549.17	397.68	323.13	279.33	250.89	231.20	216.96
12000	1100.16	599.09	433.83	352.50	304.73	273.70	252.22	236.68
13000	1191.84	649.02	469.99	381.88	330.12	296.51	273.24	256.41
14000	1283.52	698.94	506.14	411.25	355.51	319.31	294.25	276.13
15000	1375.20	748.87	542.29	440.63	380.91	342.12	315.27	295.85
16000	1466.88	798.79	578.44	470.00	406.30	364.93	336.29	315.58
17000	1558.56	848.71	614.60	499.38	431.69	387.74	357.31	335.30
18000	1650.24	898.64	650.75	528.75	457.09	410.55	378.33	355.02
19000	1741.92	948.56	686.90	558.13	482.48	433.35	399.34	374.75
20000	1833.60	998.49	723.05	587.50	507.87	456.16	420.36	394.47
21000	1925.28	1048.41	759.21	616.88	533.27	478.97	441.38	414.19
22000	2016.96	1098.34	795.36	646.25	558.66	501.78	462.40	433.92
23000	2108.64	1148.26	831.51	675.63	584.05	524.58	483.42	453.64
24000	2200.32	1198.18	867.66	705.00	609.45	547.39	504.43	473.36
25000	2292.00	1248.11	903.81	734.38	634.84	570.20	525.45	493.09
26000	2383.68	1298.03	939.97	763.75	660.23	593.01	546.47	512.81
27000	2475.36	1347.96	976.12	793.13	685.63	615.82	567.49	532.53
28000	2567.04	1397.88	1012.27	822.50	711.02	638.62	588.50	552.25
29000	2658.72	1447.80	1048.42	851.88	736.41	661.43	609.52	571.98
30000	2750.40	1497.73	1084.58	881.25	761.81	684.24	630.54	591.70
31000	2842.08	1547.65	1120.73	910.63	787.20	707.05	651.56	611.42
32000	2933.76	1597.58	1156.88	940.00	812.59	729.85	672.58	631.15
33000	3025.44	1647.50	1193.03	969.38	837.99	752.66	693.59	650.87
34000	3117.12	1697.42	1229.19	998.75	863.38	775.47	714.61	670.59
35000	3208.80	1747.35	1265.34	1028.13	888.77	798.28	735.63	690.32
40000	3667.20	1996.97	1446.10	1175.00	1015.74	912.32	840.72	788.93
45000	4125.60	2246.59	1626.86	1321.88	1142.71	1026.36	945.81	887.55
50000	4584.00	2496.21	1807.62	1468.75	1269.68	1140.39	1050.90	986.17
55000	5042.40	2745.83	1988.39	1615.63	1396.64	1254.43	1155.99	1084.78
60000	5500.80	2995.45	2169.15	1762.50	1523.61	1368.47	1261.08	1183.40
65000	5959.20	3245.07	2349.91	1909.38	1650.58	1482.51	1366.16	1282.01
70000	6417.60	3494.69	2530.67	2056.25	1777.54	1596.55	1471.25	1380.63
75000	6876.00	3744.31	2711.43	2203.13	1904.51	1710.59	1576.34	1479.25
80000	7334.40	3993.93	2892.20	2350.00	2031.48	1824.63	1681.43	1577.86
85000	7792.80	4243.55	3072.96	2496.88	2158.45	1938.67	1786.52	1676.48
90000	8251.20	4493.17	3253.72	2643.75	2285.41	2052.71	1891.61	1775.09
95000	8709.60	4742.79	3434.48	2790.63	2412.38	2166.75	1996.70	1873.71
100000	9168.00	4992.42	3615.24	2937.50	2539.35	2280.78	2101.79	1972.33
105000	9626.40	5242.04	3796.01	3084.38	2666.31	2394.82	2206.88	2070.94
110000	10084.80	5491.66	3976.77	3231.25	2793.28	2508.86	2311.97	2169.56
115000	10543.20	5741.28	4157.53	3378.13	2920.25	2622.90	2417.06	2268.17
120000	11001.60	5990.90	4338.29	3525.00	3047.22	2736.94	2522.15	2366.79
125000	11460.00	6240.52	4519.05	3671.88	3174.18	2850.98	2627.23	2465.41
130000	11918.40	6490.14	4699.82	3818.75	3301.15	2965.02	2732.32	2564.02
135000	12376.80	6739.76	4880.58	3965.63	3428.12	3079.06	2837.41	2662.64
140000	12835.20	6989.38	5061.34	4112.50	3555.08	3193.10	2942.50	2761.25
145000	13293.60	7239.00	5242.10	4259.38	3682.05	3307.13	3047.59	2859.87
150000	13752.00	7488.62	5422.86	4406.25	3809.02	3421.17	3152.68	2958.49
155000	14210.40	7738.24	5603.63	4553.13	3935.99	3535.21	3257.77	3057.10
160000	14668.80	7987.86	5784.39	4700.00	4062.95	3649.25	3362.86	3155.72

178

AMOUNT OF LOAN	NUMBER OF YEARS IN TERM							
	9	10	15	20	25	30	35	40
$ 50	.94	.91	.81	.78	.76	.76	.76	.76
100	1.88	1.81	1.62	1.55	1.52	1.51	1.51	1.51
200	3.76	3.61	3.23	3.09	3.04	3.02	3.01	3.01
300	5.63	5.41	4.84	4.63	4.56	4.53	4.51	4.51
400	7.51	7.21	6.45	6.18	6.07	6.03	6.02	6.01
500	9.38	9.01	8.06	7.72	7.59	7.54	7.52	7.51
600	11.26	10.82	9.67	9.26	9.11	9.05	9.02	9.01
700	13.13	12.62	11.28	10.81	10.63	10.55	10.53	10.51
800	15.01	14.42	12.89	12.35	12.14	12.06	12.03	12.01
900	16.89	16.22	14.50	13.89	13.66	13.57	13.53	13.52
1000	18.76	18.02	16.11	15.44	15.18	15.08	15.03	15.02
2000	37.52	36.04	32.21	30.87	30.35	30.15	30.06	30.03
3000	56.28	54.06	48.32	46.30	45.53	45.22	45.09	45.04
4000	75.03	72.08	64.42	61.74	60.70	60.29	60.12	60.05
5000	93.79	90.10	80.53	77.17	75.88	75.36	75.15	75.06
6000	112.55	108.12	96.63	92.60	91.05	90.43	90.18	90.08
7000	131.30	126.13	112.73	108.04	106.23	105.50	105.21	105.09
8000	150.06	144.15	128.84	123.47	121.40	120.57	120.24	120.10
9000	168.82	162.17	144.94	138.90	136.57	135.64	135.27	135.11
10000	187.57	180.19	161.05	154.34	151.75	150.71	150.29	150.12
11000	206.33	198.21	177.15	169.77	166.92	165.78	165.32	165.14
12000	225.09	216.23	193.26	185.20	182.10	180.86	180.35	180.15
13000	243.84	234.25	209.36	200.64	197.27	195.93	195.38	195.16
14000	262.60	252.26	225.46	216.07	212.45	211.00	210.41	210.17
15000	281.36	270.28	241.57	231.50	227.62	226.07	225.44	225.18
16000	300.12	288.30	257.67	246.93	242.79	241.14	240.47	240.19
17000	318.87	306.32	273.78	262.37	257.97	256.21	255.50	255.21
18000	337.63	324.34	289.88	277.80	273.14	271.28	270.53	270.22
19000	356.39	342.36	305.98	293.23	288.32	286.35	285.55	285.23
20000	375.14	360.38	322.09	308.67	303.49	301.42	300.58	300.24
21000	393.90	378.39	338.19	324.10	318.67	316.49	315.61	315.25
22000	412.66	396.41	354.30	339.53	333.84	331.56	330.64	330.27
23000	431.41	414.43	370.40	354.97	349.01	346.63	345.67	345.28
24000	450.17	432.45	386.51	370.40	364.19	361.71	360.70	360.29
25000	468.93	450.47	402.61	385.83	379.36	376.78	375.73	375.30
26000	487.68	468.49	418.71	401.27	394.54	391.85	390.76	390.31
27000	506.44	486.51	434.82	416.70	409.71	406.92	405.79	405.32
28000	525.20	504.52	450.92	432.13	424.89	421.99	420.81	420.34
29000	543.95	522.54	467.03	447.57	440.06	437.06	435.84	435.35
30000	562.71	540.56	483.13	463.00	455.23	452.13	450.87	450.36
31000	581.47	558.58	499.24	478.43	470.41	467.20	465.90	465.37
32000	600.23	576.60	515.34	493.86	485.58	482.27	480.93	480.38
33000	618.98	594.62	531.44	509.30	500.76	497.34	495.96	495.40
34000	637.74	612.63	547.55	524.73	515.93	512.41	510.99	510.41
35000	656.50	630.65	563.65	540.16	531.11	527.48	526.02	525.42
40000	750.28	720.75	644.17	617.33	606.98	602.84	601.16	600.48
45000	844.06	810.84	724.69	694.50	682.85	678.19	676.31	675.54
50000	937.85	900.93	805.22	771.66	758.72	753.55	751.45	750.60
55000	1031.63	991.02	885.74	848.83	834.59	828.90	826.60	825.66
60000	1125.42	1081.12	966.26	925.99	910.46	904.26	901.74	900.71
65000	1219.20	1171.21	1046.78	1003.16	986.33	979.61	976.88	975.77
70000	1312.99	1261.30	1127.30	1080.32	1062.21	1054.96	1052.03	1050.83
75000	1406.77	1351.39	1207.82	1157.49	1138.08	1130.32	1127.17	1125.89
80000	1500.56	1441.49	1288.34	1234.65	1213.95	1205.67	1202.32	1200.95
85000	1594.34	1531.58	1368.86	1311.82	1289.82	1281.03	1277.46	1276.01
90000	1688.12	1621.67	1449.38	1388.99	1365.69	1356.38	1352.61	1351.07
95000	1781.91	1711.76	1529.90	1466.15	1441.56	1431.74	1427.75	1426.13
100000	1875.69	1801.86	1610.43	1543.32	1517.43	1507.09	1502.90	1501.19
105000	1969.48	1891.95	1690.95	1620.48	1593.31	1582.44	1578.04	1576.25
110000	2063.26	1982.04	1771.47	1697.65	1669.18	1657.80	1653.19	1651.31
115000	2157.05	2072.13	1851.99	1774.81	1745.05	1733.15	1728.33	1726.36
120000	2250.83	2162.23	1932.51	1851.98	1820.92	1808.51	1803.48	1801.42
125000	2344.62	2252.32	2013.03	1929.14	1896.79	1883.86	1878.62	1876.48
130000	2438.40	2342.41	2093.55	2006.31	1972.66	1959.22	1953.76	1951.54
135000	2532.18	2432.51	2174.07	2083.48	2048.54	2034.57	2028.91	2026.60
140000	2625.97	2522.60	2254.59	2160.64	2124.41	2109.92	2104.05	2101.66
145000	2719.75	2612.69	2335.12	2237.81	2200.28	2185.28	2179.20	2176.72
150000	2813.54	2702.78	2415.64	2314.97	2276.15	2260.63	2254.34	2251.78
155000	2907.32	2792.88	2496.16	2392.14	2352.02	2335.99	2329.49	2326.84
160000	3001.11	2882.97	2576.68	2469.30	2427.89	2411.34	2404.63	2401.90

18.250% MONTHLY AMORTIZING PAYMENTS

AMOUNT OF LOAN	NUMBER OF YEARS IN TERM							
	1	2	3	4	5	6	7	8
$ 50	4.59	2.51	1.82	1.48	1.28	1.15	1.06	1.00
100	9.18	5.01	3.63	2.96	2.56	2.30	2.12	1.99
200	18.36	10.01	7.26	5.91	5.11	4.59	4.24	3.98
300	27.54	15.02	10.89	8.86	7.66	6.89	6.35	5.97
400	36.72	20.02	14.52	11.81	10.22	9.18	8.47	7.96
500	45.90	25.03	18.14	14.76	12.77	11.48	10.59	9.94
600	55.08	30.03	21.77	17.71	15.32	13.77	12.70	11.93
700	64.26	35.04	25.40	20.66	17.88	16.07	14.82	13.92
800	73.44	40.04	29.03	23.61	20.43	18.36	16.94	15.91
900	82.62	45.05	32.66	26.56	22.98	20.66	19.05	17.89
1000	91.80	50.05	36.28	29.51	25.53	22.95	21.17	19.88
2000	183.60	100.09	72.56	59.02	51.06	45.90	42.33	39.76
3000	275.40	150.14	108.84	88.52	76.59	68.85	63.50	59.63
4000	367.20	200.18	145.12	118.03	102.12	91.80	84.66	79.51
5000	459.00	250.23	181.39	147.53	127.65	114.75	105.83	99.38
6000	550.80	300.27	217.67	177.04	153.18	137.70	126.99	119.26
7000	642.60	350.32	253.95	206.55	178.71	160.65	148.16	139.13
8000	734.40	400.36	290.23	236.05	204.24	183.60	169.32	159.01
9000	826.20	450.41	326.51	265.56	229.77	206.55	190.49	178.88
10000	918.00	500.45	362.78	295.06	255.30	229.50	211.65	198.76
11000	1009.79	550.50	399.06	324.57	280.83	252.45	232.82	218.63
12000	1101.59	600.54	435.34	354.07	306.36	275.40	253.98	238.51
13000	1193.39	650.59	471.62	383.58	331.89	298.35	275.15	258.38
14000	1285.19	700.63	507.90	413.09	357.42	321.30	296.31	278.26
15000	1376.99	750.68	544.17	442.59	382.95	344.25	317.47	298.13
16000	1468.79	800.72	580.45	472.10	408.48	367.19	338.64	318.01
17000	1560.59	850.77	616.73	501.60	434.01	390.14	359.80	337.88
18000	1652.39	900.81	653.01	531.11	459.54	413.09	380.97	357.76
19000	1744.19	950.86	689.29	560.62	485.07	436.04	402.13	377.63
20000	1835.99	1000.90	725.56	590.12	510.60	458.99	423.30	397.51
21000	1927.78	1050.95	761.84	619.63	536.13	481.94	444.46	417.38
22000	2019.58	1100.99	798.12	649.13	561.66	504.89	465.63	437.26
23000	2111.38	1151.04	834.40	678.64	587.19	527.84	486.79	457.13
24000	2203.18	1201.08	870.68	708.14	612.72	550.79	507.96	477.01
25000	2294.98	1251.13	906.95	737.65	638.25	573.74	529.12	496.88
26000	2386.78	1301.17	943.23	767.16	663.78	596.69	550.29	516.76
27000	2478.58	1351.22	979.51	796.66	689.30	619.64	571.45	536.63
28000	2570.38	1401.26	1015.79	826.17	714.83	642.59	592.61	556.51
29000	2662.18	1451.31	1052.07	855.67	740.36	665.54	613.78	576.38
30000	2753.98	1501.35	1088.34	885.18	765.89	688.49	634.94	596.26
31000	2845.77	1551.40	1124.62	914.68	791.42	711.43	656.11	616.13
32000	2937.57	1601.44	1160.90	944.19	816.95	734.38	677.27	636.01
33000	3029.37	1651.49	1197.18	973.70	842.48	757.33	698.44	655.88
34000	3121.17	1701.53	1233.45	1003.20	868.01	780.28	719.60	675.76
35000	3212.97	1751.58	1269.73	1032.71	893.54	803.23	740.77	695.63
40000	3671.97	2001.80	1451.12	1180.24	1021.19	917.98	846.59	795.01
45000	4130.96	2252.03	1632.51	1327.77	1148.84	1032.73	952.41	894.38
50000	4589.96	2502.25	1813.90	1475.29	1276.49	1147.47	1058.24	993.76
55000	5048.95	2752.48	1995.29	1622.82	1404.13	1262.22	1164.06	1093.13
60000	5507.95	3002.70	2176.68	1770.35	1531.78	1376.97	1269.88	1192.51
65000	5966.94	3252.93	2358.07	1917.88	1659.43	1491.71	1375.71	1291.88
70000	6425.94	3503.15	2539.46	2065.41	1787.08	1606.46	1481.53	1391.26
75000	6884.93	3753.38	2720.85	2212.94	1914.73	1721.21	1587.35	1490.63
80000	7343.93	4003.60	2902.24	2360.47	2042.37	1835.95	1693.18	1590.01
85000	7802.92	4253.83	3083.63	2508.00	2170.02	1950.70	1799.00	1689.38
90000	8261.92	4504.05	3265.02	2655.53	2297.67	2065.45	1904.82	1788.76
95000	8720.91	4754.28	3446.41	2803.06	2425.32	2180.19	2010.64	1888.13
100000	9179.91	5004.50	3627.80	2950.58	2552.97	2294.94	2116.47	1987.51
105000	9638.90	5254.73	3809.19	3098.11	2680.62	2409.69	2222.29	2086.89
110000	10097.90	5504.95	3990.58	3245.64	2808.26	2524.43	2328.11	2186.26
115000	10556.89	5755.18	4171.97	3393.17	2935.91	2639.18	2433.94	2285.64
120000	11015.89	6005.40	4353.36	3540.70	3063.56	2753.93	2539.76	2385.01
125000	11474.88	6255.63	4534.75	3688.23	3191.21	2868.67	2645.58	2484.39
130000	11933.88	6505.85	4716.14	3835.76	3318.86	2983.42	2751.41	2583.76
135000	12392.87	6756.08	4897.53	3983.29	3446.50	3098.17	2857.23	2683.14
140000	12851.87	7006.30	5078.92	4130.83	3574.15	3212.91	2963.05	2782.51
145000	13310.86	7256.53	5260.31	4278.35	3701.80	3327.66	3068.88	2881.89
150000	13769.86	7506.75	5441.69	4425.87	3829.45	3442.41	3174.70	2981.26
155000	14228.85	7756.98	5623.08	4573.40	3957.10	3557.15	3280.52	3080.64
160000	14687.85	8007.20	5804.47	4720.93	4084.74	3671.90	3386.35	3180.01

AMOUNT OF LOAN	NUMBER OF YEARS IN TERM							
	9	10	15	20	25	30	35	40
$ 50	.95	.91	.82	.79	.77	.77	.77	.77
100	1.90	1.82	1.63	1.57	1.54	1.53	1.53	1.53
200	3.79	3.64	3.26	3.13	3.08	3.06	3.05	3.05
300	5.68	5.46	4.89	4.69	4.62	4.59	4.58	4.57
400	7.57	7.28	6.52	6.26	6.15	6.12	6.10	6.09
500	9.46	9.09	8.15	7.82	7.69	7.64	7.62	7.61
600	11.35	10.91	9.78	9.38	9.23	9.17	9.15	9.14
700	13.24	12.73	11.40	10.94	10.77	10.70	10.67	10.66
800	15.14	14.55	13.03	12.51	12.30	12.23	12.19	12.18
900	17.03	16.37	14.66	14.07	13.84	13.75	13.72	13.70
1000	18.92	18.18	16.29	15.63	15.38	15.28	15.24	15.22
2000	37.83	36.36	32.57	31.26	30.75	30.56	30.48	30.44
3000	56.75	54.54	48.86	46.88	46.13	45.83	45.71	45.66
4000	75.66	72.72	65.14	62.51	61.50	61.11	60.95	60.88
5000	94.57	90.90	81.43	78.13	76.88	76.38	76.18	76.10
6000	113.49	109.08	97.71	93.76	92.25	91.66	91.42	91.32
7000	132.40	127.26	114.00	109.39	107.63	106.93	106.65	106.54
8000	151.31	145.44	130.28	125.01	123.00	122.21	121.89	121.76
9000	170.23	163.62	146.56	140.64	138.37	137.48	137.12	136.98
10000	189.14	181.80	162.85	156.26	153.75	152.76	152.36	152.20
11000	208.05	199.98	179.13	171.89	169.12	168.03	167.59	167.42
12000	226.97	218.16	195.42	187.51	184.50	183.31	182.83	182.64
13000	245.88	236.34	211.70	203.14	199.87	198.58	198.06	197.85
14000	264.79	254.52	227.99	218.77	215.25	213.86	213.30	213.07
15000	283.71	272.70	244.27	234.39	230.62	229.13	228.53	228.29
16000	302.62	290.88	260.56	250.02	246.00	244.41	243.77	243.51
17000	321.54	309.06	276.84	265.64	261.37	259.68	259.00	258.73
18000	340.45	327.24	293.12	281.27	276.74	274.96	274.24	273.95
19000	359.36	345.42	309.41	296.89	292.12	290.23	289.47	289.17
20000	378.28	363.60	325.69	312.52	307.49	305.51	304.71	304.39
21000	397.19	381.78	341.98	328.15	322.87	320.78	319.94	319.61
22000	416.10	399.96	358.26	343.77	338.24	336.06	335.18	334.83
23000	435.02	418.14	374.55	359.40	353.62	351.33	350.42	350.05
24000	453.93	436.32	390.83	375.02	368.99	366.61	365.65	365.27
25000	472.84	454.50	407.12	390.65	384.36	381.88	380.89	380.48
26000	491.76	472.68	423.40	406.28	399.74	397.16	396.12	395.70
27000	510.67	490.86	439.68	421.90	415.11	412.43	411.36	410.92
28000	529.58	509.04	455.97	437.53	430.49	427.71	426.59	426.14
29000	548.50	527.22	472.25	453.15	445.86	442.98	441.83	441.36
30000	567.41	545.40	488.54	468.78	461.24	458.26	457.06	456.58
31000	586.33	563.58	504.82	484.40	476.61	473.53	472.30	471.80
32000	605.24	581.76	521.11	500.03	491.99	488.81	487.53	487.02
33000	624.15	599.94	537.39	515.66	507.36	504.08	502.77	502.24
34000	643.07	618.12	553.67	531.28	522.73	519.36	518.00	517.46
35000	661.98	636.30	569.96	546.91	538.11	534.63	533.24	532.68
40000	756.55	727.20	651.38	625.04	614.98	611.01	609.41	608.77
45000	851.12	818.10	732.80	703.17	691.85	687.38	685.59	684.87
50000	945.68	908.99	814.23	781.29	768.72	763.76	761.77	760.96
55000	1040.25	999.89	895.65	859.42	845.60	840.13	837.94	837.06
60000	1134.82	1090.79	977.07	937.55	922.47	916.51	914.12	913.16
65000	1229.39	1181.69	1058.49	1015.68	999.34	992.88	990.29	989.25
70000	1323.95	1272.59	1139.91	1093.81	1076.21	1069.26	1066.47	1065.35
75000	1418.52	1363.49	1221.34	1171.94	1153.08	1145.63	1142.65	1141.44
80000	1513.09	1454.39	1302.76	1250.07	1229.96	1222.01	1218.82	1217.54
85000	1607.66	1545.29	1384.18	1328.20	1306.83	1298.38	1295.00	1293.64
90000	1702.23	1636.19	1465.60	1406.33	1383.70	1374.76	1371.18	1369.73
95000	1796.79	1727.08	1547.02	1484.45	1460.57	1451.13	1447.35	1445.83
100000	1891.36	1817.98	1628.45	1562.58	1537.44	1527.51	1523.53	1521.92
105000	1985.93	1908.88	1709.87	1640.71	1614.32	1603.88	1599.70	1598.02
110000	2080.50	1999.78	1791.29	1718.84	1691.19	1680.26	1675.88	1674.12
115000	2175.06	2090.68	1872.71	1796.97	1768.06	1756.63	1752.06	1750.21
120000	2269.63	2181.58	1954.13	1875.10	1844.93	1833.01	1828.23	1826.31
125000	2364.20	2272.48	2035.56	1953.23	1921.80	1909.38	1904.41	1902.40
130000	2458.77	2363.38	2116.98	2031.36	1998.68	1985.76	1980.58	1978.50
135000	2553.34	2454.28	2198.40	2109.49	2075.55	2062.13	2056.76	2054.60
140000	2647.90	2545.17	2279.82	2187.61	2152.42	2138.51	2132.94	2130.69
145000	2742.47	2636.07	2361.24	2265.74	2229.29	2214.88	2209.11	2206.79
150000	2837.04	2726.97	2442.67	2343.87	2306.16	2291.26	2285.29	2282.88
155000	2931.61	2817.87	2524.09	2422.00	2383.03	2367.64	2361.47	2358.98
160000	3026.17	2908.77	2605.51	2500.13	2459.91	2444.01	2437.64	2435.08

AMOUNT OF LOAN	NUMBER OF YEARS IN TERM							
	1	2	3	4	5	6	7	8
$ 50	4.60	2.51	1.83	1.49	1.29	1.16	1.07	1.01
100	9.20	5.02	3.65	2.97	2.57	2.31	2.14	2.01
200	18.39	10.04	7.29	5.93	5.14	4.62	4.27	4.01
300	27.58	15.05	10.93	8.90	7.70	6.93	6.40	6.01
400	36.77	20.07	14.57	11.86	10.27	9.24	8.53	8.02
500	45.96	25.09	18.21	14.82	12.84	11.55	10.66	10.02
600	55.16	30.10	21.85	17.79	15.40	13.86	12.79	12.02
700	64.35	35.12	25.49	20.75	17.97	16.17	14.92	14.02
800	73.54	40.14	29.13	23.71	20.54	18.48	17.05	16.03
900	82.73	45.15	32.77	26.68	23.10	20.79	19.19	18.03
1000	91.92	50.17	36.41	29.64	25.67	23.10	21.32	20.03
2000	183.84	100.34	72.81	59.28	51.34	46.19	42.63	40.06
3000	275.76	150.50	109.22	88.92	77.00	69.28	63.94	60.09
4000	367.68	200.67	145.62	118.55	102.67	92.37	85.25	80.11
5000	459.60	250.84	182.02	148.19	128.34	115.46	106.56	100.14
6000	551.51	301.00	218.43	177.83	154.00	138.55	127.88	120.17
7000	643.43	351.17	254.83	207.46	179.67	161.64	149.19	140.20
8000	735.35	401.33	291.23	237.10	205.33	184.74	170.50	160.22
9000	827.27	451.50	327.64	266.74	231.00	207.83	191.81	180.25
10000	919.19	501.67	364.04	296.37	256.67	230.92	213.12	200.28
11000	1011.10	551.83	400.45	326.01	282.33	254.01	234.44	220.31
12000	1103.02	602.00	436.85	355.65	308.00	277.10	255.75	240.33
13000	1194.94	652.16	473.25	385.28	333.67	300.19	277.06	260.36
14000	1286.86	702.33	509.66	414.92	359.33	323.28	298.37	280.39
15000	1378.78	752.50	546.06	444.56	385.00	346.38	319.68	300.42
16000	1470.69	802.66	582.46	474.20	410.66	369.47	341.00	320.44
17000	1562.61	852.83	618.87	503.83	436.33	392.56	362.31	340.47
18000	1654.53	902.99	655.27	533.47	462.00	415.65	383.62	360.50
19000	1746.45	953.16	691.68	563.11	487.66	438.74	404.93	380.53
20000	1838.37	1003.33	728.08	592.74	513.33	461.83	426.24	400.55
21000	1930.29	1053.49	764.48	622.38	539.00	484.92	447.56	420.58
22000	2022.20	1103.66	800.89	652.02	564.66	508.01	468.87	440.61
23000	2114.12	1153.82	837.29	681.65	590.33	531.11	490.18	460.64
24000	2206.04	1203.99	873.69	711.29	615.99	554.20	511.49	480.66
25000	2297.96	1254.16	910.10	740.93	641.66	577.29	532.80	500.69
26000	2389.88	1304.32	946.50	770.56	667.33	600.38	554.11	520.72
27000	2481.79	1354.49	982.91	800.20	692.99	623.47	575.43	540.75
28000	2573.71	1404.65	1019.31	829.84	718.66	646.56	596.74	560.77
29000	2665.63	1454.82	1055.71	859.48	744.33	669.65	618.05	580.80
30000	2757.55	1504.99	1092.12	889.11	769.99	692.75	639.36	600.83
31000	2849.47	1555.15	1128.52	918.75	795.66	715.84	660.67	620.86
32000	2941.38	1605.32	1164.92	948.39	821.32	738.93	681.99	640.88
33000	3033.30	1655.48	1201.33	978.02	846.99	762.02	703.30	660.91
34000	3125.22	1705.65	1237.73	1007.66	872.66	785.11	724.61	680.94
35000	3217.14	1755.82	1274.13	1037.30	898.32	808.20	745.92	700.97
40000	3676.73	2006.65	1456.15	1185.48	1026.65	923.66	852.48	801.10
45000	4136.32	2257.48	1638.17	1333.67	1154.98	1039.12	959.04	901.24
50000	4595.91	2508.31	1820.19	1481.85	1283.32	1154.57	1065.60	1001.38
55000	5055.50	2759.14	2002.21	1630.04	1411.65	1270.03	1172.16	1101.51
60000	5515.09	3009.97	2184.23	1778.22	1539.98	1385.49	1278.72	1201.65
65000	5974.68	3260.80	2366.25	1926.40	1668.31	1500.94	1385.28	1301.79
70000	6434.27	3511.63	2548.27	2074.59	1796.64	1616.40	1491.84	1401.93
75000	6893.86	3762.46	2730.28	2222.77	1924.97	1731.86	1598.40	1502.06
80000	7353.45	4013.29	2912.30	2370.96	2053.30	1847.31	1704.96	1602.20
85000	7813.04	4264.12	3094.32	2519.14	2181.63	1962.77	1811.52	1702.34
90000	8272.64	4514.95	3276.34	2667.33	2309.96	2078.23	1918.08	1802.47
95000	8732.23	4765.78	3458.36	2815.51	2438.29	2193.68	2024.64	1902.61
100000	9191.82	5016.61	3640.38	2963.70	2566.63	2309.14	2131.20	2002.75
105000	9651.41	5267.44	3822.40	3111.88	2694.96	2424.60	2237.76	2102.89
110000	10111.00	5518.27	4004.41	3260.07	2823.29	2540.05	2344.32	2203.02
115000	10570.59	5769.10	4186.43	3408.25	2951.62	2655.51	2450.88	2303.16
120000	11030.18	6019.93	4368.45	3556.44	3079.95	2770.97	2557.44	2403.30
125000	11489.77	6270.76	4550.47	3704.62	3208.28	2886.42	2663.99	2503.44
130000	11949.36	6521.59	4732.49	3852.80	3336.61	3001.88	2770.55	2603.57
135000	12408.95	6772.42	4914.51	4000.99	3464.94	3117.34	2877.11	2703.71
140000	12868.54	7023.25	5096.53	4149.17	3593.27	3232.79	2983.67	2803.85
145000	13328.13	7274.08	5278.54	4297.36	3721.61	3348.25	3090.23	2903.98
150000	13787.72	7524.91	5460.56	4445.54	3849.94	3463.71	3196.79	3004.12
155000	14247.31	7775.74	5642.58	4593.73	3978.27	3579.16	3303.35	3104.26
160000	14706.90	8026.57	5824.60	4741.91	4106.60	3694.62	3409.91	3204.40

AMOUNT OF LOAN	NUMBER OF YEARS IN TERM							
	9	10	15	20	25	30	35	40
$ 50	.96	.92	.83	.80	.78	.78	.78	.78
100	1.91	1.84	1.65	1.59	1.56	1.55	1.55	1.55
200	3.82	3.67	3.30	3.17	3.12	3.10	3.09	3.09
300	5.73	5.51	4.94	4.75	4.68	4.65	4.64	4.63
400	7.63	7.34	6.59	6.33	6.23	6.20	6.18	6.18
500	9.54	9.18	8.24	7.91	7.79	7.74	7.73	7.72
600	11.45	11.01	9.88	9.50	9.35	9.29	9.27	9.26
700	13.35	12.84	11.53	11.08	10.91	10.84	10.81	10.80
800	15.26	14.68	13.18	12.66	12.46	12.39	12.36	12.35
900	17.17	16.51	14.82	14.24	14.02	13.94	13.90	13.89
1000	19.08	18.35	16.47	15.82	15.58	15.48	15.45	15.43
2000	38.15	36.69	32.94	31.64	31.15	30.96	30.89	30.86
3000	57.22	55.03	49.40	47.46	46.73	46.44	46.33	46.28
4000	76.29	73.37	65.87	63.28	62.30	61.92	61.77	61.71
5000	95.36	91.71	82.33	79.10	77.88	77.40	77.21	77.14
6000	114.43	110.05	98.80	94.92	93.45	92.88	92.66	92.56
7000	133.50	128.40	115.26	110.74	109.03	108.36	108.10	107.99
8000	152.57	146.74	131.73	126.56	124.60	123.84	123.54	123.42
9000	171.64	165.08	148.19	142.38	140.18	139.32	138.98	138.84
10000	190.71	183.42	164.66	158.19	155.75	154.80	154.42	154.27
11000	209.78	201.76	181.12	174.01	171.33	170.28	169.86	169.70
12000	228.85	220.10	197.59	189.83	186.90	185.76	185.31	185.12
13000	247.93	238.45	214.05	205.65	202.48	201.24	200.75	200.55
14000	267.00	256.79	230.52	221.47	218.05	216.72	216.19	215.98
15000	286.07	275.13	246.98	237.29	233.63	232.20	231.63	231.40
16000	305.14	293.47	263.45	253.11	249.20	247.68	247.07	246.83
17000	324.21	311.81	279.91	268.93	264.78	263.16	262.51	262.26
18000	343.28	330.15	296.38	284.75	280.35	278.64	277.96	277.68
19000	362.35	348.50	312.84	300.57	295.93	294.11	293.40	293.11
20000	381.42	366.84	329.31	316.38	311.50	309.59	308.84	308.54
21000	400.49	385.18	345.77	332.20	327.08	325.07	324.28	323.96
22000	419.56	403.52	362.24	348.02	342.65	340.55	339.72	339.39
23000	438.63	421.86	378.71	363.84	358.23	356.03	355.16	354.82
24000	457.70	440.20	395.17	379.66	373.80	371.51	370.61	370.24
25000	476.78	458.55	411.64	395.48	389.38	386.99	386.05	385.67
26000	495.85	476.89	428.10	411.30	404.95	402.47	401.49	401.10
27000	514.92	495.23	444.57	427.12	420.53	417.95	416.93	416.52
28000	533.99	513.57	461.03	442.94	436.10	433.43	432.37	431.95
29000	553.06	531.91	477.50	458.76	451.68	448.91	447.81	447.38
30000	572.13	550.25	493.96	474.57	467.25	464.39	463.26	462.80
31000	591.20	568.60	510.43	490.39	482.83	479.87	478.70	478.23
32000	610.27	586.94	526.89	506.21	498.40	495.35	494.14	493.66
33000	629.34	605.28	543.36	522.03	513.97	510.83	509.58	509.08
34000	648.41	623.62	559.82	537.85	529.55	526.31	525.02	524.51
35000	667.48	641.96	576.29	553.67	545.12	541.79	540.46	539.94
40000	762.84	733.67	658.61	632.76	623.00	619.18	617.67	617.07
45000	858.19	825.38	740.94	711.86	700.87	696.58	694.88	694.20
50000	953.55	917.09	823.27	790.95	778.75	773.98	772.09	771.34
55000	1048.90	1008.80	905.59	870.05	856.62	851.37	849.30	848.47
60000	1144.25	1100.50	987.92	949.14	934.50	928.77	926.51	925.60
65000	1239.61	1192.21	1070.25	1028.24	1012.37	1006.17	1003.71	1002.74
70000	1334.96	1283.92	1152.57	1107.33	1090.24	1083.57	1080.92	1079.87
75000	1430.32	1375.63	1234.90	1186.43	1168.12	1160.96	1158.13	1157.00
80000	1525.67	1467.34	1317.22	1265.52	1245.99	1238.36	1235.34	1234.14
85000	1621.02	1559.05	1399.55	1344.62	1323.87	1315.76	1312.55	1311.27
90000	1716.38	1650.75	1481.88	1423.71	1401.74	1393.16	1389.76	1388.40
95000	1811.73	1742.46	1564.20	1502.81	1479.61	1470.55	1466.96	1465.54
100000	1907.09	1834.17	1646.53	1581.90	1557.49	1547.95	1544.17	1542.67
105000	2002.44	1925.88	1728.85	1661.00	1635.36	1625.35	1621.38	1619.80
110000	2097.79	2017.59	1811.18	1740.09	1713.24	1702.74	1698.59	1696.94
115000	2193.15	2109.30	1893.51	1819.19	1791.11	1780.14	1775.80	1774.07
120000	2288.50	2201.00	1975.83	1898.28	1868.99	1857.54	1853.01	1851.20
125000	2383.86	2292.71	2058.16	1977.38	1946.86	1934.94	1930.21	1928.34
130000	2479.21	2384.42	2140.49	2056.47	2024.73	2012.33	2007.42	2005.47
135000	2574.57	2476.13	2222.81	2135.57	2102.61	2089.73	2084.63	2082.60
140000	2669.92	2567.84	2305.14	2214.66	2180.48	2167.13	2161.84	2159.74
145000	2765.27	2659.54	2387.46	2293.76	2258.36	2244.52	2239.05	2236.87
150000	2860.63	2751.25	2469.79	2372.85	2336.23	2321.92	2316.26	2314.00
155000	2955.98	2842.96	2552.12	2451.94	2414.11	2399.32	2393.46	2391.13
160000	3051.34	2934.67	2634.44	2531.04	2491.98	2476.72	2470.67	2468.27

AMOUNT OF LOAN	NUMBER OF YEARS IN TERM							
	1	2	3	4	5	6	7	8
$ 50	4.61	2.52	1.83	1.49	1.30	1.17	1.08	1.01
100	9.21	5.03	3.66	2.98	2.59	2.33	2.15	2.02
200	18.41	10.06	7.31	5.96	5.17	4.65	4.30	4.04
300	27.62	15.09	10.96	8.94	7.75	6.98	6.44	6.06
400	36.82	20.12	14.62	11.91	10.33	9.30	8.59	8.08
500	46.02	25.15	18.27	14.89	12.91	11.62	10.73	10.10
600	55.23	30.18	21.92	17.87	15.49	13.95	12.88	12.11
700	64.43	35.21	25.58	20.84	18.07	16.27	15.03	14.13
800	73.63	40.23	29.23	23.82	20.65	18.59	17.17	16.15
900	82.84	45.26	32.88	26.80	23.23	20.92	19.32	18.17
1000	92.04	50.29	36.53	29.77	25.81	23.24	21.46	20.19
2000	184.08	100.58	73.06	59.54	51.61	46.47	42.92	40.37
3000	276.12	150.87	109.59	89.31	77.41	69.71	64.38	60.55
4000	368.15	201.15	146.12	119.08	103.22	92.94	85.84	80.73
5000	460.19	251.44	182.65	148.85	129.02	116.17	107.30	100.91
6000	552.23	301.73	219.18	178.62	154.82	139.41	128.76	121.09
7000	644.27	352.02	255.71	208.38	180.63	162.64	150.22	141.27
8000	736.30	402.30	292.24	238.15	206.43	185.88	171.68	161.45
9000	828.34	452.59	328.77	267.92	232.23	209.11	193.14	181.63
10000	920.38	502.88	365.30	297.69	258.04	232.34	214.60	201.81
11000	1012.42	553.16	401.83	327.46	283.84	255.58	236.06	221.99
12000	1104.45	603.45	438.36	357.23	309.64	278.81	257.52	242.17
13000	1196.49	653.74	474.89	386.99	335.45	302.04	278.98	262.35
14000	1288.53	704.03	511.42	416.76	361.25	325.28	300.44	282.53
15000	1380.56	754.31	547.95	446.53	387.05	348.51	321.90	302.71
16000	1472.60	804.60	584.48	476.30	412.86	371.75	343.36	322.89
17000	1564.64	854.89	621.01	506.07	438.66	394.98	364.82	343.07
18000	1656.68	905.18	657.54	535.84	464.46	418.21	386.28	363.25
19000	1748.71	955.46	694.07	565.60	490.27	441.45	407.74	383.43
20000	1840.75	1005.75	730.60	595.37	516.07	464.68	429.20	403.61
21000	1932.79	1056.04	767.13	625.14	541.87	487.92	450.66	423.79
22000	2024.83	1106.32	803.66	654.91	567.68	511.15	472.12	443.97
23000	2116.86	1156.61	840.19	684.68	593.48	534.38	493.58	464.15
24000	2208.90	1206.90	876.72	714.45	619.28	557.62	515.04	484.33
25000	2300.94	1257.19	913.25	744.21	645.08	580.85	536.50	504.51
26000	2392.97	1307.47	949.78	773.98	670.89	604.08	557.96	524.69
27000	2485.01	1357.76	986.31	803.75	696.69	627.32	579.42	544.88
28000	2577.05	1408.05	1022.84	833.52	722.49	650.55	600.88	565.06
29000	2669.09	1458.33	1059.37	863.29	748.30	673.79	622.34	585.24
30000	2761.12	1508.62	1095.90	893.06	774.10	697.02	643.80	605.42
31000	2853.16	1558.91	1132.43	922.82	799.90	720.25	665.26	625.60
32000	2945.20	1609.20	1168.96	952.59	825.71	743.49	686.72	645.78
33000	3037.24	1659.48	1205.49	982.36	851.51	766.72	708.18	665.96
34000	3129.27	1709.77	1242.02	1012.13	877.31	789.95	729.64	686.14
35000	3221.31	1760.06	1278.55	1041.90	903.12	813.19	751.10	706.32
40000	3681.50	2011.49	1461.19	1190.74	1032.13	929.36	858.39	807.22
45000	4141.68	2262.93	1643.84	1339.58	1161.15	1045.53	965.69	908.12
50000	4601.87	2514.37	1826.49	1488.42	1290.16	1161.70	1072.99	1009.02
55000	5062.06	2765.80	2009.14	1637.26	1419.18	1277.86	1180.29	1109.93
60000	5522.24	3017.24	2191.79	1786.11	1548.20	1394.03	1287.59	1210.83
65000	5982.43	3268.68	2374.44	1934.95	1677.21	1510.20	1394.89	1311.73
70000	6442.62	3520.11	2557.09	2083.79	1806.23	1626.37	1502.19	1412.63
75000	6902.80	3771.55	2739.74	2232.63	1935.24	1742.54	1609.48	1513.53
80000	7362.99	4022.98	2922.38	2381.47	2064.26	1858.71	1716.78	1614.44
85000	7823.18	4274.42	3105.03	2530.32	2193.28	1974.88	1824.08	1715.34
90000	8283.36	4525.86	3287.68	2679.16	2322.29	2091.05	1931.38	1816.24
95000	8743.55	4777.29	3470.33	2828.00	2451.31	2207.22	2038.68	1917.14
100000	9203.74	5028.73	3652.98	2976.84	2580.32	2323.39	2145.98	2018.04
105000	9663.92	5280.16	3835.63	3125.68	2709.34	2439.56	2253.28	2118.94
110000	10124.11	5531.60	4018.28	3274.52	2838.36	2555.72	2360.57	2219.85
115000	10584.30	5783.04	4200.93	3423.37	2967.37	2671.89	2467.87	2320.75
120000	11044.48	6034.47	4383.57	3572.21	3096.39	2788.06	2575.17	2421.65
125000	11504.67	6285.91	4566.22	3721.05	3225.40	2904.23	2682.47	2522.55
130000	11964.85	6537.35	4748.87	3869.89	3354.42	3020.40	2789.77	2623.45
135000	12425.04	6788.78	4931.52	4018.73	3483.44	3136.57	2897.07	2724.36
140000	12885.23	7040.22	5114.17	4167.57	3612.45	3252.74	3004.37	2825.26
145000	13345.41	7291.65	5296.82	4316.42	3741.47	3368.91	3111.66	2926.16
150000	13805.60	7543.09	5479.47	4465.26	3870.48	3485.08	3218.96	3027.06
155000	14265.79	7794.53	5662.12	4614.10	3999.50	3601.25	3326.26	3127.96
160000	14725.97	8045.96	5844.76	4762.94	4128.51	3717.42	3433.56	3228.87

MONTHLY AMORTIZING PAYMENTS 18.750%

AMOUNT OF LOAN	\multicolumn{8}{c}{NUMBER OF YEARS IN TERM}
	9	**10**	**15**	**20**	**25**	**30**	**35**	**40**
$ 50	.97	.93	.84	.81	.79	.79	.79	.79
100	1.93	1.86	1.67	1.61	1.58	1.57	1.57	1.57
200	3.85	3.71	3.33	3.21	3.16	3.14	3.13	3.13
300	5.77	5.56	5.00	4.81	4.74	4.71	4.70	4.70
400	7.70	7.41	6.66	6.41	6.32	6.28	6.26	6.26
500	9.62	9.26	8.33	8.01	7.89	7.85	7.83	7.82
600	11.54	11.11	9.99	9.61	9.47	9.42	9.39	9.39
700	13.47	12.96	11.66	11.21	11.05	10.98	10.96	10.95
800	15.39	14.81	13.32	12.82	12.63	12.55	12.52	12.51
900	17.31	16.66	14.99	14.42	14.20	14.12	14.09	14.08
1000	19.23	18.51	16.65	16.02	15.78	15.69	15.65	15.64
2000	38.46	37.01	33.30	32.03	31.56	31.37	31.30	31.27
3000	57.69	55.52	49.95	48.04	47.33	47.06	46.95	46.91
4000	76.92	74.02	66.59	64.06	63.11	62.74	62.60	62.54
5000	96.15	92.53	83.24	80.07	78.88	78.43	78.25	78.18
6000	115.38	111.03	99.89	96.08	94.66	94.11	93.89	93.81
7000	134.61	129.53	116.53	112.09	110.43	109.79	109.54	109.44
8000	153.83	148.04	133.18	128.11	126.21	125.48	125.19	125.08
9000	173.06	166.54	149.83	144.12	141.99	141.16	140.84	140.71
10000	192.29	185.05	166.47	160.13	157.76	156.85	156.49	156.35
11000	211.52	203.55	183.12	176.14	173.54	172.53	172.14	171.98
12000	230.75	222.05	199.77	192.16	189.31	188.21	187.78	187.61
13000	249.98	240.56	216.41	208.17	205.09	203.90	203.43	203.25
14000	269.21	259.06	233.06	224.18	220.86	219.58	219.08	218.88
15000	288.43	277.57	249.71	240.19	236.64	235.27	234.73	234.52
16000	307.66	296.07	266.35	256.21	252.42	250.95	250.38	250.15
17000	326.89	314.58	283.00	272.22	268.19	266.63	266.03	265.79
18000	346.12	333.08	299.65	288.23	283.97	282.32	281.67	281.42
19000	365.35	351.58	316.29	304.25	299.74	298.00	297.32	297.05
20000	384.58	370.09	332.94	320.26	315.52	313.69	312.97	312.69
21000	403.81	388.59	349.59	336.27	331.29	329.37	328.62	328.32
22000	423.04	407.10	366.23	352.28	347.07	345.05	344.27	343.96
23000	442.26	425.60	382.88	368.30	362.84	360.74	359.91	359.59
24000	461.49	444.10	399.53	384.31	378.62	376.42	375.56	375.22
25000	480.72	462.61	416.17	400.32	394.40	392.11	391.21	390.86
26000	499.95	481.11	432.82	416.33	410.17	407.79	406.86	406.49
27000	519.18	499.62	449.47	432.35	425.95	423.48	422.51	422.13
28000	538.41	518.12	466.11	448.36	441.72	439.16	438.16	437.76
29000	557.64	536.63	482.76	464.37	457.50	454.84	453.80	453.40
30000	576.86	555.13	499.41	480.38	473.27	470.53	469.45	469.03
31000	596.09	573.63	516.05	496.40	489.05	486.21	485.10	484.66
32000	615.32	592.14	532.70	512.41	504.83	501.90	500.75	500.30
33000	634.55	610.64	549.35	528.42	520.60	517.58	516.40	515.93
34000	653.78	629.15	565.99	544.44	536.38	533.26	532.05	531.57
35000	673.01	647.65	582.64	560.45	552.15	548.95	547.69	547.20
40000	769.15	740.17	665.87	640.51	631.03	627.37	625.94	625.37
45000	865.29	832.69	749.11	720.57	709.91	705.79	704.18	703.54
50000	961.44	925.21	832.34	800.64	788.79	784.21	782.42	781.71
55000	1057.58	1017.73	915.57	880.70	867.67	862.63	860.66	859.88
60000	1153.72	1110.25	998.81	960.76	946.54	941.05	938.90	938.05
65000	1249.87	1202.77	1082.04	1040.83	1025.42	1019.47	1017.14	1016.23
70000	1346.01	1295.29	1165.27	1120.89	1104.30	1097.89	1095.38	1094.40
75000	1442.15	1387.82	1248.51	1200.95	1183.18	1176.31	1173.62	1172.57
80000	1538.30	1480.34	1331.74	1281.02	1262.06	1254.73	1251.87	1250.74
85000	1634.44	1572.86	1414.97	1361.08	1340.94	1333.15	1330.11	1328.91
90000	1730.58	1665.38	1498.21	1441.14	1419.81	1411.57	1408.35	1407.08
95000	1826.73	1757.90	1581.44	1521.21	1498.69	1489.99	1486.59	1485.25
100000	1922.87	1850.42	1664.67	1601.27	1577.57	1568.41	1564.83	1563.42
105000	2019.01	1942.94	1747.91	1681.33	1656.45	1646.83	1643.07	1641.59
110000	2115.16	2035.46	1831.14	1761.40	1735.33	1725.25	1721.31	1719.76
115000	2211.30	2127.98	1914.37	1841.46	1814.20	1803.67	1799.55	1797.93
120000	2307.44	2220.50	1997.61	1921.52	1893.08	1882.09	1877.80	1876.10
125000	2403.59	2313.02	2080.84	2001.59	1971.96	1960.52	1956.04	1954.28
130000	2499.73	2405.54	2164.07	2081.65	2050.84	2038.94	2034.28	2032.45
135000	2595.87	2498.06	2247.31	2161.71	2129.72	2117.36	2112.52	2110.62
140000	2692.02	2590.58	2330.54	2241.78	2208.60	2195.78	2190.76	2188.79
145000	2788.16	2683.11	2413.78	2321.84	2287.47	2274.20	2269.00	2266.96
150000	2884.30	2775.63	2497.01	2401.90	2366.35	2352.62	2347.24	2345.13
155000	2980.45	2868.15	2580.24	2481.97	2445.23	2431.04	2425.48	2423.30
160000	3076.59	2960.67	2663.48	2562.03	2524.11	2509.46	2503.73	2501.47

185

19.000%   MONTHLY AMORTIZING PAYMENTS

AMOUNT OF LOAN	NUMBER OF YEARS IN TERM							
	1	2	3	4	5	6	7	8
$ 50	4.61	2.53	1.84	1.50	1.30	1.17	1.09	1.02
100	9.22	5.05	3.67	3.00	2.60	2.34	2.17	2.04
200	18.44	10.09	7.34	5.99	5.19	4.68	4.33	4.07
300	27.65	15.13	11.00	8.98	7.79	7.02	6.49	6.11
400	36.87	20.17	14.67	11.97	10.38	9.36	8.65	8.14
500	46.08	25.21	18.33	14.96	12.98	11.69	10.81	10.17
600	55.30	30.25	22.00	17.95	15.57	14.03	12.97	12.21
700	64.51	35.29	25.66	20.94	18.16	16.37	15.13	14.24
800	73.73	40.33	29.33	23.93	20.76	18.71	17.29	16.27
900	82.95	45.37	33.00	26.92	23.35	21.04	19.45	18.31
1000	92.16	50.41	36.66	29.91	25.95	23.38	21.61	20.34
2000	184.32	100.82	73.32	59.81	51.89	46.76	43.22	40.67
3000	276.47	151.23	109.97	89.71	77.83	70.14	64.83	61.01
4000	368.63	201.64	146.63	119.61	103.77	93.51	86.44	81.34
5000	460.79	252.05	183.29	149.51	129.71	116.89	108.05	101.67
6000	552.94	302.46	219.94	179.41	155.65	140.27	129.65	122.01
7000	645.10	352.87	256.60	209.31	181.59	163.64	151.26	142.34
8000	737.26	403.27	293.25	239.21	207.53	187.02	172.87	162.68
9000	829.41	453.68	329.91	269.11	233.47	210.40	194.48	183.01
10000	921.57	504.09	366.57	299.01	259.41	233.77	216.09	203.34
11000	1013.73	554.50	403.22	328.91	285.35	257.15	237.69	223.68
12000	1105.88	604.91	439.88	358.81	311.29	280.53	259.30	244.01
13000	1198.04	655.32	476.53	388.71	337.23	303.90	280.91	264.35
14000	1290.20	705.73	513.19	418.61	363.17	327.28	302.52	284.68
15000	1382.35	756.13	549.85	448.51	389.11	350.66	324.13	305.01
16000	1474.51	806.54	586.50	478.41	415.05	374.03	345.73	325.35
17000	1566.67	856.95	623.16	508.31	440.99	397.41	367.34	345.68
18000	1658.82	907.36	659.81	538.21	466.93	420.79	388.95	366.01
19000	1750.98	957.77	696.47	568.11	492.88	444.16	410.56	386.35
20000	1843.14	1008.18	733.13	598.01	518.82	467.54	432.17	406.68
21000	1935.29	1058.59	769.78	627.91	544.76	490.92	453.77	427.02
22000	2027.45	1108.99	806.44	657.81	570.70	514.29	475.38	447.35
23000	2119.61	1159.40	843.09	687.71	596.64	537.67	496.99	467.68
24000	2211.76	1209.81	879.75	717.61	622.58	561.05	518.60	488.02
25000	2303.92	1260.22	916.41	747.51	648.52	584.42	540.21	508.35
26000	2396.08	1310.63	953.06	777.41	674.46	607.80	561.81	528.69
27000	2488.23	1361.04	989.72	807.31	700.40	631.18	583.42	549.02
28000	2580.39	1411.43	1026.37	837.21	726.34	654.55	605.03	569.35
29000	2672.55	1461.85	1063.03	867.11	752.28	677.93	626.64	589.69
30000	2764.70	1512.26	1099.69	897.01	778.22	701.31	648.25	610.02
31000	2856.86	1562.67	1136.34	926.91	804.16	724.68	669.85	630.35
32000	2949.02	1613.08	1173.00	956.81	830.10	748.06	691.46	650.69
33000	3041.17	1663.49	1209.65	986.71	856.04	771.44	713.07	671.02
34000	3133.33	1713.90	1246.31	1016.61	881.98	794.81	734.68	691.36
35000	3225.49	1764.31	1282.97	1046.51	907.92	818.19	756.29	711.69
40000	3686.27	2016.35	1466.25	1196.01	1037.63	935.07	864.33	813.36
45000	4147.05	2268.39	1649.53	1345.51	1167.33	1051.96	972.37	915.03
50000	4607.83	2520.44	1832.81	1495.01	1297.03	1168.84	1080.41	1016.70
55000	5068.62	2772.48	2016.09	1644.51	1426.74	1285.72	1188.45	1118.37
60000	5529.40	3024.52	2199.37	1794.01	1556.44	1402.61	1296.49	1220.04
65000	5990.18	3276.57	2382.65	1943.51	1686.14	1519.49	1404.53	1321.71
70000	6450.97	3528.61	2565.93	2093.01	1815.84	1636.38	1512.57	1423.38
75000	6911.75	3780.65	2749.21	2242.51	1945.55	1753.26	1620.61	1525.05
80000	7372.53	4032.69	2932.49	2392.01	2075.25	1870.14	1728.65	1626.71
85000	7833.31	4284.74	3115.77	2541.52	2204.95	1987.03	1836.69	1728.38
90000	8294.10	4536.78	3299.05	2691.02	2334.65	2103.91	1944.73	1830.05
95000	8754.88	4788.82	3482.33	2840.52	2464.36	2220.79	2052.77	1931.72
100000	9215.66	5040.87	3665.61	2990.02	2594.06	2337.68	2160.81	2033.39
105000	9676.45	5292.91	3848.89	3139.52	2723.76	2454.56	2268.85	2135.06
110000	10137.23	5544.95	4032.17	3289.02	2853.47	2571.44	2376.89	2236.73
115000	10598.01	5797.00	4215.45	3438.52	2983.17	2688.33	2484.93	2338.40
120000	11058.79	6049.04	4398.73	3588.02	3112.87	2805.21	2592.97	2440.07
125000	11519.58	6301.08	4582.01	3737.52	3242.57	2922.10	2701.01	2541.74
130000	11980.36	6553.13	4765.29	3887.02	3372.28	3038.98	2809.05	2643.41
135000	12441.14	6805.17	4948.57	4036.52	3501.98	3155.86	2917.09	2745.08
140000	12901.93	7057.21	5131.85	4186.02	3631.68	3272.75	3025.13	2846.75
145000	13362.71	7309.25	5315.13	4335.52	3761.38	3389.63	3133.17	2948.42
150000	13823.49	7561.30	5498.41	4485.02	3891.09	3506.51	3241.21	3050.08
155000	14284.27	7813.34	5681.69	4634.52	4020.79	3623.40	3349.25	3151.75
160000	14745.06	8065.38	5864.97	4784.02	4150.49	3740.28	3457.29	3253.42

186

MONTHLY AMORTIZING PAYMENTS 19.000%

AMOUNT OF LOAN	\multicolumn{8}{c}{NUMBER OF YEARS IN TERM}
	9	10	15	20	25	30	35	40
$ 50	.97	.94	.85	.82	.80	.80	.80	.80
100	1.94	1.87	1.69	1.63	1.60	1.59	1.59	1.59
200	3.88	3.74	3.37	3.25	3.20	3.18	3.18	3.17
300	5.82	5.61	5.05	4.87	4.80	4.77	4.76	4.76
400	7.76	7.47	6.74	6.49	6.40	6.36	6.35	6.34
500	9.70	9.34	8.42	8.11	7.99	7.95	7.93	7.93
600	11.64	11.21	10.10	9.73	9.59	9.54	9.52	9.51
700	13.58	13.07	11.79	11.35	11.19	11.13	11.10	11.09
800	15.51	14.94	13.47	12.97	12.79	12.72	12.69	12.68
900	17.45	16.81	15.15	14.59	14.38	14.31	14.27	14.26
1000	19.39	18.67	16.83	16.21	15.98	15.89	15.86	15.85
2000	38.78	37.34	33.66	32.42	31.96	31.78	31.71	31.69
3000	58.17	56.01	50.49	48.63	47.94	47.67	47.57	47.53
4000	77.55	74.67	67.32	64.83	63.91	63.56	63.42	63.37
5000	96.94	93.34	84.15	81.04	79.89	79.45	79.28	79.21
6000	116.33	112.01	100.98	97.25	95.87	95.34	95.13	95.06
7000	135.71	130.68	117.81	113.45	111.84	111.23	110.99	110.90
8000	155.10	149.34	134.64	129.66	127.82	127.12	126.84	126.74
9000	174.49	168.01	151.46	145.87	143.80	143.01	142.70	142.58
10000	193.88	186.68	168.29	162.07	159.77	158.89	158.55	158.42
11000	213.26	205.34	185.12	178.28	175.75	174.78	174.41	174.26
12000	232.65	224.01	201.95	194.49	191.73	190.67	190.26	190.11
13000	252.04	242.68	218.78	210.69	207.70	206.56	206.12	205.95
14000	271.42	261.35	235.61	226.90	223.68	222.45	221.97	221.79
15000	290.81	280.01	252.44	243.11	239.66	238.34	237.83	237.63
16000	310.20	298.68	269.27	259.31	255.63	254.23	253.68	253.47
17000	329.59	317.35	286.09	275.52	271.61	270.12	269.54	269.31
18000	348.97	336.02	302.92	291.73	287.59	286.01	285.39	285.16
19000	368.36	354.68	319.75	307.94	303.56	301.89	301.25	301.00
20000	387.75	373.35	336.58	324.14	319.54	317.78	317.10	316.84
21000	407.13	392.02	353.41	340.35	335.52	333.67	332.96	332.68
22000	426.52	410.68	370.24	356.56	351.49	349.56	348.81	348.52
23000	445.91	429.35	387.07	372.76	367.47	365.45	364.67	364.37
24000	465.29	448.02	403.90	388.97	383.45	381.34	380.52	380.21
25000	484.68	466.69	420.72	405.18	399.43	397.23	396.38	396.05
26000	504.07	485.35	437.55	421.38	415.40	413.12	412.23	411.89
27000	523.46	504.02	454.38	437.59	431.38	429.01	428.09	427.73
28000	542.84	522.69	471.21	453.80	447.36	444.89	443.94	443.57
29000	562.23	541.35	488.04	470.00	463.33	460.78	459.80	459.42
30000	581.62	560.02	504.87	486.21	479.31	476.67	475.65	475.26
31000	601.00	578.69	521.70	502.42	495.29	492.56	491.51	491.10
32000	620.39	597.36	538.53	518.62	511.26	508.45	507.36	506.94
33000	639.78	616.02	555.35	534.83	527.24	524.34	523.22	522.78
34000	659.17	634.69	572.18	551.04	543.22	540.23	539.07	538.62
35000	678.55	653.36	589.01	567.24	559.19	556.12	554.93	554.47
40000	775.49	746.69	673.16	648.28	639.08	635.56	634.20	633.67
45000	872.42	840.03	757.30	729.31	718.96	715.01	713.48	712.88
50000	969.36	933.37	841.44	810.35	798.85	794.45	792.75	792.09
55000	1066.29	1026.70	925.59	891.38	878.73	873.90	872.03	871.30
60000	1163.23	1120.04	1009.73	972.42	958.61	953.34	951.30	950.51
65000	1260.17	1213.38	1093.87	1053.45	1038.50	1032.79	1030.58	1029.72
70000	1357.10	1306.71	1178.02	1134.48	1118.38	1112.23	1109.85	1108.93
75000	1454.04	1400.05	1262.16	1215.52	1198.27	1191.67	1189.13	1188.14
80000	1550.97	1493.38	1346.31	1296.55	1278.15	1271.12	1268.40	1267.34
85000	1647.91	1586.72	1430.45	1377.59	1358.03	1350.56	1347.68	1346.55
90000	1744.84	1680.06	1514.59	1458.62	1437.92	1430.01	1426.95	1425.76
95000	1841.78	1773.39	1598.74	1539.66	1517.80	1509.45	1506.22	1504.97
100000	1938.71	1866.73	1682.88	1620.69	1597.69	1588.90	1585.50	1584.18
105000	2035.65	1960.06	1767.02	1701.72	1677.57	1668.34	1664.77	1663.39
110000	2132.58	2053.40	1851.17	1782.76	1757.45	1747.79	1744.05	1742.60
115000	2229.52	2146.74	1935.31	1863.79	1837.34	1827.23	1823.32	1821.81
120000	2326.45	2240.07	2019.46	1944.83	1917.22	1906.68	1902.60	1901.01
125000	2423.39	2333.41	2103.60	2025.86	1997.11	1986.12	1981.87	1980.22
130000	2520.33	2426.75	2187.74	2106.90	2076.99	2065.57	2061.15	2059.43
135000	2617.26	2520.08	2271.89	2187.93	2156.87	2145.01	2140.42	2138.64
140000	2714.20	2613.42	2356.03	2268.96	2236.76	2224.45	2219.70	2217.85
145000	2811.13	2706.75	2440.18	2350.00	2316.64	2303.90	2298.97	2297.06
150000	2908.07	2800.09	2524.32	2431.03	2396.53	2383.34	2378.25	2376.27
155000	3005.00	2893.43	2608.46	2512.07	2476.41	2462.79	2457.52	2455.48
160000	3101.94	2986.76	2692.61	2593.10	2556.29	2542.23	2536.80	2534.68

187

19.250% MONTHLY AMORTIZING PAYMENTS

AMOUNT OF LOAN	NUMBER OF YEARS IN TERM							
	1	2	3	4	5	6	7	8
$ 50	4.62	2.53	1.84	1.51	1.31	1.18	1.09	1.03
100	9.23	5.06	3.68	3.01	2.61	2.36	2.18	2.05
200	18.46	10.11	7.36	6.01	5.22	4.71	4.36	4.10
300	27.69	15.16	11.04	9.01	7.83	7.06	6.53	6.15
400	36.92	20.22	14.72	12.02	10.44	9.41	8.71	8.20
500	46.14	25.27	18.40	15.02	13.04	11.77	10.88	10.25
600	55.37	30.32	22.07	18.02	15.65	14.12	13.06	12.30
700	64.60	35.38	25.75	21.03	18.26	16.47	15.23	14.35
800	73.83	40.43	29.43	24.03	20.87	18.82	17.41	16.40
900	83.05	45.48	33.11	27.03	23.48	21.17	19.59	18.44
1000	92.28	50.54	36.79	30.04	26.08	23.53	21.76	20.49
2000	184.56	101.07	73.57	60.07	52.16	47.05	43.52	40.98
3000	276.83	151.60	110.35	90.10	78.24	70.57	65.28	61.47
4000	369.11	202.13	147.14	120.13	104.32	94.09	87.03	81.96
5000	461.38	252.66	183.92	150.17	130.40	117.61	108.79	102.44
6000	553.66	303.19	220.70	180.20	156.47	141.13	130.55	122.93
7000	645.94	353.72	257.48	210.23	182.55	164.65	152.30	143.42
8000	738.21	404.25	294.27	240.26	208.63	188.17	174.06	163.91
9000	830.49	454.78	331.05	270.29	234.71	211.69	195.82	184.40
10000	922.76	505.31	367.83	300.33	260.79	235.21	217.57	204.88
11000	1015.04	555.84	404.61	330.36	286.87	258.73	239.33	225.37
12000	1107.32	606.37	441.40	360.39	312.94	282.25	261.09	245.86
13000	1199.59	656.90	478.18	390.42	339.02	305.77	282.84	266.35
14000	1291.87	707.43	514.96	420.46	365.10	329.29	304.60	286.84
15000	1384.14	757.96	551.74	450.49	391.18	352.81	326.36	307.32
16000	1476.42	808.49	588.53	480.52	417.26	376.33	348.11	327.81
17000	1568.70	859.02	625.31	510.55	443.34	399.85	369.87	348.30
18000	1660.97	909.55	662.09	540.58	469.41	423.37	391.63	368.79
19000	1753.25	960.08	698.87	570.62	495.49	446.89	413.38	389.27
20000	1845.52	1010.61	735.66	600.65	521.57	470.41	435.14	409.76
21000	1937.80	1061.14	772.44	630.68	547.65	493.93	456.90	430.25
22000	2030.08	1111.67	809.22	660.71	573.73	517.45	478.66	450.74
23000	2122.35	1162.20	846.00	690.75	599.81	540.97	500.41	471.23
24000	2214.63	1212.73	882.79	720.78	625.88	564.49	522.17	491.71
25000	2306.90	1263.26	919.57	750.81	651.96	588.01	543.93	512.20
26000	2399.18	1313.79	956.35	780.84	678.04	611.53	565.68	532.69
27000	2491.46	1364.32	993.13	810.87	704.12	635.05	587.44	553.18
28000	2583.73	1414.85	1029.92	840.91	730.20	658.57	609.20	573.67
29000	2676.01	1465.38	1066.70	870.94	756.28	682.09	630.95	594.15
30000	2768.28	1515.91	1103.48	900.97	782.35	705.61	652.71	614.64
31000	2860.56	1566.44	1140.26	931.00	808.43	729.13	674.47	635.13
32000	2952.83	1616.97	1177.05	961.04	834.51	752.65	696.22	655.62
33000	3045.11	1667.50	1213.83	991.07	860.59	776.17	717.98	676.11
34000	3137.39	1718.03	1250.61	1021.10	886.67	799.69	739.74	696.59
35000	3229.66	1768.56	1287.39	1051.13	912.75	823.21	761.49	717.08
40000	3691.04	2021.21	1471.31	1201.29	1043.14	940.81	870.28	819.52
45000	4152.42	2273.86	1655.22	1351.45	1173.53	1058.41	979.06	921.96
50000	4613.80	2526.51	1839.13	1501.62	1303.92	1176.01	1087.85	1024.40
55000	5075.18	2779.16	2023.04	1651.78	1434.31	1293.61	1196.63	1126.84
60000	5536.56	3031.81	2206.96	1801.94	1564.70	1411.21	1305.41	1229.28
65000	5997.94	3284.47	2390.87	1952.10	1695.09	1528.81	1414.20	1331.72
70000	6459.32	3537.12	2574.78	2102.26	1825.49	1646.41	1522.98	1434.16
75000	6920.70	3789.77	2758.70	2252.42	1955.88	1764.01	1631.77	1536.60
80000	7382.08	4042.42	2942.61	2402.58	2086.27	1881.61	1740.55	1639.04
85000	7843.46	4295.07	3126.52	2552.74	2216.66	1999.21	1849.33	1741.48
90000	8304.84	4547.72	3310.43	2702.90	2347.05	2116.81	1958.12	1843.92
95000	8766.22	4800.37	3494.35	2853.06	2477.44	2234.41	2066.90	1946.35
100000	9227.60	5053.02	3678.26	3003.23	2607.84	2352.01	2175.69	2048.79
105000	9688.98	5305.67	3862.17	3153.39	2738.23	2469.61	2284.47	2151.23
110000	10150.36	5558.32	4046.08	3303.55	2868.62	2587.21	2393.26	2253.67
115000	10611.74	5810.97	4230.00	3453.71	2999.01	2704.81	2502.04	2356.11
120000	11073.12	6063.62	4413.91	3603.87	3129.40	2822.41	2610.82	2458.55
125000	11534.50	6316.28	4597.82	3754.03	3259.79	2940.02	2719.61	2560.99
130000	11995.88	6568.93	4781.74	3904.19	3390.18	3057.62	2828.39	2663.43
135000	12457.26	6821.58	4965.65	4054.35	3520.58	3175.22	2937.18	2765.87
140000	12918.64	7074.23	5149.56	4204.51	3650.97	3292.82	3045.96	2868.31
145000	13380.02	7326.88	5333.47	4354.67	3781.36	3410.42	3154.74	2970.75
150000	13841.40	7579.53	5517.39	4504.84	3911.75	3528.02	3263.53	3073.19
155000	14302.77	7832.18	5701.30	4655.00	4042.14	3645.62	3372.31	3175.63
160000	14764.15	8084.83	5885.21	4805.16	4172.53	3763.22	3481.10	3278.07

AMOUNT OF LOAN	NUMBER OF YEARS IN TERM							
	9	10	15	20	25	30	35	40
$ 50	.98	.95	.86	.83	.81	.81	.81	.81
100	1.96	1.89	1.71	1.65	1.62	1.61	1.61	1.61
200	3.91	3.77	3.41	3.29	3.24	3.22	3.22	3.21
300	5.87	5.65	5.11	4.93	4.86	4.83	4.82	4.82
400	7.82	7.54	6.81	6.57	6.48	6.44	6.43	6.42
500	9.78	9.42	8.51	8.21	8.09	8.05	8.04	8.03
600	11.73	11.30	10.21	9.85	9.71	9.66	9.64	9.63
700	13.69	13.19	11.91	11.49	11.33	11.27	11.25	11.24
800	15.64	15.07	13.61	13.13	12.95	12.88	12.85	12.84
900	17.60	16.95	15.32	14.77	14.57	14.49	14.46	14.45
1000	19.55	18.84	17.02	16.41	16.18	16.10	16.07	16.05
2000	39.10	37.67	34.03	32.81	32.36	32.19	32.13	32.10
3000	58.64	56.50	51.04	49.21	48.54	48.29	48.19	48.15
4000	78.19	75.33	68.05	65.61	64.72	64.38	64.25	64.20
5000	97.74	94.16	85.06	82.01	80.90	80.47	80.31	80.25
6000	117.28	112.99	102.07	98.41	97.07	96.57	96.38	96.30
7000	136.83	131.82	119.09	114.82	113.25	112.66	112.44	112.35
8000	156.37	150.65	136.10	131.22	129.43	128.76	128.50	128.40
9000	175.92	169.48	153.11	147.62	145.61	144.85	144.56	144.45
10000	195.47	188.31	170.12	164.02	161.79	160.94	160.62	160.50
11000	215.01	207.15	187.13	180.42	177.97	177.04	176.68	176.55
12000	234.56	225.98	204.14	196.82	194.14	193.13	192.75	192.60
13000	254.10	244.81	221.15	213.22	210.32	209.23	208.81	208.65
14000	273.65	263.64	238.17	229.63	226.50	225.32	224.87	224.70
15000	293.20	282.47	255.18	246.03	242.68	241.41	240.93	240.75
16000	312.74	301.30	272.19	262.43	258.86	257.51	256.99	256.80
17000	332.29	320.13	289.20	278.83	275.04	273.60	273.05	272.84
18000	351.83	338.96	306.21	295.23	291.21	289.70	289.12	288.89
19000	371.38	357.79	323.22	311.63	307.39	305.79	305.18	304.94
20000	390.93	376.62	340.23	328.04	323.57	321.88	321.24	320.99
21000	410.47	395.45	357.25	344.44	339.75	337.98	337.30	337.04
22000	430.02	414.29	374.26	360.84	355.93	354.07	353.36	353.09
23000	449.56	433.12	391.27	377.24	372.11	370.17	369.43	369.14
24000	469.11	451.95	408.28	393.64	388.28	386.26	385.49	385.19
25000	488.66	470.78	425.29	410.04	404.46	402.35	401.55	401.24
26000	508.20	489.61	442.30	426.44	420.64	418.45	417.61	417.29
27000	527.75	508.44	459.31	442.85	436.82	434.54	433.67	433.34
28000	547.30	527.27	476.33	459.25	453.00	450.64	449.73	449.39
29000	566.84	546.10	493.34	475.65	469.17	466.73	465.80	465.44
30000	586.39	564.93	510.35	492.05	485.35	482.82	481.86	481.49
31000	605.93	583.76	527.36	508.45	501.53	498.92	497.92	497.54
32000	625.48	602.59	544.37	524.85	517.71	515.01	513.98	513.59
33000	645.03	621.43	561.38	541.25	533.89	531.11	530.04	529.63
34000	664.57	640.26	578.39	557.66	550.07	547.20	546.10	545.68
35000	684.12	659.09	595.41	574.06	566.24	563.29	562.17	561.73
40000	781.85	753.24	680.46	656.07	647.14	643.76	642.48	641.98
45000	879.58	847.40	765.52	738.07	728.03	724.23	722.78	722.23
50000	977.31	941.55	850.58	820.08	808.92	804.70	803.09	802.47
55000	1075.04	1035.71	935.63	902.09	889.81	885.17	883.40	882.72
60000	1172.77	1129.86	1020.69	984.10	970.70	965.64	963.71	962.97
65000	1270.50	1224.02	1105.75	1066.10	1051.59	1046.11	1044.02	1043.22
70000	1368.23	1318.17	1190.81	1148.11	1132.48	1126.58	1124.33	1123.46
75000	1465.96	1412.32	1275.86	1230.12	1213.38	1207.05	1204.64	1203.71
80000	1563.69	1506.48	1360.92	1312.13	1294.27	1287.52	1284.95	1283.96
85000	1661.42	1600.63	1445.98	1394.13	1375.16	1367.99	1365.25	1364.20
90000	1759.15	1694.79	1531.03	1476.14	1456.05	1448.46	1445.56	1444.45
95000	1856.88	1788.94	1616.09	1558.15	1536.94	1528.93	1525.87	1524.70
100000	1954.61	1883.10	1701.15	1640.16	1617.83	1609.40	1606.18	1604.94
105000	2052.34	1977.25	1786.21	1722.16	1698.72	1689.87	1686.49	1685.19
110000	2150.07	2071.41	1871.26	1804.17	1779.62	1770.34	1766.80	1765.44
115000	2247.80	2165.56	1956.32	1886.18	1860.51	1850.81	1847.11	1845.69
120000	2345.54	2259.72	2041.38	1968.19	1941.40	1931.28	1927.42	1925.93
125000	2443.27	2353.87	2126.43	2050.19	2022.29	2011.75	2007.72	2006.18
130000	2541.00	2448.03	2211.49	2132.20	2103.18	2092.22	2088.03	2086.43
135000	2638.73	2542.18	2296.55	2214.21	2184.07	2172.69	2168.34	2166.67
140000	2736.46	2636.34	2381.61	2296.22	2264.96	2253.16	2248.65	2246.92
145000	2834.19	2730.49	2466.66	2378.22	2345.85	2333.63	2328.96	2327.17
150000	2931.92	2824.64	2551.72	2460.23	2426.75	2414.10	2409.27	2407.41
155000	3029.65	2918.80	2636.78	2542.24	2507.64	2494.57	2489.58	2487.66
160000	3127.38	3012.95	2721.83	2624.25	2588.53	2575.04	2569.89	2567.91

MONTHLY AMORTIZING PAYMENTS

AMOUNT OF LOAN	NUMBER OF YEARS IN TERM							
	1	2	3	4	5	6	7	8
$ 50	4.62	2.54	1.85	1.51	1.32	1.19	1.10	1.04
100	9.24	5.07	3.70	3.02	2.63	2.37	2.20	2.07
200	18.48	10.14	7.39	6.04	5.25	4.74	4.39	4.13
300	27.72	15.20	11.08	9.05	7.87	7.10	6.58	6.20
400	36.96	20.27	14.77	12.07	10.49	9.47	8.77	8.26
500	46.20	25.33	18.46	15.09	13.11	11.84	10.96	10.33
600	55.44	30.40	22.15	18.10	15.73	14.20	13.15	12.39
700	64.68	35.46	25.84	21.12	18.36	16.57	15.34	14.45
800	73.92	40.53	29.53	24.14	20.98	18.94	17.53	16.52
900	83.16	45.59	33.22	27.15	23.60	21.30	19.72	18.58
1000	92.40	50.66	36.91	30.17	26.22	23.67	21.91	20.65
2000	184.80	101.31	73.82	60.33	52.44	47.33	43.82	41.29
3000	277.19	151.96	110.73	90.50	78.65	71.00	65.72	61.93
4000	369.59	202.61	147.64	120.66	104.87	94.66	87.63	82.57
5000	461.98	253.26	184.55	150.83	131.09	118.32	109.54	103.22
6000	554.38	303.92	221.46	180.99	157.30	141.99	131.44	123.86
7000	646.77	354.57	258.37	211.16	183.52	165.65	153.35	144.50
8000	739.17	405.22	295.28	241.32	209.74	189.32	175.25	165.14
9000	831.56	455.87	332.19	271.49	235.95	212.98	197.16	185.79
10000	923.96	506.52	369.10	301.65	262.17	236.64	219.07	206.43
11000	1016.35	557.18	406.01	331.82	288.39	260.31	240.97	227.07
12000	1108.75	607.83	442.92	361.98	314.60	283.97	262.88	247.71
13000	1201.14	658.48	479.83	392.14	340.82	307.64	284.78	268.36
14000	1293.54	709.13	516.74	422.31	367.04	331.30	306.69	289.00
15000	1385.94	759.78	553.64	452.47	393.25	354.96	328.60	309.64
16000	1478.33	810.44	590.55	482.64	419.47	378.63	350.50	330.28
17000	1570.73	861.09	627.46	512.80	445.68	402.29	372.41	350.93
18000	1663.12	911.74	664.37	542.97	471.90	425.95	394.32	371.57
19000	1755.52	962.39	701.28	573.13	498.12	449.62	416.22	392.21
20000	1847.91	1013.04	738.19	603.30	524.33	473.28	438.13	412.85
21000	1940.31	1063.69	775.10	633.46	550.55	496.95	460.03	433.50
22000	2032.70	1114.35	812.01	663.63	576.77	520.61	481.94	454.14
23000	2125.10	1165.00	848.92	693.79	602.98	544.27	503.85	474.78
24000	2217.49	1215.65	885.83	723.96	629.20	567.94	525.75	495.42
25000	2309.89	1266.30	922.74	754.12	655.42	591.60	547.66	516.07
26000	2402.28	1316.95	959.65	784.28	681.63	615.27	569.56	536.71
27000	2494.68	1367.61	996.56	814.45	707.85	638.93	591.47	557.35
28000	2587.08	1418.26	1033.47	844.61	734.07	662.59	613.38	577.99
29000	2679.47	1468.91	1070.38	874.78	760.28	686.26	635.28	598.64
30000	2771.87	1519.56	1107.28	904.94	786.50	709.92	657.19	619.28
31000	2864.26	1570.21	1144.19	935.11	812.71	733.59	679.09	639.92
32000	2956.66	1620.87	1181.10	965.27	838.93	757.25	701.00	660.58
33000	3049.05	1671.52	1218.01	995.44	865.15	780.91	722.91	681.21
34000	3141.45	1722.17	1254.92	1025.60	891.36	804.58	744.81	701.85
35000	3233.84	1772.82	1291.83	1055.77	917.58	828.24	766.72	722.49
40000	3695.82	2026.08	1476.38	1206.59	1048.66	946.56	876.25	825.70
45000	4157.80	2279.34	1660.92	1357.41	1179.75	1064.88	985.78	928.92
50000	4619.77	2532.60	1845.47	1508.24	1310.83	1183.20	1095.31	1032.13
55000	5081.75	2785.86	2030.02	1659.06	1441.91	1301.52	1204.84	1135.34
60000	5543.73	3039.12	2214.56	1809.88	1572.99	1419.84	1314.37	1238.55
65000	6005.70	3292.38	2399.11	1960.70	1704.07	1538.16	1423.90	1341.76
70000	6467.68	3545.64	2583.66	2111.53	1835.16	1656.48	1533.43	1444.98
75000	6929.66	3798.90	2768.20	2262.35	1966.24	1774.80	1642.96	1548.19
80000	7391.63	4052.16	2952.75	2413.17	2097.32	1893.12	1752.49	1651.40
85000	7853.61	4305.41	3137.30	2564.00	2228.40	2011.44	1862.03	1754.61
90000	8315.59	4558.67	3321.84	2714.82	2359.49	2129.75	1971.56	1857.83
95000	8777.57	4811.93	3506.39	2865.64	2490.57	2248.07	2081.09	1961.04
100000	9239.54	5065.19	3690.94	3016.47	2621.65	2366.39	2190.62	2064.25
105000	9701.52	5318.45	3875.48	3167.29	2752.73	2484.71	2300.15	2167.46
110000	10163.50	5571.71	4060.03	3318.11	2883.81	2603.03	2409.68	2270.68
115000	10625.47	5824.97	4244.58	3468.93	3014.90	2721.35	2519.21	2373.89
120000	11087.45	6078.23	4429.12	3619.76	3145.98	2839.67	2628.74	2477.10
125000	11549.43	6331.49	4613.67	3770.58	3277.06	2957.99	2738.27	2580.31
130000	12011.40	6584.75	4798.22	3921.40	3408.14	3076.31	2847.80	2683.52
135000	12473.38	6838.01	4982.76	4072.23	3539.23	3194.63	2957.33	2786.74
140000	12935.36	7091.27	5167.31	4223.05	3670.31	3312.95	3066.86	2889.95
145000	13397.33	7344.53	5351.86	4373.87	3801.39	3431.27	3176.39	2993.16
150000	13859.31	7597.79	5536.40	4524.70	3932.47	3549.59	3285.92	3096.37
155000	14321.29	7851.05	5720.95	4675.52	4063.55	3667.91	3395.45	3199.59
160000	14783.26	8104.31	5905.49	4826.34	4194.64	3786.23	3504.98	3302.80

AMOUNT OF LOAN	NUMBER OF YEARS IN TERM							
	9	10	15	20	25	30	35	40
$ 50	.99	.95	.86	.83	.82	.82	.82	.82
100	1.98	1.90	1.72	1.66	1.64	1.63	1.63	1.63
200	3.95	3.80	3.44	3.32	3.28	3.26	3.26	3.26
300	5.92	5.70	5.16	4.98	4.92	4.89	4.89	4.88
400	7.89	7.60	6.88	6.64	6.56	6.52	6.51	6.51
500	9.86	9.50	8.60	8.30	8.20	8.15	8.14	8.13
600	11.83	11.40	10.32	9.96	9.83	9.78	9.77	9.76
700	13.80	13.30	12.04	11.62	11.47	11.41	11.39	11.38
800	15.77	15.20	13.76	13.28	13.11	13.04	13.02	13.01
900	17.74	17.10	15.48	14.94	14.75	14.67	14.65	14.64
1000	19.71	19.00	17.20	16.60	16.39	16.30	16.27	16.26
2000	39.42	38.00	34.39	33.20	32.77	32.60	32.54	32.52
3000	59.12	56.99	51.59	49.79	49.15	48.90	48.81	48.78
4000	78.83	75.99	68.78	66.39	65.53	65.20	65.08	65.03
5000	98.53	94.98	85.98	82.99	81.91	81.50	81.35	81.29
6000	118.24	113.98	103.17	99.58	98.29	97.80	97.62	97.55
7000	137.94	132.97	120.37	116.18	114.67	114.10	113.89	113.80
8000	157.65	151.97	137.56	132.78	131.05	130.40	130.15	130.06
9000	177.36	170.96	154.76	149.37	147.43	146.70	146.42	146.32
10000	197.06	189.96	171.95	165.97	163.81	163.00	162.69	162.58
11000	216.77	208.95	189.15	182.57	180.19	179.30	178.96	178.83
12000	236.47	227.95	206.34	199.16	196.57	195.60	195.23	195.09
13000	256.18	246.94	223.54	215.76	212.95	211.89	211.50	211.35
14000	275.88	265.94	240.73	232.36	229.33	228.19	227.77	227.60
15000	295.59	284.93	257.93	248.95	245.71	244.49	244.04	243.86
16000	315.30	303.93	275.12	265.55	262.09	260.79	260.30	260.12
17000	335.00	322.92	292.31	282.15	278.47	277.09	276.57	276.38
18000	354.71	341.92	309.51	298.74	294.85	293.39	292.84	292.63
19000	374.41	360.91	326.70	315.34	311.23	309.69	309.11	308.89
20000	394.12	379.91	343.90	331.94	327.61	325.99	325.38	325.15
21000	413.82	398.90	361.09	348.53	343.99	342.29	341.65	341.40
22000	433.53	417.90	378.29	365.13	360.37	358.59	357.92	357.66
23000	453.24	436.90	395.48	381.73	376.75	374.89	374.18	373.92
24000	472.94	455.89	412.68	398.32	393.13	391.19	390.45	390.18
25000	492.65	474.89	429.87	414.92	409.51	407.48	406.72	406.43
26000	512.35	493.88	447.07	431.52	425.89	423.78	422.99	422.69
27000	532.06	512.88	464.26	448.11	442.27	440.08	439.26	438.95
28000	551.76	531.87	481.46	464.71	458.65	456.38	455.53	455.20
29000	571.47	550.87	498.65	481.31	475.03	472.68	471.80	471.46
30000	591.17	569.86	515.85	497.90	491.41	488.98	488.07	487.72
31000	610.88	588.86	533.04	514.50	507.79	505.28	504.33	503.97
32000	630.59	607.85	550.24	531.10	524.17	521.58	520.60	520.23
33000	650.29	626.85	567.43	547.69	540.55	537.88	536.87	536.49
34000	670.00	645.84	584.62	564.29	556.93	554.18	553.14	552.75
35000	689.70	664.84	601.82	580.89	573.31	570.48	569.41	569.00
40000	788.23	759.81	687.79	663.87	655.21	651.97	650.75	650.29
45000	886.76	854.79	773.77	746.85	737.11	733.47	732.10	731.57
50000	985.29	949.77	859.74	829.84	819.01	814.96	813.44	812.86
55000	1083.82	1044.74	945.71	912.82	900.91	896.46	894.78	894.15
60000	1182.34	1139.72	1031.69	995.80	982.81	977.96	976.13	975.43
65000	1280.87	1234.69	1117.66	1078.79	1064.71	1059.45	1057.47	1056.72
70000	1379.40	1329.67	1203.63	1161.77	1146.61	1140.95	1138.81	1138.00
75000	1477.93	1424.65	1289.61	1244.75	1228.51	1222.44	1220.16	1219.29
80000	1576.46	1519.62	1375.58	1327.74	1310.41	1303.94	1301.50	1300.57
85000	1674.99	1614.60	1461.55	1410.72	1392.31	1385.44	1382.84	1381.86
90000	1773.51	1709.57	1547.53	1493.70	1474.21	1466.93	1464.19	1463.14
95000	1872.04	1804.55	1633.50	1576.69	1556.11	1548.43	1545.53	1544.43
100000	1970.57	1899.53	1719.48	1659.67	1638.01	1629.93	1626.87	1625.71
105000	2069.10	1994.50	1805.45	1742.65	1719.91	1711.42	1708.22	1707.00
110000	2167.63	2089.48	1891.42	1825.64	1801.81	1792.92	1789.56	1788.29
115000	2266.16	2184.46	1977.40	1908.62	1883.71	1874.41	1870.90	1869.57
120000	2364.68	2279.43	2063.37	1991.60	1965.61	1955.91	1952.25	1950.86
125000	2463.21	2374.41	2149.34	2074.59	2047.51	2037.41	2033.59	2032.14
130000	2561.74	2469.38	2235.32	2157.57	2129.41	2118.90	2114.93	2113.43
135000	2660.27	2564.36	2321.29	2240.55	2211.31	2200.40	2196.28	2194.71
140000	2758.80	2659.34	2407.26	2323.54	2293.21	2281.89	2277.62	2276.00
145000	2857.33	2754.31	2493.24	2406.52	2375.11	2363.39	2358.96	2357.28
150000	2955.85	2849.29	2579.21	2489.50	2457.01	2444.89	2440.31	2438.57
155000	3054.38	2944.26	2665.18	2572.49	2538.91	2526.38	2521.65	2519.85
160000	3152.91	3039.24	2751.16	2655.47	2620.81	2607.88	2602.99	2601.14

MONTHLY AMORTIZING PAYMENTS

AMOUNT OF LOAN	NUMBER OF YEARS IN TERM							
	1	2	3	4	5	6	7	8
$ 50	4.63	2.54	1.86	1.52	1.32	1.20	1.11	1.04
100	9.26	5.08	3.71	3.03	2.64	2.39	2.21	2.08
200	18.51	10.16	7.41	6.06	5.28	4.77	4.42	4.16
300	27.76	15.24	11.12	9.09	7.91	7.15	6.62	6.24
400	37.01	20.31	14.82	12.12	10.55	9.53	8.83	8.32
500	46.26	25.39	18.52	15.15	13.18	11.91	11.03	10.40
600	55.51	30.47	22.23	18.18	15.82	14.29	13.24	12.48
700	64.77	35.55	25.93	21.21	18.45	16.67	15.44	14.56
800	74.02	40.62	29.63	24.24	21.09	19.05	17.65	16.64
900	83.27	45.70	33.34	27.27	23.72	21.43	19.86	18.72
1000	92.52	50.78	37.04	30.30	26.36	23.81	22.06	20.80
2000	185.03	101.55	74.08	60.60	52.71	47.62	44.12	41.60
3000	277.55	152.33	111.11	90.90	79.07	71.43	66.17	62.40
4000	370.06	203.10	148.15	121.19	105.42	95.24	88.23	83.20
5000	462.58	253.87	185.19	151.49	131.78	119.05	110.28	103.99
6000	555.09	304.65	222.22	181.79	158.13	142.85	132.34	124.79
7000	647.61	355.42	259.26	212.09	184.49	166.66	154.40	145.59
8000	740.12	406.20	296.30	242.38	210.84	190.47	176.45	166.39
9000	832.64	456.97	333.33	272.68	237.20	214.28	198.51	187.18
10000	925.15	507.74	370.37	302.98	263.55	238.09	220.56	207.98
11000	1017.67	558.52	407.40	333.28	289.91	261.89	242.62	228.78
12000	1110.18	609.29	444.44	363.57	316.26	285.70	264.68	249.58
13000	1202.70	660.06	481.48	393.87	342.62	309.51	286.73	270.37
14000	1295.21	710.84	518.51	424.17	368.97	333.32	308.79	291.17
15000	1387.73	761.61	555.55	454.46	395.33	357.13	330.84	311.97
16000	1480.24	812.39	592.59	484.76	421.68	380.94	352.90	332.77
17000	1572.76	863.16	629.62	515.06	448.04	404.74	374.96	353.56
18000	1665.27	913.93	666.66	545.36	474.39	428.55	397.01	374.36
19000	1757.79	964.71	703.70	575.65	500.75	452.36	419.07	395.16
20000	1850.30	1015.48	740.73	605.95	527.10	476.17	441.12	415.96
21000	1942.82	1066.25	777.77	636.25	553.46	499.98	463.18	436.75
22000	2035.33	1117.03	814.80	666.55	579.81	523.78	485.24	457.55
23000	2127.85	1167.80	851.84	696.84	606.17	547.59	507.29	478.35
24000	2220.36	1218.58	888.88	727.14	632.52	571.40	529.35	499.15
25000	2312.88	1269.35	925.91	757.44	658.88	595.21	551.40	519.94
26000	2405.39	1320.12	962.95	787.74	685.23	619.02	573.46	540.74
27000	2497.91	1370.90	999.99	818.03	711.59	642.82	595.51	561.54
28000	2590.42	1421.67	1037.02	848.33	737.94	666.63	617.57	582.34
29000	2682.94	1472.44	1074.06	878.63	764.30	690.44	639.63	603.13
30000	2775.45	1523.22	1111.09	908.92	790.65	714.25	661.68	623.93
31000	2867.97	1573.99	1148.13	939.22	817.01	738.06	683.74	644.73
32000	2960.48	1624.77	1185.17	969.52	843.36	761.87	705.79	665.53
33000	3053.00	1675.54	1222.20	999.82	869.72	785.67	727.85	686.32
34000	3145.51	1726.31	1259.24	1030.11	896.07	809.48	749.91	707.12
35000	3238.03	1777.09	1296.28	1060.41	922.43	833.29	771.96	727.92
40000	3700.60	2030.96	1481.46	1211.90	1054.20	952.33	882.24	831.91
45000	4163.18	2284.82	1666.64	1363.38	1185.98	1071.37	992.52	935.90
50000	4625.75	2538.69	1851.82	1514.87	1317.75	1190.41	1102.80	1039.88
55000	5088.32	2792.56	2037.00	1666.36	1449.53	1309.45	1213.08	1143.87
60000	5550.90	3046.43	2222.18	1817.84	1581.30	1428.49	1323.36	1247.86
65000	6013.47	3300.30	2407.37	1969.33	1713.08	1547.53	1433.64	1351.85
70000	6476.05	3554.17	2592.55	2120.82	1844.85	1666.57	1543.92	1455.83
75000	6938.62	3808.04	2777.73	2272.30	1976.63	1785.62	1654.20	1559.82
80000	7401.20	4061.91	2962.91	2423.79	2108.40	1904.66	1764.48	1663.81
85000	7863.77	4315.77	3148.09	2575.28	2240.18	2023.70	1874.76	1767.80
90000	8326.35	4569.64	3333.27	2726.76	2371.95	2142.74	1985.04	1871.79
95000	8788.92	4823.51	3518.46	2878.25	2503.73	2261.78	2095.32	1975.77
100000	9251.49	5077.38	3703.64	3029.74	2635.50	2380.82	2205.60	2079.76
105000	9714.07	5331.25	3888.82	3181.22	2767.28	2499.86	2315.88	2183.75
110000	10176.64	5585.12	4074.00	3332.71	2899.05	2618.90	2426.16	2287.74
115000	10639.22	5838.99	4259.18	3484.20	3030.83	2737.94	2536.43	2391.72
120000	11101.79	6092.86	4444.36	3635.68	3162.60	2856.98	2646.71	2495.71
125000	11564.37	6346.72	4629.55	3787.17	3294.38	2976.02	2756.99	2599.70
130000	12026.94	6600.59	4814.73	3938.66	3426.15	3095.06	2867.27	2703.69
135000	12489.52	6854.46	4999.91	4090.14	3557.93	3214.10	2977.55	2807.68
140000	12952.09	7108.33	5185.09	4241.63	3689.70	3333.14	3087.83	2911.66
145000	13414.67	7362.20	5370.27	4393.12	3821.48	3452.18	3198.11	3015.65
150000	13877.24	7616.07	5555.45	4544.60	3953.25	3571.23	3308.39	3119.64
155000	14339.81	7869.94	5740.64	4696.09	4085.03	3690.27	3418.67	3223.63
160000	14802.39	8123.81	5925.82	4847.58	4216.80	3809.31	3528.95	3327.62

AMOUNT OF LOAN	NUMBER OF YEARS IN TERM							
	9	10	15	20	25	30	35	40
$ 50	1.00	.96	.87	.84	.83	.83	.83	.83
100	1.99	1.92	1.74	1.68	1.66	1.66	1.65	1.65
200	3.98	3.84	3.48	3.36	3.32	3.31	3.30	3.30
300	5.96	5.75	5.22	5.04	4.98	4.96	4.95	4.94
400	7.95	7.67	6.96	6.72	6.64	6.61	6.60	6.59
500	9.94	9.59	8.69	8.40	8.30	8.26	8.24	8.24
600	11.92	11.50	10.43	10.08	9.95	9.91	9.89	9.88
700	13.91	13.42	12.17	11.76	11.61	11.56	11.54	11.53
800	15.90	15.33	13.91	13.44	13.27	13.21	13.19	13.18
900	17.88	17.25	15.65	15.12	14.93	14.86	14.83	14.82
1000	19.87	19.17	17.38	16.80	16.59	16.51	16.48	16.47
2000	39.74	38.33	34.76	33.59	33.17	33.01	32.96	32.93
3000	59.60	57.49	52.14	50.38	49.75	49.52	49.43	49.40
4000	79.47	76.65	69.52	67.17	66.33	66.02	65.91	65.86
5000	99.33	95.81	86.90	83.97	82.92	82.53	82.38	82.33
6000	119.20	114.97	104.28	100.76	99.50	99.03	98.86	98.79
7000	139.07	134.13	121.65	117.55	116.08	115.54	115.33	115.26
8000	158.93	153.29	139.03	134.34	132.66	132.04	131.81	131.72
9000	178.80	172.45	156.41	151.14	149.24	148.55	148.29	148.19
10000	198.66	191.61	173.79	167.93	165.83	165.05	164.76	164.65
11000	218.53	210.77	191.17	184.72	182.41	181.56	181.24	181.12
12000	238.39	229.93	208.55	201.51	198.99	198.06	197.71	197.58
13000	258.26	249.09	225.93	218.30	215.57	214.56	214.19	214.05
14000	278.13	268.25	243.30	235.10	232.16	231.07	230.66	230.51
15000	297.99	287.41	260.68	251.89	248.74	247.57	247.14	246.98
16000	317.86	306.57	278.06	268.68	265.32	264.08	263.62	263.44
17000	337.72	325.73	295.44	285.47	281.90	280.58	280.09	279.91
18000	357.59	344.89	312.82	302.27	298.48	297.09	296.57	296.37
19000	377.46	364.05	330.20	319.06	315.07	313.59	313.04	312.84
20000	397.32	383.21	347.58	335.85	331.65	330.10	329.52	329.30
21000	417.19	402.37	364.95	352.64	348.23	346.60	345.99	345.77
22000	437.05	421.53	382.33	369.43	364.81	363.11	362.47	362.23
23000	456.92	440.69	399.71	386.23	381.39	379.61	378.95	378.70
24000	476.78	459.85	417.09	403.02	397.98	396.12	395.42	395.16
25000	496.65	479.01	434.47	419.81	414.56	412.62	411.90	411.63
26000	516.52	498.17	451.85	436.60	431.14	429.12	428.37	428.09
27000	536.38	517.33	469.23	453.40	447.72	445.63	444.85	444.56
28000	556.25	536.49	486.60	470.19	464.31	462.13	461.32	461.02
29000	576.11	555.65	503.98	486.98	480.89	478.64	477.80	477.49
30000	595.98	574.81	521.36	503.77	497.47	495.14	494.28	493.95
31000	615.84	593.97	538.74	520.56	514.05	511.65	510.75	510.42
32000	635.71	613.13	556.12	537.36	530.63	528.15	527.23	526.88
33000	655.58	632.29	573.50	554.15	547.22	544.66	543.70	543.34
34000	675.44	651.45	590.88	570.94	563.80	561.16	560.18	559.81
35000	695.31	670.61	608.25	587.73	580.38	577.67	576.65	576.27
40000	794.64	766.41	695.15	671.69	663.29	660.19	659.03	658.60
45000	893.97	862.21	782.04	755.66	746.20	742.71	741.41	740.92
50000	993.29	958.01	868.93	839.62	829.11	825.24	823.79	823.25
55000	1092.62	1053.81	955.83	923.58	912.02	907.76	906.17	905.57
60000	1191.95	1149.61	1042.72	1007.54	994.93	990.28	988.55	987.90
65000	1291.28	1245.41	1129.61	1091.50	1077.84	1072.80	1070.92	1070.22
70000	1390.61	1341.21	1216.50	1175.46	1160.76	1155.33	1153.30	1152.54
75000	1489.94	1437.01	1303.40	1259.42	1243.67	1237.85	1235.68	1234.87
80000	1589.27	1532.81	1390.29	1343.38	1326.58	1320.37	1318.06	1317.19
85000	1688.60	1628.61	1477.18	1427.34	1409.49	1402.90	1400.44	1399.52
90000	1787.93	1724.41	1564.07	1511.31	1492.40	1485.42	1482.82	1481.84
95000	1887.26	1820.21	1650.97	1595.27	1575.31	1567.94	1565.19	1564.17
100000	1986.58	1916.02	1737.86	1679.23	1658.22	1650.47	1647.57	1646.49
105000	2085.91	2011.82	1824.75	1763.19	1741.13	1732.99	1729.95	1728.81
110000	2185.24	2107.62	1911.65	1847.15	1824.04	1815.51	1812.33	1811.14
115000	2284.57	2203.42	1998.54	1931.11	1906.95	1898.04	1894.71	1893.46
120000	2383.90	2299.22	2085.43	2015.07	1989.86	1980.56	1977.09	1975.79
125000	2483.23	2395.02	2172.32	2099.03	2072.77	2063.08	2059.47	2058.11
130000	2582.56	2490.82	2259.22	2182.99	2155.68	2145.60	2141.84	2140.43
135000	2681.89	2586.62	2346.11	2266.96	2238.59	2228.13	2224.22	2222.76
140000	2781.22	2682.42	2433.00	2350.92	2321.51	2310.65	2306.60	2305.08
145000	2880.55	2778.22	2519.89	2434.88	2404.42	2393.17	2388.98	2387.41
150000	2979.87	2874.02	2606.79	2518.84	2487.33	2475.70	2471.36	2469.73
155000	3079.20	2969.82	2693.68	2602.80	2570.24	2558.22	2553.74	2552.06
160000	3178.53	3065.62	2780.57	2686.76	2653.15	2640.74	2636.11	2634.38

20.000% MONTHLY AMORTIZING PAYMENTS

AMOUNT OF LOAN	NUMBER OF YEARS IN TERM							
	1	2	3	4	5	6	7	8
$ 50	4.64	2.55	1.86	1.53	1.33	1.20	1.12	1.05
100	9.27	5.09	3.72	3.05	2.65	2.40	2.23	2.10
200	18.53	10.18	7.44	6.09	5.30	4.80	4.45	4.20
300	27.80	15.27	11.15	9.13	7.95	7.19	6.67	6.29
400	37.06	20.36	14.87	12.18	10.60	9.59	8.89	8.39
500	46.32	25.45	18.59	15.22	13.25	11.98	11.11	10.48
600	55.59	30.54	22.30	18.26	15.90	14.38	13.33	12.58
700	64.85	35.63	26.02	21.31	18.55	16.77	15.55	14.67
800	74.11	40.72	29.74	24.35	21.20	19.17	17.77	16.77
900	83.38	45.81	33.45	27.39	23.85	21.56	19.99	18.86
1000	92.64	50.90	37.17	30.44	26.50	23.96	22.21	20.96
2000	185.27	101.80	74.33	60.87	52.99	47.91	44.42	41.91
3000	277.91	152.69	111.50	91.30	79.49	71.86	66.62	62.86
4000	370.54	203.59	148.66	121.73	105.98	95.82	88.83	83.82
5000	463.18	254.48	185.82	152.16	132.47	119.77	111.04	104.77
6000	555.81	305.38	222.99	182.59	158.97	143.72	133.24	125.72
7000	648.45	356.28	260.15	213.02	185.46	167.67	155.45	146.68
8000	741.08	407.17	297.31	243.45	211.96	191.63	177.65	167.63
9000	833.72	458.07	334.48	273.88	238.45	215.58	199.86	188.58
10000	926.35	508.96	371.64	304.31	264.94	239.53	222.07	209.54
11000	1018.98	559.86	408.80	334.74	291.44	263.49	244.27	230.49
12000	1111.62	610.75	445.97	365.17	317.93	287.44	266.48	251.44
13000	1204.25	661.65	483.13	395.60	344.43	311.39	288.69	272.40
14000	1296.89	712.55	520.30	426.03	370.92	335.34	310.89	293.35
15000	1389.52	763.44	557.46	456.46	397.41	359.30	333.10	314.30
16000	1482.16	814.34	594.62	486.89	423.91	383.25	355.30	335.26
17000	1574.79	865.23	631.79	517.32	450.40	407.20	377.51	356.21
18000	1667.43	916.13	668.95	547.75	476.89	431.16	399.72	377.16
19000	1760.06	967.03	706.11	578.18	503.39	455.11	421.92	398.12
20000	1852.70	1017.92	743.28	608.61	529.88	479.06	444.13	419.07
21000	1945.33	1068.82	780.44	639.04	556.38	503.01	466.34	440.02
22000	2037.96	1119.71	817.60	669.47	582.87	526.97	488.54	460.98
23000	2130.60	1170.61	854.77	699.90	609.36	550.92	510.75	481.93
24000	2223.23	1221.50	891.93	730.33	635.86	574.87	532.95	502.88
25000	2315.87	1272.40	929.09	760.76	662.35	598.83	555.16	523.84
26000	2408.50	1323.30	966.26	791.19	688.85	622.78	577.37	544.79
27000	2501.14	1374.19	1003.42	821.62	715.34	646.73	599.57	565.74
28000	2593.77	1425.09	1040.59	852.06	741.83	670.68	621.78	586.69
29000	2686.41	1475.98	1077.75	882.49	768.33	694.64	643.98	607.65
30000	2779.04	1526.88	1114.91	912.92	794.82	718.59	666.19	628.60
31000	2871.67	1577.77	1152.08	943.35	821.32	742.54	688.40	649.55
32000	2964.31	1628.67	1189.24	973.78	847.81	766.50	710.60	670.51
33000	3056.94	1679.57	1226.40	1004.21	874.30	790.45	732.81	691.46
34000	3149.58	1730.46	1263.57	1034.64	900.80	814.40	755.02	712.41
35000	3242.21	1781.36	1300.73	1065.07	927.29	838.35	777.22	733.37
40000	3705.39	2035.84	1486.55	1217.22	1059.76	958.12	888.25	838.13
45000	4168.56	2290.32	1672.37	1369.37	1192.23	1077.88	999.28	942.90
50000	4631.73	2544.80	1858.18	1521.52	1324.70	1197.65	1110.31	1047.67
55000	5094.90	2799.27	2044.00	1673.67	1457.17	1317.41	1221.35	1152.43
60000	5558.08	3053.75	2229.82	1825.83	1589.64	1437.17	1332.38	1257.20
65000	6021.25	3308.23	2415.64	1977.98	1722.11	1556.94	1443.41	1361.96
70000	6484.42	3562.71	2601.46	2130.13	1854.58	1676.70	1554.44	1466.73
75000	6947.59	3817.19	2787.27	2282.28	1987.05	1796.47	1665.47	1571.50
80000	7410.77	4071.67	2973.09	2434.43	2119.52	1916.23	1776.50	1676.26
85000	7873.94	4326.15	3158.91	2586.59	2251.99	2036.00	1887.53	1781.03
90000	8337.11	4580.63	3344.73	2738.74	2384.45	2155.76	1998.56	1885.79
95000	8800.28	4835.11	3530.55	2890.89	2516.92	2275.52	2109.59	1990.56
100000	9263.46	5089.59	3716.36	3043.04	2649.39	2395.29	2220.62	2095.33
105000	9726.63	5344.06	3902.18	3195.19	2781.86	2515.05	2331.66	2200.09
110000	10189.80	5598.54	4088.00	3347.34	2914.33	2634.82	2442.69	2304.86
115000	10652.97	5853.02	4273.82	3499.50	3046.80	2754.58	2553.72	2409.62
120000	11116.15	6107.50	4459.64	3651.65	3179.27	2874.34	2664.75	2514.39
125000	11579.32	6361.98	4645.45	3803.80	3311.74	2994.11	2775.78	2619.16
130000	12042.49	6616.46	4831.27	3955.95	3444.21	3113.87	2886.81	2723.92
135000	12505.66	6870.94	5017.09	4108.10	3576.68	3233.64	2997.84	2828.69
140000	12968.84	7125.42	5202.91	4260.26	3709.15	3353.40	3108.87	2933.45
145000	13432.01	7379.90	5388.72	4412.41	3841.62	3473.16	3219.90	3038.22
150000	13895.18	7634.38	5574.54	4564.56	3974.09	3592.93	3330.93	3142.99
155000	14358.35	7888.85	5760.36	4716.71	4106.56	3712.69	3441.97	3247.75
160000	14821.53	8143.33	5946.18	4868.86	4239.03	3832.46	3553.00	3352.52

194

AMOUNT OF LOAN	NUMBER OF YEARS IN TERM							
	9	10	15	20	25	30	35	40
$ 50	1.01	.97	.88	.85	.84	.84	.84	.84
100	2.01	1.94	1.76	1.70	1.68	1.68	1.67	1.67
200	4.01	3.87	3.52	3.40	3.36	3.35	3.34	3.34
300	6.01	5.80	5.27	5.10	5.04	5.02	5.01	5.01
400	8.02	7.74	7.03	6.80	6.72	6.69	6.68	6.67
500	10.02	9.67	8.79	8.50	8.40	8.36	8.35	8.34
600	12.02	11.60	10.54	10.20	10.08	10.03	10.01	10.01
700	14.02	13.53	12.30	11.90	11.75	11.70	11.68	11.68
800	16.03	15.47	14.06	13.60	13.43	13.37	13.35	13.34
900	18.03	17.40	15.81	15.29	15.11	15.04	15.02	15.01
1000	20.03	19.33	17.57	16.99	16.79	16.72	16.69	16.68
2000	40.06	38.66	35.13	33.98	33.57	33.43	33.37	33.35
3000	60.08	57.98	52.69	50.97	50.36	50.14	50.05	50.02
4000	80.11	77.31	70.26	67.96	67.14	66.85	66.74	66.70
5000	100.14	96.63	87.82	84.95	83.93	83.56	83.42	83.37
6000	120.16	115.96	105.38	101.93	100.71	100.27	100.10	100.04
7000	140.19	135.28	122.95	118.92	117.50	116.98	116.78	116.71
8000	160.22	154.61	140.51	135.91	134.28	133.69	133.47	133.39
9000	180.24	173.94	158.07	152.90	151.07	150.40	150.15	150.06
10000	200.27	193.26	175.63	169.89	167.85	167.11	166.83	166.73
11000	220.30	212.59	193.20	186.88	184.63	183.82	183.52	183.40
12000	240.32	231.91	210.76	203.86	201.42	200.53	200.20	200.08
13000	260.35	251.24	228.32	220.85	218.20	217.24	216.88	216.75
14000	280.38	270.56	245.89	237.84	234.99	233.95	233.56	233.42
15000	300.40	289.89	263.45	254.83	251.77	250.66	250.25	250.09
16000	320.43	309.21	281.01	271.82	268.56	267.37	266.93	266.77
17000	340.46	328.54	298.58	288.81	285.34	284.08	283.61	283.44
18000	360.48	347.87	316.14	305.79	302.13	300.79	300.30	300.11
19000	380.51	367.19	333.70	322.78	318.91	317.50	316.98	316.79
20000	400.54	386.52	351.26	339.77	335.70	334.21	333.66	333.46
21000	420.56	405.84	368.83	356.76	352.48	350.92	350.34	350.13
22000	440.59	425.17	386.39	373.75	369.26	367.63	367.03	366.80
23000	460.61	444.49	403.95	390.73	386.05	384.34	383.71	383.48
24000	480.64	463.82	421.52	407.72	402.83	401.05	400.39	400.15
25000	500.67	483.14	439.08	424.71	419.62	417.76	417.07	416.82
26000	520.69	502.47	456.64	441.70	436.40	434.47	433.76	433.49
27000	540.72	521.80	474.21	458.69	453.19	451.18	450.44	450.17
28000	560.75	541.12	491.77	475.68	469.97	467.89	467.12	466.84
29000	580.77	560.45	509.33	492.66	486.76	484.60	483.81	483.51
30000	600.80	579.77	526.89	509.65	503.54	501.31	500.49	500.18
31000	620.83	599.10	544.46	526.64	520.33	518.02	517.17	516.86
32000	640.85	618.42	562.02	543.63	537.11	534.73	533.85	533.53
33000	660.88	637.75	579.58	560.62	553.89	551.44	550.54	550.20
34000	680.91	657.07	597.15	577.61	570.68	568.15	567.22	566.87
35000	700.93	676.40	614.71	594.59	587.46	584.86	583.90	583.55
40000	801.07	773.03	702.52	679.53	671.39	668.41	667.32	666.91
45000	901.20	869.66	790.34	764.48	755.31	751.96	750.73	750.27
50000	1001.33	966.28	878.15	849.42	839.23	835.51	834.14	833.64
55000	1101.46	1062.91	965.97	934.36	923.15	919.07	917.56	917.00
60000	1201.60	1159.54	1053.78	1019.30	1007.08	1002.62	1000.97	1000.36
65000	1301.73	1256.17	1141.60	1104.24	1091.00	1086.17	1084.39	1083.73
70000	1401.86	1352.79	1229.41	1189.18	1174.92	1169.72	1167.80	1167.09
75000	1501.99	1449.42	1317.23	1274.12	1258.84	1253.27	1251.21	1250.45
80000	1602.13	1546.05	1405.04	1359.06	1342.77	1336.82	1334.63	1333.82
85000	1702.26	1642.68	1492.86	1444.01	1426.69	1420.37	1418.04	1417.18
90000	1802.39	1739.31	1580.67	1528.95	1510.61	1503.92	1501.46	1500.54
95000	1902.52	1835.93	1668.49	1613.89	1594.53	1587.47	1584.87	1583.91
100000	2002.66	1932.56	1756.30	1698.83	1678.46	1671.02	1668.28	1667.27
105000	2102.79	2029.19	1844.12	1783.77	1762.38	1754.57	1751.70	1750.63
110000	2202.92	2125.82	1931.93	1868.71	1846.30	1838.13	1835.11	1834.00
115000	2303.05	2222.45	2019.75	1953.65	1930.22	1921.68	1918.53	1917.36
120000	2403.19	2319.07	2107.56	2038.59	2014.15	2005.23	2001.94	2000.72
125000	2503.32	2415.70	2195.38	2123.54	2098.07	2088.78	2085.35	2084.09
130000	2603.45	2512.33	2283.19	2208.48	2181.99	2172.33	2168.77	2167.45
135000	2703.58	2608.96	2371.01	2293.42	2265.91	2255.88	2252.18	2250.81
140000	2803.72	2705.58	2458.82	2378.36	2349.84	2339.43	2335.59	2334.17
145000	2903.85	2802.21	2546.63	2463.30	2433.76	2422.98	2419.01	2417.54
150000	3003.98	2898.84	2634.45	2548.24	2517.68	2506.53	2502.42	2500.90
155000	3104.11	2995.47	2722.26	2633.18	2601.61	2590.08	2585.84	2584.26
160000	3204.25	3092.10	2810.08	2718.12	2685.53	2673.63	2669.25	2667.63

AMOUNT OF LOAN	NUMBER OF YEARS IN TERM							
	1	2	3	4	5	6	7	8
$ 50	4.64	2.56	1.87	1.53	1.34	1.21	1.12	1.06
100	9.28	5.11	3.73	3.06	2.67	2.41	2.24	2.12
200	18.56	10.21	7.46	6.12	5.33	4.82	4.48	4.23
300	27.83	15.31	11.19	9.17	7.99	7.23	6.71	6.34
400	37.11	20.41	14.92	12.23	10.66	9.64	8.95	8.45
500	46.38	25.51	18.65	15.29	13.32	12.05	11.18	10.56
600	55.66	30.62	22.38	18.34	15.98	14.46	13.42	12.67
700	64.93	35.72	26.11	21.40	18.65	16.87	15.65	14.78
800	74.21	40.82	29.84	24.46	21.31	19.28	17.89	16.89
900	83.48	45.92	33.57	27.51	23.97	21.69	20.13	19.00
1000	92.76	51.02	37.30	30.57	26.64	24.10	22.36	21.11
2000	185.51	102.04	74.59	61.13	53.27	48.20	44.72	42.22
3000	278.27	153.06	111.88	91.70	79.90	72.30	67.08	63.33
4000	371.02	204.08	149.17	122.26	106.54	96.40	89.43	84.44
5000	463.78	255.10	186.46	152.82	133.17	120.49	111.79	105.55
6000	556.53	306.11	223.75	183.39	159.80	144.59	134.15	126.66
7000	649.28	357.13	261.04	213.95	186.44	168.69	156.50	147.77
8000	742.04	408.15	298.33	244.51	213.07	192.79	178.86	168.88
9000	834.79	459.17	335.62	275.08	239.70	216.89	201.22	189.99
10000	927.55	510.19	372.92	305.64	266.34	240.98	223.57	211.10
11000	1020.30	561.20	410.21	336.21	292.97	265.08	245.93	232.21
12000	1113.06	612.22	447.50	366.77	319.60	289.18	268.29	253.32
13000	1205.81	663.24	484.79	397.33	346.24	313.28	290.65	274.43
14000	1298.56	714.26	522.08	427.90	372.87	337.38	313.00	295.54
15000	1391.32	765.28	559.37	458.46	399.50	361.47	335.36	316.65
16000	1484.07	816.29	596.66	489.02	426.14	385.57	357.72	337.75
17000	1576.83	867.31	633.95	519.59	452.77	409.67	380.07	358.86
18000	1669.58	918.33	671.24	550.15	479.40	433.77	402.43	379.97
19000	1762.33	969.35	708.54	580.72	506.04	457.87	424.79	401.08
20000	1855.09	1020.37	745.83	611.28	532.67	481.96	447.14	422.19
21000	1947.84	1071.38	783.12	641.84	559.30	506.06	469.50	443.30
22000	2040.60	1122.40	820.41	672.41	585.93	530.16	491.86	464.41
23000	2133.35	1173.42	857.70	702.97	612.57	554.26	514.22	485.52
24000	2226.11	1224.44	894.99	733.53	639.20	578.36	536.57	506.63
25000	2318.86	1275.46	932.28	764.10	665.83	602.45	558.93	527.74
26000	2411.61	1326.47	969.57	794.66	692.47	626.55	581.29	548.85
27000	2504.37	1377.49	1006.86	825.23	719.10	650.65	603.64	569.96
28000	2597.12	1428.51	1044.16	855.79	745.73	674.75	626.00	591.07
29000	2689.88	1479.53	1081.45	886.35	772.37	698.85	648.36	612.18
30000	2782.63	1530.55	1118.74	916.92	799.00	722.94	670.71	633.29
31000	2875.39	1581.56	1156.03	947.48	825.63	747.04	693.07	654.40
32000	2968.14	1632.58	1193.32	978.04	852.27	771.14	715.43	675.50
33000	3060.89	1683.60	1230.61	1008.61	878.90	795.24	737.79	696.61
34000	3153.65	1734.62	1267.90	1039.17	905.53	819.34	760.14	717.72
35000	3246.40	1785.64	1305.19	1069.74	932.17	843.43	782.50	738.83
40000	3710.17	2040.73	1491.65	1222.55	1065.33	963.92	894.28	844.38
45000	4173.94	2295.82	1678.10	1375.37	1198.50	1084.41	1006.07	949.93
50000	4637.71	2550.91	1864.56	1528.19	1331.66	1204.90	1117.85	1055.47
55000	5101.49	2806.00	2051.01	1681.01	1464.83	1325.39	1229.64	1161.02
60000	5565.26	3061.09	2237.47	1833.83	1598.00	1445.88	1341.42	1266.57
65000	6029.03	3316.18	2423.93	1986.65	1731.16	1566.37	1453.21	1372.11
70000	6492.80	3571.27	2610.38	2139.47	1864.33	1686.86	1564.99	1477.66
75000	6956.57	3826.36	2796.84	2292.28	1997.49	1807.35	1676.78	1583.21
80000	7420.34	4081.45	2983.29	2445.10	2130.66	1927.84	1788.56	1688.75
85000	7884.11	4336.54	3169.75	2597.92	2263.83	2048.33	1900.35	1794.30
90000	8347.88	4591.63	3356.20	2750.74	2396.99	2168.82	2012.13	1899.85
95000	8811.65	4846.72	3542.66	2903.56	2530.16	2289.31	2123.92	2005.39
100000	9275.42	5101.81	3729.11	3056.38	2663.32	2409.80	2235.70	2110.94
105000	9739.20	5356.90	3915.57	3209.20	2796.49	2530.29	2347.49	2216.49
110000	10202.97	5611.99	4102.02	3362.01	2929.65	2650.78	2459.27	2322.04
115000	10666.74	5867.08	4288.48	3514.83	3062.82	2771.27	2571.06	2427.58
120000	11130.51	6122.17	4474.94	3667.65	3195.99	2891.76	2682.84	2533.13
125000	11594.28	6377.26	4661.39	3820.47	3329.15	3012.25	2794.63	2638.68
130000	12058.05	6632.35	4847.85	3973.29	3462.32	3132.74	2906.41	2744.22
135000	12521.82	6887.44	5034.30	4126.11	3595.48	3253.23	3018.20	2849.77
140000	12985.59	7142.53	5220.76	4278.93	3728.65	3373.72	3129.98	2955.32
145000	13449.36	7397.62	5407.21	4431.74	3861.82	3494.21	3241.77	3060.86
150000	13913.13	7652.71	5593.67	4584.56	3994.98	3614.70	3353.55	3166.41
155000	14376.91	7907.80	5780.12	4737.38	4128.15	3735.19	3465.34	3271.96
160000	14840.68	8162.89	5966.58	4890.20	4261.31	3855.68	3577.12	3377.50

AMOUNT OF LOAN	NUMBER OF YEARS IN TERM							
	9	**10**	**15**	**20**	**25**	**30**	**35**	**40**
$ 50	1.01	.98	.89	.86	.85	.85	.85	.85
100	2.02	1.95	1.78	1.72	1.70	1.70	1.69	1.69
200	4.04	3.90	3.55	3.44	3.40	3.39	3.38	3.38
300	6.06	5.85	5.33	5.16	5.10	5.08	5.07	5.07
400	8.08	7.80	7.10	6.88	6.80	6.77	6.76	6.76
500	10.10	9.75	8.88	8.60	8.50	8.46	8.45	8.45
600	12.12	11.70	10.65	10.32	10.20	10.15	10.14	10.13
700	14.14	13.65	12.43	12.03	11.90	11.85	11.83	11.82
800	16.16	15.60	14.20	13.75	13.59	13.54	13.52	13.51
900	18.17	17.55	15.98	15.47	15.29	15.23	15.21	15.20
1000	20.19	19.50	17.75	17.19	16.99	16.92	16.89	16.89
2000	40.38	38.99	35.50	34.37	33.98	33.84	33.78	33.77
3000	60.57	58.48	53.25	51.56	50.97	50.75	50.67	50.65
4000	80.76	77.97	71.00	68.74	67.95	67.67	67.56	67.53
5000	100.94	97.46	88.74	85.93	84.94	84.58	84.45	84.41
6000	121.13	116.95	106.49	103.11	101.93	101.50	101.34	101.29
7000	141.32	136.45	124.24	120.30	118.92	118.42	118.23	118.17
8000	161.51	155.94	141.99	137.48	135.90	135.33	135.12	135.05
9000	181.69	175.43	159.74	154.67	152.89	152.25	152.01	151.93
10000	201.88	194.92	177.48	171.85	169.88	169.16	168.90	168.81
11000	222.07	214.41	195.23	189.04	186.86	186.08	185.79	185.69
12000	242.26	233.90	212.98	206.22	203.85	203.00	202.68	202.57
13000	262.45	253.40	230.73	223.41	220.84	219.91	219.57	219.45
14000	282.63	272.89	248.48	240.59	237.83	236.83	236.46	236.33
15000	302.82	292.38	266.22	257.78	254.81	253.74	253.35	253.21
16000	323.01	311.87	283.97	274.96	271.80	270.66	270.24	270.09
17000	343.20	331.36	301.72	292.14	288.79	287.58	287.13	286.97
18000	363.38	350.85	319.47	309.33	305.77	304.49	304.02	303.85
19000	383.57	370.35	337.22	326.51	322.76	321.41	320.91	320.73
20000	403.76	389.84	354.96	343.70	339.75	338.32	337.80	337.61
21000	423.95	409.33	372.71	360.88	356.74	355.24	354.69	354.50
22000	444.14	428.82	390.46	378.07	373.72	372.16	371.58	371.38
23000	464.32	448.31	408.21	395.25	390.71	389.07	388.47	388.26
24000	484.51	467.80	425.96	412.44	407.70	405.99	405.36	405.14
25000	504.70	487.30	443.70	429.62	424.68	422.90	422.25	422.02
26000	524.89	506.79	461.45	446.81	441.67	439.82	439.14	438.90
27000	545.07	526.28	479.20	463.99	458.66	456.73	456.03	455.78
28000	565.26	545.77	496.95	481.18	475.65	473.65	472.92	472.66
29000	585.45	565.26	514.70	498.36	492.63	490.57	489.81	489.54
30000	605.64	584.75	532.44	515.55	509.62	507.48	506.70	506.42
31000	625.83	604.24	550.19	532.73	526.61	524.40	523.59	523.30
32000	646.01	623.74	567.94	549.92	543.59	541.31	540.48	540.18
33000	666.20	643.23	585.69	567.10	560.58	558.23	557.37	557.06
34000	686.39	662.72	603.44	584.28	577.57	575.15	574.26	573.94
35000	706.58	682.21	621.18	601.47	594.56	592.06	591.15	590.82
40000	807.52	779.67	709.92	687.39	679.49	676.64	675.60	675.22
45000	908.45	877.13	798.66	773.32	764.43	761.22	760.05	759.63
50000	1009.39	974.59	887.40	859.24	849.36	845.80	844.50	844.03
55000	1110.33	1072.04	976.14	945.16	934.30	930.38	928.95	928.43
60000	1211.27	1169.50	1064.88	1031.09	1019.23	1014.96	1013.40	1012.83
65000	1312.21	1266.96	1153.62	1117.01	1104.17	1099.54	1097.85	1097.24
70000	1413.15	1364.42	1242.36	1202.93	1189.11	1184.12	1182.30	1181.64
75000	1514.09	1461.88	1331.10	1288.86	1274.04	1268.70	1266.75	1266.04
80000	1615.03	1559.33	1419.84	1374.78	1358.98	1353.28	1351.20	1350.44
85000	1715.97	1656.79	1508.58	1460.70	1443.91	1437.86	1435.65	1434.85
90000	1816.90	1754.25	1597.32	1546.63	1528.85	1522.44	1520.10	1519.25
95000	1917.84	1851.71	1686.06	1632.55	1613.79	1607.02	1604.55	1603.65
100000	2018.78	1949.17	1774.80	1718.47	1698.72	1691.60	1689.00	1688.05
105000	2119.72	2046.62	1863.54	1804.40	1783.66	1776.18	1773.45	1772.46
110000	2220.66	2144.08	1952.28	1890.32	1868.59	1860.76	1857.90	1856.86
115000	2321.60	2241.54	2041.02	1976.24	1953.53	1945.34	1942.35	1941.26
120000	2422.54	2339.00	2129.76	2062.17	2038.46	2029.92	2026.80	2025.66
125000	2523.48	2436.46	2218.50	2148.09	2123.40	2114.50	2111.25	2110.07
130000	2624.41	2533.91	2307.24	2234.01	2208.34	2199.08	2195.70	2194.47
135000	2725.35	2631.37	2395.98	2319.94	2293.27	2283.65	2280.15	2278.87
140000	2826.29	2728.83	2484.72	2405.86	2378.21	2368.23	2364.60	2363.27
145000	2927.23	2826.29	2573.46	2491.78	2463.14	2452.81	2449.05	2447.67
150000	3028.17	2923.75	2662.20	2577.71	2548.08	2537.39	2533.50	2532.08
155000	3129.11	3021.20	2750.94	2663.63	2633.02	2621.97	2617.95	2616.48
160000	3230.05	3118.66	2839.68	2749.56	2717.95	2706.55	2702.40	2700.88

AMOUNT OF LOAN	NUMBER OF YEARS IN TERM							
	1	2	3	4	5	6	7	8
$ 50	4.65	2.56	1.88	1.54	1.34	1.22	1.13	1.07
100	9.29	5.12	3.75	3.07	2.68	2.43	2.26	2.13
200	18.58	10.23	7.49	6.14	5.36	4.85	4.51	4.26
300	27.87	15.35	11.23	9.21	8.04	7.28	6.76	6.38
400	37.15	20.46	14.97	12.28	10.71	9.70	9.01	8.51
500	46.44	25.58	18.71	15.35	13.39	12.13	11.26	10.64
600	55.73	30.69	22.46	18.42	16.07	14.55	13.51	12.76
700	65.02	35.80	26.20	21.49	18.75	16.98	15.76	14.89
800	74.30	40.92	29.94	24.56	21.42	19.40	18.01	17.02
900	83.59	46.03	33.68	27.63	24.10	21.82	20.26	19.14
1000	92.88	51.15	37.42	30.70	26.78	24.25	22.51	21.27
2000	185.75	102.29	74.84	61.40	53.55	48.49	45.02	42.54
3000	278.63	153.43	112.26	92.10	80.32	72.74	67.53	63.80
4000	371.50	204.57	149.68	122.79	107.10	96.98	90.04	85.07
5000	464.37	255.71	187.10	153.49	133.87	121.22	112.55	106.34
6000	557.25	306.85	224.52	184.19	160.64	145.47	135.05	127.60
7000	650.12	357.99	261.94	214.89	187.42	169.71	157.56	148.87
8000	743.00	409.13	299.36	245.58	214.19	193.95	180.07	170.13
9000	835.87	460.27	336.77	276.28	240.96	218.20	202.58	191.40
10000	928.74	511.41	374.19	306.98	267.73	242.44	225.09	212.67
11000	1021.62	562.55	411.61	337.68	294.51	266.68	247.60	233.93
12000	1114.49	613.69	449.03	368.37	321.28	290.93	270.10	255.20
13000	1207.37	664.83	486.45	399.07	348.05	315.17	292.61	276.46
14000	1300.24	715.97	523.87	429.77	374.83	339.41	315.12	297.73
15000	1393.11	767.11	561.29	460.47	401.60	363.66	337.63	319.00
16000	1485.99	818.25	598.71	491.16	428.37	387.90	360.14	340.26
17000	1578.86	869.39	636.13	521.86	455.14	412.15	382.65	361.53
18000	1671.74	920.53	673.54	552.56	481.92	436.39	405.15	382.79
19000	1764.61	971.67	710.96	583.26	508.69	460.63	427.66	404.06
20000	1857.48	1022.81	748.38	613.95	535.46	484.88	450.17	425.33
21000	1950.36	1073.95	785.80	644.65	562.24	509.12	472.68	446.59
22000	2043.23	1125.09	823.22	675.35	589.01	533.36	495.19	467.86
23000	2136.11	1176.23	860.64	706.05	615.78	557.61	517.69	489.12
24000	2228.98	1227.37	898.06	736.74	642.55	581.85	540.20	510.39
25000	2321.85	1278.51	935.48	767.44	669.33	606.09	562.71	531.66
26000	2414.73	1329.66	972.89	798.14	696.10	630.34	585.22	552.92
27000	2507.60	1380.80	1010.31	828.83	722.87	654.58	607.73	574.19
28000	2600.48	1431.94	1047.73	859.53	749.65	678.82	630.24	595.45
29000	2693.35	1483.08	1085.15	890.23	776.42	703.07	652.74	616.72
30000	2786.22	1534.22	1122.57	920.93	803.19	727.31	675.25	637.99
31000	2879.10	1585.36	1159.99	951.62	829.96	751.55	697.76	659.25
32000	2971.97	1636.50	1197.41	982.32	856.74	775.80	720.27	680.52
33000	3064.85	1687.64	1234.83	1013.02	883.51	800.04	742.78	701.78
34000	3157.72	1738.78	1272.25	1043.72	910.28	824.29	765.29	723.05
35000	3250.59	1789.92	1309.66	1074.41	937.06	848.53	787.79	744.32
40000	3714.96	2045.62	1496.76	1227.90	1070.92	969.75	900.33	850.65
45000	4179.33	2301.32	1683.85	1381.39	1204.78	1090.96	1012.88	956.98
50000	4643.70	2557.02	1870.95	1534.87	1338.65	1212.18	1125.42	1063.31
55000	5108.07	2812.73	2058.04	1688.36	1472.51	1333.40	1237.96	1169.64
60000	5572.44	3068.43	2245.14	1841.85	1606.38	1454.62	1350.50	1275.97
65000	6036.81	3324.13	2432.23	1995.34	1740.24	1575.83	1463.04	1382.30
70000	6501.18	3579.83	2619.32	2148.82	1874.11	1697.05	1575.58	1488.63
75000	6965.55	3835.53	2806.42	2302.31	2007.97	1818.27	1688.12	1594.96
80000	7429.92	4091.24	2993.51	2455.80	2141.83	1939.49	1800.66	1701.29
85000	7894.29	4346.94	3180.61	2609.28	2275.70	2060.71	1913.21	1807.62
90000	8358.66	4602.64	3367.70	2762.77	2409.56	2181.92	2025.75	1913.95
95000	8823.03	4858.34	3554.79	2916.26	2543.43	2303.14	2138.29	2020.28
100000	9287.40	5114.04	3741.89	3069.74	2677.29	2424.36	2250.83	2126.61
105000	9751.77	5369.75	3928.98	3223.23	2811.16	2545.58	2363.37	2232.94
110000	10216.14	5625.45	4116.08	3376.72	2945.02	2666.79	2475.91	2339.27
115000	10680.51	5881.15	4303.17	3530.21	3078.88	2788.01	2588.45	2445.60
120000	11144.88	6136.85	4490.27	3683.69	3212.75	2909.23	2700.99	2551.93
125000	11609.25	6392.55	4677.36	3837.18	3346.61	3030.45	2813.54	2658.26
130000	12073.62	6648.26	4864.45	3990.67	3480.48	3151.66	2926.08	2764.59
135000	12537.99	6903.96	5051.55	4144.15	3614.34	3272.88	3038.62	2870.92
140000	13002.36	7159.66	5238.64	4297.64	3748.21	3394.10	3151.16	2977.25
145000	13466.73	7415.36	5425.74	4451.13	3882.07	3515.32	3263.70	3083.58
150000	13931.10	7671.06	5612.83	4604.61	4015.93	3636.54	3376.24	3189.91
155000	14395.47	7926.77	5799.92	4758.10	4149.80	3757.75	3488.78	3296.24
160000	14859.84	8182.47	5987.02	4911.59	4283.66	3878.97	3601.32	3402.57

AMOUNT OF LOAN	NUMBER OF YEARS IN TERM							
	9	10	15	20	25	30	35	40
$ 50	1.02	.99	.90	.87	.86	.86	.86	.86
100	2.04	1.97	1.80	1.74	1.72	1.72	1.71	1.71
200	4.07	3.94	3.59	3.48	3.44	3.43	3.42	3.42
300	6.11	5.90	5.39	5.22	5.16	5.14	5.13	5.13
400	8.14	7.87	7.18	6.96	6.88	6.85	6.84	6.84
500	10.18	9.83	8.97	8.70	8.60	8.57	8.55	8.55
600	12.21	11.80	10.77	10.43	10.32	10.28	10.26	10.26
700	14.25	13.77	12.56	12.17	12.04	11.99	11.97	11.97
800	16.28	15.73	14.35	13.91	13.76	13.70	13.68	13.68
900	18.32	17.70	16.15	15.65	15.48	15.41	15.39	15.38
1000	20.35	19.66	17.94	17.39	17.20	17.13	17.10	17.09
2000	40.70	39.32	35.87	34.77	34.39	34.25	34.20	34.18
3000	61.05	58.98	53.81	52.15	51.58	51.37	51.30	51.27
4000	81.40	78.64	71.74	69.53	68.77	68.49	68.39	68.36
5000	101.75	98.30	89.67	86.91	85.96	85.61	85.49	85.45
6000	122.10	117.95	107.61	104.29	103.15	102.74	102.59	102.54
7000	142.45	137.61	125.54	121.68	120.34	119.86	119.69	119.62
8000	162.80	157.27	143.47	139.06	137.53	136.98	136.78	136.71
9000	183.15	176.93	161.41	156.44	154.72	154.10	153.88	153.80
10000	203.50	196.59	179.34	173.82	171.91	171.22	170.98	170.89
11000	223.85	216.25	197.27	191.20	189.10	188.34	188.07	187.98
12000	244.20	235.90	215.21	208.58	206.29	205.47	205.17	205.07
13000	264.55	255.56	233.14	225.97	223.48	222.59	222.27	222.15
14000	284.90	275.22	251.07	243.35	240.67	239.71	239.37	239.24
15000	305.25	294.88	269.01	260.73	257.86	256.83	256.46	256.33
16000	325.60	314.54	286.94	278.11	275.05	273.95	273.56	273.42
17000	345.95	334.19	304.87	295.49	292.24	291.08	290.66	290.51
18000	366.30	353.85	322.81	312.87	309.43	308.20	307.76	307.60
19000	386.65	373.51	340.74	330.25	326.62	325.32	324.85	324.68
20000	407.00	393.17	358.67	347.64	343.81	342.44	341.95	341.77
21000	427.35	412.83	376.61	365.02	361.00	359.56	359.05	358.86
22000	447.70	432.49	394.54	382.40	378.19	376.68	376.14	375.95
23000	468.05	452.14	412.47	399.78	395.38	393.81	393.24	393.04
24000	488.40	471.80	430.41	417.16	412.57	410.93	410.34	410.13
25000	508.74	491.46	448.34	434.54	429.76	428.05	427.44	427.21
26000	529.09	511.12	466.28	451.93	446.95	445.17	444.53	444.30
27000	549.44	530.78	484.21	469.31	464.14	462.29	461.63	461.39
28000	569.79	550.44	502.14	486.69	481.33	479.42	478.73	478.48
29000	590.14	570.09	520.08	504.07	498.52	496.54	495.82	495.57
30000	610.49	589.75	538.01	521.45	515.71	513.66	512.92	512.66
31000	630.84	609.41	555.94	538.83	532.90	530.78	530.02	529.74
32000	651.19	629.07	573.88	556.21	550.09	547.90	547.12	546.83
33000	671.54	648.73	591.81	573.60	567.28	565.02	564.21	563.92
34000	691.89	668.38	609.74	590.98	584.47	582.15	581.31	581.01
35000	712.24	688.04	627.68	608.36	601.66	599.27	598.41	598.10
40000	813.99	786.33	717.34	695.27	687.61	684.88	683.89	683.54
45000	915.74	884.63	807.01	782.17	773.56	770.49	769.38	768.98
50000	1017.48	982.92	896.68	869.08	859.51	856.10	854.87	854.42
55000	1119.23	1081.21	986.35	955.99	945.46	941.70	940.35	939.86
60000	1220.98	1179.50	1076.01	1042.90	1031.41	1027.31	1025.84	1025.31
65000	1322.73	1277.79	1165.68	1129.81	1117.36	1112.92	1111.33	1110.75
70000	1424.48	1376.08	1255.35	1216.71	1203.31	1198.53	1196.81	1196.19
75000	1526.22	1474.37	1345.02	1303.62	1289.26	1284.14	1282.30	1281.63
80000	1627.97	1572.66	1434.68	1390.53	1375.21	1369.75	1367.78	1367.07
85000	1729.72	1670.95	1524.35	1477.44	1461.16	1455.36	1453.27	1452.52
90000	1831.47	1769.25	1614.02	1564.34	1547.11	1540.97	1538.76	1537.96
95000	1933.22	1867.54	1703.68	1651.25	1633.06	1626.58	1624.24	1623.40
100000	2034.96	1965.83	1793.35	1738.16	1719.01	1712.19	1709.73	1708.84
105000	2136.71	2064.12	1883.02	1825.07	1804.96	1797.80	1795.22	1794.28
110000	2238.46	2162.41	1972.69	1911.97	1890.91	1883.40	1880.70	1879.72
115000	2340.21	2260.70	2062.35	1998.88	1976.86	1969.01	1966.19	1965.17
120000	2441.96	2358.99	2152.02	2085.79	2062.81	2054.62	2051.67	2050.61
125000	2543.70	2457.28	2241.69	2172.70	2148.76	2140.23	2137.16	2136.05
130000	2645.45	2555.57	2331.36	2259.61	2234.71	2225.84	2222.65	2221.49
135000	2747.20	2653.87	2421.02	2346.51	2320.66	2311.45	2308.13	2306.93
140000	2848.95	2752.16	2510.69	2433.42	2406.61	2397.06	2393.62	2392.38
145000	2950.69	2850.45	2600.36	2520.33	2492.57	2482.67	2479.10	2477.82
150000	3052.44	2948.74	2690.03	2607.24	2578.52	2568.28	2564.59	2563.26
155000	3154.19	3047.03	2779.69	2694.14	2664.47	2653.89	2650.08	2648.70
160000	3255.94	3145.32	2869.36	2781.05	2750.42	2739.49	2735.56	2734.14

20.750% MONTHLY AMORTIZING PAYMENTS

AMOUNT OF LOAN	NUMBER OF YEARS IN TERM							
	1	2	3	4	5	6	7	8
$ 50	4.65	2.57	1.88	1.55	1.35	1.22	1.14	1.08
100	9.30	5.13	3.76	3.09	2.70	2.44	2.27	2.15
200	18.60	10.26	7.51	6.17	5.39	4.88	4.54	4.29
300	27.90	15.38	11.27	9.25	8.08	7.32	6.80	6.43
400	37.20	20.51	15.02	12.34	10.77	9.76	9.07	8.57
500	46.50	25.64	18.78	15.42	13.46	12.20	11.33	10.72
600	55.80	30.76	22.53	18.50	16.15	14.64	13.60	12.86
700	65.10	35.89	26.29	21.59	18.84	17.08	15.87	15.00
800	74.40	41.02	30.04	24.67	21.54	19.52	18.13	17.14
900	83.70	46.14	33.80	27.75	24.23	21.96	20.40	19.29
1000	93.00	51.27	37.55	30.84	26.92	24.39	22.66	21.43
2000	185.99	102.53	75.10	61.67	53.83	48.78	45.32	42.85
3000	278.99	153.79	112.65	92.50	80.74	73.17	67.98	64.27
4000	371.98	205.06	150.19	123.33	107.66	97.56	90.64	85.70
5000	464.97	256.32	187.74	154.16	134.57	121.95	113.30	107.12
6000	557.97	307.58	225.29	184.99	161.48	146.34	135.96	128.54
7000	650.96	358.85	262.83	215.82	188.40	170.73	158.62	149.97
8000	743.96	410.11	300.38	246.66	215.31	195.12	181.28	171.39
9000	836.95	461.37	337.93	277.49	242.22	219.51	203.94	192.81
10000	929.94	512.63	375.47	308.32	269.13	243.90	226.60	214.24
11000	1022.94	563.90	413.02	339.15	296.05	268.29	249.26	235.66
12000	1115.93	615.16	450.57	369.98	322.96	292.68	271.92	257.08
13000	1208.92	666.42	488.11	400.81	349.87	317.07	294.58	278.51
14000	1301.92	717.69	525.66	431.64	376.79	341.46	317.24	299.93
15000	1394.91	768.95	563.21	462.48	403.70	365.85	339.90	321.35
16000	1487.91	820.21	600.75	493.31	430.61	390.24	362.56	342.78
17000	1580.90	871.47	638.30	524.14	457.52	414.63	385.22	364.20
18000	1673.89	922.74	675.85	554.97	484.44	439.02	407.88	385.62
19000	1766.89	974.00	713.39	585.80	511.35	463.41	430.54	407.05
20000	1859.88	1025.26	750.94	616.63	538.26	487.80	453.20	428.47
21000	1952.88	1076.53	788.49	647.46	565.18	512.19	475.86	449.89
22000	2045.87	1127.79	826.04	678.30	592.09	536.58	498.52	471.32
23000	2138.86	1179.05	863.58	709.13	619.00	560.96	521.18	492.74
24000	2231.86	1230.32	901.13	739.96	645.92	585.35	543.84	514.16
25000	2324.85	1281.58	938.68	770.79	672.83	609.74	566.50	535.59
26000	2417.84	1332.84	976.22	801.62	699.74	634.13	589.16	557.01
27000	2510.84	1384.10	1013.77	832.45	726.65	658.52	611.82	578.43
28000	2603.83	1435.37	1051.32	863.28	753.57	682.91	634.48	599.86
29000	2696.83	1486.63	1088.86	894.12	780.48	707.30	657.14	621.28
30000	2789.82	1537.89	1126.41	924.95	807.39	731.69	679.80	642.70
31000	2882.81	1589.16	1163.96	955.78	834.31	756.08	702.46	664.13
32000	2975.81	1640.42	1201.50	986.61	861.22	780.47	725.12	685.55
33000	3068.80	1691.68	1239.05	1017.44	888.13	804.86	747.78	706.97
34000	3161.80	1742.94	1276.60	1048.27	915.04	829.25	770.44	728.40
35000	3254.79	1794.21	1314.14	1079.10	941.96	853.64	793.10	749.82
40000	3719.76	2050.52	1501.88	1233.26	1076.52	975.59	906.40	856.94
45000	4184.73	2306.84	1689.61	1387.42	1211.09	1097.53	1019.70	964.05
50000	4649.70	2563.15	1877.35	1541.57	1345.65	1219.48	1133.00	1071.17
55000	5114.67	2819.47	2065.08	1695.73	1480.22	1341.43	1246.30	1178.29
60000	5579.63	3075.78	2252.81	1849.89	1614.78	1463.38	1359.60	1285.40
65000	6044.60	3332.10	2440.55	2004.05	1749.34	1585.33	1472.90	1392.52
70000	6509.57	3588.41	2628.28	2158.20	1883.91	1707.27	1586.20	1499.63
75000	6974.54	3844.73	2816.02	2312.36	2018.47	1829.22	1699.50	1606.75
80000	7439.51	4101.04	3003.75	2466.52	2153.04	1951.17	1812.80	1713.87
85000	7904.48	4357.35	3191.49	2620.67	2287.60	2073.12	1926.10	1820.98
90000	8369.45	4613.67	3379.22	2774.83	2422.17	2195.06	2039.40	1928.10
95000	8834.42	4869.98	3566.95	2928.99	2556.73	2317.01	2152.70	2035.22
100000	9299.39	5126.30	3754.69	3083.14	2691.30	2438.96	2266.00	2142.33
105000	9764.36	5382.61	3942.42	3237.30	2825.86	2560.91	2379.30	2249.45
110000	10229.33	5638.93	4130.16	3391.46	2960.43	2682.86	2492.60	2356.57
115000	10694.30	5895.24	4317.89	3545.61	3094.99	2804.80	2605.90	2463.68
120000	11159.26	6151.56	4505.62	3699.77	3229.56	2926.75	2719.20	2570.80
125000	11624.23	6407.87	4693.36	3853.93	3364.12	3048.70	2832.50	2677.91
130000	12089.20	6664.19	4881.09	4008.09	3498.68	3170.65	2945.80	2785.03
135000	12554.17	6920.50	5068.83	4162.24	3633.25	3292.59	3059.10	2892.15
140000	13019.14	7176.82	5256.56	4316.40	3767.81	3414.54	3172.40	2999.26
145000	13484.11	7433.13	5444.30	4470.56	3902.38	3536.49	3285.70	3106.38
150000	13949.08	7689.45	5632.03	4624.71	4036.94	3658.44	3399.00	3213.50
155000	14414.05	7945.76	5819.76	4778.87	4171.51	3780.38	3512.30	3320.61
160000	14879.02	8202.08	6007.50	4933.03	4306.07	3902.33	3625.60	3427.73

200

AMOUNT OF LOAN	NUMBER OF YEARS IN TERM							
	9	10	15	20	25	30	35	40
$ 50	1.03	1.00	.91	.88	.87	.87	.87	.87
100	2.06	1.99	1.82	1.76	1.74	1.74	1.74	1.73
200	4.11	3.97	3.63	3.52	3.48	3.47	3.47	3.46
300	6.16	5.95	5.44	5.28	5.22	5.20	5.20	5.19
400	8.21	7.94	7.25	7.04	6.96	6.94	6.93	6.92
500	10.26	9.92	9.06	8.79	8.70	8.67	8.66	8.65
600	12.31	11.90	10.88	10.55	10.44	10.40	10.39	10.38
700	14.36	13.88	12.69	12.31	12.18	12.13	12.12	12.11
800	16.41	15.87	14.50	14.07	13.92	13.87	13.85	13.84
900	18.47	17.85	16.31	15.83	15.66	15.60	15.58	15.57
1000	20.52	19.83	18.12	17.58	17.40	17.33	17.31	17.30
2000	41.03	39.66	36.24	35.16	34.79	34.66	34.61	34.60
3000	61.54	59.48	54.36	52.74	52.18	51.99	51.92	51.89
4000	82.05	79.31	72.48	70.32	69.58	69.32	69.22	69.19
5000	102.56	99.13	90.60	87.90	86.97	86.64	86.53	86.49
6000	123.08	118.96	108.72	105.48	104.36	103.97	103.83	103.78
7000	143.59	138.78	126.84	123.06	121.76	121.30	121.14	121.08
8000	164.10	158.61	144.96	140.64	139.15	138.63	138.44	138.38
9000	184.61	178.43	163.08	158.21	156.54	155.96	155.75	155.67
10000	205.12	198.26	181.20	175.79	173.94	173.28	173.05	172.97
11000	225.64	218.08	199.32	193.37	191.33	190.61	190.36	190.26
12000	246.15	237.91	217.44	210.95	208.72	207.94	207.66	207.56
13000	266.66	257.74	235.56	228.53	226.12	225.27	224.96	224.86
14000	287.17	277.56	253.68	246.11	243.51	242.59	242.27	242.15
15000	307.68	297.39	271.80	263.69	260.90	259.92	259.57	259.45
16000	328.20	317.21	289.92	281.27	278.30	277.25	276.88	276.75
17000	348.71	337.04	308.04	298.84	295.69	294.58	294.18	294.04
18000	369.22	356.86	326.16	316.42	313.08	311.91	311.49	311.34
19000	389.73	376.69	344.28	334.00	330.48	329.23	328.79	328.63
20000	410.24	396.51	362.40	351.58	347.87	346.56	346.10	345.93
21000	430.76	416.34	380.52	369.16	365.26	363.89	363.40	363.23
22000	451.27	436.16	398.63	386.74	382.66	381.22	380.71	380.52
23000	471.78	455.99	416.75	404.32	400.05	398.55	398.01	397.82
24000	492.29	475.82	434.87	421.90	417.44	415.87	415.31	415.12
25000	512.80	495.64	452.99	439.47	434.84	433.20	432.62	432.41
26000	533.32	515.47	471.11	457.05	452.23	450.53	449.92	449.71
27000	553.83	535.29	489.23	474.63	469.62	467.86	467.23	467.00
28000	574.34	555.12	507.35	492.21	487.02	485.18	484.53	484.30
29000	594.85	574.94	525.47	509.79	504.41	502.51	501.84	501.60
30000	615.36	594.77	543.59	527.37	521.80	519.84	519.14	518.89
31000	635.88	614.59	561.71	544.95	539.20	537.17	536.45	536.19
32000	656.39	634.42	579.83	562.53	556.59	554.50	553.75	553.49
33000	676.90	654.24	597.95	580.11	573.98	571.82	571.06	570.78
34000	697.41	674.07	616.07	597.68	591.37	589.15	588.36	588.08
35000	717.92	693.89	634.19	615.26	608.77	606.48	605.67	605.37
40000	820.48	793.02	724.79	703.16	695.73	693.12	692.19	691.86
45000	923.04	892.15	815.38	791.05	782.70	779.76	778.71	778.34
50000	1025.60	991.28	905.98	878.94	869.67	866.40	865.23	864.82
55000	1128.16	1090.40	996.58	966.84	956.63	953.04	951.76	951.30
60000	1230.72	1189.53	1087.18	1054.73	1043.60	1039.68	1038.28	1037.78
65000	1333.28	1288.66	1177.77	1142.63	1130.56	1126.31	1124.80	1124.26
70000	1435.84	1387.78	1268.37	1230.52	1217.53	1212.95	1211.33	1210.74
75000	1538.40	1486.91	1358.97	1318.41	1304.50	1299.59	1297.85	1297.23
80000	1640.96	1586.04	1449.57	1406.31	1391.46	1386.23	1384.37	1383.71
85000	1743.52	1685.17	1540.17	1494.20	1478.43	1472.87	1470.89	1470.19
90000	1846.08	1784.29	1630.76	1582.10	1565.40	1559.51	1557.42	1556.67
95000	1948.64	1883.42	1721.36	1669.99	1652.36	1646.15	1643.94	1643.15
100000	2051.20	1982.55	1811.96	1757.88	1739.33	1732.79	1730.46	1729.63
105000	2153.76	2081.67	1902.56	1845.78	1826.29	1819.43	1816.99	1816.11
110000	2256.32	2180.80	1993.15	1933.67	1913.26	1906.07	1903.51	1902.60
115000	2358.88	2279.93	2083.75	2021.57	2000.23	1992.71	1990.03	1989.08
120000	2461.44	2379.06	2174.35	2109.46	2087.19	2079.35	2076.55	2075.56
125000	2564.00	2478.18	2264.95	2197.35	2174.16	2165.98	2163.08	2162.04
130000	2666.56	2577.31	2355.54	2285.25	2261.12	2252.62	2249.60	2248.52
135000	2769.12	2676.44	2446.14	2373.14	2348.09	2339.26	2336.12	2335.00
140000	2871.68	2775.56	2536.74	2461.04	2435.06	2425.90	2422.65	2421.48
145000	2974.24	2874.69	2627.34	2548.93	2522.02	2512.54	2509.17	2507.97
150000	3076.80	2973.82	2717.93	2636.82	2608.99	2599.18	2595.69	2594.45
155000	3179.36	3072.94	2808.53	2724.72	2695.96	2685.82	2682.21	2680.93
160000	3281.92	3172.07	2899.13	2812.61	2782.92	2772.46	2768.74	2767.41

21.000% MONTHLY AMORTIZING PAYMENTS

AMOUNT OF LOAN	NUMBER OF YEARS IN TERM							
	1	2	3	4	5	6	7	8
$ 50	4.66	2.57	1.89	1.55	1.36	1.23	1.15	1.08
100	9.32	5.14	3.77	3.10	2.71	2.46	2.29	2.16
200	18.63	10.28	7.54	6.20	5.42	4.91	4.57	4.32
300	27.94	15.42	11.31	9.29	8.12	7.37	6.85	6.48
400	37.25	20.56	15.08	12.39	10.83	9.82	9.13	8.64
500	46.56	25.70	18.84	15.49	13.53	12.27	11.41	10.80
600	55.87	30.84	22.61	18.58	16.24	14.73	13.69	12.95
700	65.18	35.97	26.38	21.68	18.94	17.18	15.97	15.11
800	74.50	41.11	30.15	24.78	21.65	19.63	18.25	17.27
900	83.81	46.25	33.91	27.87	24.35	22.09	20.54	19.43
1000	93.12	51.39	37.68	30.97	27.06	24.54	22.82	21.59
2000	186.23	102.78	75.36	61.94	54.11	49.08	45.63	43.17
3000	279.35	154.16	113.03	92.90	81.17	73.61	68.44	64.75
4000	372.46	205.55	150.71	123.87	108.22	98.15	91.25	86.33
5000	465.57	256.93	188.38	154.83	135.27	122.68	114.07	107.91
6000	558.69	308.32	226.06	185.80	162.33	147.22	136.88	129.49
7000	651.80	359.70	263.73	216.76	189.38	171.76	159.69	151.07
8000	744.92	411.09	301.41	247.73	216.43	196.29	182.50	172.65
9000	838.03	462.48	339.08	278.70	243.49	220.83	205.32	194.23
10000	931.14	513.86	376.76	309.66	270.54	245.36	228.13	215.82
11000	1024.26	565.25	414.43	340.63	297.59	269.90	250.94	237.40
12000	1117.37	616.63	452.11	371.59	324.65	294.44	273.75	258.98
13000	1210.48	668.02	489.78	402.56	351.70	318.97	296.56	280.56
14000	1303.60	719.40	527.46	433.52	378.75	343.51	319.38	302.14
15000	1396.71	770.79	565.13	464.49	405.81	368.04	342.19	323.72
16000	1489.83	822.18	602.81	495.46	432.86	392.58	365.00	345.30
17000	1582.94	873.56	640.48	526.42	459.91	417.12	387.81	366.88
18000	1676.05	924.95	678.16	557.39	486.97	441.65	410.63	388.46
19000	1769.17	976.33	715.83	588.35	514.02	466.19	433.44	410.04
20000	1862.28	1027.72	753.51	619.32	541.07	490.72	456.25	431.63
21000	1955.39	1079.10	791.18	650.28	568.13	515.26	479.06	453.21
22000	2048.51	1130.49	828.86	681.25	595.18	539.80	501.87	474.79
23000	2141.62	1181.87	866.53	712.22	622.23	564.33	524.69	496.37
24000	2234.74	1233.26	904.21	743.18	649.29	588.87	547.50	517.95
25000	2327.85	1284.65	941.88	774.15	676.34	613.40	570.31	539.53
26000	2420.96	1336.03	979.56	805.11	703.39	637.94	593.12	561.11
27000	2514.08	1387.42	1017.23	836.08	730.45	662.48	615.94	582.69
28000	2607.19	1438.80	1054.91	867.04	757.50	687.01	638.75	604.27
29000	2700.30	1490.19	1092.58	898.01	784.55	711.55	661.56	625.85
30000	2793.42	1541.57	1130.26	928.98	811.61	736.08	684.37	647.44
31000	2886.53	1592.96	1167.93	959.94	838.66	760.62	707.18	669.02
32000	2979.65	1644.35	1205.61	990.91	865.71	785.16	730.00	690.60
33000	3072.76	1695.73	1243.28	1021.87	892.77	809.69	752.81	712.18
34000	3165.87	1747.12	1280.96	1052.84	919.82	834.23	775.62	733.76
35000	3258.99	1798.50	1318.63	1083.80	946.87	858.76	798.43	755.34
40000	3724.56	2055.43	1507.01	1238.63	1082.14	981.44	912.49	863.25
45000	4190.12	2312.36	1695.38	1393.46	1217.41	1104.12	1026.56	971.15
50000	4655.69	2569.29	1883.76	1548.29	1352.67	1226.80	1140.62	1079.06
55000	5121.26	2826.22	2072.13	1703.12	1487.94	1349.48	1254.68	1186.96
60000	5586.83	3083.14	2260.51	1857.95	1623.21	1472.16	1368.74	1294.87
65000	6052.40	3340.07	2448.88	2012.78	1758.47	1594.84	1482.80	1402.77
70000	6517.97	3597.00	2637.26	2167.60	1893.74	1717.52	1596.86	1510.68
75000	6983.54	3853.93	2825.64	2322.43	2029.01	1840.20	1710.92	1618.58
80000	7449.11	4110.86	3014.01	2477.26	2164.27	1962.88	1824.98	1726.49
85000	7914.68	4367.79	3202.39	2632.09	2299.54	2085.56	1939.04	1834.39
90000	8380.24	4624.71	3390.76	2786.92	2434.81	2208.24	2053.11	1942.30
95000	8845.81	4881.64	3579.14	2941.75	2570.07	2330.92	2167.17	2050.20
100000	9311.38	5138.57	3767.51	3096.57	2705.34	2453.60	2281.23	2158.11
105000	9776.95	5395.50	3955.89	3251.40	2840.61	2576.28	2395.29	2266.01
110000	10242.52	5652.43	4144.26	3406.23	2975.87	2698.96	2509.35	2373.92
115000	10708.09	5909.35	4332.64	3561.06	3111.14	2821.64	2623.41	2481.82
120000	11173.66	6166.28	4521.01	3715.89	3246.41	2944.32	2737.47	2589.73
125000	11639.23	6423.21	4709.39	3870.72	3381.67	3067.00	2851.53	2697.63
130000	12104.80	6680.14	4897.76	4025.55	3516.94	3189.68	2965.59	2805.54
135000	12570.36	6937.07	5086.14	4180.37	3652.21	3312.36	3079.66	2913.44
140000	13035.93	7194.00	5274.51	4335.20	3787.48	3435.04	3193.72	3021.35
145000	13501.50	7450.92	5462.89	4490.03	3922.74	3557.72	3307.78	3129.25
150000	13967.07	7707.85	5651.27	4644.86	4058.01	3680.40	3421.84	3237.16
155000	14432.64	7964.78	5839.64	4799.69	4193.28	3803.08	3535.90	3345.06
160000	14898.21	8221.71	6028.02	4954.52	4328.54	3925.76	3649.96	3452.97

AMOUNT OF LOAN	NUMBER OF YEARS IN TERM							
	9	**10**	**15**	**20**	**25**	**30**	**35**	**40**
$ 50	1.04	1.00	.92	.89	.88	.88	.88	.88
100	2.07	2.00	1.84	1.78	1.76	1.76	1.76	1.76
200	4.14	4.00	3.67	3.56	3.52	3.51	3.51	3.51
300	6.21	6.00	5.50	5.34	5.28	5.27	5.26	5.26
400	8.27	8.00	7.33	7.12	7.04	7.02	7.01	7.01
500	10.34	10.00	9.16	8.89	8.80	8.77	8.76	8.76
600	12.41	12.00	10.99	10.67	10.56	10.53	10.51	10.51
700	14.48	14.00	12.82	12.45	12.32	12.28	12.26	12.26
800	16.54	16.00	14.65	14.23	14.08	14.03	14.01	14.01
900	18.61	18.00	16.48	16.00	15.84	15.79	15.77	15.76
1000	20.68	20.00	18.31	17.78	17.60	17.54	17.52	17.51
2000	41.35	39.99	36.62	35.56	35.20	35.07	35.03	35.01
3000	62.03	59.98	54.92	53.33	52.79	52.61	52.54	52.52
4000	82.70	79.98	73.23	71.11	70.39	70.14	70.05	70.02
5000	103.38	99.97	91.54	88.89	87.99	87.68	87.56	87.53
6000	124.05	119.96	109.84	106.66	105.58	105.21	105.08	105.03
7000	144.73	139.96	128.15	124.44	123.18	122.74	122.59	122.53
8000	165.40	159.95	146.45	142.22	140.78	140.28	140.10	140.04
9000	186.08	179.94	164.76	159.99	158.37	157.81	157.61	157.54
10000	206.75	199.94	183.07	177.77	175.97	175.35	175.12	175.05
11000	227.43	219.93	201.37	195.55	193.57	192.88	192.64	192.55
12000	248.10	239.92	219.68	213.32	211.16	210.41	210.15	210.06
13000	268.78	259.92	237.98	231.10	228.76	227.95	227.66	227.56
14000	289.45	279.91	256.29	248.88	246.36	245.48	245.17	245.06
15000	310.13	299.90	274.60	266.65	263.95	263.02	262.68	262.57
16000	330.80	319.90	292.90	284.43	281.55	280.55	280.20	280.07
17000	351.48	339.89	311.21	302.20	299.15	298.08	297.71	297.58
18000	372.15	359.88	329.52	319.98	316.74	315.62	315.22	315.08
19000	392.83	379.88	347.82	337.76	334.34	333.15	332.73	332.59
20000	413.50	399.87	366.13	355.53	351.94	350.69	350.24	350.09
21000	434.18	419.86	384.43	373.31	369.53	368.22	367.76	367.59
22000	454.85	439.85	402.74	391.09	387.13	385.75	385.27	385.10
23000	475.53	459.85	421.05	408.86	404.73	403.29	402.78	402.60
24000	496.20	479.84	439.35	426.64	422.32	420.82	420.29	420.11
25000	516.88	499.83	457.66	444.42	439.92	438.36	437.80	437.61
26000	537.55	519.83	475.96	462.19	457.52	455.89	455.32	455.12
27000	558.23	539.82	494.27	479.97	475.11	473.42	472.83	472.62
28000	578.90	559.81	512.58	497.75	492.71	490.96	490.34	490.12
29000	599.58	579.81	530.88	515.52	510.31	508.49	507.85	507.63
30000	620.25	599.80	549.19	533.30	527.90	526.03	525.36	525.13
31000	640.93	619.79	567.49	551.07	545.50	543.56	542.88	542.64
32000	661.60	639.79	585.80	568.85	563.10	561.09	560.39	560.14
33000	682.28	659.78	604.11	586.63	580.69	578.63	577.90	577.64
34000	702.95	679.77	622.41	604.40	598.29	596.16	595.41	595.15
35000	723.63	699.77	640.72	622.18	615.89	613.70	612.92	612.65
40000	827.00	799.73	732.25	711.06	703.87	701.37	700.48	700.17
45000	930.37	899.70	823.78	799.94	791.85	789.04	788.04	787.70
50000	1033.75	999.66	915.31	888.83	879.84	876.71	875.60	875.22
55000	1137.12	1099.63	1006.84	977.71	967.82	964.38	963.16	962.74
60000	1240.50	1199.60	1098.37	1066.59	1055.80	1052.05	1050.72	1050.26
65000	1343.87	1299.56	1189.90	1155.47	1143.79	1139.72	1138.28	1137.78
70000	1447.25	1399.53	1281.43	1244.36	1231.77	1227.39	1225.84	1225.30
75000	1550.62	1499.49	1372.96	1333.24	1319.75	1315.06	1313.40	1312.82
80000	1653.99	1599.46	1464.49	1422.12	1407.74	1402.73	1400.96	1400.34
85000	1757.37	1699.42	1556.03	1511.00	1495.72	1490.40	1488.52	1487.86
90000	1860.74	1799.39	1647.56	1599.88	1583.70	1578.07	1576.08	1575.39
95000	1964.12	1899.36	1739.09	1688.77	1671.68	1665.74	1663.64	1662.91
100000	2067.49	1999.32	1830.62	1777.65	1759.67	1753.41	1751.20	1750.43
105000	2170.87	2099.29	1922.15	1866.53	1847.65	1841.08	1838.76	1837.95
110000	2274.24	2199.25	2013.68	1955.41	1935.63	1928.75	1926.32	1925.47
115000	2377.61	2299.22	2105.21	2044.29	2023.62	2016.42	2013.88	2012.99
120000	2480.99	2399.19	2196.74	2133.18	2111.60	2104.09	2101.44	2100.51
125000	2584.36	2499.15	2288.27	2222.06	2199.58	2191.76	2189.00	2188.03
130000	2687.74	2599.12	2379.80	2310.94	2287.57	2279.43	2276.56	2275.56
135000	2791.11	2699.08	2471.33	2399.82	2375.55	2367.10	2364.12	2363.08
140000	2894.49	2799.05	2562.86	2488.71	2463.53	2454.77	2451.68	2450.60
145000	2997.86	2899.01	2654.39	2577.59	2551.52	2542.44	2539.24	2538.12
150000	3101.24	2998.98	2745.92	2666.47	2639.50	2630.11	2626.80	2625.64
155000	3204.61	3098.95	2837.45	2755.35	2727.48	2717.78	2714.36	2713.16
160000	3307.98	3198.91	2928.98	2844.23	2815.47	2805.45	2801.92	2800.68

21.250% MONTHLY AMORTIZING PAYMENTS

AMOUNT OF LOAN	NUMBER OF YEARS IN TERM							
	1	2	3	4	5	6	7	8
$ 50	4.67	2.58	1.90	1.56	1.36	1.24	1.15	1.09
100	9.33	5.16	3.79	3.12	2.72	2.47	2.30	2.18
200	18.65	10.31	7.57	6.23	5.44	4.94	4.60	4.35
300	27.98	15.46	11.35	9.34	8.16	7.41	6.89	6.53
400	37.30	20.61	15.13	12.45	10.88	9.88	9.19	8.70
500	46.62	25.76	18.91	15.56	13.60	12.35	11.49	10.87
600	55.95	30.91	22.69	18.67	16.32	14.81	13.78	13.05
700	65.27	36.06	26.47	21.78	19.04	17.28	16.08	15.22
800	74.59	41.21	30.25	24.89	21.76	19.75	18.38	17.40
900	83.92	46.36	34.03	28.00	24.48	22.22	20.67	19.57
1000	93.24	51.51	37.81	31.11	27.20	24.69	22.97	21.74
2000	186.47	103.02	75.61	62.21	54.39	49.37	45.93	43.48
3000	279.71	154.53	113.42	93.31	81.59	74.05	68.90	65.22
4000	372.94	206.04	151.22	124.41	108.78	98.74	91.86	86.96
5000	466.17	257.55	189.02	155.51	135.98	123.42	114.83	108.70
6000	559.41	309.06	226.83	186.61	163.17	148.10	137.79	130.44
7000	652.64	360.56	264.63	217.71	190.36	172.79	160.76	152.18
8000	745.88	412.07	302.43	248.81	217.56	197.47	183.72	173.92
9000	839.11	463.58	340.24	279.91	244.75	222.15	206.69	195.66
10000	932.34	515.09	378.04	311.01	271.95	246.83	229.65	217.40
11000	1025.58	566.60	415.84	342.11	299.14	271.52	252.62	239.14
12000	1118.81	618.11	453.65	373.21	326.34	296.20	275.58	260.88
13000	1212.04	669.62	491.45	404.31	353.53	320.88	298.55	282.62
14000	1305.28	721.12	529.25	435.41	380.72	345.57	321.51	304.35
15000	1398.51	772.63	567.06	466.51	407.92	370.25	344.48	326.09
16000	1491.75	824.14	604.86	497.61	435.11	394.93	367.44	347.83
17000	1584.98	875.65	642.67	528.71	462.31	419.61	390.41	369.57
18000	1678.21	927.16	680.47	559.81	489.50	444.30	413.37	391.31
19000	1771.45	978.67	718.27	590.91	516.69	468.98	436.34	413.05
20000	1864.68	1030.18	756.08	622.01	543.89	493.66	459.30	434.79
21000	1957.91	1081.68	793.88	653.11	571.08	518.35	482.27	456.53
22000	2051.15	1133.19	831.68	684.21	598.28	543.03	505.23	478.27
23000	2144.38	1184.70	869.49	715.31	625.47	567.71	528.20	500.01
24000	2237.62	1236.21	907.29	746.41	652.67	592.39	551.16	521.75
25000	2330.85	1287.72	945.09	777.51	679.86	617.08	574.13	543.49
26000	2424.08	1339.23	982.90	808.61	707.05	641.76	597.09	565.23
27000	2517.32	1390.74	1020.70	839.71	734.25	666.44	620.06	586.97
28000	2610.55	1442.24	1058.50	870.81	761.44	691.13	643.02	608.70
29000	2703.79	1493.75	1096.31	901.91	788.64	715.81	665.99	630.44
30000	2797.02	1545.26	1134.11	933.01	815.83	740.49	688.95	652.18
31000	2890.25	1596.77	1171.92	964.11	843.02	765.17	711.92	673.92
32000	2983.49	1648.28	1209.72	995.22	870.22	789.86	734.88	695.66
33000	3076.72	1699.79	1247.52	1026.32	897.41	814.54	757.85	717.40
34000	3169.95	1751.29	1285.33	1057.42	924.61	839.22	780.81	739.14
35000	3263.19	1802.80	1323.13	1088.52	951.80	863.91	803.78	760.88
40000	3729.36	2060.35	1512.15	1244.02	1087.77	987.32	918.60	869.58
45000	4195.53	2317.89	1701.16	1399.52	1223.74	1110.73	1033.43	978.27
50000	4661.69	2575.43	1890.18	1555.02	1359.71	1234.15	1148.25	1086.97
55000	5127.86	2832.97	2079.20	1710.52	1495.68	1357.56	1263.08	1195.66
60000	5594.03	3090.52	2268.22	1866.02	1631.66	1480.98	1377.90	1304.36
65000	6060.20	3348.06	2457.24	2021.53	1767.63	1604.39	1492.73	1413.06
70000	6526.37	3605.60	2646.25	2177.03	1903.60	1727.81	1607.55	1521.75
75000	6992.54	3863.14	2835.27	2332.53	2039.57	1851.22	1722.38	1630.45
80000	7458.71	4120.69	3024.29	2488.03	2175.54	1974.64	1837.20	1739.15
85000	7924.88	4378.23	3213.31	2643.53	2311.51	2098.05	1952.02	1847.84
90000	8391.05	4635.77	3402.32	2799.03	2447.48	2221.46	2066.85	1956.54
95000	8857.22	4893.32	3591.34	2954.54	2583.45	2344.88	2181.67	2065.23
100000	9323.38	5150.86	3780.36	3110.04	2719.42	2468.29	2296.50	2173.93
105000	9789.55	5408.40	3969.38	3265.54	2855.39	2591.71	2411.32	2282.63
110000	10255.72	5665.94	4158.40	3421.04	2991.36	2715.12	2526.15	2391.32
115000	10721.89	5923.49	4347.41	3576.54	3127.34	2838.54	2640.97	2500.02
120000	11188.06	6181.03	4536.43	3732.04	3263.31	2961.95	2755.80	2608.72
125000	11654.23	6438.57	4725.45	3887.54	3399.28	3085.37	2870.62	2717.41
130000	12120.40	6696.11	4914.47	4043.05	3535.25	3208.78	2985.45	2826.11
135000	12586.57	6953.66	5103.48	4198.55	3671.22	3332.19	3100.27	2934.81
140000	13052.74	7211.20	5292.50	4354.05	3807.19	3455.61	3215.10	3043.50
145000	13518.91	7468.74	5481.52	4509.55	3943.16	3579.02	3329.92	3152.20
150000	13985.07	7726.28	5670.54	4665.05	4079.13	3702.44	3444.75	3260.89
155000	14451.24	7983.83	5859.56	4820.55	4215.10	3825.85	3559.57	3369.59
160000	14917.41	8241.37	6048.57	4976.06	4351.07	3949.27	3674.40	3478.29

204

AMOUNT OF LOAN	NUMBER OF YEARS IN TERM							
	9	10	15	20	25	30	35	40
$ 50	1.05	1.01	.93	.90	.90	.89	.89	.89
100	2.09	2.02	1.85	1.80	1.79	1.78	1.78	1.78
200	4.17	4.04	3.70	3.60	3.57	3.55	3.55	3.55
300	6.26	6.05	5.55	5.40	5.35	5.33	5.32	5.32
400	8.34	8.07	7.40	7.19	7.13	7.10	7.09	7.09
500	10.42	10.09	9.25	8.99	8.91	8.86	8.86	8.86
600	12.51	12.10	11.10	10.79	10.69	10.65	10.64	10.63
700	14.59	14.12	12.95	12.59	12.47	12.42	12.41	12.40
800	16.68	16.13	14.80	14.38	14.25	14.20	14.18	14.17
900	18.76	18.15	16.65	16.18	16.03	15.97	15.95	15.95
1000	20.84	20.17	18.50	17.98	17.81	17.75	17.72	17.72
2000	41.68	40.33	36.99	35.95	35.61	35.49	35.44	35.43
3000	62.52	60.49	55.48	53.93	53.41	53.23	53.16	53.14
4000	83.36	80.65	73.98	71.90	71.21	70.97	70.88	70.85
5000	104.20	100.81	92.47	89.88	89.01	88.71	88.60	88.57
6000	125.03	120.97	110.96	107.85	106.81	106.45	106.32	106.28
7000	145.87	141.14	129.46	125.83	124.61	124.19	124.04	123.99
8000	166.71	161.30	147.95	143.80	142.41	141.93	141.76	141.70
9000	187.55	181.46	166.44	161.77	160.21	159.67	159.48	159.41
10000	208.39	201.62	184.94	179.75	178.01	177.41	177.20	177.13
11000	229.23	221.78	203.43	197.72	195.81	195.15	194.92	194.84
12000	250.06	241.94	221.92	215.70	213.61	212.89	212.64	212.55
13000	270.90	262.10	240.42	233.67	231.41	230.63	230.36	230.26
14000	291.74	282.27	258.91	251.65	249.21	248.37	248.08	247.98
15000	312.58	302.43	277.40	269.62	267.01	266.11	265.80	265.69
16000	333.42	322.59	295.90	287.60	284.81	283.85	283.52	283.40
17000	354.26	342.75	314.39	305.57	302.61	301.59	301.24	301.11
18000	375.09	362.91	332.88	323.54	320.41	319.33	318.96	318.82
19000	395.93	383.07	351.38	341.52	338.21	337.07	336.67	336.54
20000	416.77	403.23	369.87	359.49	356.01	354.81	354.39	354.25
21000	437.61	423.40	388.36	377.47	373.81	372.55	372.11	371.96
22000	458.45	443.56	406.86	395.44	391.61	390.29	389.83	389.67
23000	479.29	463.72	425.35	413.42	409.41	408.03	407.55	407.39
24000	500.12	483.88	443.84	431.39	427.21	425.77	425.27	425.10
25000	520.96	504.04	462.34	449.37	445.01	443.51	442.99	442.81
26000	541.80	524.20	480.83	467.34	462.81	461.25	460.71	460.52
27000	562.64	544.36	499.32	485.31	480.61	478.99	478.43	478.23
28000	583.48	564.53	517.82	503.29	498.41	496.73	496.15	495.95
29000	604.32	584.69	536.31	521.26	516.21	514.47	513.87	513.66
30000	625.15	604.85	554.80	539.24	534.00	532.21	531.59	531.37
31000	645.99	625.01	573.30	557.21	551.81	549.95	549.31	549.08
32000	666.83	645.17	591.79	575.19	569.61	567.69	567.03	566.80
33000	687.67	665.33	610.28	593.16	587.41	585.43	584.75	584.51
34000	708.51	685.50	628.77	611.14	605.21	603.17	602.47	602.22
35000	729.35	705.66	647.27	629.11	623.01	620.92	620.19	619.93
40000	833.54	806.46	739.73	718.98	712.02	709.62	708.78	708.49
45000	937.73	907.27	832.20	808.85	801.02	798.32	797.38	797.05
50000	1041.92	1008.08	924.67	898.73	890.02	887.02	885.98	885.62
55000	1146.11	1108.89	1017.13	988.60	979.02	975.72	974.58	974.18
60000	1250.30	1209.69	1109.60	1078.47	1068.02	1064.42	1063.17	1062.74
65000	1354.50	1310.50	1202.07	1168.34	1157.02	1153.12	1151.77	1151.30
70000	1458.69	1411.31	1294.53	1258.22	1246.02	1241.83	1240.37	1239.86
75000	1562.88	1512.12	1387.00	1348.09	1335.02	1330.53	1328.97	1328.42
80000	1667.07	1612.92	1479.46	1437.96	1424.03	1419.23	1417.56	1416.98
85000	1771.26	1713.73	1571.93	1527.83	1513.03	1507.93	1506.16	1505.54
90000	1875.45	1814.54	1664.40	1617.70	1602.03	1596.63	1594.76	1594.10
95000	1979.65	1915.35	1756.86	1707.58	1691.03	1685.33	1683.35	1682.67
100000	2083.84	2016.15	1849.33	1797.45	1780.03	1774.03	1771.95	1771.23
105000	2188.03	2116.96	1941.79	1887.32	1869.03	1862.74	1860.55	1859.79
110000	2292.22	2217.77	2034.26	1977.19	1958.03	1951.44	1949.15	1948.35
115000	2396.41	2318.57	2126.73	2067.07	2047.03	2040.14	2037.74	2036.91
120000	2500.60	2419.38	2219.19	2156.94	2136.04	2128.84	2126.34	2125.47
125000	2604.80	2520.19	2311.66	2246.81	2225.04	2217.54	2214.94	2214.03
130000	2708.99	2621.00	2404.13	2336.68	2314.04	2306.24	2303.54	2302.59
135000	2813.18	2721.80	2496.59	2426.55	2403.04	2394.94	2392.13	2391.15
140000	2917.37	2822.61	2589.06	2516.43	2492.04	2483.65	2480.73	2479.72
145000	3021.56	2923.42	2681.52	2606.30	2581.04	2572.35	2569.33	2568.28
150000	3125.75	3024.23	2773.99	2696.17	2670.04	2661.05	2657.93	2656.84
155000	3229.95	3125.03	2866.46	2786.04	2759.04	2749.75	2746.52	2745.40
160000	3334.14	3225.84	2958.92	2875.92	2848.05	2838.45	2835.12	2833.96

21.500% MONTHLY AMORTIZING PAYMENTS

AMOUNT OF LOAN	NUMBER OF YEARS IN TERM							
	1	2	3	4	5	6	7	8
$ 50	4.67	2.59	1.90	1.57	1.37	1.25	1.16	1.10
100	9.34	5.17	3.80	3.13	2.74	2.49	2.32	2.19
200	18.68	10.33	7.59	6.25	5.47	4.97	4.63	4.38
300	28.01	15.49	11.38	9.38	8.21	7.45	6.94	6.57
400	37.35	20.66	15.18	12.50	10.94	9.94	9.25	8.76
500	46.68	25.82	18.97	15.62	13.67	12.42	11.56	10.95
600	56.02	30.98	22.76	18.75	16.41	14.90	13.88	13.14
700	65.35	36.15	26.56	21.87	19.14	17.39	16.19	15.33
800	74.69	41.31	30.35	24.99	21.87	19.87	18.50	17.52
900	84.02	46.47	34.14	28.12	24.61	22.35	20.81	19.71
1000	93.36	51.64	37.94	31.24	27.34	24.84	23.12	21.90
2000	186.71	103.27	75.87	62.48	54.68	49.67	46.24	43.80
3000	280.07	154.90	113.80	93.71	82.01	74.50	69.36	65.70
4000	373.42	206.53	151.73	124.95	109.35	99.33	92.48	87.60
5000	466.77	258.16	189.67	156.18	136.68	124.16	115.60	109.50
6000	560.13	309.79	227.60	187.42	164.02	148.99	138.71	131.39
7000	653.48	361.43	265.53	218.65	191.35	173.82	161.83	153.29
8000	746.84	413.06	303.46	249.89	218.69	198.65	184.95	175.19
9000	840.19	464.69	341.40	281.12	246.02	223.48	208.07	197.09
10000	933.54	516.32	379.33	312.36	273.36	248.31	231.19	218.99
11000	1026.90	567.95	417.26	343.59	300.69	273.14	254.30	240.88
12000	1120.25	619.58	455.19	374.83	328.03	297.97	277.42	262.78
13000	1213.61	671.22	493.12	406.06	355.36	322.80	300.54	284.68
14000	1306.96	722.85	531.06	437.30	382.70	347.63	323.66	306.58
15000	1400.31	774.48	568.99	468.53	410.04	372.46	346.78	328.48
16000	1493.67	826.11	606.92	499.77	437.37	397.29	369.90	350.37
17000	1587.02	877.74	644.85	531.00	464.71	422.12	393.01	372.27
18000	1680.38	929.37	682.79	562.24	492.04	446.95	416.13	394.17
19000	1773.73	981.00	720.72	593.47	519.38	471.78	439.25	416.07
20000	1867.08	1032.64	758.65	624.71	546.71	496.61	462.37	437.97
21000	1960.44	1084.27	796.58	655.95	574.05	521.44	485.49	459.86
22000	2053.79	1135.90	834.52	687.18	601.38	546.27	508.60	481.76
23000	2147.14	1187.53	872.45	718.42	628.72	571.10	531.72	503.66
24000	2240.50	1239.16	910.38	749.65	656.05	595.93	554.84	525.56
25000	2333.85	1290.79	948.31	780.89	683.39	620.76	577.96	547.46
26000	2427.21	1342.43	986.24	812.12	710.72	645.59	601.08	569.35
27000	2520.56	1394.06	1024.18	843.36	738.06	670.42	624.19	591.25
28000	2613.91	1445.69	1062.11	874.59	765.40	695.25	647.31	613.15
29000	2707.27	1497.32	1100.04	905.83	792.73	720.08	670.43	635.05
30000	2800.62	1548.95	1137.97	937.06	820.07	744.91	693.55	656.95
31000	2893.98	1600.58	1175.91	968.30	847.40	769.74	716.67	678.84
32000	2987.33	1652.22	1213.84	999.53	874.74	794.57	739.79	700.74
33000	3080.68	1703.85	1251.77	1030.77	902.07	819.40	762.90	722.64
34000	3174.04	1755.48	1289.70	1062.00	929.41	844.23	786.02	744.54
35000	3267.39	1807.11	1327.63	1093.24	956.74	869.06	809.14	766.44
40000	3734.16	2065.27	1517.30	1249.42	1093.42	993.21	924.73	875.93
45000	4200.93	2323.43	1706.96	1405.59	1230.10	1117.36	1040.32	985.42
50000	4667.70	2581.58	1896.62	1561.77	1366.77	1241.51	1155.91	1094.91
55000	5134.47	2839.74	2086.28	1717.94	1503.45	1365.67	1271.50	1204.40
60000	5601.24	3097.90	2275.94	1874.12	1640.13	1489.82	1387.09	1313.89
65000	6068.01	3356.06	2465.60	2030.30	1776.80	1613.97	1502.68	1423.38
70000	6534.78	3614.21	2655.26	2186.47	1913.48	1738.12	1618.27	1532.87
75000	7001.55	3872.37	2844.93	2342.65	2050.16	1862.27	1733.87	1642.36
80000	7468.32	4130.53	3034.59	2498.83	2186.84	1986.42	1849.46	1751.85
85000	7935.09	4388.69	3224.25	2655.00	2323.51	2110.57	1965.05	1861.34
90000	8401.86	4646.85	3413.91	2811.18	2460.19	2234.72	2080.64	1970.83
95000	8868.63	4905.00	3603.57	2967.35	2596.87	2358.87	2196.23	2080.32
100000	9335.40	5163.16	3793.23	3123.53	2733.54	2483.02	2311.82	2189.81
105000	9802.17	5421.32	3982.89	3279.71	2870.22	2607.18	2427.41	2299.30
110000	10268.94	5679.48	4172.56	3435.88	3006.90	2731.33	2543.00	2408.79
115000	10735.70	5937.64	4362.22	3592.06	3143.57	2855.48	2658.59	2518.28
120000	11202.47	6195.79	4551.88	3748.24	3280.25	2979.63	2774.18	2627.77
125000	11669.24	6453.95	4741.54	3904.41	3416.93	3103.78	2889.77	2737.26
130000	12136.01	6712.11	4931.20	4060.59	3553.60	3227.93	3005.36	2846.75
135000	12602.78	6970.27	5120.86	4216.76	3690.28	3352.08	3120.95	2956.24
140000	13069.55	7228.42	5310.52	4372.94	3826.96	3476.23	3236.54	3065.73
145000	13536.32	7486.58	5500.18	4529.12	3963.64	3600.38	3352.13	3175.22
150000	14003.09	7744.74	5689.85	4685.29	4100.31	3724.53	3467.73	3284.71
155000	14469.86	8002.90	5879.51	4841.47	4236.99	3848.69	3583.32	3394.20
160000	14936.63	8261.06	6069.17	4997.65	4373.67	3972.84	3698.91	3503.69

AMOUNT OF LOAN	NUMBER OF YEARS IN TERM							
	9	10	15	20	25	30	35	40
$ 50	1.06	1.02	.94	.91	.91	.90	.90	.90
100	2.11	2.04	1.87	1.82	1.81	1.80	1.80	1.80
200	4.21	4.07	3.74	3.64	3.61	3.59	3.59	3.59
300	6.31	6.10	5.61	5.46	5.41	5.39	5.38	5.38
400	8.41	8.14	7.48	7.27	7.21	7.18	7.18	7.17
500	10.51	10.17	9.35	9.09	9.01	8.98	8.97	8.97
600	12.61	12.20	11.21	10.91	10.81	10.77	10.76	10.76
700	14.71	14.24	13.08	12.73	12.61	12.57	12.55	12.55
800	16.81	16.27	14.95	14.54	14.41	14.36	14.35	14.34
900	18.91	18.30	16.82	16.36	16.21	16.16	16.14	16.13
1000	21.01	20.34	18.69	18.18	18.01	17.95	17.93	17.93
2000	42.01	40.67	37.37	36.35	36.01	35.90	35.86	35.85
3000	63.01	61.00	56.05	54.52	54.02	53.85	53.79	53.77
4000	84.01	81.33	74.73	72.70	72.02	71.79	71.71	71.69
5000	105.02	101.66	93.41	90.87	90.03	89.74	89.64	89.61
6000	126.02	121.99	112.09	109.04	108.03	107.69	107.57	107.53
7000	147.02	142.32	130.77	127.21	126.03	125.63	125.49	125.45
8000	168.02	162.65	149.45	145.39	144.04	143.58	143.42	143.37
9000	189.03	182.98	168.13	163.56	162.04	161.53	161.35	161.29
10000	210.03	203.31	186.81	181.73	180.05	179.47	179.28	179.21
11000	231.03	223.64	205.49	199.91	198.05	197.42	197.20	197.13
12000	252.03	243.97	224.18	218.08	216.05	215.37	215.13	215.05
13000	273.04	264.30	242.86	236.25	234.06	233.31	233.06	232.97
14000	294.04	284.63	261.54	254.42	252.06	251.26	250.98	250.89
15000	315.04	304.96	280.22	272.60	270.07	269.21	268.91	268.81
16000	336.04	325.29	298.90	290.77	288.07	287.15	286.84	286.73
17000	357.04	345.62	317.58	308.94	306.07	305.10	304.76	304.65
18000	378.05	365.95	336.26	327.12	324.08	323.05	322.69	322.57
19000	399.05	386.28	354.94	345.29	342.08	340.99	340.62	340.49
20000	420.05	406.61	373.62	363.46	360.09	358.94	358.55	358.41
21000	441.05	426.94	392.30	381.63	378.09	376.89	376.47	376.33
22000	462.06	447.27	410.98	399.81	396.10	394.83	394.40	394.25
23000	483.06	467.60	429.66	417.98	414.10	412.78	412.33	412.17
24000	504.06	487.93	448.35	436.15	432.10	430.73	430.25	430.09
25000	525.06	508.26	467.03	454.33	450.11	448.67	448.18	448.01
26000	546.07	528.59	485.71	472.50	468.11	466.62	466.11	465.93
27000	567.07	548.92	504.39	490.67	486.12	484.57	484.03	483.85
28000	588.07	569.25	523.07	508.84	504.12	502.51	501.96	501.77
29000	609.07	589.58	541.75	527.02	522.12	520.46	519.89	519.69
30000	630.07	609.92	560.43	545.19	540.13	538.41	537.82	537.61
31000	651.07	630.25	579.11	563.36	558.13	556.35	555.74	555.53
32000	672.08	650.58	597.79	581.54	576.14	574.30	573.67	573.45
33000	693.08	670.91	616.47	599.71	594.14	592.25	591.60	591.37
34000	714.08	691.24	635.15	617.88	612.14	610.19	609.52	609.29
35000	735.09	711.57	653.83	636.05	630.15	628.14	627.45	627.21
40000	840.10	813.22	747.24	726.92	720.17	717.87	717.09	716.81
45000	945.11	914.87	840.64	817.78	810.19	807.61	806.72	806.42
50000	1050.12	1016.52	934.05	908.65	900.21	897.34	896.36	896.02
55000	1155.13	1118.17	1027.45	999.51	990.23	987.07	985.99	985.62
60000	1260.14	1219.83	1120.86	1090.37	1080.25	1076.81	1075.63	1075.22
65000	1365.16	1321.48	1214.26	1181.24	1170.27	1166.54	1165.26	1164.82
70000	1470.17	1423.13	1307.66	1272.10	1260.29	1256.27	1254.90	1254.42
75000	1575.18	1524.78	1401.07	1362.97	1350.31	1346.01	1344.53	1344.02
80000	1680.19	1626.43	1494.47	1453.83	1440.33	1435.74	1434.17	1433.62
85000	1785.20	1728.08	1587.88	1544.69	1530.35	1525.47	1523.80	1523.22
90000	1890.21	1829.74	1681.28	1635.56	1620.37	1615.21	1613.44	1612.83
95000	1995.23	1931.39	1774.69	1726.42	1710.40	1704.94	1703.07	1702.43
100000	2100.24	2033.04	1868.09	1817.29	1800.42	1794.67	1792.71	1792.03
105000	2205.25	2134.69	1961.49	1908.15	1890.44	1884.41	1882.34	1881.63
110000	2310.26	2236.34	2054.90	1999.01	1980.46	1974.14	1971.98	1971.23
115000	2415.27	2337.99	2148.30	2089.88	2070.48	2063.88	2061.61	2060.83
120000	2520.28	2439.65	2241.71	2180.74	2160.50	2153.61	2151.25	2150.43
125000	2625.29	2541.30	2335.11	2271.61	2250.52	2243.34	2240.88	2240.03
130000	2730.31	2642.95	2428.52	2362.47	2340.54	2333.08	2330.52	2329.63
135000	2835.32	2744.60	2521.92	2453.33	2430.56	2422.81	2420.15	2419.24
140000	2940.33	2846.25	2615.32	2544.20	2520.58	2512.54	2509.79	2508.84
145000	3045.34	2947.90	2708.73	2635.06	2610.60	2602.28	2599.42	2598.44
150000	3150.35	3049.56	2802.13	2725.93	2700.62	2692.01	2689.06	2688.04
155000	3255.36	3151.21	2895.54	2816.79	2790.64	2781.74	2778.69	2777.64
160000	3360.38	3252.86	2988.94	2907.66	2880.66	2871.48	2868.33	2867.24

MONTHLY AMORTIZING PAYMENTS

AMOUNT OF LOAN	NUMBER OF YEARS IN TERM							
	1	2	3	4	5	6	7	8
$ 50	4.68	2.59	1.91	1.57	1.38	1.25	1.17	1.11
100	9.35	5.18	3.81	3.14	2.75	2.50	2.33	2.21
200	18.70	10.36	7.62	6.28	5.50	5.00	4.66	4.42
300	28.05	15.53	11.42	9.42	8.25	7.50	6.99	6.62
400	37.39	20.71	15.23	12.55	11.00	10.00	9.31	8.83
500	46.74	25.88	19.04	15.69	13.74	12.49	11.64	11.03
600	56.09	31.06	22.84	18.83	16.49	14.99	13.97	13.24
700	65.44	36.23	26.65	21.96	19.24	17.49	16.30	15.45
800	74.78	41.41	30.45	25.10	21.99	19.99	18.62	17.65
900	84.13	46.58	34.26	28.24	24.73	22.49	20.95	19.86
1000	93.48	51.76	38.07	31.38	27.48	24.98	23.28	22.06
2000	186.95	103.51	76.13	62.75	54.96	49.96	46.55	44.12
3000	280.43	155.27	114.19	94.12	82.44	74.94	69.82	66.18
4000	373.90	207.02	152.25	125.49	109.91	99.92	93.09	88.23
5000	467.38	258.78	190.31	156.86	137.39	124.89	116.36	110.29
6000	560.85	310.53	228.37	188.23	164.87	149.87	139.64	132.35
7000	654.32	362.29	266.43	219.60	192.34	174.85	162.91	154.41
8000	747.80	414.04	304.49	250.97	219.82	199.83	186.18	176.46
9000	841.27	465.80	342.56	282.34	247.30	224.81	209.45	198.52
10000	934.75	517.55	380.62	313.71	274.77	249.78	232.72	220.58
11000	1028.22	569.31	418.68	345.08	302.25	274.76	255.99	242.64
12000	1121.69	621.06	456.74	376.45	329.73	299.74	279.27	264.69
13000	1215.17	672.82	494.80	407.82	357.21	324.72	302.54	286.75
14000	1308.64	724.57	532.86	439.19	384.68	349.70	325.81	308.81
15000	1402.12	776.33	570.92	470.56	412.16	374.67	349.08	330.86
16000	1495.59	828.08	608.98	501.93	439.64	399.65	372.35	352.92
17000	1589.06	879.84	647.05	533.30	467.11	424.63	395.63	374.98
18000	1682.54	931.59	685.11	564.67	494.59	449.61	418.90	397.04
19000	1776.01	983.35	723.17	596.04	522.07	474.59	442.17	419.09
20000	1869.49	1035.10	761.23	627.42	549.54	499.56	465.44	441.15
21000	1962.96	1086.86	799.29	658.79	577.02	524.54	488.71	463.21
22000	2056.44	1138.61	837.35	690.16	604.50	549.52	511.98	485.27
23000	2149.91	1190.36	875.41	721.53	631.98	574.50	535.26	507.32
24000	2243.38	1242.12	913.47	752.90	659.45	599.48	558.53	529.38
25000	2336.86	1293.87	951.54	784.27	686.93	624.45	581.80	551.44
26000	2430.33	1345.63	989.60	815.64	714.41	649.43	605.07	573.49
27000	2523.81	1397.38	1027.66	847.01	741.88	674.41	628.34	595.55
28000	2617.28	1449.14	1065.72	878.38	769.36	699.39	651.62	617.61
29000	2710.75	1500.89	1103.78	909.75	796.84	724.37	674.89	639.67
30000	2804.23	1552.65	1141.84	941.12	824.31	749.34	698.16	661.72
31000	2897.70	1604.40	1179.90	972.49	851.79	774.32	721.43	683.78
32000	2991.18	1656.16	1217.96	1003.86	879.27	799.30	744.70	705.84
33000	3084.65	1707.91	1256.03	1035.23	906.74	824.28	767.97	727.90
34000	3178.12	1759.67	1294.09	1066.60	934.22	849.26	791.25	749.95
35000	3271.60	1811.42	1332.15	1097.97	961.70	874.23	814.52	772.01
40000	3738.97	2070.20	1522.45	1254.83	1099.08	999.12	930.88	882.30
45000	4206.34	2328.97	1712.76	1411.68	1236.47	1124.01	1047.24	992.58
50000	4673.71	2587.74	1903.07	1568.53	1373.85	1248.90	1163.60	1102.87
55000	5141.08	2846.52	2093.37	1725.38	1511.24	1373.79	1279.95	1213.16
60000	5608.45	3105.29	2283.68	1882.24	1648.62	1498.68	1396.31	1323.44
65000	6075.82	3364.07	2473.99	2039.09	1786.01	1623.57	1512.67	1433.73
70000	6543.19	3622.84	2664.29	2195.94	1923.39	1748.46	1629.03	1544.02
75000	7010.56	3881.61	2854.60	2352.79	2060.78	1873.35	1745.39	1654.30
80000	7477.93	4140.39	3044.90	2509.65	2198.16	1998.24	1861.75	1764.59
85000	7945.30	4399.16	3235.21	2666.50	2335.55	2123.13	1978.11	1874.88
90000	8412.67	4657.94	3425.52	2823.35	2472.93	2248.02	2094.47	1985.16
95000	8880.04	4916.71	3615.82	2980.20	2610.32	2372.91	2210.83	2095.45
100000	9347.42	5175.48	3806.13	3137.06	2747.70	2497.80	2327.19	2205.73
105000	9814.79	5434.26	3996.44	3293.91	2885.09	2622.69	2443.54	2316.02
110000	10282.16	5693.03	4186.74	3450.76	3022.47	2747.58	2559.90	2426.31
115000	10749.53	5951.80	4377.05	3607.61	3159.86	2872.47	2676.26	2536.59
120000	11216.90	6210.58	4567.35	3764.47	3297.24	2997.36	2792.62	2646.88
125000	11684.27	6469.35	4757.66	3921.32	3434.62	3122.25	2908.98	2757.17
130000	12151.64	6728.13	4947.97	4078.17	3572.01	3247.14	3025.34	2867.45
135000	12619.01	6986.90	5138.27	4235.02	3709.39	3372.03	3141.70	2977.74
140000	13086.38	7245.67	5328.58	4391.88	3846.78	3496.92	3258.06	3088.03
145000	13553.75	7504.45	5518.89	4548.73	3984.16	3621.81	3374.42	3198.31
150000	14021.13	7763.22	5709.19	4705.58	4121.55	3746.70	3490.78	3308.60
155000	14488.49	8022.00	5899.50	4862.43	4258.93	3871.59	3607.13	3418.89
160000	14955.86	8280.77	6089.80	5019.29	4396.32	3996.48	3723.49	3529.17

AMOUNT OF LOAN	NUMBER OF YEARS IN TERM							
	9	10	15	20	25	30	35	40
$ 50	1.06	1.03	.95	.92	.92	.91	.91	.91
100	2.12	2.05	1.89	1.84	1.83	1.82	1.82	1.82
200	4.24	4.10	3.78	3.68	3.65	3.64	3.63	3.63
300	6.36	6.15	5.67	5.52	5.47	5.45	5.45	5.44
400	8.47	8.20	7.55	7.35	7.29	7.27	7.26	7.26
500	10.59	10.25	9.44	9.19	9.11	9.08	9.07	9.07
600	12.71	12.30	11.33	11.03	10.93	10.90	10.89	10.88
700	14.82	14.35	13.21	12.87	12.75	12.71	12.70	12.69
800	16.94	16.40	15.10	14.70	14.57	14.53	14.51	14.51
900	19.06	18.45	16.99	16.99	16.39	16.34	16.33	16.32
1000	21.17	20.50	18.87	18.38	18.21	18.16	18.14	18.13
2000	42.34	41.00	37.74	36.75	36.42	36.31	36.27	36.26
3000	63.51	61.50	56.61	55.12	54.63	54.46	54.41	54.39
4000	84.67	82.00	75.48	73.49	72.84	72.62	72.54	72.52
5000	105.84	102.50	94.35	91.86	91.05	90.77	90.68	90.65
6000	127.01	123.00	113.22	110.23	109.25	108.92	108.81	108.77
7000	148.17	143.50	132.09	128.61	127.46	127.08	126.95	126.90
8000	169.34	164.00	150.96	146.98	145.67	145.23	145.08	145.03
9000	190.51	184.50	169.83	165.35	163.88	163.38	163.22	163.16
10000	211.67	205.00	188.69	183.72	182.09	181.54	181.35	181.29
11000	232.84	225.50	207.56	202.09	200.29	199.69	199.49	199.42
12000	254.01	246.00	226.43	220.46	218.50	217.84	217.62	217.54
13000	275.17	266.50	245.30	238.83	236.71	236.00	235.75	235.67
14000	296.34	287.00	264.17	257.21	254.92	254.15	253.89	253.80
15000	317.51	307.50	283.04	275.58	273.13	272.30	272.02	271.93
16000	338.67	328.00	301.91	293.95	291.34	290.46	290.16	290.06
17000	359.84	348.50	320.78	312.32	309.54	308.61	308.29	308.19
18000	381.01	369.00	339.65	330.69	327.75	326.76	326.43	326.31
19000	402.18	389.50	358.52	349.06	345.96	344.92	344.56	344.44
20000	423.34	410.00	377.38	367.44	364.17	363.07	362.70	362.57
21000	444.51	430.50	396.25	385.81	382.38	381.22	380.83	380.70
22000	465.68	451.00	415.12	404.18	400.58	399.38	398.97	398.83
23000	486.84	471.50	433.99	422.55	418.79	417.53	417.10	416.96
24000	508.01	492.00	452.86	440.92	437.00	435.68	435.24	435.08
25000	529.18	512.50	471.73	459.29	455.21	453.84	453.37	453.21
26000	550.34	533.00	490.60	477.66	473.42	471.99	471.50	471.34
27000	571.51	553.50	509.47	496.04	491.63	490.14	489.64	489.47
28000	592.68	574.00	528.34	514.41	509.83	508.30	507.77	507.60
29000	613.84	594.50	547.20	532.78	528.04	526.45	525.91	525.72
30000	635.01	615.00	566.07	551.15	546.25	544.60	544.04	543.85
31000	656.18	635.50	584.94	569.52	564.46	562.75	562.18	561.98
32000	677.34	656.00	603.81	587.89	582.67	580.91	580.31	580.11
33000	698.51	676.50	622.68	606.27	600.87	599.06	598.45	598.24
34000	719.68	697.00	641.55	624.64	619.08	617.21	616.58	616.37
35000	740.84	717.50	660.42	643.01	637.29	635.37	634.72	634.49
40000	846.68	819.99	754.76	734.87	728.33	726.13	725.39	725.14
45000	952.51	922.49	849.11	826.72	819.37	816.90	816.06	815.78
50000	1058.35	1024.99	943.45	918.58	910.41	907.67	906.73	906.42
55000	1164.18	1127.49	1037.80	1010.44	1001.45	998.43	997.41	997.06
60000	1270.02	1229.99	1132.14	1102.30	1092.49	1089.20	1088.08	1087.70
65000	1375.85	1332.49	1226.49	1194.15	1183.54	1179.96	1178.75	1178.34
70000	1481.68	1434.99	1320.83	1286.01	1274.58	1270.73	1269.43	1268.98
75000	1587.52	1537.49	1415.18	1377.87	1365.62	1361.50	1360.10	1359.62
80000	1693.35	1639.98	1509.52	1469.73	1456.66	1452.26	1450.77	1450.27
85000	1799.19	1742.48	1603.87	1561.59	1547.70	1543.03	1541.45	1540.91
90000	1905.02	1844.98	1698.21	1653.44	1638.74	1633.79	1632.12	1631.55
95000	2010.86	1947.48	1792.56	1745.30	1729.78	1724.56	1722.79	1722.19
100000	2116.69	2049.98	1886.90	1837.16	1820.82	1815.33	1813.46	1812.83
105000	2222.52	2152.48	1981.25	1929.02	1911.86	1906.09	1904.14	1903.47
110000	2328.36	2254.98	2075.59	2020.87	2002.90	1996.86	1994.81	1994.11
115000	2434.19	2357.48	2169.94	2112.73	2093.94	2087.63	2085.48	2084.76
120000	2540.03	2459.97	2264.28	2204.59	2184.98	2178.39	2176.16	2175.40
125000	2645.86	2562.47	2358.63	2296.45	2276.03	2269.16	2266.83	2266.04
130000	2751.69	2664.97	2452.97	2388.30	2367.07	2359.92	2357.50	2356.68
135000	2857.53	2767.47	2547.31	2480.16	2458.11	2450.69	2448.18	2447.32
140000	2963.36	2869.97	2641.66	2572.02	2549.15	2541.46	2538.85	2537.96
145000	3069.20	2972.47	2736.00	2663.88	2640.19	2632.22	2629.52	2628.60
150000	3175.03	3074.97	2830.35	2755.74	2731.23	2722.99	2720.19	2719.24
155000	3280.87	3177.46	2924.69	2847.59	2822.27	2813.75	2810.87	2809.89
160000	3386.70	3279.96	3019.04	2939.45	2913.31	2904.52	2901.54	2900.53

22.000% MONTHLY AMORTIZING PAYMENTS

AMOUNT OF LOAN	NUMBER OF YEARS IN TERM							
	1	2	3	4	5	6	7	8
$ 50	4.68	2.60	1.91	1.58	1.39	1.26	1.18	1.12
100	9.36	5.19	3.82	3.16	2.77	2.52	2.35	2.23
200	18.72	10.38	7.64	6.31	5.53	5.03	4.69	4.45
300	28.08	15.57	11.46	9.46	8.29	7.54	7.03	6.67
400	37.44	20.76	15.28	12.61	11.05	10.06	9.38	8.89
500	46.80	25.94	19.10	15.76	13.81	12.57	11.72	11.11
600	56.16	31.13	22.92	18.91	16.58	15.08	14.06	13.34
700	65.52	36.32	26.74	22.06	19.34	17.59	16.40	15.56
800	74.88	41.51	30.56	25.21	22.10	20.11	18.75	17.78
900	84.24	46.70	34.38	28.36	24.86	22.62	21.09	20.00
1000	93.60	51.88	38.20	31.51	27.62	25.13	23.43	22.22
2000	187.19	103.76	76.39	63.02	55.24	50.26	46.86	44.44
3000	280.79	155.64	114.58	94.52	82.86	75.38	70.28	66.66
4000	374.38	207.52	152.77	126.03	110.48	100.51	93.71	88.87
5000	467.98	259.40	190.96	157.54	138.10	125.64	117.13	111.09
6000	561.57	311.27	229.15	189.04	165.72	150.76	140.56	133.31
7000	655.17	363.15	267.34	220.55	193.34	175.89	163.99	155.52
8000	748.76	415.03	305.53	252.05	220.96	201.01	187.41	177.74
9000	842.35	466.91	343.72	283.56	248.58	226.14	210.84	199.96
10000	935.95	518.79	381.91	315.07	276.19	251.27	234.26	222.18
11000	1029.54	570.66	420.10	346.57	303.81	276.39	257.69	244.39
12000	1123.14	622.54	458.29	378.08	331.43	301.52	281.12	266.61
13000	1216.73	674.42	496.48	409.58	359.05	326.64	304.54	288.83
14000	1310.33	726.30	534.67	441.09	386.67	351.77	327.97	311.04
15000	1403.92	778.18	572.86	472.60	414.29	376.90	351.39	333.26
16000	1497.52	830.06	611.05	504.10	441.91	402.02	374.82	355.48
17000	1591.11	881.93	649.24	535.61	469.53	427.15	398.25	377.70
18000	1684.70	933.81	687.43	567.11	497.15	452.28	421.67	399.91
19000	1778.30	985.69	725.62	598.62	524.76	477.40	445.10	422.13
20000	1871.89	1037.57	763.81	630.13	552.38	502.53	468.52	444.35
21000	1965.49	1089.45	802.00	661.63	580.00	527.65	491.95	466.56
22000	2059.08	1141.32	840.19	693.14	607.62	552.78	515.38	488.78
23000	2152.68	1193.20	878.39	724.64	635.24	577.91	538.80	511.00
24000	2246.27	1245.08	916.58	756.15	662.86	603.03	562.23	533.21
25000	2339.86	1296.96	954.77	787.66	690.48	628.16	585.65	555.43
26000	2433.46	1348.84	992.96	819.16	718.10	653.28	609.08	577.65
27000	2527.05	1400.72	1031.15	850.67	745.72	678.41	632.51	599.87
28000	2620.65	1452.59	1069.34	882.18	773.33	703.54	655.93	622.08
29000	2714.24	1504.47	1107.53	913.68	800.95	728.66	679.36	644.30
30000	2807.84	1556.35	1145.72	945.19	828.57	753.79	702.78	666.52
31000	2901.43	1608.23	1183.91	976.69	856.19	778.91	726.21	688.73
32000	2995.03	1660.11	1222.10	1008.20	883.81	804.04	749.64	710.95
33000	3088.62	1711.98	1260.29	1039.71	911.43	829.17	773.06	733.17
34000	3182.21	1763.86	1298.48	1071.21	939.05	854.29	796.49	755.39
35000	3275.81	1815.74	1336.67	1102.72	966.67	879.42	819.91	777.60
40000	3743.78	2075.13	1527.62	1260.25	1104.76	1005.05	937.04	888.69
45000	4211.75	2334.52	1718.58	1417.78	1242.86	1130.68	1054.17	999.77
50000	4679.72	2593.91	1909.53	1575.31	1380.95	1256.31	1171.30	1110.86
55000	5147.70	2853.30	2100.48	1732.84	1519.05	1381.94	1288.43	1221.94
60000	5615.67	3112.69	2291.43	1890.37	1657.14	1507.57	1405.56	1333.03
65000	6083.64	3372.09	2482.38	2047.90	1795.23	1633.20	1522.69	1444.12
70000	6551.61	3631.48	2673.34	2205.43	1933.33	1758.83	1639.82	1555.20
75000	7019.58	3890.87	2864.29	2362.96	2071.42	1884.46	1756.95	1666.29
80000	7487.56	4150.26	3055.24	2520.49	2209.52	2010.10	1874.08	1777.37
85000	7955.53	4409.65	3246.19	2678.02	2347.61	2135.73	1991.21	1888.46
90000	8423.50	4669.04	3437.15	2835.55	2485.71	2261.36	2108.34	1999.54
95000	8891.47	4928.43	3628.10	2993.08	2623.80	2386.99	2225.47	2110.63
100000	9359.44	5187.82	3819.05	3150.61	2761.90	2512.62	2342.60	2221.71
105000	9827.41	5447.21	4010.00	3308.14	2899.99	2638.25	2459.73	2332.80
110000	10295.39	5706.60	4200.95	3465.67	3038.09	2763.88	2576.86	2443.88
115000	10763.36	5965.99	4391.91	3623.20	3176.18	2889.51	2693.99	2554.97
120000	11231.33	6225.38	4582.86	3780.73	3314.27	3015.14	2811.12	2666.05
125000	11699.30	6484.77	4773.81	3938.26	3452.37	3140.77	2928.25	2777.14
130000	12167.27	6744.17	4964.76	4095.80	3590.46	3266.40	3045.38	2888.23
135000	12635.25	7003.56	5155.72	4253.33	3728.56	3392.03	3162.51	2999.31
140000	13103.22	7262.95	5346.67	4410.86	3866.65	3517.66	3279.64	3110.40
145000	13571.19	7522.34	5537.62	4568.39	4004.75	3643.29	3396.77	3221.48
150000	14039.16	7781.73	5728.57	4725.92	4142.84	3768.92	3513.90	3332.57
155000	14507.13	8041.12	5919.53	4883.45	4280.94	3894.55	3631.03	3443.65
160000	14975.11	8300.51	6110.48	5040.98	4419.03	4020.19	3748.16	3554.74

MONTHLY AMORTIZING PAYMENTS 22.000%

AMOUNT OF LOAN	NUMBER OF YEARS IN TERM							
	9	10	15	20	25	30	35	40
$ 50	1.07	1.04	.96	.93	.93	.92	.92	.92
100	2.14	2.07	1.91	1.86	1.85	1.84	1.84	1.84
200	4.27	4.14	3.82	3.72	3.69	3.68	3.67	3.67
300	6.40	6.21	5.72	5.58	5.53	5.51	5.51	5.51
400	8.54	8.27	7.63	7.43	7.37	7.35	7.34	7.34
500	10.67	10.34	9.53	9.29	9.21	9.18	9.18	9.17
600	12.80	12.41	11.44	11.15	11.05	11.02	11.01	11.01
700	14.94	14.47	13.35	13.00	12.89	12.86	12.84	12.84
800	17.07	16.54	15.25	14.86	14.73	14.69	14.68	14.67
900	19.20	18.61	17.16	16.72	16.58	16.53	16.51	16.51
1000	21.34	20.67	19.06	18.58	18.42	18.36	18.35	18.34
2000	42.67	41.34	38.12	37.15	36.83	36.72	36.69	36.68
3000	64.00	62.01	57.18	55.72	55.24	55.08	55.03	55.01
4000	85.33	82.68	76.24	74.29	73.65	73.44	73.37	73.35
5000	106.66	103.35	95.29	92.86	92.07	91.80	91.72	91.69
6000	128.00	124.02	114.35	111.43	110.48	110.16	110.06	110.02
7000	149.33	144.69	133.41	130.00	128.89	128.52	128.40	128.36
8000	170.66	165.36	152.47	148.57	147.30	146.88	146.74	146.70
9000	191.99	186.03	171.52	167.14	165.72	165.24	165.09	165.03
10000	213.32	206.70	190.58	185.71	184.13	183.60	183.43	183.37
11000	234.66	227.37	209.64	204.28	202.54	201.96	201.77	201.70
12000	255.99	248.04	228.70	222.85	220.95	220.32	220.11	220.04
13000	277.32	268.71	247.75	241.42	239.37	238.68	238.45	238.38
14000	298.65	289.38	266.81	259.99	257.78	257.04	256.80	256.71
15000	319.98	310.05	285.87	278.56	276.19	275.40	275.14	275.05
16000	341.32	330.72	304.93	297.13	294.60	293.76	293.48	293.39
17000	362.65	351.39	323.98	315.71	313.02	312.12	311.82	311.72
18000	383.98	372.06	343.04	334.28	331.43	330.48	330.17	330.06
19000	405.31	392.73	362.10	352.85	349.84	348.84	348.51	348.40
20000	426.64	413.40	381.16	371.42	368.25	367.20	366.85	366.73
21000	447.97	434.07	400.21	389.99	386.67	385.56	385.19	385.07
22000	469.31	454.74	419.27	408.56	405.08	403.92	403.53	403.40
23000	490.64	475.41	438.33	427.13	423.49	422.28	421.88	421.74
24000	511.97	496.08	457.39	445.70	441.90	440.64	440.22	440.08
25000	533.30	516.75	476.44	464.27	460.32	459.00	458.56	458.41
26000	554.63	537.42	495.50	482.84	478.73	477.36	476.90	476.75
27000	575.97	558.09	514.56	501.41	497.14	495.72	495.25	495.09
28000	597.30	578.76	533.62	519.98	515.55	514.08	513.59	513.42
29000	618.63	599.43	552.67	538.55	533.97	532.44	531.93	531.76
30000	639.96	620.10	571.73	557.12	552.38	550.80	550.27	550.09
31000	661.29	640.77	590.79	575.69	570.79	569.16	568.61	568.43
32000	682.63	661.44	609.85	594.26	589.20	587.52	586.96	586.77
33000	703.96	682.10	628.90	612.83	607.61	605.88	605.30	605.10
34000	725.29	702.77	647.96	631.41	626.03	624.24	623.64	623.44
35000	746.62	723.44	667.02	649.98	644.44	642.60	641.98	641.78
40000	853.28	826.79	762.31	742.83	736.50	734.40	733.69	733.46
45000	959.94	930.14	857.60	835.68	828.56	826.20	825.41	825.14
50000	1066.60	1033.49	952.88	928.53	920.63	918.00	917.12	916.82
55000	1173.26	1136.84	1048.17	1021.39	1012.69	1009.80	1008.83	1008.50
60000	1279.92	1240.19	1143.46	1114.24	1104.75	1101.60	1100.54	1100.18
65000	1386.58	1343.53	1238.75	1207.09	1196.81	1193.40	1192.25	1191.87
70000	1493.24	1446.88	1334.03	1299.95	1288.87	1285.19	1283.96	1283.55
75000	1599.90	1550.23	1429.32	1392.80	1380.94	1376.99	1375.67	1375.23
80000	1706.56	1653.58	1524.61	1485.65	1473.00	1468.79	1467.38	1466.91
85000	1813.22	1756.93	1619.90	1578.51	1565.06	1560.59	1559.10	1558.59
90000	1919.88	1860.28	1715.19	1671.36	1657.12	1652.39	1650.81	1650.27
95000	2026.54	1963.63	1810.47	1764.21	1749.19	1744.19	1742.52	1741.96
100000	2133.20	2066.97	1905.76	1857.06	1841.25	1835.99	1834.23	1833.64
105000	2239.85	2170.32	2001.05	1949.92	1933.31	1927.79	1925.94	1925.32
110000	2346.51	2273.67	2096.34	2042.77	2025.37	2019.59	2017.65	2017.00
115000	2453.17	2377.02	2191.62	2135.62	2117.43	2111.39	2109.36	2108.68
120000	2559.83	2480.37	2286.91	2228.48	2209.50	2203.19	2201.07	2200.36
125000	2666.49	2583.72	2382.20	2321.33	2301.56	2294.99	2292.78	2292.05
130000	2773.15	2687.06	2477.49	2414.18	2393.62	2386.79	2384.50	2383.73
135000	2879.81	2790.41	2572.78	2507.04	2485.68	2478.58	2476.21	2475.41
140000	2986.47	2893.76	2668.06	2599.89	2577.74	2570.38	2567.92	2567.09
145000	3093.13	2997.11	2763.35	2692.74	2669.81	2662.18	2659.63	2658.77
150000	3199.79	3100.46	2858.64	2785.59	2761.87	2753.98	2751.34	2750.45
155000	3306.45	3203.81	2953.93	2878.45	2853.93	2845.78	2843.05	2842.14
160000	3413.11	3307.16	3049.21	2971.30	2945.99	2937.58	2934.76	2933.82

22.250%　MONTHLY AMORTIZING PAYMENTS

AMOUNT OF LOAN	NUMBER OF YEARS IN TERM							
	1	2	3	4	5	6	7	8
$ 50	4.69	2.61	1.92	1.59	1.39	1.27	1.18	1.12
100	9.38	5.21	3.84	3.17	2.78	2.53	2.36	2.24
200	18.75	10.41	7.67	6.33	5.56	5.06	4.72	4.48
300	28.12	15.61	11.50	9.50	8.33	7.59	7.08	6.72
400	37.49	20.81	15.33	12.66	11.11	10.11	9.44	8.96
500	46.86	26.01	19.16	15.83	13.89	12.64	11.80	11.19
600	56.23	31.21	23.00	18.99	16.66	15.17	14.15	13.43
700	65.61	36.41	26.83	22.15	19.44	17.70	16.51	15.67
800	74.98	41.61	30.66	25.32	22.21	20.22	18.87	17.91
900	84.35	46.81	34.49	28.48	24.99	22.75	21.23	20.14
1000	93.72	52.01	38.32	31.65	27.77	25.28	23.59	22.38
2000	187.43	104.01	76.64	63.29	55.53	50.55	47.17	44.76
3000	281.15	156.01	114.96	94.93	83.29	75.83	70.75	67.14
4000	374.86	208.01	153.28	126.57	111.05	101.10	94.33	89.51
5000	468.58	260.01	191.60	158.21	138.81	126.38	117.91	111.89
6000	562.29	312.02	229.92	189.86	166.57	151.65	141.49	134.27
7000	656.01	364.02	268.24	221.50	194.33	176.93	165.07	156.65
8000	749.72	416.02	306.56	253.14	222.09	202.20	188.65	179.02
9000	843.44	468.02	344.88	284.78	249.86	227.48	212.23	201.40
10000	937.15	520.02	383.20	316.42	277.62	252.75	235.81	223.78
11000	1030.87	572.02	421.52	348.07	305.38	278.03	259.39	246.16
12000	1124.58	624.03	459.84	379.71	333.14	303.30	282.97	268.53
13000	1218.30	676.03	498.16	411.35	360.90	328.58	306.55	290.91
14000	1312.01	728.03	536.48	442.99	388.66	353.85	330.13	313.29
15000	1405.73	780.03	574.80	474.63	416.42	379.13	353.71	335.67
16000	1499.44	832.03	613.12	506.28	444.18	404.40	377.29	358.04
17000	1593.16	884.03	651.44	537.92	471.95	429.68	400.87	380.42
18000	1686.87	936.04	689.76	569.56	499.71	454.95	424.46	402.80
19000	1780.59	988.04	728.08	601.20	527.47	480.22	448.04	425.17
20000	1874.30	1040.04	766.40	632.84	555.23	505.50	471.62	447.55
21000	1968.01	1092.04	804.72	664.49	582.99	530.77	495.20	469.93
22000	2061.73	1144.04	843.04	696.13	610.75	556.05	518.78	492.31
23000	2155.04	1196.04	881.36	727.77	638.51	581.32	542.36	514.68
24000	2249.16	1248.05	919.68	759.41	666.27	606.60	565.94	537.06
25000	2342.87	1300.05	958.00	791.05	694.04	631.87	589.52	559.44
26000	2436.59	1352.05	996.32	822.70	721.80	657.15	613.10	581.82
27000	2530.30	1404.05	1034.64	854.34	749.56	682.42	636.68	604.19
28000	2624.02	1456.05	1072.96	885.98	777.32	707.70	660.26	626.57
29000	2717.73	1508.05	1111.28	917.62	805.08	732.97	683.84	648.95
30000	2811.45	1560.06	1149.60	949.26	832.84	758.25	707.42	671.33
31000	2905.16	1612.06	1187.92	980.91	860.60	783.52	731.00	693.70
32000	2998.88	1664.06	1226.24	1012.55	888.36	808.80	754.58	716.08
33000	3092.59	1716.06	1264.56	1044.19	916.13	834.07	778.16	738.46
34000	3186.31	1768.06	1302.88	1075.83	943.89	859.35	801.74	760.84
35000	3280.02	1820.06	1341.20	1107.47	971.65	884.62	825.32	783.21
40000	3748.59	2080.07	1532.80	1265.68	1110.45	1010.99	943.23	895.10
45000	4217.17	2340.08	1724.40	1423.89	1249.26	1137.37	1061.13	1006.99
50000	4685.74	2600.09	1916.00	1582.10	1388.07	1263.74	1179.03	1118.87
55000	5154.32	2860.10	2107.60	1740.31	1526.87	1390.12	1296.94	1230.76
60000	5622.89	3120.11	2299.20	1898.52	1665.68	1516.49	1414.84	1342.65
65000	6091.46	3380.12	2490.80	2056.73	1804.49	1642.86	1532.74	1454.53
70000	6560.04	3640.12	2682.40	2214.94	1943.29	1769.24	1650.64	1566.42
75000	7028.61	3900.13	2874.00	2373.15	2082.10	1895.61	1768.55	1678.31
80000	7497.18	4160.14	3065.60	2531.36	2220.90	2021.98	1886.45	1790.19
85000	7965.76	4420.15	3257.20	2689.57	2359.71	2148.36	2004.35	1902.08
90000	8434.33	4680.16	3448.80	2847.78	2498.52	2274.73	2122.26	2013.97
95000	8902.91	4940.17	3640.40	3005.99	2637.32	2401.10	2240.16	2125.85
100000	9371.48	5200.17	3832.00	3164.20	2776.13	2527.48	2358.06	2237.74
105000	9840.05	5460.18	4023.60	3322.41	2914.94	2653.85	2475.96	2349.63
110000	10308.63	5720.19	4215.19	3480.62	3053.74	2780.23	2593.87	2461.51
115000	10777.20	5980.20	4406.79	3638.83	3192.55	2906.60	2711.77	2573.40
120000	11245.78	6240.21	4598.39	3797.04	3331.35	3032.97	2829.67	2685.29
125000	11714.35	6500.22	4789.99	3955.25	3470.16	3159.35	2947.57	2797.18
130000	12182.92	6760.23	4981.59	4113.46	3608.97	3285.72	3065.48	2909.06
135000	12651.49	7020.23	5173.19	4271.67	3747.77	3412.09	3183.38	3020.95
140000	13120.07	7280.24	5364.79	4429.88	3886.58	3538.47	3301.28	3132.84
145000	13588.64	7540.25	5556.39	4588.09	4025.39	3664.84	3419.19	3244.72
150000	14057.22	7800.26	5747.99	4746.30	4164.19	3791.22	3537.09	3356.61
155000	14525.79	8060.27	5939.59	4904.51	4303.00	3917.59	3654.99	3468.50
160000	14994.36	8320.28	6131.19	5062.72	4441.80	4043.96	3772.89	3580.38

AMOUNT OF LOAN	NUMBER OF YEARS IN TERM							
	9	10	15	20	25	30	35	40
$ 50	1.08	1.05	.97	.94	.94	.93	.93	.93
100	2.15	2.09	1.93	1.88	1.87	1.86	1.86	1.86
200	4.30	4.17	3.85	3.76	3.73	3.72	3.71	3.71
300	6.45	6.26	5.78	5.64	5.59	5.57	5.57	5.57
400	8.60	8.34	7.70	7.51	7.45	7.43	7.42	7.42
500	10.75	10.43	9.63	9.39	9.31	9.29	9.28	9.28
600	12.90	12.51	11.55	11.27	11.18	11.14	11.13	11.13
700	15.05	14.59	13.48	13.14	13.04	13.00	12.99	12.99
800	17.20	16.68	15.40	15.02	14.90	14.86	14.84	14.84
900	19.35	18.76	17.33	16.90	16.76	16.71	16.70	16.69
1000	21.50	20.85	19.25	18.77	18.62	18.57	18.55	18.55
2000	43.00	41.69	38.50	37.54	37.24	37.14	37.10	37.09
3000	64.50	62.53	57.74	56.31	55.86	55.70	55.65	55.64
4000	85.99	83.37	76.99	75.08	74.47	74.27	74.20	74.18
5000	107.49	104.21	96.24	93.85	93.09	92.84	92.75	92.73
6000	128.99	125.05	115.48	112.62	111.71	111.40	111.30	111.27
7000	150.49	145.89	134.73	131.39	130.32	129.97	129.85	129.82
8000	171.98	166.73	153.98	150.16	148.94	148.54	148.40	148.36
9000	193.48	187.57	173.22	168.93	167.56	167.10	166.95	166.90
10000	214.98	208.41	192.47	187.70	186.17	185.67	185.50	185.45
11000	236.48	229.25	211.72	206.47	204.79	204.24	204.05	203.99
12000	257.97	250.09	230.96	225.24	223.41	222.80	222.60	222.54
13000	279.47	270.93	250.21	244.01	242.02	241.37	241.15	241.08
14000	300.97	291.77	269.46	262.78	260.64	259.94	259.70	259.63
15000	322.47	312.61	288.70	281.55	279.26	278.50	278.25	278.17
16000	343.96	333.45	307.95	300.32	297.88	297.07	296.80	296.72
17000	365.46	354.29	327.20	319.09	316.49	315.64	315.35	315.26
18000	386.96	375.13	346.44	337.86	335.11	334.20	333.90	333.80
19000	408.46	395.97	365.69	356.63	353.73	352.77	352.45	352.35
20000	429.95	416.81	384.94	375.40	372.34	371.34	371.00	370.89
21000	451.45	437.65	404.18	394.17	390.96	389.90	389.55	389.44
22000	472.95	458.49	423.43	412.94	409.58	408.47	408.10	407.98
23000	494.45	479.33	442.68	431.71	428.19	427.04	426.65	426.53
24000	515.94	500.17	461.92	450.48	446.81	445.60	445.20	445.07
25000	537.44	521.01	481.17	469.25	465.43	464.17	463.75	463.62
26000	558.94	541.85	500.42	488.02	484.04	482.74	482.30	482.16
27000	580.44	562.69	519.66	506.79	502.66	501.30	500.85	500.70
28000	601.93	583.53	538.91	525.56	521.28	519.87	519.40	519.25
29000	623.43	604.37	558.16	544.33	539.89	538.44	537.95	537.79
30000	644.93	625.21	577.40	563.10	558.51	557.00	556.50	556.34
31000	666.43	646.05	596.65	581.87	577.13	575.57	575.05	574.88
32000	687.92	666.89	615.90	600.64	595.75	594.14	593.60	593.43
33000	709.42	687.73	635.14	619.41	614.36	612.70	612.15	611.97
34000	730.92	708.57	654.39	638.18	632.98	631.27	630.70	630.51
35000	752.42	729.41	673.64	656.95	651.60	649.84	649.25	649.06
40000	859.90	833.61	769.87	750.80	744.68	742.67	742.00	741.78
45000	967.39	937.81	866.10	844.65	837.76	835.50	834.75	834.50
50000	1074.88	1042.01	962.34	938.50	930.85	928.33	927.50	927.23
55000	1182.37	1146.21	1058.57	1032.35	1023.93	1021.17	1020.25	1019.95
60000	1289.85	1250.42	1154.80	1126.20	1117.02	1114.00	1113.00	1112.67
65000	1397.34	1354.62	1251.04	1220.05	1210.10	1206.83	1205.75	1205.39
70000	1504.83	1458.82	1347.27	1313.90	1303.19	1299.67	1298.50	1298.11
75000	1612.32	1563.02	1443.50	1407.75	1396.27	1392.50	1391.25	1390.84
80000	1719.80	1667.22	1539.74	1501.60	1489.36	1485.33	1484.00	1483.56
85000	1827.29	1771.42	1635.97	1595.45	1582.44	1578.16	1576.75	1576.28
90000	1934.78	1875.62	1732.20	1689.30	1675.52	1671.00	1669.50	1669.00
95000	2042.27	1979.82	1828.44	1783.15	1768.61	1763.83	1762.25	1761.72
100000	2149.75	2084.02	1924.67	1877.00	1861.69	1856.66	1855.00	1854.45
105000	2257.24	2188.22	2020.90	1970.85	1954.78	1949.50	1947.75	1947.17
110000	2364.73	2292.42	2117.14	2064.70	2047.86	2042.33	2040.50	2039.89
115000	2472.22	2396.62	2213.37	2158.55	2140.95	2135.16	2133.25	2132.61
120000	2579.70	2500.83	2309.60	2252.40	2234.03	2227.99	2226.00	2225.33
125000	2687.19	2605.03	2405.83	2346.25	2327.11	2320.83	2318.75	2318.06
130000	2794.68	2709.23	2502.07	2440.10	2420.20	2413.66	2411.50	2410.78
135000	2902.16	2813.43	2598.30	2533.95	2513.28	2506.49	2504.25	2503.50
140000	3009.65	2917.63	2694.53	2627.80	2606.37	2599.33	2597.00	2596.22
145000	3117.14	3021.83	2790.77	2721.65	2699.45	2692.16	2689.75	2688.94
150000	3224.63	3126.03	2887.00	2815.50	2792.54	2784.99	2782.49	2781.67
155000	3332.11	3230.23	2983.23	2909.35	2885.62	2877.82	2875.24	2874.39
160000	3439.60	3334.43	3079.47	3003.20	2978.71	2970.66	2967.99	2967.11

22.500% MONTHLY AMORTIZING PAYMENTS

AMOUNT OF LOAN	NUMBER OF YEARS IN TERM							
	1	2	3	4	5	6	7	8
$ 50	4.70	2.61	1.93	1.59	1.40	1.28	1.19	1.13
100	9.39	5.22	3.85	3.18	2.80	2.55	2.38	2.26
200	18.77	10.43	7.69	6.36	5.59	5.09	4.75	4.51
300	28.16	15.64	11.54	9.54	8.38	7.63	7.13	6.77
400	37.54	20.86	15.38	12.72	11.17	10.17	9.50	9.02
500	46.92	26.07	19.23	15.89	13.96	12.72	11.87	11.27
600	56.31	31.28	23.07	19.07	16.75	15.26	14.25	13.53
700	65.69	36.49	26.92	22.25	19.54	17.80	16.62	15.78
800	75.07	41.71	30.76	25.43	22.33	20.34	18.99	18.04
900	84.46	46.92	34.61	28.61	25.12	22.89	21.37	20.29
1000	93.84	52.13	38.45	31.78	27.91	25.43	23.74	22.54
2000	187.68	104.26	76.90	63.56	55.81	50.85	47.48	45.08
3000	281.51	156.38	115.35	95.34	83.72	76.28	71.21	67.62
4000	375.35	208.51	153.80	127.12	111.62	101.70	94.95	90.16
5000	469.18	260.63	192.25	158.90	139.52	127.12	118.68	112.70
6000	563.02	312.76	230.70	190.67	167.43	152.55	142.42	135.23
7000	656.85	364.88	269.15	222.45	195.33	177.97	166.15	157.77
8000	750.69	417.01	307.60	254.23	223.24	203.40	189.89	180.31
9000	844.52	469.13	346.05	286.01	251.14	228.82	213.63	202.85
10000	938.36	521.26	384.50	317.79	279.04	254.24	237.36	225.39
11000	1032.19	573.38	422.95	349.56	306.95	279.67	261.10	247.92
12000	1126.03	625.51	461.40	381.34	334.85	305.09	284.83	270.46
13000	1219.86	677.64	499.85	413.12	362.76	330.51	308.57	293.00
14000	1313.70	729.76	538.30	444.90	390.66	355.94	332.30	315.54
15000	1407.53	781.89	576.75	476.68	418.56	381.36	356.04	338.08
16000	1501.37	834.01	615.20	508.46	446.47	406.79	379.78	360.62
17000	1595.20	886.14	653.65	540.23	474.37	432.21	403.51	383.15
18000	1689.04	938.26	692.10	572.01	502.28	457.63	427.25	405.69
19000	1782.87	990.39	730.55	603.79	530.18	483.06	450.98	428.23
20000	1876.71	1042.51	769.00	635.57	558.08	508.48	474.72	450.77
21000	1970.54	1094.64	807.45	667.35	585.99	533.90	498.45	473.31
22000	2064.38	1146.76	845.90	699.12	613.89	559.33	522.19	495.84
23000	2158.21	1198.89	884.35	730.90	641.80	584.75	545.92	518.38
24000	2252.05	1251.01	922.80	762.68	669.70	610.18	569.66	540.92
25000	2345.88	1303.14	961.25	794.46	697.60	635.60	593.40	563.46
26000	2439.72	1355.27	999.69	826.24	725.51	661.02	617.13	586.00
27000	2533.55	1407.39	1038.14	858.02	753.41	686.45	640.87	608.53
28000	2627.39	1459.52	1076.59	889.79	781.32	711.87	664.60	631.07
29000	2721.23	1511.64	1115.04	921.57	809.22	737.29	688.34	653.61
30000	2815.06	1563.77	1153.49	953.35	837.12	762.72	712.07	676.15
31000	2908.90	1615.89	1191.94	985.13	865.03	788.14	735.81	698.69
32000	3002.73	1668.02	1230.39	1016.91	892.93	813.57	759.55	721.23
33000	3096.57	1720.14	1268.84	1048.68	920.84	838.99	783.28	743.76
34000	3190.40	1772.27	1307.29	1080.46	948.74	864.41	807.02	766.30
35000	3284.24	1824.39	1345.74	1112.24	976.64	889.84	830.75	788.84
40000	3753.41	2085.02	1537.99	1271.13	1116.16	1016.96	949.43	901.53
45000	4222.59	2345.65	1730.24	1430.02	1255.68	1144.07	1068.11	1014.22
50000	4691.76	2606.27	1922.49	1588.91	1395.20	1271.19	1186.79	1126.91
55000	5160.94	2866.90	2114.73	1747.80	1534.72	1398.31	1305.47	1239.60
60000	5630.12	3127.53	2306.98	1906.69	1674.24	1525.43	1424.14	1352.29
65000	6099.29	3388.16	2499.23	2065.58	1813.76	1652.55	1542.82	1464.98
70000	6568.47	3648.78	2691.48	2224.48	1953.28	1779.67	1661.50	1577.68
75000	7037.64	3909.41	2883.73	2383.37	2092.80	1906.79	1780.18	1690.37
80000	7506.82	4170.04	3075.97	2542.26	2232.32	2033.91	1898.86	1803.06
85000	7976.00	4430.66	3268.22	2701.15	2371.84	2161.03	2017.53	1915.75
90000	8445.17	4691.29	3460.47	2860.04	2511.36	2288.14	2136.21	2028.44
95000	8914.35	4951.92	3652.72	3018.93	2650.88	2415.26	2254.89	2141.13
100000	9383.52	5212.54	3844.97	3177.82	2790.40	2542.38	2373.57	2253.82
105000	9852.70	5473.17	4037.21	3336.71	2929.92	2669.50	2492.25	2366.51
110000	10321.88	5733.80	4229.46	3495.60	3069.44	2796.62	2610.93	2479.20
115000	10791.05	5994.43	4421.71	3654.49	3208.96	2923.74	2729.60	2591.89
120000	11260.23	6255.05	4613.96	3813.38	3348.48	3050.86	2848.28	2704.58
125000	11729.40	6515.68	4806.21	3972.27	3488.00	3177.98	2966.96	2817.27
130000	12198.58	6776.31	4998.45	4131.16	3627.52	3305.09	3085.64	2929.96
135000	12667.75	7036.93	5190.70	4290.06	3767.04	3432.21	3204.32	3042.65
140000	13136.93	7297.56	5382.95	4448.95	3906.56	3559.33	3322.99	3155.35
145000	13606.11	7558.19	5575.20	4607.84	4046.08	3686.45	3441.67	3268.04
150000	14075.28	7818.81	5767.45	4766.73	4185.60	3813.57	3560.35	3380.73
155000	14544.46	8079.44	5959.69	4925.62	4325.12	3940.69	3679.03	3493.42
160000	15013.63	8340.07	6151.94	5084.51	4464.64	4067.81	3797.71	3606.11

214

AMOUNT OF LOAN	NUMBER OF YEARS IN TERM							
	9	10	15	20	25	30	35	40
$ 50	1.09	1.06	.98	.95	.95	.94	.94	.94
100	2.17	2.11	1.95	1.90	1.89	1.88	1.88	1.88
200	4.34	4.21	3.89	3.80	3.77	3.76	3.76	3.76
300	6.50	6.31	5.84	5.70	5.65	5.64	5.63	5.63
400	8.67	8.41	7.78	7.59	7.53	7.51	7.51	7.51
500	10.84	10.51	9.72	9.49	9.42	9.39	9.38	9.38
600	13.00	12.61	11.67	11.39	11.30	11.27	11.26	11.26
700	15.17	14.71	13.61	13.28	13.18	13.15	13.14	13.13
800	17.34	16.81	15.55	15.18	15.06	15.02	15.01	15.01
900	19.50	18.92	17.50	17.08	16.94	16.90	16.89	16.88
1000	21.67	21.02	19.44	18.97	18.83	18.78	18.76	18.76
2000	43.33	42.03	38.88	37.94	37.65	37.55	37.52	37.51
3000	65.00	63.04	58.31	56.91	56.47	56.33	56.28	56.26
4000	86.66	84.05	77.75	75.88	75.29	75.10	75.04	75.02
5000	108.32	105.06	97.19	94.85	94.11	93.87	93.79	93.77
6000	129.99	126.07	116.62	113.82	112.93	112.65	112.55	112.52
7000	151.65	147.08	136.06	132.79	131.76	131.42	131.31	131.27
8000	173.31	168.09	155.49	151.76	150.58	150.19	150.07	150.03
9000	194.98	189.11	174.93	170.73	169.40	168.97	168.82	168.78
10000	216.64	210.12	194.37	189.70	188.22	187.74	187.58	187.53
11000	238.30	231.13	213.80	208.67	207.04	206.51	206.34	206.28
12000	259.97	252.14	233.24	227.64	225.86	225.29	225.10	225.04
13000	281.63	273.15	252.68	246.61	244.68	244.06	243.85	243.79
14000	303.30	294.16	272.11	265.58	263.51	262.83	262.61	262.54
15000	324.96	315.17	291.55	284.55	282.33	281.61	281.37	281.29
16000	346.62	336.18	310.98	303.52	301.15	300.38	300.13	300.05
17000	368.29	357.20	330.42	322.49	319.97	319.15	318.89	318.80
18000	389.95	378.21	349.86	341.46	338.79	337.93	337.64	337.55
19000	411.61	399.22	369.29	360.43	357.61	356.70	356.40	356.30
20000	433.28	420.23	388.73	379.40	376.44	375.47	375.16	375.06
21000	454.94	441.24	408.16	398.37	395.26	394.25	393.92	393.81
22000	476.60	462.25	427.60	417.34	414.08	413.02	412.67	412.56
23000	498.27	483.26	447.04	436.31	432.90	431.79	431.43	431.31
24000	519.93	504.27	466.47	455.28	451.72	450.57	450.19	450.07
25000	541.59	525.28	485.91	474.25	470.54	469.34	468.95	468.82
26000	563.26	546.30	505.35	493.22	489.36	488.11	487.70	487.57
27000	584.92	567.31	524.78	512.19	508.19	506.89	506.46	506.32
28000	606.59	588.32	544.22	531.16	527.01	525.66	525.22	525.08
29000	628.25	609.33	563.65	550.13	545.83	544.43	543.98	543.83
30000	649.91	630.34	583.09	569.10	564.65	563.21	562.74	562.58
31000	671.58	651.35	602.53	588.07	583.47	581.98	581.49	581.33
32000	693.24	672.36	621.96	607.04	602.29	600.75	600.25	600.09
33000	714.90	693.37	641.40	626.01	621.11	619.53	619.01	618.84
34000	736.57	714.39	660.84	644.97	639.94	638.30	637.77	637.59
35000	758.23	735.40	680.27	663.94	658.76	657.07	656.52	656.34
40000	866.55	840.45	777.45	758.79	752.87	750.94	750.31	750.11
45000	974.87	945.51	874.63	853.64	846.97	844.81	844.10	843.87
50000	1083.18	1050.56	971.81	948.49	941.08	938.67	937.89	937.63
55000	1191.50	1155.62	1068.99	1043.34	1035.19	1032.54	1031.68	1031.39
60000	1299.82	1260.68	1166.18	1138.19	1129.30	1126.41	1125.47	1125.16
65000	1408.14	1365.73	1263.36	1233.04	1223.40	1220.28	1219.25	1218.92
70000	1516.46	1470.79	1360.54	1327.88	1317.51	1314.14	1313.04	1312.68
75000	1624.77	1575.84	1457.72	1422.73	1411.62	1408.01	1406.83	1406.44
80000	1733.09	1680.90	1554.90	1517.58	1505.73	1501.88	1500.62	1500.21
85000	1841.41	1785.96	1652.08	1612.43	1599.83	1595.74	1594.41	1593.97
90000	1949.73	1891.01	1749.26	1707.28	1693.94	1689.61	1688.20	1687.73
95000	2058.05	1996.07	1846.44	1802.13	1788.05	1783.48	1781.98	1781.49
100000	2166.36	2101.12	1943.62	1896.98	1882.16	1877.34	1875.77	1875.26
105000	2274.68	2206.18	2040.80	1991.82	1976.26	1971.21	1969.56	1969.02
110000	2383.00	2311.24	2137.98	2086.67	2070.37	2065.08	2063.35	2062.78
115000	2491.32	2416.29	2235.17	2181.52	2164.48	2158.95	2157.14	2156.54
120000	2599.63	2521.35	2332.35	2276.37	2258.59	2252.81	2250.93	2250.31
125000	2707.95	2626.40	2429.53	2371.22	2352.69	2346.68	2344.71	2344.07
130000	2816.27	2731.46	2526.71	2466.07	2446.80	2440.55	2438.50	2437.83
135000	2924.59	2836.51	2623.89	2560.91	2540.91	2534.41	2532.29	2531.59
140000	3032.91	2941.57	2721.07	2655.76	2635.02	2628.28	2626.08	2625.36
145000	3141.22	3046.63	2818.25	2750.61	2729.12	2722.15	2719.87	2719.12
150000	3249.54	3151.68	2915.43	2845.46	2823.23	2816.01	2813.66	2812.88
155000	3357.86	3256.74	3012.61	2940.31	2917.34	2909.88	2907.44	2906.64
160000	3466.18	3361.79	3109.79	3035.16	3011.45	3003.75	3001.23	3000.41

215

22.750%　MONTHLY AMORTIZING PAYMENTS

AMOUNT OF LOAN	NUMBER OF YEARS IN TERM							
	1	2	3	4	5	6	7	8
$ 50	4.70	2.62	1.93	1.60	1.41	1.28	1.20	1.14
100	9.40	5.23	3.86	3.20	2.81	2.56	2.39	2.27
200	18.80	10.45	7.72	6.39	5.61	5.12	4.78	4.54
300	28.19	15.68	11.58	9.58	8.42	7.68	7.17	6.81
400	37.59	20.90	15.44	12.77	11.22	10.23	9.56	9.08
500	46.98	26.13	19.29	15.96	14.03	12.79	11.95	11.35
600	56.38	31.35	23.15	19.15	16.83	15.35	14.34	13.62
700	65.77	36.58	27.01	22.35	19.64	17.91	16.73	15.89
800	75.17	41.80	30.87	25.54	22.44	20.46	19.12	18.16
900	84.57	47.03	34.73	28.73	25.25	23.02	21.51	20.43
1000	93.96	52.25	38.58	31.92	28.05	25.58	23.90	22.70
2000	187.92	104.50	77.16	63.83	56.10	51.15	47.79	45.40
3000	281.87	156.75	115.74	95.75	84.15	76.72	71.68	68.10
4000	375.83	209.00	154.32	127.66	112.19	102.30	95.57	90.80
5000	469.78	261.25	192.90	159.58	140.24	127.87	119.46	113.50
6000	563.74	313.50	231.48	191.49	168.29	153.44	143.35	136.20
7000	657.69	365.75	270.06	223.41	196.33	179.02	167.24	158.90
8000	751.65	418.00	308.64	255.32	224.38	204.59	191.13	181.60
9000	845.61	470.25	347.22	287.24	252.43	230.16	215.03	204.30
10000	939.56	522.50	385.80	319.15	280.48	255.74	238.92	227.00
11000	1033.52	574.75	424.38	351.07	308.52	281.31	262.81	249.70
12000	1127.47	627.00	462.96	382.98	336.57	306.88	286.70	272.40
13000	1221.43	679.25	501.54	414.90	364.62	332.46	310.59	295.10
14000	1315.38	731.49	540.12	446.81	392.66	358.03	334.48	317.80
15000	1409.34	783.74	578.70	478.72	420.71	383.60	358.37	340.50
16000	1503.30	835.99	617.28	510.64	448.76	409.18	382.26	363.20
17000	1597.25	888.24	655.86	542.55	476.80	434.75	406.16	385.90
18000	1691.21	940.49	694.44	574.47	504.85	460.32	430.05	408.59
19000	1785.16	992.74	733.02	606.38	532.90	485.90	453.94	431.29
20000	1879.12	1044.99	771.60	638.30	560.95	511.47	477.83	453.99
21000	1973.07	1097.24	810.18	670.21	588.99	537.04	501.72	476.69
22000	2067.03	1149.49	848.75	702.13	617.04	562.62	525.61	499.39
23000	2160.99	1201.74	887.33	734.04	645.09	588.19	549.50	522.09
24000	2254.94	1253.99	925.91	765.96	673.13	613.76	573.39	544.79
25000	2348.90	1306.24	964.49	797.87	701.18	639.34	597.28	567.49
26000	2442.85	1358.49	1003.07	829.79	729.23	664.91	621.18	590.19
27000	2536.81	1410.74	1041.65	861.70	757.27	690.48	645.07	612.89
28000	2630.76	1462.98	1080.23	893.62	785.32	716.06	668.96	635.59
29000	2724.72	1515.23	1118.81	925.53	813.37	741.63	692.85	658.29
30000	2818.68	1567.48	1157.39	957.44	841.42	767.20	716.74	680.99
31000	2912.63	1619.73	1195.97	989.36	869.46	792.78	740.63	703.69
32000	3006.59	1671.98	1234.55	1021.27	897.51	818.35	764.52	726.39
33000	3100.54	1724.23	1273.13	1053.19	925.56	843.92	788.41	749.09
34000	3194.50	1776.48	1311.71	1085.10	953.60	869.49	812.31	771.79
35000	3288.45	1828.73	1350.29	1117.02	981.65	895.07	836.20	794.48
40000	3758.23	2089.98	1543.19	1276.56	1121.89	1022.93	955.65	907.98
45000	4228.01	2351.22	1736.08	1436.16	1262.12	1150.80	1075.11	1021.48
50000	4697.79	2612.47	1928.98	1595.74	1402.36	1278.67	1194.56	1134.98
55000	5167.57	2873.71	2121.88	1755.31	1542.59	1406.53	1314.02	1248.47
60000	5637.35	3134.96	2314.78	1914.88	1682.83	1534.40	1433.48	1361.97
65000	6107.13	3396.21	2507.68	2074.46	1823.06	1662.26	1552.93	1475.47
70000	6576.90	3657.45	2700.57	2234.03	1963.30	1790.13	1672.39	1588.96
75000	7046.68	3918.70	2893.47	2393.60	2103.53	1918.00	1791.84	1702.46
80000	7516.46	4179.95	3086.37	2553.18	2243.77	2045.86	1911.30	1815.96
85000	7986.24	4441.19	3279.27	2712.75	2384.00	2173.73	2030.76	1929.46
90000	8456.02	4702.44	3472.16	2872.32	2524.24	2301.60	2150.21	2042.95
95000	8925.80	4963.69	3665.06	3031.90	2664.47	2429.46	2269.67	2156.45
100000	9395.58	5224.93	3857.96	3191.47	2804.71	2557.33	2389.12	2269.95
105000	9865.35	5486.18	4050.86	3351.04	2944.94	2685.19	2508.58	2383.44
110000	10335.13	5747.42	4243.75	3510.62	3085.18	2813.06	2628.04	2496.94
115000	10804.91	6008.67	4436.65	3670.19	3225.41	2940.93	2747.49	2610.44
120000	11274.69	6269.92	4629.55	3829.76	3365.65	3068.79	2866.95	2723.94
125000	11744.47	6531.16	4822.45	3989.34	3505.88	3196.66	2986.40	2837.43
130000	12214.25	6792.41	5015.35	4148.91	3646.12	3324.52	3105.86	2950.93
135000	12684.03	7053.66	5208.24	4308.48	3786.35	3452.39	3225.31	3064.43
140000	13153.80	7314.90	5401.14	4468.06	3926.59	3580.26	3344.77	3177.92
145000	13623.58	7576.15	5594.04	4627.63	4066.82	3708.12	3464.23	3291.42
150000	14093.36	7837.40	5786.94	4787.20	4207.06	3835.99	3583.68	3404.92
155000	14563.14	8098.64	5979.83	4946.78	4347.29	3963.86	3703.14	3518.42
160000	15032.92	8359.89	6172.73	5106.35	4487.53	4091.72	3822.59	3631.91

AMOUNT OF LOAN	NUMBER OF YEARS IN TERM							
	9	10	15	20	25	30	35	40
$ 50	1.10	1.06	.99	.96	.96	.95	.95	.95
100	2.19	2.12	1.97	1.92	1.91	1.90	1.90	1.90
200	4.37	4.24	3.93	3.84	3.81	3.80	3.80	3.80
300	6.55	6.36	5.89	5.76	5.71	5.70	5.69	5.69
400	8.74	8.48	7.86	7.67	7.62	7.60	7.59	7.59
500	10.92	10.60	9.82	9.59	9.52	9.50	9.49	9.49
600	13.10	12.71	11.78	11.51	11.42	11.39	11.38	11.38
700	15.29	14.83	13.74	13.42	13.32	13.29	13.28	13.28
800	17.47	16.95	15.71	15.34	15.23	15.19	15.18	15.17
900	19.65	19.07	17.67	17.26	17.13	17.09	17.07	17.07
1000	21.84	21.19	19.63	19.17	19.03	18.99	18.97	18.97
2000	43.67	42.37	39.26	38.34	38.06	37.97	37.94	37.93
3000	65.50	63.55	58.88	57.51	57.08	56.95	56.90	56.89
4000	87.33	84.74	78.51	76.68	76.11	75.93	75.87	75.85
5000	109.16	105.92	98.14	95.85	95.14	94.91	94.83	94.81
6000	130.99	127.10	117.76	115.02	114.16	113.89	113.80	113.77
7000	152.82	148.28	137.39	134.19	133.19	132.87	132.76	132.73
8000	174.65	169.47	157.01	153.36	152.22	151.85	151.73	151.69
9000	196.48	190.65	176.64	172.53	171.24	170.83	170.69	170.65
10000	218.31	211.83	196.27	191.70	190.27	189.81	189.66	189.61
11000	240.14	233.01	215.89	210.87	209.29	208.79	208.62	208.57
12000	261.97	254.20	235.52	230.04	228.32	227.77	227.59	227.53
13000	283.80	275.38	255.15	249.21	247.35	246.75	246.56	246.49
14000	305.63	296.56	274.77	268.38	266.37	265.73	265.52	265.45
15000	327.46	317.75	294.40	287.55	285.40	284.71	284.49	284.41
16000	349.29	338.93	314.02	306.72	304.43	303.69	303.45	303.38
17000	371.12	360.11	333.65	325.89	323.45	322.67	322.42	322.34
18000	392.95	381.29	353.28	345.06	342.48	341.65	341.38	341.30
19000	414.78	402.48	372.90	364.23	361.51	360.63	360.35	360.26
20000	436.61	423.66	392.53	383.40	380.53	379.61	379.31	379.22
21000	458.44	444.84	412.15	402.57	399.56	398.59	398.28	398.18
22000	480.27	466.02	431.78	421.74	418.58	417.57	417.24	417.14
23000	502.10	487.21	451.41	440.91	437.61	436.55	436.21	436.10
24000	523.93	508.39	471.03	460.08	456.64	455.53	455.18	455.06
25000	545.76	529.57	490.66	479.25	475.66	474.51	474.14	474.02
26000	567.59	550.76	510.29	498.42	494.69	493.49	493.11	492.98
27000	589.42	571.94	529.91	517.59	513.72	512.47	512.07	511.94
28000	611.25	593.12	549.54	536.76	532.74	531.45	531.04	530.90
29000	633.08	614.30	569.16	555.93	551.77	550.43	550.00	549.86
30000	654.91	635.49	588.79	575.10	570.79	569.41	568.97	568.82
31000	676.74	656.67	608.42	594.27	589.82	588.39	587.93	587.78
32000	698.57	677.85	628.04	613.44	608.85	607.37	606.90	606.75
33000	720.40	699.03	647.67	632.61	627.87	626.36	625.86	625.71
34000	742.23	720.22	667.30	651.78	646.90	645.34	644.83	644.67
35000	764.06	741.40	686.92	670.95	665.93	664.32	663.80	663.63
40000	873.21	847.31	785.05	766.79	761.06	759.22	758.62	758.43
45000	982.36	953.23	883.18	862.64	856.19	854.12	853.45	853.23
50000	1091.51	1059.14	981.31	958.49	951.32	949.02	948.28	948.04
55000	1200.67	1165.05	1079.45	1054.34	1046.45	1043.92	1043.10	1042.84
60000	1309.82	1270.97	1177.58	1150.19	1141.58	1138.82	1137.93	1137.64
65000	1418.97	1376.88	1275.71	1246.04	1236.72	1233.73	1232.76	1232.45
70000	1528.12	1482.80	1373.84	1341.89	1331.85	1328.63	1327.59	1327.25
75000	1637.27	1588.71	1471.97	1437.73	1426.98	1423.53	1422.41	1422.05
80000	1746.42	1694.62	1570.10	1533.58	1522.11	1518.43	1517.24	1516.86
85000	1855.57	1800.54	1668.23	1629.43	1617.24	1613.33	1612.07	1611.66
90000	1964.72	1906.45	1766.36	1725.28	1712.37	1708.23	1706.90	1706.46
95000	2073.87	2012.36	1864.49	1821.13	1807.51	1803.13	1801.72	1801.27
100000	2183.02	2118.28	1962.62	1916.98	1902.64	1898.04	1896.55	1896.07
105000	2292.18	2224.19	2060.75	2012.83	1997.77	1992.94	1991.38	1990.87
110000	2401.33	2330.10	2158.89	2108.67	2092.90	2087.84	2086.20	2085.68
115000	2510.48	2436.02	2257.02	2204.52	2188.03	2182.74	2181.03	2180.48
120000	2619.63	2541.93	2355.15	2300.37	2283.16	2277.64	2275.86	2275.28
125000	2728.78	2647.85	2453.28	2396.22	2378.30	2372.54	2370.69	2370.08
130000	2837.93	2753.76	2551.41	2492.07	2473.43	2467.45	2465.51	2464.89
135000	2947.08	2859.67	2649.54	2587.92	2568.56	2562.35	2560.34	2559.69
140000	3056.23	2965.59	2747.67	2683.77	2663.69	2657.25	2655.17	2654.49
145000	3165.38	3071.50	2845.80	2779.61	2758.82	2752.15	2750.00	2749.30
150000	3274.53	3177.41	2943.93	2875.46	2853.95	2847.05	2844.82	2844.10
155000	3383.69	3283.33	3042.06	2971.31	2949.08	2941.95	2939.65	2938.90
160000	3492.84	3389.24	3140.19	3067.16	3044.22	3036.85	3034.48	3033.71

217

AMOUNT OF LOAN	NUMBER OF YEARS IN TERM							
	1	2	3	4	5	6	7	8
$ 50	4.71	2.62	1.94	1.61	1.41	1.29	1.21	1.15
100	9.41	5.24	3.88	3.21	2.82	2.58	2.41	2.29
200	18.82	10.48	7.75	6.42	5.64	5.15	4.81	4.58
300	28.23	15.72	11.62	9.62	8.46	7.72	7.22	6.86
400	37.64	20.95	15.49	12.83	11.28	10.29	9.62	9.15
500	47.04	26.19	19.36	16.03	14.10	12.87	12.03	11.44
600	56.45	31.43	23.23	19.24	16.92	15.44	14.43	13.72
700	65.86	36.67	27.10	22.44	19.74	18.01	16.84	16.01
800	75.27	41.90	30.97	25.65	22.56	20.58	19.24	18.29
900	84.67	47.14	34.84	28.85	25.38	23.16	21.65	20.58
1000	94.08	52.38	38.71	32.06	28.20	25.73	24.05	22.87
2000	188.16	104.75	77.42	64.11	56.39	51.45	48.10	45.73
3000	282.23	157.12	116.13	96.16	84.58	77.17	72.15	68.59
4000	376.31	209.50	154.84	128.21	112.77	102.90	96.19	91.45
5000	470.39	261.87	193.55	160.26	140.96	128.62	120.24	114.31
6000	564.46	314.24	232.26	192.31	169.15	154.34	144.29	137.17
7000	658.54	366.62	270.97	224.37	197.34	180.07	168.34	160.03
8000	752.62	418.99	309.68	256.42	225.53	205.79	192.38	182.89
9000	846.69	471.36	348.39	288.47	253.72	231.51	216.43	205.76
10000	940.77	523.74	387.10	320.52	281.91	257.24	240.48	228.62
11000	1034.84	576.11	425.81	352.57	310.10	282.96	264.52	251.48
12000	1128.92	628.48	464.52	384.62	338.29	308.68	288.57	274.34
13000	1223.00	680.86	503.23	416.67	366.48	334.41	312.62	297.20
14000	1317.07	733.23	541.94	448.73	394.67	360.13	336.67	320.06
15000	1411.15	785.60	580.65	480.78	422.86	385.85	360.71	342.92
16000	1505.23	837.98	619.36	512.83	451.05	411.57	384.76	365.78
17000	1599.30	890.35	658.07	544.88	479.24	437.30	408.81	388.65
18000	1693.38	942.72	696.78	576.93	507.43	463.02	432.85	411.51
19000	1787.46	995.10	735.49	608.98	535.62	488.74	456.90	434.37
20000	1881.53	1047.47	774.20	641.03	563.81	514.47	480.95	457.23
21000	1975.61	1099.84	812.91	673.09	592.00	540.19	505.00	480.09
22000	2069.68	1152.22	851.62	705.14	620.20	565.91	529.04	502.95
23000	2163.76	1204.59	890.33	737.19	648.39	591.64	553.09	525.81
24000	2257.84	1256.96	929.04	769.24	676.58	617.36	577.14	548.67
25000	2351.91	1309.34	967.75	801.29	704.77	643.08	601.18	571.53
26000	2445.99	1361.71	1006.46	833.34	732.96	668.81	625.23	594.40
27000	2540.07	1414.08	1045.17	865.39	761.15	694.53	649.28	617.26
28000	2634.14	1466.46	1083.88	897.45	789.34	720.25	673.33	640.12
29000	2728.22	1518.83	1122.59	929.50	817.53	745.98	697.37	662.98
30000	2822.29	1571.20	1161.30	961.55	845.72	771.70	721.42	685.84
31000	2916.37	1623.58	1200.01	993.60	873.91	797.42	745.47	708.70
32000	3010.45	1675.95	1238.72	1025.65	902.10	823.14	769.52	731.56
33000	3104.52	1728.32	1277.43	1057.70	930.29	848.87	793.56	754.42
34000	3198.60	1780.70	1316.14	1089.76	958.48	874.59	817.61	777.29
35000	3292.68	1833.07	1354.85	1121.81	986.67	900.31	841.66	800.15
40000	3763.06	2094.94	1548.39	1282.06	1127.62	1028.93	961.89	914.45
45000	4233.44	2356.80	1741.94	1442.32	1268.58	1157.54	1082.13	1028.76
50000	4703.82	2618.67	1935.49	1602.58	1409.53	1286.16	1202.36	1143.06
55000	5174.20	2880.54	2129.04	1762.84	1550.48	1414.78	1322.60	1257.37
60000	5644.58	3142.40	2322.59	1923.09	1691.43	1543.39	1442.84	1371.68
65000	6114.97	3404.27	2516.14	2083.35	1832.39	1672.01	1563.07	1485.98
70000	6585.35	3666.14	2709.69	2243.61	1973.34	1800.62	1683.31	1600.29
75000	7055.73	3928.00	2903.23	2403.87	2114.29	1929.24	1803.54	1714.59
80000	7526.11	4189.87	3096.78	2564.12	2255.24	2057.85	1923.78	1828.90
85000	7996.49	4451.74	3290.33	2724.38	2396.20	2186.47	2044.02	1943.21
90000	8466.87	4713.60	3483.88	2884.64	2537.15	2315.08	2164.25	2057.51
95000	8937.26	4975.47	3677.43	3044.89	2678.10	2443.70	2284.49	2171.82
100000	9407.64	5237.34	3870.98	3205.15	2819.05	2572.32	2404.72	2286.12
105000	9878.02	5499.20	4064.53	3365.41	2960.00	2700.93	2524.96	2400.43
110000	10348.40	5761.07	4258.07	3525.67	3100.96	2829.55	2645.20	2514.74
115000	10818.78	6022.94	4451.62	3685.92	3241.91	2958.16	2765.43	2629.04
120000	11289.16	6284.80	4645.17	3846.18	3382.86	3086.78	2885.67	2743.35
125000	11759.55	6546.67	4838.72	4006.44	3523.81	3215.39	3005.90	2857.65
130000	12229.93	6808.53	5032.27	4166.70	3664.77	3344.01	3126.14	2971.96
135000	12700.31	7070.40	5225.82	4326.95	3805.72	3472.62	3246.38	3086.27
140000	13170.69	7332.27	5419.37	4487.21	3946.67	3601.24	3366.61	3200.57
145000	13641.07	7594.13	5612.91	4647.47	4087.62	3729.86	3486.85	3314.88
150000	14111.45	7856.00	5806.46	4807.73	4228.58	3858.47	3607.08	3429.18
155000	14581.83	8117.87	6000.01	4967.98	4369.53	3987.09	3727.32	3543.49
160000	15052.22	8379.73	6193.56	5128.24	4510.48	4115.70	3847.56	3657.80

AMOUNT OF LOAN	NUMBER OF YEARS IN TERM							
	9	10	15	20	25	30	35	40
$ 50	1.10	1.07	1.00	.97	.97	.96	.96	.96
100	2.20	2.14	1.99	1.94	1.93	1.92	1.92	1.92
200	4.40	4.28	3.97	3.88	3.85	3.84	3.84	3.84
300	6.60	6.41	5.95	5.82	5.77	5.76	5.76	5.76
400	8.80	8.55	7.93	7.75	7.70	7.68	7.67	7.67
500	11.00	10.68	9.91	9.69	9.62	9.60	9.59	9.59
600	13.20	12.82	11.89	11.63	11.54	11.52	11.51	11.51
700	15.40	14.95	13.88	13.56	13.47	13.44	13.43	13.42
800	17.60	17.09	15.86	15.50	15.39	15.35	15.34	15.34
900	19.80	19.22	17.84	17.44	17.31	17.27	17.26	17.26
1000	22.00	21.36	19.82	19.38	19.24	19.19	19.18	19.17
2000	44.00	42.71	39.64	38.75	38.47	38.38	38.35	38.34
3000	66.00	64.07	59.45	58.12	57.70	57.57	57.52	57.51
4000	87.99	85.42	79.27	77.49	76.93	76.75	76.70	76.68
5000	109.99	106.78	99.09	96.86	96.16	95.94	95.87	95.85
6000	131.99	128.13	118.90	116.23	115.39	115.13	115.04	115.02
7000	153.99	149.49	138.72	135.60	134.62	134.32	134.22	134.19
8000	175.98	170.84	158.54	154.97	153.86	153.50	153.39	153.36
9000	197.98	192.20	178.35	174.34	173.09	172.69	172.56	172.52
10000	219.98	213.55	198.17	193.71	192.32	191.88	191.74	191.69
11000	241.98	234.91	217.99	213.08	211.55	211.07	210.91	210.86
12000	263.97	256.26	237.80	232.45	230.78	230.25	230.08	230.03
13000	285.97	277.62	257.62	251.82	250.01	249.44	249.26	249.20
14000	307.97	298.97	277.44	271.19	269.24	268.63	268.43	268.37
15000	329.96	320.33	297.25	290.56	288.47	287.81	287.60	287.54
16000	351.96	341.68	317.07	309.93	307.71	307.00	306.78	306.71
17000	373.96	363.04	336.89	329.30	326.94	326.19	325.95	325.87
18000	395.96	384.39	356.70	348.67	346.17	345.38	345.12	345.04
19000	417.95	405.75	376.52	368.04	365.40	364.56	364.30	364.21
20000	439.95	427.10	396.34	387.41	384.63	383.75	383.47	383.38
21000	461.95	448.46	416.15	406.78	403.86	402.94	402.64	402.55
22000	483.95	469.81	435.97	426.15	423.09	422.13	421.82	421.72
23000	505.94	491.16	455.79	445.52	442.32	441.31	440.99	440.89
24000	527.94	512.52	475.60	464.89	461.56	460.50	460.16	460.06
25000	549.94	533.87	495.42	484.26	480.79	479.69	479.34	479.22
26000	571.94	555.23	515.24	503.63	500.02	498.88	498.51	498.39
27000	593.93	576.58	535.05	523.00	519.25	518.06	517.68	517.56
28000	615.93	597.94	554.87	542.37	538.48	537.25	536.86	536.73
29000	637.93	619.29	574.69	561.74	557.71	556.44	556.03	555.90
30000	659.92	640.65	594.50	581.11	576.94	575.62	575.20	575.07
31000	681.92	662.00	614.32	600.48	596.18	594.81	594.38	594.24
32000	703.92	683.36	634.14	619.85	615.41	614.00	613.55	613.41
33000	725.92	704.71	653.95	639.22	634.64	633.19	632.72	632.57
34000	747.91	726.07	673.77	658.59	653.87	652.37	651.90	651.74
35000	769.91	747.42	693.59	677.96	673.10	671.56	671.07	670.91
40000	879.90	854.20	792.67	774.81	769.26	767.50	766.94	766.76
45000	989.88	960.97	891.75	871.66	865.41	863.43	862.80	862.60
50000	1099.87	1067.74	990.84	968.51	961.57	959.37	958.67	958.44
55000	1209.86	1174.52	1089.92	1065.36	1057.73	1055.31	1054.53	1054.29
60000	1319.84	1281.29	1189.00	1162.21	1153.88	1151.24	1150.40	1150.13
65000	1429.83	1388.07	1288.09	1259.06	1250.04	1247.18	1246.27	1245.98
70000	1539.82	1494.84	1387.17	1355.91	1346.20	1343.12	1342.13	1341.82
75000	1649.80	1601.61	1486.25	1452.76	1442.35	1439.05	1438.00	1437.66
80000	1759.79	1708.39	1585.34	1549.61	1538.51	1534.99	1533.87	1533.51
85000	1869.78	1815.16	1684.42	1646.46	1634.67	1630.93	1629.73	1629.35
90000	1979.76	1921.94	1783.50	1743.31	1730.82	1726.86	1725.60	1725.20
95000	2089.75	2028.71	1882.59	1840.16	1826.98	1822.80	1821.47	1821.04
100000	2199.74	2135.48	1981.67	1937.01	1923.13	1918.74	1917.33	1916.88
105000	2309.72	2242.26	2080.75	2033.86	2019.29	2014.67	2013.20	2012.73
110000	2419.71	2349.03	2179.83	2130.71	2115.45	2110.61	2109.06	2108.57
115000	2529.70	2455.80	2278.92	2227.56	2211.60	2206.55	2204.93	2204.41
120000	2639.68	2562.58	2378.00	2324.41	2307.76	2302.48	2300.80	2300.26
125000	2749.67	2669.35	2477.08	2421.26	2403.92	2398.42	2396.66	2396.10
130000	2859.66	2776.13	2576.17	2518.11	2500.07	2494.36	2492.53	2491.95
135000	2969.64	2882.90	2675.25	2614.96	2596.23	2590.29	2588.40	2587.79
140000	3079.63	2989.67	2774.33	2711.81	2692.39	2686.23	2684.26	2683.63
145000	3189.62	3096.45	2873.42	2808.66	2788.54	2782.16	2780.13	2779.48
150000	3299.60	3203.22	2972.50	2905.51	2884.70	2878.10	2876.00	2875.32
155000	3409.59	3310.00	3071.58	3002.36	2980.86	2974.04	2971.86	2971.17
160000	3519.58	3416.77	3170.67	3099.21	3077.01	3069.97	3067.73	3067.01

23.250%   MONTHLY AMORTIZING PAYMENTS

AMOUNT OF LOAN	NUMBER OF YEARS IN TERM							
	1	2	3	4	5	6	7	8
$ 50	4.71	2.63	1.95	1.61	1.42	1.30	1.22	1.16
100	9.42	5.25	3.89	3.22	2.84	2.59	2.43	2.31
200	18.84	10.50	7.77	6.44	5.67	5.18	4.85	4.61
300	28.26	15.75	11.66	9.66	8.51	7.77	7.27	6.91
400	37.68	21.00	15.54	12.88	11.34	10.35	9.69	9.21
500	47.10	26.25	19.43	16.10	14.17	12.94	12.11	11.52
600	56.52	31.50	23.31	19.32	17.01	15.53	14.53	13.82
700	65.94	36.75	27.19	22.54	19.84	18.12	16.95	16.12
800	75.36	42.00	31.08	25.76	22.67	20.70	19.37	18.42
900	84.78	47.25	34.96	28.97	25.51	23.29	21.79	20.73
1000	94.20	52.50	38.85	32.19	28.34	25.88	24.21	23.03
2000	188.40	105.00	77.69	64.38	56.67	51.75	48.41	46.05
3000	282.60	157.50	116.53	96.57	85.01	77.63	72.62	69.08
4000	376.79	210.00	155.37	128.76	113.34	103.50	96.82	92.10
5000	470.99	262.49	194.21	160.95	141.68	129.37	121.02	115.12
6000	565.19	314.99	233.05	193.14	170.01	155.25	145.23	138.15
7000	659.38	367.49	271.89	225.33	198.35	181.12	169.43	161.17
8000	753.58	419.99	310.73	257.51	226.68	206.99	193.63	184.19
9000	847.78	472.48	349.57	289.70	255.01	232.87	217.84	207.22
10000	941.98	524.98	388.41	321.89	283.35	258.74	242.04	230.24
11000	1036.17	577.48	427.25	354.08	311.68	284.61	266.25	253.26
12000	1130.37	629.98	466.09	386.27	340.02	310.49	290.45	276.29
13000	1224.57	682.47	504.93	418.46	368.35	336.36	314.65	299.31
14000	1318.76	734.97	543.77	450.65	396.69	362.23	338.86	322.33
15000	1412.96	787.47	582.61	482.83	425.02	388.11	363.06	345.36
16000	1507.16	839.97	621.45	515.02	453.35	413.98	387.26	368.38
17000	1601.35	892.46	660.29	547.21	481.69	439.85	411.47	391.40
18000	1695.55	944.96	699.13	579.40	510.02	465.73	435.67	414.43
19000	1789.75	997.46	737.97	611.59	538.36	491.60	459.87	437.45
20000	1883.95	1049.96	776.81	643.78	566.69	517.47	484.08	460.47
21000	1978.14	1102.45	815.65	675.97	595.03	543.35	508.28	483.50
22000	2072.34	1154.95	854.49	708.15	623.36	569.22	532.49	506.52
23000	2166.54	1207.45	893.33	740.34	651.69	595.09	556.69	529.54
24000	2260.73	1259.95	932.17	772.53	680.03	620.97	580.89	552.57
25000	2354.93	1312.44	971.01	804.72	708.36	646.84	605.10	575.59
26000	2449.13	1364.94	1009.85	836.91	736.70	672.71	629.30	598.61
27000	2543.32	1417.44	1048.69	869.10	765.03	698.59	653.50	621.64
28000	2637.52	1469.94	1087.53	901.29	793.37	724.46	677.71	644.66
29000	2731.72	1522.43	1126.37	933.47	821.70	750.33	701.91	667.69
30000	2825.92	1574.93	1165.21	965.66	850.03	776.21	726.11	690.71
31000	2920.11	1627.43	1204.05	997.85	878.37	802.08	750.32	713.73
32000	3014.31	1679.93	1242.89	1030.04	906.70	827.95	774.52	736.76
33000	3108.51	1732.42	1281.73	1062.23	935.04	853.83	798.73	759.78
34000	3202.70	1784.92	1320.57	1094.42	963.37	879.70	822.93	782.80
35000	3296.90	1837.42	1359.41	1126.61	991.71	905.57	847.13	805.83
40000	3767.89	2099.91	1553.61	1287.55	1133.38	1034.94	968.15	920.94
45000	4238.87	2362.39	1747.81	1448.49	1275.05	1164.31	1089.17	1036.06
50000	4709.86	2624.88	1942.01	1609.43	1416.72	1293.68	1210.19	1151.18
55000	5180.84	2887.37	2136.21	1770.38	1558.39	1423.04	1331.21	1266.29
60000	5651.83	3149.86	2330.41	1931.32	1700.06	1552.41	1452.22	1381.41
65000	6122.81	3412.34	2524.61	2092.26	1841.73	1681.78	1573.24	1496.53
70000	6593.80	3674.83	2718.82	2253.21	1983.41	1811.14	1694.26	1611.65
75000	7064.78	3937.32	2913.02	2414.15	2125.08	1940.51	1815.28	1726.76
80000	7535.77	4199.81	3107.22	2575.09	2266.75	2069.88	1936.30	1841.88
85000	8006.75	4462.29	3301.42	2736.04	2408.42	2199.25	2057.32	1957.00
90000	8477.74	4724.78	3495.62	2896.98	2550.09	2328.61	2178.33	2072.12
95000	8948.72	4987.27	3689.82	3057.92	2691.76	2457.98	2299.35	2187.23
100000	9419.71	5249.76	3884.02	3218.86	2833.43	2587.35	2420.37	2302.35
105000	9890.69	5512.24	4078.22	3379.81	2975.11	2716.71	2541.39	2417.47
110000	10361.68	5774.73	4272.42	3540.75	3116.78	2846.08	2662.41	2532.58
115000	10832.66	6037.22	4466.62	3701.69	3258.45	2975.45	2783.43	2647.70
120000	11303.65	6299.71	4660.82	3862.64	3400.12	3104.81	2904.44	2762.82
125000	11774.63	6562.19	4855.02	4023.58	3541.79	3234.18	3025.46	2877.94
130000	12245.62	6824.68	5049.22	4184.52	3683.46	3363.55	3146.48	2993.05
135000	12716.60	7087.17	5243.42	4345.47	3825.13	3492.92	3267.50	3108.17
140000	13187.59	7349.66	5437.63	4506.41	3966.81	3622.28	3388.52	3223.29
145000	13658.57	7612.14	5631.83	4667.35	4108.48	3751.65	3509.54	3338.41
150000	14129.56	7874.63	5826.03	4828.29	4250.15	3881.02	3630.55	3453.52
155000	14600.54	8137.12	6020.23	4989.24	4391.82	4010.38	3751.57	3568.64
160000	15071.53	8399.61	6214.43	5150.18	4533.49	4139.75	3872.59	3683.76

220

AMOUNT OF LOAN	NUMBER OF YEARS IN TERM							
	9	10	15	20	25	30	35	40
$ 50	1.11	1.08	1.01	.98	.98	.97	.97	.97
100	2.22	2.16	2.01	1.96	1.96	1.94	1.94	1.94
200	4.44	4.31	4.01	3.92	3.89	3.88	3.88	3.88
300	6.65	6.46	6.01	5.88	5.84	5.82	5.82	5.82
400	8.87	8.62	8.01	7.83	7.78	7.76	7.76	7.76
500	11.09	10.77	10.01	9.79	9.72	9.70	9.70	9.69
600	13.30	12.92	12.01	11.75	11.67	11.64	11.63	11.63
700	15.52	15.07	14.01	13.70	13.61	13.58	13.57	13.57
800	17.74	17.23	16.01	15.66	15.55	15.52	15.51	15.51
900	19.95	19.38	18.01	17.62	17.50	17.46	17.45	17.44
1000	22.17	21.53	20.01	19.58	19.44	19.40	19.39	19.38
2000	44.33	43.06	40.02	39.15	38.88	38.79	38.77	38.76
3000	66.50	64.59	60.03	58.72	58.31	58.19	58.15	58.14
4000	88.66	86.11	80.04	78.29	77.75	77.58	77.53	77.51
5000	110.83	107.64	100.04	97.86	97.19	96.98	96.91	96.89
6000	132.99	129.17	120.05	117.43	116.62	116.37	116.29	116.27
7000	155.16	150.70	140.06	137.00	136.06	135.77	135.67	135.64
8000	177.32	172.22	160.07	156.57	155.50	155.16	155.05	155.02
9000	199.49	193.75	180.07	176.14	174.93	174.55	174.44	174.40
10000	221.65	215.28	200.08	195.71	194.37	193.95	193.82	193.77
11000	243.82	236.81	220.09	215.28	213.81	213.34	213.20	213.15
12000	265.98	258.33	240.10	234.85	233.24	232.74	232.58	232.53
13000	288.15	279.86	260.10	254.42	252.68	252.13	251.96	251.91
14000	310.31	301.39	280.11	273.99	272.12	271.53	271.34	271.28
15000	332.48	322.92	300.12	293.56	291.55	290.92	290.72	290.66
16000	354.64	344.44	320.13	313.14	310.99	310.32	310.10	310.04
17000	376.81	365.97	340.13	332.71	330.42	329.71	329.48	329.41
18000	398.97	387.50	360.14	352.28	349.86	349.10	348.87	348.79
19000	421.14	409.02	380.15	371.85	369.30	368.50	368.25	368.17
20000	443.30	430.55	400.16	391.42	388.73	387.89	387.63	387.54
21000	465.47	452.08	420.16	410.99	408.17	407.29	407.01	406.92
22000	487.63	473.61	440.17	430.56	427.61	426.68	426.39	426.30
23000	509.80	495.13	460.18	450.13	447.04	446.08	445.77	445.67
24000	531.96	516.66	480.19	469.70	466.48	465.47	465.15	465.05
25000	554.13	538.19	500.19	489.27	485.92	484.86	484.53	484.43
26000	576.29	559.72	520.20	508.84	505.35	504.26	503.91	503.81
27000	598.46	581.24	540.21	528.41	524.79	523.65	523.30	523.18
28000	620.62	602.77	560.22	547.98	544.23	543.05	542.68	542.56
29000	642.79	624.30	580.22	567.55	563.66	562.44	562.06	561.94
30000	664.95	645.83	600.23	587.12	583.10	581.84	581.44	581.31
31000	687.12	667.35	620.24	606.69	602.53	601.23	600.82	600.69
32000	709.28	688.88	640.25	626.27	621.97	620.63	620.20	620.07
33000	731.45	710.41	660.25	645.84	641.41	640.02	639.58	639.44
34000	753.61	731.93	680.26	665.41	660.84	659.41	658.96	658.82
35000	775.78	753.46	700.27	684.98	680.28	678.81	678.34	678.20
40000	886.60	861.10	800.31	782.83	777.46	775.78	775.25	775.08
45000	997.43	968.74	900.34	880.68	874.64	872.75	872.16	871.97
50000	1108.25	1076.37	1000.38	978.54	971.83	969.72	969.06	968.85
55000	1219.08	1184.01	1100.42	1076.39	1069.01	1066.70	1065.97	1065.74
60000	1329.90	1291.65	1200.46	1174.24	1166.19	1163.67	1162.87	1162.62
65000	1440.73	1399.28	1300.49	1272.10	1263.37	1260.64	1259.78	1259.51
70000	1551.55	1506.92	1400.53	1369.95	1360.56	1357.61	1356.68	1356.39
75000	1662.38	1614.56	1500.57	1467.80	1457.74	1454.58	1453.59	1453.28
80000	1773.20	1722.19	1600.61	1565.66	1554.92	1551.56	1550.50	1550.16
85000	1884.03	1829.83	1700.64	1663.51	1652.10	1648.53	1647.40	1647.04
90000	1994.85	1937.47	1800.68	1761.36	1749.28	1745.50	1744.31	1743.93
95000	2105.68	2045.10	1900.72	1859.22	1846.47	1842.47	1841.21	1840.81
100000	2216.50	2152.74	2000.76	1957.07	1943.65	1939.44	1938.12	1937.70
105000	2327.33	2260.38	2100.80	2054.92	2040.83	2036.42	2035.02	2034.58
110000	2438.15	2368.01	2200.83	2152.78	2138.01	2133.39	2131.93	2131.47
115000	2548.97	2475.65	2300.87	2250.63	2235.20	2230.36	2228.83	2228.35
120000	2659.80	2583.29	2400.91	2348.48	2332.38	2327.33	2325.74	2325.24
125000	2770.62	2690.92	2500.95	2446.33	2429.56	2424.30	2422.65	2422.12
130000	2881.45	2798.56	2600.98	2544.19	2526.74	2521.27	2519.55	2519.01
135000	2992.27	2906.20	2701.02	2642.04	2623.92	2618.25	2616.46	2615.89
140000	3103.10	3013.83	2801.06	2739.89	2721.11	2715.22	2713.36	2712.78
145000	3213.92	3121.47	2901.10	2837.75	2818.29	2812.19	2810.27	2809.66
150000	3324.75	3229.11	3001.13	2935.60	2915.47	2909.16	2907.17	2906.55
155000	3435.57	3336.74	3101.17	3033.45	3012.65	3006.13	3004.08	3003.43
160000	3546.40	3444.38	3201.21	3131.31	3109.83	3103.11	3100.99	3100.31

23.500%   MONTHLY AMORTIZING PAYMENTS

AMOUNT OF LOAN	NUMBER OF YEARS IN TERM							
	1	2	3	4	5	6	7	8
$ 50	4.72	2.64	1.95	1.62	1.43	1.31	1.22	1.16
100	9.44	5.27	3.90	3.24	2.85	2.61	2.44	2.32
200	18.87	10.53	7.80	6.47	5.70	5.21	4.88	4.64
300	28.30	15.79	11.70	9.70	8.55	7.81	7.31	6.96
400	37.73	21.05	15.59	12.94	11.40	10.41	9.75	9.28
500	47.16	26.32	19.49	16.17	14.24	13.02	12.19	11.60
600	56.60	31.58	23.39	19.40	17.09	15.62	14.62	13.92
700	66.03	36.84	27.28	22.63	19.94	18.22	17.06	16.24
800	75.46	42.10	31.18	25.87	22.79	20.82	19.49	18.55
900	84.89	47.36	35.08	29.10	25.64	23.43	21.93	20.87
1000	94.32	52.63	38.98	32.33	28.48	26.03	24.37	23.19
2000	188.64	105.25	77.95	64.66	56.96	52.05	48.73	46.38
3000	282.96	157.87	116.92	96.98	85.44	78.08	73.09	69.56
4000	377.28	210.49	155.89	129.31	113.92	104.10	97.45	92.75
5000	471.59	263.11	194.86	161.64	142.40	130.13	121.81	115.94
6000	565.91	315.74	233.83	193.96	170.88	156.15	146.17	139.12
7000	660.23	368.36	272.80	226.29	199.35	182.17	170.53	162.31
8000	754.55	420.98	311.77	258.61	227.83	208.20	194.89	185.49
9000	848.87	473.60	350.74	290.94	256.31	234.22	219.25	208.68
10000	943.18	526.22	389.71	323.27	284.79	260.25	243.61	231.87
11000	1037.50	578.85	428.68	355.59	313.27	286.27	267.97	255.05
12000	1131.82	631.47	467.65	387.92	341.75	312.29	292.33	278.24
13000	1226.14	684.09	506.63	420.24	370.23	338.32	316.69	301.43
14000	1320.45	736.71	545.60	452.57	398.70	364.34	341.05	324.61
15000	1414.77	789.33	584.57	484.90	427.18	390.37	365.41	347.80
16000	1509.09	841.95	623.54	517.22	455.66	416.39	389.77	370.98
17000	1603.41	894.58	662.51	549.55	484.14	442.42	414.14	394.17
18000	1697.73	947.20	701.48	581.87	512.62	468.44	438.50	417.36
19000	1792.04	999.82	740.45	614.20	541.10	494.46	462.86	440.54
20000	1886.36	1052.44	779.42	646.53	569.57	520.49	487.22	463.73
21000	1980.68	1105.06	818.39	678.85	598.05	546.51	511.58	486.92
22000	2075.00	1157.69	857.36	711.18	626.53	572.54	535.94	510.10
23000	2169.31	1210.31	896.33	743.50	655.01	598.56	560.30	533.29
24000	2263.63	1262.93	935.30	775.83	683.49	624.58	584.66	556.47
25000	2357.95	1315.55	974.28	808.16	711.97	650.61	609.02	579.66
26000	2452.27	1368.17	1013.25	840.48	740.45	676.63	633.38	602.85
27000	2546.59	1420.80	1052.22	872.81	768.92	702.66	657.74	626.03
28000	2640.90	1473.42	1091.19	905.13	797.40	728.68	682.10	649.22
29000	2735.22	1526.04	1130.16	937.46	825.88	754.70	706.46	672.40
30000	2829.54	1578.66	1169.13	969.79	854.36	780.73	730.82	695.59
31000	2923.86	1631.28	1208.10	1002.11	882.84	806.75	755.18	718.78
32000	3018.17	1683.90	1247.07	1034.44	911.32	832.78	779.54	741.96
33000	3112.49	1736.53	1286.04	1066.76	939.79	858.80	803.90	765.15
34000	3206.81	1789.15	1325.01	1099.09	968.27	884.83	828.27	788.34
35000	3301.13	1841.77	1363.98	1131.42	996.75	910.85	852.63	811.52
40000	3772.72	2104.88	1558.84	1293.05	1139.14	1040.97	974.43	927.45
45000	4244.31	2367.99	1753.69	1454.68	1281.54	1171.09	1096.23	1043.38
50000	4715.89	2631.10	1948.55	1616.31	1423.93	1301.21	1218.03	1159.31
55000	5187.48	2894.21	2143.40	1777.94	1566.32	1431.33	1339.84	1275.25
60000	5659.07	3157.32	2338.25	1939.57	1708.71	1561.45	1461.64	1391.18
65000	6130.66	3420.43	2533.11	2101.20	1851.11	1691.57	1583.44	1507.11
70000	6602.25	3683.54	2727.96	2262.83	1993.50	1821.69	1705.25	1623.04
75000	7073.84	3946.65	2922.82	2424.46	2135.89	1951.82	1827.05	1738.97
80000	7545.43	4209.75	3117.67	2586.09	2278.28	2081.94	1948.85	1854.90
85000	8017.02	4472.86	3312.52	2747.72	2420.68	2212.06	2070.66	1970.83
90000	8488.61	4735.97	3507.38	2909.35	2563.07	2342.18	2192.46	2086.76
95000	8960.20	4999.08	3702.23	3070.98	2705.46	2472.30	2314.26	2202.69
100000	9431.78	5262.19	3897.09	3232.61	2847.85	2602.42	2436.06	2318.62
105000	9903.37	5525.30	4091.94	3394.24	2990.25	2732.54	2557.87	2434.56
110000	10374.96	5788.41	4286.79	3555.87	3132.64	2862.66	2679.67	2550.49
115000	10846.55	6051.52	4481.65	3717.50	3275.03	2992.78	2801.47	2666.42
120000	11318.14	6314.63	4676.50	3879.13	3417.42	3122.90	2923.28	2782.35
125000	11789.73	6577.74	4871.36	4040.76	3559.82	3253.02	3045.08	2898.28
130000	12261.32	6840.85	5066.21	4202.39	3702.21	3383.14	3166.88	3014.21
135000	12732.91	7103.96	5261.06	4364.02	3844.60	3513.26	3288.68	3130.14
140000	13204.50	7367.07	5455.92	4525.65	3986.99	3643.38	3410.49	3246.07
145000	13676.08	7630.18	5650.77	4687.28	4129.38	3773.50	3532.29	3362.00
150000	14147.67	7893.29	5845.63	4848.91	4271.78	3903.63	3654.09	3477.93
155000	14619.26	8156.40	6040.48	5010.54	4414.17	4033.75	3775.90	3593.87
160000	15090.85	8419.50	6235.33	5172.17	4556.56	4163.87	3897.70	3709.80

MONTHLY AMORTIZING PAYMENTS 23.500%

AMOUNT OF LOAN	NUMBER OF YEARS IN TERM							
	9	10	15	20	25	30	35	40
$ 50	1.12	1.09	1.01	.99	.99	.99	.98	.98
100	2.24	2.18	2.02	1.98	1.97	1.97	1.96	1.96
200	4.47	4.35	4.04	3.96	3.93	3.93	3.92	3.92
300	6.70	6.52	6.06	5.94	5.90	5.89	5.88	5.88
400	8.94	8.69	8.08	7.91	7.86	7.85	7.84	7.84
500	11.17	10.86	10.10	9.89	9.83	9.81	9.80	9.80
600	13.40	13.03	12.12	11.87	11.79	11.77	11.76	11.76
700	15.64	15.20	14.14	13.85	13.75	13.73	13.72	13.71
800	17.87	17.37	16.16	15.82	15.72	15.69	15.68	15.67
900	20.10	19.54	18.18	17.80	17.68	17.65	17.64	17.63
1000	22.34	21.71	20.20	19.78	19.65	19.61	19.59	19.59
2000	44.67	43.41	40.40	39.55	39.29	39.21	39.18	39.18
3000	67.00	65.11	60.60	59.32	58.93	58.81	58.77	58.76
4000	89.34	86.81	80.80	79.09	78.57	78.41	78.36	78.35
5000	111.67	108.51	101.00	98.86	98.21	98.01	97.95	97.93
6000	134.00	130.21	121.20	118.63	117.86	117.61	117.54	117.52
7000	156.34	151.91	141.40	138.41	137.50	137.22	137.13	137.10
8000	178.67	173.61	161.60	158.18	157.14	156.82	156.72	156.69
9000	201.00	195.31	181.79	177.95	176.78	176.42	176.31	176.27
10000	223.34	217.01	201.99	197.72	196.42	196.02	195.90	195.86
11000	245.67	238.71	222.19	217.49	216.06	215.62	215.48	215.44
12000	268.00	260.41	242.39	237.26	235.71	235.22	235.07	235.03
13000	290.34	282.11	262.59	257.03	255.35	254.82	254.66	254.61
14000	312.67	303.81	282.79	276.81	274.99	274.43	274.25	274.20
15000	335.00	325.51	302.99	296.58	294.63	294.03	293.84	293.78
16000	357.33	347.21	323.19	316.35	314.27	313.63	313.43	313.37
17000	379.67	368.91	343.39	336.12	333.91	333.23	333.02	332.95
18000	402.00	390.61	363.58	355.89	353.56	352.83	352.61	352.54
19000	424.33	412.31	383.78	375.66	373.20	372.43	372.20	372.12
20000	446.67	434.01	403.98	395.44	392.84	392.04	391.79	391.71
21000	469.00	455.71	424.18	415.21	412.48	411.64	411.37	411.29
22000	491.33	477.41	444.38	434.98	432.12	431.24	430.96	430.88
23000	513.67	499.11	464.58	454.75	451.76	450.84	450.55	450.46
24000	536.00	520.82	484.78	474.52	471.41	470.44	470.14	470.05
25000	558.33	542.52	504.98	494.29	491.05	490.04	489.73	489.63
26000	580.67	564.22	525.17	514.06	510.69	509.64	509.32	509.22
27000	603.00	585.92	545.37	533.84	530.33	529.25	528.91	528.80
28000	625.33	607.62	565.57	553.61	549.97	548.85	548.50	548.39
29000	647.66	629.32	585.77	573.38	569.62	568.45	568.09	567.97
30000	670.00	651.02	605.97	593.15	589.26	588.05	587.68	587.56
31000	692.33	672.72	626.17	612.92	608.90	607.65	607.26	607.14
32000	714.66	694.42	646.37	632.69	628.54	627.25	626.85	626.73
33000	737.00	716.12	666.57	652.47	648.18	646.85	646.44	646.31
34000	759.33	737.82	686.77	672.24	667.82	666.46	666.03	665.90
35000	781.66	759.52	706.96	692.01	687.47	686.06	685.62	685.48
40000	893.33	868.02	807.96	790.87	785.67	784.07	783.57	783.41
45000	1004.99	976.52	908.95	889.72	883.88	882.07	881.51	881.33
50000	1116.66	1085.03	1009.95	988.58	982.09	980.08	979.46	979.26
55000	1228.32	1193.53	1110.94	1087.44	1080.30	1078.09	1077.40	1077.19
60000	1339.99	1302.03	1211.94	1186.30	1178.51	1176.10	1175.35	1175.11
65000	1451.66	1410.53	1312.93	1285.15	1276.72	1274.10	1273.29	1273.04
70000	1563.32	1519.04	1413.92	1384.01	1374.93	1372.11	1371.24	1370.96
75000	1674.99	1627.54	1514.92	1482.87	1473.13	1470.12	1469.18	1468.89
80000	1786.65	1736.04	1615.91	1581.73	1571.34	1568.13	1567.13	1566.81
85000	1898.32	1844.54	1716.91	1680.58	1669.55	1666.14	1665.07	1664.74
90000	2009.98	1953.04	1817.90	1779.44	1767.76	1764.14	1763.02	1762.66
95000	2121.65	2061.55	1918.90	1878.30	1865.97	1862.15	1860.96	1860.59
100000	2233.31	2170.05	2019.89	1977.16	1964.18	1960.16	1958.91	1958.52
105000	2344.98	2278.55	2120.88	2076.01	2062.39	2058.17	2056.85	2056.44
110000	2456.64	2387.05	2221.88	2174.87	2160.59	2156.17	2154.80	2154.37
115000	2568.31	2495.55	2322.87	2273.73	2258.80	2254.18	2252.74	2252.29
120000	2679.98	2604.06	2423.87	2372.59	2357.01	2352.19	2350.69	2350.22
125000	2791.64	2712.56	2524.86	2471.44	2455.22	2450.20	2448.63	2448.14
130000	2903.31	2821.06	2625.85	2570.30	2553.43	2548.20	2546.58	2546.07
135000	3014.97	2929.56	2726.85	2669.16	2651.64	2646.21	2644.52	2643.99
140000	3126.64	3038.07	2827.84	2768.02	2749.85	2744.22	2742.47	2741.92
145000	3238.30	3146.57	2928.84	2866.88	2848.06	2842.23	2840.41	2839.85
150000	3349.97	3255.07	3029.83	2965.73	2946.26	2940.24	2938.36	2937.77
155000	3461.63	3363.57	3130.83	3064.59	3044.47	3038.24	3036.30	3035.70
160000	3573.30	3472.07	3231.82	3163.45	3142.68	3136.25	3134.25	3133.62

23.750% MONTHLY AMORTIZING PAYMENTS

AMOUNT OF LOAN	NUMBER OF YEARS IN TERM							
	1	2	3	4	5	6	7	8
$ 50	4.73	2.64	1.96	1.63	1.44	1.31	1.23	1.17
100	9.45	5.28	3.92	3.25	2.87	2.62	2.46	2.34
200	18.89	10.55	7.83	6.50	5.73	5.24	4.91	4.67
300	28.34	15.83	11.74	9.74	8.59	7.86	7.36	7.01
400	37.78	21.10	15.65	12.99	11.45	10.48	9.81	9.34
500	47.22	26.38	19.56	16.24	14.32	13.09	12.26	11.68
600	56.67	31.65	23.47	19.48	17.18	15.71	14.72	14.01
700	66.11	36.93	27.38	22.73	20.04	18.33	17.17	16.35
800	75.56	42.20	31.29	25.98	22.90	20.95	19.62	18.68
900	85.00	47.48	35.20	29.22	25.77	23.56	22.07	21.02
1000	94.44	52.75	39.11	32.47	28.63	26.18	24.52	23.35
2000	188.88	105.50	78.21	64.93	57.25	52.36	49.04	46.70
3000	283.32	158.24	117.31	97.40	85.87	78.53	73.56	70.05
4000	377.76	210.99	156.41	129.86	114.50	104.71	98.08	93.40
5000	472.20	263.74	195.51	162.32	143.12	130.88	122.59	116.75
6000	566.64	316.48	234.62	194.79	171.74	157.06	147.11	140.10
7000	661.08	369.23	273.72	227.25	200.37	183.23	171.63	163.45
8000	755.51	421.98	312.82	259.72	228.99	209.41	196.15	186.80
9000	849.95	474.72	351.92	292.18	257.61	235.58	220.67	210.15
10000	944.39	527.47	391.02	324.64	286.24	261.76	245.18	233.50
11000	1038.83	580.22	430.12	357.11	314.86	287.93	269.70	256.85
12000	1133.27	632.96	469.23	389.57	343.48	314.11	294.22	280.20
13000	1227.71	685.71	508.33	422.03	372.10	340.28	318.74	303.55
14000	1322.15	738.45	547.43	454.50	400.73	366.46	343.26	326.90
15000	1416.58	791.20	586.53	486.96	429.35	392.63	367.77	350.25
16000	1511.02	843.95	625.63	519.43	457.97	418.81	392.29	373.60
17000	1605.46	896.69	664.73	551.89	486.60	444.98	416.81	396.95
18000	1699.90	949.44	703.84	584.35	515.22	471.16	441.33	420.29
19000	1794.34	1002.19	742.94	616.82	543.84	497.34	465.85	443.64
20000	1888.78	1054.93	782.04	649.28	572.47	523.51	490.36	466.99
21000	1983.22	1107.68	821.14	681.74	601.09	549.69	514.88	490.34
22000	2077.66	1160.43	860.24	714.21	629.71	575.86	539.40	513.69
23000	2172.09	1213.17	899.34	746.67	658.33	602.04	563.92	537.04
24000	2266.53	1265.92	938.45	779.14	686.96	628.21	588.44	560.39
25000	2360.97	1318.67	977.55	811.60	715.58	654.39	612.95	583.74
26000	2455.41	1371.41	1016.65	844.06	744.20	680.56	637.47	607.09
27000	2549.85	1424.16	1055.75	876.53	772.83	706.74	661.99	630.44
28000	2644.29	1476.90	1094.85	908.99	801.45	732.91	686.51	653.79
29000	2738.73	1529.65	1133.95	941.45	830.07	759.09	711.03	677.14
30000	2833.16	1582.40	1173.06	973.92	858.70	785.26	735.54	700.49
31000	2927.60	1635.14	1212.16	1006.38	887.32	811.44	760.06	723.84
32000	3022.04	1687.89	1251.26	1038.85	915.94	837.61	784.58	747.19
33000	3116.48	1740.64	1290.36	1071.31	944.57	863.79	809.10	770.54
34000	3210.92	1793.38	1329.46	1103.77	973.19	889.96	833.62	793.89
35000	3305.36	1846.13	1368.56	1136.24	1001.81	916.14	858.13	817.23
40000	3777.55	2109.86	1564.07	1298.56	1144.93	1047.02	980.72	933.98
45000	4249.74	2373.59	1759.58	1460.88	1288.04	1177.89	1103.31	1050.73
50000	4721.94	2637.33	1955.09	1623.19	1431.16	1308.77	1225.90	1167.48
55000	5194.13	2901.06	2150.60	1785.51	1574.27	1439.65	1348.49	1284.22
60000	5666.32	3164.79	2346.11	1947.83	1717.39	1570.52	1471.08	1400.97
65000	6138.52	3428.52	2541.62	2110.15	1860.50	1701.40	1593.67	1517.72
70000	6610.71	3692.25	2737.12	2272.47	2003.62	1832.27	1716.26	1634.46
75000	7082.90	3955.99	2932.63	2434.79	2146.73	1963.15	1838.85	1751.21
80000	7555.10	4219.72	3128.14	2597.11	2289.85	2094.03	1961.44	1867.96
85000	8027.29	4483.45	3323.65	2759.43	2432.96	2224.90	2084.03	1984.71
90000	8499.48	4747.18	3519.16	2921.75	2576.08	2355.78	2206.62	2101.45
95000	8971.68	5010.91	3714.67	3084.06	2719.19	2486.66	2329.21	2218.20
100000	9443.87	5274.65	3910.18	3246.38	2862.31	2617.53	2451.80	2334.95
105000	9916.06	5538.38	4105.68	3408.70	3005.42	2748.41	2574.39	2451.69
110000	10388.26	5802.11	4301.19	3571.02	3148.54	2879.29	2696.98	2568.44
115000	10860.45	6065.84	4496.70	3733.34	3291.65	3010.16	2819.57	2685.19
120000	11332.64	6329.57	4692.21	3895.66	3434.77	3141.04	2942.16	2801.94
125000	11804.83	6593.31	4887.72	4057.98	3577.88	3271.91	3064.75	2918.68
130000	12277.03	6857.04	5083.23	4220.30	3721.00	3402.79	3187.34	3035.43
135000	12749.22	7120.77	5278.74	4382.62	3864.12	3533.67	3309.93	3152.18
140000	13221.42	7384.50	5474.24	4544.93	4007.23	3664.54	3432.52	3268.92
145000	13693.61	7648.23	5669.75	4707.25	4150.35	3795.42	3555.11	3385.67
150000	14165.80	7911.97	5865.26	4869.57	4293.46	3926.30	3677.70	3502.42
155000	14638.00	8175.70	6060.77	5031.89	4436.58	4057.17	3800.29	3619.17
160000	15110.19	8439.43	6256.28	5194.21	4579.69	4188.05	3922.88	3735.91

AMOUNT OF LOAN	NUMBER OF YEARS IN TERM							
	9	10	15	20	25	30	35	40
$ 50	1.13	1.10	1.02	1.00	1.00	1.00	.99	.99
100	2.26	2.19	2.04	2.00	1.99	1.99	1.98	1.98
200	4.51	4.38	4.08	4.00	3.97	3.97	3.96	3.96
300	6.76	6.57	6.12	6.00	5.96	5.95	5.94	5.94
400	9.01	8.75	8.16	7.99	7.94	7.93	7.92	7.92
500	11.26	10.94	10.20	9.99	9.93	9.91	9.90	9.90
600	13.51	13.13	12.24	11.99	11.91	11.89	11.88	11.88
700	15.76	15.32	14.28	13.99	13.90	13.87	13.86	13.86
800	18.01	17.50	16.32	15.98	15.88	15.85	15.84	15.84
900	20.26	19.69	18.36	17.98	17.87	17.83	17.82	17.82
1000	22.51	21.88	20.40	19.98	19.85	19.81	19.80	19.80
2000	45.01	43.75	40.79	39.95	39.70	39.62	39.59	39.59
3000	67.51	65.63	61.18	59.92	59.55	59.43	59.40	59.38
4000	90.01	87.50	81.57	79.90	79.39	79.24	79.19	79.18
5000	112.51	109.38	101.96	99.87	99.24	99.05	98.99	98.97
6000	135.02	131.25	122.35	119.84	119.09	118.86	118.79	118.76
7000	157.52	153.12	142.74	139.81	138.94	138.67	138.58	138.56
8000	180.02	175.00	163.13	159.79	158.78	158.48	158.38	158.35
9000	202.52	196.87	183.52	179.76	178.63	178.28	178.18	178.14
10000	225.02	218.75	203.91	199.73	198.48	198.09	197.97	197.94
11000	247.52	240.62	224.30	219.70	218.32	217.90	217.77	217.73
12000	270.03	262.49	244.69	239.68	238.17	237.71	237.57	237.52
13000	292.53	284.37	265.08	259.65	258.02	257.52	257.37	257.32
14000	315.03	306.24	285.47	279.62	277.87	277.33	277.16	277.11
15000	337.53	328.12	305.86	299.60	297.71	297.14	296.96	296.90
16000	360.03	349.99	326.25	319.57	317.56	316.95	316.76	316.70
17000	382.53	371.86	346.64	339.54	337.41	336.75	336.55	336.49
18000	405.04	393.74	367.04	359.51	357.25	356.56	356.35	356.28
19000	427.54	415.61	387.43	379.49	377.10	376.37	376.15	376.08
20000	450.04	437.49	407.82	399.46	396.95	396.18	395.94	395.87
21000	472.54	459.36	428.21	419.43	416.80	415.99	415.74	415.66
22000	495.04	481.23	448.60	439.40	436.64	435.80	435.54	435.46
23000	517.54	503.11	468.99	459.38	456.49	455.61	455.33	455.25
24000	540.05	524.98	489.38	479.35	476.34	475.42	475.13	475.04
25000	562.55	546.86	509.77	499.32	496.18	495.22	494.93	494.84
26000	585.05	568.73	530.16	519.29	516.03	515.03	514.73	514.63
27000	607.55	590.60	550.55	539.27	535.88	534.84	534.52	534.42
28000	630.05	612.48	570.94	559.24	555.73	554.65	554.32	554.22
29000	652.55	634.35	591.33	579.21	575.57	574.46	574.12	574.01
30000	675.06	656.23	611.72	599.19	595.42	594.27	593.91	593.80
31000	697.56	678.10	632.11	619.16	615.27	614.08	613.71	613.60
32000	720.06	699.97	652.50	639.13	635.11	633.89	633.51	633.39
33000	742.56	721.85	672.89	659.10	654.96	653.69	653.30	653.18
34000	765.06	743.72	693.28	679.08	674.81	673.50	673.10	672.98
35000	787.57	765.60	713.68	699.05	694.66	693.31	692.90	692.77
40000	900.07	874.97	815.63	798.91	793.89	792.36	791.88	791.74
45000	1012.58	984.34	917.58	898.78	893.13	891.40	890.87	890.70
50000	1125.09	1093.71	1019.53	998.64	992.36	990.44	989.85	989.67
55000	1237.60	1203.08	1121.49	1098.50	1091.60	1089.49	1088.84	1088.64
60000	1350.11	1312.45	1223.44	1198.37	1190.83	1188.53	1187.82	1187.60
65000	1462.62	1421.82	1325.39	1298.23	1290.07	1287.57	1286.81	1286.57
70000	1575.13	1531.19	1427.35	1398.09	1389.31	1386.62	1385.79	1385.54
75000	1687.63	1640.56	1529.30	1497.96	1488.54	1485.66	1484.78	1484.50
80000	1800.14	1749.93	1631.25	1597.82	1587.78	1584.71	1583.76	1583.47
85000	1912.65	1859.30	1733.20	1697.68	1687.01	1683.75	1682.74	1682.43
90000	2025.16	1968.67	1835.16	1797.55	1786.25	1782.79	1781.73	1781.40
95000	2137.67	2078.04	1937.11	1897.41	1885.49	1881.84	1880.71	1880.37
100000	2250.18	2187.41	2039.06	1997.27	1984.72	1980.88	1979.70	1979.33
105000	2362.69	2296.78	2141.02	2097.14	2083.96	2079.92	2078.68	2078.30
110000	2475.19	2406.15	2242.97	2197.00	2183.19	2178.97	2177.67	2177.27
115000	2587.70	2515.52	2344.92	2296.86	2282.43	2278.01	2276.65	2276.23
120000	2700.21	2624.89	2446.88	2396.73	2381.66	2377.06	2375.64	2375.20
125000	2812.72	2734.26	2548.83	2496.59	2480.90	2476.10	2474.62	2474.17
130000	2925.23	2843.63	2650.78	2596.45	2580.14	2575.14	2573.61	2573.13
135000	3037.74	2953.00	2752.73	2696.32	2679.37	2674.19	2672.59	2672.10
140000	3150.25	3062.37	2854.69	2796.18	2778.61	2773.23	2771.58	2771.07
145000	3262.75	3171.74	2956.64	2896.04	2877.84	2872.27	2870.56	2870.03
150000	3375.26	3281.11	3058.59	2995.91	2977.08	2971.32	2969.55	2969.00
155000	3487.77	3390.48	3160.55	3095.77	3076.32	3070.36	3068.53	3067.97
160000	3600.28	3499.85	3262.50	3195.63	3175.55	3169.41	3167.51	3166.93

24.000%   MONTHLY AMORTIZING PAYMENTS

AMOUNT OF LOAN	NUMBER OF YEARS IN TERM							
	1	2	3	4	5	6	7	8
$ 50	4.73	2.65	1.97	1.64	1.44	1.32	1.24	1.18
100	9.46	5.29	3.93	3.27	2.88	2.64	2.47	2.36
200	18.92	10.58	7.85	6.53	5.76	5.27	4.94	4.71
300	28.37	15.87	11.77	9.79	8.64	7.90	7.41	7.06
400	37.83	21.15	15.70	13.05	11.51	10.54	9.88	9.41
500	47.28	26.44	19.62	16.31	14.39	13.17	12.34	11.76
600	56.74	31.73	23.54	19.57	17.27	15.80	14.81	14.11
700	66.20	37.01	27.47	22.83	20.14	18.43	17.28	16.46
800	75.65	42.30	31.39	26.09	23.02	21.07	19.75	18.82
900	85.11	47.59	35.31	29.35	25.90	23.70	22.21	21.17
1000	94.56	52.88	39.24	32.61	28.77	26.33	24.68	23.52
2000	189.12	105.75	78.47	65.21	57.54	52.66	49.36	47.03
3000	283.68	158.62	117.70	97.81	86.31	78.99	74.03	70.54
4000	378.24	211.49	156.94	130.41	115.08	105.31	98.71	94.06
5000	472.80	264.36	196.17	163.01	143.84	131.64	123.38	117.57
6000	567.36	317.23	235.40	195.62	172.61	157.97	148.06	141.08
7000	661.92	370.10	274.63	228.22	201.38	184.29	172.74	164.60
8000	756.48	422.97	313.87	260.82	230.15	210.62	197.41	188.11
9000	851.04	475.84	353.10	293.42	258.92	236.95	222.09	211.62
10000	945.60	528.72	392.33	326.02	287.68	263.27	246.76	235.14
11000	1040.16	581.59	431.57	358.63	316.45	289.60	271.44	258.65
12000	1134.72	634.46	470.80	391.23	345.22	315.93	296.11	282.16
13000	1229.28	687.33	510.03	423.83	373.99	342.25	320.79	305.68
14000	1323.84	740.20	549.26	456.43	402.76	368.58	345.47	329.19
15000	1418.40	793.07	588.50	489.03	431.52	394.91	370.14	352.70
16000	1512.96	845.94	627.73	521.63	460.29	421.23	394.82	376.22
17000	1607.52	898.81	666.96	554.24	489.06	447.56	419.49	399.73
18000	1702.08	951.68	706.20	586.84	517.83	473.89	444.17	423.24
19000	1796.64	1004.56	745.43	619.44	546.60	500.21	468.85	446.75
20000	1891.20	1057.43	784.66	652.04	575.36	526.54	493.52	470.27
21000	1985.76	1110.30	823.89	684.64	604.13	552.87	518.20	493.78
22000	2080.32	1163.17	863.13	717.25	632.90	579.20	542.87	517.29
23000	2174.88	1216.04	902.36	749.85	661.67	605.52	567.55	540.81
24000	2269.44	1268.91	941.59	782.45	690.44	631.85	592.22	564.32
25000	2363.99	1321.78	980.83	815.05	719.20	658.18	616.90	587.83
26000	2458.55	1374.65	1020.06	847.65	747.97	684.50	641.58	611.35
27000	2553.11	1427.52	1059.29	880.25	776.74	710.83	666.25	634.86
28000	2647.67	1480.40	1098.52	912.86	805.51	737.16	690.93	658.37
29000	2742.23	1533.27	1137.76	945.46	834.28	763.48	715.60	681.89
30000	2836.79	1586.14	1176.99	978.06	863.04	789.81	740.28	705.40
31000	2931.35	1639.01	1216.22	1010.66	891.81	816.14	764.96	728.91
32000	3025.91	1691.88	1255.46	1043.26	920.58	842.46	789.63	752.43
33000	3120.47	1744.75	1294.69	1075.87	949.35	868.79	814.31	775.94
34000	3215.03	1797.62	1333.92	1108.47	978.12	895.12	838.98	799.45
35000	3309.59	1850.49	1373.15	1141.07	1006.88	921.44	863.66	822.96
40000	3782.39	2114.85	1569.32	1304.08	1150.72	1053.08	987.04	940.53
45000	4255.19	2379.20	1765.48	1467.09	1294.56	1184.71	1110.42	1058.10
50000	4727.98	2643.56	1961.65	1630.10	1438.40	1316.35	1233.80	1175.66
55000	5200.78	2907.92	2157.81	1793.11	1582.24	1447.98	1357.17	1293.23
60000	5673.58	3172.27	2353.98	1956.12	1726.08	1579.61	1480.55	1410.79
65000	6146.38	3436.63	2550.14	2119.12	1869.92	1711.25	1603.93	1528.36
70000	6619.18	3700.98	2746.30	2282.13	2013.76	1842.88	1727.31	1645.92
75000	7091.97	3965.34	2942.47	2445.14	2157.60	1974.52	1850.69	1763.49
80000	7564.77	4229.69	3138.63	2608.15	2301.44	2106.15	1974.07	1881.06
85000	8037.57	4494.05	3334.80	2771.16	2445.28	2237.79	2097.45	1998.62
90000	8510.37	4758.40	3530.96	2934.17	2589.12	2369.42	2220.83	2116.19
95000	8983.17	5022.76	3727.13	3097.18	2732.96	2501.05	2344.21	2233.75
100000	9455.96	5287.11	3923.29	3260.19	2876.80	2632.69	2467.59	2351.32
105000	9928.76	5551.47	4119.45	3423.20	3020.64	2764.32	2590.97	2468.88
110000	10401.56	5815.83	4315.62	3586.21	3164.48	2895.96	2714.34	2586.45
115000	10874.36	6080.18	4511.78	3749.22	3308.32	3027.59	2837.72	2704.01
120000	11347.16	6344.54	4707.95	3912.23	3452.16	3159.22	2961.10	2821.58
125000	11819.95	6608.89	4904.11	4075.23	3596.00	3290.86	3084.48	2939.15
130000	12292.75	6873.25	5100.28	4238.24	3739.84	3422.49	3207.86	3056.71
135000	12765.55	7137.60	5296.44	4401.25	3883.68	3554.13	3331.24	3174.28
140000	13238.35	7401.96	5492.60	4564.26	4027.52	3685.76	3454.62	3291.84
145000	13711.15	7666.31	5688.77	4727.27	4171.36	3817.40	3578.00	3409.41
150000	14183.94	7930.67	5884.93	4890.28	4315.20	3949.03	3701.38	3526.97
155000	14656.74	8195.03	6081.10	5053.29	4459.04	4080.66	3824.76	3644.54
160000	15129.54	8459.38	6277.26	5216.30	4602.88	4212.30	3948.13	3762.11

226

MONTHLY AMORTIZING PAYMENTS 24.000%

AMOUNT OF LOAN	\multicolumn{8}{c}{NUMBER OF YEARS IN TERM}							
	9	10	15	20	25	30	35	40
$ 50	1.14	1.11	1.03	1.01	1.01	1.01	1.01	1.01
100	2.27	2.21	2.06	2.02	2.01	2.01	2.01	2.01
200	4.54	4.41	4.12	4.04	4.02	4.01	4.01	4.01
300	6.81	6.62	6.18	6.06	6.02	6.01	6.01	6.01
400	9.07	8.82	8.24	8.07	8.03	8.01	8.01	8.01
500	11.34	11.03	10.30	10.09	10.04	10.01	10.01	10.01
600	13.61	13.23	12.35	12.11	12.04	12.01	12.01	12.01
700	15.87	15.44	14.41	14.13	14.04	14.02	14.01	14.01
800	18.14	17.64	16.47	16.14	16.05	16.02	16.01	16.01
900	20.41	19.85	18.53	18.16	18.05	18.02	18.02	18.01
1000	22.68	22.05	20.59	20.18	20.06	20.02	20.02	20.01
2000	45.35	44.10	41.17	40.35	40.11	40.04	40.04	40.01
3000	68.02	66.15	61.75	60.53	60.16	60.05	60.02	60.01
4000	90.69	88.20	82.34	80.70	80.22	80.07	80.02	80.01
5000	113.36	110.25	102.92	100.88	100.27	100.09	100.03	100.01
6000	136.03	132.29	123.50	121.05	120.32	120.10	120.03	120.01
7000	158.70	154.34	144.08	141.22	140.37	140.12	140.04	140.02
8000	181.37	176.39	164.67	161.40	160.43	160.13	160.04	160.02
9000	204.04	198.44	185.25	181.57	180.48	180.15	180.05	180.02
10000	226.71	220.49	205.83	201.75	200.53	200.17	200.05	200.02
11000	249.38	242.53	226.42	221.92	220.59	220.18	220.06	220.02
12000	272.06	264.58	247.00	242.09	240.64	240.20	240.06	240.02
13000	294.73	286.63	267.58	262.27	260.69	260.21	260.07	260.02
14000	317.40	308.68	288.16	282.44	280.74	280.23	280.07	280.03
15000	340.07	330.73	308.75	302.62	300.80	300.25	300.08	300.03
16000	362.74	352.77	329.33	322.79	320.85	320.26	320.08	320.03
17000	385.41	374.82	349.91	342.96	340.90	340.28	340.09	340.03
18000	408.08	396.87	370.49	363.14	360.95	360.29	360.09	360.03
19000	430.75	418.92	391.08	383.31	381.01	380.31	380.10	380.03
20000	453.42	440.97	411.66	403.49	401.06	400.33	400.10	400.03
21000	476.09	463.02	432.24	423.66	421.11	420.34	420.11	420.04
22000	498.76	485.06	452.83	443.83	441.17	440.36	440.11	440.04
23000	521.43	507.11	473.41	464.01	461.22	460.37	460.12	460.04
24000	544.11	529.16	493.99	484.18	481.27	480.39	480.12	480.04
25000	566.78	551.21	514.57	504.36	501.32	500.41	500.13	500.04
26000	589.45	573.26	535.16	524.53	521.38	520.42	520.13	520.04
27000	612.12	595.30	555.74	544.71	541.43	540.44	540.14	540.05
28000	634.79	617.35	576.32	564.88	561.48	560.45	560.15	560.05
29000	657.46	639.40	596.90	585.05	581.53	580.47	580.15	580.05
30000	680.13	661.45	617.49	605.23	601.59	600.49	600.15	600.05
31000	702.80	683.50	638.07	625.40	621.64	620.50	620.16	620.05
32000	725.47	705.54	658.65	645.58	641.69	640.52	640.16	640.05
33000	748.14	727.59	679.24	665.75	661.75	660.53	660.17	660.06
34000	770.81	749.64	699.82	685.92	681.80	680.55	680.17	680.06
35000	793.48	771.69	720.40	706.10	701.85	700.57	700.18	700.06
40000	906.84	881.93	823.31	806.97	802.11	800.65	800.20	800.06
45000	1020.19	992.17	926.23	907.84	902.38	900.73	900.22	900.07
50000	1133.55	1102.41	1029.14	1008.71	1002.64	1000.81	1000.25	1000.08
55000	1246.90	1212.65	1132.06	1109.58	1102.90	1100.89	1100.27	1100.09
60000	1360.26	1322.89	1234.97	1210.45	1203.17	1200.97	1200.30	1200.09
65000	1473.61	1433.13	1337.88	1311.32	1303.43	1301.05	1300.32	1300.10
70000	1586.96	1543.37	1440.80	1412.19	1403.70	1401.13	1400.35	1400.11
75000	1700.32	1653.61	1543.71	1513.06	1503.96	1501.21	1500.37	1500.12
80000	1813.67	1763.85	1646.62	1613.93	1604.22	1601.29	1600.40	1600.12
85000	1927.03	1874.09	1749.54	1714.80	1704.49	1701.37	1700.42	1700.13
90000	2040.38	1984.33	1852.45	1815.67	1804.75	1801.45	1800.44	1800.14
95000	2153.74	2094.57	1955.36	1916.54	1905.02	1901.53	1900.47	1900.15
100000	2267.09	2204.81	2058.28	2017.41	2005.28	2001.61	2000.49	2000.15
105000	2380.44	2315.06	2161.19	2118.28	2105.54	2101.69	2100.52	2100.16
110000	2493.80	2425.30	2264.11	2219.15	2205.81	2201.77	2200.54	2200.17
115000	2607.15	2535.54	2367.02	2320.02	2306.07	2301.85	2300.57	2300.18
120000	2720.51	2645.78	2469.93	2420.89	2406.33	2401.93	2400.59	2400.18
125000	2833.86	2756.02	2572.85	2521.77	2506.60	2502.01	2500.62	2500.19
130000	2947.22	2866.26	2675.76	2622.64	2606.86	2602.09	2600.64	2600.20
135000	3060.57	2976.50	2778.67	2723.51	2707.12	2702.17	2700.66	2700.21
140000	3173.92	3086.74	2881.59	2824.38	2807.39	2802.25	2800.69	2800.21
145000	3287.28	3196.98	2984.50	2925.25	2907.65	2902.33	2900.71	2900.22
150000	3400.63	3307.22	3087.42	3026.12	3007.92	3002.41	3000.74	3000.23
155000	3513.99	3417.46	3190.33	3126.99	3108.18	3102.49	3100.76	3100.24
160000	3627.34	3527.70	3293.24	3227.86	3208.44	3202.57	3200.79	3200.24

24.250% MONTHLY AMORTIZING PAYMENTS

AMOUNT OF LOAN	NUMBER OF YEARS IN TERM							
	1	2	3	4	5	6	7	8
$ 50	4.74	2.65	1.97	1.64	1.45	1.33	1.25	1.19
100	9.47	5.30	3.94	3.28	2.90	2.65	2.49	2.37
200	18.94	10.60	7.88	6.55	5.79	5.30	4.97	4.74
300	28.41	15.90	11.81	9.83	8.68	7.95	7.46	7.11
400	37.88	21.20	15.75	13.10	11.57	10.60	9.94	9.48
500	47.35	26.50	19.69	16.38	14.46	13.24	12.42	11.84
600	56.81	31.80	23.62	19.65	17.35	15.89	14.91	14.21
700	66.28	37.10	27.56	22.92	20.24	18.54	17.39	16.58
800	75.75	42.40	31.50	26.20	23.14	21.19	19.87	18.95
900	85.22	47.70	35.43	29.47	26.03	23.84	22.36	21.31
1000	94.69	53.00	39.37	32.75	28.92	26.48	24.84	23.68
2000	189.37	106.00	78.73	65.49	57.83	52.96	49.67	47.36
3000	284.05	158.99	118.10	98.23	86.74	79.44	74.51	71.04
4000	378.73	211.99	157.46	130.97	115.66	105.92	99.34	94.71
5000	473.41	264.98	196.83	163.71	144.57	132.40	124.18	118.39
6000	568.09	317.98	236.19	196.45	173.48	158.88	149.01	142.07
7000	662.77	370.98	275.55	229.19	202.40	185.36	173.84	165.75
8000	757.45	423.97	314.92	261.93	231.31	211.84	198.68	189.42
9000	852.13	476.97	354.28	294.67	260.22	238.31	223.51	213.10
10000	946.81	529.96	393.65	327.41	289.14	264.79	248.35	236.78
11000	1041.49	582.96	433.01	360.15	318.05	291.27	273.18	260.46
12000	1136.17	635.96	472.38	392.89	346.96	317.75	298.01	284.13
13000	1230.85	688.95	511.74	425.63	375.88	344.23	322.85	307.81
14000	1325.53	741.95	551.10	458.37	404.79	370.71	347.68	331.49
15000	1420.21	794.94	590.47	491.11	433.70	397.19	372.52	355.16
16000	1514.89	847.94	629.83	523.85	462.62	423.67	397.35	378.84
17000	1609.58	900.94	669.20	556.59	491.53	450.14	422.18	402.52
18000	1704.26	953.93	708.56	589.33	520.44	476.62	447.02	426.20
19000	1798.94	1006.93	747.93	622.07	549.36	503.10	471.85	449.87
20000	1893.62	1059.92	787.29	654.81	578.27	529.58	496.69	473.55
21000	1988.30	1112.92	826.65	687.55	607.18	556.06	521.52	497.23
22000	2082.98	1165.92	866.02	720.29	636.10	582.54	546.36	520.91
23000	2177.66	1218.91	905.38	753.03	665.01	609.02	571.19	544.58
24000	2272.34	1271.91	944.75	785.77	693.92	635.50	596.02	568.26
25000	2367.02	1324.90	984.11	818.51	722.84	661.98	620.86	591.94
26000	2461.70	1377.90	1023.48	851.25	751.75	688.45	645.69	615.62
27000	2556.38	1430.90	1062.84	883.99	780.66	714.93	670.53	639.29
28000	2651.06	1483.89	1102.20	916.73	809.58	741.41	695.36	662.97
29000	2745.74	1536.89	1141.57	949.47	838.49	767.89	720.19	686.65
30000	2840.42	1589.88	1180.93	982.21	867.40	794.37	745.03	710.32
31000	2935.10	1642.88	1220.30	1014.95	896.32	820.85	769.86	734.00
32000	3029.78	1695.88	1259.66	1047.69	925.23	847.33	794.70	757.68
33000	3124.47	1748.87	1299.02	1080.43	954.14	873.81	819.53	781.36
34000	3219.15	1801.87	1338.39	1113.17	983.06	900.28	844.36	805.03
35000	3313.83	1854.86	1377.75	1145.91	1011.97	926.76	869.20	828.71
40000	3787.23	2119.84	1574.57	1309.61	1156.54	1059.16	993.37	947.10
45000	4260.63	2384.82	1771.40	1473.31	1301.10	1191.55	1117.54	1065.48
50000	4734.04	2649.80	1968.22	1637.01	1445.67	1323.95	1241.71	1183.87
55000	5207.44	2914.78	2165.04	1800.72	1590.23	1456.34	1365.88	1302.26
60000	5680.84	3179.76	2361.86	1964.42	1734.80	1588.73	1490.05	1420.64
65000	6154.25	3444.74	2558.68	2128.12	1879.37	1721.13	1614.22	1539.03
70000	6627.65	3709.72	2755.50	2291.82	2023.93	1853.52	1738.39	1657.42
75000	7101.05	3974.70	2952.32	2455.52	2168.50	1985.92	1862.56	1775.80
80000	7574.45	4239.68	3149.14	2619.22	2313.07	2118.31	1986.73	1894.19
85000	8047.86	4504.66	3345.97	2782.92	2457.63	2250.70	2110.90	2012.58
90000	8521.26	4769.64	3542.79	2946.62	2602.20	2383.10	2235.07	2130.96
95000	8994.66	5034.62	3739.61	3110.32	2746.76	2515.49	2359.24	2249.35
100000	9468.07	5299.60	3936.43	3274.02	2891.33	2647.89	2483.41	2367.74
105000	9941.47	5564.58	4133.25	3437.73	3035.90	2780.28	2607.59	2486.12
110000	10414.87	5829.56	4330.07	3601.43	3180.46	2912.67	2731.76	2604.51
115000	10888.28	6094.54	4526.89	3765.13	3325.03	3045.07	2855.93	2722.90
120000	11361.68	6359.52	4723.71	3928.83	3469.60	3177.46	2980.10	2841.28
125000	11835.08	6624.50	4920.53	4092.53	3614.16	3309.86	3104.27	2959.67
130000	12308.49	6889.48	5117.36	4256.23	3758.73	3442.25	3228.44	3078.06
135000	12781.89	7154.46	5314.18	4419.93	3903.29	3574.64	3352.61	3196.44
140000	13255.29	7419.44	5511.00	4583.63	4047.86	3707.04	3476.78	3314.83
145000	13728.70	7684.42	5707.82	4747.33	4192.43	3839.43	3600.95	3433.21
150000	14202.10	7949.40	5904.64	4911.03	4336.99	3971.83	3725.12	3551.60
155000	14675.50	8214.38	6101.46	5074.74	4481.56	4104.22	3849.29	3669.99
160000	15148.90	8479.36	6298.28	5238.44	4626.13	4236.61	3973.46	3788.37

228

AMOUNT OF LOAN	NUMBER OF YEARS IN TERM							
	9	10	15	20	25	30	35	40
$ 50	1.15	1.12	1.04	1.02	1.02	1.02	1.02	1.02
100	2.29	2.23	2.08	2.04	2.03	2.03	2.03	2.03
200	4.57	4.45	4.16	4.08	4.06	4.05	4.05	4.05
300	6.86	6.67	6.24	6.12	6.08	6.07	6.07	6.07
400	9.14	8.89	8.32	8.16	8.11	8.09	8.09	8.09
500	11.43	11.12	10.39	10.19	10.13	10.12	10.11	10.11
600	13.71	13.34	12.47	12.23	12.16	12.14	12.13	12.13
700	15.99	15.56	14.55	14.27	14.19	14.16	14.15	14.15
800	18.28	17.78	16.63	16.31	16.21	16.18	16.18	16.17
900	20.56	20.01	18.70	18.34	18.24	18.21	18.20	18.19
1000	22.85	22.23	20.78	20.38	20.26	20.23	20.22	20.21
2000	45.69	44.45	41.56	40.76	40.52	40.45	40.43	40.42
3000	68.53	66.67	62.33	61.13	60.78	60.68	60.64	60.63
4000	91.37	88.90	83.11	81.51	81.04	80.90	80.86	80.84
5000	114.21	111.12	103.88	101.88	101.30	101.12	101.07	101.05
6000	137.05	133.34	124.66	122.26	121.56	121.35	121.28	121.26
7000	159.89	155.56	145.43	142.64	141.81	141.57	141.50	141.47
8000	182.73	177.79	166.21	163.01	162.07	161.79	161.71	161.68
9000	205.57	200.01	186.98	183.39	182.33	182.02	181.92	181.89
10000	228.41	222.23	207.76	203.76	202.59	202.24	202.13	202.10
11000	251.25	244.45	228.53	224.14	222.85	222.46	222.35	222.31
12000	274.09	266.68	249.31	244.51	243.11	242.69	242.56	242.52
13000	296.93	288.90	270.08	264.89	263.36	262.91	262.77	262.73
14000	319.77	311.12	290.86	285.27	283.62	283.13	282.99	282.94
15000	342.61	333.35	311.63	305.64	303.88	303.36	303.20	303.15
16000	365.45	355.57	332.41	326.02	324.14	323.58	323.41	323.36
17000	388.29	377.79	353.18	346.39	344.40	343.80	343.62	343.57
18000	411.13	400.01	373.96	366.77	364.66	364.03	363.84	363.78
19000	433.97	422.24	394.74	387.14	384.92	384.25	384.05	383.99
20000	456.81	444.46	415.51	407.52	405.17	404.47	404.26	404.20
21000	479.65	466.68	436.29	427.90	425.43	424.70	424.48	424.41
22000	502.50	488.90	457.06	448.27	445.69	444.92	444.69	444.62
23000	525.34	511.13	477.84	468.65	465.95	465.14	464.90	464.83
24000	548.18	533.35	498.61	489.02	486.21	485.37	485.11	485.04
25000	571.02	555.57	519.39	509.40	506.47	505.59	505.33	505.25
26000	593.86	577.79	540.16	529.77	526.72	525.81	525.54	525.46
27000	616.70	600.02	560.94	550.15	546.98	546.04	545.75	545.67
28000	639.54	622.24	581.71	570.53	567.24	566.26	565.97	565.88
29000	662.38	644.46	602.49	590.90	587.50	586.48	586.18	586.09
30000	685.22	666.69	623.26	611.28	607.76	606.70	606.39	606.30
31000	708.06	688.91	644.04	631.65	628.02	626.93	626.60	626.51
32000	730.90	711.13	664.81	652.03	648.28	647.15	646.82	646.72
33000	753.74	733.35	685.59	672.40	668.53	667.38	667.03	666.93
34000	776.58	755.58	706.36	692.78	688.79	687.60	687.24	687.13
35000	799.42	777.80	727.14	713.16	709.05	707.82	707.46	707.34
40000	913.62	888.91	831.02	815.03	810.34	808.94	808.52	808.39
45000	1027.83	1000.03	934.89	916.91	911.64	910.06	909.58	909.44
50000	1142.03	1111.14	1038.77	1018.79	1012.93	1011.17	1010.65	1010.49
55000	1256.23	1222.25	1142.65	1120.67	1114.22	1112.29	1111.71	1111.54
60000	1370.43	1333.37	1246.52	1222.55	1215.51	1213.41	1212.78	1212.59
65000	1484.64	1444.48	1350.40	1324.43	1316.80	1314.53	1313.84	1313.64
70000	1598.84	1555.59	1454.28	1426.31	1418.10	1415.64	1414.91	1414.68
75000	1713.04	1666.71	1558.15	1528.19	1519.39	1516.76	1515.97	1515.73
80000	1827.24	1777.82	1662.03	1630.06	1620.68	1617.88	1617.03	1616.78
85000	1941.44	1888.93	1765.90	1731.94	1721.97	1718.99	1718.10	1717.83
90000	2055.65	2000.05	1869.78	1833.82	1823.27	1820.11	1819.16	1818.88
95000	2169.85	2111.16	1973.66	1935.70	1924.56	1921.23	1920.23	1919.93
100000	2284.05	2222.27	2077.53	2037.58	2025.85	2022.34	2021.29	2020.97
105000	2398.25	2333.39	2181.41	2139.46	2127.14	2123.46	2122.36	2122.02
110000	2512.46	2444.50	2285.29	2241.34	2228.43	2224.58	2223.42	2223.07
115000	2626.66	2555.61	2389.16	2343.22	2329.73	2325.70	2324.48	2324.12
120000	2740.86	2666.73	2493.04	2445.09	2431.02	2426.81	2425.55	2425.17
125000	2855.06	2777.84	2596.92	2546.97	2532.31	2527.93	2526.61	2526.22
130000	2969.27	2888.95	2700.79	2648.85	2633.60	2629.05	2627.68	2627.27
135000	3083.47	3000.07	2804.67	2750.73	2734.90	2730.16	2728.74	2728.31
140000	3197.67	3111.18	2908.55	2852.61	2836.19	2831.28	2829.81	2829.36
145000	3311.87	3222.29	3012.42	2954.49	2937.48	2932.40	2930.87	2930.41
150000	3426.07	3333.41	3116.30	3056.37	3038.77	3033.51	3031.93	3031.46
155000	3540.28	3444.52	3220.18	3158.25	3140.06	3134.63	3133.00	3132.51
160000	3654.48	3555.63	3324.05	3260.13	3241.36	3235.75	3234.06	3233.56

AMOUNT OF LOAN	NUMBER OF YEARS IN TERM							
	1	2	3	4	5	6	7	8
$ 50	4.75	2.66	1.98	1.65	1.46	1.34	1.25	1.20
100	9.49	5.32	3.95	3.29	2.91	2.67	2.50	2.39
200	18.97	10.63	7.90	6.58	5.82	5.33	5.00	4.77
300	28.45	15.94	11.85	9.87	8.72	7.99	7.50	7.16
400	37.93	21.25	15.80	13.16	11.63	10.66	10.00	9.54
500	47.41	26.57	19.75	16.44	14.53	13.32	12.50	11.93
600	56.89	31.88	23.70	19.73	17.44	15.98	15.00	14.31
700	66.37	37.19	27.65	23.02	20.35	18.65	17.50	16.69
800	75.85	42.50	31.60	26.31	23.25	21.31	20.00	19.08
900	85.33	47.81	35.55	29.60	26.16	23.97	22.50	21.46
1000	94.81	53.13	39.50	32.88	29.06	26.64	25.00	23.85
2000	189.61	106.25	79.00	65.76	58.12	53.27	49.99	47.69
3000	284.41	159.37	118.49	98.64	87.18	79.90	74.98	71.53
4000	379.21	212.49	157.99	131.52	116.24	106.53	99.98	95.37
5000	474.01	265.61	197.48	164.40	145.30	133.16	124.97	119.21
6000	568.82	318.73	236.98	197.28	174.36	159.79	149.96	143.06
7000	663.62	371.85	276.48	230.16	203.42	186.42	174.95	166.90
8000	758.42	424.97	315.97	263.04	232.48	213.05	199.95	190.74
9000	853.22	478.09	355.47	295.91	261.54	239.69	224.94	214.58
10000	948.02	531.21	394.96	328.79	290.59	266.32	249.93	238.42
11000	1042.82	584.34	434.46	361.67	319.65	292.95	274.93	262.27
12000	1137.63	637.46	473.96	394.55	348.71	319.58	299.92	286.11
13000	1232.43	690.58	513.45	427.43	377.77	346.21	324.91	309.95
14000	1327.23	743.70	552.95	460.31	406.83	372.84	349.90	333.79
15000	1422.03	796.82	592.44	493.19	435.89	399.47	374.90	357.63
16000	1516.83	849.94	631.94	526.07	464.95	426.10	399.89	381.48
17000	1611.63	903.06	671.43	558.95	494.01	452.74	424.88	405.32
18000	1706.44	956.18	710.93	591.82	523.07	479.37	449.88	429.16
19000	1801.24	1009.30	750.43	624.70	552.12	506.00	474.87	453.00
20000	1896.04	1062.42	789.92	657.58	581.18	532.63	499.86	476.84
21000	1990.84	1115.55	829.42	690.46	610.24	559.26	524.85	500.69
22000	2085.64	1168.67	868.91	723.34	639.30	585.89	549.85	524.53
23000	2180.44	1221.79	908.41	756.22	668.36	612.52	574.84	548.37
24000	2275.25	1274.91	947.91	789.10	697.42	639.15	599.83	572.21
25000	2370.05	1328.03	987.40	821.98	726.48	665.78	624.83	596.05
26000	2464.85	1381.15	1026.90	854.86	755.54	692.42	649.82	619.90
27000	2559.65	1434.27	1066.39	887.73	784.60	719.05	674.81	643.74
28000	2654.45	1487.39	1105.89	920.61	813.65	745.68	699.80	667.58
29000	2749.26	1540.51	1145.38	953.49	842.71	772.31	724.80	691.42
30000	2844.06	1593.63	1184.88	986.37	871.77	798.94	749.79	715.26
31000	2938.86	1646.76	1224.38	1019.25	900.83	825.57	774.78	739.11
32000	3033.66	1699.88	1263.87	1052.13	929.89	852.20	799.78	762.95
33000	3128.46	1753.00	1303.37	1085.01	958.95	878.83	824.77	786.79
34000	3223.26	1806.12	1342.86	1117.89	988.01	905.47	849.76	810.63
35000	3318.07	1859.24	1382.36	1150.77	1017.07	932.10	874.75	834.47
40000	3792.07	2124.84	1579.84	1315.16	1162.36	1065.25	999.72	953.68
45000	4266.08	2390.45	1777.32	1479.55	1307.66	1198.41	1124.68	1072.89
50000	4740.09	2656.05	1974.80	1643.95	1452.95	1331.56	1249.65	1192.10
55000	5214.10	2921.66	2172.28	1808.34	1598.25	1464.72	1374.61	1311.31
60000	5688.11	3187.26	2369.76	1972.74	1743.54	1597.88	1499.58	1430.52
65000	6162.12	3452.87	2567.24	2137.13	1888.83	1731.03	1624.54	1549.73
70000	6636.13	3718.47	2764.72	2301.53	2034.13	1864.19	1749.50	1668.94
75000	7110.14	3984.08	2962.19	2465.92	2179.42	1997.34	1874.47	1788.15
80000	7584.14	4249.68	3159.67	2630.31	2324.72	2130.50	1999.43	1907.36
85000	8058.15	4515.29	3357.15	2794.71	2470.01	2263.66	2124.40	2026.57
90000	8532.16	4780.89	3554.63	2959.10	2615.31	2396.81	2249.36	2145.78
95000	9006.17	5046.50	3752.11	3123.50	2760.60	2529.97	2374.32	2264.99
100000	9480.18	5312.10	3949.59	3287.89	2905.90	2663.12	2499.29	2384.20
105000	9954.19	5577.71	4147.07	3452.29	3051.19	2796.28	2624.25	2503.41
110000	10428.20	5843.31	4344.55	3616.68	3196.49	2929.44	2749.22	2622.62
115000	10902.20	6108.92	4542.03	3781.07	3341.78	3062.59	2874.18	2741.83
120000	11376.21	6374.52	4739.51	3945.47	3487.07	3195.75	2999.15	2861.04
125000	11850.22	6640.13	4936.99	4109.86	3632.37	3328.90	3124.11	2980.25
130000	12324.23	6905.73	5134.47	4274.26	3777.66	3462.06	3249.07	3099.46
135000	12798.24	7171.34	5331.95	4438.65	3922.96	3595.21	3374.04	3218.67
140000	13272.25	7436.94	5529.43	4603.05	4068.25	3728.37	3499.00	3337.88
145000	13746.26	7702.55	5726.90	4767.44	4213.55	3861.53	3623.97	3457.09
150000	14220.27	7968.15	5924.38	4931.84	4358.84	3994.68	3748.93	3576.30
155000	14694.27	8233.76	6121.86	5096.23	4504.14	4127.84	3873.89	3695.51
160000	15168.28	8499.36	6319.34	5260.62	4649.43	4260.99	3998.86	3814.72

MONTHLY AMORTIZING PAYMENTS 24.500%

AMOUNT OF LOAN	NUMBER OF YEARS IN TERM							
	9	10	15	20	25	30	35	40
$ 50	1.16	1.12	1.05	1.03	1.03	1.03	1.03	1.03
100	2.31	2.24	2.10	2.06	2.05	2.05	2.05	2.05
200	4.61	4.48	4.20	4.12	4.10	4.09	4.09	4.09
300	6.91	6.72	6.30	6.18	6.14	6.13	6.13	6.13
400	9.21	8.96	8.39	8.24	8.19	8.18	8.17	8.17
500	11.51	11.20	10.49	10.29	10.24	10.22	10.22	10.21
600	13.81	13.44	12.59	12.35	12.28	12.26	12.26	12.26
700	16.11	15.68	14.68	14.41	14.33	14.31	14.30	14.30
800	18.41	17.92	16.78	16.47	16.38	16.35	16.34	16.34
900	20.71	20.16	18.88	18.52	18.42	18.39	18.38	18.38
1000	23.02	22.40	20.97	20.58	20.47	20.44	20.43	20.42
2000	46.03	44.80	41.94	41.16	40.93	40.87	40.85	40.84
3000	69.04	67.20	62.91	61.74	61.40	61.30	61.27	61.26
4000	92.05	89.60	83.88	82.32	81.86	81.73	81.69	81.68
5000	115.06	111.99	104.85	102.89	102.33	102.16	102.11	102.09
6000	138.07	134.39	125.81	123.47	122.79	122.59	122.53	122.51
7000	161.08	156.79	146.78	144.05	143.25	143.02	142.95	142.93
8000	184.09	179.19	167.75	164.63	163.72	163.45	163.37	163.35
9000	207.10	201.58	188.72	185.20	184.18	183.88	183.79	183.77
10000	230.11	223.98	209.69	205.78	204.65	204.31	204.21	204.18
11000	253.12	246.38	230.66	226.36	225.11	224.74	224.63	224.60
12000	276.13	268.78	251.62	246.94	245.58	245.17	245.06	245.02
13000	299.14	291.18	272.59	267.51	266.04	265.61	265.48	265.44
14000	322.15	313.57	293.56	288.09	286.50	286.04	285.90	285.86
15000	345.16	335.97	314.53	308.67	306.97	306.47	306.32	306.27
16000	368.17	358.37	335.50	329.25	327.43	326.90	326.74	326.69
17000	391.18	380.77	356.47	349.83	347.90	347.33	347.16	347.11
18000	414.20	403.16	377.43	370.40	368.36	367.76	367.58	367.53
19000	437.21	425.56	398.40	390.98	388.83	388.19	388.00	387.95
20000	460.22	447.96	419.37	411.56	409.29	408.62	408.42	408.36
21000	483.23	470.36	440.34	432.14	429.75	429.05	428.84	428.78
22000	506.24	492.76	461.31	452.71	450.22	449.48	449.26	449.20
23000	529.25	515.15	482.27	473.29	470.68	469.91	469.68	469.62
24000	552.26	537.55	503.24	493.87	491.15	490.34	490.11	490.03
25000	575.27	559.95	524.21	514.45	511.61	510.78	510.53	510.45
26000	598.28	582.35	545.18	535.02	532.08	531.21	530.95	530.87
27000	621.29	604.74	566.15	555.60	552.54	551.64	551.37	551.29
28000	644.30	627.14	587.12	576.18	573.00	572.07	571.79	571.71
29000	667.31	649.54	608.08	596.76	593.47	592.50	592.21	592.12
30000	690.32	671.94	629.05	617.33	613.93	612.93	612.63	612.54
31000	713.33	694.33	650.02	637.91	634.40	633.36	633.05	632.96
32000	736.34	716.73	670.99	658.49	654.86	653.79	653.47	653.38
33000	759.35	739.13	691.96	679.07	675.33	674.22	673.89	673.80
34000	782.36	761.53	712.93	699.65	695.79	694.65	694.31	694.21
35000	805.37	783.93	733.89	720.22	716.25	715.08	714.74	714.63
40000	920.43	895.91	838.73	823.11	818.58	817.24	816.84	816.72
45000	1035.48	1007.90	943.58	926.00	920.90	919.39	918.94	918.81
50000	1150.53	1119.89	1048.42	1028.89	1023.22	1021.55	1021.05	1020.90
55000	1265.59	1231.88	1153.26	1131.78	1125.54	1123.70	1123.15	1122.99
60000	1380.64	1343.87	1258.10	1234.66	1227.86	1225.85	1225.26	1225.08
65000	1495.69	1455.86	1362.94	1337.55	1330.18	1328.01	1327.36	1327.17
70000	1610.74	1567.85	1467.78	1440.44	1432.50	1430.16	1429.47	1429.26
75000	1725.80	1679.83	1572.62	1543.33	1534.83	1532.32	1531.57	1531.35
80000	1840.85	1791.82	1677.46	1646.22	1637.15	1634.47	1633.67	1633.44
85000	1955.90	1903.81	1782.31	1749.11	1739.47	1736.62	1735.78	1735.53
90000	2070.96	2015.80	1887.15	1851.99	1841.79	1838.78	1837.88	1837.62
95000	2186.01	2127.79	1991.99	1954.88	1944.11	1940.93	1939.99	1939.71
100000	2301.06	2239.78	2096.83	2057.77	2046.43	2043.09	2042.09	2041.80
105000	2416.11	2351.77	2201.67	2160.66	2148.75	2145.24	2144.20	2143.89
110000	2531.17	2463.76	2306.51	2263.55	2251.07	2247.39	2246.30	2245.98
115000	2646.22	2575.74	2411.35	2366.43	2353.40	2349.55	2348.40	2348.07
120000	2761.27	2687.73	2516.19	2469.32	2455.72	2451.70	2450.51	2450.15
125000	2876.33	2799.72	2621.04	2572.21	2558.04	2553.86	2552.61	2552.24
130000	2991.38	2911.71	2725.88	2675.10	2660.36	2656.01	2654.72	2654.33
135000	3106.43	3023.70	2830.72	2777.99	2762.68	2758.16	2756.82	2756.42
140000	3221.48	3135.69	2935.56	2880.88	2865.00	2860.32	2858.93	2858.51
145000	3336.54	3247.68	3040.40	2983.76	2967.33	2962.47	2961.03	2960.60
150000	3451.59	3359.66	3145.24	3086.65	3069.65	3064.63	3063.14	3062.69
155000	3566.64	3471.65	3250.08	3189.54	3171.97	3166.78	3165.24	3164.78
160000	3681.70	3583.64	3354.92	3292.43	3274.29	3268.93	3267.34	3266.87

231

24.750%   MONTHLY AMORTIZING PAYMENTS

AMOUNT OF LOAN	NUMBER OF YEARS IN TERM							
	1	2	3	4	5	6	7	8
$ 50	4.75	2.67	1.99	1.66	1.47	1.34	1.26	1.21
100	9.50	5.33	3.97	3.31	2.93	2.68	2.52	2.41
200	18.99	10.65	7.93	6.61	5.85	5.36	5.04	4.81
300	28.48	15.98	11.89	9.91	8.77	8.04	7.55	7.21
400	37.97	21.30	15.86	13.21	11.69	10.72	10.07	9.61
500	47.47	26.63	19.82	16.51	14.61	13.40	12.58	12.01
600	56.96	31.95	23.78	19.82	17.53	16.08	15.10	14.41
700	66.45	37.28	27.74	23.12	20.45	18.75	17.61	16.81
800	75.94	42.60	31.71	26.42	23.37	21.43	20.13	19.21
900	85.44	47.93	35.67	29.72	26.29	24.11	22.64	21.61
1000	94.93	53.25	39.63	33.02	29.21	26.79	25.16	24.01
2000	189.85	106.50	79.26	66.04	58.41	53.57	50.31	48.02
3000	284.77	159.74	118.89	99.06	87.62	80.36	75.46	72.03
4000	379.70	212.99	158.52	132.08	116.82	107.14	100.61	96.03
5000	474.62	266.24	198.14	165.09	146.03	133.92	125.77	120.04
6000	569.54	319.48	237.77	198.11	175.23	160.71	150.92	144.05
7000	664.47	372.73	277.40	231.13	204.44	187.49	176.07	168.05
8000	759.39	425.97	317.03	264.15	233.64	214.28	201.22	192.06
9000	854.31	479.22	356.65	297.17	262.85	241.06	226.37	216.07
10000	949.23	532.47	396.28	330.18	292.05	267.84	251.53	240.08
11000	1044.16	585.71	435.91	363.20	321.26	294.63	276.68	264.08
12000	1139.08	638.96	475.54	396.22	350.46	321.41	301.83	288.09
13000	1234.00	692.21	515.17	429.24	379.67	348.20	326.98	312.10
14000	1328.93	745.45	554.79	462.25	408.87	374.98	352.13	336.10
15000	1423.85	798.70	594.42	495.27	438.08	401.76	377.29	360.11
16000	1518.77	851.94	634.05	528.29	467.28	428.55	402.44	384.12
17000	1613.69	905.19	673.68	561.31	496.49	455.33	427.59	408.13
18000	1708.62	958.44	713.30	594.33	525.69	482.12	452.74	432.13
19000	1803.54	1011.68	752.93	627.34	554.90	508.90	477.89	456.14
20000	1898.46	1064.93	792.56	660.36	584.10	535.68	503.05	480.15
21000	1993.39	1118.17	832.19	693.38	613.31	562.47	528.20	504.15
22000	2088.31	1171.42	871.81	726.40	642.51	589.25	553.35	528.16
23000	2183.23	1224.67	911.44	759.42	671.72	616.04	578.50	552.17
24000	2278.16	1277.91	951.07	792.43	700.92	642.82	603.65	576.17
25000	2373.08	1331.16	990.70	825.45	730.13	669.60	628.81	600.18
26000	2468.00	1384.41	1030.33	858.47	759.33	696.39	653.96	624.19
27000	2562.92	1437.65	1069.95	891.49	788.54	723.17	679.11	648.20
28000	2657.85	1490.90	1109.58	924.50	817.74	749.96	704.26	672.20
29000	2752.77	1544.14	1149.21	957.52	846.95	776.74	729.41	696.21
30000	2847.69	1597.39	1188.84	990.54	876.15	803.52	754.57	720.22
31000	2942.62	1650.64	1228.46	1023.56	905.36	830.31	779.72	744.22
32000	3037.54	1703.88	1268.09	1056.58	934.56	857.09	804.87	768.23
33000	3132.46	1757.13	1307.72	1089.59	963.77	883.88	830.02	792.24
34000	3227.38	1810.37	1347.35	1122.61	992.97	910.66	855.17	816.25
35000	3322.31	1863.62	1386.98	1155.63	1022.18	937.44	880.33	840.25
40000	3796.92	2129.85	1585.11	1320.72	1168.20	1071.36	1006.09	960.29
45000	4271.54	2396.08	1783.25	1485.81	1314.23	1205.28	1131.85	1080.32
50000	4746.15	2662.31	1981.39	1650.90	1460.25	1339.20	1257.61	1200.36
55000	5220.77	2928.54	2179.53	1815.99	1606.28	1473.12	1383.37	1320.39
60000	5695.38	3194.78	2377.67	1981.08	1752.30	1607.04	1509.13	1440.43
65000	6170.00	3461.01	2575.81	2146.16	1898.33	1740.96	1634.89	1560.47
70000	6644.61	3727.24	2773.95	2311.25	2044.35	1874.88	1760.65	1680.50
75000	7119.22	3993.47	2972.06	2476.34	2190.38	2008.80	1886.41	1800.54
80000	7593.84	4259.70	3170.22	2641.43	2336.40	2142.72	2012.17	1920.57
85000	8068.45	4525.93	3368.36	2806.52	2482.42	2276.64	2137.93	2040.61
90000	8543.07	4792.16	3566.50	2971.61	2628.45	2410.56	2263.69	2160.64
95000	9017.68	5058.39	3764.64	3136.70	2774.47	2544.48	2389.45	2280.68
100000	9492.30	5324.62	3962.78	3301.79	2920.50	2678.40	2515.21	2400.71
105000	9966.91	5590.85	4160.92	3466.88	3066.52	2812.32	2640.97	2520.75
110000	10441.53	5857.08	4359.05	3631.97	3212.55	2946.24	2766.73	2640.78
115000	10916.14	6123.31	4557.19	3797.06	3358.57	3080.16	2892.49	2760.82
120000	11390.76	6389.55	4755.33	3962.15	3504.60	3214.08	3018.25	2880.85
125000	11865.37	6655.78	4953.47	4127.24	3650.62	3348.00	3144.01	3000.89
130000	12339.99	6922.01	5151.61	4292.32	3796.65	3481.92	3269.77	3120.93
135000	12814.60	7188.24	5349.75	4457.41	3942.67	3615.84	3395.53	3240.96
140000	13289.21	7454.47	5547.89	4622.50	4088.70	3749.76	3521.29	3361.00
145000	13763.83	7720.70	5746.02	4787.59	4234.72	3883.68	3647.05	3481.03
150000	14238.44	7986.93	5944.16	4952.68	4380.75	4017.60	3772.81	3601.07
155000	14713.06	8253.16	6142.30	5117.77	4526.77	4151.52	3898.57	3721.10
160000	15187.67	8519.39	6340.44	5282.86	4672.80	4285.44	4024.33	3841.14

232

MONTHLY AMORTIZING PAYMENTS 24.750%

AMOUNT OF LOAN	NUMBER OF YEARS IN TERM							
	9	10	15	20	25	30	35	40
$ 50	1.16	1.13	1.06	1.04	1.04	1.04	1.04	1.04
100	2.32	2.26	2.12	2.08	2.07	2.07	2.07	2.07
200	4.64	4.52	4.24	4.16	4.14	4.13	4.13	4.13
300	6.96	6.78	6.35	6.24	6.21	6.20	6.19	6.19
400	9.28	9.03	8.47	8.32	8.27	8.26	8.26	8.26
500	11.60	11.29	10.59	10.39	10.34	10.32	10.32	10.32
600	13.91	13.55	12.70	12.47	12.41	12.39	12.38	12.38
700	16.23	15.81	14.82	14.55	14.47	14.45	14.45	14.44
800	18.55	18.06	16.93	16.63	16.54	16.52	16.51	16.51
900	20.87	20.32	19.05	18.71	18.61	18.58	18.57	18.57
1000	23.19	22.58	21.17	20.78	20.68	20.64	20.63	20.63
2000	46.37	45.15	42.33	41.56	41.35	41.28	41.26	41.26
3000	69.55	67.72	63.49	62.34	62.02	61.92	61.89	61.88
4000	92.73	90.30	84.65	83.12	82.69	82.56	82.52	82.51
5000	115.91	112.87	105.81	103.90	103.36	103.20	103.15	103.14
6000	139.09	135.44	126.97	124.68	124.03	123.83	123.78	123.76
7000	162.27	158.02	148.14	145.46	144.70	144.47	144.41	144.39
8000	185.45	180.59	169.30	166.24	165.37	165.11	165.04	165.01
9000	208.64	203.16	190.46	187.02	186.04	185.75	185.67	185.64
10000	231.82	225.74	211.62	207.80	206.71	206.39	206.29	206.27
11000	255.00	248.31	232.78	228.58	227.38	227.03	226.92	226.89
12000	278.18	270.88	253.94	249.36	248.05	247.66	247.55	247.52
13000	301.36	293.46	275.11	270.14	268.72	268.30	268.18	268.14
14000	324.54	316.03	296.27	290.92	289.39	288.94	288.81	288.77
15000	347.72	338.60	317.43	311.70	310.06	309.58	309.44	309.40
16000	370.90	361.18	338.59	332.48	330.73	330.22	330.07	330.02
17000	394.08	383.75	359.75	353.26	351.40	350.86	350.70	350.65
18000	417.27	406.32	380.91	374.04	372.07	371.49	371.33	371.28
19000	440.45	428.90	402.07	394.82	392.74	392.13	391.95	391.90
20000	463.63	451.47	423.24	415.60	413.41	412.77	412.58	412.53
21000	486.81	474.04	444.40	436.38	434.08	433.41	433.21	433.15
22000	509.99	496.62	465.56	457.16	454.75	454.05	453.84	453.78
23000	533.17	519.19	486.72	477.94	475.42	474.69	474.47	474.41
24000	556.35	541.76	507.88	498.72	496.09	495.32	495.10	495.03
25000	579.53	564.34	529.04	519.50	516.76	515.96	515.73	515.66
26000	602.71	586.91	550.21	540.28	537.43	536.60	536.36	536.28
27000	625.90	609.48	571.37	561.06	558.10	557.24	556.99	556.91
28000	649.08	632.06	592.53	581.84	578.77	577.88	577.61	577.54
29000	672.26	654.63	613.69	602.62	599.44	598.51	598.24	598.16
30000	695.44	677.20	634.85	623.40	620.11	619.15	618.87	618.79
31000	718.62	699.78	656.01	644.18	640.78	639.79	639.50	639.42
32000	741.80	722.35	677.18	664.96	661.45	660.43	660.13	660.04
33000	764.98	744.92	698.34	685.74	682.12	681.07	680.76	680.67
34000	788.16	767.50	719.50	706.52	702.79	701.71	701.39	701.29
35000	811.34	790.07	740.66	727.30	723.46	722.34	722.02	721.92
40000	927.25	902.94	846.47	831.20	826.81	825.54	825.16	825.05
45000	1043.16	1015.80	952.28	935.10	930.17	928.73	928.31	928.18
50000	1159.06	1128.67	1058.08	1038.99	1033.52	1031.92	1031.45	1031.31
55000	1274.97	1241.54	1163.89	1142.89	1136.87	1135.11	1134.59	1134.44
60000	1390.87	1354.40	1269.70	1246.79	1240.22	1238.30	1237.74	1237.57
65000	1506.78	1467.27	1375.51	1350.69	1343.57	1341.49	1340.88	1340.70
70000	1622.68	1580.13	1481.32	1454.59	1446.92	1444.68	1444.03	1443.84
75000	1738.59	1693.00	1587.12	1558.49	1550.27	1547.88	1547.17	1546.97
80000	1854.50	1805.87	1692.93	1662.39	1653.62	1651.07	1650.32	1650.10
85000	1970.40	1918.73	1798.74	1766.29	1756.98	1754.26	1753.46	1753.23
90000	2086.31	2031.60	1904.55	1870.19	1860.33	1857.45	1856.61	1856.36
95000	2202.21	2144.47	2010.35	1974.09	1963.68	1960.64	1959.75	1959.49
100000	2318.12	2257.33	2116.16	2077.98	2067.03	2063.83	2062.89	2062.62
105000	2434.02	2370.20	2221.97	2181.88	2170.38	2167.02	2166.04	2165.75
110000	2549.93	2483.07	2327.78	2285.78	2273.73	2270.21	2269.18	2268.88
115000	2665.84	2595.93	2433.59	2389.68	2377.08	2373.41	2372.33	2372.01
120000	2781.74	2708.80	2539.39	2493.58	2480.43	2476.60	2475.47	2475.14
125000	2897.65	2821.66	2645.20	2597.48	2583.78	2579.79	2578.62	2578.27
130000	3013.55	2934.53	2751.01	2701.38	2687.14	2682.98	2681.76	2681.40
135000	3129.46	3047.40	2856.82	2805.28	2790.49	2786.17	2784.91	2784.53
140000	3245.36	3160.26	2962.63	2909.18	2893.84	2889.36	2888.05	2887.67
145000	3361.27	3273.13	3068.43	3013.08	2997.19	2992.55	2991.19	2990.80
150000	3477.18	3386.00	3174.24	3116.97	3100.54	3095.75	3094.34	3093.93
155000	3593.08	3498.86	3280.05	3220.87	3203.89	3198.94	3197.48	3197.06
160000	3708.99	3611.73	3385.86	3324.77	3307.24	3302.13	3300.63	3300.19

233

25.000% MONTHLY AMORTIZING PAYMENTS

AMOUNT OF LOAN	NUMBER OF YEARS IN TERM							
	1	2	3	4	5	6	7	8
$ 50	4.76	2.67	1.99	1.66	1.47	1.35	1.27	1.21
100	9.51	5.34	3.98	3.32	2.94	2.70	2.54	2.42
200	19.01	10.68	7.96	6.64	5.88	5.39	5.07	4.84
300	28.52	16.02	11.93	9.95	8.81	8.09	7.60	7.26
400	38.02	21.35	15.91	13.27	11.75	10.78	10.13	9.67
500	47.53	26.69	19.88	16.58	14.68	13.47	12.66	12.09
600	57.03	32.03	23.86	19.90	17.62	16.17	15.19	14.51
700	66.54	37.37	27.84	23.21	20.55	16.86	17.72	16.93
800	76.04	42.70	31.81	26.53	23.49	21.55	20.25	19.34
900	85.54	48.04	35.79	29.85	26.42	24.25	22.79	21.76
1000	95.05	53.38	39.76	33.16	29.36	26.94	25.32	24.18
2000	190.09	106.75	79.52	66.32	58.71	53.88	50.63	48.35
3000	285.14	160.12	119.28	99.48	88.06	80.82	75.94	72.52
4000	380.18	213.49	159.04	132.63	117.41	107.75	101.25	96.70
5000	475.23	266.86	198.80	165.79	146.76	134.69	126.56	120.87
6000	570.27	320.23	238.56	198.95	176.11	161.63	151.87	145.04
7000	665.31	373.61	278.32	232.10	205.46	188.57	177.19	169.21
8000	760.36	426.98	318.08	265.26	234.82	215.50	202.50	193.39
9000	855.40	480.35	357.84	298.42	264.17	242.44	227.81	217.56
10000	950.45	533.72	397.60	331.58	293.52	269.38	253.12	241.73
11000	1045.49	587.09	437.36	364.73	322.87	296.31	278.43	265.90
12000	1140.54	640.46	477.12	397.89	352.22	323.25	303.74	290.08
13000	1235.58	693.83	516.88	431.05	381.57	350.19	329.06	314.25
14000	1330.62	747.21	556.64	464.20	410.92	377.13	354.37	338.42
15000	1425.67	800.58	596.40	497.36	440.27	404.06	379.68	362.59
16000	1520.71	853.95	636.16	530.52	469.63	431.00	404.99	386.77
17000	1615.76	907.32	675.92	563.68	498.98	457.94	430.30	410.94
18000	1710.80	960.69	715.68	596.83	528.33	484.87	455.61	435.11
19000	1805.84	1014.06	755.44	629.99	557.68	511.81	480.93	459.29
20000	1900.89	1067.44	795.20	663.15	587.03	538.75	506.24	483.46
21000	1995.93	1120.81	834.96	696.30	616.38	565.69	531.55	507.63
22000	2090.98	1174.18	874.72	729.46	645.73	592.62	556.86	531.80
23000	2186.02	1227.55	914.48	762.62	675.09	619.56	582.17	555.98
24000	2281.07	1280.92	954.24	795.78	704.44	646.50	607.48	580.15
25000	2376.11	1334.29	994.00	828.93	733.79	673.43	632.80	604.32
26000	2471.15	1387.66	1033.76	862.09	763.14	700.37	658.11	628.49
27000	2566.20	1441.04	1073.52	895.25	792.49	727.31	683.42	652.67
28000	2661.24	1494.41	1113.28	928.40	821.84	754.25	708.73	676.84
29000	2756.29	1547.78	1153.04	961.56	851.19	781.18	734.04	701.01
30000	2851.33	1601.15	1192.80	994.72	880.54	808.12	759.35	725.18
31000	2946.38	1654.52	1232.56	1027.88	909.90	835.06	784.67	749.36
32000	3041.42	1707.89	1272.32	1061.03	939.25	861.99	809.98	773.53
33000	3136.46	1761.27	1312.08	1094.19	968.60	888.93	835.29	797.70
34000	3231.51	1814.64	1351.84	1127.35	997.95	915.87	860.60	821.88
35000	3326.55	1868.01	1391.60	1160.50	1027.30	942.81	885.91	846.05
40000	3801.77	2134.87	1590.40	1326.29	1174.06	1077.49	1012.47	966.91
45000	4276.99	2401.72	1789.20	1492.08	1320.81	1212.18	1139.03	1087.77
50000	4752.22	2668.58	1988.00	1657.86	1467.57	1346.86	1265.59	1208.64
55000	5227.44	2935.44	2186.80	1823.65	1614.33	1481.55	1392.14	1329.50
60000	5702.66	3202.30	2385.59	1989.43	1761.08	1616.24	1518.70	1450.36
65000	6177.88	3469.15	2584.39	2155.22	1907.84	1750.92	1645.26	1571.23
70000	6653.10	3736.01	2783.19	2321.00	2054.60	1885.61	1771.82	1692.09
75000	7128.32	4002.87	2981.99	2486.79	2201.35	2020.29	1898.38	1812.95
80000	7603.54	4269.73	3180.79	2652.58	2348.11	2154.98	2024.94	1933.82
85000	8078.76	4536.58	3379.59	2818.36	2494.87	2289.67	2151.49	2054.68
90000	8553.98	4803.44	3578.39	2984.15	2641.62	2424.35	2278.05	2175.54
95000	9029.20	5070.30	3777.19	3149.93	2788.38	2559.04	2404.61	2296.41
100000	9504.43	5337.16	3975.99	3315.72	2935.14	2693.72	2531.17	2417.27
105000	9979.65	5604.01	4174.79	3481.50	3081.89	2828.41	2657.73	2538.13
110000	10454.87	5870.87	4373.59	3647.29	3228.65	2963.09	2784.28	2659.00
115000	10930.09	6137.73	4572.38	3813.07	3375.41	3097.78	2910.84	2779.86
120000	11405.31	6404.59	4771.18	3978.86	3522.16	3232.47	3037.40	2900.72
125000	11880.53	6671.45	4969.98	4144.65	3668.92	3367.15	3163.96	3021.59
130000	12355.75	6938.30	5168.78	4310.43	3815.68	3501.84	3290.52	3142.45
135000	12830.97	7205.16	5367.58	4476.22	3962.43	3636.52	3417.08	3263.31
140000	13306.19	7472.02	5566.38	4642.00	4109.19	3771.21	3543.63	3384.18
145000	13781.41	7738.88	5765.18	4807.79	4255.95	3905.90	3670.19	3505.04
150000	14256.64	8005.73	5963.98	4973.57	4402.70	4040.58	3796.75	3625.90
155000	14731.86	8272.59	6162.78	5139.36	4549.46	4175.27	3923.31	3746.77
160000	15207.08	8539.45	6361.58	5305.15	4696.22	4309.95	4049.87	3867.63

234

AMOUNT OF LOAN	NUMBER OF YEARS IN TERM							
	9	10	15	20	25	30	35	40
$ 50	1.17	1.14	1.07	1.05	1.05	1.05	1.05	1.05
100	2.34	2.28	2.14	2.10	2.09	2.09	2.09	2.09
200	4.68	4.55	4.28	4.20	4.18	4.17	4.17	4.17
300	7.01	6.83	6.41	6.30	6.27	6.26	6.26	6.26
400	9.35	9.10	8.55	8.40	8.36	8.34	8.34	8.34
500	11.68	11.38	10.68	10.50	10.44	10.43	10.42	10.42
600	14.02	13.65	12.82	12.59	12.53	12.51	12.51	12.51
700	16.35	15.93	14.95	14.69	14.62	14.60	14.59	14.59
800	18.69	18.20	17.09	16.79	16.71	16.68	16.67	16.67
900	21.02	20.48	19.22	18.89	18.79	18.77	18.76	18.76
1000	23.36	22.75	21.36	20.99	20.88	20.85	20.84	20.84
2000	46.71	45.50	42.72	41.97	41.76	41.70	41.68	41.67
3000	70.06	68.25	64.07	62.95	62.63	62.54	62.52	62.51
4000	93.41	91.00	85.43	83.93	83.51	83.39	83.35	83.34
5000	116.77	113.75	106.78	104.92	104.39	104.23	104.19	104.18
6000	140.12	136.50	128.14	125.90	125.26	125.08	125.03	125.01
7000	163.47	159.25	149.49	146.88	146.14	145.93	145.86	145.85
8000	186.82	182.00	170.85	167.86	167.02	166.77	166.70	166.68
9000	210.17	204.75	192.20	188.84	187.89	187.62	187.54	187.51
10000	233.53	227.50	213.56	209.83	208.77	208.46	208.37	208.35
11000	256.88	250.25	234.91	230.81	229.64	229.31	229.21	229.18
12000	280.23	273.00	256.27	251.79	250.52	250.15	250.05	250.02
13000	303.58	295.75	277.62	272.77	271.40	271.00	270.89	270.85
14000	326.94	318.50	298.98	293.76	292.27	291.85	291.72	291.69
15000	350.29	341.24	320.33	314.74	313.15	312.69	312.56	312.52
16000	373.64	363.99	341.69	335.72	334.03	333.54	333.40	333.36
17000	396.99	386.74	363.04	356.70	354.90	354.38	354.23	354.19
18000	420.34	409.49	384.40	377.68	375.78	375.23	375.07	375.02
19000	443.70	432.24	405.76	398.67	396.65	396.07	395.91	395.86
20000	467.05	454.99	427.11	419.65	417.53	416.92	416.74	416.69
21000	490.40	477.74	448.47	440.63	438.41	437.77	437.58	437.53
22000	513.75	500.49	469.82	461.61	459.28	458.61	458.42	458.36
23000	537.11	523.24	491.18	482.59	480.16	479.46	479.25	479.20
24000	560.46	545.99	512.53	503.58	501.04	500.30	500.09	500.03
25000	583.81	568.74	533.89	524.56	521.91	521.15	520.93	520.86
26000	607.16	591.49	555.24	545.54	542.79	542.00	541.77	541.70
27000	630.51	614.24	576.60	566.52	563.67	562.84	562.60	562.53
28000	653.87	636.99	597.95	587.51	584.54	583.69	583.44	583.37
29000	677.22	659.73	619.31	608.49	605.42	604.53	604.28	604.20
30000	700.57	682.48	640.66	629.47	626.29	625.38	625.11	625.04
31000	723.92	705.23	662.02	650.45	647.17	646.22	645.95	645.87
32000	747.28	727.98	683.37	671.43	668.05	667.07	666.79	666.71
33000	770.63	750.73	704.73	692.42	688.92	687.92	687.62	687.54
34000	793.98	773.48	726.08	713.40	709.80	708.76	708.46	708.37
35000	817.33	796.23	747.44	734.38	730.68	729.61	729.30	729.21
40000	934.09	909.98	854.22	839.29	835.06	833.84	833.48	833.38
45000	1050.85	1023.72	960.99	944.20	939.44	938.07	937.67	937.55
50000	1167.61	1137.48	1067.77	1049.11	1043.82	1042.29	1041.85	1041.72
55000	1284.38	1251.22	1174.55	1154.02	1148.20	1146.52	1146.04	1145.90
60000	1401.14	1364.96	1281.32	1258.93	1252.58	1250.75	1250.22	1250.07
65000	1517.90	1478.71	1388.10	1363.85	1356.96	1354.98	1354.41	1354.24
70000	1634.66	1592.46	1494.88	1468.76	1461.35	1459.21	1458.59	1458.41
75000	1751.42	1706.20	1601.65	1573.67	1565.73	1563.44	1562.78	1562.58
80000	1868.18	1819.95	1708.43	1678.58	1670.11	1667.67	1666.96	1666.76
85000	1984.94	1933.70	1815.20	1783.49	1774.49	1771.90	1771.15	1770.93
90000	2101.70	2047.44	1921.98	1888.40	1878.87	1876.13	1875.33	1875.10
95000	2218.46	2161.19	2028.76	1993.31	1983.25	1980.35	1979.51	1979.27
100000	2335.22	2274.93	2135.53	2098.22	2087.64	2084.58	2083.70	2083.44
105000	2451.99	2388.68	2242.31	2203.13	2192.02	2188.81	2187.88	2187.62
110000	2568.75	2502.43	2349.09	2308.04	2296.40	2293.04	2292.07	2291.79
115000	2685.51	2616.17	2455.86	2412.95	2400.78	2397.27	2396.25	2395.96
120000	2802.27	2729.92	2562.64	2517.86	2505.16	2501.50	2500.44	2500.13
125000	2919.03	2843.67	2669.42	2622.78	2609.54	2605.73	2604.62	2604.30
130000	3035.79	2957.41	2776.19	2727.69	2713.92	2709.96	2708.81	2708.47
135000	3152.55	3071.16	2882.97	2832.60	2818.31	2814.19	2812.99	2812.65
140000	3269.31	3184.91	2989.75	2937.51	2922.69	2918.42	2917.18	2916.82
145000	3386.07	3298.65	3096.52	3042.42	3027.07	3022.64	3021.36	3020.99
150000	3502.83	3412.40	3203.30	3147.33	3131.45	3126.87	3125.55	3125.16
155000	3619.60	3526.15	3310.07	3252.24	3235.83	3231.10	3229.73	3229.33
160000	3736.36	3639.89	3416.85	3357.15	3340.21	3335.33	3333.92	3333.51

OWNERSHIP

Real Property versus Personal Property

The law of the land recognizes only two forms of property; real and personal property. That which is not personal property is considered to be real property, and that which is not real property is consider to be personal property.

In a broad sense of the term real property, real estate, realty and land are considered synonymous. A lot with the house included may be called land and the reference would include the house. However, land with a house on it or any form of construction on it is technically referred to as improved property, or improved real estate, while totally vacant land is referred to as unimproved property or unimproved real estate.

Personal Property

Personal property items are referred to as "Chattels". They include furniture, automobiles, cash, promissory notes, or anything else that is not considered real property. Then, in a broad sense of the term, all property which is movable and not attached to real property is considered to be personal property.

Real Property

Real property is the land, that which is attached to the land (improvements such as houses, fences and trees) and that which is appurtenant to the land (rights of way). Not only the surface soil of the land is included, but the minerals and water beneath, as well.

Minerals, such as gold and silver, are real property. However, once they are removed from the ground they become personal property. Farmed crops may be personal property, even before they are harvested from the land. These crops can be sold separate from the land as personal property.

Water Rights

An owner of land which borders on a river or stream is said to be a **Riparian Owner**. If his property touches or adjoins a navigable river, his property line extends to the low water mark. Ownership of the river beds of navigable streams is vested in the State.

In the case of a non-navigable stream, a riparian owner's title extends to the middle of the stream while the riparian owner across the stream owns to the middle of the bed from his side. If an owner's property adjoins ocean or tidal waters, his property line extends to the high water mark. If his property adjoins ocean beaches, his property line extends to

Water Rights (cont)

the high tide line, while the State owns the tideland.

Riparian owners are entitled to the reasonable use of water flowing adjacent to their land. However, an owner cannot erect a dam in order to divert an unreasonable amount of water to his land, as other owners along the river are entitled to reasonable use of the water.

The upper limit of earth saturated with underground water is called the **Water Table.** In areas where heavy rainfall prevails the water table can be merely a few feet beneath the earth's surface. Conversely, in desert areas the water table would be several hundred feet below the surface.

Waters that overflow a regular defined channel are referred to as **Flood Waters.** Riparian owners may dike against flood waters but cannot divert them onto another's property. **Surface Waters** are the result of a cloudburst. Property owners are responsible for absorbing their share of surface waters along with adjoining property owners.

Easements

An easement is the right to cross another's land. An easement that is appurtenant to (part of) the owner's land cannot be sold off separately and must be transferred with the title to the land to which it is appurtenant.

Trade Fixtures

When personal property becomes affixed to real estate it becomes real property. As an example: Should a tenant (lessee) secure walnut paneling to the wall of a house he is renting, he cannot legally remove this paneling without the consent of the landlord (lessor).

There is however, an exception to this rule that affixed personal property becomes real property. Items that are standard for a specific business, such as kitchen equipment for a restaurant and theatre seats for a cinema can be secured to real estate and later removed without the consent of the lessor. However, if they are so removed that damage is caused to the premises, the lessee is required to restore the property to its original condition.

To avoid problems between the parties, it is a good practice to set forth in the lease agreement what items can be removed and the responsibility of each party. Generally, in a trial dispute between lessee and lessor, the courts apply the following tests to determine if an item is real or personal property; method of attachment; adaptability of item to property; inten-

Trade Fixtures (cont.)

tion when item was attached; relationship of parties (buyer and seller, or tenant and landlord).

Estates in Property

One who has ownership of property is said to have the exclusive right to use, enjoy and profit from its possession. His ownership is referred to as an estate. An owner of an estate may have a whole interest or a part interest.

The word "estate" includes all property holdings, both real and personal. When a person dies leaving an estate, such an estate would not only include all his real estate holdings, but all jewelry, automobiles, cash, etc.

Fee Estate

Of the various forms of ownership of real estate, the most common and inclusive type of interest is a Fee Simple Estate, or additionally referred to as fee simple interest, fee simple absolute estate, fee estate, or an estate of inheritance. Each of these phrases mean the same form of ownership. In order for an estate to be a fee estate, it is required to be: freely transferable; freely inheritable; and have a definite duration.

Life Estate

A more limited form of ownership, one that is measured by the life of a person is known as a Life Estate. A life estate may be limited by the life span of the person holding the life estate (Frank gives Andy any estate until Andy dies), or a life estate may be limited to the life span of a third person (Frank gives Andy an estate until Bertha dies). In the first example, Andy cannot will his interest in the estate to another since he only holds interest in the estate during his life span. In the second example, Andy can will his interest, however it will only last until Bertha dies.

Provisions in a life estate deed will provide that upon the death of the grantee, the estate will automatically revert to the grantor or to some other person written into the deed.

Forms of Ownership

Tenants in Common

When two or more persons buy property and own it together, they are called tenants in common. In this form of ownership, if one of the tenants in common should die, his heirs will receive his interest in the property.

Forms of Ownership (cont.)

Joint Tenancy

When two or more persons own property as joint tenants, they both have an undivided interest and equal rights to the use of the property. If either dies, his interest immediately reverts to the remaining joint tenant, who is said to hold the "right of survivorship".

Community Property

Community Property is another form of ownership held by more than one person, but it is limited to husband and wife. Ownership by close relatives, other than husband and wife, would not be community property ownership. It would have to be either joint tenancy, tenancy in common, or a form of partnership.

Joint Ventures and Syndicates

These are formal arrangements whereby groups of investors pool their funds to purchase one or more properties. In a joint venture, two or more people simply agree to combine their property, efforts and skills for a business purpose.

With a syndicate, a more formal type of group venture, several investors contribute funds and receive profits, while the work of handling the investment is left to one or more general partners or a management team.

The main advantage of a group investment is that, because of the larger sums of money available, more profitable property can usually be purchased, and more leverage is attainable.

Joint ventures and syndicates are not legal terms insofar as the tax laws are concerned. Such ventures, depending on the way they are structured, are classified as corporations, partnerships and real estate investment trusts. Corporations are legal entities that exist indefinitely, independent of any one owner or investor. Through corporate structuring, an investor may sell or transfer his interest in a venture without disturbing the corporate investments. In a corporation, an investor's risk or liability is limited to the amount of his investment. The management of a corporation is vested in the controlling body referred to as the Board of Directors.

The disadvantage of corporate structuring for certain purposes is the potential for double taxation. The total profits of the corporation are taxable. Then, the corporate owner's share of the net profit is taxed once again as a part of regular income.

Partnerships exist where two or more persons operate a business as co-owners. A partnership avoids double taxation, as each partner is taxed only upon his share of the profits - the partnership as a whole is not subject to the tax laws.

Forms of Ownership (cont.)

In a General Partnership, each partner is liable for any or all of the partnership's debts, so that liability is not limited to the amount of investment. Each general partner participates in the management of the business, and the death of either partner terminates the partnership.

Because of the risk involved in a general partnership, most investors prefer a variation which is called a Limited Partnership. This latter way of structuring a joint venture has the benefits and advantages of both the corporation and the partnership for many kinds of business ventures. With a limited partnership, liability of an investor is limited to the amount of his investment, and the partnership can continue despite death or withdrawal of a limited partner. A limited partnership places management in the hands of one or more general partners, as the limited partners are forbidden to function in the operation of the business.

The Real Estate Investment Trust (REIT) is an unincorporated association which is managed by one or more trustees. Although similar to a corporation, it is not taxed in the same way because of a special exemption granted in the Federal tax laws.

To qualify as an REIT, some of the requirements are:

1. Must be managed and operated by trustees.
2. Must be beneficially owned by 100 or more investors.
3. Cannot retain property for sale to customers (such as a subdivision, housing tracts and so forth).
4. No more than five people (or less) may own more than a total of 50% of the shared assets.
5. 90% of the gross income must be from investments, rents, dividends and interest.
6. 75% of gross income must be from real estate investment.
7. 90% of taxable income must be distributed as profits, except for net capital gains.

Leases

A lease is an agreement between a tenant (lessee) and an owner (lessor) whereby the tenant agrees to pay a specified rental on a certain property for a specific period of time, whereby the tenant is given the right to use, occupy and peacefully enjoy the owner's property. In addition to being a contract, a lease is a conveyance or transfer of property rights, and it must contain the following to be legally binding: form, intention, delivery and term.

Leases (cont)

Some states allow verbal leases when the term is of one year or less. However, it is better practice to have all leases in writing to avoid any potential disputes. A lease signed by the lessor, when delivered to the lessee becomes binding when the lessee moves in and pays rent, whether or not the lessee signs the lease.

When a lessee abandons the property during the term of the lease, he is not released from his obligation. Lessor may sue for rent as it becomes due. If lessor rents abandoned premises to another party, he can only recover his actual losses from the breaker of the lease.

Death by a lessee or lessor does not cancel the lease, which is binding upon the heirs. If the lessee dies, the lessor can file a rent claim against the deceased's estate.

Lessee is required to take "reasonable care" of the property, unless the lease requires him to keep it in a specified condition.

A lessee may sublet all or part of the leased property, often for a higher rental, unless a provision in the lease prevents this. When a subletter sublets in turn to another tenant, he is said to hold a "sandwich lease".

A percentage lease is a special form usually used for retail business, where a percentage of the gross sales is used to determine the amount of rent. A minimum base rent is stipulated by the lessor, to cover periods of reduced sales. Sometimes such leases are structured as "triple net leases", wherein the tenant is responsible, not only for paying the owner a percentage of gross income, but also for real estate taxes, insurance and maintenance.

A graduated lease is a lease which provides for varying rental rates, often based on periodic re-evaluation of the property or the consumer price index.

Deeds

Deeds are written instruments used to transfer ownership interest in real estate. There are several types of deeds depending on required usage. Most commonly used, expecially in California, is the Grant Deed, by which the seller transfers, assigns, or grants (all are used interchangeably) to the buyer, title to the property described in the deed.

Warranty Deeds are similar to grand deeds, except in addition to granting title to the property described in the deed, it expressly states a warranty. This warranty not only guarantees the title of the person granting the deed, but it also warrants any defects from former owners or any condition that could affect the title.

Warranty Deeds (cont)

When sellers of real property furnish buyers with title guarantee insurance, the use of a warranty deed is seldom demanded by buyers.

Quitclaim Deeds are used to clear any defects in the title and release any interest the present or former grantors might have in the property.

The Eviction Process

The following explains the step-by-step procedure for legally evicting a tenant in the case of non-payment of rent. This procedure may vary slightly from state to state:

1. Tenant is served with a "3-Day Notice to Pay Rent or Quit the Premises" when the tenant is more than three days delinquent with his rent.

2. If, after three days, no rent is received and the tenant stays on and does not quit the premises, an "Un-lawful Detainer" is filed with the Municipal Court and a Summons is issued.

3. The Summons and Complaint is served on the tenant, who then has a right to file a plea and an answer to the Complaint. If this occurs, a trial will be held. Otherwise,

4. Default of the tenant is assumed by the court, which then issues a Default Judgment.

5. The court issues a Writ of Possession to the Sheriff or Marshall.

6. The Sheriff or Marshall evicts the tenant (physically or otherwise).

Occassionally it will be necessary to evict a tenant for other reasons than non-payment of rent, such as unauthorized pets, too much noise, or too many people living on the premises. To evict under these circumstances, you must serve the tenant with a 30-Day Notice To Terminate Tenancy. If the tenant moves out within the prescribed thirty days, there is no need to proceed further. If, however, the tenant remains on the premises after the prescribed thirty days, you must begin with procedure #2 under the eviction process above, and follow all the subsequent steps.

Eminent Domain

The right vested in the federal, state, county or local government to take private property for public use is called eminent domain. When a government exercises its right of eminent domain, it must pay just compensation to the property owner who had his property condemned. Use of eminent domain is common for the construction of freeways, public parks, and expansion of airports.

Adverse Possession

Under the law of adverse possession, it is possible for someone who never received a deed to a particular property to take possession for a certain period of time and acquire rightful ownership. In order to lawfully do so, the claimant must occupy the property openly and continuously for at least five years, pay the taxes for five consecutive years, claim the subject property adversely to the owner, and have color of title.

The adversity requirement means that the claimant must be in possession without consent of the owner and that he does not recognize the owner's title. (Payment of rent would nullify the adversity requirement because it implies the claimant recognizes the owner's title). Color of title means there is existence of an invalid deed, or other instrument which is in disfavor of the adverse possessor.

The adverse possessor may perfect title to the subject property by either final court order or quitclaim deed from the record owner.

FINANCE

Sources of Real Estate Funding

Although commercial banks rank the largest with respect to overall volume of lending for the short and long term business, commercial, and mortgage loans, savings and loan associations supply the largest percentage of real estate financing.

The function of mortgage lenders has been essentially the same over the centuries. Starting in the early days of colonial America, countrymen who were fortunate enough to save any money joined with others to pool their funds in a safe place. The accumulated savings would then be loaned to other members of the community to build or improve their property.

Savings and Loan Associations

Since those early colonial days, a lot has happened to improve these thrift institutions. Before the Great Depression there was little government regulation to watch over these associations, but the Depression brought to the surface the many inherent problems which before were not evident.

The major problem was flexibility due to the long term nature of the majority of their outstanding loans. This often caused liquidity problems when depositors suddenly decided to withdraw needed funds. The crisis was overcome in 1932 by the creation of the Federal Home Loan Bank Board. This authority, which is still in operation today, provided member associations with liquidity by offering a continuing source of funds for emergencies or additional mortgage loans.

Savings and Loan Associations (cont.)

Then in 1933, the Federal Home Loan Bank Board was given the authorization to issue federal charters to newly formed savings and loans. These charters regulated methods of operation and required certain standards of compliance. In 1934, the Federal Savings and Loan Insurance Corporation (FSLIC) was created to provide insurance on deposits for all federally chartered associations. That insurance coverage currently protects any one depositor up to $40,000.

Although the Federal Home Loan Bank Board governs federally chartered savings and loan associations, there are also state chartered associations. The majority of financing made available by these thrift institutions is in the form of conventional loans secured by residential real estate and sometimes commercial property. They also underwrite VA and FHA loans which are considered to be non-conventional loans. In addition, they make loans for construction, home improvement and on mobile homes. They are not authorized to make consumer or business loans.

Mutual Savings Banks

Their origins are similar to that of savings and loans. They exist primarily in the Northeastern and Northwestern areas of the United States. They are all state chartered and mutually owned by their depositors, although managed by an elected group of trustees.

Their investment portfolio consists of approximately 75% mortgage loans, and the balance is made up of government securities, and personal and consumer type loans.

Commercial Banks

Commercial banks are the largest of all lenders, but only an estimated 2% of their investment portfolio is in the form of loans on real property. The bulk of their financing involves business and consumer loans. Larger banks are an important source of commercial and industrial real estate financing. And can either be state or federally chartered.

State chartered banks must comply to the regulations of a state banking board or commission while national banks are under the jurisdiction of the Federal Reserve System. The Federal Deposit Insurance Corporation (FDIC) insures the deposits of its members up to $40,000. State banks can also belong to the FDIC, but most comply with state regulations.

Insurance Companies

Insurance companies were not initially created for the purpose of providing long term real estate financing. Their primary interest is to supply a

Insurance Companies (cont.)

high yield on investment funds, yet at a low risk to provide safety for policy holder's money which is available on mortgages secured by real property.

They are governed by the state in which they operate. The bulk of their lending is long term and usually on large income producing real estate including residential, commercial as well as industrial. Often they will require equity participation when large real estate projects are to be financed.

Credit Unions

The employees of many companies have formed credit unions for the benefit of their own members. They are an invaluable source of funds and credit unions pay their depositors interest on savings, and have year end profit sharing. The majority of their lendable funds are loaned to members for the purchase of cars and furniture. Recently, some have started making long term real estate loans at very reasonable interest rates.

Private Mortgage Insurance

Numerous private mortgage insurance companies are now insuring real estate loans similar to that of FHA. A portion of the loan is insured against default by the borrower, the premium of which is paid for by the borrower.

Private mortgage insurance allows lenders to make higher loan-to-value ratios, thereby allowing more buyers to purchase with less of a down payment. Furthermore, discounts or points are eliminated due to the fact that interest rates are the effective rates in the prevailing money market.

Mortgage Bankers

Mortgage Bankers function as a financial intermediary between institutional lenders and borrowers, bringing both together for a fee. This fee, or commission, is usually one to two percent of the funds appropriated. They do not fund the money directly, but appropriate the money, then administer and service the loan for a fee. This additional service fee usually falls within a range of one half to one percent of the loan proceeds, depending on the extent of the service provided. They usually represent insurance companies, savings and loan associations, and pension funds.

Mortgage Companies

Mortgage companies operate similar to mortage bankers only they represent private lenders and government backed loans, such as VA and FHA loans.

Home Loan Companies

Home loan companies also operate similarly to the above financial intermediaries, except they deal mostly in second trust deeds and represent private investors. Their fee for originating and servicing the loan is between 10 and 20 points, which is charged to the borrower.

Loan Brokers

Loan brokers function as a financial intermediary, however they can represent lenders directly or they can represent any of the above three types of companies.

Organized solutions to the variety of problems related to real estate financing would not exist today without the presence of loan brokers. They bring the borrower and lender together and monitor the many legal safeguards and other controls available to assure the security of the transaction. To fulfill their obligation, they must not only protect the individual lender, but the borrower as well.

Licensed real estate brokers are authorized to act as loan brokers in many states. In practice, some real estate brokers arrange loans, and others sell property; the two tend to specialize. The loan broker arranges financing through private lenders for prospective home buyers who do not have sufficient funds to make up the difference between a first mortgage and the total sales price. The loan broker serves the real estate salesman as a clearing house of available loans, freeing him to concentrate on his basic objective . . . sales.

Loan brokers serve the borrower by arranging funds for specific needs that might otherwise not be available. One such instance would be when a prospective home buyer does not have the difference between the first mortgage and the total sales price. Another would be when a homeowner requires funds for an emergency but doesn't have adequate credit or collateral except for his home. In either event, the loan broker could arrange for secondary financing through a private lender.

Loan broker services are not restricted to arranging first and second loans through private lenders. They usually represent most institutional lenders, plus union, private pension and trust funds, and surplus corporate funds. A first mortgage or trust deed may be financed through an institutional lender with the broker negotiating the most favorable loan possible on behalf of the borrower.

If time is of the essence, the broker may advise arranging a second mortgage through a private lender. When the broker receives and approves an application for such a loan, he seeks out a lender usually from a list of available contacts.

Loan Brokers (cont.)

At this time, the role of the loan broker as an intermediary between two laymen becomes particularly important. As a professional with knowledge of economic trends and real estate values, he advises how much may be safely borrowed, arranges title searches and escrow services, provides title and fire insurance, and secures all other safeguards.

It is also the responsibility of the loan broker to protect the borrower against illegal charges. Real estate loan brokers provide their borrowers with a full disclosure of finance and interest charges. These disclosures are in writing and outline all charges such as the annual interest, broker's loan fee, and all escrow fees. Upon completion of the transaction, a borrower knows exactly the proceeds of the loan as well as the charges.

Serving the lender, whether private or institutional, the real estate loan broker has generated a large volume of business. This generation of second mortgages and trust deeds has made possible the purchase of homes by hundreds of thousands of families who otherwise could not afford them. This has increased the demand for first trust deeds and mortgages, contributing to an increase in overall mortgage activity and to an expansion of the overall economy.

The loan broker, along with his fellow real estate brokers, is closer to the broad source of demand for financing than a specific institution. He acts informally as a "field man" to generate this additional volume.

To the private lender the loan broker has become a source of sound real estate investment opportunities yielding a fair rate of return. These investments have the advantage of being secured by real property that has been appraised by experienced people. They usually are short term, provide reasonable liquidity, and yield an annual rate of return of 10 to 13% interest.

Brokers not only serve lenders as a medium of investment, but provide a number of services for their protection. They investigate and appraise the property involved, create and record the loan documents, and set up the mechanics for making the transaction convenient. At the option of the lender, they may assist in making collections.

Investing through a loan broker provides the lender with unusual flexibility. He may choose a first mortgage or trust deed, offering longer term stability as a lesser rate of interest. Or he may choose a second mortgage or trust deed for higher interest over a shorter period.

Loan Brokers (cont)

Should the holder of a mortgage or trust deed find it impractical to hold it to maturity, he may sell it at a discount, either to a broker or to a private investor through a broker. In some circumstances the broker may advise the owner of a note to keep it and borrow with the note as collateral. When he borrows on the note, immediate cash is realized as it would be if he had sold it, but ownership is still retained. The privilege of realizing most of the principal and the balance of the interest is still available.

Thus the real estate loan broker not only helps arrange the investment, but also is in a position to assist with any problems that may arise out of an unforseen need for liquidity.

Financial Instruments

Mortgages

A mortgage or trust deed from a lender is referred to as conventional financing when VA and FHA government backed loans are not involved. Both are agreements between borrower and lender creating liens against real property. In other words, the agreement states that, should the borrower default on the loan, a mortgage or trust deed will allow the lender to sell the property in order to satisfy the loan obligation.

The two parties involved in a mortgage are referred to as the **Mortgagor,** who is the property owner or borrower, and the **Mortgagee,** or lender. There are two parts to a mortgage instrument: the **Mortgage Note,** which is evidence of the debt; and the **Mortgage Contract,** which is security for the debt. The note promises to repay the loan, while the Contract promises to convey title of the property to the **Mortgagee** in case of default.

Should the Mortgagor fail to make payments, the property can then be sold through court action known as "foreclosure". The foreclosure process is quite lengthy and complex. First, the Mortgagee must obtain from the court a foreclosure judgment, which orders the sheriff to sell the property to the bidder (over and above that which is due the lender). The property is then put up for public auction. Should a successful bid be made, the bidder receives from the sheriff a document known as the **Certificate of Sale**. The highest bidder must then hold the certificate for one year before he will be issued the deed to the property. If, within that year, the Mortgagor pays the bidder sufficient monies (bid price plus interest), the Mortgagor then retains ownership of the property and the foreclosure sale is nullified. The period during which a Mortgagor is entitled to redeem his property is referred to as the **Mortgagor's Equity of Redemption.**

Trust Deeds

Trust deeds are similar to mortgages except that: a) an additional third party is involved, and b) the foreclosure period is shorter, without a court action.

With a trust deed, the property owner or borrower is called the **Trustor**, and the lender is the **Beneficiary**. The intermediate third party whose function is to hold title to the property for the security of the lender is called the **Trustee**.

Should the Trustor default on his loan obligation, the subject property will be sold by the Trustee at public auction through a "power of sale" clause contained in all trust deeds, without court procedure.

Foreclosure is initiated by a **Notice of Default,** which is recorded by the Trustee, with a copy sent to the Trustor. After three months, a **Notice of Sale** is posted on the property, and an advertisement for sale is carried in local newspapers once a week for three weeks. If during this period, the trustor fails to pay the Beneficiary sufficient funds to halt the foreclosure (overdue loan payments, plus interest, penalties and fees), the sale will then be conducted by the Trustee. Proceeds from the foreclosure sale are disbursed to the Beneficiary, then to any other lien holders.

Second Mortgages and Trust Deeds

An owner of real property is entitled to arrange more than one loan against the same property, which then stands as security against default for the payment of the second loan. This "junior" or "subordinate" loan is called a "second" because it is second in priority to a first loan with respect to a claim upon the proceeds in the event of a foreclosure sale.

During the course of many real estate transactions, secondary financing becomes necessary in order to consummate the deal when conventional financing, along with the down payment, may be insufficient to accommodate the full purchase price. If the savings and loan will loan only 80% of the purchase price, and the buyer can only put up 10% as a down payment, the remaining 10% balance can be obtained through such additional financing. Often, a secondary loan is carried by the seller himself, in the form of a second mortgage or trust deed. This type of loan is referred to as a **Purchase Money Second** when the seller of real property carries back a loan to accommodate the sale of his property.

Unlike a Purchase Money Second, a **Hard Money Second** is a loan secured by a second trust deed or mortgage whereas the owner of real property receives hard cash dollars in return for a second mortgage or trust deed.

Second Mortgages and Trust Deeds (cont.)

Most secondary financing involves a term of from three to five years, and carries interest rates slightly higher than first mortgages and trust deeds. Monthly payments are typically one percent of the amount financed (i.e., a secondary loan for $10,000 will have monthly payments of $100). Secondary financing can be structured to the buyer's advantage through reduction of monthly payments and/or an increase in the term of the loan beyond the accepted five year term.

Land Contract

Also referred to as Contract of Sale of Conditional Sales Contract. This form of agreement in the sale of real property is strictly a contract between buyer and seller, without a financial intermediary involved. The buyer agrees to purchase a property and pays principal and interest to the seller along with a down payment. The title to the property remains vested with the seller until the conditions of the contract are fulfilled. The buyer retains possession of the property. Should the buyer default on the agreement, the property reverts back to the seller and the buyer loses his interest invested in the property.

This form of financing real property is ideal during "tight money" conditions as interest rates on a land contract can be set between buyer and seller, often at lesser rates than current market rates. Furthermore, a more lenient down payment may be required by the seller or less restrictive credit requirements can be offered because no financial intermediary is involved in this type of transaction.

VA Loans

This is a government backed loan extended to qualified veterans, entitling them to borrow money for homes, mobile homes and farms with 100% financing at interest rates below market rates. The VA Loan is underwritten and processed by conventional lenders, but a portion of the loan is guaranteed by the Veterans Administration against default.

In order to protect the veteran himself and assist the lender in approving or disapproving the loan, the Veterans Administration will have the property appraised and then will issue a Certificate of Reasonable Value (CRV). A veteran may purchase a home at whatever price he wishes to pay, but a VA loan cannot be secured for more than the value of the CRV, with any amount in excess of that paid in cash by the veteran.

Although a portion of the loan is guaranteed by the VA, the veteran must repay the lender and, if he defaults, he will lose the property. Any loss incurred by the lender will be compensated by the VA, but the veteran must eventually repay the government.

FHA LOANS

These government-backed loans, under the supervision of the Federal Housing Administration, are not restricted to veterans but are also available to other individuals who meet the requirements of the FHA. An FHA loan is underwritten and processed by conventional lending institutions, as with the VA loan, and the lender is similarly insured against default by the buyer. Thus, the lender is enabled to grant longer and more lenient terms, so that FHA loans offer a lower interest rate and smaller down payment than conventional financing.

Points and Fees

When a lending institution has been collecting for some time on a particular mortgage, and the payments have been regularly made on time, the loan is referred to as a "seasoned loan", meaning that it represents an A-1 credit situation. When a FHA or VA loan is seasoned, the lending institution which did the underwriting of the loan may decide to sell it for less than the remaining principal amount owing, in order to receive cash which then can be lent out at a higher rate of interest. It is to their advantage to do this because of the low interest rates fixed by the Federal Government on these guaranteed loans. The loan is discounted to increase the yield because otherwise, with the low interest rates, it would be difficult to attract buyers. (A loan may also be sold without a discount, of course. It is to the lender's advantage to sell a loan if he can then, lend out the proceeds at a higher rate of interest.)

The mortgage market is a critical part of the economy, and the low interest rates of government backed loans might not attract investors as they may seek higher yields elsewhere, unless the discount points are used to make the mortgage loan attractive to the investor.

A discount point represents 1/8% additional yield on a mortgage. Thus, if a FHA or VA loan at 8½% is discounted 4 points, or ½% (4 x 1/8), this means that the loan is sold by the mortgagee to an investor for an amount which will enable the investor to earn 9% on his money.

Loan fees are charged to the Mortgagor or Trustor to cover the lender's expenses. These are expenses that include credit investigations, loan application evaluation, and appraisal of the subject property.

Assuming a Mortgage

When a buyer of real property assumes a mortgage (or trust deed), a formal agreement between buyer and lender is executed. Often, the new buyer will be faced with an increase in the interest rate, along with an assumption fee, subject to approval of his credit.

Assuming a Mortgage (cont)

The actual assumption transfers the responsibility of payment of the mortgage to the new owner from the seller. Savings and loan associations and commercial banks will usually insist on formal assumptions of the existing mortgage because they most often include due-on-sale clauses in their mortgage instruments. NOTE: Existing VA and FHA loans can usually be assumed by a new buyer without credit qualification or change in interest rate, mainly because they do not have due-on-sale clauses written into the mortgage.

Taking Subject to Mortgage

A property is taken subject to a mortgage when there is no formal agreement between the lender and the new purchaser of the property. This can technically only occur when the note contains no due-on-sale clause, as in the case of VA, FHA, and most insurance company loans. Therefore, when there is not a due-on-sale clause, the lender's consent to the transfer is not necessary.

When the buyer takes subject to a mortgage, the primary responsibility for payment of the mortgage is with the original maker of the note. Since the lender only has a contractual agreement with the original borrower, the new owner is not technically obligated to pay off the mortgage debt because he never agreed to it in writing. The only time there is reason for concern by the seller is when the new buyer has a thin equity position in the property.

In the event of default, the lender would foreclose and then sell the property. If there are enough proceeds from the sale to satisfy the balance owing on the mortgage, the original borrower will be released from all obligations on the mortgage. If the property does not yield sufficient proceeds to cover the loan balance, the lender may have legal recourse to recover the deficiency, depending on the individual state laws where the property is located.

APPRAISAL

An appraisal of real estate is an opinion, or estimate, of the value of a property, made by gathering and analyzing the essential data as of a specific date. The appraisal is based upon the "highest and best use" of that property, that use which will produce the greatest net return. Such an estimate must take into consideration zoning laws, government regulations and the demand for that type of property in the area.

The appraisal of real property is done by various methods, and the final opinion of value is given by weighing the values from each method used, i.e., by comparison.

Appraisal (cont)

Appraisal of real estate is an art and not a science: the appraiser is actually arriving at a range of values wherein the subject property may be expected to sell. Although three different appraisers may come up with three different opinions of value, each opinion will probably fall within a close range.

General Factors That Influence Value

The general factors which go into determining the value of a property are simply those of supply and demand. If land of that type is scarce or limited, the property value increases. A corollary of this principle is that value increases in areas of expanding population, or when property has special attributes, such that a larger number of people seek it out. Examples of this principle can be portrayed by the variance in land values throughout the United States. Land in populated areas of California, the Southwest and Florida has gone up in value substantially more than in areas of the east and mideast. This is primarily due to a better climate in these areas which causes a migration to these areas from other areas of the country. In other words, more people are seeking out similar types of property.

The utility, or usefulness of the property is then taken into account. I once saw a home that had been added-onto in such a way that it was necessary to go through the kitchen and main bathroom in order to get to the master bedroom. This bizarre arrangement was obviously entered into as a way of making improvement costs lower, but it also substantially altered the usefulness (and thus the appraised value) of that residence. Other such features, comical or otherwise, can affect the value upwards or downwards.

Finally the transferability of a property will strongly affect its value. When a property is tied up in an estate, or is heavily encumbered with liens or other difficulites, a buyer may look forward to having his monies tied up in escrow for months beyond what is normal, perhaps a year or more. Such encumbrances substantially reduce the value of the property, since it cannot easily be sold at all!

Selective Factors Influencing Value

Here, we can make a list of certain "wanted" or unwanted attributes affecting the appraised value of any particular property.

* In a residential neighborhood, curving streets, cul de sacs, and uneven elevations of terrain, especially where this creates a view, will tend to increase values.

Selective Factors Influencing Value (cont.)

* Proximity to such amenities as a lake, parks, shopping centers, schools and transportation will increase the value of residential homes.

* Fireplaces, patios, sundecks, views, tastefully color-coordinated interiors and exteriors and other such luxury items, will tend to increase the value of a residence. In contrast, the absence of such qualities in an otherwise prime neighborhood may lower the value.

* Areas adjacent to manufacturing facilities and truck terminals tend to become slums eventually, reducing property value. Even before such deterioration takes place, the appraised valuation is affected.

* Overcrowding of the land (i.e., buildings too close together), where no plans have been made for grass and trees, is another situation which tends to breed decay. Such poor land usage eventually creates tenements where crime, arson and other threatening factors arise.

* In commercial or business property, the availability of parking, pedestrian count, traffic count, corner versus mid-block location, and directional growth of the city will all affect the appraised value of a particular property.

Methods of Appraisal: Market Data Approach

There are three basic methods for appraising real estate. The most widely used is the "market date" or "comparable sales" approach. With this method, recent sales of comparable properties in the area are considered and compared to the subject property, and the value is then adjusted upward or downward according to the amenities, construction type, quality and individual location.

A simple example of the comparable method approach would be to compare the subject property with three properties which have sold within six months and are located within the same tract, and are essentially without any meaningful differences. Assume all these comparables have sold for between 50,000 and 51,000 dollars and that the subject property has a swimming pool, while the comparables do not. You determine that a swiming pool is worth about $10,000, therefore the subject property is worth about $61,000 ($51,000 plus $10,000 for the pool).

Reproduction Cost Method

The Reproduction, or "Replacement Cost" method of appraisal has three steps: 1. Determine today's cost of replacing all improvements on the property; 2. Deduct for all factors of depreciation to determine current appraised value of the improvements; 3. Add the current value to the

Reproduction Cost Method (cont.)

value of the land. (The land is not depreciated since it is generally considered irreplacable, indestructible and immovable).

Let us assume that the subject property consists of a standard brick home on a 60' x 150' lot, and the home is thirty years old. If today's construction costs are $35 per square foot and your property contains 1500 square feet of living space, it would cost 1500 x $35 or $52,500 to replace the improvement. Now you must deduct an allowable amount for thirty years of physical depreciation on the house. Assume in this case that it would take $3,000 to completely put the house in A-one condition. Then, if the current appraised value is $52,500 you would subtract $3,000 resulting in a true appraised depreciated value of the improvement of $49,500. If comparable vacant lots in that area are curently selling for $10,000, then your total appraised value of that property is $49,500 plus $10,000 for the land, or $59,500.

The reproduction cost method is predominatly used when appraising service properties such as public buildings, schools, and hospitals, and fairly new buildings of all types where the depreciation allowance is a minor factor in the overall appraisal.

Capitalization or "Income" Method

This approach to the appraisal of real estate is primarily used to determine the value of income property. Here the Net Operating Income of the property is used to determine its fair market value. Debt service and amount of down payment are not considered in this calculation.

This appraisal technique depends upon what the appraiser considers a suitable rate of return for investment capital in that particular area. Obviously, if you are investing in a high risk area, you must receive a higher return on your investment. Conversely, prime property carries a lower risk factor to the investor and thus a lower rate of return.

This rate of return upon invested capital is called the "Capitalization" or "Cap" Rate, and must be arbitrarily determined by the appraiser. The cap rate normally varies from 8% in the best neighborhoods to 12% in low income (high risk) areas, but this percentage must be adjusted based upon the "going rate" for that type of property.

The appraiser determines the rate within the 8% to 12% range by considering the risk of the investment along with the type of property and the quality of the income.

The Net Operating Income (NOI) is used to determine appraised value using this capitalization approach. To arrive at Net Operating Income,

Capitalization or "Income" Method (cont.)

you must first calculate the gross income (based upon 100% occupancy) and then deduct all operating expenses, including potential losses from bad debts and vacancy losses. Property taxes are then deducted, as well as management expenses, insurance, maintenance cost and repairs, replacement reserves, and so on.

If you want to appraise a property using this approach and you have calculated the net operating income for that property at $25,000, while the cap rate for that type of property in that area is 10% (average), the appraised value would equal the NOI of $25,000 divided by 10% or $250,000.

Appraisal by Gross Income Multiplier

This method of determining value cannot be classed as a professional approach, but it is often used as a quick off-the-cuff calculation by brokers and in advertisements, for comparing like properties. You will often see income properties advertised in the newspapers denoting a sales price as "eight times the gross". What this means is that the sales price of that particular property is eight times the gross income (income before deduction of expenses). For example, if gross income is $20,000, then the selling price would be $20,000 times 8, or $160,000.

This is merely a fast and simple method of determining an approximate value of income producing property, with respect only to gross income.

As with capitalization rate, the gross income multiplier is determined by the appraiser within a range of values, taking into consideration the "going rate" for that area. This going rate is normally between 4 and 12, with the lower number representing the less desirable locations.

So if the gross income equals $20,000 annually:

Multiplier	Value
Worst Area equals 4 Times	Gross Income equals $80,000
Average Area equals 7 Times	Gross Income equals $140,000
Best Area Equals 11 Times	Gross Income equals $220,000

The Gross Income Multiplier is mostly used as an immediate gauge to determine whether a property deserves further attention. It gives only a ball-park estimate, it does not reflect net income, and is not a reliable rule of thumb for arriving at an accurate appraised value.

Depreciation

In real estate, it is the loss in value for any cause from reproduction cost new. It is usually measured by estimating the difference between the current reproduction cost new and the estimated value of improvements as of the date of appraisal.

It should be noted that differences exist between "book" depreciation as calculated by an accountant and estimated loss in value determined by an appraisal.

For income tax purposes, a depreciation allowance can be deducted from operating profits of income property (this is where the term "tax shelter" came into existance - the owners of income property are sheltering, or protecting income through depreciation allowances).

While an owner may receive a positive cash income from an individual property, in most cases that income will be tax free after a suitable depreciation allowance is deducted from it. In other instances where an owner may not have positive cash flow, he can still apply a depreciation allowance and show a sizable tax loss. Then, that tax loss can be applied towards the taxpayer's income from other sources, thereby reducing his overall tax liability.

Essentially, any property held for the production of income can be depreciated, such as apartment buildings, rented homes, and whatever carpeting, furniture, appliances, and other equipment the owner may furnish.

Land is not depreciable. Therefore, to calculate depreciation on an apartment building, as we have said, the owner must determine how much of the property value can be allocated to the building.

The most acceptable method is to use the latest tax bill on the property. The tax bill will note the assessed value for both the building and the land. Add the sums given for both, then divide the total into the amount allocated to the building alone. The result will be a percentage figure. Multiply the percentage figure by the price paid for the property and the result will be that portion of the total value of the property which can be depreciated.

Example to determine amount of depreciation from tax bill

Assessed Improvements + Assessed Land Value = Total Assessment

| $50,000 | + | $10,000 | = | $60,000 |

Therefore: $50,000 divided by $60,000 equals .83 or 83%

Depreciation (cont.)

If you paid $250,000 for the property, then multiply this figure times .83 resulting in a depreciable allowance of $207,500 allocated to the improvement, less the value of the land which cannot be depreciated.

Now that we have determined the amount which can be depreciated ($207,500), you must decide the remaining economic life or useful life of the property.

Although the Internal Revenue Service has set various guidelines regarding useful life, for our purposes the following will suit most buildings.

1. Wood frame with brick veneer type buildings have a useful life of 25 to 30 years.

2. Concrete and block, 40 to 45 years.

3. Frame buildings, 25 years.

4. Brick buildings, 20 to 25 years.

5. Concrete and steel buildings have a useful life of 50 years.

Straight-Line Depreciation

This method offers an equal amount of depreciation each year over the usual life of an asset. If the depreciable property is valued at $80,000, with an estimated useful life of 40 years, then the straight line method will give a $2,000 per year deduction ($80,000 divided by 40 years equals $2,000 or 2.5% of the total allowable depreciation per year.)

125% Declining Balance Depreciation

This method is for "used" residential income property, as opposed to new construction. It offers 125% (1.25) of the straight line deduction, but the increase rate is applicable only to the remaining balance each year, not to the original cost. This method results in higher deductions during the early years and reduced deductions during the later years of useful life.

Using this method, the first year's depreciation is calculated at 125% of the straight line rate, or (for the property described in the previous example) 1.25 times $2,000 or $2,500.

The second year, depreciation is based upon the $80,000 cost minus the $2,500 already taken, or $77,500. The straight line yearly rate for this new value would be 2.5% of $77,500, or $1,937.50. Because you are using the declining balance method, you will now increase the deduction by a factor of 125%. $1,937.50 times 1.25 is $2,421.88, total depreciation for year number two.

150% Declining Balance Depreciation

This method is exactly like the preceeding one, except that the larger depreciation rate of 150% is allowed on the declining balance. This method may only be used by an investor who qualifies under the tax laws as a "first user". This means either that the owner was himself responsible for the building construction, or else he acquired the building before the units were leased or occupied.

Sum of the Years Digits Depreciation

This method is also available only to the "first user". Depreciation is calculated as follows: if the depreciable value of the property is $110,000 with a useful life of 10 years, the sum of the digits of those years (i.e. 1 plus 2 plus 3 ... plus 10) or a total of 55 years is the denominator of your multiplier, and the number of years is the numerator. In this case, your multiplier is 10/55 or .18. This, times the original value of $110,000 is your depreciation allowance for the first year. For year number two, 9/55 or .16 is used, for the third year 8/55, and so on.

Options

An option is a contract. Defined, it is an agreement in writing, whereby the owner (optionor) gives to another (optionee) the exclusive right upon certain conditions for a limited period of time to purchase or lease his property.

An option requires a consideration to be valid. One dollar is sufficient. If an option agreement is not exercised prior to its expiration date, it automatically expires.

When an option is extended or renewed for an additional term, there must be additional consideration given.

Options are assignable like any other agreement of sale.

The purpose of an option is to give the holder, in return for his paid consideration, a period of time to make up his mind whether he will elect to purchase or lease the subject property. During the term of the option, the property is withdrawn from other buyers. Should the optionee decline to exercise the option, the consideration paid for the option is forfeited. If he does in fact exercise his option, the consideration paid can be applied, depending on the written terms, toward the purchase price.

Listing Agreements

Real estate agents work through agreements called "listings" - formal written agreements entered into for the purpose of securing clients to buy, lease, or rent property. A listing is an employment contract between the

Listing Agreement (cont)

owner and the agent, authorizing the agent to perform the service of selling the property. The following are the most common listing agreements:

a) **Exclusive Listing** - An exclusive right-to-sell listing is preferred by most agents, as it protects the broker's commission. With an exclusive listing, the broker receives his commission whether he is the selling agent or not.

b) **Exclusive Agency Listing** - This form of listing allows the agent to sell the property over a specified time, however, it reserves the right of the owner (seller) to sell the property himself without the payment of a commission. The seller is obligated to pay a commission to the exclusive agency listing broker if anyone other then the seller finds a buyer.

c) **Multiple Listing** - This is a modified form of the exclusive right-to-sell, where the owner authorizes the agent to place the property with a large group of cooperating, licensed brokers, referred to as "Multiple Listing Service". The multiple listing broadens the market for the property, since it reaches a greater number of agents, and, therefore, buyers. The advantage to the agent is that it increases the number of properties he can show, and thus, his potential sales.

d) **Open Listing** - This is a non-exclusive form of listing which simply entitles the first agent who procures a buyer to receive the commission. The seller can have numerous open listings with several agents. This is the reason this type of listing is unpopular among real estate brokers. With an open listing, little advertising or marketing effort will usually be extended by the broker, since there is no exclusive commission protection for an agent who is trying to make a sale.

e) **Net Listing** - Although legal, it is not often used by real estate brokers as it allows the selling agent to retain, as his commission, any amount in excess of what the seller wanted for his property.

Real Estate Purchase Contract and Deposit Receipt . . .

Clauses to Consider

*Purchaser to pay $ . . . . cash down payment, including the above deposit, plus the normal closing costs.

*This offer is subject to Purchaser obtaining a new first deed of trust (or mortgage) in the amount of $ . . . . payable at approximately $ . . . . per month including interest at . . . . . % per annum. Loan origination fee not to exceed . . . . . . points.

*Seller to carry a note secured by a second deed of trust (or mortgage) in the amount of $ . . . . payable at $ . . . . per month or more , including interest at . . . . . % per annum, with the entire balance due . . . . . years from date of this note. (Or upon sale or transfer of the property).
*"Or more" clause allows the purchaser an early pay-off of the loan.

*Seller to deliver to escrow all copies of leases and rental agreements within . . . . . days from acceptance of this agreement.

*This offer subject to Purchaser's approval of a Pest Control Report made by a company of his choice within . . . . . days from acceptance of this agreement.

*The purchase price includes all furniture and personal property used in the operation of the subject property including . . . .

*Purchaser to take possession of the subject property immediately upon recordation of the deed.

Land Description

Land is described by two methods, Government Survey and Metes and Bounds. Most commonly used is the government survey method which divides areas of a state using fixed imaginary lines (See diagram "A"). Land of the state is divided into townships which are 6 miles by 6 miles square consisting of 36 sections.

The State of California, for example, utilizes three sets of meridians and baselines. The Humboldt base and Meridian Lines refers to the northwest sector of the State. The Mount Diablo Base and Meridian Lines refer to the San Francisco Bay area, while the San Bernardino Base and Meridian Lines refer to Southern California.

Townships are again 6 miles by 6 miles square and are designated in relation to any given base and meridian line. In diagram "B", assuming we are using the San Bernardino Base and Meridian Lines, the first row of townships north of the base line is designated as T I N , all being townships located 1 North; the second row, Townships 2 North; the third row Townships 3 North, etc. You will also note that the first row of

Land Description (cont)

townships south of the baseline shows Townships 1 South, the second row, Townships 2 South, etc.

In this example, using the San Bernardino Base and Meridian Lines, the townships running south will continue numerically until they reach the southern border of the state. The townships running north will continue until they meet the townships running south from the Mount Diablo Base Line.

Before we can locate any given townships, we must first describe range and township lines. Range lines run north and south parallel to the meridian line. Township lines run east and west parallel to the base line. Now, to locate any given township, as in T2S, R2W, it would be Township 2 South, Range 2 West, San Bernardino Base and Meridian Lines, County of San Bernardino, State of California. Essentially this designation is stating that this particular township is located two rows south of the Base Line and two rows west of the Meridian Line of San Bernardino Base and Meridian Lines, State of California.

Sections (See Diagram "C")

Within a township are 36 sections, each one mile square. Sections are located and identified by numbers running one to thirty six. If you were to describe Section sixteen of a particular township, it would be described as follows: Section 16, Township 2 South, Range 2 West, San Bernardino Base and Meridian, County of San Bernardino, State of California.

Fractional Sections

Within a section there are 640 acres. If an owner of an entire section wishes to sell the whole section, it could be described as; Section 4, Township 3 South, Range 1 West, San Bernardino Base and Meridian Line, County of San Bernardino, State of California.

If that same owner decides to sell only the south half, the description in the deed will be as follows:

The south half of Section 4, Township 3 South, Range 1 West, San Bernardino Base and Meridian Lines, County of San Bernardino, State of California.

Metes and Bounds

The second method for describing land is referred to as Metes and Bounds. This method is primarily used when describing irregularly shaped land. An example of this method would be as follows:

Metes and Bounds (cont)

Beginning at a point located at the NW corner of the SW¼ of the NW¼ of Section 4; thence South ¾ of a mile, thence East ½ mile, thence in a straight line to the point of beginning.

To diagram the above description, you would first read backward from the first semicolon, the largest piece of Section 4 first as follows: Section 4; the NW¼, SW¼, and the NW corner of that SW¼.

The starting point is denoted as point "A" from where you will draw a straight line south ¾ of a mile. From this point you go East ½ of a mile along the bottom line of that section, then in a straight line back to the point of beginning.

To compute the number of acres in the above description simply calculate the area designated within the dotted line in diagram "E", then take half of that area for your final answer. Example: Our area is ¾ of a mile deep and ½ of a mile wide, and since 640 acres equal a full section, we multiply ½ x ¾ which equals .375. Divide this by 2 which results in .1875. Multiply this by 640 acres and the answer is 120 acres.

Land Description

One acre equals 43,560 feet.

If you have a lot 120' x 200', you have 24,000 square feet. To determine the acres you have, divide 24,000 square feet by 43,560. 43,560 ÷ 24,000 = .551. An acre is approximately 209' square.

Map of California
Designating Meridian and Base Lines
Diagram "A"

Humboldt Meridian
Mount Diablo Meridian

Humboldt
Base Line

Mount Diablo
Base Line

San Bernardino
Base Line

San Bernardino
Meridian

Diagram "B"
Land Description
"Township"

Meridian line

Range lines run
parallel to meridian lines

T3N R3W	T3N R2W	T3N R1W	T3N R1E	T3N R2E	T3N R3E
T2N R3W	T2N R2W	T2N R1W	T2N R1E	T2N R2E	T2N R3E
T1N R3W	T1N R2W	T1N R1W	T1N R1E	T1N R2E	T1N R3E
T1S R3W	T1S R2W	T1S R1W	T1S R1E	T1S R2E	T1S R3E
T2S R3W	T2S R2W	T2S R1W	T2S R1E	T2S R2E	T2S R3E
T3S R3W	T3S R2W	T3S R1W	T3S R1E	T3S R2E	T3S R3E

Base Line

Township lines run
parallel to base line

1 mi.

1 mi.

Township = 6 miles x 6 miles
= 36 Sections of 1 sq. mile each
1 Section = 1 mile x 1 mile

Diagram "C"

6	5	4	3	2	1
7	8	9	10	11	12
18	17	16	15	14	13
19	20	21	22	23	24
30	29	28	27	26	25
31	32	33	34	35	36

Diagram "D"

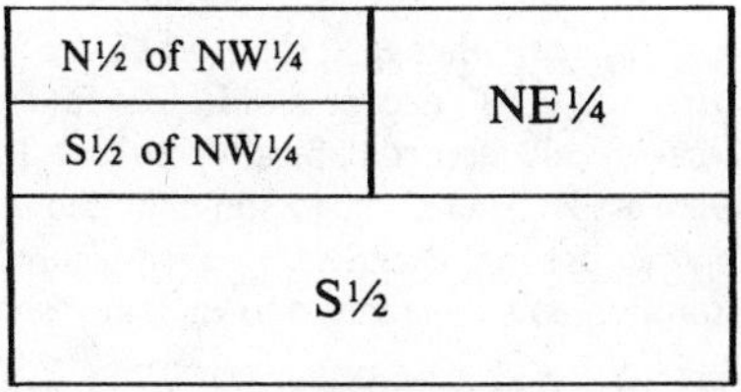
N½ of NW¼
S½ of NW¼
NE¼
S½

Zoning Symbols

C = Commercial zoning

M = Manufacturing/Industrial

P = Parking

R = Residential

Zoning Classification

A = Agricultural

C, C1, C2 = Light Commercial

C3 = Commercial, regional shopping center

C4 = Commercial (unlimited, i.e. service stations)

E = Estates

I = Industrial

M, M1, M2 = Industrial, manufacturing

M3 = Heavy manufacturing or industrial

P = Parking

R1 = Single family residence

R2 = Duplex

R3 = Multi-family housing

R4 = High density multi-family

T = Trailor park

MATHEMATICS OF REAL ESTATE

Many people, including newcomers to real estate investment, find their use of arithmetic after leaving school has been limited to balancing their checkbook and counting their change at the store. They feel ill prepared to deal with the percentages and decimals which are fundamentally used in real estate. All that is really needed to recall these basic fundamentals is to brush-up on these skills. Therefore, to stimulate those of you with a rusty memory for fractions and decimals, I have prepared some sample problems with a solution and explanation to each problem.

1. Problem: If a property sold for $80,000 and the broker's commission was 6% of the selling price, of which the salesperson was to receive 60%, how much would be the salesman's commission?

$80,000
  x .06
_____
$ 4,800.00 Broker's commission

$ 4,800
  x .60
_____
$ 2,880.00 Salesman's commission

2. Problem: If you purchase an apartment complex for $120,000 with a down payment of $24,000 and it yields a net income of $300 per month, what percentage are you receiving on your investment? Answer - 15%

Explanation: First of all the $120,000 purchase price is irrevelant to this problem because we are only interested in the return on the invested monies of $24,000. So first we will determine how much $300 per month amounts to in a year. $300 x 12 months = $3,600 annual net income. Now we can reword the question: If you purchase a $120,000 apartment with a down payment of $24,000 and it brings a net income of $3,600 annually, what percent are you earning on your investment? We now divide the $24,000 down payment into $3,600. Result is 15% annual return on investment. In other words, you would be receiving fifteen cents per year on each dollar invested.

3. Problem: If you received $200 per month on an investment and your return was equal to 5%, how much money did you invest? Answer is $48,000.

Explanation: Again, the percentage of return on real estate investments is always figured on a yearly basis. If 5% is the yearly percentage return, then the yearly return in dollars would be $200 x 12 months which is $2,400. To clarify further we can reword the question: If you received

Mathematics of Real Estate (cont.)

$2,400 per year on an investment and your return was 5% per year, how much money did you invest? With a percentage problem the unknown sum, which in this problem is the amount you invested, is always 100%. Now the problem tells us that 5% and $2,400 are equal to each other. Next would be to determine what 1% amounts to in dollars since we know that 5% equals $2,400, which gives you $480. Therefore if 1% is equal to $480, then 100% (the unknown sum would be 100 x $480 or $48,000).

4. Problem: If a loan for $4,800 is paid off at the rate of $25.00 per month, how many years will it take to pay the loan off? Answer is 16 years.

Explanation: Again we have to convert the problem to a yearly basis. $25.00 per month x 12 months equals $300 per year. This time our problem is not dealing with percentages but with whole dollars. Therefore, we must divide the smaller amount into the larger. $300 divided into $4,800 results in 16 years.

5. Problem: If you purchased a lot with front footage of 70.21 feet and depth of 170.64 feet for $3 per square foot, what would be the purchase price? Answer is $35,942.

Solution: 70.21 front footage x 170.64 feet deep = 11,980.63 sq. feet.

  11,980.63 sq. ft.
  x $3   cost per sq. ft.
  _____
  $35,941.89 purchase price

If the same lot sold for $500 per frontage foot, what would be the selling price? 70.21 front feet x $500 = $35,105 selling price.

6. Problem: If you have a lot with front footage of 80 feet and a depth of 150 feet, how many acres do you have? Answer is .28 acres or 28/100 of an acre.

Solution: First you have to know that an acre of land equals 43,560 square feet. Now we have to determine how many square feet our lot has. Multiply frontage by depth 80' x 150' which equals 12,000 square feet. Now we can divide our lot of 12,000 square feet by one acre, or 43,560 square feet.

  12,000 divided by 43,560 = .2754 acres.

In other words, we have almost 28/100's of an acre, or just over a quarter of an acre.

Fractions

A fraction is simply a portion of a whole number, such as 1/4, 1/3, 1/2, 3/4, or 7/8. In a fraction, the number above the line is called the numerator; the denominator is the number below the line. In the fraction 1/3, 1 is the numerator and 3 is the denominator. When a whole number is mixed with a fraction, such as 3-1/2, it's called a mixed number. Changing mixed numbers to fractions is done by multiplying the whole number by the denominator, adding the numerator to the product, then writing the denominator under the sum.

Example: $3 - 1/2 = 3 \times 2 + 1 = 7/2$
             $6 \ 1/4 = 6 \times 4 + 1 = 25/4$

To change a fraction into a mixed number, or a decimal, divide the numerator by the denominator.

Example: $2/5 = 2$ divided by $5 = .40$
                 $3/4 = 3$ divided by $4 = .75$

To add fractions, a common denominator has to be found. To add 3/4, 1/2, and 1/5, first find the lowest common denominator for all the fractions. Example: The fractions 3/4, 1/2, and 1/5, the lowest common denominator is 20, being the lowest figure into which 2, 4, and 5 will divide into evenly. So $3/4 = 15/20$; $1/2 = 10/20$; $1/5 = 4/20$. Now the second step is to add the numerators and put the sum over the common denominator. So $15/20 + 10/20 + 4/20 = 29/20$. Then, in the final step we reduce the result to its lowest terms; $29/20 = 1-9/20$.

To subtract fractions, as in 1/4 from 2/3, we need to find the least common denominator (12) and change both fractions to fractions which have this common denominator; $1/4 = 3/12$; $2/3 = 8/12$. Now, we subtract the numerators and put the result over the common denominator: $8/12 -3/12 = 5/12$. Third, we would reduce to lowest terms, but 5/12 cannot be reduced any further so 5/12 is our final result.

To multiply fractions, as in 1/4 x 2/3, we first multiply the numerators ($1 \times 2 = 2$). Next, multiply the two denominators ($4 \times 3 = 12$). Third, place the product of the numerators over the product of the denominators and reduct to lowest terms ($2/12 = 1/6$).

Problem: Multiply 9 x 2/3. In this problem, whole numbers are considered to have (1) for a denominator. So, the problem becomes 9/1 x 2/3 and following the above steps we have $9/1 \times 2/3 = 18/3 = 6$.

To divide fractions, as in 3/4 by 1/3, you first have to invert the divisor (the fraction you are dividing by has to be turned over) then multiply; therefore 3/4 divided by $1/3 = 3/4 \times 3/1 = 9/4 = 2-1/4$.

Decimals

A decimal is part of a whole number and could also be considered a fraction that has 10, 100, 1000 or some other multiple of 10 as its denominator. However, in a decimal the denominator is not written: A decimal point is used to indicate what the denominator is. Example: .7 = 7/10; .07 = 7/100; .007 = 7/1000 and 2.7 = 27/10; and 2.75 = 2-75/100 or 2-3/4.   '

To add and subtract decimals, you need only to write the numbers in a column being sure to align the decimal points under each other.

Problem: Add 6.4, 87.21 and 646.372.

Solution:
```
        6.4
       87.21
   +  646.372
   ---------
      739.982
```

Problem: Subtract 67.432 from 98.6

Solution:
```
       98.6
    -  67.432
   ---------
       31.168
```

To multiply decimals you use the same principles as multiplying whole numbers. Then, to locate the proper placement of the decimal point in the result, add the number of decimal places there are in the numbers you are multiplying and count off this total, from the right to the left, in the result.

Problem: Multiply 64 x .876

Solution:

.876	(3 decimal places to right of decimal point)
x 64	(0 decimal places to right of decimal point)
3504	
5256	
56.064	(3 decimal places from the right)

Problem: Multiply .75 x .672

Solution:

.672	(3 decimal places to right of decimal point)
.75	(2 decimal places to right of decimal point)
3360	
4704	
.50400	(5 decimal places from the right)

Decimals (cont.)

To divide decimals you use the same principles as in dividing whole numbers. Then, to locate the proper placement of the decimal point in the result use the following steps.

First, relocate the decimal point in the divisor (the number you are dividing by) which is outside the bracket, enough spaces to the right to bringing it to the end of the number. (If dividing by .25, you would move decimal point 2 places to the right).

Second, relocate the decimal point of the dividend (the number you are dividing into) which is inside the bracket the same number of spaces as you moved the decimal point in the divisor.

Third, you divide and locate the decimal point in the result, referred to as the quotient, directly above the decimal point in the dividend after relocating it as you did in the second step.

Problem: Divide 74.2 by .35

Solution: .35 after first step becomes 35. (divisor)
                74.2 after second step becomes 7420. (divident)

```
              212.
       .35 )  74.20.
              70
              42
              35
              ‾‾
              70
              70
              ‿
```

Percentages

A percentage is a part of a whole number, such as 25%, which is equal to the fraction 1/4; 50% which is equal to 1/2; and 2/3 which is equal to 66-2/3% of a whole thing. A percentage could also be a fraction which always has 100 as its denominator, as in 25% equals 25/100; 1% equals 1/100 or .01.

Any percentage can be changed to a fraction or to a decimal and vice versa.

In order to change a percentage to a decimal remove the percent sign and relocate the decimal point two places to the left. Example: 1% equals .01, 5% equals .05, 10% equals .10, 4 1/2% equals .045 which equals 4.5%.

Percentages

To change a percentage to a fraction, put 100 under it and reduce to lowest terms, as in 10% equals 10/100, which equals 1/10; 20% equals 20/100, which equals 1/5.

To change a decimal to a percentage, relocate the decimal point two places to the right and add the percent sign as in .10 equals 10%; .01 equals 1%; .0425 equals 4.25%.

To change a fraction to a percentage, first change it to a decimal by dividing the numerator by the denominator, and write the result which is the quotient in percent form.

Problem: Change 1/5 to a percentage.

Solution:

```
        .20
   5 ) 1.00
        10
```

So .20 equals 20%.

Median Sales Price of New Private One-Family Residences sold by region
1965 - 1978

Year	U.S.	N.E.	N. Cen	South	West
1965	20,000	21,500	21,600	17,500	21,600
1966	21,400	23,500	23,200	18,200	23,200
1967	22,700	25,400	25,100	19,400	24,100
1968	24,700	27,700	27,400	21,500	25,100
1969	25,600	31,600	27,600	22,800	25,300
1970	23,400	30,300	24,400	20,300	24,000
1971	25,200	30,600	27,200	22,500	25,500
1972	27,600	31,400	29,300	25,800	27,500
1973	32,500	37,100	32,900	30,900	32,400
1974	35,900	40,100	36,100	34,500	35,800
1975	39,300	44,000	39,600	37,300	40,600
1976	44,200	47,300	44,800	40,500	47,200
1977	48,800	51,600	51,500	44,100	53,500
1978	55,700	58,100	59,200	50,300	61,300

*Statistical Abstract of the United States - 100th Edition

History of the Consumer Price Index - 1967 equals 100

1965	1970	1972	1973	1974	1975	1976	1977	1978	1979 May	1980 Feb.
94.5	116.3	125.3	133.1	147.7	161.2	170.5	181.5	195.4	214.1	236.5

Metric - English Distance Conversions

	Mile	Yard	Foot	Inch
1 km	0.6214	1,093.64	3,280.9	
1 m	0.00062	1.0936	3.2809	39.371
1 dm		0.1094	0.3281	3.9371
1 cm		0.0109	0.328	0.3937
1 mm			0.0033	0.0394

	km	m	dm	cm	mm
1 mile	1.6093	1609.33			
1 yard		0.9144	9.1438	91.438	914.38
1 foot		0.3048	3.0479	30.479	304.79
1 inch		0.0254	0.254	2.54	24.4

m = meter   cm = centimeter
km = kilometer   mm = millimeter
dm = decimeter

English Distance Measurements

1 Link = 7.92 Inches   1 Rod = 16 1/2 Feet
1 Yard = 4.545 Links   1 Chain = 100 Links = 66 Feet = 4 Rods

1 Furlong = 660 Feet = 1/8 Mile = 40 Rods
1 Mile = 8 Furlongs = 5280 Feet = 320 Rods = 80 Chains
1 Sq. Rod = 272¼ Sq. Feet = 30¼ Sq. Yards
1 Acre = 43,560 Sq. Feet or Approximately 209' x 209'
1 Acre = 160 Sq. Rods

Monthly Payment Factors for 30-year FHA Loans

Interest Rate	P & I Payment Factor per $1000 of Loan Amount	MMI Factor per $1000 of Loan Amount	Total Monthly Payment Factor per $1000 of Loan Amount
10.00	8.78	.4156	9.1956
10.25	8.97	.4157	9.3857
10.50	9.15	.4157	9.5657
10.75	9.34	.4158	9.7558
11.00	9.53	.4158	9.9458
11.25	9.72	.4159	10.1359
11.50	9.91	.4159	10.3259
11.75	10.10	.4159	10.5159
12.00	10.29	.4160	10.7060
12.25	10.48	.4160	10.8960
12.50	10.68	.4160	11.0960
12.75	10.87	.4161	11.2861
13.00	11.07	.4161	11.4861
13.25	11.26	.4161	11.6761
13.50	11.46	.4162	11.8762
13.75	11.66	.4162	12.0762
14.00	11.85	.4162	12.2662
14.25	12.05	.4162	12.4662
14.50	12.25	.4163	12.6663
14.75	12.45	.4163	12.8663
15.00	12.65	.4163	13.0663
15.25	12.85	.4163	13.2663
15.50	13.05	.4163	13.4663
15.75	13.25	.4164	13.6664
16.00	13.45	.4164	13.8664
16.25	13.65	.4164	14.0664
16.50	13.86	.4164	14.2764
16.75	14.06	.4164	14.4764
17.00	14.26	.4164	14.6764
17.25	14.46	.4165	14.8765
17.50	14.67	.4165	15.0865
17.75	14.87	.4165	15.2865
18.00	15.08	.4165	15.4965
18.25	15.28	.4165	15.6965
18.50	15.48	.4165	15.8965
18.75	15.69	.4165	16.1065
19.00	15.89	.4165	16.3065
19.25	16.10	.4165	16.5165
19.50	16.30	.4165	16.7165
19.75	16.51	.4165	16.9265
20.00	16.72	.4165	17.1365

Multiply these factors by each $1000 of the loan amount to get the monthly payment

Multiply these factors by each $1000 of the loan amount to get the monthly payment

Monthly Payment Factors for 35-year FHA Loans

Interest Rate	P & I Payment Factor per $1000 of Loan Amount	MMI Factor per $1000 of Loan Amount	Total Monthly Payment Factor per $1000 of Loan Amount
10.00	8.60	.4160	9.0160
10.25	8.79	.4161	9.2061
10.50	8.99	.4161	9.4061
10.75	9.18	.4161	9.5961
11.00	9.37	.4162	9.7862
11.25	9.57	.4162	9.9862
11.50	9.77	.4162	10.1862
11.75	9.96	.4163	10.3763
12.00	10.16	.4163	10.5763
12.25	10.36	.4163	10.7763
12.50	10.56	.4163	10.9763
12.75	10.76	.4163	11.1763
13.00	10.96	.4164	11.3764
13.25	11.16	.4164	11.5764
13.50	11.36	.4164	11.7764
13.75	11.56	.4164	11.9764
14.00	11.76	.4164	12.1764
14.25	11.96	.4165	12.3765
14.50	12.17	.4165	12.5865
14.75	12.37	.4165	12.7865
15.00	12.57	.4165	12.9865
15.25	12.78	.4165	13.1965
15.50	12.98	.4165	13.3965
15.75	13.19	.4165	13.6065
16.00	13.39	.4165	13.8065
16.25	13.59	.4166	14.0066
16.50	13.80	.4166	14.2166
16.75	14.00	.4166	14.4166
17.00	14.21	.4166	14.6266
17.25	14.42	.4166	14.8366
17.50	14.62	.4166	15.0366
17.75	14.83	.4166	15.2466
18.00	15.03	.4166	15.4466
18.25	15.24	.4166	15.6566
18.50	15.45	.4166	15.8666
18.75	15.65	.4166	16.0666
19.00	15.86	.4166	16.2766
19.25	16.07	.4166	16.4866
19.50	16.27	.4166	16.6866
19.75	16.48	.4166	16.8966
20.00	16.69	.4166	17.1066

Multiply these factors by each $1000 of the loan amount to get the monthly payment

Multiply these factors by each $1000 of the loan amount to get the monthly payment

Monthly Payment Factors for 40-year FHA Loans

Interest Rate	P & I Payment Factor per $1000 of Loan Amount	MMI Factor per $1000 of Loan Amount	Total Monthly Payment Factor per $1000 of Loan Amount
10.00	8.50	.4163	8.9163
10.25	8.69	.4163	9.1063
10.50	8.89	.4163	9.3063
10.75	9.09	.4164	9.5064
11.00	9.29	.4164	9.7064
11.25	9.49	.4164	9.9064
11.50	9.69	.4164	10.1064
11.75	9.89	.4164	10.3064
12.00	10.09	.4165	10.5065
12.25	10.29	.4165	10.7065
12.50	10.49	.4165	10.9065
12.75	10.70	.4165	11.1165
13.00	10.90	.4165	11.3165
13.25	11.10	.4165	11.5165
13.50	11.31	.4165	11.7265
13.75	11.51	.4165	11.9265
14.00	11.72	.4165	12.1365
14.25	11.92	.4166	12.3366
14.50	12.13	.4166	12.5466
14.75	12.33	.4166	12.7466
15.00	12.54	.4166	12.9566
15.25	12.74	.4166	13.1566
15.50	12.95	.4166	13.3666
15.75	13.16	.4166	13.5766
16.00	13.36	.4166	13.7766
16.25	13.57	.4166	13.9866
16.50	13.77	.4166	14.1866
16.75	13.98	.4166	14.3966
17.00	14.19	.4166	14.6066
17.25	14.40	.4166	14.8166
17.50	14.60	.4166	15.0166
17.75	14.81	.4166	15.2266
18.00	15.02	.4166	15.4366
18.25	15.22	.4166	15.6366
18.50	15.43	.4166	15.8466
18.75	15.64	.4166	16.0566
19.00	15.85	.4166	16.2666
19.25	16.05	.4166	16.4666
19.50	16.26	.4166	16.6766
19.75	16.47	.4166	16.8866
20.00	16.68	.4166	17.0966

Multiply these factors by each $1000 of the loan amount to get the monthly payment

Multiply these factors by each $1000 of the loan amount to get the monthly payment

PRORATIONS FROM JAN. 1st TO PRORATION DATE

DATE	JAN Days Past	JAN % of 365	FEB Days Past	FEB % of 365	MAR Days Past	MAR % of 365	APR Days Past	APR % of 365	MAY Days Past	MAY % of 365	JUN Days Past	JUN % of 365	DATE
1	1	.27	32	8.77	60	16.44	91	24.93	121	33.15	152	41.64	1
2	2	.55	33	9.04	61	16.71	92	25.21	122	33.42	153	41.92	2
3	3	.82	34	9.32	62	16.99	93	25.48	123	33.70	154	42.19	3
4	4	1.10	35	9.59	63	17.26	94	25.75	124	33.97	155	42.47	4
5	5	1.37	36	9.86	64	17.53	95	26.03	125	34.25	156	42.74	5
6	6	1.64	37	10.14	65	17.81	96	26.30	126	34.52	157	43.01	6
7	7	1.92	38	10.41	66	18.08	97	26.58	127	34.79	158	43.29	7
8	8	2.19	39	10.68	67	18.36	98	26.85	128	35.07	159	43.56	8
9	9	2.47	40	10.96	68	18.63	99	27.12	129	35.34	160	43.84	9
10	10	2.74	41	11.23	69	18.90	100	27.40	130	35.62	161	44.11	10
11	11	3.01	42	11.51	70	19.18	101	27.67	131	35.89	162	44.38	11
12	12	3.29	43	11.78	71	19.45	102	27.95	132	36.16	163	44.66	12
13	13	3.56	44	12.05	72	19.73	103	28.22	133	36.44	164	44.93	13
14	14	3.84	45	12.33	73	20.00	104	28.49	134	36.71	165	45.21	14
15	15	4.11	46	12.60	74	20.27	105	28.77	135	36.99	166	45.48	15
16	16	4.38	47	12.88	75	20.55	106	29.04	136	37.26	167	45.75	16
17	17	4.66	48	13.15	76	20.82	107	29.32	137	37.53	168	46.03	17
18	18	4.93	49	13.42	77	21.10	108	29.59	138	37.81	169	46.30	18
19	19	5.21	50	13.70	78	21.37	109	29.86	139	38.08	170	46.58	19
20	20	5.48	51	13.97	79	21.64	110	30.14	140	38.36	171	46.85	20
21	21	5.75	52	14.25	80	21.92	111	30.41	141	38.63	172	47.12	21
22	22	6.03	53	14.52	81	22.19	112	30.68	142	38.90	173	47.40	22
23	23	6.30	54	14.79	82	22.47	113	30.96	143	39.18	174	47.67	23
24	24	6.58	55	15.07	83	22.74	114	31.23	144	39.45	175	47.95	24
25	25	6.85	56	15.34	84	23.01	115	31.51	145	39.73	176	48.22	25
26	26	7.12	57	15.62	85	23.29	116	31.78	146	40.00	177	48.49	26
27	27	7.40	58	15.89	86	23.56	117	32.05	147	40.27	178	48.77	27
28	28	7.67	59	16.16	87	23.84	118	32.33	148	40.55	179	49.04	28
29	29	7.95			88	24.11	119	32.60	149	40.82	180	49.32	29
30	30	8.22			89	24.38	120	32.88	150	41.10	181	49.59	30
31	31	8.49			90	24.66			151	41.37			31

PRORATIONS FROM PRORATION DATE TO DEC. 31st

DATE	JAN Days to Come	JAN % of 365	FEB Days to Come	FEB % of 365	MAR Days to Come	MAR % of 365	APR Days to Come	APR % of 365	MAY Days to Come	MAY % of 365	JUN Days to Come	JUN % of 365	DATE
1	365	100.00	334	91.51	306	83.84	275	75.34	245	67.12	214	58.63	1
2	364	99.73	333	91.23	305	83.56	274	75.07	244	66.85	213	58.36	2
3	363	99.45	332	90.96	304	83.29	273	74.79	243	66.58	212	58.08	3
4	362	99.18	331	90.68	303	83.01	272	74.52	242	66.30	211	57.81	4
5	361	98.90	330	90.41	302	82.74	271	74.25	241	66.03	210	57.53	5
6	360	98.63	329	90.14	301	82.47	270	73.97	240	65.75	209	57.26	6
7	359	98.36	328	89.86	300	82.19	269	73.70	239	65.48	208	56.99	7
8	358	98.08	327	89.59	299	81.92	268	73.42	238	65.21	207	56.71	8
9	357	97.81	326	89.32	298	81.64	267	73.15	237	64.93	206	56.44	9
10	356	97.53	325	89.04	297	81.37	266	72.88	236	64.66	205	56.16	10
11	355	97.26	324	88.77	296	81.10	265	72.60	235	64.38	204	55.89	11
12	354	96.99	323	88.49	295	80.82	264	72.33	234	64.11	203	55.62	12
13	353	96.71	322	88.22	294	80.55	263	72.05	233	63.84	202	55.34	13
14	352	96.44	321	87.95	293	80.27	262	71.78	232	63.56	201	55.07	14
15	351	96.16	320	87.67	292	80.00	261	71.51	231	63.29	200	54.79	15
16	350	95.89	319	87.40	291	79.73	260	71.23	230	63.01	199	54.52	16
17	349	95.62	318	87.12	290	79.45	259	70.96	229	62.74	198	54.25	17
18	348	95.34	317	86.85	289	79.18	258	70.68	228	62.47	197	53.97	18
19	347	95.07	316	86.58	288	78.90	257	70.41	227	62.19	196	53.70	19
20	346	94.79	315	86.30	287	78.63	256	70.14	226	61.92	195	53.42	20
21	345	94.52	314	86.03	286	78.36	255	69.86	225	61.64	194	53.15	21
22	344	94.25	313	85.75	285	78.08	254	69.59	224	61.37	193	52.88	22
23	343	93.97	312	85.48	284	77.81	253	69.32	223	61.10	192	52.60	23
24	342	93.70	311	85.21	283	77.53	252	69.04	222	60.82	191	52.33	24
25	341	93.42	310	84.93	282	77.26	251	68.77	221	60.55	190	52.05	25
26	340	93.15	309	84.66	281	76.99	250	68.49	220	60.27	189	51.78	26
27	339	92.88	308	84.38	280	76.71	249	68.22	219	60.00	188	51.51	27
28	338	92.60	307	84.11	279	76.44	248	67.95	218	59.73	187	51.23	28
29	337	92.33			278	76.16	247	67.67	217	59.45	186	50.96	29
30	336	92.05			277	75.89	246	67.40	216	59.18	185	50.68	30
31	335	91.78			276	75.62			215	58.90	184		31

PRORATIONS FROM JAN. 1st TO PRORATION DATE

DATE	JUL Days Past	JUL % of 365	AUG Days Past	AUG % of 365	SEP Days Past	SEP % of 365	OCT Days Past	OCT % of 365	NOV Days Past	NOV % of 365	DEC Days Past	DEC % of 365	DATE
1	182	49.86	213	58.36	244	66.85	274	75.07	305	83.56	335	91.78	1
2	183	50.14	214	58.63	245	67.12	275	75.34	306	83.84	336	92.05	2
3	184	50.41	215	58.90	246	67.40	276	75.62	307	84.11	337	92.33	3
4	185	50.68	216	59.18	247	67.67	277	75.89	308	84.38	338	92.60	4
5	186	50.96	217	59.45	248	67.95	278	76.16	309	84.66	339	92.88	5
6	187	51.23	218	59.73	249	68.22	279	76.44	310	84.93	340	93.15	6
7	188	51.51	219	60.00	250	68.49	280	76.71	311	85.21	341	93.42	7
8	189	51.78	220	60.27	251	68.77	281	76.99	312	85.48	342	93.70	8
9	190	52.05	221	60.55	252	69.04	282	77.26	313	85.75	343	93.97	9
10	191	52.33	222	60.82	253	69.32	283	77.53	314	86.03	344	94.25	10
11	192	52.60	223	61.10	254	69.59	284	77.81	315	86.30	345	94.52	11
12	193	52.88	224	61.37	255	69.86	285	78.08	316	86.58	346	94.79	12
13	194	53.15	225	61.64	256	70.14	286	78.36	317	86.85	347	95.07	13
14	195	53.42	226	61.92	257	70.41	287	78.63	318	87.12	348	95.34	14
15	196	53.70	227	62.19	258	70.68	288	78.90	319	87.40	349	95.62	15
16	197	53.97	228	62.47	259	70.96	289	79.18	320	87.67	350	95.89	16
17	198	54.25	229	62.74	260	71.23	290	79.45	321	87.95	351	96.16	17
18	199	54.52	230	63.01	261	71.51	291	79.73	322	88.22	352	96.44	18
19	200	54.79	231	63.29	262	71.78	292	80.00	323	88.49	353	96.71	19
20	201	55.07	232	63.56	263	72.05	293	80.27	324	88.77	354	96.99	20
21	202	55.34	233	63.84	264	72.33	294	80.55	325	89.04	355	97.26	21
22	203	55.62	234	64.11	265	72.60	295	80.82	326	89.32	356	97.53	22
23	204	55.89	235	64.38	266	72.88	296	81.10	327	89.59	357	97.81	23
24	205	56.16	236	64.66	267	73.15	297	81.37	328	89.86	358	98.08	24
25	206	56.44	237	64.93	268	73.42	298	81.64	329	90.14	359	98.36	25
26	207	56.71	238	65.21	269	73.70	299	81.92	330	90.41	360	98.63	26
27	208	56.99	239	65.48	270	73.97	300	82.19	331	90.68	361	98.90	27
28	209	57.26	240	65.75	271	74.25	301	82.47	332	90.96	362	99.18	28
29	210	57.53	241	66.03	272	74.52	302	82.74	333	91.23	363	99.45	29
30	211	57.81	242	66.30	273	74.79	303	83.01	334	91.51	364	99.73	30
31	212	58.08	243	66.58			304	83.29			365	100.00	31

PRORATIONS FROM PRORATION DATE TO DEC. 31st

DATE	JUL Days to Come	JUL % of 365	AUG Days to Come	AUG % of 365	SEP Days to Come	SEP % of 365	OCT Days to Come	OCT % of 365	NOV Days to Come	NOV % of 365	DEC Days to Come	DEC % of 365	DATE
1	184	50.41	153	41.92	122	33.42	92	25.21	61	16.71	31	8.49	1
2	183	50.14	152	41.64	121	33.15	91	24.93	60	16.44	30	8.22	2
3	182	49.86	151	41.37	120	32.88	90	24.66	59	16.16	29	7.95	3
4	181	49.59	150	41.10	119	32.60	89	24.38	58	15.89	28	7.67	4
5	180	49.32	149	40.82	118	32.33	88	24.11	57	15.62	27	7.40	5
6	179	49.04	148	40.55	117	32.05	87	23.84	56	15.34	26	7.12	6
7	178	48.77	147	40.27	116	31.78	86	23.56	55	15.07	25	6.85	7
8	177	48.49	146	40.00	115	31.51	85	23.29	54	14.79	24	6.58	8
9	176	48.22	145	39.73	114	31.23	84	23.01	53	14.52	23	6.30	9
10	175	47.95	144	39.45	113	30.96	83	22.74	52	14.25	22	6.03	10
11	174	47.67	143	39.18	112	30.68	82	22.47	51	13.97	21	5.75	11
12	173	47.40	142	38.90	111	30.41	81	22.19	50	13.70	20	5.48	12
13	172	47.12	141	38.63	110	30.14	80	21.92	49	13.42	19	5.21	13
14	171	46.85	140	38.36	109	29.86	79	21.64	48	13.15	18	4.93	14
15	170	46.58	139	38.08	108	29.59	78	21.37	47	12.88	17	4.66	15
16	169	46.30	138	37.81	107	29.32	77	21.10	46	12.60	16	4.38	16
17	168	46.03	137	37.53	106	29.04	76	20.82	45	12.33	15	4.11	17
18	167	45.75	136	37.26	105	28.77	75	20.55	44	12.05	14	3.84	18
19	166	45.48	135	36.99	104	28.49	74	20.27	43	11.78	13	3.56	19
20	165	45.21	134	36.71	103	28.22	73	20.00	42	11.51	12	3.29	20
21	164	44.93	133	36.44	102	27.95	72	19.73	41	11.23	11	3.01	21
22	163	44.66	132	36.16	101	27.67	71	19.45	40	10.96	10	2.74	22
23	162	44.38	131	35.89	100	27.40	70	19.18	39	10.68	9	2.47	23
24	161	44.11	130	35.62	99	27.12	69	18.90	38	10.41	8	2.19	24
25	160	43.84	129	35.34	98	26.85	68	18.63	37	10.14	7	1.92	25
26	159	43.56	128	35.07	97	26.58	67	18.36	36	9.86	6	1.64	26
27	158	43.29	127	34.79	96	26.30	66	18.08	35	9.59	5	1.37	27
28	157	43.01	126	34.52	95	26.03	65	17.81	34	9.32	4	1.10	28
29	156	42.74	125	34.25	94	25.75	64	17.53	33	9.04	3	.82	29
30	155	42.47	124	33.97	93	25.48	63	17.26	32	8.77	2	.55	30
31	154	42.19	123	33.70			62	16.99			1	.27	31

NOTES

NOTES

NOTES